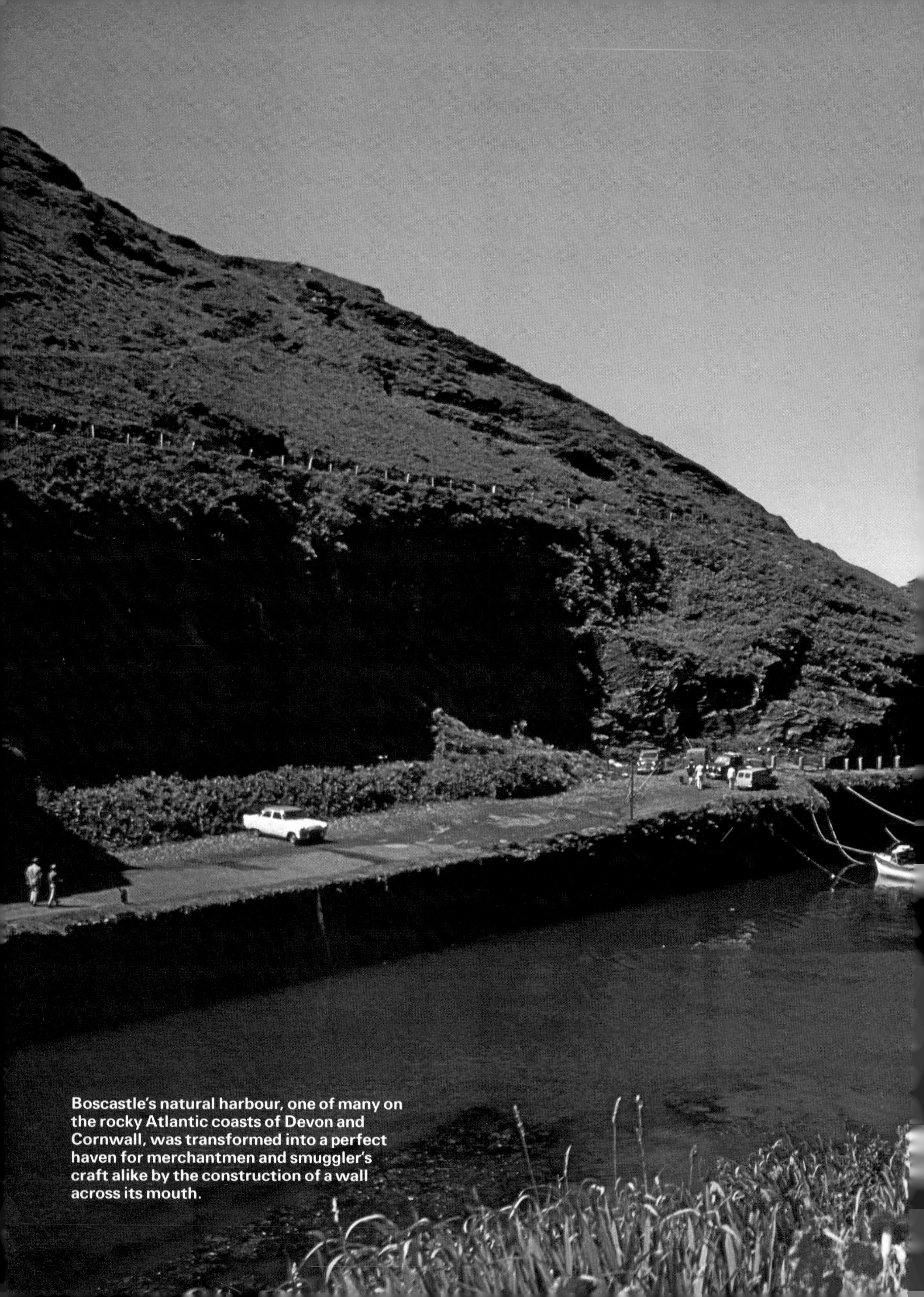

Boscastle's natural harbour, one of many on the rocky Atlantic coasts of Devon and Cornwall, was transformed into a perfect haven for merchantmen and smuggler's craft alike by the construction of a wall across its mouth.

Bridges of stone and wood span the River Eye as it threads its way between the cottages of Lower Slaughter, a lovely village where the magic of water adds another dimension to the typical beauty of Cotswold scenery.

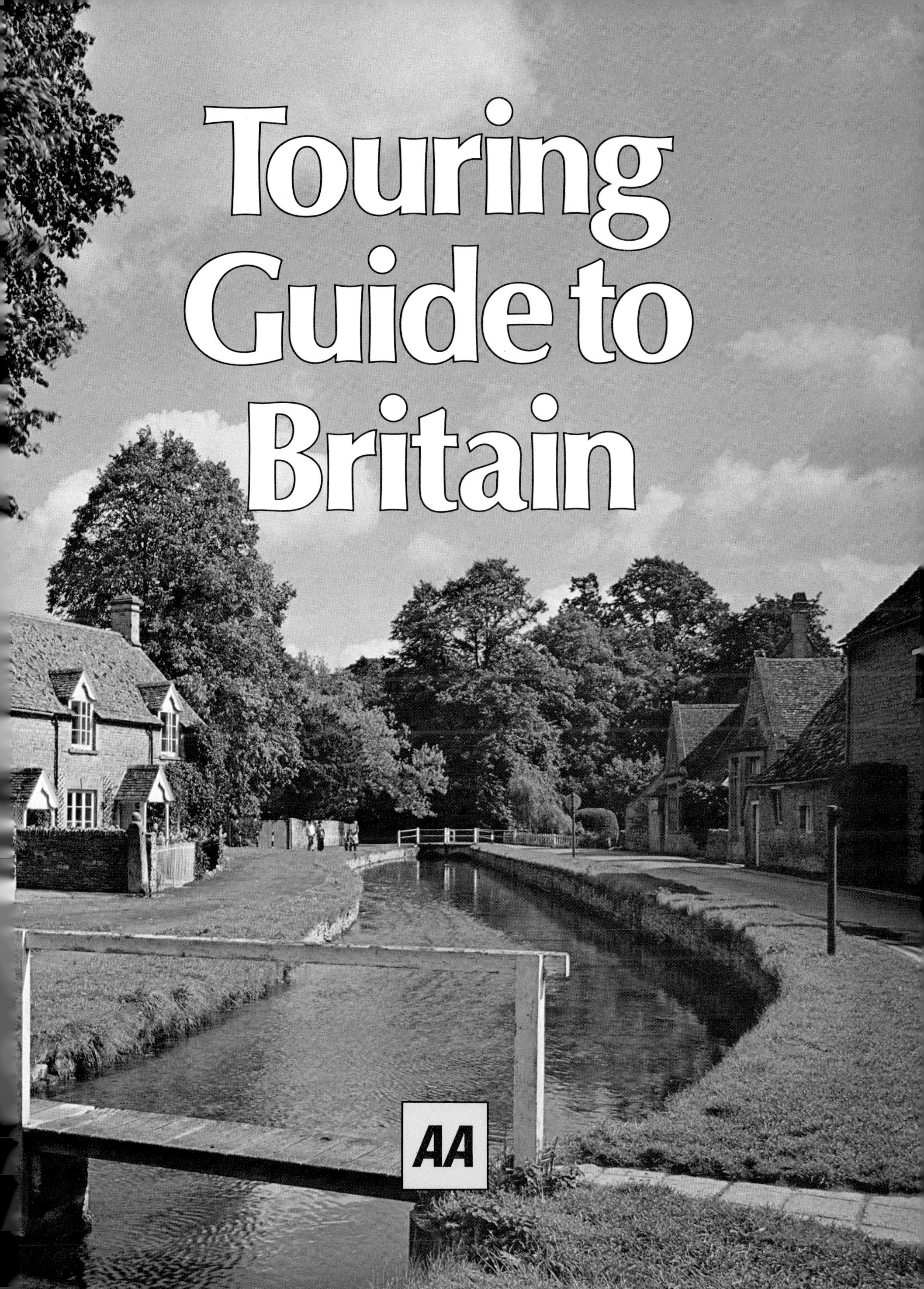

Touring Guide to Britain
AA

Set between peaceful Coniston Water and the rugged Langdale Pikes, the lakes and forests of Tarn Hows offer some of the finest scenery of the English Lakes.

CONTENTS

Produced by the Publications Division of The Automobile Association
Editor Russell P O Beach
Art Editor Dave Austin
Assistant Editor Michael Cady
Assistant Designer Robert Johnson
Design concept by M A Preedy, MSIAD

Tour routes compiled and driven by the Publications Research Unit of The Automobile Association
Index compiled by Linda Beach
Photographs by: Martyn Adelman, Martin Boddy, the British Tourist Authority S & O Mathews, Jarrold Colour Publications Ltd, and Woodmansterne Ltd

All maps by the Cartographic Department, Publications Division of The Automobile Association
Based on the Ordnance Survey Maps, with the permission of the Controller of HM Stationery Office

Phototypeset by Jarrold & Sons Ltd of Norwich, England
Printed and bound by New Interlitho SpA, Milan, Italy
Colour separations by Rito of Zurich, Switzerland

First edition 1978
Reprinted 1979
First edition (revised) 1979
Reprinted 1980, 1981 (twice), 1982, 1983, 1985
ISBN 0 86145 110 4 (softback) AA Ref 52401
ISBN 0 86145 287 9 (hardback) AA Ref 53552

Published by The Automobile Association, Fanum House, Basing View, Basingstoke, Hampshire RG21 2EA

KEY TO TOURS AND TOUR REGIONS

The Touring Guide to Britain contains 112 selected tours in some of the most picturesque and interesting places accessible to the motoring public. It is divided into the six geographical regions shown on the key maps here and overleaf, and has been designed for ease of use in a moving vehicle. Included in each self-contained tour are a colour map, photographs of interesting places on the route, and text presented in a way that makes this book different from any other of its kind. Places of interest, shown as black type on the maps, are described as they occur on the road and linked in sequence by route directions. This precise wayfinding information is set in *italic* type so that the navigator can easily identify it from the rest of the text. Castles, stately homes, and other places of interest described in the tours are not necessarily open to the public, although they may have been at the time of publication. Properties administered by the National Trust, National Trust for Scotland, and Ancient Monuments Scheme (NT, NTS, and AM) are usually open most times of the year, but there are many exceptions. It is a good idea to check that such places still receive visitors before planning a stop.

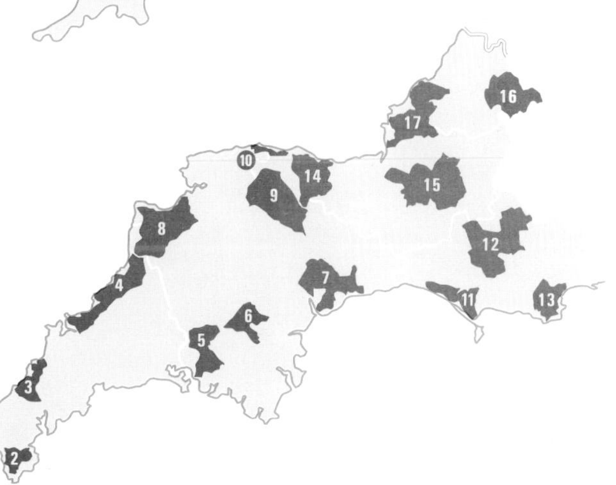

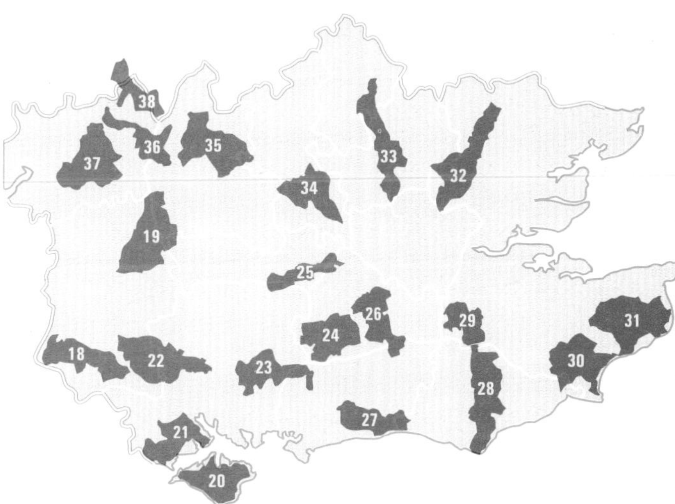

THE WEST COUNTRY
PAGES 8-43

SOUTH AND SOUTH EAST ENGLAND
PAGES 44-87

SYMBOLS AND ABBREVIATIONS

MAPS

- Main Tour Route
- Detour/Diversion from Main Tour Route
- Motorway
- Motorway Access
- Motorway Service Area
- Motorway & Junction Under Construction
- A-class Road (A466)
- B-class Road (B423)
- Unclassified Road (unclass)
- Dual Carriageway (A48)
- Road Under Construction

- Airport
- Battlefield
- Bridge
- Castle
- Church as Route Landmark
- Ferry
- Folly/Tower
- Forestry Commission Land
- Gazetteer Placename *River Leven*/Chelford
- Industrial Site (Old & New)
- Level Crossing

- Lighthouse
- Marshland
- Memorial/Monument
- Miscellaneous Places of Interest & Route Landmarks
- National Boundary
- National Trust Property
- National Trust for Scotland Property
- Non-gazetteer Placenames Ded
- Notable Religious Site
- Picnic Site

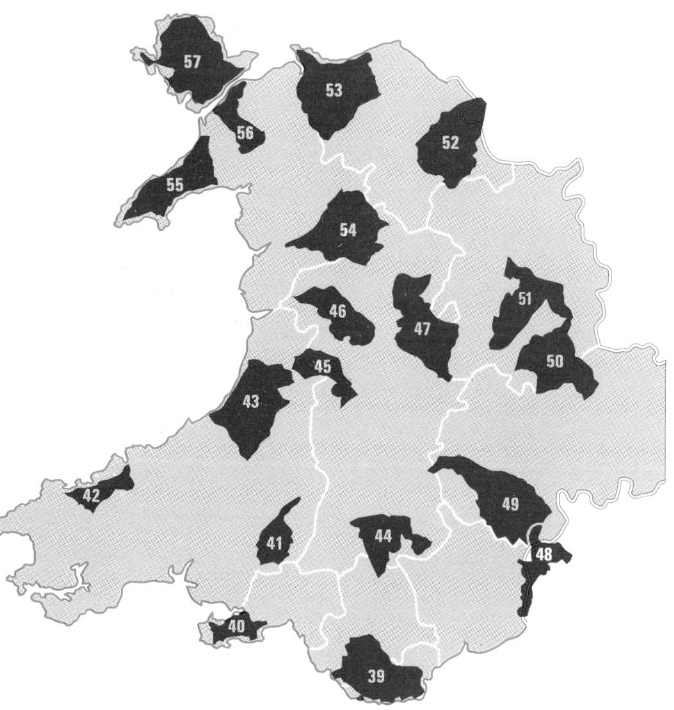

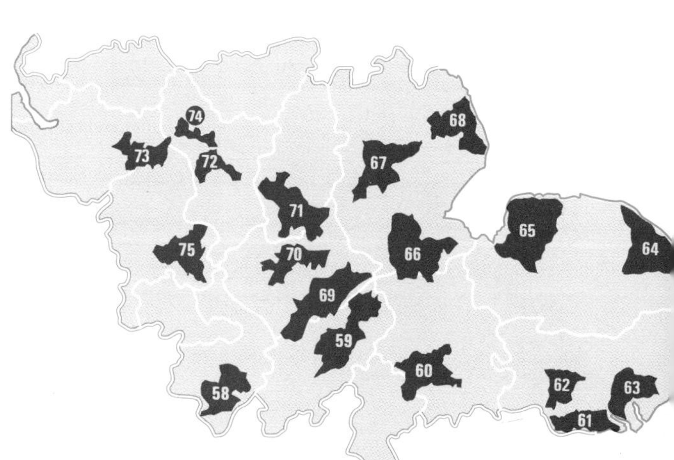

WALES AND THE MARCHER LANDS
PAGES 88-127

CENTRAL AND EASTERN ENGLAND
PAGES 128-165

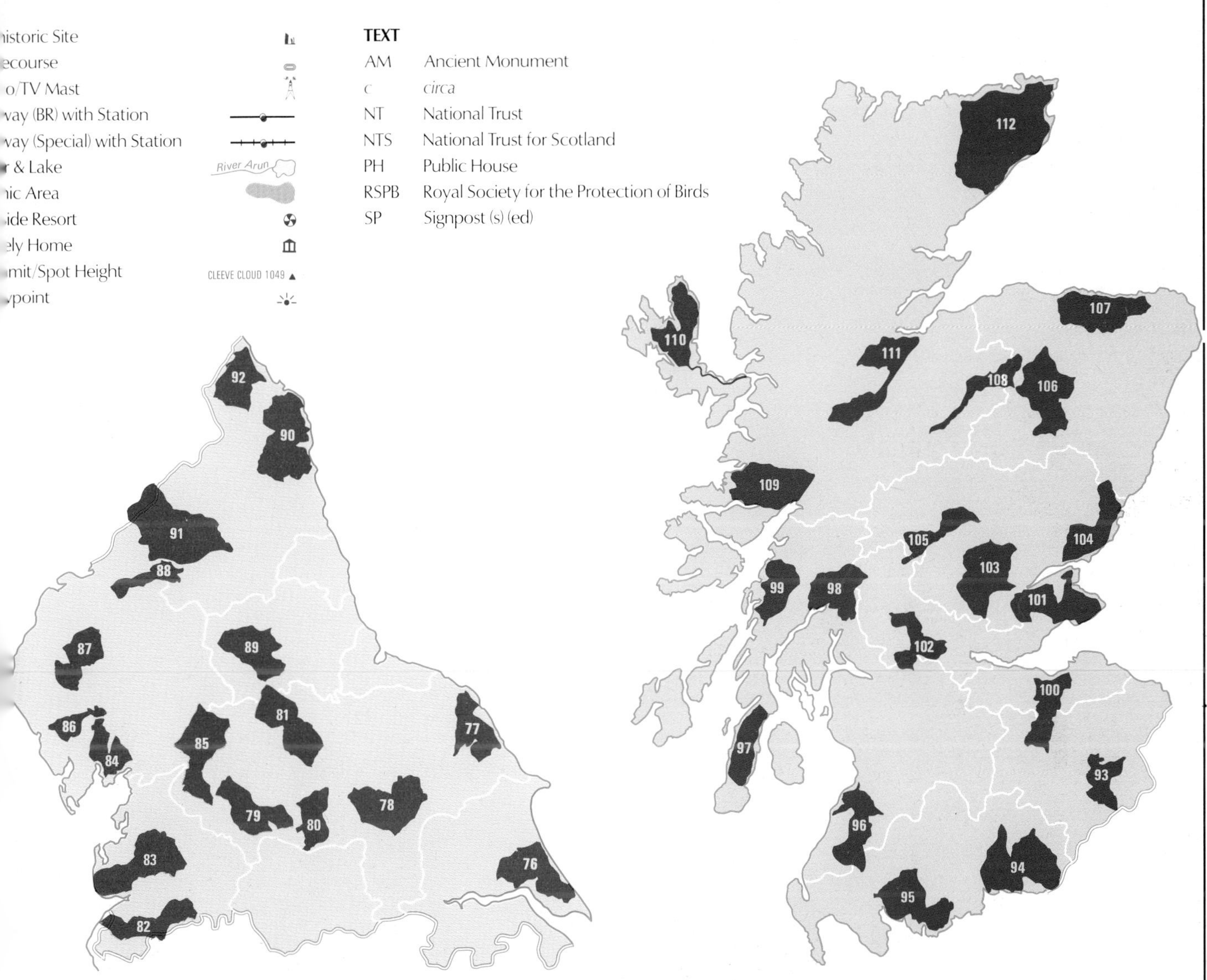

THE NORTH COUNTRY
PAGES 166-201

SCOTLAND
PAGES 202-243

Ruined engine houses, like the one at Wheal Coates near St Agnes, are forceful reminders of the men who once struggled to extract precious mineral ores from primitive mines deep beneath the rural landscapes of Cornwall.

The West Country

PENZANCE, Cornwall SW43
The most westerly town in England, Penzance enjoys a mild climate all year round. The town grew to prosperity through tin mining, and possibly smuggling, and was immortalized by Gilbert and Sullivan in *The Pirates of Penzance*. Evidence of its popularity in Regency times can be seen in the fine period buildings still standing in Chapel Street. Also here is a private museum with exhibits from the ship *Association*, which was wrecked off the Scillies in 1707. There is a natural history museum in Penlee Park, and many exotic plants grow in Morab Gardens. About 2 miles inland are the Trengwainton Gardens (NT), with their exceptional collections of magnolias, rhododendrons and other shrubs. It was here that magnolias flowered for the first time in the British Isles.

MOUNT'S BAY, Cornwall SW52
Mount's Bay curves in a series of wide coves and inlets between the Land's End peninsula in the west and The Lizard in the east. In spite of playing host to many visitors each year it is still a place of isolated bays and deserted, cliff-fringed beaches.

Leave Penzance on the A3077 'Newlyn', road skirting the harbour to Newlyn.

NEWLYN, Cornwall SW42
This busy fishing port used to be famous for its artist colony. Many of the painters moved north to St Ives, but a few still live and work among the quaint old cottages and fish-cellars. The Passmore Edwards picture gallery shows some of the colony's work.

From Newlyn continue along the A3077 and reach a bridge. Once over the bridge, turn left on to an unclassified road which hugs the coast to Mousehole.

TOUR 1 43 MILES

THE PENWITH PENINSULA

Storm-tumbled cliffs haunted by gulls and mermaid legends guard the wild Atlantic shoreline of Penwith. On the other side of Land's End is the great bight of Mount's Bay, where the 'nightmen' of folksong fame crept from secluded coves with 'baccy for the parson and brandy for the squire'.

The fairytale structure of St Michael's Mount dominates Mount's Bay.

MOUSEHOLE, Cornwall SW42
Largely unchanged by time, Mousehole preserves the original character of old Cornwall in its granite houses and working harbour.

Turn left, drive to the harbour, and turn right then right again. Leave Mousehole SP 'Paul', turn inland, and climb to Paul.

PAUL, Cornwall SW42
Dorothy Penreath, one of the last people to speak the ancient Cornish language is buried here. Inside the 15th-century church are several pieces of old armour.

Turn left past Paul Church and after ½ mile meet a T-junction. Turn left on to the B3315 and continue for 1¾ miles. A detour can be taken from the main route by turning left on to an unclassified road through the Lamorna Valley to Lamorna Cove.

LAMORNA COVE, Cornwall SW42
Huge granite boulders and the rocky outcrops of this spectacular cove contrast with the gentler surrounding countryside. A granite quay and pier were built here in the last century to export granite from the quarries near by. Nowadays the cove is visited for its lovely scenery by tourists and artists.

Continue on the B3315 for 3¼ miles, meet a T-junction, and turn left. Descend steeply, then climb to the edge of Treen.

TREEN, Cornwall SW32
This tiny village stands near the end of a fortified headland known as Treen Castle (NT). Outside the local inn is a sign telling how in 1824 a nephew of Oliver Goldsmith overturned the 60 ton Logan Rock, a famous rocking stone, and how he was made to replace it at his own expense. Treen is the central point for walks to some of Cornwall's most beautiful and spectacular scenery.

TRERYN DINAS, Cornwall SW32
It is believed that the defences of this excellent iron-age cliff castle were started between the 3rd and 2nd centuries BC. A huge bank and ditch cuts off the headland, and at the extreme tip of the rocks jutting out to sea is a bank faced with heavy mason. Access is by footpath from Treen.

LOGAN ROCK, Cornwall SW32
Pronounced 'loggan', the name of this curious rocking stone is derived from the Cornish verb *log*, meaning to move. It is reached by footpath from the village of Treen.

From the edge of Treen, remain on the B3315 for ¾ mile. A detour from the main route can be taken by turning left on to an unclassified road for Porthcurno and the Minack Theatre

PORTHCURNO AND THE MINACK THEATRE, Cornwall SW32
The first transatlantic cable was brought ashore in this modern village. Porthcurno has an exceptionally good beach of almost white sand, and just to the west is the unique Minack Theatre – built out of living stone on the edge of the cliffs by Miss Rowena Cade in 1931. The auditorium is formed from ridges cut into the sloping rock, with the natural bedding adapted to make seats facing south and east over a stage that hangs above the sea.

Continue with the 'Land's End' road and after ½ mile turn left, still with the B3315. After 2¼ miles turn left on to the A30 'Land's End' road, and drive for about ½ mile to Land's End.

LAND'S END, Cornwall SW32
Famous as England's most westerly point, Land's End is about 873 miles from the equally famous John O'Groats in Scotland. On a fine day the Isles of Scilly are visible 28 miles away to the west. Much of the countryside here is in a designated area of outstanding natural beauty.

LONGSHIPS LIGHTHOUSE, Cornwall SW32
Some 2 miles out to sea from Land's End the Longships Lighthouse rises 50ft high from a 60ft rock. Waves have been known to lash as high as the lantern during severe storms.

Wave torn rocks and the distant Longships Lighthouse starkly outlined against sunset at Land's End.

Ruined mine buildings, ike the Carn Galver Mine ıt Morvah, add much o Cornwall's andscape.

A short detour can be taken by turning left in St Just on to an unclassified road to Cape Cornwall.

CAPE CORNWALL, Cornwall SW33
Features of this quiet, unspoilt headland of granite and slate – apart from its natural beauty – include a prehistoric burial ground and a ruined chapel.

From St Just continue on the B3306 to Pendeen.

On the headland at St Ives is a fishermen's chapel.

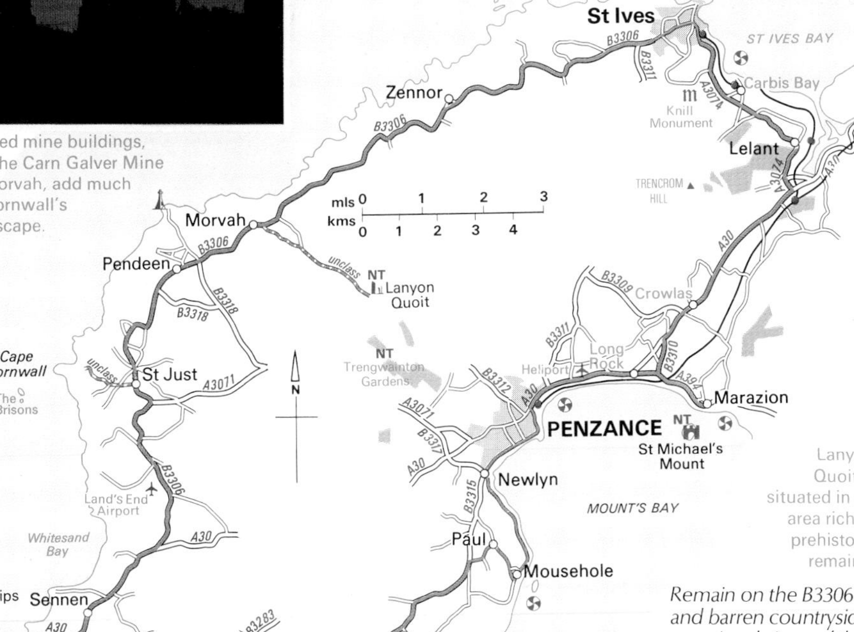

Lanyon Quoit is situated in an area rich in prehistoric remains.

ave Land's End and return along the 30, past the 'Porthcurno' road, to ennen.

NNEN, Cornwall SW32
ccording to legend Sennen, a small lage with a past rich in local story, was the battleground for the st Cornish fight against invading anes. The 15th-century church ntains a medieval statue of the rgin Mary and is the most westerly urch in England. Sennen Cove ers good sand, excellent bathing, d superb scenery.

ave Sennen on the A30. After 1¾ les turn left on to the B3306, SP 'St t' and pass Land's End Airport. er 3 miles turn left on to the A3071 d enter St Just.

JUST, Cornwall SW33
o known as St Just-in-Penwith, village is noted for the contents ts old church. Among these is a l painting, an interesting inscribed ne of 5th-century date, and the ft of a 9th-century Hiberno-Saxon ss. St Just itself is enchanting.

PENDEEN, Cornwall SW33
Two buildings of particular interest can be seen here. One is a 15th-century farmhouse with a façade added in 1670, and the other is a modern church modelled on Scotland's Iona Cathedral. All around are rugged cliffs and the derelict remains of old mine workings.

Leave Pendeen and continue along the B3306 to Morvah.

MORVAH, Cornwall SW43
This little mining and farming village is attractively set on the edge of the Penwirth moorland. About 1 mile south of the village are Chun Castle and Chun Quoit, respectively a circular iron-age fort built of stone and the remains of a large neolithic dolmen, or tomb chamber.

Shortly beyond Morvah a detour can be taken right along an unclassified road for 2 miles to Lanyon Quoit.

LANYON QUOIT, Cornwall SW43
Perhaps the best known and most visited of Cornwall's megaliths, this neolithic tomb (NT) resembles a huge three-legged stone table.

Remain on the B3306 through rocky and barren countryside, with occasional views of the coast; skirt the village of Zennor.

ZENNOR, Cornwall SW43
Zennor is famous for a mermaid carving cut into one of the benches in its 15th-century church. Seals are common along this coast, and it is probable that their 'singing' is largely responsible for the mermaid legends that are so much a part of Western folk lore. At one time the village was a prosperous tin-mining community, and it became briefly famous in the 1920s when there was a local scandal involving Virginia Woolf. This famous authoress lived in a local house called the Eagle's Nest (which still stands), and writer DH Lawrence lived near by in a cottage near the cliff top. A folk museum in the village is well worth visiting.

Continue on to B3306 to St Ives.

ST IVES, Cornwall SW54
Until her recent death the sculptress Barbara Hepworth was the leading light in a famous artists' community that lived and worked in this attractive fishing village. Quaint old houses and winding alleys cluster beneath the 120ft rough-hewn granite spire of the church, a fine building dating from the 15th century.

Leave St Ives on the A3074 and follow SP 'Hayle'. Pass Carbis Bay on the left and continue into Lelant.

LELANT, Cornwall SW53
Lelant, a touring centre on the River Hayle, has a Norman and perpendicular-style church with a 17th-century sundial.

At Lelant turn right and in ½ mile keep forward SP 'Penzance'. Reach the A30 and turn right to Crowlas. Continue with the A30, and in ¾ mile turn left on to the B3310 SP 'Helston'. After a further ½ mile turn left on to the A394 and cross a railway bridge to Marazion.

MARAZION, Cornwall SW53
Good bathing and fishing can be enjoyed in this ancient port, and the marshland between Marazion and Ludgvan is the habitat for many species of bird. Marvellous views of famous St Michael's Mount can be enjoyed from here.

ST MICHAEL'S MOUNT Cornwall SW53
This little granite island (NT) rises to a 250ft summit from the waters of Mount's Bay and is accessible by foot via a causeway at low tide, or by boat from Marazion. Its splendid castle (NT) and priory (NT), both founded by Edward the Confessor in the 11th-century, stand high above a small harbour and hamlet. Inside the 14th-century chapel is an excellent collection of armour and furniture.

Return along the A394 and rejoin the A30 at Long Rock. Pass Penzance Heliport on the right and return to Penzance.

TOUR 2 45 MILES

COVES OF THE LIZARD

Wreckers once used the jagged reefs and towering cliffs of the Lizard to cripple their prey. All round the peninsula's coast are stern little villages in rocky bays, towering stacks and pinnacles of multi-hued serpentine, and the constant boom of waves crashing into hidden caves.

HELSTON, Cornwall SW62
In Elizabethan times Helston was one of Cornwall's 4 stannary or coinage towns, where all the smelted tin mined in the area was brought to be tested for quality and taxed. Even earlier it had been a busy port, until the Loe Bar formed across the mouth of the Cober River in the 13th century. Well-preserved Regency houses can be seen along Cross Street, and behind the early Victorian Guildhall is an interesting museum with many old implements, including a cider press. Local people would say that May 8 is the best day to visit the town, for that is the time of the Furry, or Floral Dance. From early in the morning the inhabitants dance through the winding streets and in and out of houses to celebrate the time a dragon dropped a rock on the town without causing any damage. About $1\frac{1}{4}$ miles south west of Helston, on the B3304, is a footpath leading left to Loe Pool.

LOE POOL, Cornwall SW62
Loe Pool, Cornwall's biggest lake, was formed 600 years ago when a bar cut the River Cober off from the sea. This natural dam consists of gravel and a type of flint not seen anywhere else in the area. A conduit takes water from the lake to prevent flooding, but in former times people who lived here had periodically to seek permission from the lord of the manor to make a cut in the bar. The lake is rich in fish, and its shoreline is attractively wooded.

Leave Helston on the A3083 SP 'Lizard'. Pass Culdrose Airfield and turn left on to the B3293, SP 'St Keverne'. The airfield entrance is close by on the left.

CULDROSE ROYAL NAVAL AIR STATION, Cornwall SW62
Navy search craft operate over a wide area of West Country water from this air-to-sea-rescue base. The public are only admitted to an aircraft viewing area.

Continue to the Mawgan Cross war memorial and branch left over crossroads on to an unclassified road for Mawgan. Bear left SP 'Manaccan, Helford' and continue through St Martin's Green to Newtown. Keep left, then in 250yds turn left again. After another $1\frac{1}{2}$ miles meet crossroads and go forwards, then in $\frac{3}{4}$ mile turn left and descend to Helford.

HELFORD, Cornwall SW72
This lovely little village on the wooded banks of the Helford River is a favourite haunt of anglers and yachtsmen. The river is dotted with small villages and creeks, and a passenger ferry sails from here to Helford Passage – where there is a bright, attractive inn.

Leave Helford and return along the same road for $\frac{3}{4}$ mile. Turn left on to an unclassified road for St Anthony.

ST ANTHONY, Cornwall SW72
The church of St Anthony in Meneage stands only 30yds from the sea. Its chancel and parts of the south wall are Norman, and tradition holds that it was built by shipwrecked Norman sailors as a thank-offering to St Anthony for saving them from drowning. The tranquil scenery of Gillan Creek presents a charming, timeless picture of Cornish maritime life.

Drive alongside the creek to leave St Anthony, and after 1 mile turn left on to an unclassified road, SP 'St Keverne'. Climb to the edge of Gillan, keep right on to a byroad, and continue into the large village of St Keverne.

A fisherman's cottage in Cadgwith.

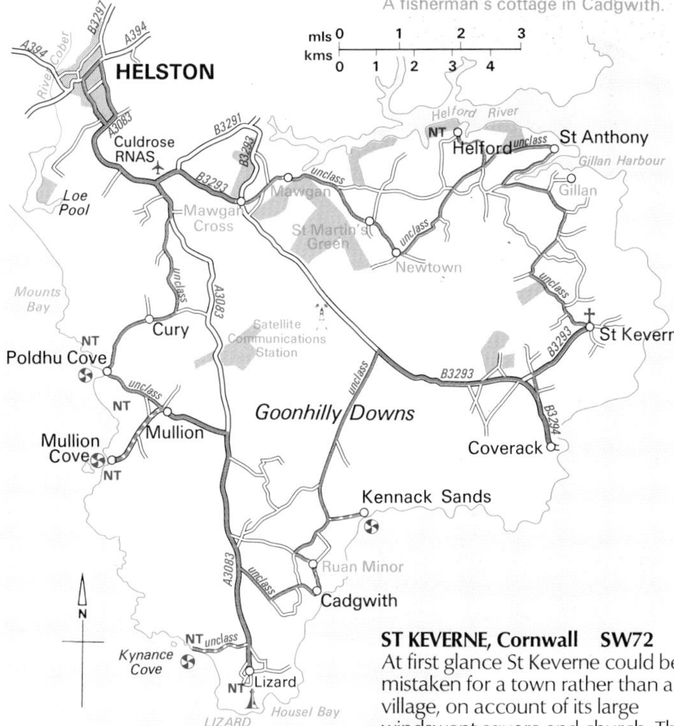

The sheltered waters and hidden creeks of Helford River once made ideal bases for the secret activities of smugglers.

ST KEVERNE, Cornwall SW72
At first glance St Keverne could be mistaken for a town rather than a village, on account of its large windswept square and church. The latter dates from the 15th century and carries an unusual octagonal spire which has been a welcome landmark for sailors for hundreds of years. Just 3 miles offshore are the treacherous Manacle Rocks, which have made shipwrecks a gruesome part of the village's history. Over 400 victims are buried at the church, including 126 people who died when the *Primrose* was wrecked in 1809. Close to the village is a bronze-age burial chamber known as the Three Brothers of Grugwith.

Leave St Keverne on the B3293 'Coverack and Helston' road. After $1\frac{1}{4}$ miles turn left on to an unclassified road and later join the B3294. From here descend into Coverack.

COVERACK, Cornwall SW71
Smugglers once frequented this small fishing village, and wreckers lured unsuspecting vessels on to the nearby Manacle Rocks to plunder their cargoes. Nowadays Coverack has a lifeboat station that was established after a particularly bad series of disasters. The harbour is overlooked by thatched cottages.

Climb out of Coverack on the B3294 and B3293 'Helston' roads, and continue for 4 miles. Meet crossroads and turn left on to an unclassified road SP 'Cadgwith'. Views to the right take in Goonhilly Downs Satellite Communications Station.

GOONHILLY DOWNS, Cornwall
Goonhilly Downs, a small windswept moor only about 7 square miles in area, was once covered by oak forests. Nowadays there is nothing here but a bleak stretch of gorse and heather dominated by the huge radio aerials of the Satellite Communications Station.

Drive over Goonhilly Downs for 3 miles and meet a T-junction. A detour from the main route leads left to Kennack Sands.

ioonhilly Downs Satellite :ommunications Station receives gnals from all over the world.

ENNACK SANDS, Cornwall SW71
Vide firm sands, wave-ribbed and otted with large shallow pools at w tide, make this a perfect beach or families with children.

ontinue for $\frac{3}{4}$ mile, meet crossroads, nd turn left for Ruan Minor. At the llage turn right and make descent (1 4) to Cadgwith.

ADGWITH, Cornwall SW71
adgwith's attractive thatched ottages overlook a stone strand otted with beached boats and the araphernalia of a working fishing ommunity. All along the coast are ndy coves, and to the south is the eat tidal chasm the Devil's Frying an. This was formed when a vast a cave collapsed, and is at its enic best in stormy weather.

ave Cadgwith, continue with an nclassified road SP 'Lizard', and cend. In $\frac{3}{4}$ mile turn right, then after other $\frac{3}{4}$ mile turn left on to the 3083. Continue straight into Lizard.

ZARD, Cornwall SW61
nile from Lizard is the headland of ard Point, the southernmost tip of ovely peninsula that has become nous for its outstanding natural auty (NT). In the heather and bogs the interior rivulets and streams to chatter down to the beach ough small valleys and, casionally, as miniature falls over edge of the cliffs. Many rare nts grow here, and some of the area is leased to the Cornwall Naturalists' Trust. Splendid walks extend along the clifftops of the Point. To the east the countryside is sheltered from the full force of Atlantic gales and is lush and green, but round the Point to the west everything becomes wilder and more desolate. Much of the land on this side is pitted with holes left by people digging for the mineral serpentine, a lovely stone prized for the rich shades of greens, reds and purple released by cutting and polishing. Magnificent views from Lizard Point extend many miles along the Cornish coast to Rame Head, (near Plymouth), and when ideal conditions prevail, as far as Bolt Head in the South Hams district of Devon. This superb vantage point forms an ideal site for the Lizard Lighthouse.

Leave Lizard by returning along the A3083 SP 'Helston'. After $\frac{1}{2}$ mile a detour can be made from the main route along a toll road to breathtaking Kynance Cove.

KYNANCE COVE, Cornwall SW61
Serpentine is seen at its very best in Kynance Cove, where spectacular formations of the mineral rise in pillars, stacks, and pyramids from a flat surface of firm sand. An infinity of shades from red through to green, blue and purple lace exposed rock surfaces and ornament the insides of sea-bored caves. High above the surrealistic beach is a stark promontory that affords wonderful views along the coast. Slightly inland is a softer landscape of grass and flowers alongside small streams that eventually trickle from the cliff edge to the beach far below.

Continue with the main tour route on the A3083, and after $3\frac{1}{2}$ miles turn left on to the B3296 for Mullion. A possible detour from the main route leads left along the B3296 to lovely Mullion Cove.

Sea, rocks, and sand combine to create a spectacular seascape at Kynance Cove.

MULLION COVE, Cornwall SW61
Almost as dramatic as Kynance, this superb cove is fringed by steep, cave-pocked cliffs that form a splendid counterpoint to rocky Mullion Island, just offshore. The small harbour (NT) here is used by local fishermen and visiting skin divers.

MULLION, Cornwall SW61
Here the local rock changes from the colourful serpentine to greenstone, a very hard mineral that will spark when struck with steel. The village itself is large, with several shops, and boasts a fine 15th-century church. Notable bench ends inside the latter date from the 16th-century and depict a jester, a monk, Instruments of the Passion, and a few profiles.

From Mullion keep left (one-way) and turn right down an unclassified road for Poldhu Cove.

POLDHU COVE, Cornwall SW61
A pleasant beach fringes the sheltered waters of this inlet. On top of the cliffs, which are composed of an unstable slate and clay mixture known as killas, the Marconi Memorial commemorates the first successful transatlantic radio signal in 1901. Some 22 years later this same spot was used for the testing of a short-wave beam system. At the beginning of the century the headland was covered in masts, aerials, wire, and sheds. All that remains now is the simple stone memorial and a few foundations.

Continue from Poldhu Cove, cross a bridge, and ascend to Cury.

CURY, Cornwall SW62
The village church of St Corentin is set in a high windy churchyard and probably dates back to Norman times. It has since been added to.

Continue through the village and in $\frac{1}{2}$ mile turn left, SP 'Helston'. In $1\frac{3}{4}$ miles turn left again to rejoin the A3083. Return to Helston.

Mullion Cove is protected from Atlantic breakers by its sturdy harbour walls.

NEWQUAY, Cornwall SW86
Magnificent beaches, fine scenery, and a wide range of amenities for the holiday-maker have made Newquay one of the most popular seaside resorts in Cornwall. The original iron-age settlement was to the north east at Porth Island, where today's tourists admire the grand cliffs and splendid caves. Since the first train arrived here in 1875 tourism has been the main factor in Newquay's growth. The railway originally came to bring china clay and tin to the port, but the harbour proved too small and shallow for large cargo ships. Because of this the harbour has retained some of its original character and preserved a number of old structures. Another area of historic charm is St Columb Minor, once the mother parish of Newquay but now just a suburb. Amongst its old and attractive cottages is the church of St Columba, whose 115ft pinnacled and lichen-covered 15th-century tower is considered one of the finest in the country. Visitors can enjoy the amusement park in Trenance Garden, which also boasts the only zoo in Cornwall, and the mile-long main beach is close to the town. Between Newquay and the surfing beach at Fistral is the rock-strewn promontory of Towan Head, which affords magnificent views.

Leave Newquay on the A392 SP 'Truro, St Austell' and continue to Quintrel Downs. Drive over a level crossing, then meet crossroads and go forward on to the A3058. After $\frac{3}{4}$ mile turn right on to a narrow unclassified road SP 'Newlyn East'. Continue for 1 mile to Trerice Manor, on the left.

TRERICE MANOR, Cornwall SW85
With its grey curving gables and E-shaped entrance front, Trerice Manor (NT) has hardly changed since it was first built by Sir John Arundell in 1573. Sir John, a member of an old and influential Cornish family, spent a great deal of time soldiering in the Low Countries. When he returned to his native Cornwall he did not entirely forget foreign parts, as the design of the house shows. Excellent plasterwork on the ceilings and fire-places is acknowledged as the most outstanding feature of the interior.

Leave Trerice Manor and continue for 1 mile, then meet crossroads and turn left. In $\frac{1}{2}$ mile a detour can be taken from the main route by turning left on to an unclassified road and driving for $\frac{1}{2}$ mile to the Lappa Valley Railway.

LAPPA VALLEY RAILWAY, Cornwall SW85
This narrow-gauge line once formed part of a Great Western route between Newquay and Chacewater. Today the steam locomotives that run on its 15-inch track haul tourist trains through a 2-mile circuit of lovely countryside. A stop is usually made at East Wheal Rose Halt, where passengers can disembark to explore the site of an old silver and lead mine.

Continue to St Newlyn East.

TOUR 3 — 40 MILES

ATLANTIC SEASCAPES

Long, foam-capped rollers crash on to ideal surfing beaches between the craggy headlands and promontories of Cornwall's Atlantic coast. Away from the shore is the gentle rise and fall of downland, scored by deep lanes and scattered with the beautifully decayed remains of mine buildings.

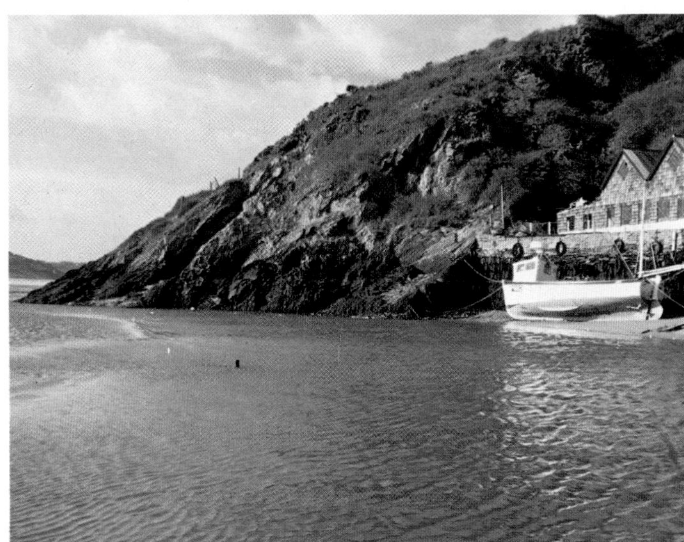

The estuary of the River Gannel opens out to form Crantock Beach.

ST NEWLYN EAST, Cornwall SW85
Known as St Newlyn East to distinguish it from the port of Newlyn near Penzance, this attractive village was probably the original settlement of Saint Newelina, the Cornish martyr to whom the parish church is dedicated. Beautiful examples of Norman and medieval carving can be seen inside the church, including particularly fine pieces of 14th-century work.

Leave St Newlyn East SP 'Truro, Redruth' and continue for 1 mile to Fiddler's Green. Turn left, then after $1\frac{1}{4}$ miles meet crossroads. Go forward, then turn right on to the A30 for Zelah. In $\frac{1}{2}$ mile meet crossroads and turn left on to an unclassified road SP 'Shortlanesend'. Continue for 2 miles to reach the Shortlanesend Inn, and join the B3284 for Truro.

TRURO, Cornwall SW84
Cathedral city of Cornwall and the county's unofficial capital, Truro stands where the rivers Allen and Kenwyn join to form the large Fal-estuary inlet known as the Truro River. Until 1752 the town was one of Cornwall's 4 stannery or coinage towns, to which all smelted tin had to be brought to be tested for quality and taxed. During this time it developed into an important centre for the export of mineral ores, and in the 18th century it became a focus of social life to rival even Bath, the country's then most fashionable town. Among the fine Georgian structures surviving from the period is the outstanding Lemon Street, which was laid out c1795 and is complemented by Walsingham Place, a beautiful early 19th-century crescent just off Victoria Place. The former Assembly Rooms date from c1770 and were the main gathering place for 18th-century society. One of Cornwall's oldest and most famous potteries, Lake's, still works in Chapel Street, and is open to visitors. Edward VII, then the Prince of Wales laid the cathedral's foundation stone in 1880. Various types of Cornish granite were used in the building's construction, and it stands on the site of the 16th-century church of St Mary. Part of the older building is retained in the east end. The Truro Museum, in River Street, is considered to be the finest in Cornwall and has a number of exhibits depicting the history of the local mineral industries.

Leave Truro following SP 'Redruth' on the A390. In 4 miles meet a roundabout and take the 2nd exit. Continue for a further $2\frac{1}{4}$ miles to another roundabout and take the 3rd exit on to the B3277 SP 'St Agnes'. Continue to St Agnes.

One of the Wheal Coates engine houses on the cliffs at Chapel Porth near St Agnes.

Atlantic waves have sculpted the natural arch at Perranporth.

ST AGNES, Cornwall SW75
St Agnes is one of those Cornish villages that has retained its charm and character despite the burden of two centuries of mining and one century of tourism. Decaying engine houses and wildflower-covered burrows bear silent witness to the mineral booms of years gone by, and ; mile north is Trevaunance Cove – a lovely place with excellent sands and reminders of a different industry. Many futile attempts have been made to build a harbour here. Remains of 18th-century piers from the last try can be seen at the western end of the cove, and today's holiday makers bask where great schooners were once built and launched. St Agnes itself fits snugly round the parish church, which was rebuilt in Cornish style during the mid-19th century but is unusual in having a slender spire. Most Cornish churches have towers. Among the pleasant streets and by-ways of the village is the quaint Stippy-Stappy, a steep and stepped row of slate-roofed cottages leading down Town Hill. The well-known beauty spot of St Agnes Beacon lies to the west.

T AGNES BEACON, ornwall SW75
is said that 32 church towers and 3 miles of coast can be seen from 28ft St Agnes Beacon (NT), perhaps he most prominent landmark in the rea. Much of the surrounding area art NT) has been worked for inerals in times past, but the many ining scars and old buildings add a elancholy beauty rather than the nse of desecration that usually ervades industrial sites. Bolster's yke, a 2-mile earthwork on the eacon, is named after a legendary ant who is supposed to have lived ere in ancient times.

/HEAL COATES ENGINE HOUSE, ornwall SW74
Wheal Coates engine house (NT) ands precariously on a forbidding ff to the west of St Agnes Beacon. nce it contained an engine which ovided the essential services of nding, pumping, and ventilation r the mine below; now it is being stored as an important relic of rnwall's past.

ave St Agnes on the B3285 rranporth road and continue for miles to Trevellas. Drive through evellas and in 1 mile descend into rranporth.

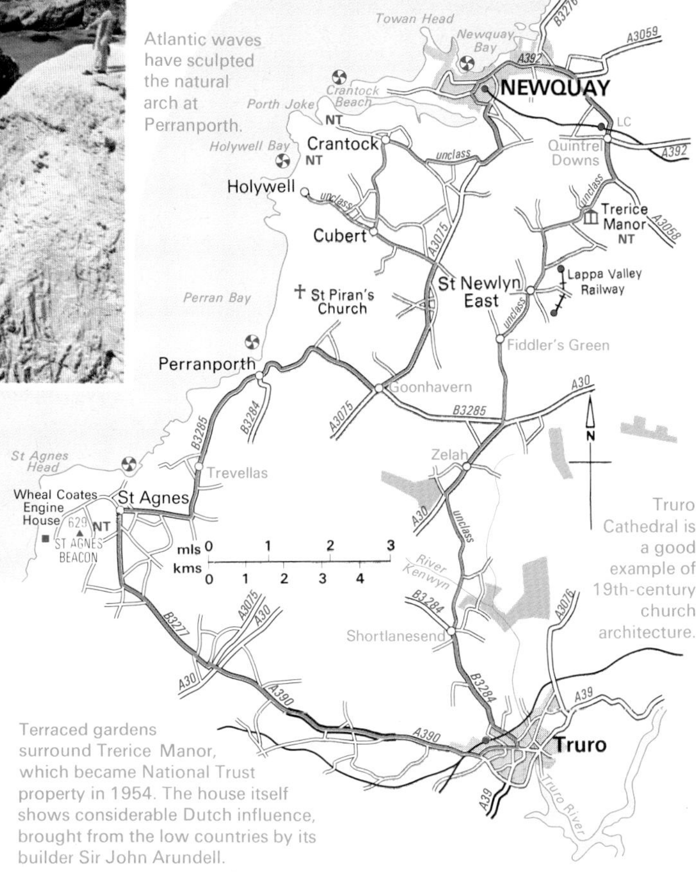

Terraced gardens surround Trerice Manor, which became National Trust property in 1954. The house itself shows considerable Dutch influence, brought from the low countries by its builder Sir John Arundell.

PERRANPORTH, Cornwall SW75
Terraces of hotels and guesthouses rise from the sea-level centre of this popular resort, which is among the more modern Cornish towns. Even though it lacks the quaint cottages and blue-jerseyed fishermen the public has been taught to expect of the west, visitors find a more than ample attraction in the magnificent bay that sweeps away to the north. This boasts a 3-mile stretch of smooth golden sand, one of the longest beaches in England, and is reputed to be where surfing was introduced into Britain. Near by, on the road to Goonhavern, is the 2,000-year old hilltop fort of St Piran's Round (AM). Nearby Penhale Point offers spectacular rock scenery, and the sands of the local bathing beach have been blown into large dunes.

ST PIRAN'S CHURCH, Cornwall SW75
Perranporth is in the parish of *Perranzabuloe* which means 'St Piran in the Sand'. St Piran is thought to have come to Cornwall from Ireland in the 6th-century, and legend has it that he wasn't always sober. However, he is said to have taught the Cornish the art of smelting and was adopted as the patron saint of tinners. He built his church north of Perranporth on the Penhale Sands, but by the 11th century shifting dunes had closed in and completely enveloped the little building. It wasn't until the 19th century that it was excavated, and nowadays it is housed in a concrete shell to protect it from further damage. The mile-long walk over easy ground to see the church is well worth the effort.

Truro Cathedral is a good example of 19th-century church architecture.

Leave Perranporth on the B3285 SP 'Newquay'. Continue for 2 miles to Goonhavern, then turn left on to the A3075. In 2¼ miles turn left on to an unclassified road for Cubert.

CUBERT, Cornwall SW75
High above the sandy landscape round Cubert is the tower of the church, a local landmark curiously shaped like a bishop's hat. Although restored in 1852 the interior of the church preserves fine Norman and 14th-century carvings and a font. In a café in the village centre are the granite remains of a 17th-century Cornish cider press.

A pleasant detour from the main route can be taken to Holywell, some 1¼ miles from Cubert.

HOLYWELL, Cornwall SW75
The large beach at Holywell Bay is quieter than most on this coastline and offers good bathing except at low tide. At the north end is a freshwater spring that gave the place its name, one of the holy wells of Cornwall. It can only be reached at low tide via steps cut into the cliff. Magnificent views can be enjoyed from Penhale Point.

Leave Cubert on an unclassified road for 'Crantock'. Continue for 1½ miles to reach Crantock.

CRANTOCK, Cornwall SW76
A plaque records that the old stocks in the churchyard here were last used in 1817 on a 'Smuggler's son and a vagabond'. This is not surprising since the village was once notorious for its involvement in contraband. The church itself is a showpiece of Edwardian restoration. Attractive countryside (NT) lines the steep-sided Gannel Estuary, which flows past the vast and increasingly popular sands of Crantock Beach.

Leave Crantock on an unclassified road SP 'Newquay'. In ¾ mile turn left on to another unclassified road and continue for 1 mile to the A3075. Turn left and return to Newquay.

TOUR 4 81 MILES

BETWEEN BODMIN AND THE SEA

Majestic cliffs indented by tiny harbours are typical of north Cornwall. So also are the long sands of Bude Bay, the eerie enchantment of Arthur's Castle at Tintagel, and the dark counterpoint of Bodmin Moor rising inland.

WADEBRIDGE, Cornwall SW97
One of the finest medieval bridges in England can be seen here. Built c 1485 and widened in 1849, it spans the River Camel with 17 arches and measures 320ft long. It is thought that packs of wool may have been sunk into the river bed to make firm bases for the piers. Also of interest is the Cornish Motor Museum, which has vintage cars and traction engines amongst its many displays.

Leave Wadebridge on the A39 'Bude' road and drive for ½ mile before turning left on to the B3314 SP 'Port Isaac'. After 3 miles turn left again on to an unclassified road SP 'Rock'. In a further 1½ miles turn right. A detour from the main route can be made by continuing ahead for 1 mile to Rock.

ROCK, Cornwall SW97
Rock is separated from Padstow by the lovely Camel Estuary. The small Church of St Michael, at nearby Porthilly, was dug from drifting sand and houses a simple Norman font.

Continue along the main tour route and pass through Trebetherick to reach Polzeath.

POLZEATH, Cornwall SW97
Safe bathing and excellent sands that offer some of the best surfing in Cornwall are the main attractions of Polzeath. The village stands on Padstow Bay and the wide Camel estuary, within easy reach of beautiful walking country (NT) round Portquin. Fine views over Portquin Bay can be enjoyed from Pentire Head, to the north.

Leave Polzeath and ascend sharply. After 2 miles branch left on to a road SP 'Port Isaac'. In ½ mile turn left on to the B3314 for St Endellion.

ST ENDELLION, Cornwall SW97
Although inland from sheltered Portquin Bay, St Endellion occupies an exposed site and often feels the full force of the gales for which this part of the country is known. Its beautiful compact church was built from Lundy Island granite. Inside, under the 18th-century tower arch, are several quaint bell-ringer's rhymes. A number of amusing and somewhat irreverent Georgian epitaphs can be seen on old gravestones in the churchyard.

Leave St Endellion and continue along the B3314 for 1 mile, then turn left on to the B3267 for Port Isaac.

PORT ISAAC, Cornwall SW98
In the old part of this outstandingly picturesque fishing village the houses huddle together along a steep coombe and down to the harbour.

From Port Isaac continue on an unclassified road and descend to Port Gaverne. Pass through the village and curve inland. After 2 miles rejoin the B3314 and continue to Delabole.

DELABOLE, Cornwall SX08
At one time most of the roofs in Cornwall came from the ancient slate quarry in this village, which is estimated to have been worked continuously for at least 300 years. A path through the old village gives impressive views into the vast excavations left by this once flourishing industry.

Since the 19th century Boscastle has declined as a port but developed as a resort.

Leave Delabole and continue on the B3314 for 1¾ miles, then turn left on to an unclassified road SP 'Tintagel'. After ½ mile keep forward to join the B3263. Just before the village of Trewarmett a road to the left offers a pleasant detour to Trebarwith Strand.

TREBARWITH STRAND, Cornwall SX08
The good beach in this cove is crossed by a natural slate causeway, which leads down to the water's edge from the high-water line.

Continue through Trewarmett on the main tour route and drive to Tintagel.

TINTAGEL, Cornwall SX08
The name Tintagel is highly evocative of the Arthurian legends, but the only King Arthur's Hall here nowadays is the modern home of the Fellowship of the Round Table. The local post office (NT) is a superb slate-built structure that dates from the 14th century and was originally a small manor house. Norman workmanship is very evident in the local church, but its origins are probably farther back in Saxon time. A Norman font and Roman milestone can be seen inside.

TINTAGEL CASTLE, Cornwall SX08
High on the jagged, broken cliffs nea Tintagel is a romantically ruined cas (AM) that, according to legend, was the birthplace of King Arthur. Its remains post-date that giant of Western folklore by some 7 centuri but traces of a Celtic monastery (AM founded early enough to have accommodated him can be seen cl by. The castle itself was built on its wave-lashed promontory by Regina Earl of Cornwall and illegitimate sor Henry I, in the 12th century. Views from here take in the great slate caverns on the other side of Tintag Cove, and a waterfall that plunges down the face of the cliff.

From the Wharncliffe Hotel in Tintag follow the B3263 'Boscastle' road, an after about ¾ mile reach Bossiney. Leave Bossiney on the B3263, then continue for another ½ mile to reach Rocky Valley and St Nectan's Kieve Waterfall.

Tintagel Castle is divided in two by a breathtaking chasm.

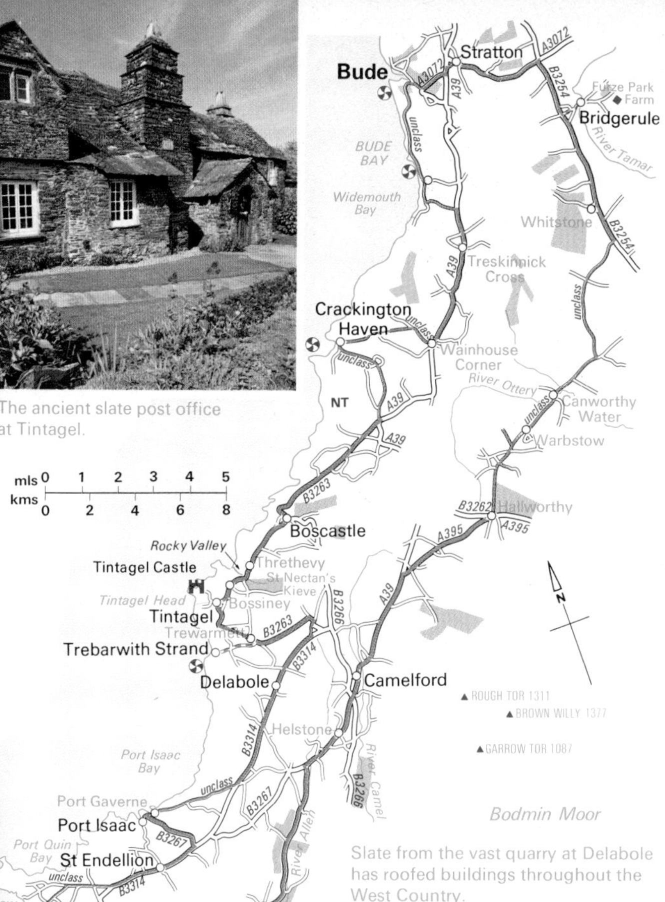

The ancient slate post office at Tintagel.

Rockpools are a feature of Widemouth Bay, which is situated to the south of Bude.

Slate from the vast quarry at Delabole has roofed buildings throughout the West Country.

OCKY VALLEY, Cornwall SX08
rees, stone, and water all contribute ieir own particular magic to the vonderful scenery of Rocky Valley, a eep cut sloping down to the sea. bout 1 mile along the valley is its ıost magnificent feature, the 40ft vaterfall of St Nectan's Kieve. Nectan r Knighton) was a Celtic hermit iint said to have had an oratory eside the kieve (basin).

ontinue on the B3263, pass through rethevy, and after $1\frac{3}{4}$ miles turn left ı to a road SP 'Bude'. Descend eeply through a hairpin bend to ıscastle.

OSCASTLE, Cornwall SX09
ıe combined Valency and Jordan vers meet incoming tides with amatic effect at Boscastle, articularly when the moon is full ıd the rivers are running at full ate. A long mole has been built to otect the strong-walled harbour ainst the worst effects of the nflict, but even on a relatively lm day the sea is thrown high over e stones. A local blowhole amply monstrates the force of the water. scastle itself is an attractive village ranged round a long, broad street at climbs steeply through ıodland. Close to the harbour is a ches' museum of interesting (and en gruesome) relics associated th magic and witchcraft. At one ıe the local seal population was verely reduced by hunters, but this lustry is now controlled.

Leave Boscastle, cross a river bridge, and ascend (1 in 6). After $2\frac{3}{4}$ miles join the A39 and immediately turn left on to an unclassified road SP 'Crackington Haven'. Later descend steeply into the village of Crackington Haven.

CRACKINGTON HAVEN, Cornwall SX19
This tiny seaside village stands on a rugged stretch of coast and has a good surfing beach. High Cliff, to the south, drops 700ft in a series of weathered faces and terraces.

Leave Crackington Haven and ascend. After 3 miles reach the village of Wainhouse Corner and turn left on to the A39. Continue past Treskinnick Cross, then $1\frac{1}{4}$ miles farther turn left on to an unclassified road SP 'Widemouth'. After $\frac{3}{4}$ mile follow the wide sweep of Widemouth Bay to Bude.

BUDE, Cornwall SS20
One of Bude's main attractions is its huge surfing beach, where strong winds that have caused hundreds of wrecks over the centuries provide a constant supply of rollers ideal for the sport. The town itself is sheltered from the full force of the weather by ridges of downland between it and the sea. See also tour 8.

Leave Bude by turning away from the coast on the A3072 'Bideford' road. After $1\frac{1}{4}$ miles turn left on to the A39, continue for $\frac{1}{4}$ mile, then turn right and rejoin the A3072, SP 'Holsworthy'. Drive into Stratton.

STRATTON, Cornwall SS20
This picturesque grouping of attractive houses and thatched cottages has a peaceful atmosphere that belies its turbulent history. In 1643 a Civil War battle was fought here; the Tree Inn was the headquarters of Sir Bevil Grenville before he led his Cavaliers to victory at Stamford Hill, just north of the village. Local legend recalls Anthony Payne, a 7ft giant who was born in the Tree Inn and was a retainer in Sir Bevil's household. The village church dates from the 15th century and houses good 16th-century brasses. See also tour 8.

Leave Stratton by continuing on the A3072 'Holsworthy' road. After about 2 miles turn right on to the B3254 SP 'Launceston'. After $1\frac{1}{4}$ miles a pleasant detour from the main route can be made by turning left on to an unclassified road for Bridgerule.

BRIDGERULE, Cornwall SS20
Furze Farm Park at Bridgerule features 30 different breeds of cattle and sheep, an agricultural museum, a pets' corner, blacksmith's shop, cider hall and an old dairy. Visitors can enjoy the additional attractions of sideshows and tractor rides during the summer season.

Continuing on the main route, drive along the B3254 to Whitstone and $\frac{3}{4}$ mile beyond the village turn right on to an unclassified road SP 'Week St Mary'. Continue for $1\frac{1}{4}$ miles, meet crossroads, and drive straight on towards Canworthy Water. After 2 miles on this narrow road turn right to Canworthy Water. Keep straight on and after 1 mile ascend to Warbstow. Continue to Hallworthy, turn right on to the A395, and in another $2\frac{3}{4}$ miles turn left on to the A39 SP 'Wadebridge'. Continue to Camelford.

CAMELFORD, Cornwall SX18
One of the more obscure Arthurian legends places Camelford as having been the site of Camelot, the fabulous city of King Arthur and his Knights of the Round Table. Slaughter Bridge, which crosses the Camel River 1 mile north of the town, is one of several contenders for the title 'Arthur's last battleground'.

Leave Camelford on the A39 and keep straight on. Pass through Helstone, crossing the River Allen at Knightsmill, and continue to St Kew Highway.

ST KEW HIGHWAY, Cornwall SX07
Old stocks are preserved in the porch of the village church, and inside is a very fine Elizabethan pulpit decorated with ornamental panels. Also here is a stone inscribed with characters of the Celtic Ogham script, an ancient form of writing.

Remain on the A39 and return to Wadebridge.

TOUR 5 56 MILES

PLYMOUTH AND THE WESTERN MOOR

This is the country of Drake and Raleigh, of large adventures in small boats and salty tales that the historians have somehow missed. North are the water-sculpted tors and heathy slopes of western Dartmoor, a place of vast spaces patterned with the shadows of clouds.

PLYMOUTH, Devon SX45
Sandwiched between the estuaries of the Plym and the Tamar, this popular yachting resort and important maritime city is the venue for national sailing championships and a stop-off point for round-the-world yachtsmen. It has been a naval base since the 16th century, and in the 17th the Pilgrim Fathers sailed from its Sutton Harbour to the New World of America in the *Mayflower*. Their last glimpses of England would have included much of the present-day Barbican – Plymouth's Elizabethan quarter. Today Sutton Harbour is busy with large and small boats, and the delightful craft and antique shops of the Barbican make it an exciting district of modern Plymouth as well as a fascinating historic memorial. Most of the city centre was rebuilt after appalling war damage, and the area where Royal Parade is bisected by spacious Armada Way includes one of the finest shopping complexes in Europe. The 200ft Civic Centre affords excellent cross-town views from its roof deck (open in summer). A prominent statue of Sir Francis Drake shares the Hoe with Smeaton's Tower (open), which is the re-erected base of the old Eddystone Lighthouse. This was removed from the rocks in 1881 because of serious erosion. Near by are the 17th-century Royal Citadel (AM) and the outstanding aquarium of the Marine Biological Association. Rising from the waters of the sound, almost in front of the Hoe, is the rocky, tree-scattered hump of Drake's Island (NT). The city's Church of St Andrew is the largest in Devon and dates from the 15th century. Close by is Prysten House, which is the city's oldest building (open) and is thought to have been built by monks from nearby Plympton. Across the estuary is the beautiful house and park of Mount Edgcumbe, which can be reached via the Cremyll Passenger Ferry from Plymouth.

MOUNT EDGCUMBE HOUSE & PARK, Cornwall SX45
This beautiful Tudor mansion (open) was severely damaged during World War II but has since been completely restored. Its lovely gardens and parkland offer extensive views of Plymouth Sound.

West of the city and linked to it by car ferry is the town of Torpoint.

TORPOINT, Cornwall SX45
Situated on the Hamoaze, the estuary of the River Tamar, this small town boasts a fine 18th-century house (NT) which is particularly noted for its very good 19th-century entrance way.

DEVONPORT, Devon SX45
Although Devonport started life with an identity of its own, the establishment of the important naval dockyard on the Hamoaze in 1691 resulted in its rapid development into the navy quarter of neighbouring Plymouth. Its fine 19th-century town hall was by the architect John Foulston, and older foundations include the Gun Wharf of 1718 and the Royal Naval Hospital, also of the 18th century.

THE TAMAR BRIDGES, Devon SX45
Spanning the Tamar river north-west of Plymouth city centre are two famous bridges that have opened up the West Country to tourism. The oldest is the Royal Albert, a railway bridge designed by the brilliant engineer Brunel and completed in 1859. Close by is a modern, single-span suspension road bridge with a lightness and grace that contrast sharply with the heavy solidity of its elderly neighbour.

Sir Francis Drake's statue stands on Plymouth Hoe.

Leave Plymouth with SP 'Exeter A38' and enter the Plympton roundabout. Take the 2nd exit on to the A374 road and cross the River Plym. After $\frac{1}{2}$ mile pass a right turn leading to Saltram House.

SALTRAM HOUSE, Devon SX55
This fine Tudor house (NT) has an 18th-century façade and contains a saloon and dining room by designer Robert Adam. Features of the lovely garden include an 18th-century summer house and a quaint orangery dating from 1773.

Continue on the A374 for a further $\frac{3}{4}$ mile and meet a mini-roundabout. A short detour from the main route to the village of Plympton can be made from here by keeping forward.

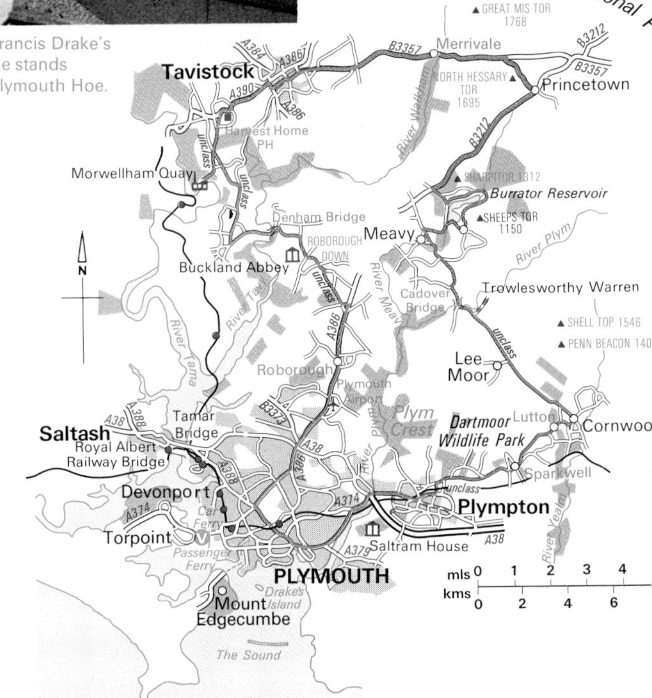

For many hundreds of years the vast Tamar estuary protected the West Country peoples from invasion.

PLYMPTON, Devon SX55
In medieval times Plymouth was an insignificant little hamlet called Sutton, and Plympton an important town with a wealthy priory. Since then the elder community has become a suburb of the successful younger. A Norman keep on a mound affords goods views.

From the mini-roundabout on the main route turn left SP 'Exeter', and in another $\frac{1}{2}$ mile turn left again SP 'Sparkwell' and 'Cornwood'. In $\frac{1}{4}$ mile meet a T-junction, turn right, and continue to Sparkwell. Beyond the village reach the Dartmoor Wildlife Park on the left.

DARTMOOR WILDLIFE PARK, Devon SX55
A fine collection of British and European animals can be seen in the 25-acre zoo park. Excellent all-round views of the grounds are afforded by a tall observation tower.

Continue through Lutton to Cornwood.

CORNWOOD, Devon SX65
Woodlands known as the Hawns and Dendles surround this pleasant village, which is attractively sited in the Yealm Valley and makes a good touring centre for west Dartmoor. Dendles Wood incorporates a national nature reserve, and there are numerous bronze-age enclosures and hut circles in the district. The family seats of the Raleighs and Drakes stand near by.

Drive to crossroads in the village and turn left SP 'Tavistock'. Begin a gradual ascent on to Lee Moor, with Penn Beacon prominent to the right.

orwellham Quay is linked to Tavistock y an unusual underground canal.

E MOOR, Devon SX56
olossal conical mountains of white aste dominate the landscape here, oclaiming Lee Moor as Devon's incipal source of china clay.

gin a descent from Lee Moor with 546ft Shell Top to the right. Later ach a track leading right to owlesworthy Warren nature trail.

OWLESWORTHY WARREN, von SX56
is 1½-mile nature trail flanks the uth-west corner of Dartmoor ngside the River Plym. Prehistoric t circles can be seen near the er's headwaters.

ntinue the descent and shortly ar right across the River Plym at dover Bridge. Ascend, and at the mmit turn right SP 'Sheepstor, avy'. Descend into Meavy Valley, ssing the river to reach the edge of avy. A short detour can be made the village by turning left here.

AVY, Devon SX56
stream from which this delightful age takes its name winds through odlands over a rocky bed and rs over a small waterfall. Beside Norman church on the village en is an ancient oak which is litionally held to be the church's temporary.

Cox Tor is situated north of the B3357 road between Tavistock and Merrivale.

Continue forward (away from Meavy) on the main drive SP 'Dousland, Princetown' and in ½ mile turn sharp right SP 'Sheepstor'. In ¾ mile turn right again and cross the dam of Burrator Reservoir. In another ¾ mile turn left. A short detour to Sheepstor village can be made by bearing right here.

SHEEPSTOR & THE BURRATOR RESERVOIR, Devon SX56
This enchanting hamlet is centred round an appealing little granite church. The picturesque Burrator Reservoir offers a dramatic backcloth, its sparkling waters reflecting the massive height of Sheeps Tor and the wooded slopes that rise from the opposite shore.

Skirt the reservoir on a narrow road and after 3 miles turn sharp right SP 'Princetown'. Ascend, and in ¾ mile meet crossroads and turn right again on to the B3212. Climb on to the wide, open moorland of Dartmoor National Park to reach Princetown. On the approach to Princetown are views left of 1,695ft North Hessary Tor and a BBC transmitter.

DARTMOOR NATIONAL PARK (WEST), Devon
Much of this tour is in the south-western part of this vast area, and near Princetown it climbs on to the rugged uplands of the moor itself. The landscape is dramatic and full of contrast, where jagged granite tors rise ghostlike out of dangerous moorland mists. Among the bracken-clad slopes are peat bogs constantly replenished by the highest rainfall in Devon, though here and there great plantations of conifers are helping to dry the ground and bring back the forests that once stood here. Prehistoric crosses and hut circles are common in these parts. See also tour 6.

PRINCETOWN, Devon SX57
Sir Thomas Tyrwhitt founded the great convict prison here in 1806 and named the town in honour of his friend, the Prince Regent. Forced labour built many of the roads that allow modern motorists to tour comfortably through remote parts of the moor, and the town church was built by prisoners in 1883.

At Princetown turn left on to the B3357 'Tavistock' road, shortly passing the prison, then in 1 mile meet a T-junction and turn left again. Great Mis Tor rises to 1,768ft to the right, and views ahead encompass the Tamar estuary and Bodmin Moor. Gradually descend from Dartmoor itself and pass Merrivale Quarry in the Walkham Valley to leave the Dartmoor National Park and enter Tavistock.

Buckland Abbey contains many items connected with Sir Francis Drake, including a portrait of Elizabeth I in panelled Drake's Drawing Room.

TAVISTOCK, Devon SX47
Light engineering and timber-working firms in this pleasant little market town continue an industrial tradition that started at least as far back as the 14th century. At that time tin mining was the big money maker, but cloth came into its own in the 15th century and the discovery of copper brought a new mineral boom in the 19th. Despite this activity the town remains unspoilt, an ideal touring base on the western fringe of the extensive Dartmoor National Park.

Leave Tavistock on the A390 'Liskeard' road. In 2½ miles reach the Harvest Home PH and branch left on to an unclassified road SP 'Bere Alston, Morwellham'. In 1 mile meet crossroads and go forward, SP 'Morwellham'. Follow a long descent to Morwellham Quay.

MORWELLHAM QUAY, Devon SX46
This quay was once a busy copper-loading port on the River Tamar. Surviving installations now form part of a major industrial museum featuring the history of the port in particular and the development of the Devon copper mines in general.

Return to the crossroads and turn sharp right SP 'Bere Alston'. Continue along a high ridge between the Tamar and Tavy valleys, and after 2¾ miles turn sharp left SP 'Denham Bridge, Plymouth'. After a long descent cross the River Tavy at Denham Bridge and immediately turn right SP 'Plymouth'. Ascend to a T-junction and turn right SP 'Buckland Abbey'. In ½ mile meet crossroads and turn right, then turn left passing the entrance to Buckland Abbey on the right.

BUCKLAND ABBEY, Devon SX46
Originally built by Cistercian monks in 1278, Buckland Abbey was considerably altered and adapted as a dwelling place by the Grenville family. The present house (NT) was sold to Sir Francis Drake in 1581, and nowadays contains a Drake Museum full of relics associated with the great sailor.

In 1¾ miles drive to crossroads at the edge of Roborough Down and turn left. Meet a T-junction and turn right on to the A386 (no SP) for Plymouth. Pass through Roborough, with Plym Forest to the left, and skirt Plymouth Airport. Return to the city centre.

TOUR 6 — 48 MILES

BELOW THE HIGH MOOR

Below the desolate summits of the high moor is a gentler country, where small rivers tumble through deep wooded valleys, and mellow old towns maintain a pace of life long gone elsewhere in England. Here were the tin, wool, and market centres of Dartmoor - the focuses of Devonshire life.

DARTMOOR NATIONAL PARK (EAST), Devon
The south-eastern edge of the vast national park that surrounds Dartmoor proper is a kinder country than the wild, high plateau farther inland. Here are wind-haunted heathlands clad with bracken and heather, where granite outcrops raise strange weathered silhouettes against the sky and the remains of prehistoric settlements survive underfoot. Country lanes strung with picturesque villages of thatch and stone lead into lush river valleys and round the flanks of the occasional 1,000ft-plus hills. See also tour 5.

ASHBURTON, Devon SX76
Once an important tin and cloth centre on a popular coaching route, Ashburton is attractively sited on the River Yeo and makes an ideal base from which to tour this side of the national park. Its cobbled streets and old tile-hung houses impart their own particular charm to the town, and the fine local church features a characteristic Devon stair turret.

From Ashburton follow SP 'Buckland' along an unclassified road and shortly turn left across the River Ashburn. Ascend, and pass beneath the slopes of Buckland Beacon.

BUCKLAND BEACON, Devon SX77
At the summit of this 1,282ft hill, which commands good all-round views, is the Ten Commandments Stone, carved by a local stonemason.

BUCKLAND-IN-THE-MOOR, Devon SX77
Although visited by many people as one of the county's show villages, Buckland-in-the-Moor remains unspoilt. Its 15th- and 16th-century church contains a notable rood-screen, and the church clock has an unusual dial on which the hours are marked by the letters 'My Dear Mother' instead of numbers.

Continue for 1 mile, meet a T-junction, and turn left SP 'Widecombe'. Descend into the attractive East Webburn Valley and cross the river, then ascend to another T-junction. Turn right, and in 1 mile enter Widecombe-in-the- Moor.

WIDECOMBE-IN-THE-MOOR, Devon SX77
Probably the best known and by far the most commercialized of the Dartmoor villages, Widecombe stands at 800ft and is dominated by the 120ft tower of its fine 14th-century church - often referred to as the Cathedral of the Moor. Adjacent are the Church House (NT) and the green, where the Widdecombe Fair of song fame is held on the second Tuesday in September.

Leave by the 'Bovey Tracey' road, bearing right past the green, and ascend on to open moorland. Later pass 1,560ft Rippon Tor on the right and enjoy magnificent views over South Devon to Torbay. To the left are 1,350ft Saddle Tor and the famous Haytor Rocks.

Ancient farmsteads shelter in many of Dartmoor's deep coombs.

HAYTOR ROCKS, Devon SX77
These rocks rise 100ft above the surrounding moorland heights and form one of the most spectacular crags in the national park. They are easily accessible by car, simple to climb, and afford superb views of the coastline and the rich, cultivated lowlands of Devon. During the 19th century stone worked from nearby quarries was loaded on to a tramway and hauled some 6 miles to a canal wharf at Teigngrace by horses. The track is still visible in places.

Descend to the Bovey Valley and after 3 miles meet crossroads by the Edgemoor Hotel. Turn left, and in $\frac{1}{2}$ mile turn left again on to the B3344 SP 'Manaton'. Shortly pass the Yarner Wood National Nature Reserve on the left.

YARNER WOOD NATIONAL NATURE RESERVE, Devon SX77
This reserve protects the mature stands of oak, holly, birch, and rowan that make up an unspoilt woodland rich with birdlife. A nature trail has been laid out here, and the necessary visitors' permits are available from the entrance lodge.

The church at Widecombe-in-the-Moor.

Continue a winding climb across the slopes of Trendlebere Down and enter dense woodland surrounding Becka Fa

BECKA FALLS, Devon SX78
Best seen after heavy rain, these falls are created by the picturesque Becka Brook as it leaps and plunges 70ft down a series of great boulders.

Continue on the B3344 to Manaton.

MANATON, Devon SX78
Once the home of novelist John Galsworthy, Manaton is a scattered moorland hamlet with a typical 15th-century church. A notable feature of the latter is its fine rood-screen, which extends right across the building. The town itself has a pleasant green surrounded by trees and overlooked by the thatched Church House. About $1\frac{1}{2}$ miles south west of the town is Hound Tor, where there is a medieval settlement of long houses inhabited from Saxon times to cAD1300. Bowerman's Nose, an outcrop of rock weathered into a curiously distinctive shape, can be seen $\frac{3}{4}$ mile to the south.

Continue for $\frac{3}{4}$ mile from Manaton Church and meet a T-junction. Turn right on to the unclassified 'North Bovey' road, descend steeply, and after $1\frac{1}{2}$ miles cross the River Bovey. Ascend into North Bovey.

NORTH BOVEY, Devon SX78
Many people consider this east Dartmoor village to be the most picturesque in Devon. The River Bovey countryside that surrounds it enchanting, and the unspoilt village green is complemented by the delightful Ring of Bells Inn. Inside the church is a fine screen with statuett

Turn left to leave the village, and in $\frac{1}{4}$ mile descend and bear right SP 'Princetown'. Recross the river, ascen sharply, and bear right. In $1\frac{1}{4}$ miles meet a T-junction and turn left on to the B3212 SP 'Princetown'. Ascend o to open moorland and after 2 miles reach an unclassified left turn leading to Grimspound and 1,737ft Hameldown Tor.

GRIMSPOUND, Devon SX78
This fine example of a bronze-age shepherd settlement consists of 24 small hut circles in a walled enclosure with a paved entrance. S Arthur Conan Doyle used the brooding atmosphere of the area ir *The Hound of the Baskervilles.*

Continue on the B3212 and climb tc road summit of 1,426ft near the Warren House Inn.

WARREN HOUSE INN, Devon SX
A traditional welcome in the form a peat fire that has been burning continously for over 100 years wait here. The inn takes its name from one of the park's many rabbit warrens. A footpath leads to the headstream of the West Webburr and the remains of artificial ravines dug by long-dead tin miners.

Continue to the village of Postbridg

Bowerman's Nose stands south of Manaton.

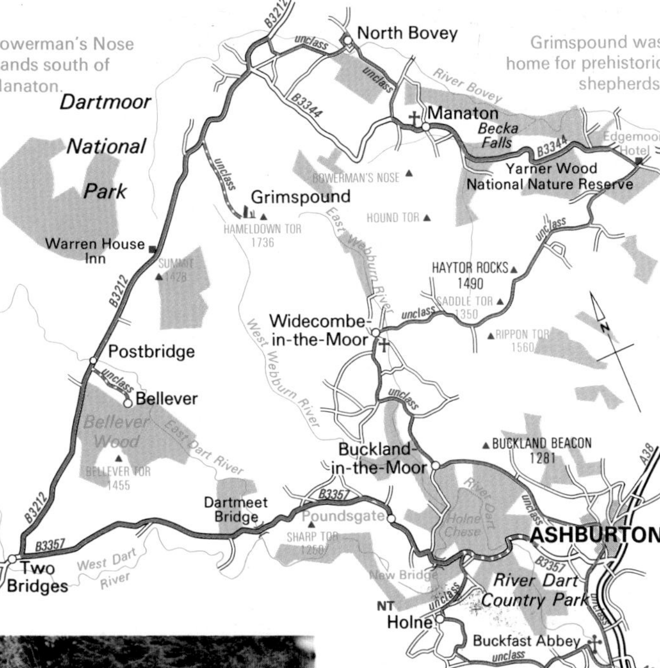

Grimspound was home for prehistoric shepherds.

…ckland-in-the-Moor's cottages are …lt to weather the roughest storms.

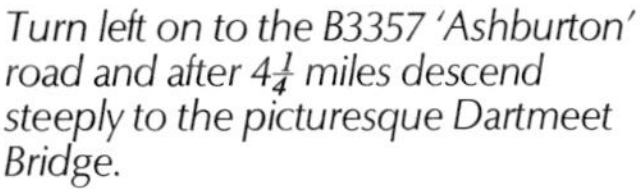

…STBRIDGE, Devon SX67
…small touring centre for the moor, …stbridge derives its name from a …dge that once carried the earliest …rtmoor post road between Exeter …d south Cornwall across the East …rt River. A few yards south is the …gest and by far the most …pressive of Dartmoor's clapper …dges. This primitive-looking …ucture is massively constructed …m huge granite slabs, and is …ught to have been built when the …er moor was opened up for …ning and farming some time …ring the 13th century.

…yond the bridge a detour can be …en from the main route by turning …along an unclassified road and …sing Bellever Wood to reach …ever picnic site and nature trail.

BELLEVER, Devon SX67
Numerous hut circles and other prehistoric monuments survive in this area. Also here are 2 fascinating nature trails laid out for visitors by the Forestry Commission.

Continue on the main route with the B3212 and reach the edge of Two Bridges.

TWO BRIDGES, Devon SX67
A pub and little else stands at this junction of the only 2 major routes across central Dartmoor. North east is Crockern Tor, where the so-called Tinner's Parliament once met at irregular intervals to enact special laws governing the stannary towns where tin was valued and taxed. Wistman's Wood, a forest nature reserve some $1\frac{1}{2}$ miles north near the West Dart River, features a mature stand of rare dwarf oaks.

Turn left on to the B3357 'Ashburton' road and after $4\frac{1}{4}$ miles descend steeply to the picturesque Dartmeet Bridge.

DARTMEET BRIDGE, Devon SX67
Here, where the East and West Dart Rivers join forces to descend through a deep valley to Dartmouth, is one of the most popular beauty spots in the national park. Footpaths which wind through the valley allow some of the spectacular gorge-like scenery to be seen at close range.

Ascend (1 in 5) to the neighbourhood of 1,250ft Sharp Tor for fine views down the valley, and continue to Poundsgate. Descend steeply to cross the river at Newbridge, where there is a picnic site, and enter the woods of Holne Chase. In $\frac{1}{2}$ mile turn right on to an unclassified road. A detour from the main route to the River Dart Country Park can be made here by continuing forward on the B3357 for $1\frac{3}{4}$ miles.

RIVER DART COUNTRY PARK, Devon SX77
Oak coppice, marshland, and valley bogs make up the varied landscape of this country park, which adjoins Holne Woods (NT) and occupies both banks of the River Dart.

Continue on the main route to Holne.

HOLNE, Devon SX76
In 1819 the attractive late-Georgian rectory above the River Dart here was the birthplace of novelist Charles Kingsley. Holne Church dates from c1300 and houses a good screen featuring a wealth of detail. An hour glass is incorporated in the carved pulpit. A fine walk leads west of the village along the Sandy Way to the source of the River Avon.

Follow SP 'Buckfastleigh' along a narrow road and in $\frac{1}{2}$ mile bear right. In a farther $\frac{1}{2}$ mile descend (1 in 5), and at the bottom keep left. In $1\frac{1}{2}$ miles meet crossroads and turn left SP 'Buckfast, Totnes'. In $\frac{1}{4}$ mile bear right then immediately left, and in $\frac{3}{4}$ mile enter Buckfast village to pass the famous abbey.

BUCKFAST ABBEY, Devon SX76
Buckfast Abbey was founded in the 10th century, refounded 2 centuries later, and rebuilt on the old foundations by the Benedictine monks themselves between 1907 and 1938. A magnificent mosaic pavement has been laid inside the church. Near by is the House of Shells museum, which demonstrates the use of shells in arts and crafts.

Continue for $\frac{1}{2}$ mile to meet a T-junction. A short detour can be made from the main route by turning right into Buckfastleigh here.

BUCKFASTLEIGH, Devon SX76
A long flight of steps leading to the church in this old wool town affords excellent views. Inside the church, which has an early-English chancel, is a notable Norman font.

DART VALLEY RAILWAY, Devon SX76
The northern terminus of this revived steam line, originally built in 1872 to serve the mining and farming industries, is in Buckfastleigh. Great Western rolling stock and a number of locomotives from that company are stored here. The 14-mile round trip to Totnes Riverside (where passengers cannot join or leave trains) takes 63 minutes and affords excellent views of the superb Dart Valley countryside.

Follow the main route by turning left at the T-junction before the detour. Cross the River Dart by Dart Bridge, turn left again, and in $1\frac{3}{4}$ miles meet a T-junction. Turn left on to the B3357, then shortly right on to an unclassified road. Return to Ashburton.

TOUR 7 73 MILES

THE HILLS OF EAST DEVON

East Devon is a mild, well-rounded collection of contrasts. Gracious Regency coastal resorts rub shoulders with working fishing villages, sub-tropical gardens grow alongside native woodlands, and little stone farms fringe the parkland estates of great country houses.

EXMOUTH, Devon SY08
Situated on the estuary of the River Exe, this pleasant town is the oldest and one of the largest seaside resorts in Devon. Its sandy beaches offer safe and sheltered bathing, and extensive coastal views can be enjoyed from The Maer, a tussocky piece of land above the esplanade. Local tourist facilities include a small zoo and an open-air swimming pool. Good Georgian houses can be seen in The Beacon, and a picturesque group near by includes quaint almshouses and a tiny chapel. A passenger ferry makes frequent estuary crossings between Exmouth and its sister town of Starcross.

A LA RONDE, Devon SY08
This unusual circular house (open) stands north of the Exeter road and was built in 1798 by a Miss Jane Parminter. Its rooms are arranged around an octagonal hall, and the curious Shell Gallery is imaginatively decorated with shells, feathers, and fascinating pictures made from a variety of natural objects.

Leave Exmouth on the A376 and pass through attractive woodland scenery to Budleigh Salterton.

BUDLEIGH SALTERTON, Devon SY08
During the 13th century this Ottermouth village was a salt-panning community supplying the local priory. At the mouth of the river is a shingle beach backed by red sandstone cliffs, and less than a mile away are the challenging fairways of the best golf course in south Devon. Several Georgian houses can be seen in the town, and a small but interesting museum called the Fairlynch Arts Centre is in an 18th-century thatched house.

Continue along the A376 SP 'East Budleigh'. After 2 miles meet crossroads and turn left on to an unclassified road. Enter East Budleigh.

EAST BUDLEIGH, Devon SY08
Typical of many Devon communities, this charming little village has delightful thatched cottages and seems hardly to have been touched by time.

A miniature railway provides a mobile viewpoint from which to enjoy the varied scenery of Bicton Gardens.

HAYES BARTON, Devon SY08
Nestling in a wooded dale about 1 mile west of East Budleigh is the thatched 16th-century house of Hayes Barton (not open), birthplace of the famous adventurer Sir Walter Raleigh in 1552.

Meet East Budleigh Church and turn right to shortly rejoin the A376. Proceed to the next crossroads, where there is an obelisk.

The Exeter Ship Canal has carried water-borne traffic since 1566.

Ottery St Mary's 14th-century church

THE OBELISK, Devon SY08
This curious and rather attractive white-stone cross is dated 1743 and carries route directions couched in biblical terms and phrases.

A possible detour leads 1 mile to the right, across the River Otter, to Otterton.

OTTERTON, Devon SY08
Fine thatched cottages and a handsome chestnut grove combine to make this one of the most picturesque villages in the area. At one time it was the centre of the Honiton lace industry.

Keep forward on the A376 and after $\frac{1}{2}$ mile reach the entrance to Bicton Gardens on the left.

BICTON GARDENS, Devon SY08
These gardens (open) form part of Lord Clinton's estate and are among the most beautiful in Britain. Le Nôtre, the designer of the superb gardens of Versailles in France, laid out the fine lawns of the Italian Garden in 1735. Other features include a narrow-gauge woodland railway and a large children's adventure playground.

After $1\frac{1}{2}$ miles turn right on to the A3052 and enter Newton Poppleford. Cross the River Otter and ascend alongside Harpford Wood to a road summit offering views ahead of 734ft Beacon Hill. Shortly turn right on to the B3176 SP 'Sidmouth' and skirt tree-topped Bulverton Hill on the right before descending into Sidmouth.

SIDMOUTH, Devon SY18
Created as a resort from almost nothing in the 18th century, Sidmouth boasts a shingle beach backed by spectacular red cliffs and is still a popular holiday town. Rows of architecturally outstanding Regency terraces are reminders of the prosperous recent past, while elsewhere are the more ancient Old Chancel and Manor House. The former incorporates medieval parts of the old parish church, and the latter now houses a museum. On either side of the town are Peak Hill to the west and Salcombe Hill to the east, both of which offer exceptional views of the coastline. Peak Hill shelters the Royal Glen, a former residence of Queen Victoria. Every August the town is host to a well-known International Folk Song and Dance Festival.

Follow SP 'Honiton' on the B3175 ar drive to Sidford.

SIDFORD, Devon SY18
Although rebuilt and widened in 1930, Sidford's bridge still displays the pleasing lines of the old high-backed packhorse bridge that stoc here from c1100. Porch House, which dates from the 16th century said to have hidden Charles II after the Battle of Worcester.

Turn right on to the A3052 and clin Orleigh Hill, which offers magnificer views across the Sid Valley. Cross th road summit, then after $\frac{1}{2}$ mile turn right on to an unclassified road for Branscombe.

3RANSCOMBE, Devon SY18
t is difficult to find the centre of this /illage, which sprawls along steep anes in a shallow wooded valley, but ts situation makes it one of the oveliest in Devon. Features of the ıpper village include thatched roofs, ın old smithy, and a Norman to later hurch. Some 300 acres of the eautiful Branscombe Estate is wned by the National Trust.

ollow SP 'Beer', reach the top of an scent, and turn left SP 'Honiton'. Continue for 1 mile then turn left on o the A3052. After ¾ mile pass the hree Horseshoes Inn before turning ght on to the B3174. After 2 miles ass the road to the Farway Countryside Park on the right.

ARWAY COUNTRYSIDE PARK, Devon SY19
1uch of this 70-acre park is reserved in its natural state, though ne or two places have been repared as picnic sites. Attractions part from the scenery include pony des and nature trails.

½ mile bear right on to an nclassified road and cross Farway ill, with fine views into the Coly alley on the right. After ¾ mile keep rward on to the 'Honiton' road. each a golf course and turn left, then escend into Honiton.

ONITON, Devon ST10
is town gave its name to Honiton ce, a material which is now oduced in neighbouring villages d can still be bought in some local ops. Examples can be seen in a nall museum housed in the old apel beside the parish church. arwood House, Honiton's oldest ilding, dates from 1619 and ntains one of many antique shops at thrive in this acknowledged ntre of the trade. A 17th-century ıck marble tomb to Thomas arwood, physician to Queen zabeth I, can be seen in the local urch. Visitors to the local pottery n watch work being thrown on the eel and hand painted. An unusual ilding known as Copper Castle nds by the side of old toll gates on e village outskirts.

rn left into Honiton High Street (the eter road), proceed for ¾ mile, then n left on to the A375 SP 'Sidmouth'. cend Gittisham Hill and continue to Hare and Hounds Inn. Turn right to the B3174 and descend into ery St Mary, beside the River Otter.

TERY ST MARY, Devon SY09
rious literary figures are associated h this pleasant River Otter town. poet Samuel Taylor Coleridge s born here in 1772, and satirist lliam Thackeray set his novel *dennis* here (though he changed name to Clavering St Mary). The gnificent collegiate church was delled on Exeter Cathedral by hop Grandson, and dates largely m 1337. Notable features include n 14th-century stalls and a curious abethan clock. An annual carnival eld in the town on November 5.

Branscombe Mouth is an unspoilt beach protected by the National Trust.

Leave Ottery St Mary along Hind Street (the B3176) and cross the river to reach Cadhay House.

CADHAY HOUSE, Devon SY09
Considered one of the finest examples of Tudor building in Devon, this superb house (open sometimes) was built in 1550 by a lawyer called John Haydon.

Continue to Fairmile, cross the A30, and follow SP 'Cullompton'. Continue to Clyst Hydon through farming country, and at the end of the village turn right. In ¾ mile turn left on to an unclassified road, then after a further 2 miles meet a junction with the B3185 and turn left then immediately right for Hele. Pass under the M5 motorway, drive over a level crossing and the River Culm, then turn left. After 1½ miles keep forward on the B3185 and recross the River Culm near paper mills. In ¾ mile turn right on to the unclassified 'Killerton Road'; Killerton Gardens are on the right.

KILLERTON GARDENS, Devon SS90
In 1944 Sir Richard Acland gave his family home and its superb gardens (both open) to the National Trust. The care and dedication with which the Aclands tended their gardens since they first came here in 1778 is still evident in the beautiful hillside arboretum and 200-year-old beech trees that can be enjoyed here.

Follow SP 'Poltimore' then 'Exeter' and descend into the city of Exeter.

EXETER, Devon SX99
In recent years the centre of this long-established city and county town has been developed into a massive shopping complex. The modern buildings, pedestrian ways and arcades of the new Exeter have been built with an eye to beauty as well as convenience, and are liberally dotted with decorative pavements, flower beds and baskets, and greensward. The old city, farther down the hill towards the River Exe itself, contains many interesting old buildings. The most imposing structure is undoubtedly the cathedral, which is noted for its fine proportions and the beauty of its two Norman transeptal towers. The present building stands on the site of an 11th-century church, and the towers date from the 12th century. Among its most famous features is the elegant gothic fan-vaulting inside, claimed to be the finest and most extensive in the world. Town Quay features the Exeter Maritime Museum, which preserves over 75 sail-, oar-, and steam-propelled vessels, while down in the Canal Basin near famous Exeter Wharf is the fine Custom House. This was built in 1681 and illustrates the first use of brickwork in the city. Other features not to be missed are the superb 11th- to 16th-century rooms of St Nicholas Priory, Rougemont Museum and the castle remains and the Albert Memorial Museum in Queen Street. Also inviting exploration in the city's maze of little lanes and winding old streets are a host of ancient pubs, inns, and fascinating shops.

Follow SP 'Exmouth B3182' to leave the city by Topsham Road. In 2 miles meet a roundabout and keep forward on to an unclassified road SP 'Topsham'. Drive to Topsham.

TOPSHAM, Devon SX98
Once an important seaport, Topsham stands on the Exe estuary and features several 17th- and 18th-century Dutch-gabled houses. These fine buildings, mainly in the Strand, are reminders of a flourishing trade with Holland. One of them contains a local history museum in its sail loft.

Continue along an unclassified road and meet a T-junction in Clyst St George. Turn left and continue to reach a roundabout at Clyst St Mary, and take the 3rd exit on to the A3052 'Lyme Regis' road. In 4¾ miles reach the Halfway Inn and turn right on to the B3180 for the return to Exmouth.

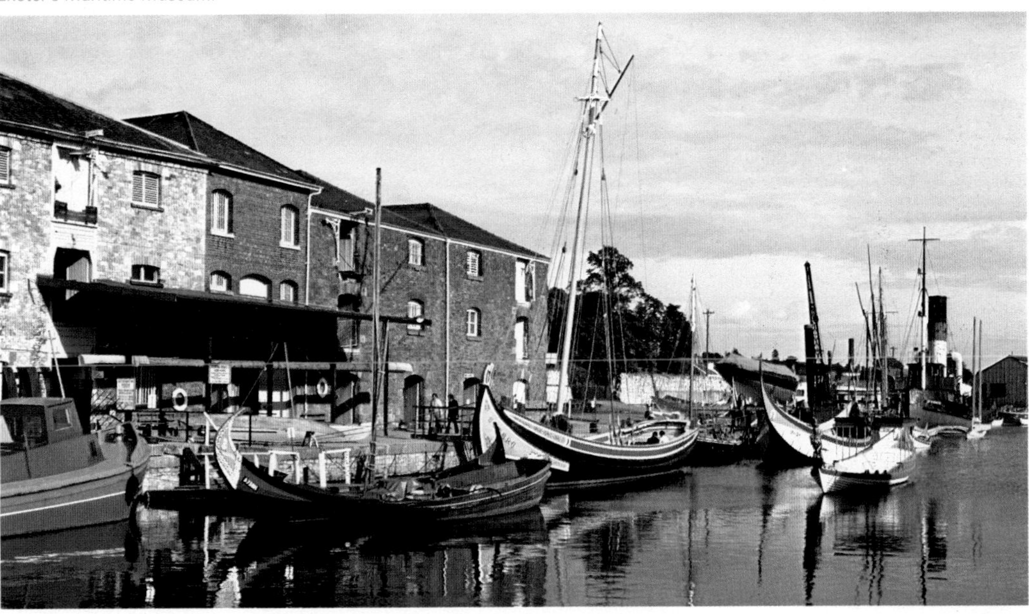

Portuguese fishing boats are displayed along with many other vessels at Exeter's Maritime Museum.

BUDE, Cornwall SS20
One of Bude's main attractions is its huge surfing beach, where strong winds that have caused hundreds of wrecks over the centuries provide a constant supply of rollers ideal for the sport. The town itself is sheltered from the full force of the weather by ridges of downland between it and the sea. Visitors interested in sun and sea bathing are catered for by Summerleaze beach, a sheltered area of sand at the mouth of the River Neet. Here a large swimming pool that is naturally refilled every high tide accommodates swimmers who want to avoid being hit on the head by a surfboard. A notable 3-mile scenic walk extends along clifftops south of Bude, visiting Compass Point and Efford Beacon for their excellent views. Bude's so-called Castle was built in 1840 and now houses the local council offices. See also tour 4.

Leave by the A3072 'Bideford' road. After $1\frac{1}{4}$ miles turn left on to the A39, pass the edge of Stratton, and drive to Kilkhampton.

KILKHAMPTON, Cornwall SS21
The main feature of the village is the 12th- to 15th-century church, which contains no fewer than 157 carved bench-ends dating from the 16th century. The Norman doorway is elaborately carved, and there is a splendid barrel roof.

Continue for 3 miles. A detour from the main route can be made by turning left on to an unclassified road to reach Morwenstow.

MORWENSTOW, Cornwall SS21
Henna Cliff rears 450ft above the waves about $\frac{1}{4}$ mile from Morwenstow village church, on the other side of a grassy coomb. It is the highest cliff in Cornwall and forms part of an awesome range that once proved useful to the wreckers, who signalled ships on to the rocks in order to plunder their cargoes. The church itself stands a little aloof from the tiny village, and features attractive Romanesque zig-zag work over the porch. During the 19th century the local vicar, Robert Hawker, wrote the ballad *Song of the Western Men*.

Continue on the A39 for 2 miles. At Welcombe Cross a detour can be made from the main route to reach Welcombe and Welcombe Mouth by turning left on to an unclassified road.

WELCOMBE, Devon SS21
Situated near the Cornish border, this village stands in a remote glen that leads to a wild stretch of cliff-bound coast at Morwenstow Bay. The cliff strata here has been violently contorted by unimaginable stresses to form really spectacular coastal scenery. A fine waterfall can be seen at Marsland Mouth, and picturesque Welcombe Cove is well worth visiting.

A small stream tumbles into Bideford Bay at Buck's Mills.

TOUR 8 72 MILES

NORTH DEVON CLIFFTOPS

Bude's long beach is a brief calm before the great geological storm that lies ahead. Just north are soaring cliffs violently twisted and fractured by massive forces, where small streams from the lush hinterland plunge hundreds of feet to the shore as waterfalls, or dash over boulder beds through deep wooded ravines.

Atlantic waves break constantly on Bude's magnificent beach, creating ideal conditions for surfers.

From Welcombe Cross proceed on the A39 for 1 mile to pass the West Country Inn, then branch left on to an unclassified road SP 'Stoke'. Cross a short stretch of moorland to reach Tosberry Cross, and bear left then right to reach Stoke.

STOKE, Devon SS22
Hartland's 14th-century church stands here, raising its magnificent tower 128ft into the air to form a local landmark. Inside are a carved Norman font and a rood screen.

Continue for $\frac{1}{2}$ mile and descend steeply to Hartland Quay.

HARTLAND QUAY, Devon SS22
The quay that stood here has long since been washed away by storms, but the fine beach is a constant attraction. Some of the most exciting shorescapes of the north Devon and Cornwall coasts are formed by the strangely twisted and fractured strata of the local cliffs. A clifftop path leads 1 mile south to Speke's Mill Mouth waterfall, perhaps the most spectacular of several cliff waterfalls in the district.

Return to Stoke and follow SP 'Hartland, Bideford'. After $\frac{1}{2}$ mile a road to the left leads to Hartland Point.

HARTLAND POINT, Devon SS22
Although only 3 miles from Hartland Quay, the beautiful 350ft cliffs here are red instead of grey. This spectacular coast has an ugly history and has been the death of many a helpless and storm-battered ship. Because of this the point carries a small white lighthouse which emits the strongest light of any on Britain's coast. The mainly flat and sparsely populated hinterland is unspectacular, but much of it has been included in a designated area of outstanding natural beauty.

Return to Hartland.

HARTLAND, Devon SS22
To the west of this pleasant little town is the 18th-century house of Hartland Abbey. The abbey itself wa founded in the 12th century and ha entirely vanished. A coomb leads from here to the sea.

From Hartland proceed on the B3248 'Bideford, Clovelly' road for 3 miles and turn left on to an unclassified road. After another $\frac{1}{2}$ mile turn left again on to the B3237 and drive to th carpark for Clovelly.

CLOVELLY, Devon SS32
Clovelly is one of the West Country most picturesque fishing villages. N cars are allowed here because the steep cobbled street, lined with lovely old houses, descends 400ft to the sea in a series of steps. Donkeys are used to transport visitors' luggage, and zig-zag steps allow pedestrian access down the woode cliffs to the tiny quay and a pebble beach. The idyllic surroundings of the village tend to soothe away the normal healthy respect for the ope sea, but a local lifeboat station that has saved 350 lives is a sobering reminder that the tranquillity is not permanent. The village, discovered by holidaymakers in the mid-19th century, is popular with artists and enjoys a climate as mild as that of the south Devon coast. Local gardens bloom well beyond their normal season. An attractive 2-mi walk leads west from the harbour a magnificent range of 400ft cliffs.

Return along the B3237, then in $1\frac{1}{4}$ miles turn left on to the A39 'Bideford' road to reach Buck's Cros An unclassified road to the left lead through a wooded glen to Buck's Mills.

BUCK'S MILLS, Devon SS32
This unspoilt fishing village of thatched cottages nestles at the bottom of a wooded valley, on a section of coast noted for its picturesque cliff scenery.

After another 5 miles on the A39 t left on to the B3236 to reach Abbotsham.

ABBOTSHAM, Devon SS42
Nearly 2 miles of low, rocky shore along Bideford Bay are accessible from this village. Abbotsham Chu features a good 15th-century bar roof bearing trade emblems and coats of arms, and preserves carv bench-ends and a Norman font.

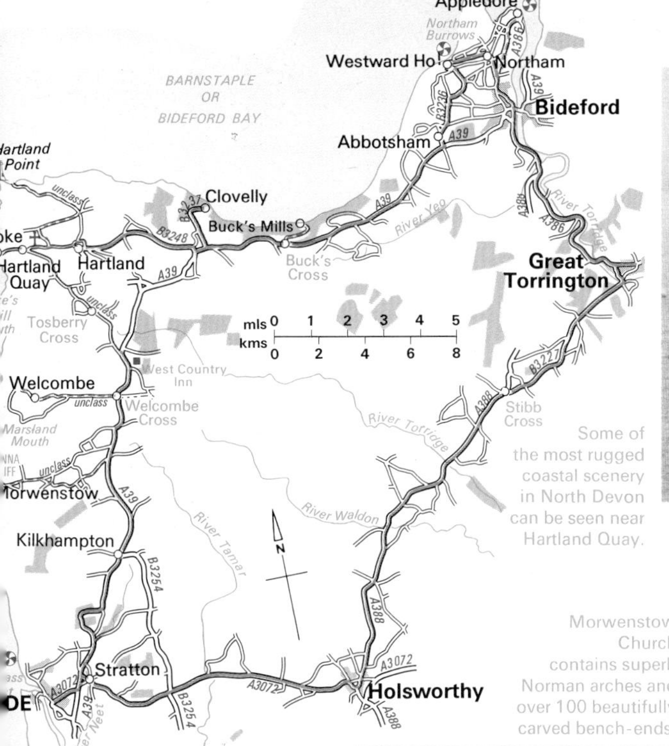

Some of the most rugged coastal scenery in North Devon can be seen near Hartland Quay.

Morwenstow Church contains superb Norman arches and over 100 beautifully carved bench-ends.

ontinue along the B3236 to reach /estward Ho!

/ESTWARD HO!, Devon SS42

amed after the famous novel by harles Kingsley, this popular seaside sort offers a well-known golf ourse and 3 miles of sandy beach. 'est of the town the sands merge to rocks scattered with teeming ools, ideal ground for the infant aturalist. North-west is the 650-acre panse of Northam Burrows, which protected from the Atlantic by a markable pebble ridge.

ontinue to Northam.

ORTHAM, Devon SS42

ramatic views extending from artmoor to the Bristol Channel can enjoyed from the crest of Bay ew Road in Northam, a village ose to the attractive Torridge tuary. An inscribed stone at Bloody orner recalls King Alfred's ccessful last battle against Hubba e Dane in the 9th century.

detour can be made to pretty pledore by turning left on to the 386.

PLEDORE, Devon SS43

bbled streets leading to a quay d a sandy beach contribute to the at charm of this village, which has eral attractive Georgian houses d cottages. Its tranquillity is nehow maintained despite the ablishment in 1970 of Europe's gest covered shipbuilding dock on Torridge estuary.

ow the main route on the A386 drive to Bideford.

EFORD, Devon SS42

ween c1550 and 1750 this town the principal port of north von and the home of a renowned ship-building industry. Sir Richard Grenville, who obtained a charter for the town from Queen Elizabeth I, crewed his ship *Revenge* entirely with Bideford men. That brave little vessel will always be famous for its stand against 15 Spanish ships in the Azores. The mile-long, tree-lined quay remains lively, and the estuary is popular with yachtsmen and small-boat sailors. Bridgeland Road preserves evidence of a once prosperous past in the shape of 17th-century merchants' houses. Predating these is the bridge over the River Torridge, a 15th-century structure unusual in that none of its 24 arches is of the same width. It has been considerably renovated and widened to take the burden of 20th-century traffic. The Royal Hotel, across the river, was originally a merchant's house and dates from 1688. It was here that Charles Kingsley wrote part of *Westward Ho!*

Leave Bideford following SP 'Torrington' and drive beside the River Torridge to reach Great Torrington.

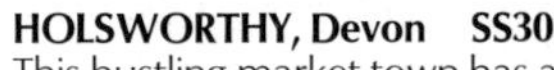

GREAT TORRINGTON, Devon SS41

The church in this hilltop market town was rebuilt in 1651, 6 years after it and 200 Royalist soldiers imprisoned inside were blown up by gunpowder. The tragedy was caused by Roundhead troops using the church as a gunpowder store as well as a prison. A fine 17th-century pulpit can be seen inside the building. The well-known Dartington glass is made in the town, and visitors to the factory can watch the highly skilled glassblowers at work. About 1 mile south-east of Great Torrington is Rosemoor Garden (open), where hybrid rhododendrons, eucalyptus, roses, and ornamental trees and shrubs can be seen. Within easy reach of the town are the two magnificent vantage points of Castle Hill and Furzebeam. The former rises to the south and affords views over the graceful loops of the River Torridge, while the gorse-covered crag of Furzebeam juts out into the river valley to the north and is separated from the town by an attractive narrow ravine.

Follow SP 'Holsworthy, Bude' on the B3227 to leave Great Torrington. After 6 miles enter Stibb Cross, then keep forward on to the A388 for Holsworthy.

HOLSWORTHY, Devon SS30

This bustling market town has a dubious claim to fame as the last place in England where a man was punished by being sent to the stocks. The mainly 13th-century church here has a pinnacled 15th-century tower and a carillion which plays one of a number of tunes on the hour.

Leave Holsworthy on the A3072 SP 'Bude'. Later cross the River Tamar and reach Stratton.

STRATTON, Cornwall SS20

An ancient town that was probably founded by the Romans, Stratton is made up of old and sometimes thatched buildings lining a steep main street. The Tree Inn was once a manor, and in 1643 it served as the home and headquarters of Sir Bevil Grenville before he led the Royalists to victory at the battle of Stamford Hill, $\frac{1}{2}$ mile north-west. Features of the local church include a pinnacled 15th-century tower, a barrel roof with carved bosses, a fine 16th-century brass, and a window by the talented artist and designer Burne-Jones. See also tour 4.

Follow SP 'Bude' on the A3072 for the return to Bude.

Clovelly is one of the most popular of Devon's picturesque fishing villages.

TOUR 9 56 MILES

ALONG THE EXE VALLEY

From its wild moorland source the Exe struggles through a mile of peat before finding its deep valley to the fertile heartlands of North Devon. All along its route are sleepy little red-stone villages that burst into activity once a week when the local hunt meets.

BAMPTON, Devon SS92
This small market town is situated by the River Batherm near its junction with the Exe. Ponies culled from the wild herds that roam the moor are sold in the October Pony Fair. The excellence of the limestone quarried to the south of the town is almost legendary. Today these quarries are of geological rather than commercial interest, and their situation affords fine views of the town. St Michael's Church, built c1300, was rebuilt with a north aisle in the 15th century. Inside are notable carved rood and tower screens and a pulpit dating from the 16th-century.

Leave Bampton on the B3222 SP 'Dulverton', then join the A396 at Exbridge. Turn immediately left to rejoin the B3222, cross the River Exe, and proceed through the valley of the River Barle to Dulverton.

DULVERTON, Somerset SS92
The River Barle is spanned here by an attractive 3-arched bridge and is known for its excellent trout and salmon fishing. Dulverton itself is a shopping centre and the general administrative centre for the south-east area of Exmoor, a status that makes it a prime touring base. Everywhere is the sight and sound of water, a fact succinctly commented upon by Lord Tennyson in 1891 when he called Dulverton 'a land of bubbling streams'. Fine views of the town are available from the shade of a giant sycamore, which is some 250 years old and obscures a modest church. Local painters exhibit their works each summer in Exmoor House by the bridge.

Turn left on to the B3223 'Lynton' road and enter the Exmoor National Park.

EXMOOR NATIONAL PARK (SOUTH), Devon & Somerset
Much of this tour runs through the southern area of the Exmoor National Park, a place of dense mixed forests and wild open moors dominated in the north by the River Exe and in the south by the River Barle. Once a year the Exmoor ponies are herded and culled, some being freed and others taken to be sold at the famous local pony fairs. Pure-bred Exmoors are bay, dun, or brown, with no white or other markings of any kind, and have a characteristic oatmeal colour to the muzzle and inside ears. These animals, untainted by domestic stock, are hardy, agile creatures. The possibilities for recreation in the park are unlimited. Superb walks start from almost any point along the route, and those worried about getting lost in the vast expanse of the moor can follow specially marked trails. Care must be taken to avoid the deep, sphagnum- filled bogs; broken-in Exmoor ponies are good for trekking the moor because they know the area and recognize the smell of the boglands. The only other large herd animal found here is the red deer, a lovely, shy animal which is best sought for in secluded spots during the early morning or late evening. See also tours 10 and 14.

Continue on the B3223. After a short distance reach a left turn leading to Tarr Steps for a pleasant detour from the main route.

TARR STEPS, Somerset SS83
Tarr Steps (AM, NT) is the local name for a superb old clapper bridge. Peacefully situated on the edge of Exmoor, near Dulverton, it spans the tumbling River Barle and comprises 20 piers topped by a stone footway raised some 3ft above water level. The piers are large blocks of stone placed on the river bed, and the top is made up of several giant slabs that must have taken incredible effort to position. This fascinating monument to the ingenuity of ancient man is believed to have been built before the Norman Conquest. A lane leads from the Steps to Hawkridge.

Back on the main route, continue along the B3223 to reach Winsford Hill and the Caratacus Stone, on the right.

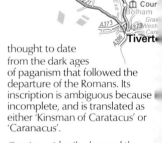

Tarr Steps' enormous slabs have bee washed away many times, but ha always been replaced in th original positior

WINSFORD HILL & THE CARATACUS STONE, Somerset SS83
Heather-clad Winsford Hill (NT) rises between Exmoor's two major rivers. Its wooded lower slopes rise to a clear summit from which the marked contrast between the River Barle woodlands and the empty slopes that rise from the Exe can be truly appreciated. The Caratacus Stone, an inscribed tablet on the hill, is thought to date from the dark ages of paganism that followed the departure of the Romans. Its inscription is ambiguous because incomplete, and is translated as either 'Kinsman of Caratacus' or 'Caranacus'.

Exmoor is a beautiful mixture of rolling farmland and open moor.

Continue $1\frac{1}{4}$ miles beyond the Winsford Hill road summit to a left turn that offers a pleasant detour to Withypool.

WITHYPOOL, Somerset SS83
Beautifully situated on the River B and much favoured by game anglers, this tiny village has one o the two legal commons existing i the national park (the other is at Brendon). A fine old bridge spans river here, and nearby Withypoo features a stone circle among neolithic burial mounds.

Continue for $1\frac{1}{2}$ miles (on the mai route), meet crossroads, and turn right on to an unclassified road to descend into Exford.

EXFORD, Somerset SS83
Hunting and horses are the bread and butter of this well-kept Exe-Valley village. The kennels of the Devon and Somerset Stag Hounds are based here, and horses are very much in evidence at all times. Exford's annual Horse Show is generally held on the 2nd Wednesday in August. The nucleus of the village is an attractive grouping of cottages, shops, and hotels around the local cricket and football field. Other buildings are dotted amid the rural outskirts, and the modest little church contains an interesting 15th-century screen.

ollow the B3224 'Lynton' road for ' mile, rejoin the B3223, and continue o Simonsbath.

ulverton's Market House dates from 366.

MONSBATH, Somerset SS73
ted 1,100ft above sea level, monsbath is the highest village in e park and stands at the centre of hat used to be the Royal Exmoor orest. Deer were once ommonplace here, but today these nid creatures are rarely seen. The 0-year-old church administers the rgest parish in the park.

urn left on to an unclassified road SP outh Molton' and climb to 1,500ft. ontinue forward to join the B3226, en after $1\frac{1}{2}$ miles join the A361 and oceed to South Molton.

OUTH MOLTON, Devon SS72
own to have existed as a Saxon lony cAD700, this lovely little town s just south of Exmoor and is an ricultural centre for the region. tween the middle ages and the d-19th century it became a iving wool town; it was also a ach stop on the route to nstaple and Bideford, and the arest town to the iron and copper nes of North Molton. A square of gant Georgian houses is mplemented by the town's grand th-century Guildhall and 19th-ntury Assembly Rooms, all built h the profits from wool and nerals. Disaster struck when the lustries collapsed, and the town's pulation was reduced by half. ce 1961 it has been the ntre for a busy livestock market, l every summer brings in more tors wanting to be entertained and accommodated. Opposite the square an avenue of pollarded lime trees leads to the local church, which houses an excellently-carved pulpit and carries a 15th-century tower. A small museum behind the Guildhall displays examples of pewterware, a cider press, and an intriguing old fire engine dating from 1736.

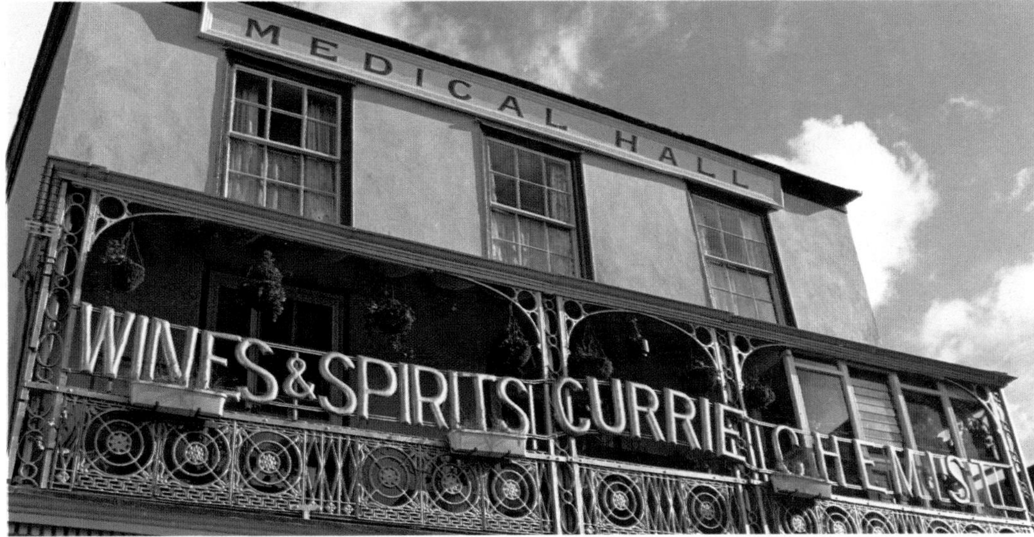

The Medical Hall in South Molton.

Continue on the A361 'Bampton, Taunton' road and cross the rivers Mole and Yeo to Bish Mill. Branch right on to the B3221 SP 'Tiverton' and continue through woodland and hilly farming country to Tiverton.

TIVERTON, Devon SS91
This prosperous industrial and agricultural town stands on the River Exe and its tributary, the River Lowman. After the conquest of the south-west in the 7th century it became one of the first Saxon settlements, and later during the 17th- and 18th-century heyday of the clothing industry the town became the principal industrial area in the county. Architecturally, the town has benefited greatly from the prosperity of its inhabitants. Rich wool merchants have bequeathed such fine buildings as St Peter's Church, Blundell's School, and three sets of almshouses. The church, particularly noted for the richly-carved Greenway Chapel and its organ, stands in front of a 12th-century castle which preserves its towers and gateway despite being incorporated in a private house (open on application). Blundell's School is famous in having taught such illustrious persons as R D Blackmore, author of *Lorna Doone*, and Frederick Temple, Archbishop of Canterbury from 1896 to 1902. St George's Church was built in 1773 and is reputed to be one of the finest Georgian churches in Devon. Also of interest is the local Folk Museum, which is housed in a 19th-century school building and displays a particularly good selection of farm implements. The 19th-century Grand Western Canal begins at the south-east edge of the town and extends for 11 miles. It was originally intended to link the Bristol Channel with the English Channel, but the project was never completed and the towpath now forms a famous scenic walk.

From Tiverton take the A396 'Bampton' road and continue to a roundabout at Bolham. Turn right here for a short detour to Knightshayes Court.

KNIGHTSHAYES COURT, Devon SS91
The 19th-century house that stands here is pleasant enough to look at, but it is totally put in the shade by some of the most beautiful gardens in Devon. Protected by both the National Trust and Knightshayes Garden Trust, the grounds have a woodland theme and are particularly noted for their splendid rhododendrons. There is something of interest here at all times of the year, summer or winter.

On the main route, continue along the A396 for the return to Bampton.

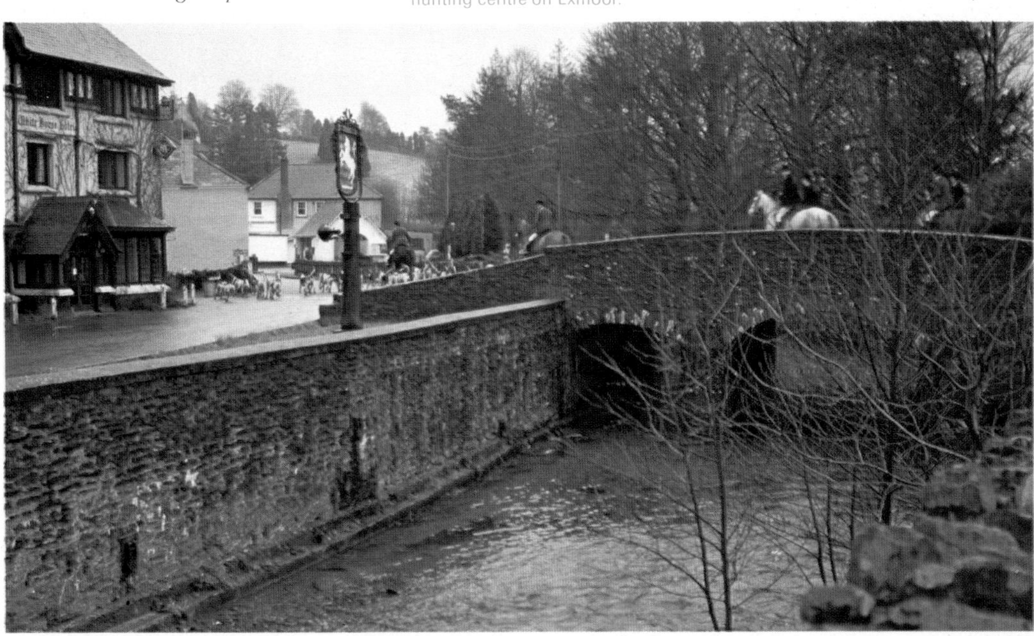

Exford is the most important stag hunting centre on Exmoor.

LYNTON, Devon SS74
This pleasant and very popular resort is sited high on a cliff some 500ft above its sister village of Lynmouth. Tree-covered Summerhouse Hill shields it from the blustery sea gales, and a solid ring of hills protects it from the worst of Exmoor's rain. The Victorians were quick to recognize these attributes as being suited to seaside holidays, and since then the resort has attracted a constant stream of visitors. Victorian architecture predominates here, and a typical eccentricity of that era is the water-powered cliff lift. This was donated by a lawyer named George Newnes in 1890, and has been restored to working order. Newnes also built the Town Hall, behind which rise the flower-strewn slopes of viewpoint Hollerday Hill. Miles of coastline and the Exmoor hills can be seen from here. Other features of Lynton include a Catholic church containing rare and beautiful marble work, and the Lyn and Exmoor Museum in old St Vincent's Cottage. The local cliffs afford views across the Bristol Channel to Wales, and the magnificent Valley of the Rocks is accessible by footpath.

VALLEY OF THE ROCKS, Devon SS74
The poet Robert Southey described this fantastic place of jagged tors and breathtaking coastal scenery with the words '. . . rock reeling upon rock, stone piled upon stone, a huge terrific reeling mass'.

Descend Lynmouth Hill (1 in 4) to Lynmouth and turn right on to the A39 'Barnstaple' road for Watersmeet.

WATERSMEET, Devon SS74
As its name suggests, this National Trust beauty spot is the place where the tumbling waters of the East Lyn River converge with the Hoaroak Water, which cascades down a rocky bed in a series of waterfalls. It is best to leave the car and explore the cool beauty of this wooded gorge on foot.

Continue alongside the Hoaroak Water for ½ mile then turn left on to the B3223 SP 'Simonsbath'. Cross Hillsford Bridge, and in ¾ mile go round a hairpin bend and drive forward on to an unclassified road SP 'Brendon Valley'. Pass Brendon Church, with views of the tree-covered slopes that characterize this area, then descend through the oak-wooded valley of the East Lyn River for Brendon.

BRENDON, Devon SS74
This picturesque village is situated on the banks of the East Lyn, which is spanned here by an attractive medieval packhorse bridge.

Continue alongside the East Lyn River to Malmsmead

MALMSMEAD, Devon SS74
Ponies can be hired here for a 2½-mile trek along the deep valley of Badgworthy Water, leading to the legendary Doone Country. The journey can just as easily be undertaken on foot.

TOUR 10 34 MILES

INTO THE DOONE COUNTRY

Before they come here many people half believe Blackmore's romantic novel 'Lorna Doone' to be a true historical account. By the time they leave, the region's gorse and heather covered moors, wooded ravines, and exquisite little stone villages have convinced them of it.

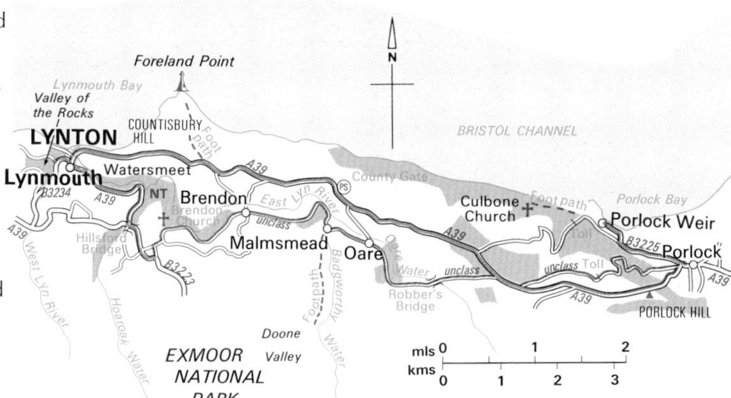

DOONE VALLEY, Devon & Somerset
R D Blackmore immortalized isolated and beautiful Hoccombe Combe as 'Doone Valley' in his famous novel *Lorna Doone*. Thanks to his brilliantly emotive style this has become one of the most romantic places in the country, and many visitors go away firmly believing that the whole tale was actually a true historical account. Tales of a villainous Doone family who terrorized the moorfolk have been told here since 1790. It appears that Blackmore seized on these as a handy base for his novel, and although he did not concentrate on authentic landscape description, several features can be identified from his text. Lanke Combe enters the valley from the west and has miniature versions of features attributed to Doone Valley by the author, including the famous waterslide. Records show that the remains of several buildings in this area belonged to a medieval settlement, but the name Doone is not mentioned. With or without the legend, this is a beautiful area that should not be missed.

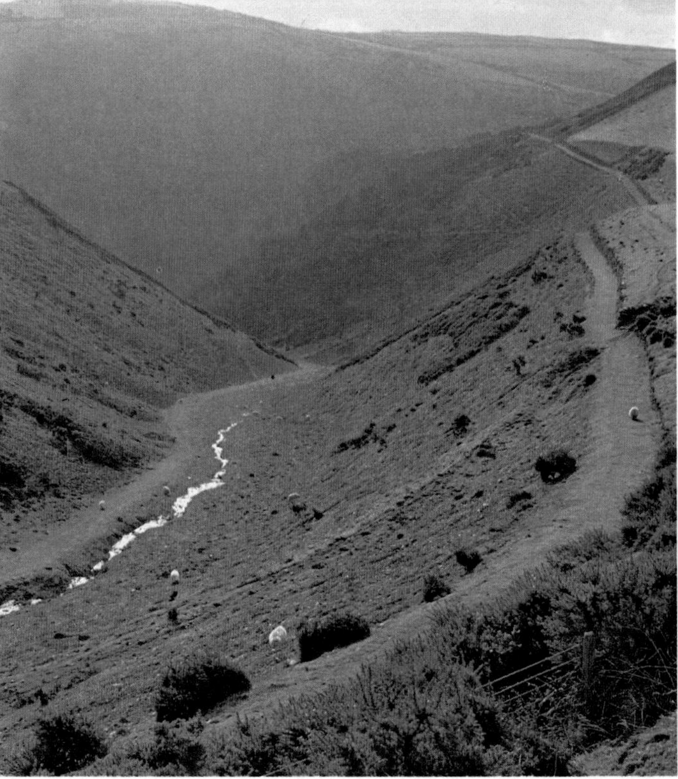

EXMOOR NATIONAL PARK (NORTH), Devon & Somerset
In its northern reaches this vast national park meets the sea with magnificent results. Rugged hogs-back cliffs stretch continuously from Lynton to Porlock, falling steeply to the waters of the Bristol Channel and affording views across to the coast of South Wales. Lush coombs wind deep into rambling moorland, scattered here and there with tiny hamlets and picturesque villages. The burgeoning life of the valleys makes a striking contrast with the remote and heather-clad wastelands through which they cut, but together these opposites form a landscape that could be nowhere else but Exmoor. Agriculture and forestry play a large part in the park's life, and the rich patchwork of farmland in areas like the Porlock Vale are sharp reminders that this is more than just a place of outstanding natural beauty. Wildlife abounds on Exmoor. The shy red dee that haunt its wooded coombs are unique in being direct descendants of the wild deer that once roamed prehistoric Britain. Common mammals thrive in a variety of habitats, and the park boasts many species of birds. Vestiges of prehistoric ages can be found in the form of earthworks, tumuli, standing stones, and barrows. Of particular note is the stone circle on Porlock Hill, but there are many other fascinating examples easily reached from Lynton. See also tours 9 and 14

From Malmsmead cross a river bridg into Somerset and continue to Oare.

OARE, Somerset SS84
This tiny Oare Valley hamlet stands by the Oare Water and has strong connexions with the fiction of R D Blackmore. It was here that his heroine Lorna was married, and he that she almost met an untimely end. The village church is a lovely little 15th-century building well suited to the magical tale that has been woven around it. Inside are 19th-century boxpews and a curiou piscina shaped like a man's head. Exceptionally fine coomb scenery with wooded valleys and steep screes surrounds the area.

Follow the road SP 'Oareford, Robber's Bridge' for 1½ miles. Cross the bridge and continue the steep ascent to join the A39. Proceed alor a scenic moorland road, with fine views across the Bristol Channel, an reach Porlock Hill.

PORLOCK HILL, Somerset SS84
The notorious incline of this hill as i rises from Porlock is one of the steepest in Britain, and the breathtaking view from its summit surpasses many. A prehistoric ston circle survives close by.

Make a steep and winding descent (1 in 4) into Porlock.

Rain and mist add extra dimensions c beauty and mystery to Northern Exmoor.

ORLOCK, Somerset SS84
axon Kings chose the site of this nchanting coastal village as a base rom which to hunt in Exmoor Forest, nd nowadays it serves as an ideal ouring centre. A famous riding chool is established here, and it is lifficult to venture far without neeting horses and riders. Notable uildings in Porlock include 15th-entury Doverhay Manor House and mainly 13th-century red-stone hurch containing the tomb of one ohn Harrington, who is said to have ought at Agincourt. This remarkable onument is topped by almost life-ze effigies of Harrington and his ife. Like many of its neighbours orlock attracted an artistic following ent on recording its delights in paint nd verse. Robert Southey the poet as obviously disenchanted with the eather when he stayed at the Ship n and wrote: 'Porlock, I shall forget ee not, here by the unwelcome immer rain confined . . . .'

ave the village on the B3225 and ive to Porlock Weir.

Lynmouth Bay is overlooked by the cliff mass of Blackhead and the ancient earthworks on Wind Hill.

lbone Church occupies a delightfully oded position beside a stream.

RLOCK WEIR & CULBONE IURCH, Somerset SS84
years gone by Porlock was a iving port, but all that remains day is the miniature harbour of this ique little Porlock Bay hamlet. asure craft make good use of its eltered waters, and its shingle ach is backed by cliffs cloaked h thick woodland. A pleasant lk leads from here to Culbone, ere can be seen the smallest glish church still in regular use. The lding displays Norman and later les, and measures only 33 by 13½ft. ide are old benches and a 14th-ntury screen, while all around are ods and pits once used by a arcoal-burning community.

urn to Porlock and take the nmouth' road, then branch right on n unclassified road SP 'Alternative ute via Toll Road' and climb dually to open moorland. Meet a in road and turn right on to the 9, re-entering Devon at County e with a picnic site to the left. After other 2½ miles reach a footpath ling right to Foreland Point.

FORELAND POINT AND LIGHTHOUSE, Devon SS75
The footpath to this lighthouse runs through magnificent coastal scenery (NT) and affords extensive views of the Bristol Channel.

Continue to Countisbury Hill.

COUNTISBURY HILL, Devon SS74
Stagecoach drivers had to change horses at the ancient inn on top of this exceptionally steep hill. Prehistoric earthworks (NT) overlook the inn and sea to the west, and superb cliff walks can be made beyond the small local church.

Descend Countisbury Hill (1 in 4) to Lynmouth.

LYNMOUTH, Devon SS74
In 1812 the poet Shelley and his 16-year-old bride were captivated by the beautiful little fishing village that stood here. Since then tourism and a rash of boarding houses have given it a new lease of commercial life, but the basic framework of towering cliffs and swirling river estuaries remains. Disastrous floods that made national headlines in 1952 swept away part of the quay, a great deal of the resort, and a curious edifice known as the Rhenish Tower. Afterwards the East and West Lyn rivers were widened, and strong walls built to prevent a recurrence of the tragedy. This tidying up included the rebuilding of the tower, which is supposed to resemble a type found in Germany and was originally constructed to store salt water for indoor bathing. The picturesque lower town is a medley of colour-washed cottages clustered amid gardens bright with roses, fuchsias, and other shrubs.

Ascend Lynmouth Hill and return to Lynton.

of season Porlock Weir once more omes a quiet fishing hamlet.

THOMAS HARDY'S WESSEX

Hardy's novels featured many places, thinly disguised, from his beloved Dorset. Here the visitor can find his barren island and wind-blasted heaths, earthworks overlooking thatch and stone villages from the tops of green downs, and salt lagoons held behind by giant shingle banks.

WEYMOUTH, Dorset SY67
Weymouth's early claim to fame was as the only safe port for miles around, but the town became fashionable for seaside holidays after King George III began coming here in 1789. Georgian terraces still line the wide Esplanade, and quaint little back streets wind round the old harbour. Local waters are busy with the comings and goings of cross-Channel ferries, cargo boats, and pleasure craft, and a sandy beach offers sun and sea bathing. Among Weymouth's places of interest are the Museum of Local History and No. 3 Trinity Street. The latter is actually two 17th-century cottages with contemporary furnishings (open).

Leave Weymouth by the A354 SP 'Portland'. Cross Small Mouth, the only outlet for the waters of the Fleet, with Chesil Bank (or Beach) to the right.

CHESIL BANK, Dorset SY67
This 20- to 30ft-high pebble ridge is 200yds wide and extends approximately 12 miles from Portland to Abbotsbury. It is separated from the mainland by a channel and tidal lagoon called the East and West Fleet, and joins the mainland at Abbotsbury. Severe storms are commonplace along the coast here, and bathing from the bank is dangerous.

ISLE OF PORTLAND, Dorset SY67
Dorsetman Thomas Hardy referred to this small, almost treeless limestone peninsula as 'The Rock of Gibraltar' and used it in his novels as the 'Isle of Slingers'. Up until the 19th century it was of small importance, but then convict labour from the local prison was used to build the important naval harbour and breakwater that stand here today. The prison is now a Borstal institution. An old lighthouse on Portland Bill now serves as a bird-watching station. The interior of the island is pitted with excavations left by the extraction of the prized Portland Stone, which was used by Wren for St Paul's Cathedral. All round the coast are the deserted quays where it was loaded before road transport became a practicable possibility.

Continue on the A354 to Fortuneswell and Portland Castle.

FORTUNESWELL, Dorset SY67
North of the village high cliffs drop to the waters of Portland Harbour. Close by is the highest point in the peninsula, a 490ft eminence bristling with the 19th-century forts and batteries of vast Verne Citadel.

PORTLAND CASTLE, Dorset SY67
Built by Henry VIII in 1520, this massive fortress (AM) was part of a defensive chain that stretched from Kent in the east to Cornwall in the west. Its 14ft thick walls were built to absorb cannon fire.

Weymouth Harbour is used extensively by cargo and passenger vessels from the Channel Islands.

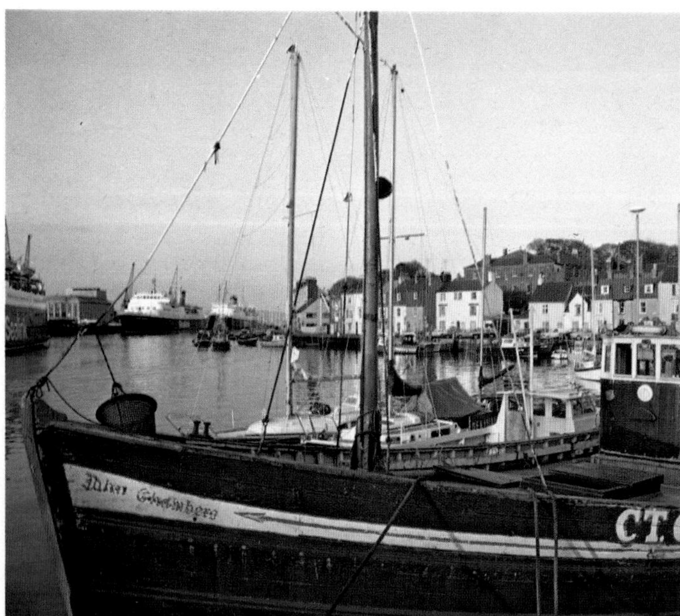

Chesil Bank stretches for 12 miles from Fortuneswe on the Isle of Portland to Abbotsbur

The statue of Thomas Hardy in Dorchester.

Leave Fortuneswell and climb steeply with SP 'Portland Bill'. Fine views can be enjoyed from the carpark at the top of the ascent. Reach Easton.

EASTON, Dorset SY67
Thatched Avice's Cottage, a 17th-century Portland Island dwelling now containing a museum, was featured as the heroine's home in Thomas Hardy's novel *The Well Beloved*. Near by is the single pentagonal tower of Bow and Arrow Castle, said to have been built by William Rufus in the 11th-century. It derives its name from the many small loopholes which pierce the walls. Pennsylvania Castle was built during the 19th century for the Governor of Portland, grandson to the founder of America's Pennsylvania state.

Proceed to Southwell. Reach the Eight Kings (PH) and turn left for Portland Bill.

PORTLAND BILL AND LIGHTHOUS Dorset SY66
This barren mass of limestone rises only 20ft above the sea at the southern tip of the Isle. Nearby Pulp Rock is a pinnacle rising from the se in a series of crags and caves. For years its labyrinthine tunnels were used by smugglers.

Return to the Eight Kings (PH) and turn left to reach Weston, passing o of the Portland stone quarries on th way.

WESTON, Dorset SY67
Portland stone, a superb material made famous by architect Sir Christopher Wren while he was rebuilding London after the Great Fire, is quarried near this village.

Drive through Weston, climb to th top of Portland Hill, and turn left. Descend into Fortuneswell and cro to the mainland. After another 1 m join the B3157 SP 'Bridport' and proceed through Chickerell to reac Portesham.

PORTESHAM, Dorset SY68
This village has an attractive green and stands at the foot of hills dotted with ancient monuments. Those nearest include burial mounds and standing stones.

Proceed on the B3157 to reach Abbotsbury.

ABBOTSBURY, Dorset SY58
A notable 15th-century tithe barn and gateway survives from the ancient Benedictine monastery that stood here, and the 15th- to 16th-century church has a pulpit bearing the marks of Civil War bullets. Abbotsbury Gardens, 17 beautiful acres of rare sub-tropical plants, can be visited 1½ miles west of the village. Excellent views are afforded by Chapel Hill, which is named after the 15th-century chapel that still stands on its exposed summit.

ABBOTSBURY SWANNERY, Dorset SY58
Swans, once considered a table delicacy, were bred here as long ago as 1393 to provide food for the monastery at Abbotsbury village. The swannery (open) lies ½ mile south of the village in the lagoon formed by Chesil Bank. Some 560 swans and various species of geese, ducks, and other water birds live here.

Leave Abbotsbury on the 'Bridport' road and ascend steep Abbotsbury Hill for excellent views over low-hedged fields to the sea. Continue through Swyre to reach Burton Bradstock.

BURTON BRADSTOCK, Dorset ST48
The restored 15th-century church in this picturesque thatched village has an embattled central tower. Unusually stratified cliffs of geological interest can be seen to the east.

Leave Burton Bradstock and proceed for 2 miles; a short detour can be made to West Bay.

WEST BAY, Dorset SY49
A port since the 13th century, West Bay is still used for fishing but additionally caters for small cargo boats and pleasure craft. At one time it served as a harbour for Bridport, which lies 1½ miles north, but nowadays it supplements its port business with resort facilities such as piers and a promenade.

Continue on B3157 to reach Bridport.

BRIDPORT, Dorset SY49
For over 750 years Bridport has been associated with rope and net making, and it is still Europe's principal centre for the production of fishing nets, lines, and cordage. These fascinating local trades are featured in a permanent exhibition at Bridport Museum and Art Gallery. Also here are exhibits showing the archaeology, geology, and natural history of the area. After the battle of Worcester in 1651 Charles II came here to hide, rather incautiously, in 'the best inn in town'; this now contains a shop.

Excavations at Maiden Castle in 1937 revealed the bones of men killed whilst defending the fort against the Romans.

Leave Bridport on the A35 'Dorchester' road and enjoy fine views from Askerswell Down. Proceed to the Nine Stones.

NINE STONES, Dorset SY69
This ancient stone circle (AM) stands ½ mile west of Winterbourne Abbas and is the most notable of many tumuli and configurations of stones in the Dorchester area.

Continue through Winterbourne Abbas. At the end of the village bear right on to the B3159 SP 'Weymouth', then immediately right again on to an unclassified road SP 'Hardy Monument'. Climb on to heathland and turn left to reach the monument.

Dorchester Museum displays many exhibits in elegant Victorian surroundings.

HARDY MONUMENT, Dorset SY68
Admiral Hardy, who was beside Lord Nelson at his death during the battle of Trafalgar, is commemorated here by an obelisk on top of Black Down. Tremendous views can be enjoyed from the hill top (NT).

Continue for 2 miles meet a T-junction, and turn right on to the B3159 to enter Martinstown. Drive to the end of the village and branch left on to an unclassified road. Proceed for 1¼ miles, meet a T-junction, and turn right on to A35. Continue to Dorchester.

DORCHESTER, Dorset SY69
Thomas Hardy was born 2 miles north-east of Dorchester in a cottage (NT, open by appointment), at Higher Bockhampton. The town itself is featured in several of his novels as 'Casterbridge', and the original manuscript of *The Mayor of Casterbridge* can be seen among other relics in the County Museum. Excellent finds from periods before and after the Romans founded their major walled town of *Durnovaria* here cAD43 are also displayed, and foundations of a Roman villa complete with tessellated pavement can be seen at Colliton Park. After the Monmouth rebellion Judge Jeffries held his notorious 'Bloody Assize' at the Antelope Hotel in 1685, sentencing 292 local men to various degrees of punishment for their treachery. Up to 74 of them were hanged in the town, and their heads were impaled on the railings of St Peter's Church as a grim warning against treason. The rest were deported. Much later in 1834 the infant trades union movement was dealt a public blow at the trial of 6 agricultural workers later to become known as the Tolpuddle Martyrs. They were tried in the courtroom of the old Shire Hall, now a Tolpuddle memorial (open), and were sentenced to transportation for joining forces to request a wage increase for local farmworkers. Also of interest in the town are the Dorset Military Museum, in The Keep, and the oddly-named 17th-century Napper's Mite almshouses.

Leave Dorchester on the A354 'Weymouth' road. An unclassified road on the right leads to Maiden Castle.

MAIDEN CASTLE, Dorset SY68
Situated 2 miles south west of Dorchester, this vast prehistoric hillfort (AM) occupies 120 acres of land and is the finest of its kind in Britain. It was large enough to have accommodated 5,000 people, and probably developed from a simple bank and ditch defence against neighbouring tribes. After successfully storming it the Romans used the castle as a base and built a temple cAD367 within its ramparts.

Continue along the A354 and drive over downland. Pass through Broadwey and return to Weymouth.

SHAFTESBURY, Dorset ST82
Situated on the edge of a 700ft plateau, Shaftesbury is an ancient town full of quaint corners and little eccentricities. Its most famous street, cobbled Gold Hill, plunges down the hillside with a graceful abandon. Thomas Hardy used the original town name Shaston when featuring it in his novels. Shaftesbury's history began with the abbey established here c880, a foundation that became the burial place of Edward the Martyr and grew to be one of the richest in the area until destroyed at the Dissolution in the 16th century. Only slight remains now exist (AM, open sometimes), but various relics are preserved in the Abbey Ruins Museum. In the Grosvenor Hotel is the famous Chevy Chase sideboard, which was carved from a single piece of oak in the 13th century.

Take the A30 'Sherborne, Yeovil' road and descend to the Blackmore Vale. Continue for 5 miles to reach East Stour, then turn left on to the B3092 and enter the Stour Valley. Continue to Marnhull.

MARNHULL, Dorset ST71
Thomas Hardy called this village Marlott and made it the birthplace of his heroine in *Tess of the d'Urbervilles*. The 14th-century church has an attractive pinnacled tower overlooking Blackmore Vale.

Continue to Sturminster Newton.

STURMINSTER NEWTON, Dorset ST71
The most important livestock market in the southern part of the Blackmore Vale is held here. A fine six-arched medieval bridge spans the Stour, and 1 mile east is 14th-century Fiddleford Mill, which has been restored to full working order.

TOUR 12 — 78 MILES

FARMLAND AND FOREST

Gentle hills and farmland watered by several rivers characterize the fertile Blackmore Vale. In contrast are the rolling grass and woodlands of Cranborne Chase, a vast area that was once the private hunting preserve of kings.

Gold Hill, Shaftesbury's most picturesque street, overlooks the Blackmoor Vale.

Continue through Sturminster Newton on the 'Blandford' road. Cross a bridge and turn right on to the A357, then pass through agricultural country to reach unfenced Lydlinch Common. Continue for $\frac{3}{4}$ mile and turn left on to an unclassified road SP 'Stourton Caundle'. Pass the edge of Stourton Caundle and proceed to Purse Caundle.

PURSE CAUNDLE, Dorset ST61
Purse Caundle Manor is an excellent medieval house (open), notable for its great hall and chamber, and beautiful oriel window.

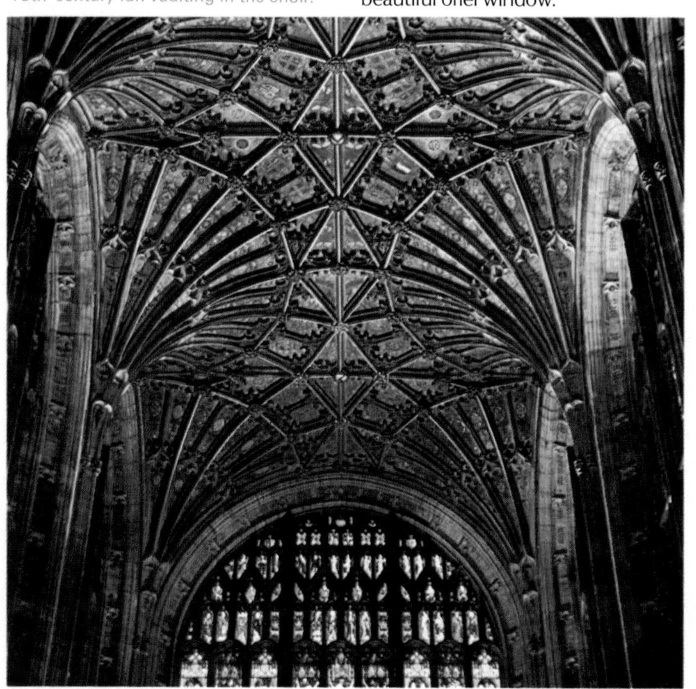

Sherborne Abbey has beautiful 15th-century fan vaulting in the choir.

Proceed for $\frac{1}{4}$ mile and turn left on to the A30 SP 'Sherborne'. Continue to Milborne Port.

MILBORNE PORT, Dorset ST61
Although stone is the predominant building material in this area, beautiful Venn House was brick built in Queen Anne style c1700. The local church preserves Saxon work, and a fine tympanum over the south door.

Proceed on the A30 to Sherborne.

SHERBORNE, Dorset ST61
Winding streets of mellow stone-built houses dating from the 15th century onwards weave a fascinating web across this beautiful and historic town. From AD705 to 1075 Sherborne was a cathedral city, but the great church was adopted by a slightly later monastery that flourished until the Dissolution in the 16th century. Many of the foundation's buildings were adopted by other bodies and survive in a good state of preservation. Some were occupied by the famous Sherborne School, and the Abbey Gatehouse now accommodates the Sherborne Museum of local history. Over all stands the Norman to 15th-century Abbey Church, a magnificent building best known for its superb fan vaulting. The older of the town's two castles stands $\frac{1}{2}$ mile east and dates from the 12th and 13th centuries. It was reduced to a picturesque heap of ruins (AM) in the Civil War. Sherborne's 16th-century castle was built for Sir Walter Raleigh, and contains fine furniture, paintings, and porcelain (open). It is set in 20-acre grounds designed by the 18th-century garden landscaper Capability Brown.

Follow SP 'Dorchester' to leave Sherborne on the A352. Pass through wooded country and continue through Middlemarsh. Make a winding ascent on the outer slopes to 860ft High Stoy to pass through a gap in the hills and reach Minterne Magna.

MINTERNE MAGNA, Dorset ST60
Features of the attractive wild shrub garden that occupies 29 acres of ground round Minterne House (open) include bamboo-lined walks, great banks of Himalayan and Chinese rhododendrons, and a beautiful collection of azaleas.

Continue for 2 miles and branch left to enter Cerne Abbas. The turf-cut Giant can be seen to the left.

CERNE ABBAS GIANT, Dorset ST60
This 180ft long figure (NT) is believed to be associated with fertility rites and may date from before the Roman occupation.

CERNE ABBAS, Dorset ST60
The village of Cerne Abbas derives its name from a Benedictine abbey founded here in 987. Remains of this include a beautiful 15th-century guesthouse, and the contemporary tithe barn has been converted into a house. Early examples of heraldic stained glass can be seen in the windows of the local church.

In Cerne Abbas centre turn left on to an unclassified road, then turn right on to the 'Piddletrenthide' road to reach that village.

PIDDLETRENTHIDE, Dorset SY79
Attractive yellow-stone houses are scattered for nearly a mile along the banks of the River Piddle, or Trent. The 15th-century church has one of the finest towers in Dorset.

Turn right onto the B3143 and continue through Piddlehinton. Continue for $1\frac{1}{2}$ miles and turn left on to the B3142 to pass Waterston Manor Gardens and reach Puddletown.

PUDDLETOWN, Dorset SY79
Thomas Hardy's Weatherbury in *Far from the Madding Crowd*, this village is one of the most attractive in Dorset and features a beautiful 15th-century church with an unusual panelled roof. Elizabethan and later Waterston Manor stands 2 miles northwest and was described by Hardy as Bathsheba's house in *Far from the Madding Crowd*. Between the village and Wareham are stretches of moorland that were part of the novel's Egdon Heath.

ATHELHAMPTON HOUSE Dorset SY79
Standing in 10 acres of formal landscape and water gardens about 1 mile east of Puddletown is the notable 15th- and 16th-century Athelhampton House, one of England's finest medieval houses (open).

Leave Puddletown and turn left on to the A354 SP 'Blandford'. Continue to Milborne St Andrew, then take an unclassified valley road to the left and drive to Milton Abbas.

Milton Abbas was built by the owner of Milton Abbey to replace a village which he demolished because it spoilt his view.

BULBARROW HILL, Dorset ST70
Excellent views over much of Dorset can be enjoyed from this 902ft hill, which is an official AA Viewpoint and one of the highest summits in this part of the country.

Follow SP 'Blandford', pass the outskirts of Winterbourne Stickland, and join the A354. Cross the River Stour to reach Blandford Forum.

ILTON ABBAS, Dorset ST80
et in unspoilt rural surroundings, is peaceful village of thatched and hitewashed cottages was designed nd built from scratch during the 3th century. It was probably the first tegrally planned village in Britain. ne Brewery Farm Museum is oused in the old brewery and ntains antique agricultural nplements, bygones, old otographs, and other relics.

om the foot of the village follow the ilton' road past Milton Abbey.

ILTON ABBEY, Dorset ST70
e beautiful abbey church dates m the 14th and 15th centuries d stands in front of a hill mounted by a Norman chapel. xt to Milton Abbey is 15th-century bot's Hall, which was orporated in a mansion by hitects Sir William Chambers and nes Wyatt. The huge 18th-century nsion here now is of exceptional erest and houses a school. It is en during the summer months.

ach Hilton and proceed for ¾ mile. nch right to reach Bulbarrow Hill.

BLANDFORD FORUM, Dorset ST80
All but 50 or so of the town's houses were destroyed by a terrible fire in 1731, which explains why handsome brick and stone architecture of the late 18th century is so much in evidence. Earlier survivals include the Ryves Almshouses of 1682, Dale House of 1689, and the early 17th-century Old House. Much of the countryside round Blandford is rich arable and dairy-farming land, watered by the beautiful River Stour to the south and fringed by the lovely countryside of Cranborne Chase to the north and west.

CRANBORNE CHASE, Dorset
Now an area of rolling grasslands scattered with fine beechwoods, the Chase covers over 100 square miles between Shaftesbury and Salisbury and was once a royal hunting forest. Subsequently the local hunting rights passed into the hands of the earls of Salisbury and Shaftesbury.

Bulbarrow Hill is situated in a part of Dorset which is designated as an area of outstanding natural beauty.

Leave Blandford Forum on the A350 SP 'Warminster'. Continue along the Stour Valley for 2¾ miles and pass through Stourpaine. Just past the village on the left are the hills of Hambledon and Hod.

HAMBLEDON AND HOD HILLS, Dorset ST81
Grass-covered Hambledon Hill rises to 622ft and is topped by earthworks raised at various times between the stone age and the Roman conquest. Its steep flanks, worth climbing for the tremendous views, were used by General Wolfe to train troops before embarking to take Quebec. To the south east is slightly lower Hod Hill, which features ancient earthworks and traces of a Roman camp that was built and manned cAD63.

Continue to Iwerne Minster.

IWERNE MINSTER, Dorset ST81
The local Norman to 17th-century church has an attractive stone spire. Just outside the village is the site of a Roman villa.

From Iwerne Minster war memorial turn right on to the unclassified 'Tarrant Gunville' road. Climb on to the heights of Cranborne Chase and turn left on to the Shaftesbury road. Excellent views across Blackmore Vale can be enjoyed from this section of route. Continue for 2½ miles, meet crossroads, and turn right for Ashmore.

ASHMORE, Dorset ST91
Georgian houses mingle with flint, stone, and brick cottages round a duckpond and 19th-century church in this charming village. The village itself stands at 700ft in the chalk hills of Cranborne Chase and is the highest in Dorset. To the north is a summit, topped by a prehistoric earthwork, which commands views across the Chase to the Solent channel and the Isle of Wight.

Keep left of Ashmore village pond and join the B3081 to enter Wiltshire for a short distance. On the right is tree-capped Win Green, a 910ft hill which is accessible by track and is the highest point on Cranborne Chase. Re-enter Dorset and descend Zig-Zag Hill to enter Shaftesbury.

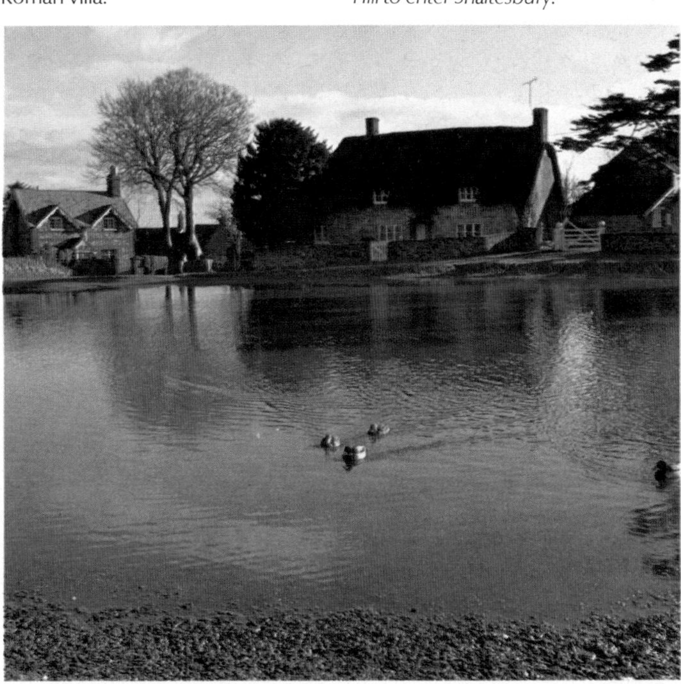

The atmosphere of rural tranquillity at Ashmore is enhanced by a duckpond.

TOUR 13 — 40 MILES

THE ISLE OF PURBECK

Superb views over this exceptionally beautiful peninsula can be enjoyed from high downs that drop sheer to the sea as massive limestone cliffs on the south side. East is the superb haven of Poole Harbour, which insinuates little creeks between heathery promontories and long, tree-covered spits.

THE ISLE OF PURBECK, Dorset
Most of this tour stays within the confines of the Isle of Purbeck, a wild and lovely peninsula that extends from Poole Harbour to Lulworth Cove and is crossed to the west by the Purbeck Hills. Like much of Dorset this is Thomas Hardy country, and reminders of the author and his many novels are everywhere. It is also a designated area of outstanding natural beauty.

SWANAGE, Dorset SZ07
This busy resort stands between towering downs that end as cliff-girded promontories on both sides of the sandy bay. Winding, switchback streets weave down to a shopping and amusement area concentrated on the only level piece of ground in the town – the sea front. Farther round the bay is the small pier and quay, where the Bournemouth ferry docks and anglers fish. An attractive group of old buildings clusters round the Mill Pond, off the Main Street.

DURLSTON COUNTRY PARK, Dorset SZ07
Accessible from Swanage by road or a 1-mile footpath, this fascinating area of wild clifftop has many unusual features. Imposing Durlston Castle is built of Purbeck stone and occupies a lovely site near the headland. On Durlston Head itself is a 40-ton globe map of the world, fashioned from Portland stone quarried in the district, and $\frac{1}{4}$ mile away near the Anvil Lighthouse are the Tilly Whim caves – old quarries once used by smugglers.

Leave Swanage on the A351 SP 'Wareham'. In $1\frac{1}{2}$ miles turn left on to the B3069 to pass through Langton Matravers, a picturesque hillside village of local stone. Climb to 400ft and turn left on to an unclassified road for Worth Matravers.

WORTH MATRAVERS, Dorset SY97
This village is an enchanting combination of steep streets and stone cottages, surrounded by lovely Dorsetshire countryside. A rough road south leads to the tiny Norman chapel and fine views of lonely St Alban's (or Aldhelm's) Head, while a toll road to the west leads to cliff-encircled Chapman's Pool.

From Worth Matravers take the 'Kingston' road and continue for $1\frac{1}{4}$ miles to a T-junction. Turn left to rejoin the B3069, and continue to Kingston, with good views to Corfe Castle.

KINGSTON, Dorset SY97
Features of 19th-century Kingston Church, considered one of the finest in the area, include black Purbeck marble pillars and a beautiful stone-vaulted chancel.

From Kingston a pleasant detour from the main route can be taken via a toll road to 600ft Swyre Head. In clear weather both the Isle of Portland and Isle of Wight can be seen from here. On the main route, however, leave Kingston with the B3069 and make a sharp, winding descent to meet the A351. Turn left along the road to enter Corfe Castle.

Corfe Castle dominates its surroundings.
The River Frome flows to the south of Wareham.

CORFE CASTLE, Dorset SY98
Dominated by the picturesquely ruined stronghold from which it takes its name, this Purbeck-stone village owes its existence to the curiously symmetrical hill on which the castle stands. The mound rises exactly in the centre of a gap in the Purbeck Hills and was probably first fortified by King Alfred against the Danes. When the Normans came they occupied the site and began the magnificent 12th- to 15th-century castle (open) whose remains can be seen today. After the Civil War Cromwell made sure that it could never again be used against him by blowing it up with gunpowder. A river curls round the base of the steep hill. On the village side is a deep moat spanned by a bridge, and in a garden off the main street is a perfect replica of the village and castle in miniature. Various old relics from the village can be seen in the local museum, and an interesting (though very informal) fossil museum occupies a shed near the castle gates.

Ammonites are the most easily identified of many fossil types found in Dorset.

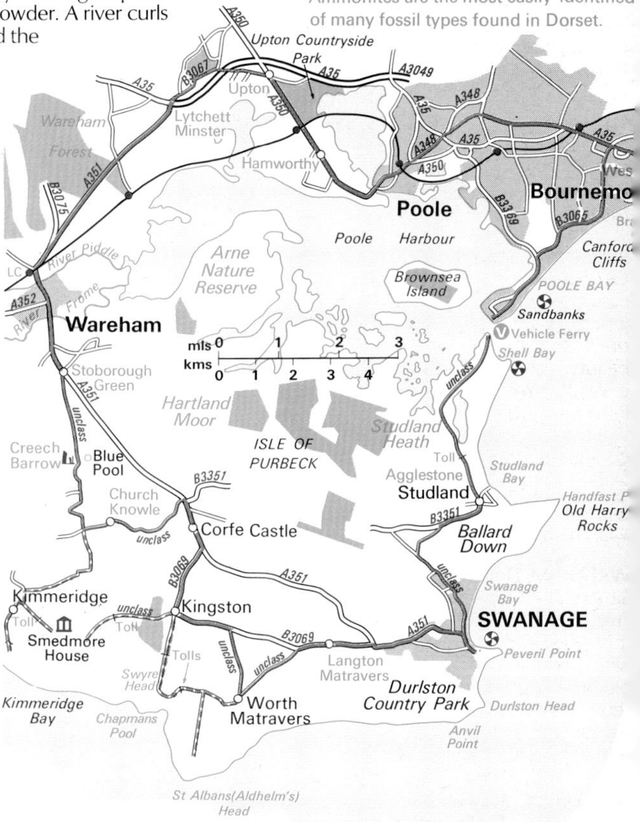

Continue along the 'Wareham' road and just past the castle turn left and skirt the castle hill to reach Church Knowle. Drive through Church Knowle and meet crossroads. A detour can be taken from the main route by turning left and following to roads through the estate of Smedmore House to Kimmeridge and Kimmeridge Bay.

KIMMERIDGE, Dorset SY97
Thatched and slate-roofed cottages make up this tiny village, which is situated near the shallow bay from which it takes its name. A toll road leads to the coast.

KIMMERIDGE BAY, Dorset SY97
Very low cliffs of black shale ring this wide, sandless bay, and the beach is littered with great chunks of rock literally packed with fossil ammonites. A condition of entry to the beach nowadays is that hammers and chisels should be left behind. A well sunk here in 1959 produces some 10,000 tons of crude oil each year.

SMEDMORE HOUSE, Dorset SY97
Nearly all the land round Kimmeridge village and bay forms part of the Smedmore estate, and it is by permission of the big house that visitors are allowed on to the toll roads that lead to the attractive coast. The house itself (open) shows a combination of Jacobean, Queen Anne, and Georgian styles. Inside is a good collection of antique dolls.

To continue on the main route, turn right at the crossroads outside Church Knowle and cross the Purbeck Hills. Left are views of Creech Barrow and to the right is the attractive Blue Pool.

BLUE POOL, Dorset SY98
Once an ugly scar left by the extraction of clay, this flooded pit (open) has been transformed into one of the county's most famous beauty spots by the re-establishment of coniferous woodland on its banks. Particles of clay suspended in the water make it brilliant blue when conditions are right.

Continue to Stoborough Green and turn left on to the A351 to reach Wareham.

WAREHAM, Dorset SY98
Situated between the tidal River Frome and the River Trent (or Piddle), this quiet port has an ancient quay which now serves anglers and pleasure craft. In Saxon times the settlement was defended by earthworks, and their grass-covered remains still almost encircle the town. Much of Wareham was rebuilt after a great fire in 1762, which explains why so many attractive Georgian houses can be seen here. The parish church preserves original Saxon work and contains an effigy of Lawrence of Arabia. To the north of the town are the sandy heathlands and coniferous plantations of 3,500-acre Wareham Forest, which covers much of the isolated area described by Thomas Hardy as 'Egdon Heath' in his novels. The area is one of high fire risk so great care must be taken with lighted cigarettes.

Leave Wareham on the A351 SP 'Bournemouth' and continue for 4 miles to a roundabout. Take the 2nd exit SP 'Lytchett Minster B3067' and pass through Lytchett Minster to reach Upton. At Upton turn right on to the A350 to reach the Upton Countryside Park on the left.

UPTON COUNTRYSIDE PARK, Dorset SY99
Features of this extensive parkland area beside Holne Bay include a planned and marked nature trail and picnic site.

Kimmeridge Bay, which is famous for its fossils, is overlooked by a ruined tower that was built in the early 19th century.

Continue on the A350 and pass through residential Hamworthy before crossing a bridge to reach Poole Old Town.

POOLE, Dorset SZ09
Elizabeth I granted Poole county status which it kept until the late 19th century, and today it is a busy mixture of industrial centre and tourist resort. Its good beach and sheltered harbour have made it popular with holidaymakers, and its position in a lovely and historic area of heaths and pinewoods makes it ideal as a touring base. Many fine old buildings stand in Poole's historic precinct, including the 18th-century Guildhall and a medieval merchant's house called Scaplen's. Both buildings contain local interest museums.

POOLE HARBOUR & BROWNSEA ISLAND, Dorset SZ08
Archaeological evidence suggests that Phoenician sailors were using this vast harbour as early as 800BC. It is the second largest natural harbour in the world, and has a coastline that measures over 100 miles if all its indentations are considered. Its largest island is Brownsea, which is accessible by boat from Poole Quay and is famous as the site of Lord Baden-Powell's first scout camp. Part of its wild heath, wood, and reed-fringed marshland is protected as a nature reserve (NT) and is a haven for many forms of wildlife, including the rare red squirrel.

Leave Poole town centre on the A348 SP 'Ringwood' and proceed for 1 mile to a roundabout. Go forward into Constitution Hill road and continue through residential areas to reach Bournemouth.

BOURNEMOUTH, Dorset SZ09
In 1840 a marine-resort village was laid out here, and with its natural advantages grew quickly to become one of Britain's largest seaside resorts. Among its assets are a mild climate, 6 miles of sandy beach, attractive sandstone cliffs, and deep ravines that provide pleasant wooded walks to the shore. Facilities for shopping and entertainment are excellent, and the cultural interest of the town is amply demonstrated by the world-famous Bournemouth Symphony Orchestra. Three major places of interest are the British Typewriter Museum, the Rothesay Museum, and the Russell-Cotes Art Gallery and Museum. Attractive gardens follow the Bourne stream from high in the town to the bustling seafront.

Return along the A35 'Poole' road, pass through Westbourne and turn left into Avenue Road (B3065). Continue to Branksome Chine, then turn inland to drive through the residential Canford Cliffs area.

CANFORD CLIFFS, Dorset SZ08
A special feature of this residential area is the Compton Acres Gardens (open), which are reputed to be amongst the finest in Europe.

Continue along Haven Road, and descend to Poole Harbour and Sandbanks.

SANDBANKS, Dorset SZ08
The sandy beaches of this mile-long peninsula are backed by dunes, and a car ferry operates from Haven Point for Studland and Swanage.

Cross the entrance of Poole Harbour by ferry, then follow an unclassified road to Studland.

STUDLAND, Dorset SZ08
Built mainly of red brick, this village contains a fine Norman church and offers 2 miles of sandy beach sheltered by dunes. Moorland extends west from here to Wareham, and on the heathland 1 mile north west is a 500-ton ironstone rock known as the Agglestone.

BALLARD DOWNS AND OLD HARRY ROCKS, Dorset SZ08
Views from Studland Bay extend to the headland of Handfast Point and the isolated chalk stacks of the Old Harry Rocks. A little farther south the great bulk of Ballard Down shelters Swanage from the sea and offers good coastal views.

From Studland turn inland on the B3351. In 1 mile turn left on to an unclassified road SP 'Swanage' and climb over Ballard Down to return to Swanage.

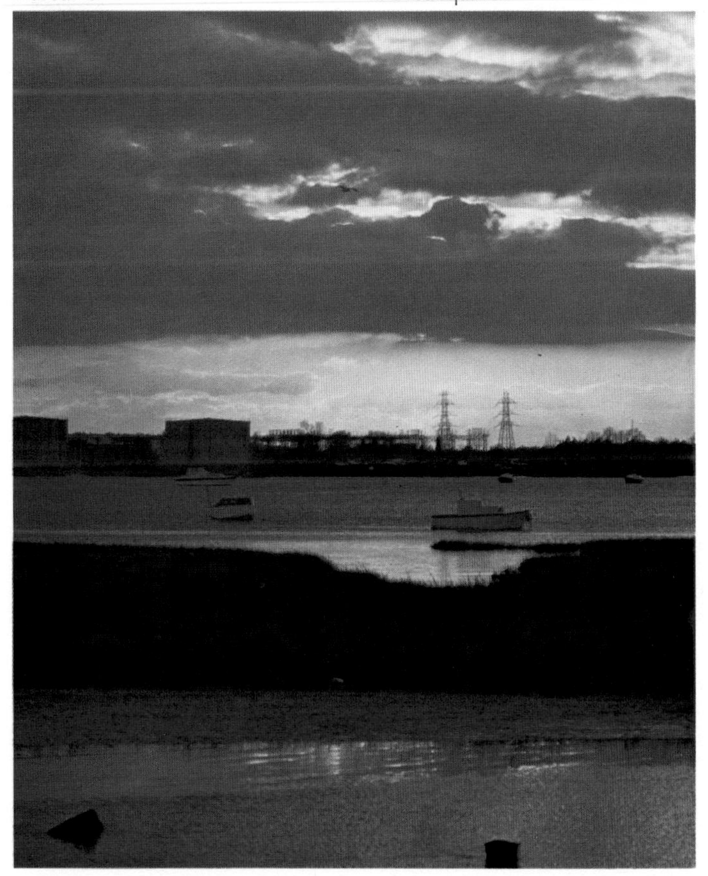

The less sightly aspects of 20th-century life are softened by sunset at Poole Harbour.

TOUR 14 — 59 MILES

OVER THE BRENDON HILLS

Where Exmoor merges into the Brendon Hills the landscape changes from wild heathland to a tapestry of fields and forest. Wooded byways and patches of moor open on to panoramic seascapes fringed with busy resorts and unspoiled villages.

MINEHEAD, Somerset SS94
The natural beauty of its surroundings combined with its delightful situation and mild climate have made this a popular seaside resort with holidaymakers from all over the country. The Esplanade commands a wide sweep of the bay, where the sands are good and bathing is safe. A prominent feature of the high ground behind the town is North Hill, which overlooks the quaint little harbour some hundreds of feet below and affords fine views across the Bristol Channel. On the landward slope is the parish church, where years ago a light burned constantly to guide travellers on the moor and lead ships to the harbour. During these times Minehead harbour was a busy Channel port second only to Bristol, but now it is just the pleasant holiday town it appears to be. Among its attractions are the beautifully-kept Blenheim Gardens, where there is a model town which is floodlit in the evening.

WEST SOMERSET RAILWAY, Somerset SS94
Britain's longest private line, this railway was re-opened in 1976 and runs 25 miles from the coast at Minehead to the lovely interior of Somerset. The trains are steam hauled and provide a nostalgic way to enjoy the scenery. Refreshments and souvenirs are available at the Minehead terminus.

Leave Minehead on the A39 'Porlock' road and enter the Exmoor National Park area. In $2\frac{1}{2}$ miles turn right on to an unclassified road and drive to Selworthy.

EXMOOR NATIONAL PARK (EAST), Somerset
East Exmoor and its associated area is a gentler landscape than the rugged central moor. Open moorland contrasts colourfully with the intensively farmed Brendon slopes, and both natural and planted forests lap occasional rocky summits that afford good all-round views. To the north is the beautiful Bristol Channel coast, while inland are National Trust villages that include some of the most picturesque communities in the entire west country. See also tours 9 and 10.

SELWORTHY, Somerset SS94
This charming village (NT) is one of the most frequented beauty spots in north Somerset, and is grouped round a walnut-shaped green attractively edged with flowers and overlooked by several old cottages. Also of note are the 15th-century almshouses and an old tithe barn, while over all is the sturdy square tower of the 16th-century church. This handsome building is renowned for the particularly fine wagon roof in its south aisle. Majestic Selworthy Beacon (NT) rises to 1,012ft north of the village and is a good viewpoint.

Return to the A39 'Porlock' road, turn right, and after a little while skirt Allerford.

Beyond Luccombe well-tended countryside gives way to open moorland which rises to the summit of 1,705ft Dunkery Beacon.

ALLERFORD, Somerset SS94
Quaint cottages and the remains of a manor house can be seen here; of particular note is Allerford's much-photographed double-arched packhorse bridge.

Continue on the A39 for $\frac{1}{2}$ mile, then turn left on to an unclassified road SP 'West Luccombe'. After this village pass another packhorse bridge to the right. After 1 mile meet crossroads and turn right. A detour can be taken from the main route to Luccombe village by keeping straight ahead.

LUCCOMBE, Somerset SS94
Access to this secluded little village (NT), whose name means 'closed-in combe', is by a narrow winding lane. The village church has a good tower, and the churchyard is entered through a charming lychgate.

On the main route, begin the long ascent of Dunkery Hill.

HOLNICOTE ESTATE, Somerset SS84
The rolling moorland and dense forest round Dunkery Hill are part of the East Holnicote Estate (NT), which incorporates some of the loveliest scenery in the Exmoor National Park. About half its 12,420 acres fall within the Exmoor boundaries, and the whole forms a band 6 miles deep along the wild Bristol Channel coastline. Features include various prehistoric remains, 4 ancient packhorse bridges, and such notable villages as picturesque Selworthy and Luccombe (both NT).

Continue the ascent of Dunkery Hill through progressively wilder scenery and reach a road summit of 1,450ft. A footpath leads from the carpark here to the 1,705 ft viewpoint of Dunkery Beacon.

DUNKERY BEACON, Somerset SS84
Dunkery Beacon (NT), the highest point on Exmoor, is surrounded by some of the most breathtaking scenery in the national park. It was once a link in a chain of fire-beacon sites across the west country. The top is nowadays shared by a cairn commemorating the gift of the hill to the National Trust, the remains of several tumuli, and an official AA viewpoint marker. The Cloutsham Nature Trail (open all year) starts from Webber's Post and covers some 3 miles of varied habitat.

Stay on the unclassified road and descend for $2\frac{1}{2}$ miles to the main road. Join the B3224, reach Wheddon Cross, and proceed along an unclassified road SP 'Taunton'. Drive to Heath Poult Cross and on to the Brendon Hills.

BRENDON HILLS, Somerset
Undulating slopes with a rich patchwork of forest and farmland are the distinctive characteristics of this gentle range. Farmers, and more recently the Forestry Commission, have transformed the landscape from moorland into a semi-cultivated countryside of symmetrical fields bordered by beech hedges and interspersed with acres of dark conifers. In earlier times small hillside mining villages sprang up to work local deposits of iron ore, but the last Brendon iron mine closed down in 1883. Vestiges of an even earlier age can be seen along the Ridgeway, which is studded with round barrows dating from the bronze age.

From the crossroads at Heath Poult Cross turn right and continue for 5 miles, with the River Exe to the right and River Haddeo to the left. Descend into the Exe Valley and turn left on to the A396, SP 'Tiverton'. Reach Exebridge and turn left on to an unclassified road SP 'Morebath'. After $1\frac{1}{2}$ miles turn left on to the B3190 'Watchet' road, and pass Morebath; 4 miles beyond the village Wimbleball Reservoir lies to the left.

The packhorse bridge at Allerford.

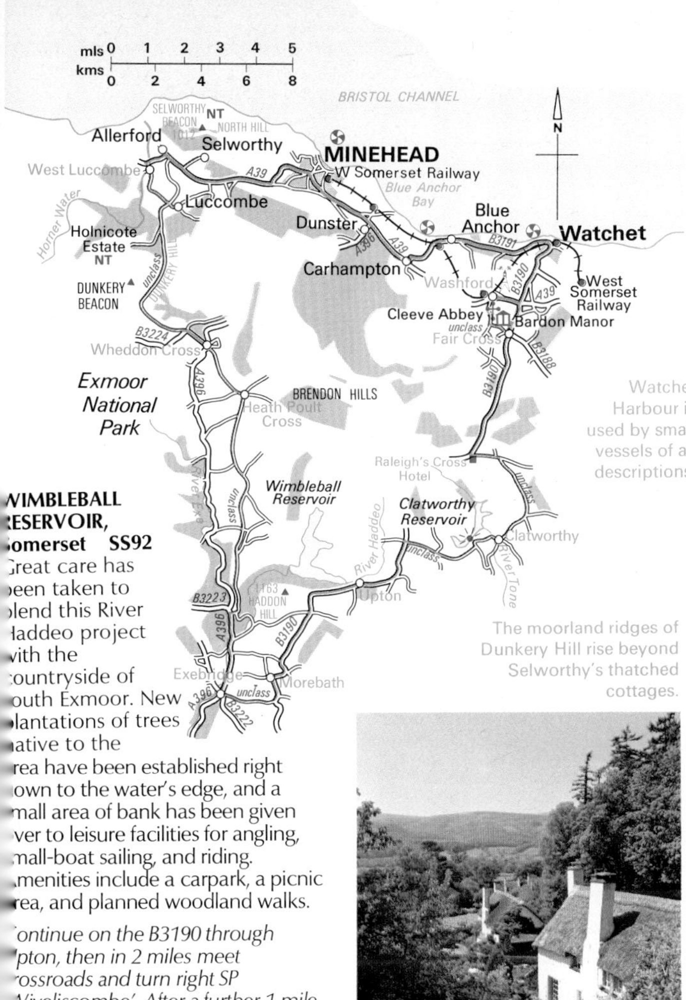

Watchet Harbour is used by small vessels of all descriptions.

The moorland ridges of Dunkery Hill rise beyond Selworthy's thatched cottages.

WIMBLEBALL RESERVOIR, Somerset SS92
Great care has been taken to blend this River Haddeo project with the countryside of south Exmoor. New plantations of trees native to the area have been established right down to the water's edge, and a small area of bank has been given over to leisure facilities for angling, small-boat sailing, and riding. Amenities include a carpark, a picnic area, and planned woodland walks.

Continue on the B3190 through Upton, then in 2 miles meet crossroads and turn right SP 'Wiveliscombe'. After a further 1 mile branch left and drive over crossroads to skirt Clatworthy Reservoir.

CLATWORTHY RESERVOIR, Somerset ST03
Like its close neighbour Wimbleball, this beautiful upland reservoir has been integrated with the local scenery and is a haven for all kinds of wildlife. A large carpark gives access to a 10-acre public viewing area with picnic facilities.

Continue, and later cross the River Tone before reaching Clatworthy village. Keep left through the village SP 'Brompton Ralph', and after 1 mile meet crossroads. Turn left SP 'Raleigh's Cross', then after a further 2 miles meet a T-junction and turn left. Reach Raleigh's Cross Hotel and turn right on to the B3190 SP 'Watchet'. Continue over high ground, with excellent views of the Bristol Channel, and descend to crossroads at Fair Cross. A detour can be made from the main route to Bardon Manor by staying on the B3190 for a further ½ mile.

BARDON MANOR, Somerset ST04
Features of this beautiful and unspoilt 14th-century manor house (open) include a notable Saxon fireplace in the main hall, a cockpit, and a ghost. West Country artists exhibit their paintings and handicrafts here.

Continue with the main route by turning left at Fair Cross crossroads on to an unclassified road SP 'Washford'. This is the entrance to Cleeve Abbey.

CLEEVE ABBEY, Somerset ST04
Remains of this 13th-century Cistercian abbey (AM), founded in 1188, include a refectory with traceried windows, a timbered roof, and some fine wall paintings. The picturesque gatehouse and painted chamber are of particular note.

Continue to Washford, then turn right on to the A39 for ¾ mile. Meet crossroads and turn left on to the B3190 for Watchet.

WATCHET, Somerset ST04
Coleridge found the main character for his long, moralistic poem *The Rime of the Ancient Mariner* in this historic seaport, which now doubles as a popular resort. The Esplanade offers a grandstand view of the bustling harbour, and the local beaches offer plenty of opportunities for the fossil hunter. Behind the town are the lofty heights of the Brendon and Quantock hill ranges.

Leave Watchet on the B3191 and continue, with views of the Bristol Channel, to Blue Anchor.

BLUE ANCHOR, Somerset ST04
In front of this small hamlet is a clean white beach which sweeps round the alabaster rocks of Blue Anchor Bay in a brilliant arc. The area is well known for its fossils.

Continue on the B3191 to Carhampton.

The ancient village of Dunster is dominated by its romantic castle.

CARHAMPTON, Somerset ST04
This little village dates back to 833, when it was the site of a Danish victory. Its restored church contains a magnificent painted screen which dates from the 15th century and stretches across the entire breadth of the building. Each January the villagers re-enact the old ceremony of Wassailing the Apple Trees, an ancient custom involving a toast to the largest apple tree in the cider orchards and a libation of cider thrown on its trunk. The whole procedure has more than a suggestion of ancient fertility rites. Close to the church lychgate is an old pub called the Butcher's Arms, which has the date 1638 worked in sheep's knuckle bones in the cobbled floor.

At Carhampton turn right on to the A39 'Minehead' road and after 1½ miles turn left on to the A396 SP 'Tiverton'. Continue into Dunster.

DUNSTER, Somerset SS94
Dunster is a beautiful medieval village that has often been described as a 'perfect relic of feudal times'. Its unspoilt condition is largely due to its constant ownership by one family, the Luttrells, for some 600 years until 1950. The castle (NT) was the family seat and is well worth visiting. Its oak-panelled halls display magnificent ceilings and fascinating relics. In the centre of the village is the octagonal Yarn Market, which was built in 1609, when Dunster was an important cloth centre. Not far away is the lovely Luttrell Arms, which is said to have stood for three centuries and was originally the house of the Abbot of Cleeve. Among its many features are an interesting 15th- century porch and a fine chamber displaying a wealth of carved oak. The parish church is by far the finest in this part of the country. Both it and its associated buildings are of a particularly warm pink sandstone, and the whole harmonious group is set in a tranquil rural scene. Nearby the River Avill is spanned by ancient Gallox packhorse bridge (AM).

Return along the A396 for ½ mile and turn left to rejoin the A39. Return to Minehead.

WELLS, Somerset ST54
Wells is a delightful cathedral city situated at the foot of the Mendip Hills. The west front of its fine 13th-to 15th-century cathedral is adorned with statues, and inside are a graceful branching staircase and a 14th-century clock. With its associated buildings the cathedral forms part of England's largest medieval ecclesiastical precinct. The Vicar's Close preserves picturesque 14th-century houses, and across the cathedral green is the moated Bishop's Palace (open), where Wells' famous swans ring a bell near the drawbridge for food. Other interesting old buildings include a medieval tithe barn (AM) and the 15th-century parish church. Wells Museum includes a display on the Mendip Caves.

An interesting detour from the main route to the caves of Wookey Hole can be made at Wells: leave the city on the A371 'Cheddar' road and in $\frac{1}{4}$ mile turn right on to the unclassified 'Wookey Hole' road. Continue for $1\frac{1}{2}$ miles to Wookey Hole. Please note that route directions for the main tour start after the following entry.

WOOKEY HOLE, Somerset ST54
Inhabited for some 650 years from 250BC this gigantic system was hollowed out of the Mendip limestone by the River Axe. Finds relating to the period of habitation can be seen in the associated museum. The old mill at the cave entrance demonstrates the art of paper making, and is a store for Madame Tussaud's waxwork museum and Lady Bangor's fairground collection.

Leave Wells by the A39 'Glastonbury' road and continue to Glastonbury.

GLASTONBURY, Somerset ST43
High above the skyline of this ancient town is the 520ft pinnacle of Glastonbury Tor, a mystical place associated in myth with fabulous Avalon and the Celtic Otherworld. Glastonbury was probably founded in Celtic times, but according to legend it was created by Joseph of Arimathea. Other traditions connect St Patrick and King Arthur with the abbey, and it is said that Arthur is actually buried here. The well preserved remains that exist today date from the 12th and 13th centuries, and include St Mary's Church, the abbey church, and a number of monastic buildings (open). By far the best preserved is the superb Abbot's Kitchen. Features of the town itself include 2 medieval churches, the George and Pilgrim Inn, and a 15th- century abbey courthouse known as the Tribunal (open). The latter now houses late prehistoric finds from lake dwellings at Meare and Godney.

Leave Glastonbury on the B3151 SP 'Meare' and proceed through low-lying country to Meare.

TOUR 15 72 MILES

THE POLDEN AND MENDIP RANGES

Low-lying areas of unpopulated countryside are dominated by the bare Mendip summits and lower Polden Hills. Here are the cradle of early English Christianity, the supposed site of King Arthur's fabulous Camelot, and old battlefields that have seen decisive turning points in the country's history.

Over 400 statues survive on the west front of Wells Cathedral. They were made during the 13th century and were inspired by sculpture in Continental cathedrals.

MEARE, Somerset ST44
From c300BC to cAD100 a lake settlement of houses on stilts and brushwood existed here. Few traces of this survive, but excavations have yielded many interesting finds that are displayed in Taunton and Glastonbury Museums. A 14th-century building known as the Fish House (AM) was used by the monks of Glastonbury to house their fishermen, and the contemporary manor house was a summer residence for the abbots.

Continue on the B3151 for $1\frac{1}{4}$ miles and turn left on to an unclassified road SP 'Shapwick, Bridgwater'. Meet a T-junction and turn left again. Continue across level, wooded countryside to Shapwick. By Shapwick Church turn right on to the 'Bridgwater' road and ascend the gradual slope of the Polden Hills.

Glastonbury Tor is reputed to be one of England's most magical places.

THE POLDEN HILLS, Somerset
These low hills (part NT), rising to less than 300ft at their highest point, extend from Glastonbury to a point near Bridgwater and dominate the surrounding marshy levels.

About $\frac{3}{4}$ mile from Shapwick cross a main road, then continue for $\frac{1}{2}$ mile and turn right on to the A39. Proceed along a low ridge for 5 miles, then descend and bear sharp left over the King's Sedgemoor Drain. Cross the M5 and enter Bridgwater.

BRIDGWATER, Somerset ST33
It was here that the rebellious Duke of Monmouth proclaimed himself King in 1685, prior to suffering a crushing defeat 3 miles south east at Sedgemoor. Before the battle began Monmouth surveyed the field from the tower of the local church.

From Bridgwater follow SP 'Langport' on the A372 and recross the M5. Drive across Sedgemoor.

SEDGEMOOR, Somerset ST33
In the 17th century the last battle on English soil was fought here when James II met James Duke of Monmouth. The King won a decisive victory at the expense of the lives of some 1,400 of Monmouth's followers. The rebels who survived were subsequently dealt with by the travelling 'Bloody Assize' of the notorious Judge Jeffries.

Continue through Weston Zoyland, then after another $2\frac{1}{4}$ miles skirt Middlezoy. Proceed for 1 mile, then turn right on to the A361 and follow SP 'Taunton' to enter Othery. Procee for $1\frac{3}{4}$ miles to Burrow Bridge.

BURROW BRIDGE & BURROW MUMP, Somerset ST33
Wide views are afforded by the hill, or mump (NT), here; an extensive collection of Victorian engines is housed in an old pumping station (open) near by.

Cross the River Parrett and immediately turn left (no SP) on to a unclassified road. Follow SP 'Stathe, Langport', reach Stathe, and follow S 'Curry Rivel'. After $\frac{3}{4}$ mile branch rig continue for 1 mile, and ascend Red Hill (NT) for excellent views over Sedgemoor. At the road summit be right. Proceed for $\frac{3}{4}$ mile and turn lef on to the A378 to enter Curry Rivel. Continue for $\frac{1}{4}$ mile and turn right o to an unclassified road SP 'Drayton, Muchelney'. Proceed through Drayton to reach Muchelney.

MUCHELNEY, Somerset ST42
The Benedictine abbey whose extensive remains (AM) survive her was not the first foundation on the site. Excavations have revealed a ra Saxon chapel, dating from around the 7th century, beneath ruined Norman monastic buildings. Priest' House is a good 14th-century thatched building (NT).

Leave Muchelney by bearing left wi SP 'Langport'. Continue for 1 mile, meet a T-junction, and turn right to enter Huish Episcopi.

Vells Cathedral's
4th-century
stronomical
lock.

Turn right by Somerton Church into unclassified New Street SP 'Ilchester, Yeovil'. Continue for $\frac{1}{2}$ mile and turn right on to the B3151. After $\frac{3}{4}$ mile turn right then left across the A372. Proceed for $1\frac{1}{2}$ miles and turn right, then enter a mini-roundabout and take the 1st exit on to an unclassified road SP 'Yeovilton, Wincanton'. A possible detour from the main route to Ilchester leads ahead from the mini-roundabout.

ILCHESTER, Somerset ST52
In Roman times this quiet River Yeo town was an important military station. Its superb Town Hall houses a 13th-century mace - the oldest staff of office in England.

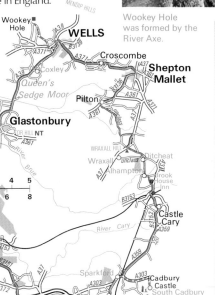

Wookey Hole was formed by the River Axe.

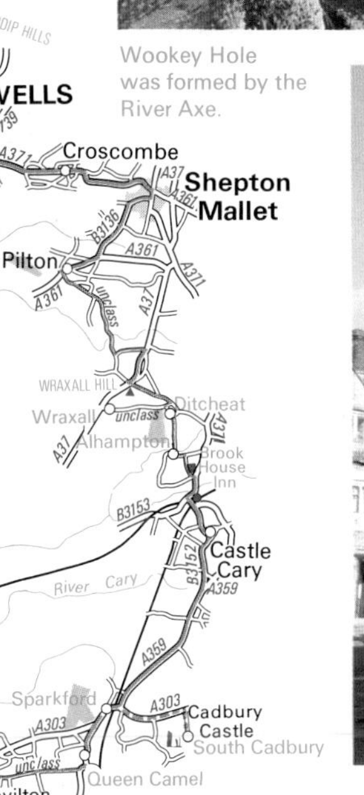

The Market Cross in Somerton was rebuilt in 1673.

'UISH EPISCOPI, Somerset ST42
lass by Burne-Jones and a fine orman doorway are features of the cal church, but its crowning glory is 15th-century tower considered to e the finest in the county.

ontinue and turn right on to the 372 'Wincanton, Yeovil' road, assing the edge of Long Sutton.

)NG SUTTON, Somerset ST42
is attractive village is grouped und a notable 15th-century urch and boasts a 17th-century anor house.

oceed for $\frac{1}{2}$ mile and turn left on to e B3165 SP 'Somerton'. Continue $2\frac{1}{4}$ miles and turn right SP hester' to enter Somerton.

)MERTON, Somerset ST42
merton was the capital of merset under the West Saxons d is particularly known for its ractive market place. All around e square and along the back eets are handsome old buildings, luding the Town Hall of c1700 and e 17th-century Hext Almshouses. merton Church carries a gnificent tie-beam roof dating m the 15th century.

On the main route, continue for $1\frac{1}{2}$ miles from the mini-roundabout and pass the entrance to the Royal Navy Air Station to reach the Fleet Air Arm Museum at Yeovilton.

YEOVILTON, Somerset ST52
Yeovilton's Fleet Air Arm Museum portrays the development of naval aviation since 1903 and displays over 40 historic aircraft.

Proceed for $\frac{1}{4}$ mile and turn right on to the 'Queen Camel' road. Continue for $2\frac{1}{2}$ miles and go forward on to the A359 SP 'Sparkford, Frome' to enter Queen Camel. Proceed for $\frac{3}{4}$ mile and turn right on to the A303 to enter Sparkford. Here a detour can be taken from the main route to Cadbury Castle along the A303: proceed for $1\frac{1}{2}$ miles and turn right on to an unclassified road for South Cadbury.

CADBURY CASTLE, Somerset ST62
Once it was thought that the myths linking this hilltop fort with King Arthur's Camelot had been disproved by excavations revealing evidence of stone- and bronze-age occupation. However, digging in 1966 suggested that the site had been re-defended during Arthur's period. The Saxon King Ethelred (the Unready) established a mint here.

From Sparkford bear right to cross a railway bridge, then turn immediately left on to the A359 'Frome' road. Continue for $3\frac{1}{4}$ miles and branch left on to the B3152 SP 'Castle Cary'. Continue $1\frac{1}{2}$ miles to enter Castle Cary.

CASTLE CARY, Somerset ST63
Several fine old houses and a pretty duckpond are grouped together at the heart of this pleasant small town. The local lock-up, an unusual circular structure once used for the restriction of petty mischief makers, dates from the 18th century.

Leave Castle Cary with SP 'Bath, Bristol (A371)'. After 1 mile turn left on to the A371 SP 'Shepton Mallet'. Shortly bear right across a railway bridge, then proceed for $\frac{1}{2}$ mile to the Brook House Inn and turn left on to an unclassified road SP 'Alhampton, Ditcheat'. Proceed for 1 mile to enter Alhampton and bear right SP 'Ditcheat, Glastonbury'. Proceed for 1 mile to Ditcheat, meet a T-junction, and turn left (no SP). Continue to the Manor House Inn and turn right, then shortly bear left SP 'East Pennard'. Proceed to Wraxall, meet crossroads, and turn right on to the A37 'Shepton Mallet' road. Ascend Wraxall Hill and meet crossroads. Turn left on to an unclassified road SP 'East Pennard', then continue for $\frac{1}{2}$ mile and turn right SP 'Pilton' to reach Pilton.

PILTON, Somerset ST54
One of the most picturesque villages in the area, lovely Pilton has an ancient cruciform tithe barn (AM) and a church with a magnificent 15th-century roof.

Meet crossroads in Pilton and turn left, then reach the church and turn left SP 'Shepton Mallet'. Meet a T-junction and turn right on to the A361. Proceed for 1 mile, then turn left on to the B3136 for Shepton Mallet.

SHEPTON MALLET, Somerset ST64
Wool from flocks grazing the windswept Mendip Hills made the fortune of this pleasant market town. Several good 17th- and 18th-century buildings survive from this period, plus a fine church with an intricately carved nave roof.

Leave the town with SP 'Wells A371' to enter Croscombe.

CROSCOMBE, Somerset ST54
Steep wooded hills surround this stone-built village, which has an old church containing amazing 17th-century pastoral and heraldic carvings in rich black oak.

Continue along the A371 to re-enter Wells.

Dodington House
Tormarton
Burton
Cotswolds
Castle Combe
Yatton Keynell
Dyrham Park
Tog Hill
Pennsylvania
Biddestone
Chippenham
Corsham
Bowood House
Lacock
Little Solsbury Hill
Batheaston
Race Course
Bathford
Beanacre
Great Chalfield Manor
University
BATH
Plough Inn
Melksham
Broughton Gifford
Holt
Bradford-on-Avon
Barton Farm Country Park
mls 0 1 2 3 4 5
kms 0 2 4 6 8

TOUR 16 54 MILES

FROM THE CITY OF ELEGANCE

High in the hills that provided the stone for Britain's most elegant city are the Cotswold wool towns. Sturdy manor houses and fine churches seem to grow from the mellow rock, and everywhere are the grass-grown scars of old quarry workings.

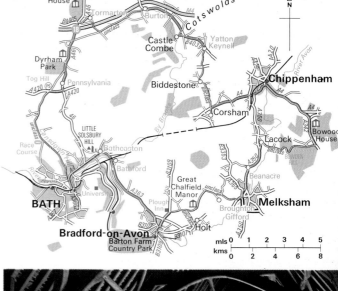

BATH, Avon ST76
Justly spoken of as England's most elegant city, Bath is a spa resort of Georgian terraces, crescents, and squares arranged round spacious landscaped parks in the Avon Valley. Warm local stone is set off by trim lawns and mature trees, and the source of the city's prosperity still bubbles into cisterns and baths built by the Romans some 2,000 years ago. Many centuries after the invaders left *Aquae Sulis* to salvage their crashing empire, the dandified high society of Georgian England resumed the sophisticating process. Beau Nash and other arbiters of fashion came here to gossip with royalty and 'take the waters', and the legions of the wealthy occupied magnificent houses built for them by John Wood and his son. Bath today mainly reflects the cultured tastes of the 17th and 18th centuries, but it also contains relics from more distant periods. The ancient baths themselves receive half a million gallons of water at a constant 49°C each day, and their history is interestingly related in an associated museum. Overlooking the baths is the city's splendid 15th-century Abbey Church, while near by is the Pump Room (open) where people came to cure everything from boredom to gout. Rebuilt in 1795, this popular meeting place offers a choice of coffee or spa water in a genteel atmosphere heightened by chandelier lighting, chamber music, and the occasional sedan chair. The work of the Woods is everywhere, but some of the best examples can be seen in the Circus, the superb Royal Crescent (No. 1 is open), and the Assembly Rooms (open). A very good museum of costume is housed in the latter. Several museums and similar foundations can be visited in the city, but by far the best are the Holburne of Menstrie Museum, the Victoria Art Gallery and the Bath Carriage Museum.

Leave Bath on the A4 'Chippenham' road and follow the Avon Valley to Batheaston, with views of Little Solsbury Hill to the left.

LITTLE SOLSBURY HILL, Avon ST76
A fine iron-age hillfort (NT) featuring ramparts faced with dry-stone walling, stands on this flat-topped 625ft hill.

Beyond Batheaston branch right on to the A363 'Bradford-on-Avon' road. Skirt Bathford and climb along wooded slopes before crossing pleasant farmland to reach Bradford-on-Avon.

BRADFORD-ON-AVON & BARTON FARM COUNTRY PARK, Wilts ST86
The disused Kennet and Avon Canal connects here with the River Avon, which itself is spanned by a 17th-century bridge incorporating a small contemporary lock-up. A tall but tiny Saxon church rescued from obscurity here in the 19th century has turned out to be one of the most important buildings of its age in Britain. Old weavers' cottages stand in Dutch Barton Street, and Barton Farm Country Park contains a superbly preserved 14th-century tithe barn (AM). The Park itself is an unspoilt area of country between the canal and the river.

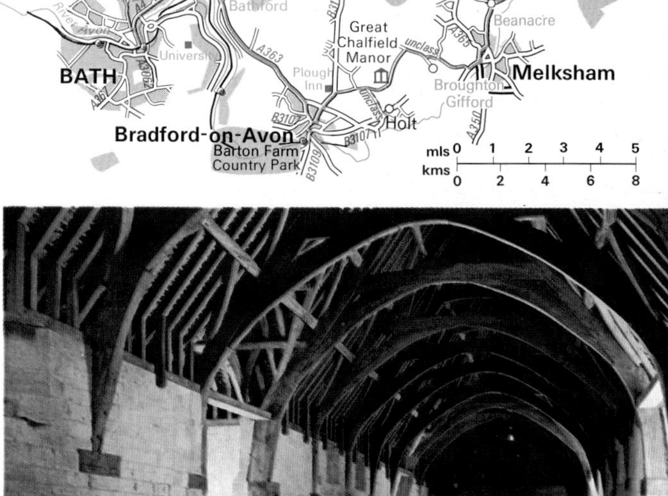

Bradford-on-Avon's tithe barn houses a collection of agricultural machinery beneath its enormous roof timbers.

Leave the town on the B3109 'Chippenham, Corsham' road. After 1 mile reach the Plough Inn and turn right on to an unclassified road SP 'Great Chalfield, Holt'. After another 1 mile branch left on to a narrow road through attractive farmland. The road to the right offers a pleasant detour to Holt.

John Wood the Younger built Bath's magnificent Royal Crescent, which is a half-ellipse of 30 houses, between 1767 and 1774. The overall style is based on the drawings of the architect Palladio.

HOLT, Wilts ST86
Local weavers once brought their disputes to The Courts to be settled but this 17th-century building now enjoys a peaceful retirement amid fine gardens (NT). Features of the latter include topiary work, a lily pond, and an arboretum.

Proceed for 1 mile to Great Chalfield Manor.

GREAT CHALFIELD MANOR, Wilts ST86
Built in the 15th century, this magnificent stone-built house (NT) features a great hall and is encircled by a moat.

Continue to a T-junction and turn right (no SP) to enter Broughton Gifford. Pass the large village green o the left, then bear left on to the 'Melksham' road. Proceed for 1¼ miles and turn left on to the B310 After ½ mile meet a roundabout and take the 1st exit SP 'Chippenham', continue to Melksham. For Melksha town centre take the 2nd exit.

MELKSHAM, Wilts ST96
The River Avon is spanned here by an 18th-century bridge, and an attractive group comprising a converted tithe barn and 17th- an 18th-century houses stands near t church. Nowadays the town is an expanding industrial centre.

Continue with SP 'Chippenham A350', passing through Beanacre w 17th- century Beanacre Manor on t left. Proceed for 1½ miles and turn right on to the unclassified 'Lacock' road to enter Lacock, then turn righ SP 'Bowden Hill, Calne'.

LACOCK, Wilts ST96
A wide architectural range from medieval times to the 19th century has been preserved in the stone, half-timbered, and thatched buildings of this delightful village (NT). Its abbey was the last religious house to be suppressed at the Dissolution in 1539, and was later converted into a private dwelling incorporating many of its medieval buildings. Over the centuries its ancient structure has acquired an octagonal Tudor tower and 17th-century gothic hall. The abbey gatehouse contains a museum of work by W H Fox-Talbot, a 19th-century pioneer of photography who once owned the abbey. Elsewhere in the village is a great tithe barn with 8 massive bays, and a small 14th-century lock-up known as the Cruck House.

About $\frac{1}{4}$ mile past Lacock Abbey cross the River Avon and begin the ascent of 580ft Bowden Hill. Proceed, with fine views of the Avon Valley, and meet a T-junction on the outskirts of Sandy Lane. Turn left on to the A342 and continue for $1\frac{1}{2}$ miles to pass the entrance to Bowood House.

BOWOOD HOUSE, Wilts ST96
The magnificent Georgian house of Bowood, with its superb art collection, is complemented by its extensive grounds, laid out by Capability Brown.

Descend to join the A4, and drive along the Avon Valley to Chippenham.

CHIPPENHAM, Wilts ST97
Situated on the River Avon near the edge of the Cotswold Hills, this pleasant industrial town was a market centre for centuries. Several attractive half-timbered houses and an old lock-up are preserved here.

Leave Chippenham on the A4 'Bath' road, and proceed for $3\frac{1}{2}$ miles. Meet crossroads and turn left on to an unclassified road for Corsham, on the edge of the Cotswold Hills.

THE COTSWOLDS
The Cotswolds extend from north of Bath to north of Oxfordshire, nowhere exceeding 30 miles in breadth but rising to 1,000ft in some places. From the 12th century the whole area benefited from the profits of wool, and a legacy of that wealth survives in the beautiful old cottages, houses, mansions, and churches which are such a feature of the district.

CORSHAM, Wilts ST87
This developing town has an old heart of Bath limestone and a scattering of buildings from various periods. Of particular note are the 16th-century Flemish Cottages and 17th-century Hungerford Almshouses. Magnificent Corsham Court (open) was extended in Georgian times and shows work by architect John Nash and by Capability Brown, better known as a brilliant landscape gardener. Inside are good pieces of Chippendale furniture and superb paintings.

Leave Corsham with SP 'Chippenham' and after $\frac{1}{2}$ mile meet crossroads. Drive forward over the A4 on to the 'Biddestone, Yatton Keynell' road, and proceed for $1\frac{3}{4}$ miles to enter Biddestone.

BIDDESTONE, Wilts ST87
Stone houses surround an attractive green and pond in this pretty Cotswold village. The 17th-century manor house (not open) has a brick gazebo, or garden house, and can be seen from the road.

Bear right on to the 'Yatton Keynell' road and after $\frac{3}{4}$ mile cross the main road SP 'Castle Combe'. After another $1\frac{1}{4}$ miles enter Yatton Keynell, turn left on to the B4039 and follow SP 'Castle Combe'. Proceed for $1\frac{3}{4}$ miles, and turn left again on to an unclassified road for Castle Combe village. Parking in the village is severely restricted, so it is advisable to stop at one of the car parks along this road and walk.

Weathered stone houses are grouped around an ancient market cross in Castle Combe.

CASTLE COMBE, Wilts ST87
Built of Cotswold stone deep in a stream-threaded combe, this old weaving centre is acknowledged as one of England's most picturesque villages. Numerous old buildings unalloyed by the brashness of concrete and brick present a homogeneous completeness round the canopied 13th-century market cross. Close to the centre is the 17th-century manor house, now an hotel.

Return to the B4039 and turn left SP 'Acton Turville'. Proceed for $2\frac{1}{2}$ miles to pass through Burton, and at the end of the village turn left on to the unclassified 'Pucklechurch' road.

Winter sunlight on Biddestone Village.

Continue for $2\frac{3}{4}$ miles and meet crossroads. Turn right SP 'Tormarton'. In $\frac{1}{2}$ mile cross the M4 motorway, and after a short distance keep forward to enter Tormarton. Branch left (no SP) past the Portcullis Inn, and in $\frac{1}{4}$ mile meet crossroads. Turn left SP 'Codrington' and proceed for $\frac{1}{2}$ mile to another crossroads. Turn left on to the A46 'Bath' road, with the entrance to Dodington House immediately opposite.

DODINGTON HOUSE, Avon ST78
Designed by James Wyatt in 1813, this Palladian mansion (open) is almost perfectly square and stands in 700 acres of parkland laid out by Capability Brown. Features of the park include 2 lakes, a carriage museum, and a children's farm.

Continue, shortly recrossing the M4, and drive along a high ridge. After $1\frac{3}{4}$ miles reach Dyrham Park on the right.

DYRHAM PARK, Avon ST77
Dyrham Park (NT) was built on the site of a Tudor house between 1692 and 1702 for William Blathwayt, Secretary of State and Secretary for War. The east front of the house has a monumental façade of warm Bath stone, while the simpler west elevation of Cotswold stone is flanked by single-storey pavilions. Contemporary Dutch influence manifests itself inside in the form of Delftware, paintings and leather hangings.

Proceed for $1\frac{3}{4}$ miles, pass through Pennsylvania, then in $\frac{1}{2}$ mile meet traffic lights and turn right on to the A420 'Bristol' road. In $\frac{3}{4}$ mile reach the start of a descent, meet crossroads, and turn left on to an unclassified road (no SP). In 1 mile descend steeply, then near the top of the following ascent turn left SP 'Lansdown, Bath'. Reach the top of a 700ft ridge and pass Bath racecourse. Return to Bath.

TOUR 17 — 81 MILES

BEACHES AND GORGES

In many ways tiny Avon is the envy of much larger counties. Its port city of Bristol is one of the most historic in England, its resort offers miles of sandy beaches, and its interior is riddled by limestone cave systems that extend deep into Somerset.

WESTON-SUPER-MARE, Avon ST36
Good beaches and lavish entertainment facilities are features of this large Bristol Channel resort. Among many places of interest are a small zoo, a marine lake with boating, an aquarium, and a model village. The resort's wide seafront road is lined by several public gardens and overlooks the low Flat Holme and Steep Holme offshore islands. Both these are particularly rich in birdlife. An iron-age earthwork (AM) can be seen 1 mile north on Worlebury Hill.

Leave Weston-super-Mare on the A370 'Bristol' road. Pass through suburbs and cross flat countryside to reach Congresbury. Turn left, cross the River Yeo, then turn left again on to the B3133 SP 'Yatton, Clevedon'. Continue to Yatton, then proceed through low countryside and pass through Kenn. Cross the M5 and drive to the clock tower in Clevedon. A brief detour can be made to visit Clevedon Court and Countryside Museum: turn right on to the B3130, then after $\frac{1}{2}$ mile meet crossroads and turn right again.

CLEVEDON COURT, Avon ST47
This superb 14th-century house is one of the oldest of its type to have survived anywhere in Britain. It carries an even older 13th-century tower and is considered typical of its period, with a screen passage dividing the buttery and kitchen from the great hall and the lord of the manor's living quarters. During the 18th and 19th centuries it became a popular meeting place for the avant-garde of the day. Its excellent terraced gardens (NT) feature the Clevedon Craft Centre and Countryside Museum, where visitors can watch displays of wood carving and turning at weekends.

CLEVEDON, Avon ST47
Situated at a junction of hill ranges, this quiet Severn-estuary resort offers 3 miles of coastline backed by downland. The 40ft tides in this part of the country were too much for the local pier, which collapsed in 1970.

Continue along the main route from the clock tower in Clevedon with SP 'Seafront B3130'. Proceed for $\frac{1}{2}$ mile, then bear right to join the sea front. In a further $\frac{1}{2}$ mile bear left, pass the pier, and keep forward for $1\frac{1}{2}$ miles to meet a T-junction, then turn left on to the B3124, SP 'Portishead'. Continue for $\frac{1}{2}$ mile to the Walton-in-Gordano crossroads. Turn left on to an unclassified road (no SP). Continue high above the Bristol Channel, then enter a built-up area and turn left into Nore Road (no SP). Continue above the coast for $1\frac{1}{2}$ miles to pass the AA Portishead viewpoint. Pass Battery Point and descend into Portishead.

PORTISHEAD, Avon ST47
Portishead is a small resort and dock situated on the lower slopes of a wooded hillside overlooking the Bristol Channel.

Birnbeck Pier at Weston-super-Mare.

Leave Portishead on the A369 'Bristol' road. After $2\frac{3}{4}$ miles reach the M5 junction roundabout and take 4th exit SP 'Clifton' (toll) to enter hill country. Continue to Abbot's Leigh.

ABBOT'S LEIGH, Avon ST57
Set deep in the shelter of Leigh Woods, this village was once the property of the Abbey of St Augustine in Bristol. Good views of the Clifton Suspension Bridge can be enjoyed from the well-wooded ravine of Nightingale Valley, which is off the A369.

Continue for $1\frac{1}{4}$ miles and turn left on to the B3129 SP 'Clifton'. In $1\frac{1}{2}$ miles reach the Clifton Suspension Bridge.

CLIFTON SUSPENSION BRIDGE AND AVON GORGE, Avon ST57
Here, where the sheer limestone cliffs of the Avon Gorge constrict that river to a silver ribbon some 245ft below, is the spectacular suspension bridge by the brilliant 19th-century engineer Isambard Kingdom Brunel. This was the last of his many great and innovatory works.

Clevedon Court, though much altered, preserves many 14th-century features, including the south entrance.

Cross the bridge and in 200yds turn left SP 'Motorway M5'. After a short distance turn left again into Clifton Down Road. After $\frac{1}{4}$ mile meet crossroads and turn left on to the B4468 SP 'Weston'. The right turn here leads to Bristol Zoo. Descend Bridge Valley Road into the Avon Gorge. At the bottom turn left on to the A4, pass underneath the suspension bridge, and after $\frac{1}{4}$ mile keep left SP 'City Centre' to remain in Hotwell Road. Enter Bristol city centre.

BRISTOL, Avon ST57
During the 16th century ships out of Bristol sailed to every part of the known world in search of new markets and exotic produce, opening up international trading routes in a way never before imagined. In 1843 Brunel launched his SS *Great Britain*, the largest iron ship of the time, and in 1970 its rusting hulk was rescued from the Falkland Islands and returned to the Bristol dry dock in which it was originally built. Extensive renovation has restored it as a proud memorial (open) to its great designer and the city of its birth. Nowadays the city's dock area is at Avonmouth, which is more fitted to coping with the vast ships of 20th-century world traffic. Bristol's many lovely old buildings include a cathedral that was founded as an Augustinian monastery and contains examples of Norman, early-English, gothic and Victorian architecture. St Mary Redcliffe, one of the city's finest churches, was built and extended between the 13th and 15th centuries and carries a massive tower with a 285ft spire. The 16th-century Red Lodge (open) houses interesting oak carvings and furnishings of contemporary and later date, and the Georgian House (open) features furniture from the 18th century. Outside the Corn Exchange are the original metal 'nails' upon which merchantmen once put their payments, hence the expression 'to pay cash on the nail'. Various displays and exhibitions can be seen in St Nicholas' Church and the City Museum and Art Gallery.

Follow SP 'Weston (A370)' to cross the impressive Cumberland Basin and Avon bridges, then keep forward to join the A370 'Long Ashton' bypass. Proceed through pleasant countryside and pass the villages of Flax Bourton and Backwell (Farleigh). Drive $1\frac{1}{2}$ miles beyond Backwell (West Town), meet crossroads, and turn left on to an unclassified road SP 'Bristol Airport'. Ascend deep and thickly-wooded Brockley Combe, then emerge to meet a T-junction. Turn right on to the A38 'Taunton' road and pass Bristol Airport on the right. Descend Red Hill, cross the River Yeo, then after another $\frac{1}{2}$ mile branch left on to an unclassified road SP 'Burrington, Blagdon'. Ahead are views of Beacon Batch Hill. After 1 mile turn right on to the A368 SP 'Burrington Combe'. Proceed for $\frac{1}{4}$ mile and turn left on to the B3134. Ascend to Burrington Combe.

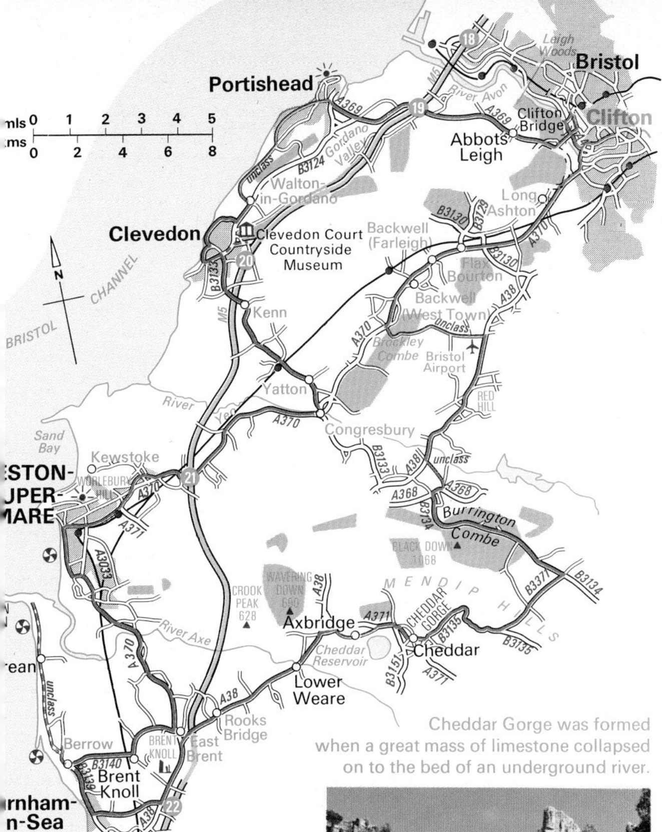

RINGTON COMBE,
nerset ST45
n above this secluded village is 5ft Beacon Batch, the summit of k Down and the highest point of bleak Mendip range. Access to village is via a dramatic gorge.

nb to over 900ft, with glimpses to left of Blagdon Lake, then cross n farmland for several miles. Meet ssroads and turn right on to the 71 SP 'Cheddar'. Proceed through n scenery, then descend into a low valley and turn right on to the 35. Make the long winding cent of Cheddar Gorge.

EDDAR GORGE & VILLAGE,
nerset ST45
ry year many thousands of ple come here to drive through spectacular rock scenery of eddar Gorge. Curiously athered limestone outcrops, ened in many places by the ge of precariously rooted shrubs, g over the road from 450ft cliffs. derground the region is neycombed by caves and holes, many of which feature rd crystalline formations created water action. Particularly good mples can be seen in Cox's and gh's caverns (open). Various naeological finds are displayed in Cheddar Caves Museum, and eddar village has a Museum of tor Transport.

ve Cheddar with SP 'Bristol' and eston-super-Mare'. Continue for ile and turn right on to the A371, Axbridge, Weston'. On the left is popular yachting centre of eddar Reservoir. Branch left and e into Axbridge.

Cheddar Gorge was formed when a great mass of limestone collapsed on to the bed of an underground river.

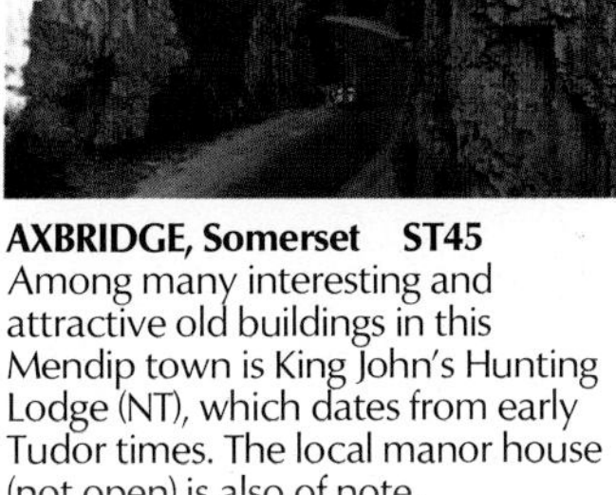

AXBRIDGE, Somerset ST45
Among many interesting and attractive old buildings in this Mendip town is King John's Hunting Lodge (NT), which dates from early Tudor times. The local manor house (not open) is also of note.

Drive to the end of Axbridge and follow SP 'Taunton, Exeter (A38)'. Meet a roundabout and take the 1st exit. Continue for $\frac{1}{2}$ mile, then turn left on to the A38 and proceed across the flat ground of the Axe Valley. Views of 690ft Wavering Down and 628ft Crook Peak can be enjoyed to the right. Continue to Lower Weare.

LOWER WEARE, Somerset ST45
Collections of waterfowl and a variety of small pets can be seen here at the Ambleside Water Gardens and Aviaries. Particular features of the gardens are their attractive ponds and varied shrubs.

The SS *Great Britain* at Bristol.

Continue and pass through Rooks Bridge with the isolated 457ft mound of Brent Knoll increasingly prominent ahead. Cross the M5, then in $\frac{1}{2}$ mile meet a roundabout and keep left. After another $1\frac{1}{2}$ miles meet another roundabout and take the 3rd exit on to the B3140 SP 'Burnham-on-Sea'. Proceed for $1\frac{1}{2}$ miles, then meet another roundabout and keep forward to enter Burnham-on-Sea.

BURNHAM-ON-SEA,
Somerset ST34
This little red-brick town is expanding to cope with holidaymakers who come to enjoy its miles of sandy beach in larger numbers every year. Bridgwater Bay Nature Reserve lies a little to the south west.

Turn right SP 'Berrow, Brean'. After $1\frac{1}{2}$ miles reach Berrow and turn right SP 'Weston-super-Mare'. A detour from the main route to Brean can be made here by keeping forward on to an unclassified road.

Evening light on the vast sands at Burnham-on-Sea.

BREAN & BREAN DOWN,
Somerset ST25
At the base of 320ft Brean Down (NT), adjacent to 7 miles of sandy beaches, is the Brean Down Bird Sanctuary (open). Many species from all over the world can be seen here.

On the main route, proceed to Brent Knoll.

BRENT KNOLL, Somerset ST35
This isolated village takes its name from a nearby 457ft hill surmounted by an ancient camp. Inside the 15th-century church are bench ends bearing animal carvings that depict the tale of a greedy abbot who once tried to seize revenue from an unfortunate parish priest.

Meet a T-junction in the village and turn left. Skirt the base of Brent Knoll to reach East Brent, then meet crossroads and turn left on to the A370. Continue for 3 miles to re-enter Avon and pass the edge of Bleadon. After 2 miles meet a T-junction, turn right and return to Weston-super-Mare.

Rye, one of the most picturesque towns on the south coast, was an important Cinque Port until its harbour silted up. It remains as a superb example of a medieval maritime town, with many of its oldest buildings intact in quaint old streets that have changed little in generations.

South and South East England

TOUR 18 — 75 MILES

ON THE WILTSHIRE DOWNS

The grandeur of this tour is in the cathedral city of Salisbury and some of the county's finest stately homes. The beauty is in its fertile river valleys, and soft downland slopes that enfold timeless villages and open up panoramic views from their tree-crowned summits.

SALISBURY, Wilts SU12
The ancient city of Salisbury first came to importance following the abandonment of nearby Old Sarum in the 13th century. The bishop's see was transferred from the old to the new site, and in 1220 the cathedral was refounded in an early-English style that made it seem to soar from the ground rather than sit solidly on it. This illusion is accentuated by numerous slim columns of Purbeck stone and a magnificent 404ft spire that was added in the 14th century and is still the tallest in the country. The Cathedral Close preserves a beauty and atmosphere all of its own, and contains fine buildings dating from the 14th to the 18th centuries. Elsewhere in the town are 16th-century Joiner's Hall (NT), the 14th-century Poultry Cross (AM), and a great number of old inns. Interesting displays illustrating local history can be seen in the Salisbury and South Wiltshire Museum. See also tour 22.

From Salisbury follow SP 'Yeovil A30' and drive to Wilton.

WILTON, Wilts SU03
Wilton is an interesting town best known as an important carpet-making centre. Good Georgian houses can be seen in Kinsbury Square, and a curious country cross stands near the market house of 1738. Wilton House (open) was built on the site of Wilton Abbey in the 1540s, but was completely rebuilt by Inigo Jones after a serious fire. Subsequent work includes alterations by architect James Wyatt. Features of the lovely grounds (open) include fine cedars and a Palladian-style bridge over the Nadder.

Meet a roundabout and take the 1st exit, passing Wilton House on the left. In ½ mile reach the end of the town and turn right on to an unclassified road SP 'Great Wishford'. Go forward for 2¾ miles, with Grovely Woods to the left, then turn right into Great Wishford.

Salisbury's cathedral has been a source of inspiration for many artists, including John Constable.

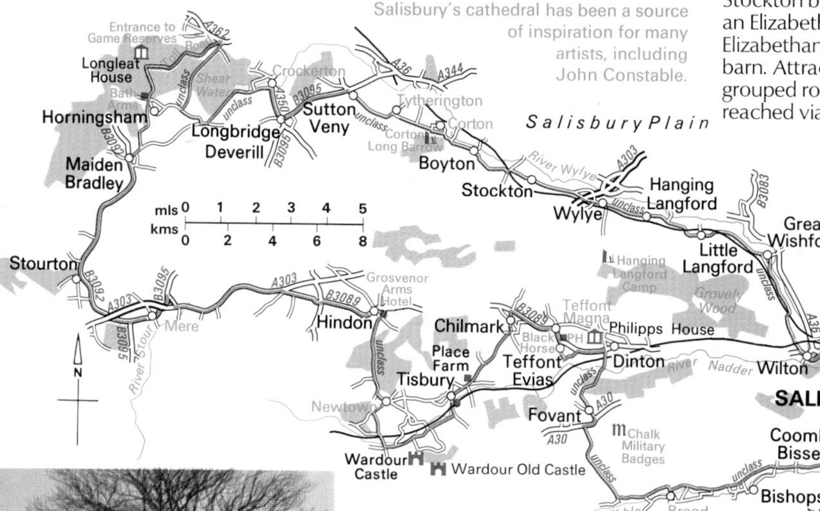

GREAT WISHFORD, Wilts SU03
This delightful village is set in the Wylye Valley and has a church with a 15th-century crenellated tower. On Oak Apple Day (May 29) the villagers reaffirm their right to collect kindling from Grovely Woods.

Drive to the village church, turn left, and shortly afterwards turn right. Continue to Little Langford.

LITTLE LANGFORD, Wilts SU03
Noted architect T H Wyatt rebuilt the local church in 1864, using material from the previous building. About ½ mile south west of the village is the notable iron-age hillfort of Grovely Castle.

Continue to Hanging Langford.

The bridge in the grounds of Wilton House was built in 1737 to a Palladian pattern.

HANGING LANGFORD, Wilts SU03
Hanging Langford clings precariously to the lower flanks of hills at the edge of Grovely Wood. Some 2 miles south west of the hamlet is an earthwork that has yielded evidence of prolonged occupation.

Keep forward and drive to Wylye.

WYLYE, Wilts SU03
Lovely flint-and-stone chequerwork cottages dating from the 17th century can be seen in this village, which stands on the Wylye River at the edge of Salisbury Plain.

SALISBURY PLAIN, Wilts
Most of the undulating 240 square miles of this windswept plateau is under cultivation, although some parts have been given over to military use. Many of its low chalk hills feature prehistoric burial mounds and other monuments. The borders of the plain are defined by the rivers Avon, Bourne, and Wylye. See tour 22 for Stonehenge.

From Wylye keep forward on the unclassified road SP 'Sutton Veny'. Drive along the Wylye Valley to Stockton.

STOCKTON, Wilts ST93
Stockton boasts thatched cottages, an Elizabethan mansion, and an Elizabethan farmhouse with a great barn. Attractive almshouses are grouped round a common courtyard reached via an arched entry.

After 1 mile cross the railway line and turn right for Boyton.

BOYTON, Wilts ST93
Flint and stone chequerwork common to this area can be seen in 13th-century and later Boyton Church, which was restored by the 19th-century architect T H Wyatt.

Drive through Corton and Tytherington, then keep left for Sutton Veny.

SUTTON VENY, Wilts ST94
The ruined church of Sutton Veny dates from the 13th century and lies east of its 19th-century successor. Also here is a manor house dating from the 14th century.

Meet crossroads at the far end of the village and turn left on to the B3095. Drive to Longbridge Deverill.

Overlooking the lake at Stourhead is the Pantheon, which contains casts of statues.

ONGBRIDGE DEVERILL, Vilts ST84
ohn Thynne of Longleat House built ne charming group of 17th-century lmshouses here. His funeral helm angs with two others in the tower f the local church.

Meet crossroads and turn right on to ne A350. Proceed for $\frac{3}{4}$ mile to the dge of Crockerton and turn left on to n unclassified road SP 'Horningsham'. ontinue through woodland, and nortly pass Shear Water on the right. fter $1\frac{1}{4}$ miles approach a T-junction nd turn right. Take the next turning ght SP 'Longleat' and 'Heaven's ate'. Drive to the outskirts of orningsham and turn right. Run ongside Longleat Estate, passing the eaven's Gate viewpoint. After miles, before the main road, turn t to enter Longleat Park (toll).

ONGLEAT HOUSE, Wilts ST84
is great Elizabethan mansion pen), the seat of the Marquess of th, stands on the site of a 13th-ntury priory and is a treasure ouse of old furniture, paintings, ooks, and interior decoration. It was ne of England's first unified designs, nd the grounds were landscaped by e brilliant 18th-century designer pability Brown. The estate cludes a large safari park (open), e first of its kind in Europe.

ave the park with SP 'Way Out' and arminster' via the Horningsham te.

ORNINGSHAM, Wilts ST84
e thatched noncomformist eeting House here, said to be one the oldest of its kind in England, ay date from the 16th century.

ive to the Bath Arms (PH), meet ossroads, and go forward SP aftesbury' and 'Maiden Bradley'. In miles meet a T-junction and turn ht for Maiden Bradley.

AIDEN BRADLEY, Wilts ST83
ooded downland hills rise to 945ft ng Knoll above this pretty village, which may be seen a number of ractive old houses.

Meet crossroads and turn left on to the B3092 SP 'Mere', passing the outskirts of Stourton.

STOURTON, Wilts ST73
Good paintings and Chippendale furniture can be seen inside Stourhead House (NT), but this famous 18th-century mansion is best known for its superb grounds. These were laid out by Henry Hoare, who owned the estate, and show one of Europe's finest layouts of this period. In the park are classical garden temples and a delightful lake.

Continue past Mere, drive under a road bridge, and turn right SP 'Andover' to join the A303. Continue through open countryside for $3\frac{1}{2}$ miles then turn right on to the B3089 SP 'Salisbury'. Continue to the A350 and turn left, then turn immediately right for Hindon.

HINDON, Wilts ST93
Created by bishops of Winchester in the 13th century, this village was handsomely rebuilt by Wyatt after a fire and is an example of good 19th-century restoration.

Proceed from the Grosvenor Arms Hotel and turn right on to an unclassified road SP 'Tisbury'. Meet crossroads and turn right (no SP). Follow a narrow byroad to Newtown. Turn right SP 'Semley', then turn left SP 'Donhead' and 'Wardour'. Descend, and in $\frac{1}{2}$ mile cross a railway. Shortly turn left SP 'Tisbury' and continue past the grounds of Wardour Castle.

WARDOUR CASTLE, Wilts ST92
New Wardour Castle (open), the largest Georgian house in Wiltshire, was begun in 1769 for the 8th Lord Arundell. Its private chapel is larger than many a parish church, and very richly decorated.

WARDOUR OLD CASTLE, Wilts ST92
Wardour Old Castle (AM) dates from the end of the 14th-century. It stands on a wooded bank overlooking an 18th-century artificial lake and is uniquely hexagonal in shape.

Keep forward for Tisbury.

TISBURY, Wilts ST92
In the 7th century this village stood on an important Saxon track. Its cruciform church dates from the 12th century and shares the churchyard with a giant yew, 36ft in circumference, that is reputed to be more than 1,000 years old.

Turn right at the post office SP 'Salisbury'. Continue to the end of the village and turn right again. Proceed for $\frac{1}{4}$ mile and branch left SP 'Chilmark', passing Place Farm on the left.

PLACE FARM, Wilts ST92
Formerly an abbey grange, this farm comprises a group of 14th to 15th-century domestic buildings. Of particular note is the 200ft-long tithe barn, which is the largest in England.

Drive to Chilmark.

CHILMARK, Wilts ST93
The creamy stone from Chilmark's quarries (closed) was used in Wilton House, Salisbury Cathedral, and the spire of Chichester Cathedral.

Turn left SP 'Salisbury', then right. Continue to the main road and turn right again, on to the B3089 for Teffont Magna. Keep right into the village, drive to the Black Horse (PH), and turn right on to an unclassified road. Continue with SP 'Tisbury' into Teffont Evias.

TEFFONT EVIAS, Wilts ST93
Twin Teffont Magna and Teffont Evias stand close together in the beautiful Nadder Valley. The former boasts the delightful Fitz House of 1700, and the latter a Tudor mansion that was once the home of Sir James Ley, who became Lord Chief Justice of England and was immortalized by Milton in a sonnet.

In $\frac{1}{4}$ mile turn left with SP 'Salisbury' and cross a river bridge. Ascend to a main road and turn right to re-join the B3089. After $\frac{3}{4}$ mile meet crossroads at the outskirts of Dinton and turn right on to an unclassified road for Fovant. A slight detour can be made to Philipps House by turning left at the crossroads.

PHILIPPS HOUSE, Wilts SU03
Designed by Sir Jeffry Wyatville in 1816, this splendid neo-Grecian mansion (NT) stands in 200-acre Dinton Park and is let as a holiday home (open by appointment).

DINTON, Wilts SU03
Three notable National Trust properties are to be found on the outskirts of this hillside village. Besides Philipps House there is the Tudor to 18th-century Hyde's House (not open) and ivy-covered Little Clarendon, which dates from the 15th-century (open on application).

On the main route, continue into Fovant.

FOVANT, Wilts SU02
Huge regimental badges were cut in the chalk downs by soldiers stationed here during World War I. A memorial brass of 1492 can be seen in the local church.

Drive to the end of the village and turn right on to the A30. In $\frac{1}{2}$ mile turn left on to an unclassified road SP 'Broad Chalke'. Ascend on to the downs, and after $1\frac{1}{2}$ miles turn left. Drive to Broad Chalke, bear right then left through the village, and proceed to Bishopstone.

BISHOPSTONE, Wilts SU02
Remarkable furnishings can be seen inside the local church, a beautiful cruciform building with superb stone vaulting and windows.

Continue to Coombe Bissett.

COOMBE BISSETT, Wilts SU12
Just downstream from the fine 18th-century bridge that spans the river here is a picturesque packhorse bridge. Its wooden parapets are new, but the mounting stone is very old. Traces of every century from Norman times to the present day can be seen in the fabric of the attractive local church.

Turn left on to the A354 and return to Salisbury.

A picturesque old mill stands beside the River Ebble in Coombe Bissett.

IN SEARCH OF ANCIENT MAN

Near Uffington the great turf-cut figure of a horse leaps across a downland slope beneath the ramparts of a prehistoric hillfort. Elsewhere in the Vale of the White Horse are the massive stones of Wayland's Smithy, the enigmatic mound of Silbury Hill, and dozens of hilltop tumuli.

Tithe barns like the one at Great Coxwell were specially built to store the tithe, or one tenth of all produce, which was once levied from all land holders.

SWINDON, Wilts SU18
In 1900 Old and New Swindon were combined to form Wiltshire's largest town. The small old town is still recognisable in fragments such as the remains of Holy Rood Church in the grounds of a 17th-century house, The Lawn, the old Town Hall, the Market Square, and in Apsley House – which now contains a museum. New Swindon grew out of the Great Western Railway's decision to site its repair and locomotive works here, and much of its history is detailed in the fascinating Great Western Railway Museum.

Leave the County Roundabout with SP 'Oxford A420'. In $1\frac{1}{4}$ miles meet another roundabout and turn left on to the A361 SP 'Stow'. In 1 mile meet traffic signals in Stratton St Margaret and turn left, then right, and continue to Highworth.

HIGHWORTH, Wilts SU29
Several 17th-century houses and an impressive church with a good west tower are features of this old hilltop village. A stone-built Zion Congregational church of 1825 stands in the High Street.

Continue on the A361. Later pass the village of Inglesham and a riverside park on the left.

INGLESHAM, Wilts SU29
The tiny church in Inglesham stands where the River Thames meets the derelict Severn Canal and the River Coln. Inside are attractive box pews, a 15th-century screen, and a beautiful late Saxon carving of the Madonna and Child.

Continue on the A361. Cross the Thames via the old Halfpenny Bridge and drive into Lechlade.

LECHLADE, Glos SU29
Lechlade marks the upper limit for large craft using the River Thames. The old Halfpenny Bridge spans the river here, and St John's Bridge stands $\frac{1}{2}$ mile to the east. The local church is noted for the curious figures on its tower buttresses.

Turn right, then right again, on to the A417 Faringdon road. In $\frac{3}{4}$ mile by the nearside of the Trout Inn, turn left on to the B4449 SP 'Bampton'. A detour from the main route can be made here to Buscot village and Buscot Park by keeping forward on the A417.

BUSCOT, Oxon SU29
Almost 4,000 acres of Buscot village and Park, including lovely woods and farmlands that run down to the Thames, are owned or protected by the National Trust. The late 18th-century house contains a noted collection of paintings, and the attractive grounds feature a water garden by landscaper Harold Peto. The Old Parsonage is an early 18th-century house in 10-acre grounds.

Continue along the B4449 and cross the River Leach. After $1\frac{1}{4}$ miles reach an unclassified right turn leading to Kelmscott village.

KELMSCOTT, Oxon SU29
Poet and painter William Morris lived in Kelmscott's Elizabethan manor house and is buried in the local churchyard. The village itself is a charming collection of greystone buildings standing on the banks of the upper Thames.

Continue along the B4449 for a further $2\frac{3}{4}$ miles and meet a T-junction. Turn right on to the A4095 SP 'Faringdon' and shortly cross the historic Radcot Bridge.

RADCOT, Oxon SU29
Many centuries ago the forces of Richard II and Henry IV met in battle at the 14th-century bridge here, and 300 years later Prince Rupert's cavalry defeated Cromwell's parliamentarian horsemen in nearby Garrison Field.

Continue to Faringdon.

FARINGDON, Oxon SU29
Poet Laureate Henry Pye built Faringdon House in 1870, and Lord Berners added a folly to its park in 1935 to help relieve local unemployment. Faringdon Church lost its spire in the Civil War. The town itself is a market centre known for its dairy produce.

Follow SP 'Swindon A420', and after $\frac{1}{2}$ mile turn right into Highworth Road (B4019). After another $1\frac{1}{4}$ miles turn left on to an unclassified road for Great Coxwell.

GREAT COXWELL, Oxon SU29
William Morris thought the great 13th-century tithe barn (NT) at Coxwell's Court Farm 'as noble as a cathedral'. Measuring 152ft long by 51ft high and 44ft wide, this huge stone building is certainly one of the finest of its kind in England today.

Turn left (no SP), then in $\frac{1}{2}$ mile meet a T-junction and turn right on to the A420. Take the 1st turning left on to an unclassified road for Little Coxwell and drive to the triangle at the far en of that village. Turn right here and continue to Fernham. Turn left on to the B4508, then in $\frac{1}{4}$ mile branch righ on to an unclassified road for Uffington, in the Vale of the White Horse.

UFFINGTON, Oxon SU38
Good views can be enjoyed from here of the famous 374ft-long prehistoric white horse cut into the chalk slopes of 856ft White Horse Hill.

Drive to the nearside of the village and turn right, then take the 2nd turning right SP 'White Horse Hill'. In 1 mile cross the main road and ascend White Horse Hill to reach Uffington Castle and associated monuments.

UFFINGTON CASTLE, THE RIDGEWAY, & WAYLAND'S SMITH Oxon SU38 & SU28
The iron-age hillfort (AM) of Uffingt stands on the ancient Ridgeway above the famous White Horse in the Berkshire Downs. The Ridgewa is a pre-Roman track that follows the crest of the downs and is now the route of a long-distance footpath. Just off it in a grove of tre is the megalithic long barrow of Wayland's Smithy (AM). This excellent example has lost part of i earth mound, so its chambers are open to view. Wayland is a smith i Norse mythology, and tradition wa that anyone who left a horse and coin here overnight would find his mount shod in the morning.

Wayland's Smithy is one of many outstanding prehistoric monuments which stand near the Ridgeway.

It is quite likely that the exact reason for the construction of henge monuments like Avebury will never be known.

ollow exit signs from Uffington 'astle, descend to a main road, and ırn right on to the B4507 with further iews of the White Horse to the right. fter another 2 miles meet crossroads nd turn right on to an unclassified ɔad SP 'Lambourn'. Ascend on to the erkshire Downs and in $4\frac{1}{4}$ miles turn ght on to the B4001 for Lambourn. ontinue across the Lambourn owns to Lambourn.

AMBOURN, Berks SU37
acehorses are trained on downland allops near this lovely village, and e crystal Lambourn River is erything a chalk trout stream ould be. The local cruciform urch, which dates from Norman nes, houses several old brasses and e village stocks.

eet crossroads and turn right on to e B4000, then drive to the next ning left SP 'Baydon'. A short tour can be made from the main ute to Ashdown House by keeping aight ahead on the B4000 for miles.

HDOWN HOUSE, Oxon SU28
hdown House (NT) was built from alk-rock blocks in the latter half of e 17th century. More than a arter of its interior is taken up by a ıgnificent staircase.

ı the main route, turn left from the 000 on to the 'Baydon' road and in miles meet a T-junction. Turn right d continue to Baydon.

YDON, Wilts SU27
3th-century font can be seen in ydon Church, which has Norman gins but acquired its west tower r. Baydon House farmhouse is of 18th-century date.

n left and continue to the vnland village of Aldbourne.

OBOURNE, Wilts SU27
bourne, one of Wiltshire's most active villages, lies south east of a -time hunting area known as bourne Chase.

n left on to the A419 SP ngerford', then in $1\frac{3}{4}$ miles turn t on to an unclassified road and tinue to Ramsbury.

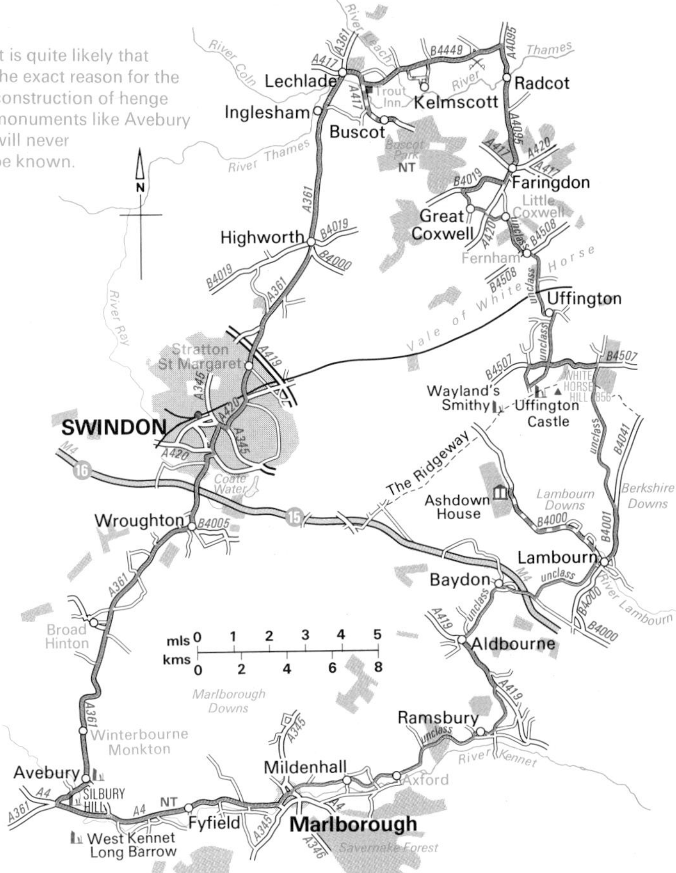

RAMSBURY, Wilts SU27
Excellent Jacobean and Georgian buildings can be seen in this charming River Kennet village, and the church contains ancient sculptured stones.

Turn right and keep forward through the village to Axford and Mildenhall.

MILDENHALL, Wilts SU26
Mildenhall, pronounced 'Minall', lies on the River Kennet to the north of Savernake Forest. A late Celtic vessel known as the Marlborough Bucket was unearthed at Folly Farm, which stands near by on the site of the Roman town *Cunetio*.

Continue to Marlborough.

MARLBOROUGH, Wilts SU16
High downs rise to the north and south of this historic River Kennet town. Legend has it that Merlin, the magician of King Arthur's court, was buried under the town's castle mound. The town may well be old enough for this claim, but many of its more ancient foundations were damaged or destroyed by a series of bad fires and by the Civil War. Its High Street, one of the widest in England, is a reminder of the way things used to be. William Morris was a pupil at the famous 19th-century Marlborough College.

Leave Marlborough on the A4 SP 'Chippenham' and drive to Fyfield.

FYFIELD, Wilts SU16
To the north of this attractive village is the high Fyfield Down nature reserve, which is as much protected for its prehistoric monuments as for its abundant wildlife. South of Fyfield are the sarsen stones of the Grey Wethers (NT), and about 1 mile north east of the village at Lockeridge Dene is a dolmen known as the Devil's Den.

Continue on the A4 to Silbury Hill.

SILBURY HILL & THE WEST KENNET LONG BARROW, Wilts SU16
Situated close to the A4 road near Avebury, these superb prehistoric monuments are among the best known in Europe. Silbury Hill (AM), an enormous artificial mound that covers almost 6 acres, is still as enigmatic as when 18th-century Cornish miners employed to explore it by the Duke of Northumberland emerged baffled and empty-handed. A footpath from the A4 leads $\frac{3}{4}$ mile to the West Kennet Long Barrow (AM), the finest monument of its kind in England. Excavations during the 19th century uncovered skeletons and pottery in the tomb's passage and end chamber, but the side chambers remained undiscovered until 1955.

Drive to the Beckhampton roundabout and take the 3rd exit to leave by the A361 SP 'Swindon'. In 1 mile keep left for Avebury.

AVEBURY, Wilts SU06
Many experts consider Avebury the most significant prehistoric monument (AM) in Europe. It is certainly one of the largest stone circles in the world, comprising 100 standing-stone positions enclosing some 28 acres of land. Inside the large outer circle, which has quite a few gaps due to superstitious destruction in the past, are two smaller rings about 300ft in diameter. At one time a 50ft-wide avenue of stones ran 1 mile to connect with a pair of concentric circles on Overton Hill. The village itself is a collection of handsome old buildings between the stones and the banks of the monument, featuring a small museum of archaeology and a multi-period church. Avebury Manor is a good 16th-century house (open) surrounded by fine gardens.

Continue on the 'Swindon' road to Winterbourne Monkton, with views of the Marlborough Downs to the right. Later descend to Wroughton.

WROUGHTON, Wilts SU18
Yet another of Wiltshire's white horses was cut into the slopes of a local hillside in 1838. Wroughton's church stands amid fine yew trees and contains many good tablets to the old Benet family.

Drive to the end of the village and turn left for the return to Swindon.

Enigmatic Silbury Hill keeps the secret of its purpose.

TOUR 20 76 MILES

A MINIATURE LANDSCAPE

The Isle of Wight has everything offered by the mainland, but smaller. Here are high downs and soaring cliffs; long beaches fringed by farm and forestland; fishing villages and resorts popularized by royalty in the past and popular with sun seekers today.

COWES, Isle of Wight SZ49
This busy island port has a good harbour on the River Medina and is connected to East Cowes by floating bridge and ferry. The headquarters of the Royal Yacht Squadron is based at Cowes Castle, and the town is well known as England's premier yachting centre.

Leave Cowes following SP 'Gurnard' on the B3325. In $\frac{3}{4}$ mile keep forward on to an unclassified road for Gurnard. Reach the Gurnard Hotel, keep forward, then meet a T-junction and turn right into Lower Church Road. Continue to the next T-junction, turn left SP 'Yarmouth', and in a further $1\frac{1}{2}$ miles meet another T-junction. Turn right and in another $1\frac{1}{2}$ miles turn right again for Porchfield. Continue through wooded countryside and after $1\frac{1}{2}$ miles turn right for Newtown.

NEWTOWN, Isle of Wight SZ49
Sited midway between Newport and Yarmouth, Newtown was created in the 13th century by the bishops of Winchester and stands on the beautiful Newtown River estuary (NT). The 18th-century Old Town Hall (NT) is notable.

In $\frac{1}{2}$ mile meet a T-junction and turn right, then in another $\frac{3}{4}$ mile meet another T-junction and turn right again on to the A3054. Proceed to Shalfleet.

SHALFLEET, Isle of Wight SZ48
Shalfleet's church displays very strong Norman features, particularly in the squat west tower and the good south doorway with its contemporary tympanum.

Continue to Yarmouth.

YARMOUTH, Isle of Wight SZ38
This Yar-estuary town is better known as a sailing centre than as a resort. Henry VIII built one of his many coastal defence forts (AM) here, and the triangular Fort Victoria of 1853 stands in grounds being developed as a country park at the time of printing.

Following SP 'Freshwater', cross the Yar bridge, and in 1 mile bear right. Pass through Colwell Bay and continue to the small resort of Totland. Join the B3322 'Alum Bay' road and in $\frac{1}{4}$ mile reach a war memorial. Bear right to Alum Bay.

ALUM BAY & THE NEEDLES, Isle of Wight SZ38
Sandstone cliffs famous for their multi-coloured strata fringe this lovely bay. The isolated rock stacks of The Needles stretch out into the sea to the south-west, with Scratchell's Bay and a 200ft chalk arch beyond.

Return, and in $\frac{1}{2}$ mile branch right on to an unclassified road SP 'Freshwater Bay'. To the right is Tennyson Down (NT), one of the West Wight Downs.

WEST WIGHT DOWNS, Isle of Wight SZ38
The high, gentle folds of the West Wight Downs (NT) occupy most of the island's south-west corner.

The brass cannons overlooking the Solent at Cowes are fired to start yacht races.

Continue to Freshwater Bay and join the A3055 SP 'Chale'. Bear right and ascend, skirting Compton Bay, and drive along a beautiful clifftop road that affords some of the finest views in the island. Later pass the edge of Brook village.

BROOK, Isle of Wight SZ38
Brook House dates from the 18th century, and Brook Chine (NT) is a beautiful cleft with 40 acres of grazing and 300 yards of superb seashore.

Continue through pleasant open country with good views. In $2\frac{1}{4}$ miles pass thickly-wooded Grange Chine to the right, with Brighstone Forest to the left and Brighstone Bay to the right. St Catherine's Point and St Catherine's Hill are prominent ahead before the tour enters Chale.

CHALE, Isle of Wight SZ47
Chale Abbey preserves a 14th-century hall, and the local church commands magnificent views of The Needles.

Drive to Chale Church and keep forward SP 'Ventnor'. In $\frac{1}{2}$ mile turn right on to an unclassified road for Blackgang. A footpath from this point leads to Blackgang Chine.

BLACKGANG CHINE & ST CATHERINE'S HILL, Isle of Wight SZ47
It is thought that this dramatic chine derived its name from a gang of smugglers, but nowadays it harbours nobody more sinister than tourists visiting the model village. Inland is 773ft St Catherine's Hill (NT), which affords excellent views and features 14th-century St Catherine's Oratory.

From Blackgang Chine return to the main route and turn right on to the A3055 SP 'Ventnor'. Pass under St Catherine's Hill and continue to Niton.

NITON, Isle of Wight SZ57
As a child Queen Victoria stayed at the Royal Sandrock Hotel in Niton, a respectable small resort that was once the haunt of smugglers.

Turn right (in Niton) and continue along Undercliff to St Lawrence.

ST LAWRENCE, Isle of Wight SZ57
Old St Lawrence's was Britain's smallest church until it acquired a porch and bell tower in 1842.

Continue to Ventnor.

VENTNOR, Isle of Wight SZ57
A paper recommending the local climate for the cure of certain illnesses transformed Ventnor from a fishing village to a focus of 19th-century society.

Follow SP 'Shanklin' and ascend, with fine sea views to the right. In $\frac{3}{4}$ mile a detour can be made from the main route to the delightful village of Bonchurch by turning right on to an unclassified road.

BONCHURCH & ST BONIFACE DOWN, Isle of Wight SZ57
The writers Dickens, Thackeray, and Macaulay all stayed in this delightful village, and the poet Swinburne lived at East Dene House. The village itself stands just below the island's highest point, 785ft Boniface Down (NT), and has a Victorian church.

Continue on the main drive, pass the Landslip viewpoint to the right of the road and reach Shanklin.

SHANKLIN, Isle of Wight SZ58
A group of thatched buildings, the Crab Inn, and St Blasius's Church are all that remain of the fishing village that stood here before the seaside holiday fad took over. The town's excellent sea-bathing, superb sandy beach, and good sunshine records attract increasing numbers of visitors every year.

Continue through Shanklin and Lake to Sandown.

SANDOWN, Isle of Wight SZ58
The assets that contributed to the development of Shanklin have also made Sandown a popular holiday resort. Additional attractions includ the Museum of Isle of Wight Geolog and a good zoo.

Turn right on to the B3395 SP 'Bembridge' and drive to Yaverland.

YAVERLAND, Isle of Wight SZ68
Yaverland Manor House (not open) is the finest 17th-century building o its kind in the island.

Meet a T-junction and turn right. In mile it is possible to make a detour from the main route by turning righ to the downs of Culver and Bembric

Until its collapse in 1764 one of the Needles was 120ft high.

lum Bay is famous for its multi-
oloured cliffs.

Vhippingham's
ermanic-looking church.

ULVER & BEMBRIDGE DOWNS,
e of Wight SZ68
overing some 104 acres of east ight, these fine downs (NT) rise to a 3ft summit and drop sharply wards the coast. Culver Down atures a bronze-age round barrow.

ontinue with the main tour to skirt mbridge Airport and at the far side eet crossroads. Turn left on to an classified road and in ¼ mile pass a otpath on the left leading to mbridge Windmill.

MBRIDGE WINDMILL,
e of Wight SZ68
uated near one end of Bembridge gh Street, this stone-built mill (NT) s a wooden roof and was erected 700. Today it is the only windmill on the island, and is maintained working order.

ntinue into Bembridge.

BEMBRIDGE, Isle of Wight SZ68
Original drawings and manuscripts by Ruskin can be seen at the Ruskin Art Gallery and Museum in Bembridge School. Yachtsmen favour the nearby natural harbour at the mouth of the Eastern Yar.

Follow the B3395 'St Helens' road and in 1½ miles meet a T-junction. Turn right on to the B3330 into St Helens, then turn left SP 'Ryde' for Nettlestone. At Nettlestone branch right on to the B3340 SP 'Seaview'. On the right is the entrance to a tropical bird garden. In ½ mile keep left, then meet a T-junction and turn left, then immediately left again. Turn right into Seafield Road for Seaview.

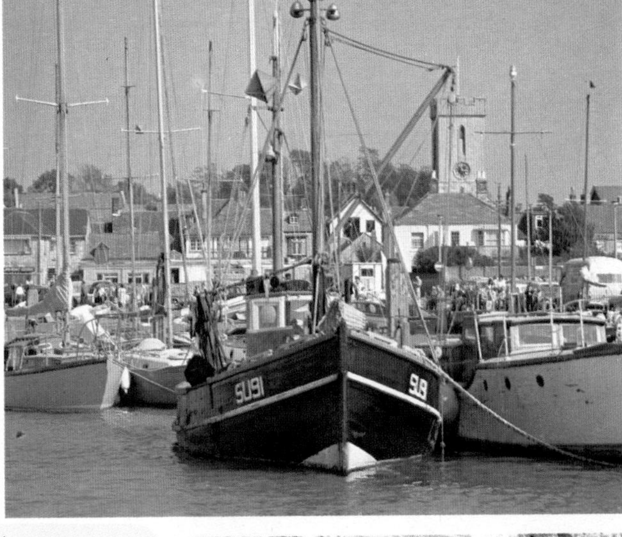

Yarmouth Harbour, crowded with yachts and other sailing craft.

SEAVIEW, Isle of Wight SZ69
Much of the unspoiled fishing village is still evident in Seaview, a quiet resort offering good beaches and excellent shore angling.

Continue to a T-junction and turn right, then keep left on to an unclassified road and drive along the shoreline. In ½ mile pass through a toll gate, and 1 mile farther turn right on to the B3330. After a short distance turn right on to the A3055 for Ryde.

RYDE, Isle of Wight SZ59
Most visitors to the island enter at Ryde, a busy port that was a small fishing and smuggling village until the 18th century.

Follow SP 'Newport' to join the A3054 and pass through Binstead.

BINSTEAD, Isle of Wight SZ59
New Quarr Abbey stands near the 12th-century remains of its predecessor at Binstead, and the local church still shows some of its 13th-century origins in spite of Victorian restoration.

Keep forward through Wootton Bridge. In 1½ miles turn right SP 'East Cowes'. Meet a T-junction and turn right on to the A3021, then in 1¼ miles turn left on to an unclassified road SP 'Whippingham Church'. Continue to Whippingham.

The Indian-style Durbar Room at Osborne House was built in 1891 to accommodate state banquets.

WHIPPINGHAM, Isle of Wight SZ59
Prince Albert built the ornate church here in 1860, and Queen Victoria was a regular member of the congregation whenever the Royal Family was in residence on the island.

Pass Whippingham Church and continue to a T-junction. Turn left into Victoria Grove, then at the next T-junction turn left again to join the A3021 for East Cowes. Return along the A3021 'Ryde' road, passing the entrance to Osborne House to the left on the outskirts of the town.

OSBORNE HOUSE, Isle of Wight SZ59
Queen Victoria and the Prince Consort built Osborne House as a retreat from the pomp and ceremony of Windsor, and Her Majesty died here in 1901. The State apartments (open) remain as they were in her day.

Continue, and in 2 miles keep right SP 'Newport', and after another ½ mile turn right on to the A3054. Proceed to Newport.

NEWPORT, Isle of Wight SZ48
Situated at the head of the Medina estuary, this town is the capital of the island and stands on a site that has been occupied at least since Roman times. Mighty Carisbrooke Castle stands on the foundations of a Roman fort 1 mile south west. The 12th-century remains of the castle include a Norman keep and a 16th-century treadmill that used to be worked by prisoners to raise water. Today it is turned by a donkey for display purposes, and forms a fascinating exhibit in the Isle of Wight Museum.

Follow the A3020 'Cowes' road and pass Parkhurst Prison, backed by Parkhurst Forest.

PARKHURST FOREST, Isle of Wight SZ49
Parkhurst Forest is the largest stretch of woodland on the island, and one of the last British refuges of the native red squirrel.

Drive to Northwood and branch left on to the B3325. Continue to a T-junction and turn right to return to Cowes.

LYMINGTON, Hants SZ39
Early wealth came to Lymington from its saltworks, but these were closed in the 19th century and the town now makes a comfortable living as a busy holiday resort, yachting centre, and Isle of Wight ferry terminal. Its wide High Street, lined with 18th- and 19th- century houses, climbs from the waterfront to a church with a huge tower crowned by an exotic cupola of 18th century date.

Follow SP 'Beaulieu B3054', cross the Lymington River, and climb into the New Forest. Cross Beaulieu Heath to the pleasant picnic spot of Hatchet Pond. Turn right, then 1 mile farther turn sharp right again on to the unclassified 'Buckler's Hard' road.

BUCKLER'S HARD, Hants SU40
This small Beaulieu River village thrived for several centuries as a shipbuilding yard. A fascinating little maritime museum recalls those times, and the deep estuary is put to peaceful use by yacht owners. The short village street of 18th-century houses was the creation of the 2nd Duke of Montagu, who planned a town and docks here to receive produce from his own extensive foreign estates.

THE SOLENT, Hants
Much of this tour is in sight of The Solent, a narrow and very busy channel that separates the coast of Hampshire from that of the Isle of Wight. It was formed by the submersion of an ancient river valley whose headstream was the Frome and tributaries the Itchen and Test. Most of the coast on the Hampshire side is designated an area of outstanding natural beauty.

Return along the 'Beaulieu' road and after 2 miles turn right on to the B3054. Enter Beaulieu.

BEAULIEU, Hants SU30
Beaulieu's idyllic position among the woods and hills of South Hampshire is enhanced by the superb ruins of its abbey (open). Largely destroyed at the Dissolution, this important foundation retains a beauty that 'mocks the spoilers still' and preserves its great gatehouse (open) as the home of Lord Montagu. Ruined walls pierced by graceful door and window apertures surround trim lawns that were once the floors of large monastic buildings. Elsewhere in the grounds is the well-known National Motor Museum (open), which features an excellent collection of veteran and vintage cars, cycles, and motorcycles.

Continue through woodlands along the 'Hythe' road for 1 mile, then turn right and immediately right again on to the unclassified 'Lepe' road. Pass Fawley refinery on the left, drive through woodland, and enter Exbury.

Huge timbers from New Forest trees were once left to weather in the wide street at Buckler's Hard before being used to build ships.

TOUR 21 — 74 MILES

THE FOREST AND THE SEA

Here the woods and heaths of the New Forest meet the lovely Solent shore. Ponies and semi-wild cattle graze through oak-fringed glades where kings once hunted, and wander at will wherever there are no grids to bar them entry.

A beech glade near Knightswood Oak.

EXBURY, Hants SU40
The gardens of Exbury estate are famous for their magnificent rhododendron and azalea displays in late spring (house not open). The village itself stands near the creeks and saltmarshes of the Beaulieu River estuary, in an area of the Solent shore designated as being of outstanding natural beauty.

Turn left into the village and after another 2 miles bear left, with views across The Solent to the Isle of Wight. Continue to the foreshore at Lepe, now part of a country park, then turn inland. After $\frac{3}{4}$ mile turn right on to the Calshot road. Drive for another $2\frac{1}{2}$ miles, meet a T-junction, and turn right on to the B3053 to enter Calshot.

CALSHOT, Hants SU40
Immediately obvious in this otherwise pleasant little place is the intrusive chimney of its power station. Rather more pleasing to the eye is the low, round tower of Calshot Castle, a coastal fort built by Henry VIII. It occupies a commanding position on a promontory at the end of a long shingle beach. Calshot foreshore is part of a country park.

Return along the B3053 SP 'Southampton' and drive to the edge of Fawley.

SOUTHAMPTON WATER, Hants
Between Calshot and Eling, the route of this tour is never far from the shores of Southampton Water, a maritime highway busy with the traffic of tankers, tugs, liners, ferries and pleasure craft. Southampton port, at its head, has long been one of the most commercially and strategically important harbours in the country. The Crusaders embarked here, the *Mayflower* set sail from the local docks, and Philip II of Spain landed here on his way to marry Mary Tudor in Winchester Cathedral. Today the Water guides great vessels from all over the world into the haven of England's premier passenger port.

FAWLEY, Hants SU40
Esso's petroleum refinery, which dominates Fawley, is an unlovely building but has some claim to fame through sheer size.

Drive to the next roundabout and follow SP 'Hythe' on to an unclassified road. After 1 mile turn right into Frost Lane and descend, over a level crossing, to the shores of Southampton Water. Continue to Hythe.

HYTHE, Hants SU40
Excellent views of Southampton docks and the shore are afforded by the Hythe ferry. Ship-spotting enthusiasts will find the village pier a handy vantage point.

Leave Hythe Pier with SP 'Totton', then after $\frac{1}{2}$ mile meet a T-junction and turn right. Continue for 2 miles, then on the nearside of the next roundabout turn sharp right on to the 'Marchwood' road. Continue to Marchwood.

MARCHWOOD, Hants SU31
Marchwood Power Station is considered architecturally among the very best in Britain.

Continue from Marchwood and after 2 miles meet crossroads. Turn right on to the 'Eling' road and continue to Eling.

ELING, Hants SU31
Situated on a creek off the head of Southampton Water, this ancient port is protected from through traffi by a toll-bridge reputed to be the smallest of its kind in Britain.

Cross the toll-bridge and follow SP 'Lyndhurst' to join the A35. Pass through Ashurst and enter the New Forest. Continue over heathland to reach Lyndhurst.

THE NEW FOREST, Hants
This district between the River Avor and Southampton Water comprise some 92,000 acres of undulating forest and heathland threaded by small streams and scattered with ponds. Many species of trees thrive in the mixture of clays, peat, and gravels here, affording cover to various species of deer and the famous New Forest ponies. Parts of the forest are nature reserves.

xhibits on display at the Montagu Motor luseum include historic record-reakers.

The boats in Lymington Harbour sprout a forest of masts.

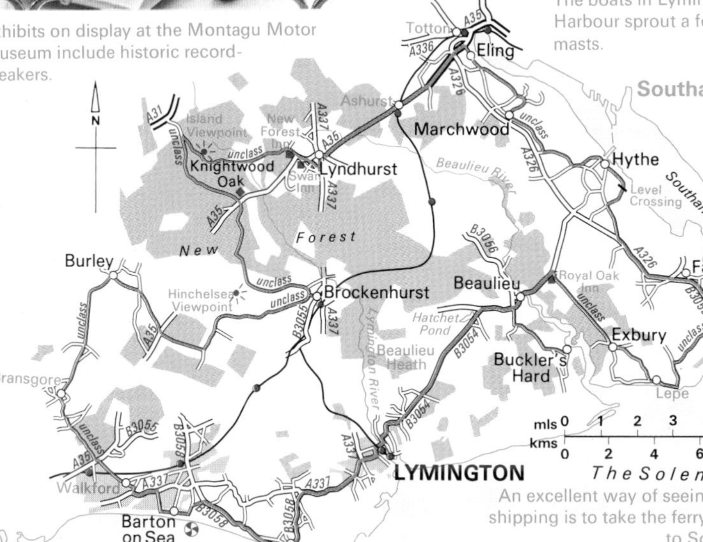

An excellent way of seeing the Solent shipping is to take the ferry from Hythe to Southampton.

NDHURST, Hants SU20
ndhurst is the capital of the New rest and an extremely popular urist centre. Woodlands lap the undaries of the town, and it is not usual to meet one of the area's mi-wild ponies or cows ambling ough the streets. The Victorian rish church features stained glass Burne-Jones, William Morris and ers, and a large mural by ghton. Alice Liddel, on whom the oine of *Alice in Wonderland* was ed, is buried here. West of the rch is the Queen's House, where Verderers' Court still sits to minister the forest.

ow the 'Bournemouth' road to the n Inn and turn right on to the lassified 'Emery Down' road. After ile reach the New Forest Inn and left SP 'Ringwood'. Continue ng one of the forest's most active byways. After 3 miles pass Island Viewpoint and a common he left, then turn sharp left (no SP) -enter fine woodlands along the lerwood Ornamental Drive. After rther 2 miles reach the htswood Oak on the left.

GHTSWOOD OAK, ts SU20
huge Knightswood Oak has a of more than 21ft and is ught to be 600 years old.

Keep forward from the Knightswood Oak and cross a main road to drive along the Rhinefield Ornamental Drive, bordered by fine conifers and rhododendrons. Cross heathland and pass through the outskirts of Brockenhurst. Turn left across a ford and drive to the town centre.

BROCKENHURST, Hants SU20
Many people find this handsome, lively village an ideal base from which to explore the New Forest. The local church is of Norman origin and claims to be the oldest foundation in the forest. *Domesday* records a church on this site, and the enormous yew in the churchyard may well have been planted over 1,000 years ago. Brusher Mills, a famous New Forest snake-catcher responsible for the demise of over 3,000 adders, is buried here.

Recross the ford and follow SP 'Burley' across wide heathland with picnic areas and good views. Pass Hinchesiea Viewpoint on the right and in $4\frac{3}{4}$ miles enter Burley.

BURLEY, Hants SU20
Nearby Castle Hill rises to 300ft and affords good views over this pretty village. An intriguing collection of souvenirs, trophies, and weapons can be seen in the local Queen's Head Inn.

The Knightswood Oak stands near Lyndhurst.

Continue along the 'Bransgore' road, cross more heathland, and reach the Crown Inn in Bransgore. Turn left here SP 'Lymington' and cross pleasant countryside. After 2 miles turn left and right across a main road, with the Cat and Fiddle Inn on the right. Drive beyond Walkford and turn left on to the A337. After $\frac{3}{4}$ mile turn right on to the unclassified 'Barton on Sea' road. Continue for $\frac{1}{2}$ mile and turn left, then meet a T-junction and turn right to enter Barton on Sea.

BARTON ON SEA, Hants SZ29
This modern resort's low clay cliffs form part of the Barton Beds, a geological series noted for its fossil shell, bone, and shark remains. Good views from the clifftop greensward extend to the chalk stacks of the Needles, and Isle of Wight.

Reach the end of the Promenade and turn left to follow SP 'Milford on Sea' across heaths and commons. Turn right on to the B3058 and drive to Milford on Sea.

MILFORD ON SEA, Hants SZ29
A popular resort since Victorian times, Milford on Sea offers good bathing from its sand and shingle beach and excellent views across the Solent to the Isle of Wight. All Saints' Church has a picture by Perugino at the west end of the south aisle. On a promontory about $2\frac{1}{2}$ miles south east is Hurst Castle.

HURST CASTLE, Hants SZ38
Built by Henry VIII in 1544, this fort (AM) was later occupied by Cromwell's forces and served as a prison for Charles I in 1648. Restoration work was carried out in 1873, and access today is by foot along a shingle promontory or by boat from Keyhaven.

From Milford on Sea, continue along the B3058 'Lymington' road and turn right on to the A337 before re-entering Lymington.

TOUR 22 — 71 MILES

SANCTITY IN STONE

Centuries before Christianity the primitive peoples of England raised the huge megaliths of Stonehenge. Much later came the cathedrals, the Norman permanence of Winchester and soaring early-English completeness of Salisbury.

WINCHESTER, Hants SU42
Venta Belgarum to the Romans, this one-time capital of Wessex boasts an 11th-century and later cathedral that is the second longest in Europe. Inside are richly-carved chantry chapels, the oldest iron grille in England, and coffins holding the bones of Saxon kings. Survivals from the distant 13th century include excellent stretches of the city walls, the hall of Pilgrims' School, and the 13th-century and later Deanery. Winchester College, founded by William of Wykeham in 1382, retains much of its original structure and stands near the ruined Bishop's Palace of Wolvesey Castle. Castle Hall dates from the 13th century, and 16th-century Godbegot House stands on the site of a palace built by King Canute. Close to the centre of town the River Itchen rushes through a lovely old mill (NT) of 1744 before winding through attractive gardens alongside the medieval walls.

Follow SP 'Stockbridge' to leave Winchester on the A272, and in $4\frac{3}{4}$ miles reach the Rack and Manger Inn. Turn right on to an unclassified road SP 'Crawley'. After another 1 mile reach a pond and turn left into Crawley village.

CRAWLEY, Hants SU43
Almost too perfect to be true, this picture-book village has timber-framed cottages, an old pub, and a duckpond. Its homely church has Norman features, and its Court dates from the late 19th century.

Drive to the far end of the village and keep left, then in $1\frac{1}{4}$ miles turn right to rejoin the A272. Proceed to Stockbridge Down.

STOCKBRIDGE DOWN, Hants SU33
Situated on the north side of the A272, this lovely area of open downland (NT) features a group of bronze-age round barrows and the south-west ditch and rampart of iron-age Woolbury Camp hillfort.

Later descend and enter the Test Valley, then continue to the edge of Stockbridge.

STOCKBRIDGE, Hants SU33
People from all over the world come here to fish the Test, one of the most sought-after game rivers in the country. Stockbridge itself is a one-street town of mainly Victorian buildings. The Town Hall, the Grosvenor Hotel, and the White Hart Inn are all early 19th-century, and only the 13th-century chancel of the old church remains.

Meet a roundabout and take the 2nd exit on to the A30, then drive to the next roundabout and branch left on to the A3057 SP 'Andover'. In $\frac{3}{4}$ mile turn left on to an unclassified road SP 'Longstock', then cross a bridge and cross the River Test to Longstock.

LONGSTOCK, Hants SU33
Thatched cottages strung out along a narrow, winding lane form the spine of this pretty village. Medieval tiles can be seen behind the altar of the 19th-century church, which is also notable for its beautiful chancel arch.

Turn left, then at the end of the village turn right (no SP) on to a narrow by-road. In $\frac{3}{4}$ mile meet a T-junction and turn right. Continue across open downland, then in another $\frac{3}{4}$ mile bear left SP 'Grateley'. Pass Danebury Ring on the left.

DANEBURY RING, Hants SU33
At the top of a 469ft hill is Danebury Ring, an iron-age camp that has been thoroughly excavated in recent years. It has been acquired by the County Council as a public amenity area.

In 2 miles meet a main road and turn left on to the A343. Pass the Army Aviation Centre, then after $1\frac{1}{2}$ miles reach Middle Wallop. Meet crossroads and turn right on to the B3084 for Over Wallop.

OVER WALLOP, Hants SU23
Although St Peter's Church in Over Wallop displays 12th- and 13th-century traces, much of its old structure has been hidden by Victorian restoration. Inside is a 15th-century font.

In $3\frac{1}{2}$ miles pass Quarley Hill to the right and turn left on to an unclassified road SP 'Amesbury'. In $\frac{1}{4}$ mile bear right and drive through pleasant wooded country, then cross the River Bourne to enter Cholderton. Turn left on to the A338 and in 200 yards turn right on to an unclassified road. After another $1\frac{1}{2}$ miles turn left on to the A303, then follow a fast main road by-passing Amesbury.

Danebury Ring consists of thre lines of ramparts an ditches and enclose 13 acre

In Saxon times Winchester was the capital of England.

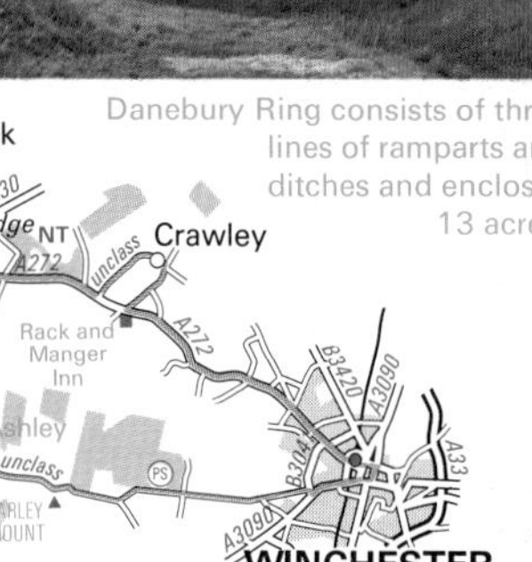

The church at King's Sombor

AMESBURY, Wilts SU14
At Amesbury the Avon is crossed b a five-arched Palladian bridge whic complements the stately flow of th river. Amesbury Abbey is of the 19 century and stands in a park in which beech clumps have been planted to represent the positions o English and French ships at Trafalga The Church of SS Mary and Melor a flint-built Norman structure containing a contemporary font fashioned from Purbeck marble.

Meet a roundabout and keep forward, then in $1\frac{3}{4}$ miles turn right to the A344 SP 'Devizes'. Continue Stonehenge.

Stonehenge is probably the most famous prehistoric monument in the world.

STONEHENGE, Wilts SU14
Almost nothing is known about this most famous of all prehistoric megalithic monuments. From time :o time the public imagination is :aught by theories of sun-worship ites and primitive astronomical :omputers, but it is likely that these ıave as little factual base as the neo-lruidical ceremonies enacted here every Midsummer's Night Eve.)riginally Stonehenge (AM) :omprised an encircling ditch and ɔank dating from the stone age, but his simple base was later developed nto circles of sarsen stones around a ıorseshoe of trilithons enclosing the nigmatic Welsh bluestones (see our 42). Several stones still stand vhere they were first erected ıousands of years ago, and the ırgest measures almost 30ft high om its deeply buried base to its top. ⁄Iuch of the surrounding land elongs to the National Trust.

'ontinue on the A344 and in ½ miles turn left on to the A360 SP alisbury'. In 1 mile meet a ɔundabout and keep forward, assing Normanton Down.

ORMANTON DOWN, Vilts SU14
the Normanton Down area there e no fewer than 26 round barrows ' various types, and a single long ırrow dating from an earlier period. :cavations of this remarkable group ıve shown them to be Wessex 'aves dating from the early bronze ʒe. Hundreds of other examples ırvive near Stonehenge.

ɔllow an undulating road across part Salisbury Plain, and after 3 miles eet crossroads. Turn left on to an ıclassified road SP 'Woodford'. ɔntinue to Middle Woodford.

IDDLE WOODFORD, 'ilts SU13
ɔst of Middle Woodford Church ıs rebuilt in Victorian times, ɔugh the great flint and rubble wer is a survival from earlier days. ɔale House, where Charles II once l and from which he rode forth to ɛw Stonehenge, also has 19th-ntury additions.

Middle Woodford meet a unction and turn right to follow the 'er Avon to Lower Woodford.

LOWER WOODFORD, Wilts SU13
High downs rise on either side of this tiny village, which is the lowest of three Woodfords strung along the Avon Valley. The only building of any real note here is the manor house (not open), but the local countryside is enchanting.

In 2 miles cross a river bridge and turn left, then immediately turn right and shortly pass the earthworks of Old Sarum.

OLD SARUM, Wilts SU13
In Roman times this important centre was linked by the Port Way to *Calleva Atrebatum*, a significant garrison town near Silchester in Hampshire. After a while Old Sarum became the site of a great cathedral, but a combination of water shortage, military troubles, and exposure to inclement weather prompted a move to Salisbury in 1220. The cathedral was demolished in 1331 and the materials transported to the new site for the superb building that stands today.

Reach the main road and turn right on to the A345. Continue to Salisbury.

SALISBURY, Wilts SU12
Salisbury's 404ft cathedral spire, the tallest in England, dominates most approaches to this lovely city. The cathedral itself is a perfect example of early-English architecture, set amid an enchanting medley of houses in the ancient cathedral close. Many other old buildings survive in the city. See Tour 18 for further details.

From Salisbury follow SP 'Southampton' to leave on the A36. In 1½ miles turn right on to an unclassified road and ascend. Near the road summit pass the Green Dragon (PH) and continue to Alderbury.

ALDERBURY, Wilts SU12
Alderbury House is said to be built of stone from the old belfry of Salisbury Cathedral. The small farm at nearby Ivychurch is on the site of a Norman priory, and local St Mary's Church is of Victorian date.

At Alderbury turn left for 'West Grimstead'. Drive to that village and keep forward SP 'West Dean', and in 3 miles meet a junction and turn right for West Dean.

WEST DEAN, Wilts SU22
Half hidden among trees at the top of a hill are remains of the old St Mary's Church of West Dean. New St Mary's was built of flint and brick in 1866. Close to the ruins is a good 16th-century barn.

Turn right SP 'Lockerley', then beyond East Dean go over a level crossing and continue to Lockerley. In ½ mile bear right, and ¼ mile farther pass under a railway bridge. Drive to the nearside of a green and turn left SP 'Dunbridge'. At Dunbridge turn left on to the B3084 and drive over a level crossing and river bridge. In ½ mile turn right on to an unclassified road SP 'Mottisfont Village'. Meet a T-junction and turn right. Pass the entrance to 18th-century Mottisfont Abbey.

MOTTISFONT, Hants SU32
Remains of a 12th-century priory are incorporated in 18th-century Mottisfont Abbey (NT), which houses an excellent collection of paintings by Rex Whistler.

Cross the River Test then later meet the main road and turn left on to the A3057. Follow the Test Valley to King's Somborne.

KING'S SOMBORNE, Hants SU33
A ring of bells in the Church of SS Peter and Paul is inscribed 'completed in the Jubilee Year of Queen Victoria, 1887'. The building itself is of ancient foundation but was much restored in 1885. The architect Sir Edwin Lutyens designed modern Marsh Court.

In King's Somborne turn right on to an unclassified road SP 'Winchester', then take the next turning left. After another ¾ mile turn right for Ashley, then climb through well-wooded country to Farley Mount. This country park has an excellent picnic site. Meet a fork junction and bear left to follow a pleasant by-road. Go forward over all crossroads for 3 miles, then turn left on to the A3090 to re-enter Winchester.

The River Test is renowned for its trout fishing.

TOUR 23 75 MILES

HAMPSHIRE DOWNS AND SUSSEX LANES

West of Petersfield are the rolling chalk downs of Hampshire, bare summits rising from wooded flanks watered by trout streams. East are the great wooded commons, winding lanes, and picturesque villages of Sussex.

PETERSFIELD, Hants SU72
In its early years Petersfield's prosperity was based on the wool trade, but as this began to decline it became an important coaching centre on the busy London to Portsmouth road. Today it is a thriving country town full of fine old houses in evocatively-named streets. A once-gilded equestrian statue of William III guards the central square, where a market is held every Wednesday. The extensive waters of Heath Pond lie south east of the town on the B2146.

Leave Petersfield on the A3 'Guildford' road and continue to Durford Heath.

DURFORD HEATH, W Sussex SU72
The 58-acre expanse of Durford Heath (NT) includes 4 acres of Rogate Common and the track bed of a disused railway.

Continue along the A3 for $\frac{3}{4}$ mile. Reach the Jolly Drover Inn and turn right on to an unclassified road SP 'Rogate' to enter Sussex. After $\frac{1}{4}$ mile turn left on to the Fernhurst road and drive through wooded country to Milland.

MILLAND, W Sussex SU82
Although close to the Portsmouth road, this straggling village preserves an air of remoteness and seclusion. St Luke's Church of 1878 stands in front of the primitive Old Church which it replaced.

Continue beyond Milland for $1\frac{1}{2}$ miles and turn right with SP 'The Old Cottage'. Ascend to Woolbeding and Pound Commons (NT).

WOOLBEDING COMMON, W Sussex SU82
Woolbeding Common, part of a 1,084-acre estate (NT), includes some 400 acres of common heath and woodland open to public access.

Descend past Woolbeding's Saxon church.

Cowdray House was built c1500.

WOOLBEDING, W Sussex SU82
Domesday describes Woolbeding as 'a perfect manor containing a church, mill, meadow, and wood.' The mill has gone, but the village is as delightful as that ancient description suggests. All Hallows' Church boasts a good Saxon nave.

Cross the River Rother, meet the A272, and turn left to enter Midhurst.

MIDHURST, W Sussex SU82
This small market town stands on the south bank of the River Rother, at the centre of one of Sussex's most beautiful regions. South lie the downs, and north are the picturesque ruins of Cowdray House (see Easebourne).

Leave Midhurst by the A286 'Guildford' road, cross the river, and turn left through Easebourne.

EASEBOURNE, W Sussex SU82
Formerly more important than Midhurst, immaculate Easebourne is very much an estate village. Among its many well-kept houses are Sycamore Cottage in Easebourne Lane, and The Priory, attached to the south side of St Mary's Church. Tudor Cowdray House (open) was ruined by fire in 1793.

Leave Easebourne and climb through woodland to the 530ft Henley Common viewpoint. Continue to Fernhurst.

FERNHURST, W Sussex SU92
Almost certainly the last stronghold of the Sussex iron-smelting industry, this large village has settled into attractive rural retirement amid the woods and valleys of the Weald.

Midhurst's mainly 19th-century church looks over a town that preserves beautiful buildings from many periods of architecture.

Meet crossroads in Fernhurst and turn left on to an unclassified road. Drive through wooded country with SP 'Linchmere', and after 1 mile branch right SP 'Liphook'. Enter Linchmere.

LINCHMERE, W Sussex SU83
Linchmere boasts a tiny green outside the enlarged hill chapel that serves as its church. Magnificent views from here extend over a deep valley flanked by steep slopes.

After Linchmere turn left on to the B2131 to re-enter Hampshire. Enter Liphook.

LIPHOOK, Hants SU83
Most of Liphook straggles untidily along the main Portsmouth road, but here and there it preserves something of a village atmosphere. Bohunt Manor (open) stands in a lovely woodland and water garden.

A detour from the main route can be made here by turning left on to the unclassified 'Midhurst' road and driving for $1\frac{1}{2}$ miles to Hollycombe.

HOLLYCOMBE, W Sussex SU82
The Hollycombe Working Steam Museum and Woodland Garden (open) has a remarkable collection of equipment ranging from old fairground rides to a 2ft-gauge railway through woodland banks of rhododendrons and azaleas. Attractions include traction engine rides and demonstrations of steam ploughing, threshing, and rolling.

At the Royal Anchor Hotel in Liphook (on the main route), turn right then sharp left to follow SP 'Longmoor, Greatham' through Longmoor Camp and Woolmer Forest. Continue to Greatham. In Greatham turn left on to the A325 and follow SP 'Alton'. Reach a church and after another $\frac{1}{4}$ mile turn right on to the B3006 and drive on to the east Hampshire Downs for Empshott. Continue along the B3006 to Selborne.

SELBORNE & SELBORNE HILL, Hants SU73
It is not just the beauty of its scenery or the architectural distinction of some of its houses that have made this lovely village famous. It is also featured in Gilbert White's classic field study entitled *The Natural History of Selborne*. White, who was born in the Vicarage in 1720, made one of the first and best studies of wildlife inter-action within a defined area. He died in The Wakes, a fine house that now contains an interesting Gilbert White Museum (open). Visitors today can still see the church meadows and high beech hangers where he made many of his observations, and climb the steep Zig-Zag Path to the excellent viewpoint of Selborne Hill (NT).

In $3\frac{1}{4}$ miles turn left on to an unclassified road for Chawton. A short detour can be made from the main route here by keeping forward on the B3006 to Alton.

'he Gilbert
Vhite Museum
at Selborne.

LTON, Hants
J73

years
one by this
storic market
wn grew quietly
osperous on
ewing and the manufacture of
oollen cloth. Fine Georgian
uildings grace the main street, and
Tudor cottage that was once the
ome of the poet Spenser is in
nery Street. Exhibits in the Curtis
useum include a collection of craft
ols and other bygones.

ontinue along the main tour route d enter Chawton.

HAWTON, Hants SU73

Chawton is the unassuming little th-century cottage where novelist ne Austen once lived. Now a Jane isten Museum (open), this was her me from 1809 till her death, and her later books were written here.

ach a roundabout at the end of awton and take the 2nd exit on to A31. Climb to 600ft at Four Marks d follow a pleasant road through hop's Sutton to New Alresford.

W ALRESFORD, Hants SU53

uring the medieval period New esford grew to be one of the greatest wool towns in the untry. Aptly-named Broad Street, nsidered the finest village street in mpshire, leads downhill to ttered Old Alresford. At the rth-west end of the village is the ge and picturesque parish pond.

hort detour can be made from the in route by turning left into Station ad to visit the Mid Hants Railway.

MID HANTS RAILWAY, Hants SU53

The original Watercress Line, as this railway has come to be known, was threatened with closure in 1973 and initial efforts to keep the whole line open were not successful. In 1975 the Winchester & Alton Railway Company raised enough money to open 3 miles of track between Alresford and Ropley. All associated buildings in the 10 miles to Alton were also acquired, and it is hoped that the track will soon be opened for the full distance.

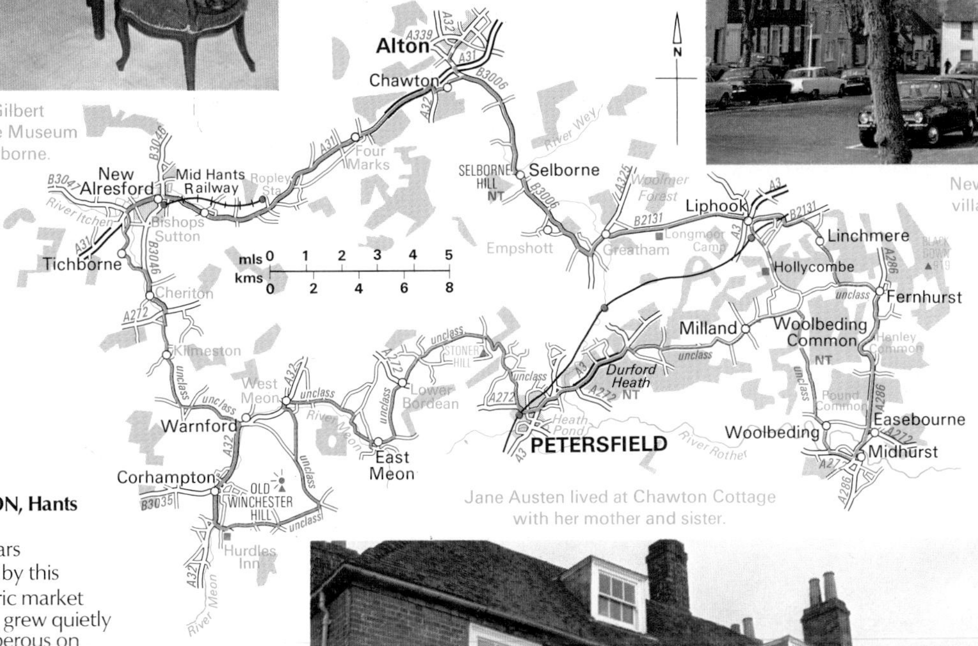

Jane Austen lived at Chawton Cottage with her mother and sister.

Leave Alresford on the Winchester road and after ½ mile meet crossroads. Turn left on to an unclassified road to Tichborne.

TICHBORNE, Hants SU53

Tichborne is a delightful collection of thatched 16th- and 17th-century houses with an unspoilt little church and a 19th-century manor house. Some 800 years ago the ailing lady of the manor, distressed by the poverty of the villagers, begged her husband to help them. Mockingly he agreed to set aside part of his estate to provide corn for the poor in perpetuity, but that would be only so much land as she could crawl round while one torch burned. Tradition has it that she managed to encompass an amazing 23 acres of ground before the flame – and her life – expired. The land concerned still known as The Crawls, and every year the villages receive a dole of 30cwt of flour blessed by the local priest.

Continue for 1 mile past the village, meet a T-junction, and turn right on to the B3046 for Cheriton. Follow SP 'Petersfield' for ½ mile, then cross a main road on to the unclassified 'Droxford' road. Drive through Kilmeston, climb rolling hills, then later turn left on to the 'Warnford' road for a descent to the Meon Valley. Continue to Warnford.

WARNFORD, Hants SU62

This beautiful Meon Valley village has a 12th- to 17th-century church with a massive Norman tower. Ruins of a 13th-century building, misleadingly known as King John's House, can be seen in Warnford Park.

New Alresford's Broad Street, said to be the finest village street in Hampshire, is lined with attractive Georgian houses and lime trees.

Meet a T-junction and turn right on to the A32 'Fareham' road. Cross the River Meon and continue into Corhampton.

CORHAMPTON, Hants SU62

This pleasant River Meon village boasts a rare Saxon church with a contemporary sundial. The walls of the ancient nave slant crazily to the south, but the building is quite safe.

After another mile turn left on to the B2150 'Waterlooville' road, then pass the Hurdles Inn and take the next turning left (no SP). Follow SP 'East Meon' over crossroads and after another ½ mile bear left. Cross downland to meet a T-junction and turn left again on to the 'West Meon' road. Continue to the slopes of Old Winchester Hill.

OLD WINCHESTER HILL, Hants SU62

Why this noted beauty spot should be so named is a mystery, for the city of Winchester lies a good 12 miles to the west. The hill's windswept summit rises to nearly 700ft, affording excellent views over half the county, and a 1¾-mile nature trail has been laid out on its flanks.

Branch right on to a narrow road and later turn right on to the A32. Drive into West Meon and turn right on to the unclassified 'East Meon' road. Continue along the attractive Meon Valley to the edge of East Meon.

EAST MEON, Hants SU62

'Father of angling' Izaak Walton once fished here, and the village is still a popular trout centre. The Norman church is arguably the finest of its kind in Hampshire.

Follow SP 'Petersfield' and in ½ mile turn left on to the narrow 'Lower Bordean' road. Later cross the A272 into the very narrow 'Colemore' road and follow SP 'Petersfield' to a T-junction. Turn right, descend the attractive Stoner Hill, and return to Petersfield.

TOUR 24 55 MILES

ALONG THE HOG'S BACK

Some of the finest views in the south of England can be enjoyed from the great chalk ridge of the Hog's Back, which itself can be seen across miles of flat farm land scattered with small woods and copses. This is the country of the yellowhammer and skylark, of thorn-covered slopes and the gnarled creepers of old man's beard.

GUILDFORD, Surrey TQ04
Medieval kings built a great castle in this ancient town and merchants later developed it into an important centre of the wool industry. Nowadays the castle has vanished except for a 3-storey keep (open) in flower gardens, but the prosperity of wool is reflected in many fine old buildings. Charles Dickens thought the steep High Street 'the most beautiful in the kingdom'. At its summit is the 16th-century Grammar School, the contemporary Hospital (open), and an 18th-century church. Farther down, the ornate clock of the 17th-century Guildhall hangs over the pavement near the Saxon tower of St Mary's Church, and the 19th-century Church of St Nicholas makes an interesting contrast at the bottom of the hill. The River Wey features an interesting 18th-century riverside crane powered by a 20ft treadmill. New buildings include Sir Edward Maufe's controversial cathedral on Stag Hill.

Leave Guildford town centre with SP 'Other Routes' and after 1 mile turn left on to the A3 bypass SP 'Petersfield'. After 1½ miles drive under a road bridge, and in another mile pass the turning for Compton and Loseley House on the left. A short detour from the main route can be taken along the B3000 to the pleasant village of Compton and Loseley House.

COMPTON, Surrey SU94
A gallery devoted entirely to Victorian painter and sculptor G F Watts displays some 200 of his works in this small village. He is commemorated by a mortuary chapel which features vivid interior decoration by his widow.

LOSELEY HOUSE, Surrey SU94
Sir William More, a kinsman of the ill-fated Sir Thomas More, used stone from Waverley Abbey to build this magnificent Elizabethan mansion (open) near Compton. Fine ceilings are complemented by panelling from King Henry VIII's Nonsuch Palace, and every room is appointed with furniture and hangings from many periods.

Continue along the A3 for another ½ mile, then turn right on to the B3000 SP 'Farnham'. Proceed to Puttenham.

PUTTENHAM, Surrey SU94
A handsomely aged church with a 15th-century tower enhances the quiet charm of this small village.

In the village turn left on to an unclassified road and continue along the southern slopes of the Hog's Back to Seale.

THE HOG'S BACK, Surrey
At its highest point this great whaleback ridge of chalk, an outlier of the North Downs, rises to 505ft above sea level. It stretches from Guildford to Farnham, with parking and picnic areas along its length.

The Hog's Back is criss-crossed by quiet country lanes.

Drive past the church in Seale and turn left. Proceed for ½ mile and meet crossroads, then turn left for The Sands. Cross a main road SP 'Tilford' and pass 534ft Crooksbury Hill on the left. Continue to crossroads and turn left again SP 'Elstead'. After a short distance turn left on to the B3001 and take the next turning right on to an unclassified road for Tilford.

TILFORD, Surrey SU84
Features of this pleasant village include two partly medieval bridges over the River Wey, the graceful lines of 18th-century Tilford House (not open), and a huge old tree known as King John's Oak. The latter is said to be many centuries old. The village is noted for its Bach music festivals.

Cross the River Wey twice with SP 'Frensham' and after ¼ mile turn left. Continue for another 1½ miles and turn left on to the A287 SP 'Hindhead'. Proceed through Frensham.

Guildford's fine 17th-century clock hangs high above the main street and can be seen for many yards in both directions.

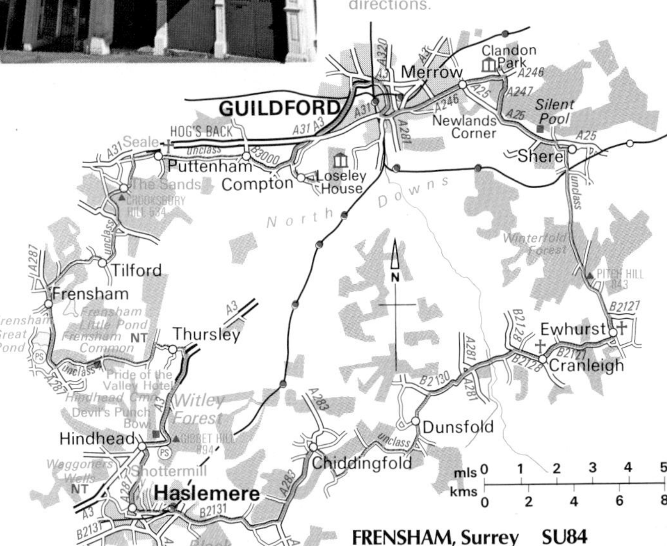

FRENSHAM, Surrey SU84
Frensham's lovely ponds are surrounded by woods and heathland on the Hampshire-Surrey border. The Great Pond covers 108 acres, and the Little Pond is resplendent with water lilies in late spring and summer. The 900-acre gorse and heather common (NT) features a line of large prehistoric bowl barrows, and much of the area is now protected as a country park. Frensham's restored church has a Norman font and, under the tower, a great copper cauldron reputed to be over 400 years old. Tradition holds that it belonged to a local witch called Mother Ludlam, and an 18th-century writer tells of it having been filled with ale to entertain the village 'at the wedding of poor maids'.

Cross Frensham Common to reach Frensham Great Pond and a picnic site. Proceed for ¾ mile and turn left on to an unclassified road SP 'Thursley'. After 1½ miles reach the Pride of the Valley Hotel. Cross the main road and after 1¾ miles turn right for Thursley.

THURSLEY, Surrey SU93
Old houses and charming cottages straggle along a winding lane to the village church which has a sundial on its shingled spire. A curious epitaph to an unknown sailor murdered by three ruffians at Hindhead in 1786 can be seen on a tombstone in the churchyard.

Continue for $\frac{1}{2}$ mile and turn right on to the A3 'Hindhead' road. Drive over Hindhead Common, with the Devil's Punch Bowl on the right and Gibbet Hill, a picnic site, and Witley Forest on the left. Enter Hindhead.

Four great beams inside Thursley Church support its shingled steeple.

HINDHEAD, Surrey SU83
ounded in the 19th century on the ighest town site in Surrey, lindhead offers some of the most eautiful surroundings in the county. he noted viewpoint of Gibbet Hill NT) rises to 894ft in the north east, ne deep combe of the Devil's Punch owl cuts through a sandstone ridge ear by, and all around is Witley orest. Off the B3002 $1\frac{1}{2}$ miles south est is the beauty spot of Vaggoner's Wells (NT).

ollow SP 'Haslemere, A287' and escend to Shottermill, then keep rward on the B2131 for Haslemere.

ASLEMERE, Surrey SU93
aslemere stands in dense woods at ne northern foot of 918ft-high ackdown. For centuries the town as been a centre for craftsmen, and day the tradition is maintained at e Dolmetsch musical instrument orkshops and museum (open). dworth, home of the great 19th- ntury poet Tennyson, stands on e slopes of Black Down. A number 17th-century tiled houses survive hind a raised walk in the town, nd the 19th-century Educational useum of Sir John Hutchinson ands in the High Street (open). The wn's annual music festival, usually ld in July, is invariably devoted to e Baroque period.

ave Haslemere on the B2131 SP tworth', with Black Down on the ht. After $2\frac{1}{2}$ miles bear left SP hiddingfold', and after a further $\frac{3}{4}$ le meet a T-junction. Turn left on to A283 for Chiddingfold.

CHIDDINGFOLD, Surrey SU93
In medieval times this large village was very famous for its fine quality glass. Despite its large size it is one of the loveliest Wealden villages. At its heart is a pretty green with a thorn tree said to be 500 years old, a pond complete with ducks and water lilies, and the delightful 14th-century Crown Inn.

Drive to the Crown Inn and turn right on to an unclassified road SP 'Dunsfold'. Reach the far side of the green and bear right, then continue for 1 mile, turn left, and proceed to Dunsfold.

DUNSFOLD, Surrey TQ03
A modern lychgate and a tunnel of clipped yews lead to Dunsfold Church, which dates from the 13th century and has an attractive Tudor porch. Its pews may be the oldest still used in England.

One mile beyond Dunsfold turn right on to the B2130 SP 'Cranleigh'. Continue for 1 mile, then bear left and after $\frac{1}{4}$ mile turn right. Drive over staggered crossroads and continue for $1\frac{1}{4}$ miles. Turn right on to the B2128 and drive into Cranleigh.

CRANLEIGH, Surrey TQ03
Cranleigh is more than a village, and yet not quite large enough to call a town. Its pleasant green has a rural aspect, but the long main street lined with maples planted by Canadian soldiers in World War I might have been borrowed from a much larger place. In 1859 a surgeon called Napper and the local rector together founded the first cottage hospital.

Clandon Park was designed by a Venetian architect in the Palladian style.

Drive to the end of the village and turn left on to the B2127. After $2\frac{1}{4}$ miles turn left again into Ewhurst.

EWHURST, Surrey TQ04
Climbers come to Ewhurst to test their mettle on Pitch Hill, a sandstone outcrop that rises 1 mile to the north of the village. Ewhurst Mill has not worked for a century and was once a haunt of smugglers.

Keep forward in Ewhurst, on to the unclassified 'Shere' road. After $\frac{3}{4}$ mile bear left and cross Pitch Hill, with Winterfold Forest on the left, and drive into Shere.

SHERE, Surrey TQ04
Situated on the River Tillingbourne under the edge of the North Downs, this enchanting village has long proved an attraction to artists. The church, which figures in the *Domesday Book*, has a Norman tower with a medieval shingled spire. The White Horse Inn has a frame of ancient ship's timbers.

Drive to a T-junction and turn left SP 'Guildford'. Continue to the next T-junction and turn left again to join the A25. After $\frac{1}{2}$ mile, off the main road to the right, is the Silent Pool.

SILENT POOL, Surrey TQ04
According to legend King John watched a local girl bathing here. She drowned herself in a fit of shame, and anybody visiting this quiet, tree-encircled water might easily imagine that her spirit lingers here still.

Ascend to Newlands Corner.

NEWLANDS CORNER, Surrey TQ04
This famous 567ft high North Downs beauty spot offers views across the Weald to the South Downs.

At Newlands Corner turn right on to the A247 SP 'Woking'. Descend for 1 mile and meet crossroads. Turn left on to the A246. By keeping straight ahead a short detour can be taken from the main route to Clandon Park.

CLANDON PARK, Surrey TQ05
Built in the early 1730s, this classical mansion (NT) features noteworthy plaster decoration, and stands in gardens refashioned by Capability Brown. A famous collection of china, furniture and needlework bequeathed to the nation by Mrs Hannah Gubbay in 1969 is displayed in these elegant surroundings.

Continue on the A246 to Merrow.

MERROW, Surrey TQ05
A footpath that starts between the church and inn at Merrow runs across gentle downland to a summit which affords views into 8 or 9 counties, depending on the weather.

Continue along the A246 and return to Guildford.

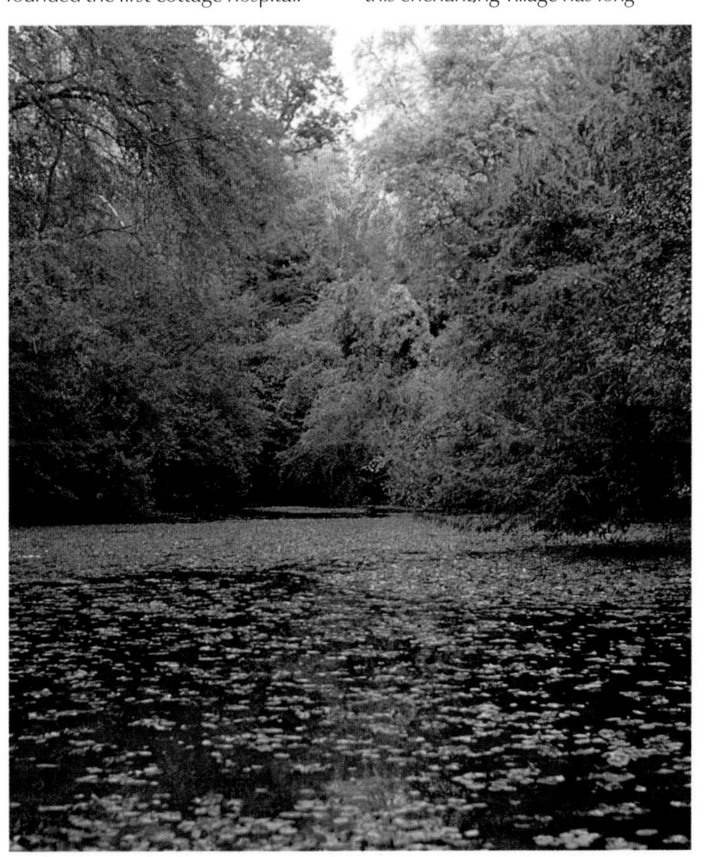

ee-shrouded Silent Pool is connected in legend with King John.

WOKINGHAM, Berks SU86
Wokingham boasted a bell foundry in the 14th century, and the silk industry flourished here in Elizabethan days. Rose Street preserves timbered houses and the Rose Inn, where poets.Dean Swift, Pope, and Gay spent a wet afternoon together. Gay utilized the time in composing verses to the landlord's daughter, Molly Mog. Several almshouses exist in and around the town, and Lucas Hospital of 1665 – at Luckely – is considered particularly fine.

Follow SP 'Reading, A329' to leave Wokingham via Broad Street. In $\frac{1}{4}$ mile approach the clock tower, then turn left on to the B3349 SP 'Arborfield' and go over a level crossing. After $2\frac{1}{2}$ miles turn right for Arborfield Cross.

ARBORFIELD CROSS, Berks SU76
To the left of Arborfield Cross, off the A327, is Arborfield Garrison. Nearby Moat House contains the Royal Electrical and Mechanical Engineers' Museum, which is open to the public at most times.

Turn right and immediately left on to an unclassified road SP 'Swallowfield'. Continue for 2 miles and turn right. Swallowfield Park is on the right.

SWALLOWFIELD PARK, Berks SU76
Swallowfield Park lies almost on the Hampshire border, at the meeting of the rivers Loddon and Blackwater. Swallowfield Park house was rebuilt in the late 17th century and remodelled by William Atkinson in 1820.

At the park gates turn left across the Blackwater River to reach Swallowfield. Turn left SP 'Basingstoke' and proceed through Swallowfield. Meet the A33 main road and turn left for Riseley. Bear right and later approach the Duke of Wellington Monument outside Stratfield Saye Park. A detour from the main route can be made by continuing for $\frac{1}{2}$ mile to an unclassified right turn leading to Stratfield Saye Park.

STRATFIELD SAYE PARK, Hants SU66
This rather unstately stately home (open) was built in the reign of Charles I and purchased by the 1st Duke of Wellington in 1817. The duke intended to use the £600,000 voted to him by a grateful nation to build a new house in the superb park, but funds did not permit this and so the great soldier set about making the existing building as comfortable and convenient as he could. Central heating was installed in the passageways, and there were 'new-fangled' water closets of blue-patterned china in every room. It has been the home of the dukes of Wellington ever since.

On the main route, drive to the Wellington Monument and turn left on to an unclassified road, SP 'Eversley', cross Heckfield Heath, and continue for $\frac{1}{2}$ mile. Cross a main road to join the B3011, then after $\frac{1}{2}$ mile branch left on to an unclassified road. Continue, cross the River Whitewater, then after $2\frac{1}{2}$ miles meet crossroads and drive forward. A short detour can be made to the village of Eversley by turning left here and continuing for $\frac{1}{2}$ mile.

TOUR 25 61 MILES

ROYAL PARKS AND HAMPSHIRE WOODS

Close to Windsor is the semi-cultivated countryside of royal parkland; farther away, near the Duke of Wellington's country estate, are dark ranks of conifer plantations and the lighter greens of oak and birch tangled with honeysuckle.

Eversley's ancient origins are suggested by the picturesque nameplate on its village green.

EVERSLEY, Hants SU76
St Mary's Church at Eversley was built in the 18th century, and is distinguished in having had naturalist Charles Kingsley as rector. The north aisle was built in his memory. Bramshill House, a Jacobean mansion regarded as one of the finest in the country, is now the Police Staff College.

Join the A327 for Eversley Cross and drive to The Chequers (PH). Turn left on to the B3016 SP 'Wokingham' and continue to Finchampstead.

FINCHAMPSTEAD, Berks SU76
Finchampstead's pride is the splendid avenue of Wellingtonia pines which runs 1 mile east to Crowthorne. Its church has a white-painted body of Norman date and carries an 18th-century tower built in red brick. The whole building stands on a prehistoric earthwork, as if aloof from the village.

Turn right, then after $\frac{1}{4}$ mile meet a war memorial and turn right on to the B3348 SP 'Crowthorne'. Pass Finchampstead Ridges on the right.

FINCHAMPSTEAD RIDGES, Berks SU86
This 60-acre heather and woodland National Trust property offers excellent views over Berkshire, Hampshire, and Surrey countryside.

Continue, enter a roundabout, and take the first exit on to the A321. After 1 mile turn right on to the unclassified Nine Mile Ride.

NINE MILE RIDE, Berks SU86
Nine Mile Ride follows the line of a Roman road through delightfully wooded country. At the Bracknell end, to the south, is the 20-acre iron-age hillfort of Caesar's Camp, part of which is now a public recreation ground with a picnic site.

After $2\frac{3}{4}$ miles go over staggered crossroads SP 'Bagshot'. Continue, passing Caesar's Camp (see Nine Mile Ride), and at the end of the road turn right on to the A322. Proceed for $1\frac{1}{2}$ miles and pass a picnic site, then turn left on to the A332 'Ascot' road. Continue for $1\frac{3}{4}$ miles and bear right. Approach a roundabout and leave by the 3rd exit on to the A329, with Ascot racecourse on the left, and enter Ascot.

ASCOT, Berks SU96
Ascot has strong Queen Anne connections. It was she who instituted the Royal Ascot race meeting in 1711, a fashionable event still held in June and patronized by members of the Royal Family. The Ascot Gold Cup was presented for the first time in 1807.

Continue to Virginia Water, which can be seen on the left.

VIRGINIA WATER, Surrey SU96
This $1\frac{1}{2}$-mile-long artificial lake, laid out by Thomas Sandby for George III, is situated at the south-east corner of Windsor Great Park and is well known for its beauty. Colonnades brought from the Roman port of Leptis Magna stand on its bank in contrast to a 100ft totem pole set up in 1958 to mark the centenary of British Columbia. The nearby Valley and Heather Gardens are most invitir

Continue to the main road and turn left on to the A30. Pass the Wheatsheaf Hotel and proceed for $1\frac{1}{4}$ miles, then turn left on to an unclassified road for Savill Gardens (lef

THE SAVILL GARDENS, Berks SU97
Windsor Great Park is noted for its magnificent horticultural areas, but none is more popular than the wooded 20-acre Savill Garden. Its variety of rare flowers is accessible to the public during the summer.

Continue to The Sun (PH) and go forward for $\frac{1}{2}$ mile before turning righ for Englefield Green.

ENGLEFIELD GREEN, Surrey SU97
This large residential district lies within easy reach of delightful Windsor Great Park. Its 250-year-old Barley Mow Inn was once a popular coaching stop. Late 19th-century Royal Holloway College stands among gardens and playing fields between Englefield Green and the railway. It was one of the first women's colleges ever built and became a constituent college of London University in 1900.

Cross a main road and pass a left turr to Cooper's Hill RAF Memorial.

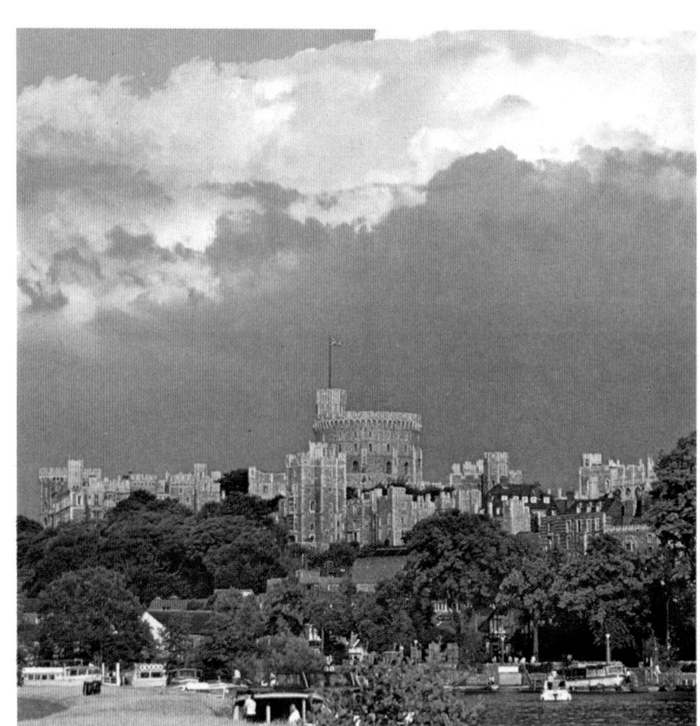
Windsor Castle has dominated its surroundings ever since William the Conqueror started it in the 11th centur

n equestrian statue of George III by ulptor Richard Westmacott stands on granite base at the end of the Long alk in Windsor Great Park.

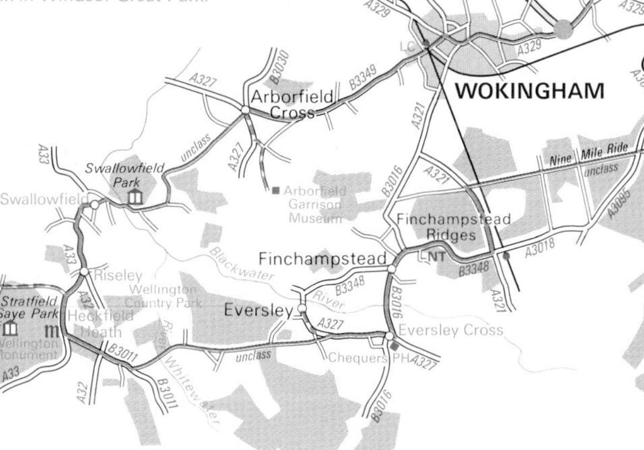

OOPER'S HILL RAF MEMORIAL, rrey SU97
e Commonwealth Air Forces morial on Cooper's Hill mmemorates 20,000 allied airmen o died, with no known grave, in orld War II. The site, which gives ws of Windsor Castle and seven unties, overlooks Runnymede.

ss a main road, passing the oper's Hill turning, then after 300 ls bear left and descend Tite Hill to edge of Egham. Enter a ndabout and leave by the 1st exit ejoin the A30. After another ¾ mile er another roundabout and leave he 3rd exit on to the A308. ntinue to Staines.

AINES, Surrey TQ07
old market town of Staines, at junction of the rivers Colne and mes, is entered via a superb road ge built by Rennie and opened William IV. The new by-pass sses by a modern bridge. West of local church the London Stone ks the limit of the City of don's former jurisdiction. Sir lter Raleigh was brought here to ried because at that time London in the grip of the plague.

Return along the A308 SP 'Windsor'. In 1 mile meet a roundabout and take the 3rd exit to pass Runnymede.

RUNNYMEDE, Surrey TQ07
About ½ mile north-west of Egham are the 60-acre riverside meadows of Runnymede. It was here in 1215 that King John was prevailed upon by his barons to seal the draft of Magna Carta, from which seed – almost by accident – grew the English ideal of personal liberty. Overlooking the meadows is Cooper's Hill, which is crowned by the RAF Memorial and has the American Bar Association's Magna Carta Memorial at its foot. Halfway up its slopes is a memorial to the assassinated US President, John F Kennedy.

Continue through Old Windsor.

OLD WINDSOR, Berks SU97
Old Windsor parish stretches from the River Thames to Virginia Water, including the semi-wild countryside of the Great Park and parts of Windsor Forest. Edward the Confessor had his palace here before the new Windsor of today existed, and William the Conqueror held a Great Council (Witan) here in 1070 – just 4 years after the Norman invasion of Britain.

Keep left in Old Windsor; to the left lies Windsor Great Park. Later enter a roundabout and leave by the 3rd exit, into King's Road, to enter Windsor.

WINDSOR, Berks SU97
Windsor is a largely Georgian and Victorian town that owes its existence to its magnificent castle. William the Conqueror first appreciated the site's strategic importance over Old Windsor and built a palisaded fort within a moat. Practically every English monarch who has taken the throne in the 900 years since then has contributed to its development, and today it is the largest inhabited castle in the world.

Leave the town with SP 'Bagshot A332', to return along King's Road. In ¾ mile enter a roundabout and leave by the 2nd exit to enter Windsor Great Park.

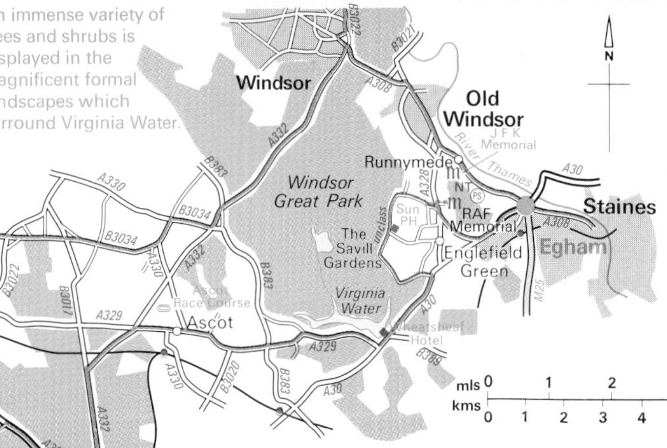

An immense variety of trees and shrubs is displayed in the magnificent formal landscapes which surround Virginia Water.

Windsor
Old Windsor
Runnymede
Windsor Great Park
The Savill Gardens
RAF Memorial
Englefield Green
Egham
Staines
Virginia Water
Ascot
Binfield
mls 0 1 2 3
kms 0 1 2 3 4

Sumptuously decorated rooms full of splendid furniture are features of the seat of the dukes of Wellington, at Stratfield Saye Park.

WINDSOR GREAT PARK, Berks SU97
Within the boundaries formed by Home Park and the castle to the north, and by all that remains of Windsor Forest's royal chase to the south and west, Windsor Great Park encompasses an area of almost 5,000 acres. Ancient King's Oak, near Forest Gate, is claimed to be the largest in the park. Legend has it that antlered Herne the Hunter meets here with his ghastly pack before chasing across the night skies. Most of the park is accessible by well-kept footpaths.

Continue for 4 miles before bearing right, then turn left SP 'Ascot'. After another ¼ mile meet crossroads and turn right on to the B3034 SP 'Winkfield'. After ¾ mile turn left on to the A330 SP 'Ascot'. After ½ mile turn right on to the B3034, then go forward over all crossroads to join the A3095. Continue for ¼ mile then turn left to rejoin the B3034 and continue for 1 mile. Cross a humpback bridge, keep left, and enter Binfield.

BINFIELD, Berks SU87
Alexander Pope sang in the choir of the local church as a boy. Among the church's treasures is a fine old hour glass.

Approach crossroads and turn left on to an unclassified road. After ½ mile bear right. Continue to the main road and turn right on to the A329 for the return to Wokingham.

TOUR 26 71 MILES

THE EDGE OF THE NORTH DOWNS

Much of this is National Trust country, protected for its outstanding beauty. Valley woodlands and high, empty commons in Surrey rise to soaring outliers of the West Sussex downs, which roll summit after windy summit into the chalklands of south Kent.

EPSOM, Surrey TQ26
In the 18th century this pleasant market town was famous for the medicinal springs that gave their name to Epsom Salts; even before that it was known for horse racing. The popularity of the spa has waned, but that of the turf is still in good heart. Among the town's more notable buildings are 19th-century Durdans and 17th-century Waterloo House.

Leave Epsom from the southern end of the High Street, enter a roundabout, and take the 2nd exit to join the B280. Cross Epsom Common, with a picnic site to the right, and after $1\frac{1}{2}$ miles approach traffic lights. A detour from the main tour route can be made by turning right at these lights for Chessington Zoo.

CHESSINGTON ZOO, Gt London TQ16
In 1931 Reginald Stuart Goddard founded this famous zoo in the grounds of Burnt Stub Manor, the successor to a house burned by Cromwellian troops. The existing house contains the zoo's administrative offices and restaurant.

On the main route, continue forward from the traffic lights for 2 miles and turn left on to the A244 for Oxshott. Turn right on to an unclassified road for Stoke D'Abernon.

STOKE D'ABERNON, Surrey TQ15
Preserved in the local church is Sir John d'Abernon's brass of 1277, thought to be the earliest memorial of its kind in the country. The old manor house is Tudor at heart, but received a brick face-lift sometime during the 18th century.

Turn right on to the A245 for Cobham.

Charles II's affection for Nell Gwynne is immortalized by this pub sign at Ockley.

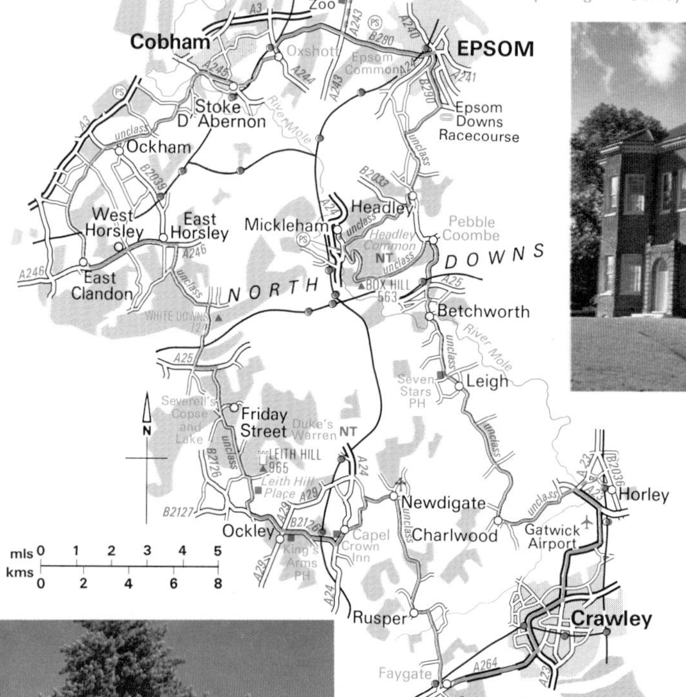

Left: Leith Hill Forest is a delightful mixture of woodland and heath. Below: 18th century Leith Hill Tower.

COBHAM, Surrey TQ16
An inscription on the bridge here tells of an earlier structure raised by Queen Matilda, wife of Henry I, because one of her ladies drowned while crossing the pool.

At Cobham, turn left on to an unclassified road SP 'Downside and Ockham'. Cross the river bridge, then turn right and follow SP 'Ockham'.

OCKHAM, Surrey TQ05
Hidden among the trees of Ockham Park, close to the great house, is the village church. This is well known for its lovely 13th-century east window of 7 lancets, sometimes known as the Seven Sisters.

Drive to the war memorial and turn right on to the B2039. Take the next turning left on to an unclassified road. Meet crossroads and go forward for 3 miles to East Clandon.

Robert Adam was responsible for m of the fine rooms in Georg Hatchlands, near East Clan

EAST CLANDON, Surrey TQ05
Timber cottages and large old barn give this place an enviable air of timelessness and peace, but the mainly 13th-century church has been poorly restored. Admiral Boscawen built 18th-century Hatchlands (NT) for his retirement, but died before he could enjoy it.

Turn left to join the A246 and continue to West Horsley.

WEST HORSLEY, Surrey TQ05
A church stood at West Horsley before the Normans came, but the massive tower dates from the 12th century. The body of the building shows traces of almost every subsequent century, including ver good 15th-century screens. Sir Walter Raleigh's remains are said lie under the south chapel.

Continue to East Horsley.

EAST HORSLEY, Surrey TQ05
The curious 19th-century mansion known as East Horsley Towers houses offices of the Electricity Board. Much older is the local par church, which was altered considerably in the 13th century restored almost out of recognitior the 19th. Beautiful recumbent figu of Thomas and Catherine Cornwa and several interesting old brasse can be seen inside.

Continue for $\frac{1}{2}$ mile, turn right on to an unclassified road SP 'Shere', and after another $\frac{1}{2}$ mile bear left with SP 'Dorking'. Ascend through woodland 'o the summit of the North Downs, and after $1\frac{1}{2}$ miles meet crossroads and turn right SP 'Abinger'. Descend '1 in 6) White Downs Hill and :ontinue for 1 mile, then turn left on o the A25. After $\frac{1}{2}$ mile turn right on o an unclassified road and ascend for $1\frac{1}{4}$ miles. A short detour can be made 'om the main tour route by turning harp left to Friday Street.

IORTH DOWNS
his range of chalk hills starts near arnham in Surrey and extends across Kent to the white cliffs of)over, culminating in a 900ft summit ear Woldingham.

RIDAY STREET, Surrey TQ14
)ld cottages and a single street ading to a lake fringed with pine nd oak are the main features of this llage. The Stephen Langton Inn ecalls a prelate of that name who layed a leading role in the signing of lagna Carta. Severell's Copse (NT) omprises 59 acres of woodland retching from the lake to Leith Hill.

eturn to the T-junction on the main oute, turn left, then keep forward SP eith Hill'. After $1\frac{1}{2}$ miles pass a otpath leading left to Leith Hill.

ITH HILL, Surrey TQ14
uch of the wooded countryside uth of Friday Street is protected by e National Trust, including Leith ll, Duke's Warren, and the estate Leith Hill Place. The hill itself carries picturesque tower whose top is)29ft above sea level – the highest int in Surrey.

ntinue for $2\frac{1}{2}$ miles to join the 126, then keep left for Ockley.

CKLEY, Surrey TQ13
e local village green is sited on the urse of the great Roman Stane reet. The local church enjoys a lightful setting, and the King's ms Inn has an unusual sign owing Nell Gwynne in the brace of King Charles II.

n left on to the A29. After the gs Arms (PH) turn right on to the 126. Continue for $1\frac{1}{2}$ miles, then n left on to the A24 to enter Capel. proach the Crown Inn and turn it on to an unclassified road SP wdigate'.

WDIGATE, Surrey TQ24
ical of Wealden villages in eral, Newdigate stands in an area was once covered by dense st. The forest has all but ppeared, but some of the great s that grew hereabouts can be ed to the massive pillars and es of the local church tower.

r Newdigate and drive to Rusper.

PER, W Sussex TQ23
eral half-timbered and tile-hung ages survive in this pretty village, St Mary Magdalene's Church sts a sturdy 16th-century tower.

Bear left SP 'Crawley', continue for $\frac{1}{2}$ mile, then turn right for Faygate. At Faygate turn left SP 'Crawley'. Meet a main road and turn left on to the A264. To the right is St Leonard's Forest.

ST LEONARD'S FOREST, W Sussex TQ23
The forests of St Leonard's and Worth, along with various scattered woodlands, are among the only sizeable remnants left of the vast prehistoric Forest of Anderida.

After $2\frac{3}{4}$ miles turn left on to the A23 Crawley bypass. Follow SP 'London' through Crawley suburbs.

CRAWLEY, W Sussex TQ23
The planning of this new town is not without merit. Its industrial estates are well separated from the residential areas, and some of the worst effects of high-density building have been avoided by the imaginative use of open spaces with green lawns.

Continue with SP 'London' to pass Gatwick Airport.

GATWICK AIRPORT, W Sussex TQ24
Access to Gatwick, London's second airport after Heathrow, is via the A23 London-to-Brighton road, or the adjoining main-line railway station. The spectators' enclosure includes parking facilities.

Continue for 1 mile, enter a roundabout, and leave by the 1st exit on to an unclassified road leading to Charlwood and Leigh. A detour can be made from the main tour route by taking the 3rd exit from this roundabout into Horley.

HORLEY, Surrey TQ24
A knight's effigy of c1315 and a 15th-century brass can be seen in the local church, and the half-timbered Six Bells Inn is very old. Some 3 miles south of Horley is Tinsley Green, the venue for an international marbles championship which began as a competition between two local men for the hand of a girl in marriage.

On the main tour, continue to Charlwood.

CHARLWOOD, Surrey TQ24
The 11th- to 15-century church in Charlwood is noted for its screen work and wall paintings.

Continue to Leigh.

LEIGH, Surrey TQ24
Charming old houses in this village are complemented by a green and a 15th-century church famous for its memorial brasses. Particularly good examples of the latter are those to the Ardernes, who lived in the area during the 15th century.

Pass through Leigh and after $\frac{1}{4}$ mile turn right at the Seven Stars (PH) for Betchworth, crossing the River Mole.

The lake at Friday Street is part of the National Trust property of Leith Hill.

BETCHWORTH, Surrey TQ24
High trees border the River Mole here, and the church preserves a great Norman chest of solid oak beneath its tower.

Meet a T-junction and turn left then right SP 'Walton-on-the-Hill'. Continue to a roundabout and take the 2nd exit on to the B2032. Climb (1 in 6) Pebble Hill to the downs. At the summit turn left on to the B2033 SP 'Box Hill'. Bear left on to an unclassified road for Box Hill and picnic site.

BOX HILL, Surrey TQ15
Named after the box trees that grow on its flanks, 563ft Box Hill (NT) is a noted viewpoint and designated area of outstanding natural beauty, including both wood and downland scenery.

Descend to the bottom of the hill. Approach a T-junction and turn right SP 'Mickleham'. Within $\frac{1}{4}$ mile turn right again on to an unclassified road SP 'Headley'. A detour can be made from the main tour by driving ahead for Mickleham.

MICKLEHAM, Surrey TQ15
Playwright George Meredith was born here in 1864. Yews from a Druid's Grove folly stand in the grounds of 18th-century Norbury Park.

Meet a T-junction and turn right on to the B2033. Headley Heath (NT) lies away to the right. Ascend and turn left on to an unclassified road for Headley SP 'Epsom'.

HEADLEY, Surrey TQ25
Yews mark the spot where Headley's 14th-century church was pulled down in the last century, and the spire of its 19th-century successor serves as a Surrey landmark. The church bell is a good 500 years old.

After $1\frac{3}{4}$ miles meet crossroads and turn right. Pass Epsom Downs racecourse.

EPSOM DOWNS RACECOURSE, Surrey TQ26
The course here has been the home of good racing since the reign of James I, and has been the venue for the Derby, perhaps Britain's most famous race, since 1780.

Turn left on to the B290 and return to Epsom.

Derby Day at Epsom racecourse attracts racing enthusiasts from all walks of life.

TOUR 27 53 MILES

RESORTS AND DOWNLAND VILLAGES

High above the bright, mercurial resorts of the Sussex coast are the tranquil hamlets of the South Downs. Here change is gradual, a process to be approached with the caution born from centuries of experience.

WORTHING, W Sussex TQ10
Until the 1760s Worthing was little more than a fishing hamlet, but by the end of that century the patronage of George III's family had encouraged the smart set and the inevitable speculators to take an interest in the new town. Sadly there were no lasting major developments of any great merit, although the usual 18th-century terraces preserve something of the old gentility. Today Worthing is a popular seaside resort with a pier and an extensive pebble beach.

Leave Worthing by the A259 'Brighton' road, with occasional views of the sea to the right. Pass through South Lancing and by Shoreham Airport. Cross the River Adur and enter Shoreham-by-Sea.

Brighton's elegant pier dates from the 19th century.

SHOREHAM-BY-SEA W Sussex TQ20
Sand at low tide, good fishing in the River Adur, and a busy harbour are features of this popular seaside town. Saxon workmanship can be seen in the mainly Norman structure of St Nicholas' Church. An old chequered-flint house in the town contains the Marlipins Museum of local relics.

Continue on the A259 to Southwick.

SOUTHWICK, W Sussex TQ20
Situated on the eastern part of Shoreham Harbour, with the South Downs to the north, Southwick forms part of the Shoreham conurbation and has all but lost its own identity. Roman remains excavated from a villa $\frac{1}{4}$ mile north of the station can be seen in the museum at Hove.

Continue along the A259 to Portslade-by-Sea.

PORTSLADE-BY-SEA, E Sussex TQ20
The 'by Sea' part of Portslade is a fairly recent seaside development of the original village, which lies 1 mile inland and has a church with Norman origins. North of the churchyard are remains of a 12th-century flint-built manor house.

Continue along the A259 to Hove.

HOVE, E Sussex TQ20
Elegant Hove is so much a part of Brighton these days that it scarcely bothers to lay claim to an identity of its own. It has a good beach, several excellent Regency terraces, a superb modern church, and a museum.

Continue into Brighton.

BRIGHTON, E Sussex TQ30
This famous resort developed as a result of the 18th-century health fad for sea bathing. Its success was assured by the patronage of George IV in 1784, and the many superb terraces preserved there today prove its continued prosperity. As with all playgrounds of the wealthy the town has a number of eccentricities. The most impressive of these is the Royal Pavilion, a magnificent Oriental-style palace built for the Prince Regent by Henry Holland in 1787. Various museums, galleries, and theatres exist in the town, and visitors are offered all the usual distractions of the British seaside holiday. An excellent aquarium can be visited near Palace Pier, and the Volk's Electric Railway – the first of its kind in the world – runs from here to the Black Rock area. Old Brighton is preserved in the winding streets of The Lanes, which contrast with the new conference centre and up-to-the-minute marina (under construction at time of printing).

Return along the seafront towards Hove, passing the King Alfred Sports Centre, and meet traffic lights. Turn right here into Hove Street and follow SP 'London'. After $1\frac{3}{4}$ miles turn right on to the A2038 and enter West Blatchington.

WEST BLATCHINGTON, E Sussex TQ20
An early 18th-century windmill and 19th-century St Peter's Church are all that remain of the village that originally stood in this highly-developed area.

Warehouses and sea-going vessels of all descriptions are an integral part of Portslade-by-Sea's character.

Brighton Pavilion has been remodel several times since it was first bu Architect John Nash was larg responsible for its final appearan

Continue to ascend the A2038. Meet crossroads and turn left on to an unclassified road SP 'Devil's Dyke'. After ½ mile keep left and ascend through open downland to Devil's Dyke.

DEVIL'S DYKE, W Sussex TQ21
Devil's Dyke is a cleft in the 711ft crest of the South Downs (see below). According to local legend the devil tried to carve a large nick to let the sea in, but failed. The spot has become popular with hang-glider enthusiasts.

THE SOUTH DOWNS
Stretching west from Beachy Head into Hampshire, the South Downs range is all that remains of a huge chalk backbone that connected England with the Continent. Some 7,000 years ago the Atlantic forced its way through to join up with the North Sea. Access for rambling and riding is available via numerous footpaths and bridleways.

Return, and after ½ mile turn left SP 'Poynings' to pass the Dyke Golf Club. After ¾ mile turn left, with views of 664ft Newtimber Hill on the right. After a further ½ mile turn sharp left and descend into Poynings.

osiac pavements are a feature of the oman remains at Bignor.

OYNINGS, W Sussex TQ21
oynings is a charming downland lage with an old church that was dowed by Michael de Poynings, no died in 1369. The Rectory is of rly 19th-century date.

rn left and follow the foot of the uth Downs to Fulking.

LKING, W Sussex TQ21
ocks of sheep graze the sides of the wnland fold in which this ancient mlet stands, and slake their rsts at a chalk spring. A like service offered to humankind by the asant Shepherd and Dog Inn.

ntinue to Edburton.

BURTON, W Sussex TQ21
pectacularly sheer downland arpment towers above this tiny ce, making it seem even smaller n it is. The village boasts a ately-owned craft pottery and a non-smoking concern. Prehistoric tle Rings stands on Edburton Hill.

ve Edburton with 708ft Truleigh to the left and continue to the 37. Turn left on to the A2037 for per Beeding.

UPPER BEEDING, W Sussex TQ11
Upper Beeding lies at the north end of a gap in the downs made by the River Adur. It has a narrow main street lined with old cottages.

Leaving Upper Beeding, turn right on to the A283 SP 'Steyning', and cross the River Adur into Bramber.

BRAMBER, W Sussex TQ11
Before the River Adur silted up this place was a large port. Its massive Norman castle was dismantled after the Civil War, leaving only a gateway and easily-traceable sections of wall (NT). An unusual museum is the House of Pipes, which features some 25,000 tobacco pipes from all over the world.

Continue along the A283 to Steyning.

STEYNING, W Sussex TQ11
Steyning enjoys a magnificent position at the foot of the South Downs and has a late-Norman church. In Mouse Lane is a 15th-century poorhouse, and an old market house stands in the High Street. The Grammar School of 1614 can be seen in Church Street.

Leave Steyning on the A283. On the left is Steyning Round Hill, which gives views over the Adur Valley. Continue, skirting Wiston Park and Wiston.

WISTON, W Sussex TQ11
It is well worth stopping in this lovely village at the foot of downland near Chanctonbury. Unfortunately its 14th-century church and Elizabethan manor house were badly treated by 19th-century restorers, but the overall atmosphere is of peaceful antiquity.

Continue on the A283. In 1 mile pass an unclassified left turn leading along a wooded glade to the footpath for Chanctonbury Ring.

CHANCTONBURY RING, W Sussex TQ11
The extensive prehistoric earthworks of Chanctonbury Ring occupy a 783ft downland summit which affords views over some 30 miles of countryside. Near by is a 19th-century dewpond.

Continue along the A283 to the edge of Washington, enter a roundabout, and leave by the 2nd exit for Storrington. Left of the road are 626ft Chantry Hill and 549ft Harrow Hill.

STORRINGTON, W Sussex TQ01
Kithurst Hill rises to 697ft above this straggling village and forms an excellent viewpoint. Celtic field patterns are preserved on its slopes, and close by is 28-acre Sullington Warren nature reserve (NT). A large tithe barn of 1685 stands at Manor Farm.

In 1 mile pass an unclassified left turn leading to Parham House.

The nave of Steyning's parish church is a superb example of Norman architecture.

PARHAM HOUSE, W Sussex TQ01
This delightfully unpretentious Elizabethan house has a 158ft long gallery and contains fine furnishings and pictures (open).

Continue on the A283 for 1 mile farther then turn left on to an unclassified road SP 'Greatham'. In 2¼ miles cross the River Arun to Coldwaltham. Turn left on to the A29 into Watersfield, then in ½ mile turn right on to the B2138 'Petworth' road. Take the next turning left on to an unclassified road for West Burton.

WEST BURTON, W Sussex SU91
Fine views of the South Downs escarpment can be enjoyed from here. Coke's House dates from the 16th century.

An unclassified road on the right leads to Bignor.

BIGNOR, W Sussex SU91
Several notable old houses here include the famous Old Shop, an unusual yeoman's house of the 15th century. The Roman villa sites here are the largest and best known in the country.

On the main tour, turn left SP 'Bury' and in 1 mile turn right on to the A29 SP 'Bognor'. Ascend Bury Hill, meet a roundabout, and take the 2nd exit on to the A284 SP 'Littlehampton'. Skirt the grounds of Arundel Park and in 2¼ miles turn left on to an unclassified road to enter Arundel.

ARUNDEL, W Sussex TQ00
Looming large over Arundel to guard a gap made in the downs by the River Arun valley is ancient and much-restored Arundel Castle, seat of the Duke of Norfolk. Behind its heavy grey walls are rooms rich in furnishings and art treasures, many of which are open to the public. A prominent town existed here before the Norman conquest, but comparatively few ancient houses remain. The only real rivals to the castle are the 14th-century Church of St Nicholas and the superb Church of Our Lady and St Philip Neri.

Continue on the A27 'Worthing' road, and in 5 miles pass an unclassified right turn to Highdown Hill.

HIGHDOWN HILL, W Sussex TQ00
Between the South Downs and the sea, about 1 mile south of the A27, is 266ft Highdown Hill (NT). This 50-acre site is of great archaeological importance for its late bronze-age, early iron-age and Saxon cemeterys which have yielded many finds.

Continue on the A27 towards Worthing. Meet a roundabout and take the 2nd exit. After ¾ mile meet another roundabout and take the 3rd exit for the return to Worthing.

Arundel Castle, one of the most impressive Norman and medieval strongholds in the south of England, is the home of the dukes of Norfolk, hereditary Earls Marshal of England.

TOUR 28 80 MILES

THE SUSSEX WEALD

Suspended between the North and South Downs is the high, broken patchwork of the Sussex Weald, a place of charming towns and villages on hillsides once cloaked by the vast, prehistoric Forest of Anderida.

EASTBOURNE, E Sussex TV69
Consistently top of the seaside sunshine league tables, the thriving resort of Eastbourne has been popular since the beginning of the 19th century.

Leave Eastbourne seafront along the B2103 'Beachy Head' road, with fine views towards the cliffs of Beachy Head. Ascend, and turn left on to an unclassified road to reach the summit of this cliff range.

BEACHY HEAD, E Sussex TV59
Beachy Head, the vast chalk promontory that marks where the South Downs are halted by the sea, is the starting point of the South Downs Way. This path runs west to beyond South Harting on the Hampshire border.

Continue past the Belle Tout lighthouse to Birling Gap.

BIRLING GAP, E Sussex TV59
For centuries Birling Gap was a landing place favoured by smugglers but today the rocky shingle and sand beach is more popular with bathers. Between Birling Gap and Seaford are the great chalk cliffs known as the Seven Sisters.

Follow the tour inland to Eastdean.

EASTDEAN, E Sussex TV59
Cottages and a small shop overlook Eastdean's sloping triangular green, and the local church houses a curious copy of a Norman font.

Turn left on to the A259 'Seaford' road, ascend steeply, then at the summit turn right on to the B2105 'Jevington' road for Friston.

FRISTON, E Sussex TV59
This downland village lies in a hilly area now popular with glider pilots. At one time its small Church of St Mary served as a landmark for mariners and smugglers alike.

Continue, with downland to the right and Friston Forest to the left. Also to the right is 659ft Willingdon Hill. Reach Jevington.

JEVINGTON, E Sussex TQ50
A sturdy Anglo-Saxon tower is carried by Jevington's flint-built church, and in the churchyard is the copper model of a square-rigged schooner once sailed by a Chinaman buried here.

Beyond Jevington descend through Wannock, with 702ft Windover Hill to the left.

WINDOVER HILL, E Sussex TQ50
A gentle climb to the summit of this hill is rewarded by excellent views, not the least of which takes in the prehistoric Long Man of Wilmington. Nobody knows who or what this giant turf-cut figure represents.

Continue to Polegate.

POLEGATE, E Sussex TQ50
Victorian St John's Church, like much of the rest of Polegate's architecture, is unremarkable but homely. The most notable building here is an early 19th-century windmill with all its sails intact.

At Polegate turn left on to the A22, SP 'London'. Pass through the flat countryside of Wilmington Wood. In 2½ miles a detour from the main route is possible by turning right on to the A295 and driving to Hailsham.

HAILSHAM, E Sussex TQ50
The market at Hailsham is one of the largest in Sussex and continues a tradition that reaches back to Norman times.

In ¼ mile (beyond the Hailsham turning) turn left on to an unclassified road to Michelham Priory. Cross the River Cuckmere before reaching the priory.

MICHELHAM PRIORY, E Sussex TQ50
Remains of this small Augustinian priory (open), founded in 1229 for 12 canons and a prior, include a Tudor mansion, a 14th-century gatehouse, and an attractive bridge over the moat.

Continue to the B2108, turn right, and then turn immediately left, SP 'London'. Turn left on to the A22, then right on to the unclassified 'Horam' road. Join the A267 and enter Horam. Continue on the 'Tunbridge Wells' road and pass through woodland scenery before reaching Cross-in-Hand, on The Weald.

Towering chalk cliffs dwarf the lighthouse at Beachy Head.

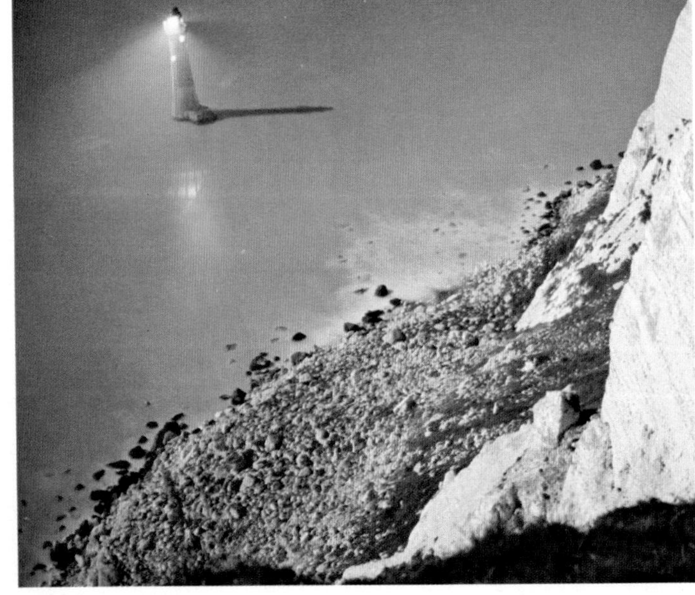

THE WEALD
The Weald is a high area of broken country suspended between the hills of the North and South Downs. Its towns and villages are rightly famous for their great character and beauty, and several wooded areas exist as reminders of the great Forest of Anderida that once cloaked these long, grassy slopes.

CROSS-IN-HAND, E Sussex TQ52
A working windmill stands in this charming village, which is sited at over 500ft on the Sussex Weald. Holy Cross Priory is partly in use as an old people's home, but the house and grounds may still be visited.

Cross high wooded country to Five Ashes. After ½ mile (beyond Five Ashes), turn left on to an unclassified road. Later join the B2101 and enter Rotherfield, at the edge of Ashdown Forest.

ROTHERFIELD, E Sussex TQ52
Situated at the edge of Ashdown Forest, this village stands at 500ft near the source of the River Rother.

Keep forward, then branch right on to an unclassified road to leave by North Street. Drive to the A26. Turn right SP 'Tunbridge Wells', and pass through Eridge Green.

ERIDGE GREEN, E Sussex TQ53
Pretty estate cottages stand behind the local Victorian church, and near by is the sandstone outcrop of Bowles Rocks where trainee mountaineers practise.

Continue for 1 mile through Broadwater Forest, then turn left on to an unclassified road SP 'Groombridge'. After ½ mile turn right SP 'High Rocks', then in a further ½ mile bear right and pass High Rocks on the right.

HIGH ROCKS, E Sussex TQ53
Perhaps the largest sandstone outcrop in the area is High Rocks, which is used extensively by climbers.

Continue for 1½ miles. Meet crossroads and turn right on to Major York's road. On the far side of Tunbridge Wells Common turn left on to the A26 and enter Royal Tunbridge Wells.

ROYAL TUNBRIDGE WELLS, Kent TQ53
In 1606 Lord North discovered chalybeate springs in the forest that stood here. Subsequently the town of Tunbridge Wells was founded, though building did not begin in earnest until the 1630s. By the end of that century it was a flourishing spa, and has remained so to the present day. Visitors to the picturesque raised parade known as the Pantiles may still 'take the waters'. See also tour 29.

From the town follow SP 'Eastbourne A267' and re-enter E Sussex for Frant.

FRANT, E Sussex TQ53
Houses cluster round a large green here, and the 19th-century church contains fine stained glass of earlier date.

Turn left on to an unclassified road SP 'Bells Yew Green' and at the latter tur right on to the B2169 'Lamberhurst' road. Return to Kent, drive through woodland, then pass a left turn leading to the ruins of Bayham Abbe

BAYHAM ABBEY, E Sussex TQ63
Claimed to be the most impressive group of monastic remains in Susse this picturesque ruin (NT) dates fron the 13th century and comprises a church, monastery buildings, and tl former gatehouse – all easily identifiable (open).

After a further ½ mile pass a left turn leading to The Owl House.

THE OWL HOUSE, Kent TQ63
Once the haunt of wool smugglers, this small half-timbered building (open) dates from the 16th century and stands in beautiful grounds. Features of the latter include woodland lakes and splendid collections of flowering shrubs.

In 1¼ miles turn left on to the B2100 and enter Lamberhurst.

LAMBERHURST, Kent TQ63
Although strung out along the bus Tunbridge Wells to Hastings road, this old village has managed to ret its own identity and features a fine 14th-century church.

About 1 mile south, off the A21, is Scotney Old Castle.

he weathered and fissured surfaces of
ıch sandstone outcrops as Bowles
ocks, near Eridge Green, make ideal
ursery faces for trainee mountaineers.
l round the rocks are expanses of sand
at have been worn from their surfaces.

COTNEY CASTLE, Kent TQ63
uins of this 14th-century tower and
ı attached 17th-century house (NT)
and in a landscaped and moated
arden planted with trees and
owering shrubs (open). Apart from
e interest of the buildings
emselves, the gardens are
nong the finest in the country.

*om Lamberhurst return along the
100 'Wadhurst' road and re-enter
ussex. In 3 miles turn left on to the
099 to visit Wadhurst.*

ADHURST, E Sussex TQ63
e churchyard of SS Peter and Paul
tures 30 iron grave slabs, a
werful indication of Wadhurst's
e-time importance as an iron-
elting centre.

*$\frac{1}{4}$ miles turn right on to the B2181
'Burwash Common'. Pass through
odland to Stonegate.*

ONEGATE, E Sussex TQ62
s small village has a modern
ırch and is attractively grouped
nd a junction of minor roads and
es.

*tonegate turn left on to the
lassified 'Burwash' road and after
ther $\frac{3}{4}$ mile turn right. Drive over a
l crossing and cross the River
ıer to enter Burwash.*

WASH, E Sussex TQ62
ırwash churchyard is a cast-iron
e slab that is claimed to be the
st in the country. Pleasant old
dings in the High Street include
ber-framed cottages.

*t a junction with the A265 and
right. Reach the war memorial
turn left on to an unclassified road
Voods Corner'. In $\frac{1}{2}$ mile pass a
turn leading to Bateman's.*

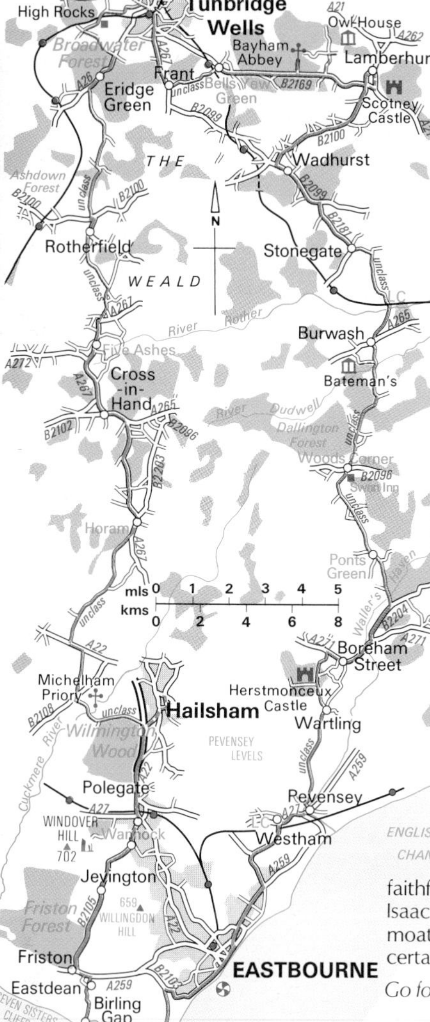

BATEMAN'S, E Sussex TQ62
Built in 1634 for a local ironmaster, this lovely house (NT) is best known as the one-time home of writer Rudyard Kipling. Much of the neighbourhood is featured in his *Puck of Pook's Hill.*

Climb to 646ft, cross the River Dudwell, and drive through Dallington Forest. Reach Woods Corner, and at the Swan Inn turn right then left on to the 'Pont's Green' road. Later follow SP 'Ninfield' and descend. Meet the B2204 and turn right SP 'Hailsham'. Later turn right on to the A271 for Boreham Street.

BOREHAM STREET, E Sussex TQ61
This village has an appealing character enhanced by attractive houses and the White Friars Hotel. Inside the latter is a 16th-century chimney breast.

Continue through Boreham Street and in $\frac{1}{2}$ mile turn left on to an unclassified road passing Herstmonceux Castle.

HERSTMONCEUX CASTLE, E Sussex TQ61
Home of the Royal Greenwich Observatory since 1948, this fortified 15th-century manor house was dismantled in the 18th century but faithfully restored in the 1930s. The Isaac Newton Telescope Building and moated grounds can be visited at certain times.

Go forward to Wartling.

WARTLING, E Sussex TQ60
Wartling boasts a church with box pews, an 18th-century pulpit, and a wealth of fascinating Georgian monuments. The neighbouring countryside is dominated by intrusive radar installations.

At Wartling bear right on to the 'Pevensey' road and cross the flat Pevensey Levels. Meet the A27 and turn right into Pevensey.

PEVENSEY, E Sussex TQ60
William the Conqueror disembarked here in 1066, and later built a stout castle within ancient Roman walls that had once been shaded by the vast Forest of Anderida. The village itself preserves Tudor shops and houses.

Continue along the A27 to Westham.

WESTHAM, E Sussex TQ60
It is probable that the local church was once part of the ancient Hospital of St Cross, most of which stood outside the west gate of Pevensey Castle. Close by is a pair of 15th-century houses.

Turn left on to the B2191 SP 'Eastbourne'. Drive over a level crossing and later join the A259 to return to Eastbourne.

Rudyard Kipling lived at Bateman's from 1902 until his death in 1936. The interior of the house is preserved much as he left it.

High Rocks is one of many sandstone outcrops situated near Tunbridge Wells.

Herstmonceux Castle was built when brick was newly fashionable in England.

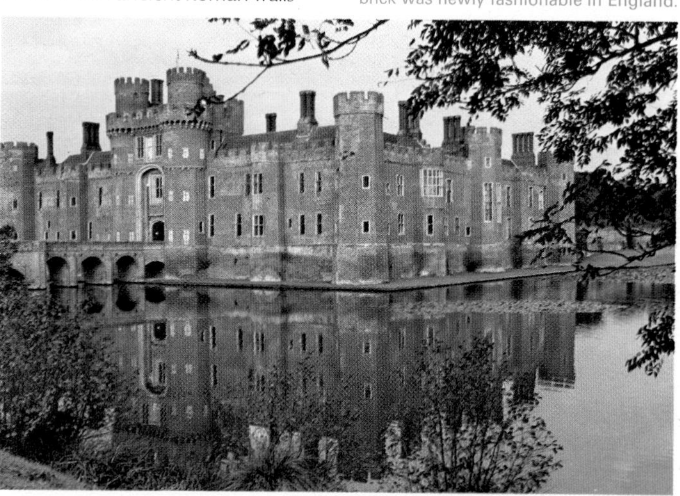

TOUR 29 51 MILES

THE WEALD OF WEST KENT

Since medieval times the wealthy have come to West Kent to build their great houses amongst the woods and weathered rocks of the High Weald. Below is a different world of rich valleys full of twisty lanes, fruit orchards, and the smell of growing hops.

SEVENOAKS, Kent TQ55
Tradition has it that this town was named from a clump of 7 oaks that once grew here. The original trees have long gone, but in 1955 new ones were taken from Knole Park and planted on the common. It was Knole Park that brought prosperity to Sevenoaks in the 15th century when Archbishop Bourchier acquired it and rebuilt the manor house as a palace for archbishops of Canterbury. Nowadays the town is largely residential, with an air of confident ease typical of long-established communities. Cricket has been played on The Vyne wicket since 1734.

Leave Sevenoaks with SP 'Bromley A21'. After 1 mile turn left on to the A25 SP 'Westerham and Redhill', with fine views towards the steep wooded escarpment of the North Downs to the right. Continue into the village of Sundridge.

SUNDRIDGE, Kent TQ45
Sundridge's pride is the 15th-century timbered hall-house in its main street. The great hall is several storeys high, and its original stone hearth is still to be seen. The house was restored in 1923. Nearby Ovenden House dates from 1745, and 13th-century Sundridge Church contains a number of good brasses.

Keep forward and enter Brasted.

BRASTED, Kent TQ45
In spite of modern traffic the main village street still retains much of its character. At one point it opens on to a small green fringed by half-timbered houses. Brasted Place, in a fine park adjoining the village, was built by Robert Adam in 1784 and subsequently became the home of Napoleon III. About $1\frac{1}{2}$ miles south of the village is 600-acre Brasted Chart (NT), which offers pleasant walks and drives.

Continue along the A25 to Westerham, passing Quebec House on entering the village.

QUEBEC HOUSE, Kent TQ45
On the eastern outskirts of Westerham village is early 17th-century Quebec House (NT), famous as the boyhood home of General Wolfe. Relics of this hero of the Battle of Quebec, who died winning the victory that made Canada British, are preserved inside the house. His statue stands in Westerham High Street.

Continue into Westerham village.

WESTERHAM, Kent TQ45
General Wolfe was born in the vicarage here in 1727. He stayed at the George and Dragon in 1758, during what was to prove his last visit to the town. Another famous person with Westerham connexions was Sir Winston Churchill, whose statue stands on the tiny green. Westerham Hill is an 800ft- high viewpoint crossed by the Pilgrims' Way.

Continue on the 'Redhill' road. At the end of the village turn left on to the unclassified road for Squerryes Court.

SQUERRYES COURT, Kent TQ45
The Warde family have lived in this 17th-century mansion from the time of General Wolfe to the present day, and it was here in 1741 that Wolfe received his commission. A room is set aside for Wolfe mementos, and other parts of the house feature fine paintings and tapestries.

This statue of General Wolf
stands on the green i
Westerham

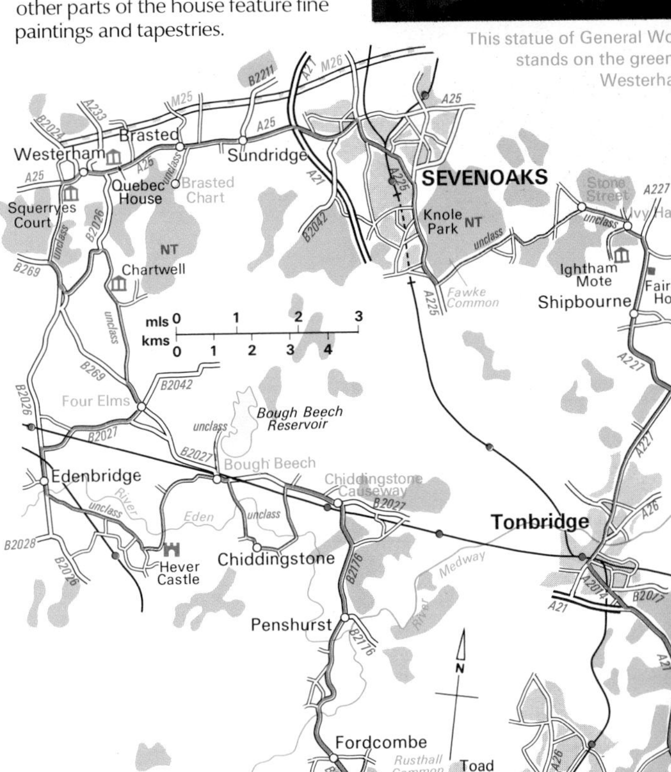

Left: care was taken to preserve the appearance of Hever Castle during restoration. Below: beautiful Italian statuary is a feature of the grounds at Hever Castle.

Ascend through thickly-wooded country and turn left on to the B26 'Edenbridge' road, with fine views across the Weald. In $\frac{3}{4}$ mile turn le on to the B2026 'Westerham' road Climb on to wooded Crockhamhi Common. After the common turn right on to an unclassified road to Chartwell.

CHARTWELL, Kent TQ45
Chartwell will always be associate with Winston Churchill. It was his country home from 1922 until his death, and part of it now houses Churchill museum. Other rooms arranged much as they must hav been in his lifetime. The Churchilliana on display include photographs illustrating every st of his life, gifts given to him by ot world leaders, and his Nobel Priz good many of his paintings are t seen in the house, and in his stud at the end of the garden.

3eyond Chartwell descend to the Eden Valley and turn left on to the 3269 'Tonbridge' road. At Four Elms urn right on to the B2042 SP Edenbridge', and shortly join the 32027. After $1\frac{1}{2}$ miles turn left on to he B2026 into Edenbridge, and drive along the main street.

DENBRIDGE, Kent TQ44
everal old buildings survive in denbridge main street, particularly etween the 16th-century Crown nn and the bridge over the River den. The mainly 13th-century hurch carries a massive tower rowned by a spire of later date.

ross the River Eden, take the first urning on the left, and proceed along n unclassified road to Hever Castle.

IEVER CASTLE, Kent TQ44
Tudor times 13th-century Hever astle was the home of the Boleyns, hose daughter Anne married enry VIII and bore him the future Queen Elizabeth I. The building egan life as a fortified farmhouse, ut was made into a crenellated ansion at the beginning of the 15th entury. The fortunes of the house aned with the fall of the Boleyns, nd by the beginning of this century had once more reverted to use as farmhouse. It took a wealthy merican, William Waldorf Astor, to store it to its present magnificence. e superb gardens feature Tudor-yle flower beds and a 35-acre lake. oth house and gardens are open to e public.

ave the castle and continue to ugh Beech. A detour can be made m here to Bough Beech Reservoir: n left on to the B2027, cross a lway bridge, then turn right on to unclassified road to the reservoir.

OUGH BEECH RESERVOIR, nt TQ44
is reservoir is the haunt of migrant aders, ducks, wintering divers, be and geese. Access is by written rmission only.

ve Bough Beech and join the 027 for 200 yards, then turn right to the unclassified 'Chiddingstone' d. Drive to crossroads and turn left Chiddingstone. Ahead, at the ssroads, is the entrance to ddingstone Castle.

IDDINGSTONE, Kent TQ54
iddingstone, a National Trust age, has a beautifully preserved eet lined with half-timbered 16th-l 17th-century houses that were bably built with iron-industry ney. At the top of the street is n-century Chiddingstone Castle. Chiding Stone, from which village takes its name, is a large dstone rock behind the street. gging wives were once brought to be chided by the assembled ge population.

r ½ mile (beyond the village) ch left. In $1\frac{3}{4}$ miles turn right on e B2027 for Chiddingstone seway. Pass the local church and right to follow the B2176. Enter hurst.

PENSHURST, Kent TQ54
At the centre of Penshurst, behind a screen of tall trees, is 14th-century Penshurst Place. The Sidney family and their descendants have lived here for more than 400 years, and Sir Philip Sidney – diplomat, courtier, and poet – was born here in 1554. The family became Earls of Leicester, and the village contains the original Leicester Square.

Leave Penshurst and follow the B2188 'Tunbridge Wells' road through the Medway Valley to Fordcombe.

FORDCOMBE, Kent TQ54
This 19th-century picture village of half-timbered and tile-hung cottages is grouped round a pleasant green. It was built at the instigation of Lord Hardinge, whose seat was near by at South Park.

Beyond Fordcombe turn left on to the A264. Cross Rusthall Common and note a left turn leading to Toad Rock.

TOAD ROCK, Kent TQ53
Amongst the many eroded sandstone outcrops in the Tunbridge Wells area is Toad Rock, on Rusthall Common, which has been weathered to look like a toad. Other unusual rock formations are to be found at nearby Happy Valley.

In ¼ mile reach the Spa Hotel and turn right on to Major York's road. Proceed to the far side of the common (carpark for the Pantiles) and turn left on to the A26 into Royal Tunbridge Wells.

ROYAL TUNBRIDGE WELLS, Kent TQ53
Extensive parks and gardens impart a quiet charm to this elegant Regency town. The 17th-century Church of St Charles the Martyr is the oldest here and Holy Trinity dates from the 19th century. The latter was built by Decimus Burton, who also laid out lovely Calverley Park. Medicinal waters discovered by Lord North in 1606 – the main reason for the foundation of the town – may still be drunk at the Pantiles, an 18th-century raised promenade fringed with lime trees. See also tour 28.

Leave the town with SP 'Hastings' to join the A264. Later turn left on to the A21 'Sevenoaks' road. Pass woodland and branch left on to the A2014. Later turn right and enter Tonbridge.

TONBRIDGE, Kent TQ54
A settlement has existed here at least since Anglo-Saxon times. The River Medway played an important part in the town's early prosperity, and the later introduction of the railway increased its importance as a centre of communication. Today Tonbridge is a mixture of market town and rail depot built round a ruined Norman to 14th-century castle on a mound.

Cross the River Medway and follow SP 'Gravesend, A227'. Ascend to Shipbourne.

The variety of architectural styles in the houses at Chiddingstone creates a beautiful village landscape.

SHIPBOURNE, Kent TQ55
Most of the Victorian village that makes up Shipbourne lies to the west of the green. St Giles' Church was reconstructed in the 1880s.

Beyond the village pass Fairlawne House.

FAIRLAWNE HOUSE, Kent TQ55
Situated just ¾ mile north of Shipbourne, this splendid house (unfortunately not open to the public) dates from the 18th century and features a Great Room designed by the architect Gibbs.

Pass Fairlawne House and ascend. At the top of the hill turn left on to an unclassified road SP 'Ivy Hatch'. Take the next turning left and descend a narrow lane to Ightham Mote.

IGHTHAM MOTE, Kent TQ55
Medieval Ightham Mote, a small manor house set in lovely meadowland, is considered to be the most complete of its kind in Britain (open at certain times). Its low bulk is encircled by a moat, and its fine wooded grounds feature a tree-fringed lake. Peacocks are kept in the gardens.

Return to Ivy Hatch and keep left on the 'Seal' road. After a short way turn left again and drive to the village of Stone Street. Bear left on the 'Fawke Common, Riverhill' road and continue through heaths and woodland. Later cross Fawke Common, meet a main road and turn right on to the A225. Descend, and reach the entrance to Knole Park on the right.

KNOLE PARK, Kent TQ55
In 1456 Thomas Bourchier, then Archbishop of Canterbury, bought an ordinary manor house called Knole Park. He and his successors developed this humble beginning into a great palace, but when Archbishop Warham died in 1532 Henry VIII seized the estate for himself. Elizabeth I granted it to Sir Thomas Sackville in 1566, who died while improvement work on the interior of the house was still in progress. Knole Park (open) looks much as it must have done then.

Return to Sevenoaks.

Kent is renowned for oast houses like this one near Bough Beech.

TOUR 30 73 MILES

AMONG THE COASTAL MARSHES

Towards the sea the Wealden hills flatten to Romney Marsh, a place of frogs and sheep where church towers can be seen for miles and the threat of flood is constant. At the sea's edge England's Napoleonic defences crumble peacefully, while massive walls repulse the ocean's eternal barrage.

ASHFORD, Kent TR04
For hundreds of years Ashford has been a market town for Romney Marsh and the Weald of Kent. Its prime situation at the meeting of the two rivers Stour (East and Great) has made it a natural focus in the past, and its proximity to London has meant new growth as a population 'overspill' town. Today it is an important shopping and touring centre a mere 14 miles from the ancient city of Canterbury and within easy reach of the south Kent beaches. The town's industrial development began in the 19th century with the establishment of large railway works, and this period is well represented by old locomotives and rolling stock preserved at the South Eastern Steam Centre, near Willesborough Crossing. Medieval, Tudor and Georgian houses have survived despite development, and the 15th-century parish church retains much of its original character. The Intelligence Corps Museum at Templar Barracks displays a fascinating array of mementos.

Leave Ashford on the A28 'Tenterden road to reach Great Chart.

GREAT CHART, Kent TQ94
A 14th-century church with a 16th-century pest house in the south corner of its churchyard can be seen here. This long, narrow structure is a timber framed building once used to isolate victims of plagues. Court Lodge, a complete 13th-century stone house, stands to the west of the church.

Continue on the A28, crossing pleasant countryside to reach Bethersden.

BETHERSDEN, Kent TQ94
Marble from this village was used for the altar stairs at Canterbury Cathedral, but many humbler buildings also display its splendour. The quarries are now worked out. Brass memorials to forbears of the 17th-century poet William Lovelace can be seen in the local 14th-century church.

Continue through High Halden to Tenterden.

TENTERDEN, Kent TQ83
Typical Wealden houses, *ie* buildings faced with tiles and weather boards, line the broad, grass-verged High Street of this delightful town. Its high situation makes its 15th-century church tower (made of the famous Bethersden marble) visible across the Weald and from many miles out to sea. At one time the tower was used as a beacon to guide shipping. In the 15th century Henry VI admitted Tenterden to the Confederation of Cinque Ports, but the course of the River Rother later changed and the town port was replaced by nearby Smallhythe. Shipbuilding became a major local concern in the 16th century. Later industry included Britain's first light railway in 1872, the Kent and East Sussex. This has been revived and operates with steam locomotives.

Continue on the A28, drive over a level crossing, and pass the Rolvenden station of the Kent and East Sussex Railway on the left. Drive into Rolvenden.

ROLVENDEN, Kent TQ83
Surrounded by well-wooded country, this pleasant combination of weather-boarded (Kentish clad) houses and grass verges is typical of the county. The large 14th-century church preserves two squire's pews, and the restored postmill is a perfect example. Great Maytham Hall, now converted into flats, was designed by Sir Edwin Lutyens in 1910 and stands in gardens (open) that were laid out by landscaper Gertrude Jekyll.

Attractive gardens stretch along the banks of the River Rother at Rye.

Drive to the church and turn left on to the unclassified 'Wittersham' road. Pass through Rolvenden Layne and cross the Rother Levels. Climb on to the Isle of Oxney, an isolated area of high ground. A detour can be made from the main tour route by turning left on to the B2082 to reach Smallhythe Place. Otherwise turn right on to the B2082 and drive to Wittersham.

SMALLHYTHE PLACE, Kent TQ83
Half-timbered Smallhythe Place dates from 1480 and was once the home of actress Dame Ellen Terry. It is now a museum displaying her personal relics (NT). The adjacent 15th-century Priest's House shares its grounds with the Barn Theatre.

WITTERSHAM, Kent TQ82
Wittersham is a quiet, charming village on the central ridge of the Isle of Oxney, between the River Rother and the Royal Military Canal. During the middle ages the tower of its 14th-century church was used as a shipping beacon. Inside the church is a finely carved lectern of late medieval origin. Wealden buildings comprising a windmill, oast houses, and a timbered cottage make an attractive group 1 mile east.

Proceed on the B2082 to cross the River Rother and continue over the Rother Levels. Pass through Iden, meet the A268, and pass through Playden to reach Rye (near the Royal Military Canal).

ROYAL MILITARY CANAL
Originally a defence against an expected Napoleonic invasion, this canal between Rye and Hythe now offers peaceful towpath walks and boat-hire facilities.

RYE, E Sussex TQ92
On a small hill rising out of fenland by the River Rother, this collection of attractive old buildings and cobbled streets was one of two Ancient Towns attached to the Cinque Ports. As such it was heavily fortified against the medieval French. This maritime importance seems odd today, but at that time Rye was almost encircled by sea. Its influence declined when the harbour silted up in the 16th century, and today the sea has receded. Many historic buildings have survived here, the oldest being probably the Norman and later church, which features a 16th-century clock with an 18ft free-swinging pendulum. Near by is the 13th-century Ypres Tower, which was built as a castle and used as a prison from the 16th to 19th centuries. Nowadays it holds nothing more sinister than a museum of local history. Weather-boarded and tile-hung houses, generally with timber frames, can be seen in Mermaid Street, Church Square, Watchbell Street, and High Street. The Mermaid Inn opened in 1420 and is possibly the oldest in the country. From the same century are The Flushing Inn, Stone House, Old Hospital, and Fletcher's House. Peacock's School was built in 1636, and 18th-century Lamb House (NT) was the home of novelist Henry James. Parts of the town walls remain, but 14th-century Landgate (AM) is the only original entry. The town stands on a small hill.

A detour can be made from the main tour route to Camber Castle by taking the A259 'Hastings' road.

CAMBER CASTLE, E Sussex TQ91
This ruined 16th-century coastal defence fort was one of several built in Kent by Henry VIII as a deterrent to the French navy.

The weather-boarded buildings in Tenterden's superb High Street are typical of the Kentish Weald.

[R]olvenden's [p]ainstakingly [r]estored windmill.

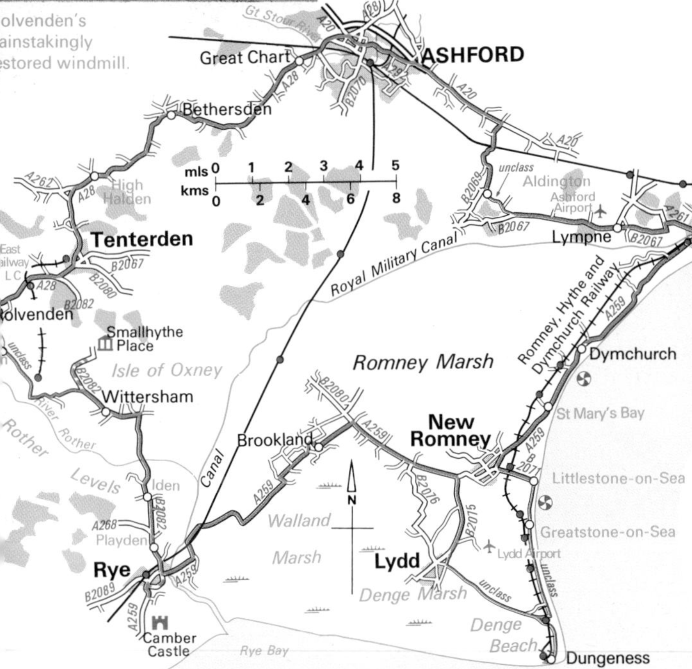

[Fr]om Rye follow SP 'Folkestone A259' [to] reach Brookland, crossing the flat [ex]panse of Walland Marsh on the [wa]y. Water is drained from the land [by] channels that crisscross the area on [bo]th sides of the route.

[BR]OOKLAND, Kent TQ92
[Th]e 13th- to 15th-century church at [Br]ookland displays an unusual wood [an]d shingle belfry, and houses a [No]rman font thought to be unique [in] Britain. The latter is decorated with [sig]ns of the Zodiac and little [vig]nettes depicting various seasonal [act]ivities.

[Co]ntinue on the A259 for $1\frac{1}{2}$ miles, [me]et crossroads, and turn right. In 4 [mil]es turn right again on to the B2075 [Ly]dd' road to reach Lydd.

[LY]DD, Kent TR02
[Lik]e Rye, Lydd was once a coastal [tow]n, but it now lies a good 3 miles [inla]nd. Its 14th-century church has a [lo]ft tower and has been described [as t]he 'Cathedral of Romney Marsh'. [A n]ew 140-acre water sports centre [is b]eing developed here.

[Pro]ceed to the edge of Lydd, cross a [rail]way bridge, then branch left on to [the] unclassified 'Dungeness' road. [Sho]rtly turn left again. To the right of [the] road are Denge Marsh and Denge [Bea]ch. After 3 miles (beyond Lydd) [turn] right to reach Dungeness.

DUNGENESS, Kent TR01
This desolate shingle promontory is the site of a nuclear power station that can be seen for miles over featureless Denge Marsh. A slender lighthouse was built here in 1961 because the old one would be obscured by the power station. The original still stands, slightly inland from its successor. Much of the promontory is taken by a 12,000-acre nature reserve frequented by seabirds and shoreline wildlife.

ROMNEY, HYTHE, AND DYMCHURCH RAILWAY, Kent
Dungeness is the western terminus of a $13\frac{1}{2}$-mile narrow-gauge line which is claimed to be the world's smallest public railway. Steam trains run from Hythe, through New Romney, and along the seaward fringe of Romney Marsh to Dungeness.

Return along the unclassified road for 1 mile, then turn right and follow SP to reach Greatstone and Littlestone-on-Sea. At Littlestone-on-Sea turn left on to the B2071 to reach New Romney.

NEW ROMNEY, Kent TR02
One of the ancient Cinque Ports but now 1 mile inland from the sea, New Romney's harbour was destroyed in 1287 by a violent storm which changed the course of the River Rother. Thanks to William Morris the town's Norman and later church was rescued from insensitive restoration in 1878.

Continue through New Romney and turn right on to the A259 'Folkestone' road to cross Romney Marsh.

ROMNEY MARSH, Kent TR03
Most of this 204-square-mile tract has been reclaimed from the sea by drainage work started in Roman times. Flooding is an ever-present

Innumerable drainage ditches prevent Romney Marsh reverting to its natural state.

threat, as much of the area is still below sea level at high tide, but the land is too fertile to waste and the Marsh is famous for its wool. Tulip-growing is a newly developed local industry.

Continue through St Mary's Bay to reach Dymchurch.

DYMCHURCH, Kent TR12
Situated on the edge of Romney Marsh, this old port is guarded by an ancient sea wall and was once a centre for smugglers. It is now a resort with vast stretches of sand and a variety of historic buildings. One of several Martello towers (AM) along the coast, built as defences against Napoleon, has been restored to house a museum.

Continue beside the sea wall to Hythe.

Amongst the steam locomotives which operate on the Romney, Hythe, and Dymchurch Railway are two miniature versions of Canadian Pacific engines.

HYTHE, Kent TR13
This Cinque Port is now a well-known resort. Just north is Saltwood Castle, a well-preserved medieval garrison fort complete with battlement walk, undercroft, armoury, and torture chamber (open). See also tour 31.

Leave Hythe by the A261 'Ashford' road and in 1 mile turn left on to the B2067 'Lympne' road. Proceed to Lympne.

LYMPNE, Kent TR13
Views over Romney Marsh and the Channel extend from Lympne Castle, which was built and variously extended from Norman times to the 15th century. The Port Lympne Wildlife Sanctuary protects many different animals.

Leave Lympne on the 'Tenterden' road, and in $2\frac{1}{4}$ miles bear right on to the unclassified 'Aldington' road. Continue to Aldington and turn right in the village on to the B2069 'Ashford' road. Pass through pleasant woodland and cross a railway. After $\frac{3}{4}$ mile (from the railway) turn left on to the A20. Follow SP 'Ashford' to finish the tour.

TOUR 31 — 74 MILES

FROM THE SEA TO THE NORTH DOWNS

At Dover soaring cliffs of dazzling white chalk mark the end of the North Downs' rolling march to the sea. Inland the massive towers of Canterbury Cathedral commemorate the halt of paganism, and the rebirth of Christianity in Kent.

FOLKESTONE, Kent TR23
A popular holiday resort and a harbour for cross-Channel steamers, this ancient port still has a fishing fleet and fish market. A wide grassy promenade known as The Leas extends along the cliff top, and attractively wooded walks slope down to the beach. Spade House, the one-time home of writer H G Wells, now contains a museum.

Follow SP 'Hythe, A259' to Sandgate.

SANDGATE, Kent TR23
The castle here belongs to a series built by Henry VIII after his religious break with Rome, when the threat of invasion seemed very real. Shorncliffe Camp, established on the plateau above Sandgate at the beginning of the 19th century, was founded to cope with the later threat of Napoleon's navy.

Continue to Hythe.

HYTHE, Kent TR13
This ancient Cinque Port was very prosperous in the 12th and 13th centuries; its wealth today is assured by its popularity as a resort. Near by is the Royal Military Canal, which was built in 1804 as a defence against Napoleon but nowadays serves as a valuable leisure amenity. A terminus of the Romney, Hythe, and Dymchurch narrow-gauge railway is in the town. See also tour 30.

Follow SP 'Ashford' and 'London' to Hythe Station, past the Royal Military Canal. Return along the 'Folkestone' road, before taking the B2065 'Elham' road and climbing to high ground. Fine views of the North Downs can be enjoyed from here. Continue, and cross the A20 to Etchinghill and Lyminge.

LYMINGE, Kent TR14
There has been a Christian community at Lyminge since 633, when King Ethelbert's daughter and Bishop Paulinus founded their abbey here. Fragments of walling from the original buildings are incorporated in the Church of SS Mary and Ethelburga. Most of Lyminge is Victorian; the half-timbered Old Robus and 18th-century Old Rectory are notable exceptions.

Drive to the far end of the village and turn left on to an unclassified road SP 'Rhodes Minnis' passing through Sibton Park. In ½ mile (beyond Rhodes Minnis) branch left and climb through Lyminge Forest on to the North Downs. Cross the B2068 and turn right for Elmsted.

ELMSTED, Kent TR14
Flint-built St James's Church in Elmsted is of Norman and later date and carries a medieval west tower. Inside is a late medieval half-timbered altar screen.

At Elmsted Church turn left, SP 'Wye', and continue to Hastingleigh.

HASTINGLEIGH, Kent TR04
Norman and later St Mary's Church stands aloof from the village, half hidden from view by the fall of the downs.

Continue on the 'Wye' road to Wye Downs nature reserve.

WYE DOWNS AND NATURE RESERVE, Kent TR04
Wye and Crundale Downs rise some 2 miles south-east of Wye and form part of the North Downs. The escarpment, covered with shrubs and woodland, is a nature reserve.

Continue to Wye.

Fishermen take aboard a net on the beach at Hythe.

THE NORTH DOWNS
This chalk range runs west from the White Cliffs of Dover to the Hog's Back near Guildford, and culminates in a 900ft hill at Woldingham.

WYE, Kent TR04
Archbishop of Canterbury John Kempe founded a college of priests here in 1447, but King Henry VIII put paid to its religious teaching and it later served as a grammar school. Since 1900 it has been the agriculture school of London University. Other features of the town include a racecourse, a Georgian mill house, and 18th-century Olantigh—a venue for summer music festivals.

Follow SP 'Ashford' and cross the Great Stour River. Drive over a level crossing and turn right on to the 'Canterbury' road. After ¾ mile turn right on to the A28 and drive along the Great Stour Valley to Godmersham.

Exquisite stained glass in Canterbury Cathedral depicts Thomas à Becket and the miraculous cures associated with hi[s] name.

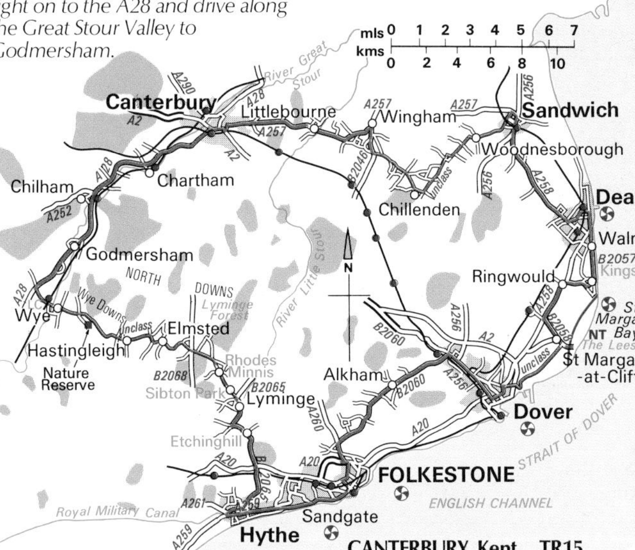

GODMERSHAM, Kent TR05
A monument to Edward Knight, a close relative of novelist Jane Austen and owner of 18th-century Godmersham Park, can be seen in the local Norman and later church. Landscaped grounds surround the big house.

Continue to the outskirts of Chilham.

CHILHAM, Kent TR05
Chilham village is gathered respectfully around a square at the gate of its castle, which was built for Henry II in 1174. The 300-acre grounds (open) feature wood and lakeside walks, plus the Kent Battle of Britain Museum.

Continue to the edge of Chartham.

CHARTHAM, Kent TR15
This large Stour valley village is a well-known angling centre. St Mary's Church is of 13th-century date and boasts one of the oldest sets of bells in the country. East of the village is a medieval chapel on a farm.

Continue to Canterbury.

CANTERBURY, Kent TR15
When the Romans came here they took over a Belgic Stourside community and developed it into the town of *Durovernum Cantioru[m]*, later to become a Christian community. When the Romans le[f]t the area was swept by waves of invaders who had little time for Christianity, but in the year 597 St Augustine's mission arrived to convert King Ethelbert of Kent and restore the town's dilapidated churches. Shortly afterwards Canterbury became the Metropolitan City of the Church o[f] England. Long stretches of the city wall survive on Roman foundation[s] and the present cathedral dates fr[om] 1070. This fine structure is best known as the place where Archbishop Thomas à Becket was murdered for his denial of the kin[g's] authority over the church. Canterbury Castle has the 3rd larg[est] Norman keep in Britain. King's Sc[hool] is thought to be the oldest extant.

Follow SP 'Dover' then 'Sandwich' [to] leave Canterbury on the A257. Continue to Littlebourne.

LITTLEBOURNE, Kent TR25
Close to the local flint church is a[n] ancient thatched barn. Neat sing[le]

A number of Chilham's ancient houses were partly refaced in brick during the 18th century.

ıis portrait of the 1st Earl of Sandwich ıngs in the Guildhall at Sandwich.

›rey cottages dating from the 17th ›ntury stand at the end of the ˡlage green.

›ntinue to Wingham.

'INGHAM, Kent TR25
ːeresting buildings in this town ːlude Debridge House and ingham Court, both of which date ·m the 18th century. Many of the ːal buildings are picturesquely half ıbered, and the Red Lion dates ·m the 15th century.

ːrn right on to the B2046 ·lkestone' road, and in 1 mile turn · on to an unclassified road SP ıillenden'.

ILLENDEN, Kent TR25
ˑe local church retains a good ıny Norman features. Chillenden ındmill, built in 1868 and restored 1958, stands ½ mile north of the ·age.

ːet crossroads, turn left, and leave ıillenden by the 'oodnesborough' road.

OODNESBOROUGH, ıt TR35
ˑ church here suffered heavy ːoration in the 19th century, ː it retains a charming 18th-ıtury cupola on the west tower. ıth-east of the church is a 17th-ıtury brick cottage.

ıtinue to Sandwich.

SANDWICH, Kent TR35
This, the oldest of the Cinque Ports, is now separated from the sea by 2 miles of sand-dunes. Among its many outstanding old buildings are the medieval Barbican, Fishgate, and a variety of houses and inns. St Bartholomew's Hospital guest house dates from the 15th century, and both the Guildhall and Manwood Court were built in the 16th. The Old House is a fine example of Tudor design. Much of the old beach between the town and Sandwich Bay is occupied by Sandwich Golf Course, which is famous the world over.

Leave Sandwich by the A256 'Dover' road and later turn left on to the A258 'Deal' road. Enter Deal.

Below: Dover's wonderfully preserved Roman lighthouse is thought to date from the 1st century. Right: the unmistakable White Cliffs of Dover would have been a familiar landmark to Roman sailors.

DEAL, Kent TR35
Henry VIII built a castle (AM) in the shape of a six-petalled flower at Deal, though considerable protection was already offered by the notorious Goodwin Sands. These vast, shifting beds lie just 5 miles offshore and have caused hundreds of wrecks. In its early history the town was a limb of the Cinque Ports, but most of its development dates from the end of the 17th century. Local exhibits can be seen in the town museum, and collections from all over the world are shown in the Maritime Museum.

Proceed along the seafront on the 'Dover' road and branch left on to the B2057, SP 'Kingsdown'. Pass 16th-century Walmer Castle.

WALMER, Kent TR35
The Henrian Castle (AM) here stands in attractive gardens and is the official residence of the Lord Warden of the Cinque Ports. The Duke of Wellington died here in 1852 and a number of his possessions are on display inside. Walmer Lifeboat is famous for the many rescues it has made from the Goodwin Sands.

Continue to the small resort of Kingsdown and turn inland SP 'Dover'. Drive to Ringwould, overlooking The Leas (NT).

RINGWOULD, Kent TR34
Several bronze-age barrows can be seen near Ringwould on Free Down. The 12th- to 14th-century church has an attractive 17th-century tower.

Join the A258 'Dover' road for a short distance and turn left on to the B2058 for St Margaret's at Cliffe.

ST MARGARET'S AT CLIFFE, Kent TR34
A superb windmill, the last to be built in Kent, stands near the clifftop lighthouse here, and a variety of old buildings line the twisty main street.

A short detour can be taken from the main route to St Margaret's Bay by keeping forward for 1 mile.

ST MARGARET'S BAY, Kent TR34
This sheltered little bay, completely enclosed by towering chalk cliffs, is a popular starting point for cross-Channel swimmers. A narrow beach peters out to weed-bearded boulders and large pools in the chalk bedrock on each side.

Return to St Margaret's at Cliffe, turn right into unclassified Reach Road, and continue to a fine viewpoint overlooking Dover Harbour. Pass a footpath to the Blériot Memorial and turn left on to the A258. Enter Dover.

DOVER, Kent TR34
Formerly the Roman walled city of *Dubris*, Dover was chief of the Cinque Ports and has a magnificent castle (AM) built on a site occupied since prehistoric times. Its strategic position gives it total command of the harbour, and successive English kings spent vast sums on its development. It was last used for military purposes during World War II. The Pharos, a surprisingly well-preserved Roman lighthouse, stands within the castle walls near the exceptionally fine Saxon Church of St Mary de Castro. Dover Town Hall incorporates the 13th-century Hall of Maison Dieu, and nearby Maison Dieu House dates from 1663. The oldest and best-preserved wall paintings north of the Alps can be seen in the Roman Painted House. A granite memorial in North Fall meadow marks the landing of Louis Blériot in 1909, after his historic cross-Channel flight.

Follow SP 'Canterbury (A2)' to leave Dover by London Road (A256). Pass a railway bridge and 1 mile farther on turn left on to the B2060 'Alkham' road. Proceed to Alkham.

ALKHAM, Kent TR24
Stone stalls and a coffin lid with a 12th-century inscription are important features of Alkham's attractive old church.

Climb through a North Downs valley and turn left on to the A260 for the return to Folkestone.

EPPING AND THE VILLAGES OF ESSEX

Most of the great forest that covered West Essex in Norman times has been cut down, though Epping and Hatfield remain. The magic of Essex today is its village life, which has a timeless quality that echoes the tranquillity of forest communities in ancient days.

WOODFORD GREEN, Gt London TQ49
Sir Winston Churchill was MP for Wanstead and Woodford from 1924 to 1964. His statue on Woodford Green is by David McFall.

From Woodford Green follow the A11 'Epping' road, and in $\frac{3}{4}$ mile turn left on to the A110 SP 'North Chingford'. In another $\frac{3}{4}$ mile turn right on to an unclassified road into Forest Side. Continue to a T-junction and turn right into Ranger's Road (A1069) to pass the Royal Forest Hotel and Queen Elizabeth's Hunting Lodge.

QUEEN ELIZABETH'S HUNTING LODGE, Gt London TQ49
Queen Elizabeth's Hunting Lodge is a wood-and-plaster building thought to have been erected towards the end of the 15th century so that the sovereign of the day could enjoy a grandstand view of the chase. After having served as a keeper's lodge for a number of years it now houses the Epping Forest Museum.

EPPING FOREST, Essex
Epping Forest owes its creation to the Norman Conquest. It was maintained as a royal hunting area through the reigns of various monarchs, and in the reign of King Charles I its bounds were fixed to embrace some 60,000 acres. In 1882 what was left of it was formally opened as a publicly-owned area by Queen Victoria.

Enter Epping Forest and in $\frac{3}{4}$ mile meet a T-junction. Turn left on to the A11 and in $1\frac{1}{4}$ miles meet a roundabout. Leave by the 1st exit on to an unclassified road SP 'High Beach', then bear right SP 'King's Oak' for High Beach.

HIGH BEACH, Essex TQ49
It is arguable whether this village is named 'Beech' after the area's principal tree or 'Beach' denoting a gravel bank. Either would seem to be appropriate. The poet Tennyson spent his early manhood here.

Beyond the King's Oak (PH) the Epping Forest Conservation Centre lies to the right. Continue to the next road junction and turn right, then descend and in $\frac{3}{4}$ mile cross the main road. Continue for 1 mile and turn right SP 'Epping' to pass through Upshire. Ascend to re-enter the forest, then meet a T-junction and turn left to rejoin the A11. Continue to Epping.

EPPING, Essex TL40
Epping lies outside the forest and has managed to retain its own identity as a small market town of some charm, despite the proximity of London. Winchelsea House and Epping Place, in the High Road, are both of 18th-century date.

Drive to the green at the end of the town and branch left on to the B181, SP 'Roydon'. In $1\frac{1}{4}$ miles bear right. After $\frac{3}{4}$ mile, having passed over Cobbin's Brook, reach a T-junction and turn left. Continue through Epping Green to Roydon.

ROYDON, Essex TL40
About $1\frac{1}{2}$ miles south-west of Roydon are the ruins of Tudor Nether Hall, a Manor house that belonged to the Coltes family. It was here that Thomas More came to woo and win the elder daughter of John Coltes. Preserved in the village itself are the old parish cage, stocks, and a whipping post.

The two upper floors of Queen Elizabeth's Hunting Lodge were originally designed without infilling between the beams, thus enabling an uninterrupted view of the hunt.

This superb brass is one of 15 preserved in Sawbridgeworth's 14th-century church.

Turn left with SP 'Hertford' and shortly cross the River Stort and a level crossing to enter Hertfordshire. In $\frac{3}{4}$ mile turn right with SP 'Chelmsford' to join the A414. After 5 miles pass through High Wych, then in $\frac{3}{4}$ mile meet a T-junction and turn left on to the A11 to Sawbridgeworth.

SAWBRIDGEWORTH, Herts TL41
A number of fine Georgian and older buildings survive in this small town, and to the south is Pishiobury – a fine house built by James Wyatt in 1782. Ancient brasses are preserved in St Mary's Church.

Meet crossroads and turn right on to the A414, SP 'Chelmsford'. Drive over a level crossing and proceed to Hatfield Heath. Turn left on to the B183 SP 'Takeley' for Hatfield Broad Oak.

HATFIELD BROAD OAK, Essex TL51
Notable features in this markedly-pretty village include a Norman and later church, 18th-century almshouses, and several distinctive Georgian houses.

Keep left and in $1\frac{1}{4}$ miles turn left on to an unclassified road SP 'Hatfield Forest'. In $\frac{3}{4}$ mile keep forward and skirt the Hatfield Forest Country Park.

HATFIELD FOREST, Essex
Once a part of the ancient Royal Forests of Essex, 1,049-acre Hatfield Forest is now protected by the National Trust and offers splendid woodland walks along its chases an rides. Additional amenities include boating and fishing.

Continue, and later turn right on to the A120 for Takeley.

TAKELEY, Essex TL52
Takeley, on the line of the old Roma Stane Street, has an interesting Norman and later church with Roman masonry in the fabric of its walls. Inside is a modern font surmounted by a 6ft-high medieval cover. Good timbered houses and 17th-century barns can be seen in the village.

Drive to traffic signals and turn left of the A120 on to an unclassified road 'Broxted'. In $1\frac{1}{2}$ miles note Stansted Airport to the left. In another $1\frac{1}{4}$ mile turn right into Molehill Green. Continue with SP 'Thaxted' and pass through Broxted.

BROXTED, Essex TL52
Broxted's church shows a happy blend of 13th- and 15th-century styles, with the nave and chancel from the earlier period and a belfry and north aisle from the later. Church Hall is of late 16th- to mid 17th-century date.

Beyond the village join the B1051 fo Thaxted.

THAXTED, Essex TL63
Many old houses survive to remin the visitor that this was once a ver prosperous town. The 15th-centur church was clearly built by a community with a great deal of money to spend. The timbered Guildhall dates from the 16th century and incorporates an earlie ancient lock-up. Several old almshouses and a tower windmill can be seen in the area.

Turn left on to the A130 and contir through the village. At the end me the Fox and Hounds (PH) and turn right on to the B1051 for Great Sampford.

GREAT SAMPFORD, Essex TL63
This pretty village has attractive gabled houses, and opposite the Bull Inn is an Elizabethan manor house. A large pond and three-cornered green complete the picture.

Turn right again on to the B1053 a continue to Finchingfield.

An essential part of Finchingfield's charm is its typically English village green.

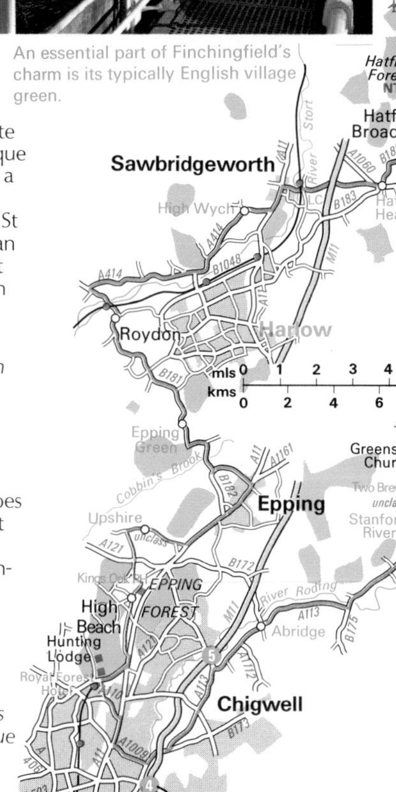

The massive timbers of Greensted Church are a unique survival.

Great Dunmow's 16th-century Clock House.

'INCHINGFIELD, Essex TL63

'ossibly the most photographed village in Essex, Finchingfield is a picture-book community complete with a church on a hill, a picturesque windmill, quaint old cottages, and a charming green enlivened by the noisy population of its duckpond. St John's Church has a sturdy Norman tower that indicates its origins, but the main body of the building is an attractive mixture of styles from subsequent periods.

Drive to the war memorial and turn right on to the B1057 for Great Bardfield.

REAT BARDFIELD, Essex TL63

major feature of this old market town is a restored windmill that goes by the name 'Gibraltar'. A pleasant mixture of old cottages and shops complemented by the mainly 14th-century church is surveyed by a timber-framed 16th- and 17th-century hall from its hill above the River Pant.

rn right SP 'Dunmow' and continue to Bran End. After $2\frac{1}{2}$ miles n left on to the A130 and continue Dunmow.

GREAT DUNMOW, Essex TL62

The Dunmow Flitch trial is held here every 4 years to find a man and wife who have not had a domestic brawl or wished to be unmarried for 12 months and a day. A flitch of bacon is presented to the couple able to prove this enviable state of affairs. The town, a quiet enough place even without this incentive, boasts a large church and a rather small square.

Turn left again SP 'Chelmsford', then in $\frac{3}{4}$ mile turn right on to the B184 SP 'Ongar'. Continue to High Roding and Leaden Roding.

THE RODINGS, Essex TL51

A number of attractive villages in the Roding Valley share this suffix. These include High Roding, with its thatched and gabled cottages and a 13th-century church, and Leaden Roding.

Reach the King William IV (PH) in Leaden Roding and turn right on to the A414. In 1 mile turn left on to the B184 for Fyfield. From Fyfield drive for $2\frac{1}{2}$ miles, enter a roundabout, and leave by the 2nd exit on to the A128 into Chipping Ongar.

CHIPPING ONGAR, Essex TL50

Chipping Ongar began as a market town beneath the walls of a Norman castle. Only the mound and moat of the castle remain, but the contemporary Church of St Martin of Tours still flourishes. Explorer David Livingstone was a pupil pastor of the town's 19th-century Congregational Church.

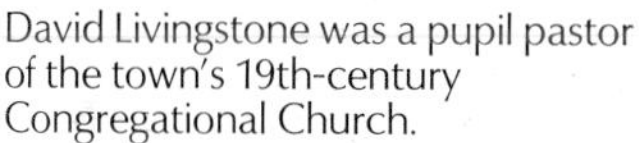

Drive to the end of the High Street and turn right on to an unclassified road SP 'Greensted'. Pass the Two Brewers (PH) and after 1 mile pass Greensted Church on the right.

GREENSTED CHURCH, Essex TL50

St Andrew's Church is famous as the only surviving example of a Saxon log church extant. The body of King Edmund is known to have been rested here in 1013, but the building is probably much older than that.

In a further $\frac{1}{2}$ mile turn left SP 'Stanford Rivers' and follow a narrow road, then in $1\frac{1}{4}$ miles meet crossroads and turn left again. Drive to a T-junction, turn right on to the A113 SP 'London', and in 3 miles enter a roundabout. Leave by the 2nd exit for Abridge and continue to Chigwell.

CHIGWELL, Essex TQ49

Novelist Charles Dickens used the 17th-century King's Head in Chigwell as The Maypole in his book *Barnaby Rudge*. The town's grammar school was founded in 1629 by Archbishop Harsnett, whose memorial brass can be seen inside local St Mary's Church.

After another $1\frac{3}{4}$ miles meet a T-junction and turn right, then in $\frac{3}{4}$ mile meet traffic signals and turn right again on to the A1009 SP 'Woodford Green'. Return to Woodford Green.

ping Forest's many acres of varied enery provide one of East London's st valuable leisure amenities.

TOUR 33 90 MILES

AN UNSUSPECTED COUNTRYSIDE

Major highways following ancient Roman routes carry new towns and overspill developments deep into the countryside north of London. Between them, unsuspected by their traffic, are quiet rural areas where wood and parkland insulate splendid mansions from the modern rush.

BARNET, Gt London TQ29
Several charmingly-rural areas have survived here in spite of the capital's appetite for building land. Mill Hill has picturesque weather-boarded houses set neatly on the green ridge from which it takes its name. A 2-mile expanse of unspoilt countryside extends from Cockfosters to Monken Hadley, and Hadley Woods are delightful.

Leave Barnet Church with SP 'Hatfield, A1000'. After $\frac{1}{2}$ mile pass through Hadley Green.

HADLEY GREEN, Gt London TQ29
Hadley Common and Hadley Green meet at St Mary's Church, a 15th-century building of flint and ironstone, topped by an 18th-century copper beacon. Various Georgian houses and cottages cluster round the fringes of the green in a very village-like way.

Continue to Potters Bar, passing the Battle of Barnet (1471) Obelisk to the right. Meet crossroads and drive forward to pass the BBC radio station at Brookman's Park. In 2 miles bear left for Hatfield. Enter a roundabout and go forward. After a short distance pass the entrance to Hatfield House (right).

HATFIELD, Herts TL20
Ancient Hatfield preserves many interesting buildings from its long history as a market town, not the least of which is the Tudor palace of Cardinal Moreton. Even this, however, with its Elizabeth I and Mary associations, is overshadowed by the famous and spectacular pile of Hatfield House (open). A chapel of the owners of the house, can be seen in the local church.

Proceed through Old Hatfield and meet traffic lights. Turn right here SP 'Hertford', then within $\frac{1}{2}$ mile cross a flyover and turn left to join the A414. A detour can be made from the main tour route by keeping forward on the A1000 and crossing the River Lee to Welwyn Garden City.

WELWYN GARDEN CITY, Herts TL21
Although not the earliest of its kind in England (that honour belongs to Letchworth), Welwyn Garden City was begun in 1919 and represents an attempt to influence the living conditions of ordinary people.

Continue with the A414. In 2 miles enter a roundabout and leave by the 1st exit. After about 1 mile reach Cole Green and take the 2nd turning left on to an unclassified road SP 'Welwyn, B1000'. Continue for $1\frac{1}{4}$ miles and turn left to join the B1000. In another $\frac{1}{2}$ mile turn right on to an unclassified road across the River Mimram SP 'Archers Green'. At the end of this turn right for Tewin.

Hatfield House, which was built between 1608 and 1612, is one of the most outstanding examples of Jacobean architecture in England.

TEWIN, Herts TL21
Tewin lies in wooded countryside above the charming River Mimram, east of the impressive 19th-century Digswell railway viaduct. Close by is beautifully-preserved Elizabethan Queen Hoo Hall.

Proceed to the green in Tewin and keep left for Burnham Green. Drive over crossroads for Woolmer Green.

WOOLMER GREEN, Herts TL21
Local St Michael's Church, built in the late 19th century, was meant to incorporate a tower that was never erected.

Turn right on to the B197 and follow part of the old Great North Road to Knebworth.

KNEBWORTH, Herts TL22
Several examples of the accomplished early 20th-century architect Lutyens' work can be seen in New Knebworth, including the Church of St Martin, Golf Club House, and 'Homewod'.

Meet crossroads and turn left on to ar unclassified road SP 'Old Knebworth'. Pass under a railway bridge and turn right. After 1 mile Knebworth House lies to the right.

KNEBWORTH HOUSE, Herts TL22
Among many fine paintings and relics displayed in this large house (open) are manuscripts belonging to historian Edward Bulwer Lytton, who lived here. The origins of the house itself are in the 15th century, but the building shows considerable later influence.

Keep left with the 'Codicote' road and in $\frac{1}{2}$ mile turn right SP 'Kimpton and Whitwell'. Continue, then turn right on to the B656 SP 'Hitchin' and shortly pass the Vanstone Garden Centre on the left. Continue for $4\frac{1}{2}$ miles, passing a road on the right leading to St Ippollitts.

ST IPPOLLITTS, Herts TL12
By all accounts St Ippollitts was a man skilled in the treatment of horses. The local church was rebuilt in 1879 from old materials. The Olive Branch is an attractive inn.

Continue into Hitchin.

HITCHIN, Herts TL12
Tilehouse Street and Bridge Street preserve the best of Hitchin's older houses, but many other features survive in this medieval wool town. The ancient market square and moated Hitchin Priory, the latter dating from the 1770s, are reminders of a prosperous past. Features of the town church include a fine old porch and good screenwork.

Leave the town by the A600 Bedford road. Continue to Henlow Camp.

HENLOW CAMP, Beds TL13
Long-renowned as a flying centre, Henlow Camp is an RAF establishment situated some 2 miles south of the village from which it derives its name.

Drive to a roundabout and go forward. In $1\frac{1}{4}$ miles meet crossroads and turn right on to an unclassified road for Clifton.

CLIFTON, Beds TL13
A large 16th-century alabaster monument to Sir Michael Fisher and his wife is in Clifton Church.

Turn left, then immediately right, SP 'Stanford'. In $\frac{1}{4}$ mile pass the church and turn left. Cross the River Ivel Navigation, proceed for $\frac{1}{2}$ mile, and keep right for Stanford. Turn right on to the B658 SP 'Sandy' and keep straight on for Caldecote. Meet crossroads and turn left on to an unclassified road for Ickwell Green.

ICKWELL GREEN, Beds TL14
Perhaps best known for the May Day revels still held round the enormous maypole that rises from its large green, this pretty village boasts several thatched cottages and a smithy where Georgian clockmaker Thomas Tompion once worked.

Turn left SP 'Old Warden' and in $\frac{1}{2}$ mile meet a T-junction. Turn right and pass Old Warden Airfield.

OLD WARDEN AIRFIELD, Beds TL14
Historical aircraft and veteran cars can be seen in the Shuttleworth Collection at this small airfield, and flying displays are given occasionally.

Take the 'Shefford' road through Old Warden.

OLD WARDEN, Beds TL14
The first Warden pear was grown in this pretty village of thatched cottages and ancient sunken lanes. Old Warden Park house was built f Sir Joseph Shuttleworth in 1872.

After $\frac{1}{2}$ mile meet a T-junction and turn left. Continue for 1 mile, pass under a railway bridge, and turn left. Follow SP 'Shefford' and eventually rejoin the A600. Cross a river and enter Shefford village.

SHEFFORD, Beds TL13
Southill Park, a notable Regency house to the north of Shefford, was rebuilt by Henry Holland in 1800. It was once the home of Admiral Byn who was unjustly shot for neglect duty after losing a battle in 1757.

Proceed to traffic signals and turn rig on to the A507 SP 'Ampthill'. In $3\frac{1}{4}$ miles turn left on to an unclassified road SP 'Silsoe'. In 1 mile turn left on to the A6 for Silsoe.

SILSOE, Beds TL03
Silsoe's church is of early 19th-century date, but is a successful attempt at a traditional English church style. Nearby Wrest Park House was built in 1834.

Continue to Barton-in-the-Clay.

BARTON-IN-THE-CLAY, Beds TL
A 16th-century painting of St Nicholas is preserved in the village church. A viewpoint known as the Clappers, including 136 acres of lovely National Trust property crowned by Clappers Wood, rises the west.

Turn left on to the B655, SP 'Hexton Climb on to the Barton Hills and dr to Hexton.

A winter scene at Hadley Green.

Dramatist and critic George Bernard Shaw lived in this Victorian house at Ayot St Lawrence for 44 years.

The Shuttleworth collection at Old Warden Airfield.

‑EXTON, Herts TL13
‑ature lends a dramatic hand to the ‑ppearance of Hexton. All around ‑e the undulating Barton Hills, and ‑ the village itself the main street is ‑ned with laburnums. The 19th-‑entury St Faith's Church is guarded ‑y giant yews.

‑eet crossroads and turn right on to ‑ unclassified road leading to Lilley.

‑LLEY, Herts TL12
‑omas Jekyll successfully copied a ‑aditional style when he designed ‑e attractive local church in 1870.

‑ep forward over all crossroads and ‑ter Whitwell.

‑HITWELL, Herts TL12
‑ck-and-timber cottages and a ‑arming old inn called The Bull ‑ake up this pretty village, set in ‑spoiled countryside.

‑rn right on to the B651 SP 'St ‑bans', and ascend to the edge of ‑mpton.

‑MPTON, Herts TL11
‑e large flint Church of SS Peter and ‑ul stands at the north-eastern end ‑this village and is thought to date ‑m the early 14th century.

Turn left, then right, and in 1 mile turn left on to an unclassfied road for Ayot St Lawrence. Turn left into the village, then pass the church and Ayot House on the left.

AYOT ST LAWRENCE, Herts TL11
Author George Bernard Shaw lived at Ayot St Lawrence from 1906 to his death in 1950 and his house – Shaw's Corner (NT) – is preserved as it was in his lifetime. His ashes were scattered in the garden.

Keep right and after 1 mile meet a T-junction. Turn right, then in a further 1½ miles meet another T-junction and turn right on to the A6129. Meet a roundabout and leave by the 1st exit on to the B651 into Wheathampstead.

WHEATHAMPSTEAD, Herts TL11
Modern industry has come to Wheathampstead, and many of its old cottages are now shops. Sarah Jennings, later the Duchess of Marlborough, is said to have been born at nearby Water End Farm. Features of the village itself include a 13th-century church and the 15th-century Bull Inn.

Continue along the B651 to Sandridge.

SANDRIDGE, Herts TL11
Roman bricks and masonry were used to build a chancel arch in the local Church of St Leonard. Also in the building is a good 14th-century stone rood screen.

Turn left on to an unclassified road SP 'Colney Heath'. In 1½ miles enter a roundabout and turn left. In 1 mile cross the main road, then in a further mile turn right across the dual carriageway and left on to the B6426 for Colney Heath.

COLNEY HEATH, Herts TL20
The local church is a clever 19th-century copy of Norman design. Its outer staircase makes its disguise all the more credible.

Meet a roundabout and take the 3rd exit on to the B556 SP 'London, Colney'. In 2 miles enter another roundabout and take the 2nd exit SP 'Radlett'. A detour may be made from the main tour route by leaving the last-mentioned roundabout by the 1st exit on to the A6, then driving for ½ mile to Salisbury Hall.

SALISBURY HALL, Herts TL10
Red-brick Salisbury Hall was built by Sir John Cuttes, treasurer to Henry VIII, and is encircled by a moat.

Continue to the next roundabout and turn left on to the B5378 for Shenley.

SHENLEY, Herts TL10
Nicholas Hawksmoor, the great architect, lived at Porter's Park until his death in 1736. His house now serves as a hospital. Preserved on the village green is the old parish lock-up, once used for petty criminals.

Drive to the end of the village and go forward on to an unclassified road. In 2¼ miles join one-way traffic and follow SP 'Barnet'. Cross a flyover, then turn right and in 1 mile turn left on to the A411. Return to Barnet.

The pavilion in the grounds of Wrest Park at Silsoe dates from 1709.

TOUR 34 68 MILES

THE BUCKINGHAM CHILTERNS

Great rounded hills crowned with beeches enfold valleys where pure chalk streams are home to the speckled trout. Here and there steeples rise dark against the green flanks, proclaiming downland villages famous for their beauty.

UXBRIDGE, Gt London TQ08
Uxbridge stands on the banks of the River Colne and the Grand Union Canal. Its George Inn, Old Crown and Treaty House all featured in an historic meeting between Charles I and Parliament in 1645. St Margaret's Church dates from the 14th and 15th centuries, but its tower was rebuilt in 1820. The Market House dates from 1789.

Follow SP 'Denham' then 'Beaconsfield' to leave Uxbridge on the A4020, crossing the Grand Union Canal and the River Colne. Proceed to the Denham roundabout and take the 3rd exit on to the A40. Denham village lies off the road to the right.

DENHAM, Bucks TQ08
Denham is a most attractive village of fine houses, old inns, and ancient brick and timber cottages. St Mary's Church, which dates from the 15th century, contains wall paintings of the Day of Judgement and a 13th-century font. The local Wesleyan Chapel was built in 1820. At the end of the main street is 17th-century Denham Place, which stands in grounds landscaped by Capability Brown. Savay Farm is a 14th-century hall house.

Continue for 2 miles, with the River Misbourne to the right of the road, and meet traffic signals. Turn right on to the A413, SP 'Amersham' and proceed for 2¼ miles. Go forward to skirt Chalfont St Peter.

Go forward to skirt Chalfont St Giles. A detour from the main route to Milton's Cottage can be made by driving to the Pheasant Inn and turning left on to an unclassified road.

MILTON'S COTTAGE, Bucks SU99
Milton lived in this timber-framed and brick cottage (open) during the plague year of 1665. He completed *Paradise Lost* here and began *Paradise Regained.*

CHALFONT ST GILES, Bucks SU99
St Giles' Church has a 13th-century heart in Victorian dress. Bertram Mills, of circus fame, is buried in the churchyard. The village has a small green bordered by ancient brick and timber cottages.

Continue to Amersham.

Ancient beech trees provide spreading canopies of dappled shade on many of the Chiltern summits.

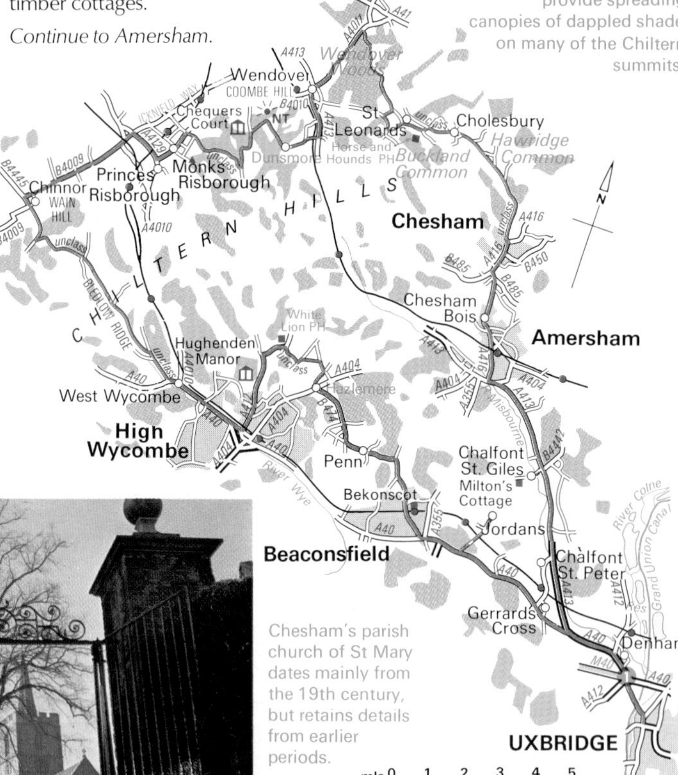

Chesham's parish church of St Mary dates mainly from the 19th century, but retains details from earlier periods.

CHALFONT ST PETER, Bucks SU99
A complete contrast in building styles is offered by two local churches. One is a Victorianized 18th-century structure and the other a 20th-century creation. The once-fashionable gothic-revival style is evident in Chalfont House, which was built for General Churchill.

AMERSHAM, Bucks SU99
Amersham is a lovely collection of old houses, quaint cottages, and ancient inns in the Misbourne Valley. Sir William Drake built the Town Hall in 1682, some 15 years after the almshouses bearing his name. Beech woods grace the Chiltern countryside around the town.

Meet traffic signals by the Crown Hotel and turn right into Church Street. Within 1 mile approach more traffic signals and turn left on to the A416 for Chesham Bois.

CHESHAM BOIS, Bucks SU99
St Leonard's at Chesham Bois is a 19th-century restoration, but the arch of its south entrance may have been part of a medieval church. Memorial brasses can be seen inside.

Continue on the A416 to Chesham.

CHESHAM, Bucks SP90
Chesham stands in the Chess Valley, with attractive Chiltern countryside to the north-west. Georgian houses and cottages exist here, and the Town Hall shows influences from both the 18th and 19th centuries. The George Inn in the High Street dates from 1715.

In Chesham bear left then right with one-way traffic SP 'Berkhamsted'. Meet a roundabout, drive forward for about a ¼ mile, and turn right. Continue to a T-junction and turn left. Within ½ mile keep forward to an unclassified road SP 'Tring'. In 1¾ miles bear left to climb on to the Chilterns.

THE CHILTERN HILLS
Wooded in the west but mostly windswept and bare near Ivinghoe in the east, the Chiltern Hills extend in majestic line from Goring in the Thames Valley to a point near Hitchin, and culminate in 835ft Coombe Hill above Wendover. Many of the chalk 'downs' are crowned with ancient beech groves. The North Bucks Way, a 30-mile walk from Wolverton to Chequers, has been opened for public use.

Keep forward to Hawridge Common and continue to Cholesbury.

CHOLESBURY, Bucks SP90
Cholesbury Common boasts a fine tower windmill which started life as smock mill in 1863. Its form was revised after it had been declared unsafe in 1884, and it has now been converted into a private house. Iron age Cholesbury Camp covers 15 acres near by.

Continue to Buckland Common, then drive to the Horse and Hound (PH) and keep left. Take the next turning right to St Leonards.

ST LEONARDS, Bucks SP90
The Church of St Leonard, rebuilt after the Civil War and restored in 1845, has plastered walls and carries a squat bell turret surmounted by a spire.

Follow the 'Aston Clinton' road. Descend Aston Hill through Wendover Woods to meet the A4011. Turn left and pass through Halton to reach Wendover.

WENDOVER, Bucks SP80
Many delightful brick and timber cottages survive here, plus a collection of quaint inns which includes the Red Lion Hotel, where Oliver Cromwell slept in 1642. Bosworth House, in the main street, is of 17th-century origin. Both the local windmill and a watermill have been converted into houses. The ancient Icknield Way crosses the Chilterns near by on its way from east to south-west England.

Turn left on to the A413 SP 'Amersham'. Within $\frac{1}{4}$ mile turn left again, then continue for $1\frac{1}{2}$ miles and turn right on to an unclassified road. Ascend to Dunsmore, go forward with SP 'Kimble', and follow the narrow road over a shoulder of Coombe Hill.

COOMBE HILL, Bucks SP80
About $1\frac{1}{2}$ miles west of Wendover is Coombe Hill (NT) – 106 acres of downland in the highest part of the Chilterns. Excellent views include Aylesbury and the Chequers Woods.

Descend to Chequers Court.

CHEQUERS COURT, Bucks SP80
Chequers is a notable 16th-century house that was given to the nation by Lord Lee of Fareham, as a thank-offering for the ending of World War I. About 3 miles from Princes Risborough in hundreds of acres of parkland, it is the Prime Minister's official country residence and contains valuable Cromwellian relics.

Turn left SP 'Great Missenden'. In $\frac{1}{4}$ miles turn sharp right SP 'Princes Risborough', and in 1 mile descend Longdown Hill. Turn left on to the A4010 for Monks Risborough.

MONKS RISBOROUGH, Bucks SP80
A well-known local landmark is the 80ft chalk cross cut on a slope overlooking the Icknield Way. Its upkeep was traditionally the duty of the earls of Buckingham.

Continue to Princes Risborough.

PRINCES RISBOROUGH, Bucks SP80
Among several picturesque old houses surviving here is a 17th- and 18th-century manor house (NT).

In Princes Risborough turn right on to the A4129 SP 'Thame'. In 1 mile meet crossroads and turn left on to the B4009. Proceed to Chinnor along the line of the Icknield Way.

Above: this pastel of John Milton at the age of 62 hangs in Milton's Cottage. Right: this picturesque, creeper hung cottage is where the poet ended his days in blindness and loneliness, a disillusioned old man.

CHINNOR, Oxon SP70
A Chiltern village with a cement works sounds incongruous, even to 20th-century ears, but Chinnor has just such an industry. Its moated manor house and attractive church are more typical of the area.

Meet crossroads and turn left, then within $\frac{1}{4}$ mile go forward along an unclassified road with SP 'Bledlow Ridge'. Wain Hill viewpoint lies to the left.

WAIN HILL, Bucks SP70
Cut into the solid chalk slope of Wain Hill is the 75ft-long Bledlow Cross, one of two turf-cut crosses in the county.

In $\frac{1}{2}$ mile ascend Chinnor Hill and turn sharp left for the climb to Bledlow Ridge.

BLEDLOW RIDGE, Bucks SU79
The climb to Bledlow Ridge is steep, but well worth the effort for it commands breathtaking views.

Descend to West Wycombe.

WEST WYCOMBE, Bucks SU89
This town has a beautifully-preserved main street (NT) which enshrines architecture dating from the 15th to 19th centuries. The town's Church of St Laurence stands isolated on a 600ft-high hill at the site of a village which has long gone. Artificial chalk caves (NT) in the area once housed the notorious Hell Fire Club founded by Sir Francis Dashwood, who owned the mansion in West Wycombe Park (NT).

Join the A40 and drive through the village to High Wycombe.

HIGH WYCOMBE, Bucks SU89
High Wycombe has been important since Roman times, and once earned a very good living from wool and lace. It is now well known for the manufacture of furniture, particularly chairs, and has a museum dealing solely with the craft in Castle Hill House. The Guildhall and octagonal Little Market House are scheduled as Ancient Monuments.

Leave High Wycombe following SP 'Great Missenden, A4128' and cross the River Wye. Within $1\frac{1}{2}$ miles reach Hughenden Manor on the left.

HUGHENDEN MANOR, Bucks SU89
Hughenden Manor was the home of Disraeli, Prime Minister of Great Britain under Queen Victoria. It was remodelled in 1862 and now houses a museum.

After about $\frac{1}{2}$ mile turn right. Ascend for $\frac{3}{4}$ mile and approach the White Lion (PH). Turn right again into unclassified Cryers Hill Lane and proceed to a T-junction. Turn left SP 'Penn' and in 1 mile turn right. In $\frac{1}{2}$ mile approach traffic signals at Hazlemere and drive straight over crossroads on to the B474 SP 'Beaconsfield'. Go forward to Penn.

PENN, Bucks SU99
Penn is in one of the loveliest parts of the Chilterns. Village inn and church stand side by side overlooking the green in the company of fine Georgian houses, and the view from the churchyard is exceptional.

Continue through Penn to the outskirts of Beaconsfield and Bekonscot Model Village.

BEKONSCOT MODEL VILLAGE, Bucks SU99
Situated in Warwick Road, Beaconsfield New Town, this model has cottages, churches, waterways, a railway, an airport, farms, and fields, at the scale of one inch to one foot.

Continue into Beaconsfield.

BEACONSFIELD, Bucks SU99
Beaconsfield has a green bordered by roads of Queen Anne and Georgian houses, and ancient inns with notable histories. The half-timbered Royal Saracen's Head and Royal White Hart were once coaching stops. Although St Mary's Church is medieval in origin it wears a Victorian face; the poet Edmund Waller lies buried here.

Turn left on to the A40 and follow SP 'London'. Continue for $\frac{1}{2}$ mile, enter a roundabout, and leave by the 1st exit. After another $\frac{1}{2}$ mile pass an unclassified left turn which leads to Jordans.

JORDANS, Bucks SU99
The most famous of all Quaker Meeting Houses stands here. It was built in 1688 and is only a few years younger than Old Jordans Farm, where Quaker meetings were held prior to its completion.

Continue along the A40 to the outskirts of Gerrards Cross.

GERRARDS CROSS, Bucks TQ08
This largely residential district has a Byzantine-style church of 1859 and a few Georgian houses.

Continue along the A40 and enter Denham roundabout. Leave by the A4020 exit and return to Uxbridge.

A painted ceiling dominates the Blue Drawing Room in 18th-century West Wycombe Park.

OXFORD, Oxon SP50
This ancient and world renowned university town stands on three main waterways – the River Cherwell, the River Thames (known locally as the Isis), and the Oxford Canal. It is first mentioned in the Saxon Chronicle of 912, but all the indications are that there was a thriving community on the site at least 200 years earlier. Organized teaching has existed at Oxford since the 12th century, and the collegiate system became established in the 13th century as the various religious orders consolidated. Town and gown were often at loggerheads in medieval times, particularly when university privileges conflicted with the interests of local merchants. Charles I established his parliament here, and Oxford served as the Royalist headquarters during that troubled time of civil war. The town's street plan forms an intriguing network centred on Carfax, a junction of four streets and the centre of the old community. Perhaps the most notable of the four is High Street, which is known locally as 'The High'. At the east end is Magdalen, one of the richest colleges in Oxford, and a little closer to Carfax is St Edmund Hall – a unique relic of a residential society founded for graduates in 1220. The High's centrepiece is the University Church of St Mary the Virgin, which is instantly recognizable by its beautiful 14th-century spire. Wren designed the Sheldonian Theatre, at the east end of Broad Street, and the 19th-century bulk of Ashmolean Museum displays a varied array of fascinating and often valuable collections.

From Oxford follow SP 'The East A420'. Pass through Headington.

HEADINGTON, Oxon SP50
Stone for many of the Oxford colleges was worked in the once-famous Headington quarries. The village church dates from the 12th century and incorporates a fine Norman chancel arch. Morris dancing is a long-standing local tradition, and Headington's own troupe of dancers performs annually on Whit Monday.

Continue to a roundabout and take the 2nd exit into unclassified Bayswater Road. After ¾ mile turn right, SP 'Stanton St John'. Drive forward to a T-junction and turn right, then left, into Stanton St John.

STANTON ST JOHN, Oxon SP50
John White, the chief founder of Massachusetts in New England, was born here in 1575. Milton's grandfather also lived here. The village has thatched farms, stone cottages, an ancient manor house, and a lovely old church.

Drive to the church, turn left, then follow SP 'Oakley'. Enter that village.

TOUR 35 71 MILES

NORTH OF THE SPIRED CITY

Just a few miles from the city of learning and dreaming spires are the vast victory estate of Blenheim, an ancient Saxon demesne that was the playground of the high aristocracy, and the gentle contours of the Vale of Oxford.

OAKLEY, Bucks SP61
Oakley House stands at the south end of the village and is of 17th-century date. Early 13th-century St Mary's Church contains a number of old coffin-lid monuments.

From Oakley approach a main road and turn right on to the B4011. Take the next turning left on to an unclassified road for Brill.

BRILL, Bucks SP61
Isolated Brill is a lovely village which stands at 700ft above the Vale of Aylesbury. Its two greens are fringed with charming cottages and almshouses, and its Tudor manor house radiates the warmth of mellow red brick. Brill windmill (open) dates from 1668 and may be one of the oldest postmills to have survived anywhere in Great Britain.

Proceed to the Sun Hotel, turn left into Windmill Street, and pass the old windmill. Later ascend, then descend to join the B4011 to Blackthorn. After 1 mile turn left on to the A41 for Bicester.

BICESTER, Oxon SP52
The site of Roman Alchester lies a mile to the south of Bicester, and the modern A421 follows the line of an old Roman road close by. No Roman remains have been found at Bicester itself, but the *castra* element in its name suggests that there was once a garrison here. If that was the case then the military tradition continues, for nowadays it is the base for one of the largest army depots in the country. Local roadsides have wide grass verges for the convenience of the many horseriders hereabouts.

Follow SP 'Oxford, A421', then turn right on to the A4095 SP 'Chipping Norton'. Proceed for 1 mile, then go forward on to the B4030 to Middleton Stoney. Cross a main road and continue to the outskirts of Lower Heyford.

LOWER HEYFORD, Oxon SP42
Set on a slope overlooking a wide valley and the River Cherwell, Lower Heyford has a 13th-century church which carries a 15th-century tower and is entered via a 15th-century porch complete with sundial. The font dates from the 17th century.

Cross the Oxford Canal and River Cherwell. (Rousham House is on the left).

ROUSHAM HOUSE, Oxon SP42
Near the River Cherwell is Rousham House, a 17th- and 18th-century building which boasts the only garden layout by William Kent to have survived intact (open).

New College, Oxford, was founded by William of Wykeham in 1379. Architect James Wyatt restored the chapel buildings in the 18th century.

Continue to the Hopcrofts Holt Hotel, and turn right on to the A423 for Deddington.

DEDDINGTON, Oxon SP43
One of many small market towns on the lovely River Cherwell, Deddington is built of honey-coloured local stone and is rich in Civil War associations. Many of these may be 'local colour', but King Charles I is reputed to have slept at 16th-century Castle Farm while in the area. The local church is of 14th-century date and has a very fine north porch. Its tower was rebuilt in 1635 after the first attempt fell down.

Turn left on to the B4031 'Chipping Norton' road and pass through Hampton. After 3 miles keep left and join the A361. After ½ mile turn left on to the B4022 SP 'Enstone'. Continue for 1 mile and turn left again on to an unclassified road for Great Tew.

GREAT TEW, Oxon SP32
Delightful cottages of thatch and stone combine with the old village stocks here to present a truly traditional picture of rural England. A number of interesting monuments can be seen in the church, and the manor house has been rebuilt in its original gardens.

After ½ mile turn right SP 'Little Tew'. Drive to crossroads and turn left to rejoin the B4022. After a further 3 miles drive over staggered crossroads and skirt Enstone. Proceed to Charlbury.

CHARLBURY, Oxon SP31
Charlbury has outgrown its village origins and perhaps lost a little of its charm in doing so. Elizabeth I's favourite the Earl of Leicester once lived at Cornbury Park, but the mansion there now owes almost everything to the 17th and 18th centuries. Ditchley Park, a fine 18th-century house by James Gibbs, lies 2½ miles to the north-east and serves as an Anglo-American conference centre. Wychwood Forest lies just across the River Evenlode.

Continue along the B4022, crossing the River Evenlode, with Wychwood Forest to the right. Later turn right into Witney.

WITNEY, Oxon SP31
The name 'Witney' is synonymous with blanket making, an industry that has grown from the town's close proximity to rich wool country and the availability of ready power from the River Windrush. *Domesday* records that two mills stood here, and doubtless there were others even before that. The main street extends for almost a mile to a green set with lime trees and graced with fine houses built with the profits of wool and weaving. Prosperity is similarly mirrored in the 17th-century Butter Cross, which stands on 13 stone pillars and displays both a clock tower and a sundial. The old Blanket Hall of 1720 displays a curious one-handed clock. Witney'

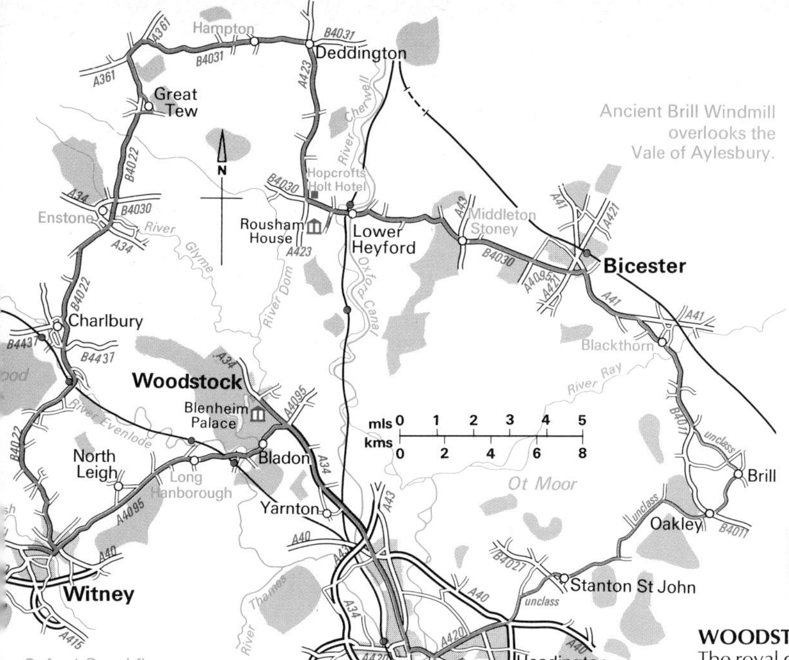

Ancient Brill Windmill overlooks the Vale of Aylesbury.

e Oxford Canal flows
rough Lower Heyford.

ırch carries a 156ft-high spire that ves as a landmark for many miles.

ırn along the A4095 'Bicester' d to the outskirts of North Leigh.

RTH LEIGH, Oxon SP31
tures of North Leigh include a sed windmill and a church with a on tower. Inside the church is a om' painting and an unusual ection of coffin plates. North-east e village are superb Roman ains (AM) on one of the best villa in this country.

tinue on the A4095 and pass ugh Long Hanborough to Bladon.

DON, Oxon SP41
Vinston Churchill, his wife, and his parents are buried in Bladon chyard. The church itself is a orian reconstruction of a ding that had previously ıpied the site for many centuries.

e 1 mile farther and approach a ıdabout. Turn left on to the A34 lenheim Palace and Woodstock.

HEIM PALACE, Oxon SP41
Churchill, 1st Duke of borough, won more than a ry when he crushed the French enheim in 1704. Queen Anne ded him and his heirs forever Royal Manor of Woodstock with Hundred of Wootton, while a no less grateful parliament voted him half a million pounds to pay for the building of Blenheim Palace. The duchess rejected plans for the house drawn up by Wren and chose instead Sir John Vanbrugh's suitably grandiose scheme. The gardens were originally laid out by Henry Wise, and the grounds – later modified by Capability Brown – cover 2,500 acres and include a vast lake, Triumphal Way, and sunken Italian garden. The palace itself is an Eldorado of art treasures and fine furnishings. One-time prime minister and war leader Sir Winston Churchill was born here in 1874.

WOODSTOCK, Oxon SP 41
The royal demesne of Woodstock was from Saxon to Tudor times the site of a great country manor that served as the playground of royalty. Various members of the high aristocracy were born here, some installed their mistresses or hunted here, and several died here. Elizabeth I was imprisoned here by Mary for a while, but the tables were resoundingly turned when the Virgin Queen returned in triumph after her accession to the throne. Woodstock House was, unfortunately, a total casualty of the Civil War and has all but vanished. In the town itself is a grand town hall that was built in 1766 by Sir William Chambers with money donated by the Duke of Marlborough. Tradition has it that the very famous Bear Inn dates back to 1237. There are a great number of very old and attractive stone houses in the streets of Woodstock.

Return along the A34 towards Oxford. After $3\frac{1}{2}$ miles meet an unclassified right turn leading to Yarnton.

YARNTON, Oxon SP41
Yarnton's manor house was built in 1612 and has since been well restored. Above its porch are the Spencer Arms. The local church, which dates from the 13th century, carries a 17th-century tower and contains a fine Jacobean screen.

Continue along the A34 for the return to Oxford.

Blenheim Palace, which covers 3 acres of ground, was built for the Duke of Marlborough between 1705 and 1722.

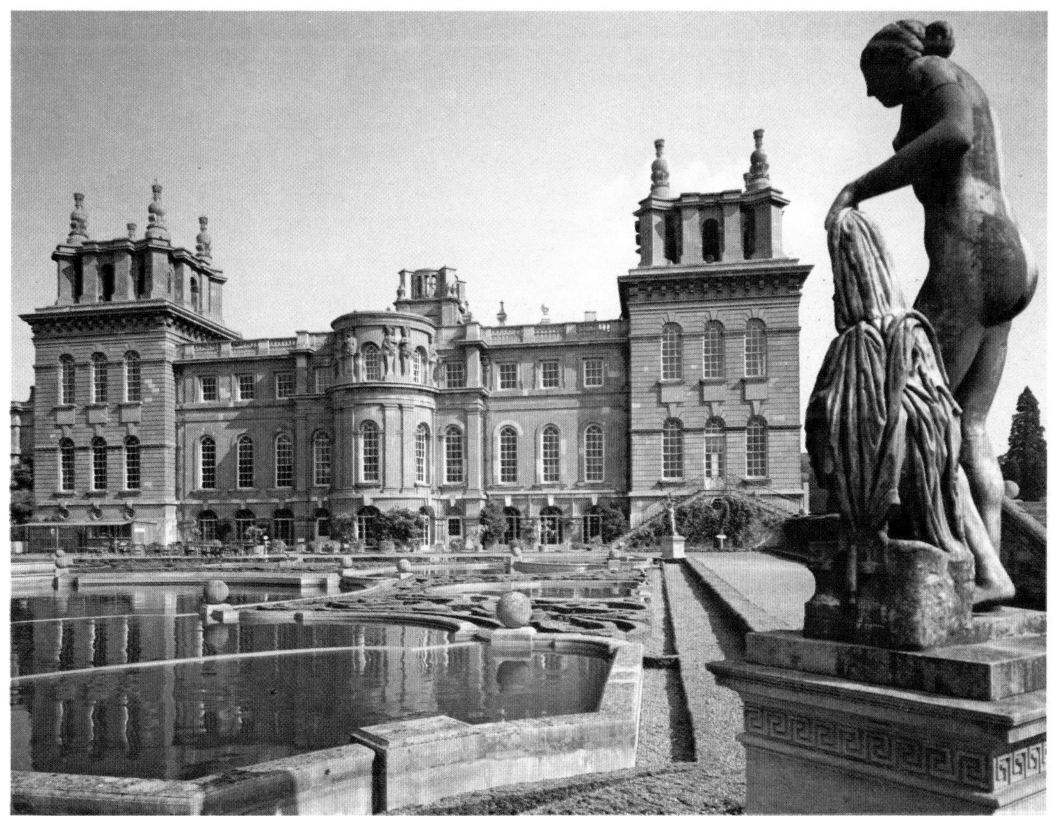

TOUR 36 71 MILES

AMONG THE COTSWOLDS

Wool and stone shaped this landscape. Mellow rock torn from hillsides cropped smooth by generations of sheep was built into great churches, houses, towns and villages by local skill applied with the profits from wool, medieval England's greatest resource.

BURFORD, Oxon SP21
Like so many other wool towns in this part of the country, Burford is centred on a charming main street lined with honey-coloured buildings of local stone. The excellence of this building material is apparent in the fact that Sir Christopher Wren would specify no other for St Paul's Cathedral. The town's main street descends a steep hillside and crosses the River Windrush via a fine old bridge. Buildings of particular interest include 15th-century almshouses, the Great House of 1690, and basically Norman church which claims to be the second largest in Oxfordshire. Features of this splendid building include an imposing tower and spire, and somewhat macabre Civil War associations. In 1649 several Cromwellian mutineers were trapped in the building by their own forces, and on capture 3 of the imprisoned men were shot near the churchyard. A restored Elizabethan house now known as The Priory was once the home of Speaker Lenthall, who defied Charles I in the House of Commons.

From the Bull Hotel in Burford follow the unclassified road to Asthall.

ASTHALL, Oxon SP21
The banks of the Windrush afford a delightful view of Asthall Manor, a striking Elizabethan house with mullioned windows and an overall atmosphere of permanence. Alongside is the parish church, which is of Norman origin and features two interesting arches in the north chapel.

Meet a T-junction and turn right SP 'Witney'. Ascend, then turn left on to the B4047 and proceed for $1\frac{3}{4}$ miles to the White Hart (PH). Turn left here on to the unclassified 'Leafield' road. Descend and cross the River Windrush, then turn right into Minster Lovell.

MINSTER LOVELL, Oxon SP31
Clustered stone-built cottages and the fine, partly-timbered Swan Inn nestle together to form this quaint little Windrush village. Of special note are the ruins of a 15th-century hall (AM), which boasts two gruesome legends. The first is of Lord Francis Lovell, who is supposed to have hidden in a secret room after the Lambert Simnel Rising of 1487. His whereabouts was known to only one servant, who died suddenly leaving the unfortunate Lord Francis incarcerated until his skeleton was reputedly discovered in 1718. A similar tale recounts the story of an unfortunate young Lovell bride who decided to hide in a large chest on her Christmas wedding night and became trapped.

Return to the T-junction and turn right for Leafield. Drive to the war memorial, turn left, then continue to the Fox Inn and bear right. Shortly pass the Leafield Radio Station. Continue to Shipton-under-Wychwood and turn right on to the A361 to enter the village.

The peaceful ruins of Minster Lovell Hall are haunted by macabre legends involving death by starvation and suffocation.

SHIPTON-UNDER-WYCHWOOD, Oxon SP21
Restored Shipton Court is of Elizabethan origin and one of the finest buildings in the village; unfortunately it is closed to the public. More easily accessible is a fountain which was raised to the memory of 19 Shipton men who died in the wreck of the ship *Cosipatrick* in 1874. The Shaven Crown Inn has a Tudor gateway.

The church doorway at Windrush is decorated with the carved heads of many exotic beasts.

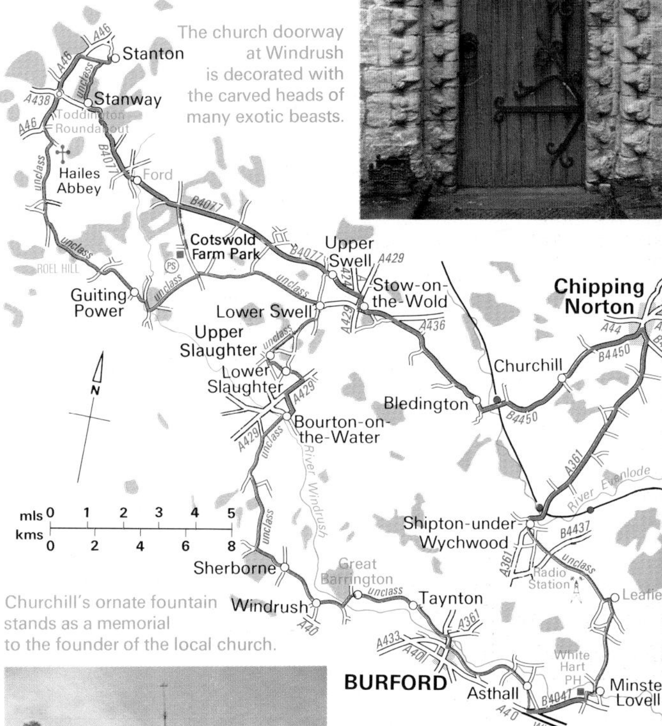

Churchill's ornate fountain stands as a memorial to the founder of the local church.

Cross the River Evenlode and continue to Chipping Norton.

CHIPPING NORTON, Oxon SP32
The 'Chipping' element of this name means 'market', and for a considerable period the 'market at Norton' was the commercial centre for the Evenlode Valley. When the Cotswolds became one giant sheepwalk the town assumed new importance as a gathering place for wool merchants and other traders. Much of the town's attraction today is due to its many survivals from a prosperous past. Among these are numerous 18th-century houses and a 'wool' church that is among the finest in the county. Almshouses of the 17th century and a treadmill that still operates are reminders of the other side of any boom – human exploitation. The Hart and the Crow were both once coaching inns.

Follow the B4450 'Stow' road and drive to Churchill.

CHURCHILL, Oxon SP22
Two famous men were born here ir the 18th century – William Hasting 1st Governor-General of India, and 'The Father of Geology' William Smith, who was the first man to ma the rock strata of England and identify fossils peculiar to each laye A restored church of 1826 crowns nearby hilltop and displays a fine tower which can be seen for miles around. An unusual square-shape fountain with open arches and pinnacles rising from a basin of flowing water stands as a memoria to Squire Langston, the original builder of the church.

Continue to Bledington.

BLEDINGTON, Glos SP22
Situated on the River Evenlode, Bledington boasts its own Victoria maypole and a fine Norman churc containing good examples of old glass. Nearby Maugersbury Hill for an excellent viewpoint.

Later join the A436 for Stow-on-the Wold.

STOW-ON-THE-WOLD, Glos SP12
'Stow-on-the-Wold where the wind blows cold' is a local saying that aptly describes this, the highest hilltop town in the Cotswolds. It is set on a ridge between the upper valleys of the rivers Windrush and Evenlode and has an enormous market square with stocks and a 14th-century cross. This is the focal point of the town. Inside the local church is a splendid 17th-century painting of the Crucifixion by Belgian artist, de Craeyer. Hundreds of Royalists were imprisoned here after a Civil War battle fought in 1646.

Follow SP 'Tewkesbury' to join the B4077 and proceed to Upper Swell.

UPPER SWELL, Glos SP12
This charming and unspoilt village comprises a cluster of houses and a tiny church. Its main feature is a fine manor house.

About 4½ miles farther a road on the left leads to Cotswold Farm Park.

COTSWOLD FARM PARK, Glos SP12
Rare breeds of British farm animals are kept here in an authentic farmyard setting in beautiful countryside on the Cotswold Hills. Major attractions include a pet's corner, young stock, and rides round the park in a pony-drawn trap.

Continue on the B4077 through Ford. Descend to Stanway.

STANWAY, Glos SP03
Magnificent wooded hills surround this attractive small village, which has a tithe barn mentioned in the Domesday Book. Stanway House, a focal point for the community, is approached through an imposing gateway in the style of Inigo Jones.

Meet crossroads and turn right on to an unclassified road, passing the grounds of Stanway House. In 1¼ miles turn right and drive to Stanton.

STANTON, Glos SP03
Larch woods on Shenbarrow Hill shelter this unspoilt village, which is often described as the most attractive in the Cotswolds. Elizabethan Stanton Court and 16th-century Warren House are old manor houses of particular note, and thatched barns add the softness of straw or reed to the picture. Watching over all is the homely sentinel of the restored church.

Return and in ¼ mile bear right SP 'Cheltenham'. In ½ mile turn left on to the A46 and continue to the Toddington roundabout. Keep forward at the roundabout, then in 1 mile take the 2nd turning on the left on to an unclassified road for Hailes Abbey.

HAILES ABBEY, Glos SP02
For many years the 13th-century Cistercian foundation was a thriving centre of learning and religion, attracting pilgrims from all over the country. Nowadays it is a collection of ruins (AM, NT) with a small site museum in which tiles, bosses, and various early relics are preserved.

Return for 200 yds and turn left on to Roel Hill, which affords fine views of the surrounding countryside. Meet a T-junction and turn left, then turn right and continue to Guiting Power.

GUITING POWER, Glos SP02
This picturesque village is attractively situated on the upper reaches of the River Windrush.

In ½ mile meet a T-junction and turn right SP 'Andoversford', then take the next turning left SP 'Stow'. Continue along a quiet country road to Lower Swell.

LOWER SWELL, Glos SP12
Huge copper beeches and stone walls line the route into Lower Swell. In the village the small River Dikler flows past attractive bankside cottages and a working smithy. An elegant Georgian pillar topped by an urn stands on the village green and inside the local church are fine examples of Norman carving.

Turn right on to the A436 SP 'The Slaughters', then turn left on to an unclassified road for Upper Slaughter.

UPPER SLAUGHTER, Glos SP12
An outstanding 3-gabled Elizabethan mansion (open), with 15 tall chimneys and an avenue of mature trees, dominates this beautiful Cotswold village. Also here are a fine 17th- century parsonage and an attractive, partly Norman church.

Lower Slaughter's 19th-century brick mill contrasts sharply with the stone houses elsewhere in the village.

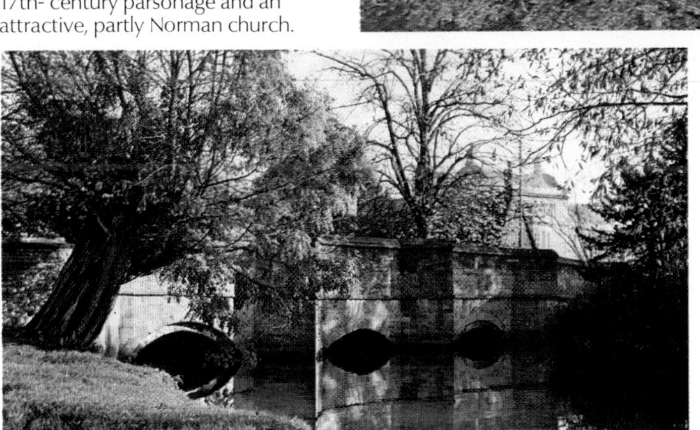

Pollarded willows and the enchantment of running water combine with the mellowness of old Cotswold stone in Burford's ancient river bridge, which spans the Windrush.

Drive to the end of the village and turn left, then continue to the neighbouring village of Lower Slaughter.

LOWER SLAUGHTER, Glos SP12
As the River Eye winds its peaceful course between the rows of charming cottages which flank both its banks in this village it is spanned by many bridges, stone and wooden, and shaded by the dark-green umbrellas of stately yew trees. This scene of rural tranquillity is completed by a church with a 12th-century arcade.

Cross a bridge and turn right, then at the end of the village turn right again on to the A429. In ½ mile turn left on to the B4068 for Bourton-on-the-Water.

BOURTON-ON-THE-WATER, Glos SP12
This Cotswold-stone village – with its churches, shops, houses, sloping lawns alongside the River Windrush, and watermill – is reproduced at one-ninth actual size in the garden of the Old New Inn. Elsewhere in the village are the Birdland Zoo Gardens, some 3½ acres of grounds featuring over 600 exotic species.

Meet crossroads in the village and follow the unclassified 'Sherborne' road. Cross the river and bear right. Ascend, and in 3½ miles turn left for Sherborne.

SHERBORNE, Glos SP11
Number 88, the last cottage on the Windrush road, was once an old chapel and retains a fine Norman doorway. Sherborne House shares extensive grounds with Lodge Park, a charming 19th-century building that was erected as a grandstand for the audiences of deer coursing.

Leave Sherborne and continue to Windrush.

WINDRUSH, Glos SP11
This village is named after the River Windrush. The local church faces a triangular patch of green surrounded by tall trees and has a Norman doorway considered to be one of the best of its type.

Keep left and continue for ¾ mile, then meet a T-junction and turn left for Great Barrington. Drive to the war memorial and bear right for Taynton.

TAYNTON, Oxon SP21
Taynton's thatched grey-stone houses nestle together with a 700-year-old church on timbered slopes above the River Windrush. Stone for the building of Blenheim Palace was supplied by the famous quarries in this area.

In the village turn right on to the A424, then the A361. Cross a river and re-enter Burford.

TOUR 37 70 MILES

GOLD IN THE COTSWOLD COUNTRYSIDE

Here is a mature countryside, first civilized by the Romans, later smoothed by the wealth of medieval clothiers, and finally polished by Regency high fashion. Everywhere is the honey colour of Cotswold stone, giving the name of Gloucestershire's rich Golden Valley another meaning.

The 19th-century lir of Sudeley Cas are complement by beauti formal garde

CHELTENHAM SPA, Glos SO92
Cheltenham started life as a typical Cotswold village, but in 1715 a mineral spring was discovered here. A pump room was built in 1738, George III gave the place his personal approval, and within half a century architects were commissioned to design a new town. The result attracted many people of education and means, who came as much for Cheltenham's fashionable elegance and taste as for its water's vaunted medicinal properties. The architect Papworth was responsible for much that is best in Cheltenham, and Forbes built the famous Pittville Pump Room. Schools flourished too, including the Cheltenham College for Boys of 1841, and the Cheltenham Ladies' College of 1853. Composer Gustav Holst was a pupil at the town's grammar school. Each March Prestbury Park is host to the Cheltenham Gold Cup horse race.

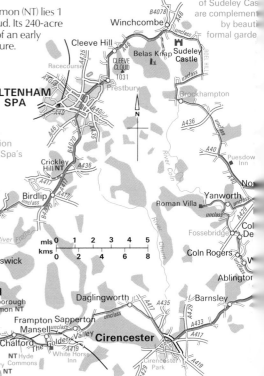

An Ionic temple was the inspiration for Cheltenham Spa's 19th-century Pump Room.

Follow SP 'Stroud A46' then SP 'Birdlip B4070' to leave Cheltenham, then climb Leckhampton Hill. At the top meet the main road and turn right, then enter a roundabout and leave by the 1st exit on to the A417. The 2nd exit leads to delightful Crickley Hill and can be taken as a diversion from the main tour.

CRICKLEY HILL, Glos SO91
This National Trust property comprises 36½ acres of beautiful Cotswold escarpment and an interesting iron-age promontory fort.

Continue along the A417, with magnificent views across the Severn Valley to the Malvern Hills, and enter Birdlip.

BIRDLIP, Glos SO91
Birdlip stands on the edge of the Cotswolds, at an altitude of 900ft. Several mosaic pavements and a well-preserved hypocaust system have been uncovered at the site of a Roman villa to the west.

Turn right on to the B4070, then turn left. After ¾ mile branch right on to the unclassified 'Painswick' road. In 2½ miles meet a T-junction and turn left on to the A46. Continue to Painswick.

PAINSWICK, Glos SO80
Years ago Painswick was an important centre of the cloth industry. This prosperity is evident in its many old houses and inns, amongst which are the tall-chimneyed Court House (associated with Charles I) and 18th-century Painswick House. One of the country's few original bowling greens has been preserved at the Falcon Inn, and a few old cloth mills have survived south of the town. St Mary's Churchyard boasts almost a hundred yews that are kept tidy in a traditional annual clipping ceremony.

Follow the Painswick Valley to Stroud.

STROUD, Glos SO80
Situated on the modest River Frome and the Stroudwater Canal, this town was once reckoned to produce the finest broadcloth in the country. It still makes most of the baize for the world's billiard tables, and has an excellent reputation for its scarlet dyes. A number of 18th-century mills and typical Cotswold cottages have survived, and the 16th-century town hall has been restored.

Follow SP 'Cirencester A419' passing the wide expanse of Rodborough Common.

RODBOROUGH COMMON, Glos SO80
Rodborough Common (NT) lies 1 mile south of Stroud. Its 240-acre site includes part of an early agricultural enclosure.

Painswick's carefully clipped churchyard yews were planted at the end of the 18th century.

After Rodborough Common continue to Brimscombe.

BRIMSCOMBE, Glos SO80
Most of the key buildings in Brimscombe are of relatively recen date. Holy Trinity Church was built 1840, the Atlantis Hotel first saw lig of day as a rectory in 1842, and bo Hope Mill and Port Mill are of 19th-century origin. A few earlier buildir survive at Bourne Mill.

Continue along the pleasant Golde Valley to Chalford.

CHALFORD, Glos SO80
Views from Chalford's steep and narrow streets encompass the ferti Golden Valley, the River Frome, ar stretches of the disused Stroud Canal. An old round house which originally served as a lock-keeper's cottage now houses an interesting museum of canal relics. Thoughts past prosperity are woken by the local mills and wool masters' hous

'HE GOLDEN VALLEY, Glos
he original Golden Valley runs from)orstone to Pontrilas in lerefordshire. The Gloucestershire iolden Valley cradles the River rome and, like its namesake, is nown for peaceful villages and nspoilt countryside.

After 2 miles (from Chalford) reach ie White Horse Inn and turn left on) an unclassified road for Frampton Aansell.

RAMPTON MANSELL, Glos SO90
nportant buildings in this village llow Cotswold tradition by dating ainly from the years of wool osperity. Manor Farmhouse is of e late 17th century, and St Luke's hurch was built in 1844.

ontinue to Sapperton.

APPERTON, Glos SO90
ews from the local churchyard tend along the length of the olden Valley. Cotswold-stone ttages in the area date back to the th century, and Daneway House mile north-west) can claim even eater antiquity, with parts dating at st from the 13th century. The ames and Severn Canal runs rough here via a $2\frac{1}{2}$-mile tunnel rough which 18th- and 19th-ntury bargees propelled their craft lying on their backs and pushing ainst the walls or roof with their t. This was commonly known as gging it'.

rn right, then meet a T-junction d turn left. After 1 mile turn right to glingworth.

AGLINGWORTH, Glos SO90
xon work has survived in the local urch in spite of major 19th-ntury rebuilding.

ntinue, and $\frac{1}{2}$ mile beyond the age turn right on to the A417 for encester.

RENCESTER, Glos SP00
Roman times Cirencester was *rinium Dobunorum*, the second gest town in England and the us of several major highways. hen the Romans withdrew the vn declined, but wool later osted it and wool money paid for Church of St John the Baptist, one he largest of its kind in the ntry. Cirencester House, seat of Earl of Bathurst, shares its 3,000-e park with a folly which tradition ntains was partly designed by xander Pope.

ow SP 'Burford A433' to leave encester. Drive to Barnsley.

RNSLEY, Glos SP00
church at Barnsley was restored he 19th century, but its 16th-tury tower and two ancient ved tables survived. Sir Isaac vton's library was discovered at nsley Park after it had been oved from Thame Park.

tinue to Bibury.

BIBURY, Glos SP10
William Morris thought Bibury 'the most beautiful village in England'. Most of its stone-built houses have gardens that run down to the River Coln, and the Arlington Row (NT) of river-fronted cottages is famous. Near Arlington Mill, which houses a museum, is a bird sanctuary. Bibury Court Hotel is of Jacobean origin, and The Swan – at the end of the street – is a pleasant coaching inn.

Drive to the Swan Inn and take an unclassified road through the Coln Valley to Ablington.

ABLINGTON, Glos SP10
This lovely River Coln community has a late 16th-century manor house with an impressive barn. There is a prehistoric long barrow near by.

After Ablington turn left to cross a river bridge over the Coln. Later turn right into Winson.

WINSON, Glos SP00
Winson Manor dates from 1740, but Manor Farm is of slightly earlier origin. Most of the village cottages are of 17th- or 18th-century date, and the church is early-Norman.

Drive through the village and turn right for Coln Rogers.

COLN ROGERS, Glos SP00
The nave and chancel of local St Andrew's Church are Saxon. Both the Old Rectory, at the south end of the village, and Lower Farm, belong to the 17th century.

Proceed to Coln St Dennis.

COLN ST DENNIS, Glos SP01
Coln St Dennis has a Norman church and a 19th-century rectory. The hotel at Fosse Bridge, a $\frac{1}{4}$ mile to the north-west, is also of 19th-century date. Colnpen is a 300ft long barrow near by.

Turn left for Fossebridge, left again on to the A429, then right on to an unclassified road. Follow SP 'Chedworth Roman Villa'.

CHEDWORTH ROMAN VILLA, Glos SP01
Chedworth Roman Villa dates from the 2nd to 4th centuries, and was rediscovered in 1864. It has various rooms and two bath suites laid out around two courtyards. The site has an excellent museum.

Return for $1\frac{1}{2}$ miles into Yanworth.

YANWORTH, Glos SP01
Traces of wall paintings, fragments of medieval glass, and a Norman font can be seen in Yanworth's 12th-century church.

Continue for 2 miles to the main road. Turn left on to the A429 and drive to the outskirts of Northleach.

NORTHLEACH, Glos SP11
Northleach stands on high ground, east of the Roman Fosse Way, between the Coln and Windrush valleys. Its attractive stone-built cottages and almshouses are dominated by a magnificent wool church. An old gaol still stands.

Continue to traffic signals, turn left on to the A40 'Cheltenham' road, then after $2\frac{3}{4}$ miles pass the Puesdown Inn. After a further $\frac{3}{4}$ mile meet crossroads and turn right on to the unclassified 'Brockhampton' road. Proceed for $2\frac{1}{4}$ miles and cross the main road for Brockhampton. After $\frac{1}{4}$ mile meet crossroads and turn right SP 'Charlton Abbots'. Drive to the next crossroads and turn right SP 'Guiting Power'. Ascend and turn left along Roel Hill, passing Sudeley Castle.

SUDELEY CASTLE, Glos SP02
Catherine Parr, the last of Henry VIII's wives, lived in this medieval castle (open). In 1858 it was reconstructed by Sir Gilbert Scott, who also designed Catherine's tomb to replace one destroyed during the Civil War.

Continue into Winchcombe.

WINCHCOMBE, Glos SP02
Ancient Winchcombe was once capital of the Kingdom of Mercia. The site of its abbey, founded in 797 and destroyed by Henry VIII, is being excavated. The 700-year-old George Inn was once used by pilgrims.

Mellow stone houses nestle amongst rolling Cotswold scenery at Bibury.

Follow the A46 'Cheltenham' road. After $\frac{1}{2}$ mile reach an unclassified left turn leading to prehistoric Belas Knap.

BELAS KNAP, Glos SP02
About 2 miles south-south-west of Winchcombe is the 180ft-long Belas Knap long barrow (AM). This was restored in 1930 and is considered one of the finest of its type extant.

Continue along the A46, with extensive views from the highest area in the Cotswolds.

CLEEVE HILL, Glos SO92
Early 20th-century St Peter's Church shares Cleeve Hill with 17th-century Cockbury Court and 18th-century Hayes. The area is dominated by lofty Cleeve Cloud.

CLEEVE CLOUD, Glos SO92
Overshadowing Cleeve Hill is the massive 1,031ft bulk of Cleeve Cloud, one of the highest points in the Cotswolds. Magnificent views can be enjoyed from its summit.

Continue the descent through Prestbury to Cheltenham, passing the racecourse and airfield on the way.

Several architectural styles are incorporated to glorious effect in Cirencester's parish church.

TOUR 38 

IN THE VALE OF RED HORSE

Relics of ancient man dot the North Cotswold Hills above vales of almost legendary richness, where English fruit and vegetables are raised round villages that grew fat on the profits of wool. Great men lived and died here; great rivers continue to flow.

MORETON-IN-MARSH, Glos SP23
Moreton-in-Marsh is a pleasant small market town under the edge of the north Cotswolds. Among many interesting old inns here are the White Hart, where Charles I slept in 1643, and the famous Redesdale Arms coaching stop. The town's curfew tower carries a 17th-century clock and incorporates an old lock-up once used for local miscreants.

Follow SP 'A44 Oxford' from Moreton-in-Marsh and continue to the Four Shire Stone, on the left of the road.

FOUR SHIRE STONE, Glos SP23
About 2 miles east of Moreton-in-Marsh is the famous Four Shire Stone, where Gloucestershire met Oxfordshire, Warwickshire, and an isolated part of Worcestershire before the county reorganization of the 1970s.

Pass Four Shire Stone and in $\frac{3}{4}$ mile turn right on to an unclassified road for Chastleton.

CHASTLETON, Oxon SP22
Chastleton House is of Cotswold stone and was built by wealthy wool merchant Walter Jones in 1603. His descendants are still in ownership. On the top floor of the house are state rooms and a long gallery, which contain many items of original furniture (open).

Go through Chastleton and after $\frac{1}{2}$ mile turn left. Cross a cattle grid and turn right on to the A44. Pass the Cross Hands (PH) and turn left on to an unclassified road. Proceed to the Rollright Stones.

ROLLRIGHT STONES, Oxon SP23
This important bronze-age monument (AM) comprises two configurations of stones. The circle, nicknamed 'The King's Men', measures a full 100ft across and is close to 'The Whispering Knights' group and an isolated outlier called the 'King's Stone'.

After $\frac{3}{4}$ mile turn left on to the A34 and descend to Long Compton.

LONG COMPTON, Warwicks SP23
A little thatched gatehouse tops the churchyard gate at Long Compton. The church itself is of Norman and later date and preserves an old stone figure of a lady in the porch.

Continue to Shipston-on-Stour

SHIPSTON-ON-STOUR Warwicks SP24
Situated on the edge of the Cotswolds in the Vale of Red Horse, this old wool town has attractive Georgian houses and inns complemented by a 19th-century church incorporating the 500-year-old tower of its predecessor.

Turn left on to the B4035 'Campden' road. Proceed for $1\frac{3}{4}$ miles, cross a main road, and continue for a further $1\frac{1}{2}$ miles through Charingworth. Enter Ebrington.

EBRINGTON, Glos SP14
Delightful cottages of stone and thatch enhance the undoubted appeal of this beautiful Cotswold village. Ebrington Manor shows a great deal of restoration to its basically 17th-century structure.

Drive to the end of the village and keep right, then right again on to an unclassified road SP 'To the Hidcotes'. After $2\frac{1}{4}$ miles turn right for Hidcote Bartrim.

Bidford-on-Avon
Welford-on-Avon
Long Marston
Cleeve Prior
South Littleton
Bretforton
Mickleton
Hidcote Bartrim
Weston Subedge
Willersey
Broadway
Broadway Tower
Snowshill
Ebrington
Charingworth
Shipston on Stour
Chipping Campden
Broad Campden
Blockley
MORETON-IN-MARSH
Four Shire Stone
Bourton on the Hill
Long Compton
Rollright Stones
Cross Hands PH
Little Rollright
Chastleton
River Avon
River Stour
mls 0 1 2 3 4 5
kms 0 2 4 6 8

HIDCOTE BARTRIM, Glos SP14
Hidcote Bartrim boasts a late 17th-century manor surrounded by lovely formal gardens (NT).

Return to the T-junction and turn left, then take the next turning on the right SP 'Mickleton'. Meet the main road and turn right on to the A46 to enter Mickleton.

The Curfew Towe[r] in Moreton-in[-] Marsh is possibl[y] the oldest buildin[g] in the tow[n]

MICKLETON, Glos SP14
Medford House is a superb exampl[e] of Renaissance architecture, and th[e] village itself preserves thatched and timber-framed buildings. Tudor House is an attractive building that probably a good 100 years later tha[n] its name suggests. St Lawrence's Church dates from the 12th centur[y]

Drive through the village and turn le[ft]. After $\frac{1}{2}$ mile continue on to the unclassified road for Long Marston.

LONG MARSTON, Warwicks SP[1]
King's Lodge in Long Marston has associations with King Charles II, w[h]is said to have come here in disgui[se] after the Battle of Worcester. The b[ell] in the village church hangs in a tur[ret] built on great oak beams resting o[n] the floor of the nave. The village its[elf] is a delightful grouping of timber a[nd] thatch cottages in leafy country lanes. It has its own traditional mo[rris] dancing troupe.

Continue to Welford-on-Avon

WELFORD-ON-AVON, Warwicks SP15
Welford-on-Avon's Norman chur[ch] has an ancient lychgate and stand[s] among charming timber-and-that[ch] cottages near a new maypole.

The Rollright Stones have been a Cotswolds feature for thousands of years.

Go forward and later cross the River Avon, then turn left on to the A439 and drive to Bidford-on-Avon.

BIDFORD-ON-AVON, Warwicks SP15
Traditionally this unspoilt village was the birthplace of playwright William Shakespeare. There is little doubt that Tudor Corner House was once the Falcon Inn beloved of both Shakespeare and his contemporary Ben Jonson. Latterly the inn has erved as a workhouse and as a roup of cottages. A fine 15th-entury bridge spans the Avon.

urn left on to the A4085 SP roadway', and cross a bridge. After mile turn right for Cleeve Prior.

LEEVE PRIOR, Herefs & Worcs SP04
he name of this village derives from e priors of Worcester, who were nce lords of the manor here. Tall himneys and a priest's hole that nce hid Charles I's banker are atures of the Jacobean manor ouse. Stone-built cottages overlook e triangular green, and the 15th-ntury King's Arms still offers omfort to the traveller.

ontinue to South Littleton.

OUTH LITTLETON, erefs & Worcs SP04
orth, Middle, and South Littleton e a picturesque group of tiny Avon alley villages. North Middleton has manor house, a tithe barn, a ovecote, and a church that is nsidered to be of great chitectural merit. South Littleton asts a beautiful early 18th-century use.

ontinue along the same road for a ther 1 mile, then go over a level ossing and turn left on to the classified 'Bretforton' road. ntinue to Bretforton.

ETFORTON, refs & Worcs SP04
ree tributaries of the Avon drain lovely countryside round this cient village. Of particular note e are the 600-year-old Fleece Inn d medieval Grange Farm. The er, changed greatly from its ginal form by successive owners, e shelter to Prince Rupert in 1645. country's largest collection of ecotes survives here, including eral very old examples and one t has been made into a cottage.

the B4035 and continue to ston-Subedge.

STON-SUBEDGE, Glos SP14
eral appealing 17th-century ses preserved in the main street is village include Latimer's, a icularly fine example associated the historic bishop of that e. Bank House and Riknild are of note. Slightly later than these e Manor House, and the 'old' tory was built in the 19th ury.

t a T-junction, turn right on to the , and pass through Willersey.

Chipping Campden's arched Market Hall was built in 1627.

WILLERSEY, Glos SP13
The 6 bells of Willersey's Church of St Peter were re-cast from the original 3 in 1712 and rung the following year to celebrate the Treaty of Utrecht. Various medieval styles can be seen in the building itself. Willersey House was once a farmhouse in the village, but in 1912 was dismantled and rebuilt at the top of a hill in its present enlarged form.

Later meet a T-junction and turn right on to the A44 into Broadway.

BROADWAY, Herefs & Worcs SP13
Broadway's wide main street is lined with fine houses and pretty cottages built in Cotswold stone.
St Eadburgha's Norman and later church is somewhat self-effacingly hidden away at one end of the community, and the 17th-century Lygon Arms coaching inn shows a narrow frontage to the street.

Drive to the end of the green and turn left on to an unclassified road to Snowshill. Ascend, then bear right into the village.

SNOWSHILL, Glos SP03
Secluded Snowshill is a hillside village of ancient Cotswold cottages grouped round a handsome 19th-century church. Its manor house (NT) dates from the 16th century, but subsequent periods have left their marks in various alterations and additions. Inside are collections of clocks, toys, and musical instruments.

Continue to the church and turn left. Ascend to the top of the incline and meet crossroads. Go forward SP 'Chipping Campden, Broadway Tower'. After $1\frac{3}{4}$ miles turn left and proceed to Broadway Tower.

BROADWAY TOWER, Herefs & Worcs SP13
Lady Coventry built this picturesque folly tower in the 18th century, and it now forms the nucleus of a 30-acre country park. Its lofty situation at over 1,000ft gives views over several counties, and in very clear weather it is possible to pick out such landmarks as Tewkesbury Abbey, Worcester Cathedral, and Warwick.

Continue for $\frac{1}{2}$ mile, cross a main road with SP 'Mickleton', and after $\frac{3}{4}$ mile turn right. Continue for $2\frac{1}{2}$ miles and meet a T-junction. Turn right on to the B4081 for Chipping Campden.

Welford-on-Avon is a picturebook village set in a pastoral landscape.

CHIPPING CAMPDEN, Glos SP13
Wool made Chipping Campden rich, and the handiwork of the merchants who prospered here can be seen in the fine gabled stone houses, the 14th-century Woolstaplers Hall, and the 15th-century wool church. Near the church are remains of the once-beautiful Campden House, whose owner burned it down in 1645 rather than see it fall into Parliamentarian hands.

Drive through the town and turn left with the B4081 SP 'Broad Campden'. After $\frac{1}{4}$ mile turn left again on to an unclassified road for Broad Campden.

BROAD CAMPDEN, Glos SP13
Features of this village include an 18th-century Friends' Meeting House that has been restored and the much older Chapel House – a 12th-century chapel recently converted into a private dwelling.

Keep right through the village and climb to Blockley.

BLOCKLEY, Glos SP13
Blockley's architecture follows the usual basic pattern for the area, with a high street of 18th- and 19th-century houses complementing a Norman church.

Turn left, continue for a short distance, then turn right on to the B4479. Proceed for $1\frac{1}{2}$ miles, meet a T-junction, and turn left on to the A44. Pass through Bourton-on-the-Hill.

BOURTON-ON-THE-HILL, Glos SP13
A fine example of a Winchester bushel can be seen in Bourton's Norman and later church. The village itself stands on a hill and is made up of cottages standing in attractively-terraced gardens. Bourton House is of 18th-century date and has a superb 16th-century tithe barn.

Return to Moreton-in-Marsh.

Llyn Ogwen lies in a steep-sided valley cut millions of years ago by the immense glaciers which shaped the face of Snowdonia as we see it today. This majestic lake is the gateway to what is surely the most spectacular mountain pass in North Wales.

Wales and the Marcher Lands

TOUR 39 67 MILES

BESIDE THE BRISTOL CHANNEL

For many centuries the Bristol Channel has admitted traders and invaders to the heartlands of the Severn Valley, and more recently it has provided a route for the export of Welsh coal. Picturesquely ruined castles recall troubled times; great harbours proclaim the industrial prosperity of today.

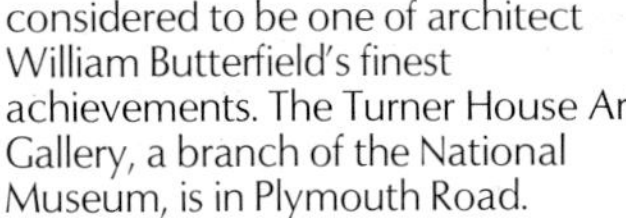

CARDIFF, S Glam ST17
Utilitarian in parts, though not depressingly so, Cardiff displays the mixture of dignity and pragmatism to be expected from the capital city and cultural centre of Wales. Massive expansion resulted in the town becoming the world's principal coal port by the start of the 20th century, and much of its present-day appearance can be directly attributed to this era. One family particularly involved in the city's growth was the Butes, who built the vast docks, sank a fortune into the development of the town as a living and working community, and restored the castle. The latter, an appealing mixture of genuine period remains and 19th-century reconstruction, was the brainchild of the 3rd Marquess, working with architect William Burges. Inside the perimeter walls the handsome Norman keep surmounts a motte surrounded by a defensive moat. In direct contrast, and well distant in a 'gothick' complex, are 19th-century living quarters that reveal the full expression of romantic medievalism so loved by Bute and the famous Burges. Cardiff's principal buildings stand quite close to the castle in Cathay's Park and include the City Hall and County Hall, the University College and the National Museum of Wales. The Llandaf district is situated north-west of the city centre and can be reached through some of Cardiff's elegant parks. Here, in a village-like setting, is the city's cathedral, an historic building which was almost destroyed by the ravages of time but is now fully restored to its old splendour. Its south-east tower and spire form a delicate and familiar local landmark. Other interesting features in the town include quaint Victorian arcades and the famous Cardiff Arms Park Rugby Ground, where beer and brawn are parts of a sporting ritual that demonstrates the indomitable Welsh character and holds all Wales in its grip.

Leave Cardiff via the A4160 'Penarth' road. After 3 miles enter a roundabout and leave by the 1st exit. After a further 1 mile enter Penarth.

The Norman keep and later, 19th-century, buildings at Cardiff Castle stand within walls that date partly from Roman times.

Real gold adds splendour to the 19th-century buildings at Cardiff Castle.

Ogmore Castle was founded by a Norman knight called William de Londres.

PENARTH, S Glam ST17
During the second half of the 19th century Penarth was adopted by well-to-do Victorians and transformed into a seaside resort. Gardens and lawns lend quiet charm to the pleasant atmosphere of the town, and the old harbour has found a new lease of life with water ski-ing and sailing enthusiasts. Dangerous currents make bathing hazardous. St Augustine's Church, on the headland, was built in 1865 and is considered to be one of architect William Butterfield's finest achievements. The Turner House Art Gallery, a branch of the National Museum, is in Plymouth Road.

Enter a roundabout and leave by the 2nd exit on to an unclassified road. Descend Beach Road to the Esplanade and drive forward into Raisdale Road. Cross a railway bridge, meet crossroads, and turn left. After ¼ mile turn left on to the B4267 SP 'Sully, Barry'. After 1 mile turn left on to the unclassified 'Swanbridge' road and pass Sully Island.

SWANBRIDGE, S Glam ST16
At low tide Sully Island becomes accessible from here. Views from t 'island' encompass much of the Bristol Channel and are constantly changing with the coming and go of Bristol's sea traffic.

Return to the B4267 and turn left. F the edge of Sully and after 1 mile tu left on to the A4055 and enter Barr After 1 mile turn right under a railw bridge, then keep forward at ensui roundabouts SP 'Barry Island'. Pass Barry Station, bear left, and shortly turn left to reach Barry Island.

BARRY, S Glam ST16
In the 19th century Barry's population expanded from 500 tc

staggering 12,665, and side by side with the development of docks that were to become among the largest n the world came the popularization of the Barry Island holiday resort. Nowadays the resort has everything or the holiday-maker, including fun airs, gardens etc; Park Road leads to Porthkerry Country Park, passing scant remains of Barry Castle on the way. Scrapped British Rail steam ocomotives rust away in a metal breaker's yard here.

Return across the causeway and keep orward on the A4050 'Cardiff' road. Enter a roundabout and leave by the st exit SP 'Cowbridge'. Enter the next oundabout and leave by the 1st exit P 'Llantwit Major'. After a mile turn eft on to the unclassified 'Rhoose' oad. After $\frac{3}{4}$ mile enter a roundabout nd leave by the 1st exit. Shortly pass Cardiff Airport on the right and ontinue, with views left across the ristol Channel, to Rhoose.

HOOSE, S Glam ST06
hoose, a small village within rather oisy range of Cardiff Airport, has ecently become a popular resort.

ontinue through Aberthaw. After mile meet a T-junction and turn left n to the B4265. Cross the River Thaw nd enter St Athan.

T ATHAN, S Glam ST06
wo 14th-century effigies and a ndow commemorating the oronation of George VI can be seen St Athan's medieval church.

ontinue on the B4265 to Boverton, n left on to an unclassified road, d continue to Llantwit Major.

ANTWIT MAJOR, S Glam SS96
nce this quiet place was one of the ost important and influential ntres of learning in British ristendom. The school founded re by 5th-century St Illtud racted scholars from distant parts d fostered some of the greatest nds of early Welsh history. A faint ho of the foundation survives in 13th- and 15th-century Church St Illtud – a remarkable structure med by two churches joined end end. Inside are a richly-carved se Tree, depicting Christ's descent n the line of David, and a ection of ancient stone crosses. her features of the town include old dovecote and monastery eway, a 15th-century town hall, Old Swann Inn, and the osing Great House (open to the blic on application).

s through the village and turn left to the B4265. Continue through cal Vale of Glamorgan scenery to ride's Major.

RIDE'S MAJOR, M Glam SS87
dieval tombs of the Butler family Dunraven are preserved in the l church, which carries a massive lemented tower.

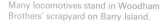

Many locomotives stand in Woodham Brothers' scrapyard on Barry Island.

Turn left on to the B4524 'Southerndown' road, and continue to Southerndown.

SOUTHERNDOWN, M Glam SS87
This small resort is a good starting point for exhilarating walks to Ogmore-by-Sea and the windy headland of Trwyn-y-Witch (Witches Nose). Curious blowholes and wave-carved caves are features of the local cliffs.

Continue to Ogmore-by-Sea.

OGMORE-BY-SEA, M Glam SS87
Sandy beaches and pleasant cliff walks make this a popular Bristol Channel resort; at low tide a more sinister side is revealed in the shape of Tusker Rock – notorious cause of dozens of shipwrecks.

Continue through enchanting wooded scenery to Ogmore Castle, on the other side of the River Ogmore from Candleston Castle.

OGMORE CASTLE, M Glam SS87
This Norman castle (AM), on the River Ogmore, has a somewhat battered stone keep that is one of the earliest of its type.

CANDLESTON CASTLE, M Glam SS87
A footpath and stepping stones across the River Ogmore lead from Ogmore Castle to the tree-shrouded and dilapidated remains of Candleston. During the 15th century it overlooked a wide fertile plain, which has since been overwhelmed by sand dunes.

Continue on the B4524. After $1\frac{1}{2}$ miles meet a junction and keep forward on to the B4265, passing the edge of Ewenny.

EWENNY, M Glam SS97
In 1141 Maurice de Londres, of Ogmore Castle, founded a priory here. Its remains (AM) are in beautiful surroundings and comprise the virtually complete 13th-century circuit walls, fragments of various buildings, and a Norman church considered to be the finest of its kind in Wales. Massive defensive details are reminders of the precarious balance that existed between war and peace in medieval Wales.

Cross the Ewenny River and in 1 mile cross the A48 to enter Bridgend.

Stryt Lydan Barn at St Fagan's Folk Museum originally stood in the one-time Welsh county of Flintshire.

BRIDGEND, M Glam SS97
This large industrial town is split into the districts of Nolton and Newcastle by the River Ogmore. Newcastle derives its name from the town's 12th-century castle (AM).

Follow SP 'Blackmill, A4061' to leave Bridgend. After $1\frac{1}{2}$ miles turn right on to an unclassified road SP 'Coity'. Drive to Coity, turn left on to the 'Bryncethin' road, and pass the entrance to Coity Castle.

COITY, M Glam SS98
Coity Castle (AM) dominates the centre of its namesake village. Nearby St Mary's Church contains several interesting monuments, and features a beautiful east window made by William Morris' company.

Leave Coity and ascend with hill views. Descend to join the B4280, turn right on to the A4061 under a railway bridge, and bear right into Bryncethin. Continue along the wooded Ogmore Valley to Blackmill, and turn right on to the A4093 'Tonyrefail' road. Continue through farm and moorland scenery to the edge of Tonyrefail. Turn right on to the unclassified 'Thomastown, Llantrisant' road, and after $1\frac{1}{4}$ miles turn right again on to the A4119. Follow the Ely River, then beyond Coed Ely Colliery pass Llantrisant Forest and enter Llantrisant.

LLANTRISANT, M Glam ST08
Both church and castle command dominating hilltop sites above the steep attractive streets of Llantrisant. The Royal Mint was moved here in 1967.

Enter the roundabout in Llantrisant and take the 2nd exit on to the A4119 SP 'Cardiff'. After $\frac{1}{2}$ mile bear left and in $1\frac{1}{2}$ miles meet the Groesfaen crossroads. Turn right on to the unclassified 'Peterston-Super-Ely' road. Pass under the M4 motorway, then after $1\frac{1}{2}$ miles meet crossroads and turn left SP 'St Brides-super-Ely'. After 1 mile turn left on to the St Fagan's road. After another 2 miles meet crossroads and turn right to enter St Fagan's.

ST FAGAN'S, S Glam ST17
Attractive thatched cottages and a waterside church are charming features of this River Ely village, but St Fagan's is best known for the amazing collection of buildings that has been gathered round its castle to form the National Folk Museum of Wales. Complete buildings of many different periods have been rescued from all over Wales and painstakingly rebuilt in the grounds. Even the furnished interiors are authentic, and in some cases the buildings still fulfil their original functions.

Turn left, following the river, and keep forward through the Cardiff suburbs. Finish the tour by returning to the city centre.

SWANSEA, W Glam SS69
Almost three centuries of intensive industrialization have left indelible scars upon the Swansea landscape. The lower Swansea Valley presents a view of unparalleled devastation, and it is said that pollution was once so bad even weeds would not grow in the sterile ground. Not all of Swansea is built over or barren; over 900 acres of tended parkland bring the country into the city. Bombing during World War II flattened the town's centre and destroyed much of Swansea's tangible history, but scant remains of a 14th-century fortified manor house (AM) can be seen in Wind Street, and 15th-century St Mary's Church was rebuilt in 1955. In 1919 the former Technical College became a university which has since expanded to occupy several buildings in the town. Close to Swansea, in complete contrast, is the lovely Gower Peninsula.

THE GOWER PENINSULA, W Glam
Virtually on Swansea's doorstep, this small 18- by 5-mile peninsula contains some of the most unspoilt and beautiful scenery in South Wales. Cliffs fringing excellent beaches on the southern coast are considered to be among the finest in Britain, and the soft agricultural landscape of the interior is scored by numerous thickly-wooded valleys. Ancient remains point to the Gower's one-time colonization by the Celts and Romans, and reminders of later times are everywhere in the shapes of ruined castles.

Leave Swansea on the A4067 SP 'Mumbles and Gower'. Pass the university, and after $1\frac{1}{4}$ miles follow SP ahead for 'Mumbles'. After $1\frac{1}{2}$ miles reach Oystermouth.

OYSTERMOUTH, W Glam SS68
Picturesque Oystermouth Castle is a 13th-century ruin which occupies the summit of a small hill above a holiday and residential area.

Detour straight ahead on the B4433 to reach The Mumbles seaside resort.

THE MUMBLES, W Glam SS68
In 1807 a horse-drawn tramway was opened between Swansea and The Mumbles as the first passenger-carrying railway in the world. The line was closed in 1960, but The Mumbles remains a popular resort offering a good beach, a pier, and the facilities for a variety of water-based leisure activities. Mumbles Head is the starting point for delightful walks to Bracelet Bay.

From Oystermouth turn right on to the B4593 SP 'Langland'. In $\frac{1}{4}$ mile reach the church and turn left, then in $\frac{1}{2}$ mile meet crossroads and keep forward along an unclassified road. Descend to Langland Bay.

LANGLAND BAY, W Glam SS68
A sandy beach and views which extend across the Bristol Channel to Somerset are the main features of this popular little bay.

TOUR 40 55 MILES

SWANSEA AND THE GOLDEN GOWER

The counties of Glamorgan form an area of contrasts, where astonishing scenes of industrial dereliction rub shoulders with the rural and coastal beauty of the Gower Peninsula, the green lung of Swansea.

Drive to the carpark at Langland Bay and turn right into Brynfield Road. After $\frac{1}{2}$ mile go forward on to the B4593. Descend to pass Caswell Bay, then continue forward along an unclassified road and ascend inland. After $\frac{3}{4}$ mile meet a T-junction and turn left. Follow the road as it turns right to reach Bishopston.

BISHOPSTON, W Glam SS58
An interesting old church survives in this village, but the main attraction here is the local scenery. Lovely Bishopston Valley leads down to Pwll-du Bay and Head, and marvellous cliff ranges extend along the coast (NT) to the west.

Continue from Bishopston, and after $1\frac{1}{4}$ miles turn left on to the B4436 SP 'Port Eynon'. Drive through Kittle and after $\frac{1}{2}$ mile turn right. After $\frac{3}{4}$ mile turn left on to the A4118 SP 'Parkmill and Port Eynon'. Continue to Parkmill.

Swansea Docks have their origin in the 14th century, when a charter confirmed the town's right to build ships.

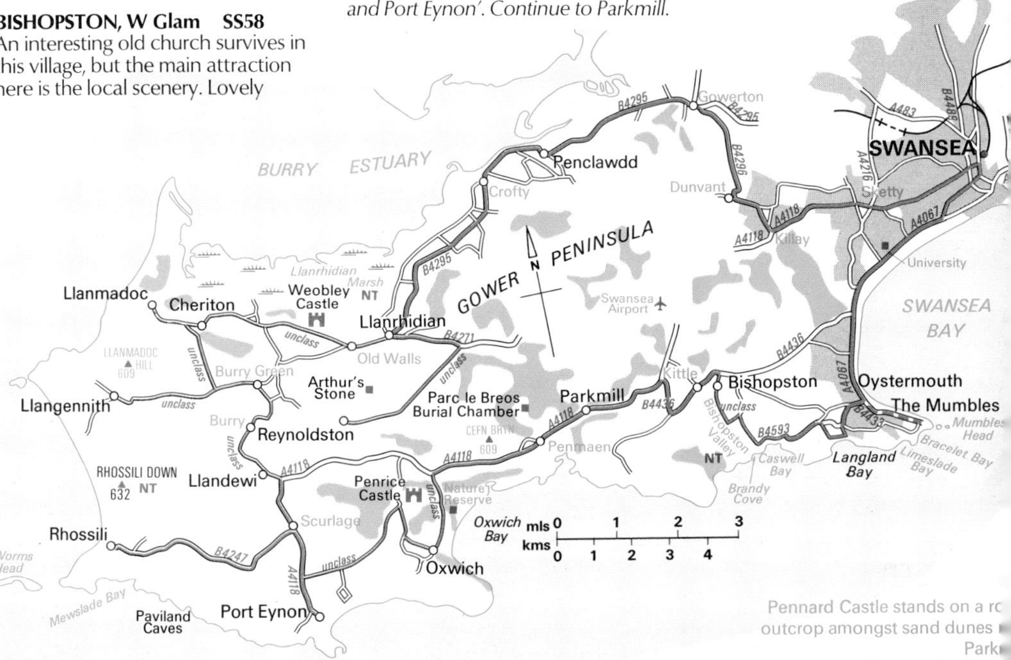

Pennard Castle stands on a ro outcrop amongst sand dunes Park

PARKMILL, W Glam SS58
Ilston Stream flows through Parkmill and continues past the ruins of Pennard Castle to its outlet at beautiful Threecliff Bay (NT). Extensive wind-sculpted sand-dunes hereabouts are known to have buried two churches and threatened to engulf the castle. Near by is the prehistoric Parc Le Breos tomb.

PARC LE BREOS BURIAL CHAMBER, W Glam SS58
This fine example of megalithic tomb architecture (AM) can be reached on foot along a path from Parkmill.

Continue through Penmaen and pass the ridge of 609ft Cefn Bryn on the right. Several paths afford access to this eminence, which makes a fine viewpoint. After 1¾ miles reach the entrance to Penrice Castle.

PENRICE CASTLE, W Glam SS48
Open only by written application, ruined Penrice Castle dates from the 13th century and was built to replace an earlier structure which occupied the mound near Penrice Church.

Leave the castle and turn left on to the unclassified 'Oxwich' road. Descend through pleasant woods to marshland behind Oxwich Bay.

OXWICH BAY, W Glam SS58
Sand-dunes and marshlands behind Oxwich Bay comprise a large National Nature Reserve which protects a wide variety of flora and fauna. Access is restricted to permit holders, but Oxwich Bay itself has superb sands and excellent scenery that can be enjoyed by anyone.

Continue into Oxwich.

OXWICH, W Glam SS48
Thatched and whitewashed cottages more suggestive of England than South Wales are a feature of Oxwich, and the pleasant local church stands shaded by sycamores at the village edge. Inside the church is the lovely de la Mare tomb, installed by the Norman-rooted family who once owned Oxwich Castle (AM). The castle was rebuilt as a Tudor manor house in 1541, but still incorporates relics from the original 14th-century stronghold. At time of publication the structure was closed for repairs.

Drive to the crossroads in Oxwich and turn right. After ½ mile reach a junction and turn right SP 'Port Eynon'. After ¾ mile reach another junction and turn left SP 'Horton'. After 2 miles meet crossroads and continue straight across. Within 1 mile turn left on to the A4118 and descend to Port Eynon.

PORT EYNON, W Glam SS48
Situated at the bottom of a steep hill and noted as a surfing centre, Port Eynon preserves several thatched cottages and lies east of breathtaking cliff scenery (NT).

Close to Port Eynon are the fascinating Paviland Caves.

PAVILAND CAVES, W Glam SS48
Hidden in the cliffs to the west of Port Eynon are the famous Paviland Caves, which have yielded the bones of prehistoric animals and a unique ceremonial burial of a young paleolithic man.

Return along the A4118 from Port Eynon and after 1¾ miles reach Scurlage. Turn left on to the B4247 and continue to Rhossili, below Rhossili Down.

RHOSSILI AND RHOSSILI DOWN, W Glam SS48
Golden sand stretches round the whole 3-mile arc of Rhossili Bay from spectacular Worm's Head (NT), where there is a large sea-bird colony. Behind the village is Rhossili Down (NT), which rises to 632ft and is known for its distinctive flora.

Return along the B4247 to Scurlage and turn left on to the A4118. After 1 mile go forward along an unclassified road SP 'Llandewi and Burry'. Continue to Llandewi.

LLANDEWI, W Glam SS48
Features of this tiny village include a lovely rural setting and a primitive little church which preserves an ancient font in its well-scrubbed interior.

Leave Llandewi and continue through Burry to reach Burry Green. At Burry Green turn left and enter Llangennith.

LLANGENNITH, W Glam SS49
During the 6th century St Cenydd founded a monastery here. This was adopted by Norman monks in the 12th century, and today a few remains of its buildings are preserved in the structures of College Farm. The nearby church is sited on a sloping green and displays the best example of a saddle back-roofed tower in the Gower Peninsula. Nearby Llanmadoc Hill, which is crowned by a hillfort called the Bulwark, affords excellent views.

Return along the 'Burry Green' road. After 1½ miles turn left and drive to Cheriton. Just before Cheriton, slightly off the route, is Llanmadoc village.

LLANMADOC, W Glam SS49
Reached via a lane from Cheriton, this small village has a medieval church displaying many interesting features, not the least of which is a triangular door. Near by are the wild and wind-haunted expanses of Whiteford Burrows (NT).

On the main route, drive to Cheriton.

CHERITON, W. Glam SS49
David Davis, a former rector, executed much of the woodwork displayed in the local church. Many ancient features are preserved in the structure of the tiny 13th-century building itself.

From Cheriton continue east to Weobley Castle.

Planned additions to 14th-century Weobley Castle were never built because of financial difficulties.

WEOBLEY CASTLE, W Glam SS49
Medieval Weobley Castle (AM) overlooks Llanrhidian Marsh from a lovely setting that belies its war-like function. It was built during the 13th and 14th centuries, and is more a fortified manor house than a castle.

Continue through Old Walls and enter Llanrhidian.

LLANRHIDIAN, W Glam SS49
A mysteriously-carved stone stands in the church porch here, and near by are two ancient upright stones of equally enigmatic purpose. Llanrhidian Marshes (NT), more typical of East Anglia than Wales, are rich in wildlife.

Drive to the end of the village and turn right on to the B4271 SP 'Swansea'. After 1¼ miles turn right on to an unclassified road for a short detour to Reynoldston.

REYNOLDSTON AND ARTHUR'S STONE, W Glam SS48
Reynoldston's Victorian church stands on the west flank of Cefn Bryn mountain and contains various 17th- and 18th-century monuments. Arthur's Stone, on the ridge of Cefn Bryn, is a prehistoric tomb covered by an enormous capstone.

Return to Llanrhidian and turn right on to the B4295. Pass through Crofty to enter Penclawdd.

PENCLAWDD, W Glam SS59
Cockle gathering on the nearby sands is a traditional occupation of the Penclawdd women, but the famous pony-drawn carts on which they carried their spoils are not as much in evidence as they were before the last war.

Continue to Gowerton. Meet crossroads and go forward, then bear right on to the B4296. Reach Dunvant and turn left into the suburbs of Swansea. Follow SP 'Swansea' to Killay and join the A4118. Continue through Sketty to Swansea town centre.

The outline of Worm's Head resembles a recumbent dragon – hence its name.

TOUR 41 88 MILES

ON THE BLACK MOUNTAIN

Infinite shades of green colour this tour: pale hillsides rise from ruined Talley Abbey; lush farmland borders the winding Afon Tywi; and the light-shifting subtlety of moorland sedges surrounds the giant Llyn Brianne Reservoir and climbs the Black Mountain.

Coarse grass and moorland sedges blanket the undulating ridges of the Black Mountain, which is traversed by twisting mountain roads.

LLANDEILO, Dyfed SN62
This riverside market town stands amid rich farming land and is a good centre for fishing and touring. Many places of interest exist in the surrounding area. A 19th-century stone bridge in the town arches over the River Tywi in a magnificent single span of 145ft. Llandeilo's church, virtually rebuilt between 1848 and 1851, contains two attractive cross heads of Celtic origin.

Leave Llandeilo on the A40 'Llandovery' road and in $\frac{1}{2}$ mile reach the B4302 turnoff on the left. This may be taken as a detour to picturesque Talley by turning left and driving 6 miles through the hamlets of Maerdy and Halfway. After Halfway a left turn leads into Talley village.

TALLEY, Dyfed SN63
Neat cottages and an attractive church protectively cluster round the remains of once-famous Talley Abbey, deep in the green folds of the Dyfed hills. Little of the abbey's 12th-century fabric has survived pillaging for building material that has gone on unchecked through the centuries, but an undeniable air of sanctity still exists. A path through the yard of the adjacent church leads to the two lakes of Talley, where clouds of dragonflies hover over the placid waters during the summer months.

Continue along the A40 (on the main route) from the start of the Talley detour and pass through pleasant hill scenery to Llandovery.

LLANDOVERY, Dyfed SN73
Llandovery's name means 'Church amid the waters' and derives from its position at the confluence of the Bran, Gwydderig, and Tywi. The town has been a place of some significance at least since Roman times, a fact highlighted by the siting of Llanfair-ar-y-Bryn Church within the ramparts of a Roman fort. Roman tiles are incorporated in the fabric of the church. A monument to William Williams, a local man who is most remembered as being the composer of the hymn *Guide Me O Thou Great Jehovah* stands in the churchyard. Another notable inhabitant of Llandovery was Rhys Pritchard, who wrote a collection of simple verses collectively called *The Welshman's Candle*. This work became as popular in Wales as Bunyan's *Pilgrim's Progress* did in England. A reminder of the town's important connexions with cattle droving is the building which houses Lloyd's Bank. Until 1909 this was the Black Ox Bank, founded in 1799 by a drover named David Jones. The nearby Market Hall is a low 19th-century building capped by an extraordinary pepper-pot turret. Llandovery College, a public school founded in 1848, was created for the express purpose of providing an education entirely in the Welsh language. Overgrown remains of a Norman castle surmount a mound above the cattle market.

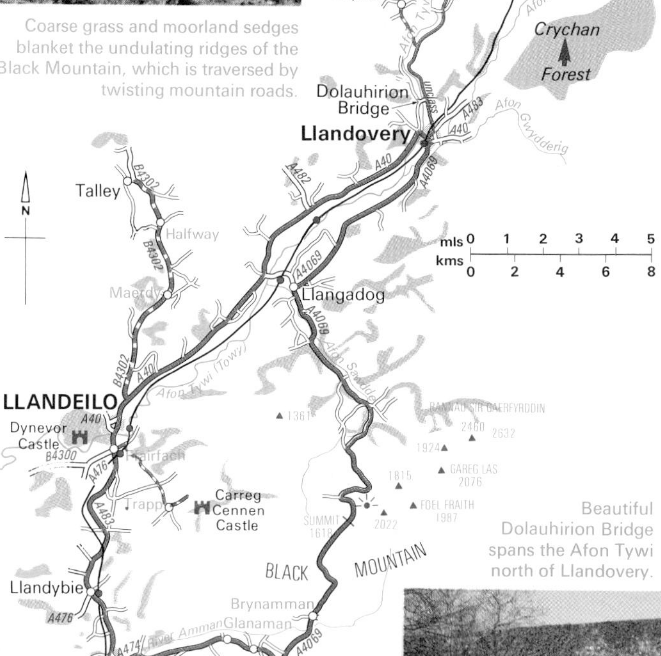

Rhys ap Gruffydd founded Talley Abbe during the 12th century.

Drive over the level crossing in Llandovery and turn left on to the A483 SP 'Builth Wells'. In $\frac{1}{4}$ mile mee crossroads and turn left on to the unclassified 'Rhandirmwyn' road. In $1\frac{3}{4}$ miles reach the bridge at Dolauhirion.

DOLAUHIRION BRIDGE, Dyfed SN73
Designed by William Edwards and built in 1773, this splendid bridge spans the Tywi in a single graceful arch of 84ft.

Continue through increasingly spectacular scenery, with Crychan Forest behind a high ridge to the eas

CRYCHAN FOREST, Dyfed & Powys SN84
This large forest is named after the little Afon Crychan. The forest itself extends almost from Llandove to Llanwrtyd Wells and is bounded the east by the moorland of Mynyc Eppynt.

About $1\frac{3}{4}$ miles from Dolauhirion a left turn from the main tour route leads to Cilycwm village.

Beautiful Dolauhirion Bridge spans the Afon Tywi north of Llandovery.

CILYCWM, Dyfed SN74
Situated in one of the tributary valleys of the Tywi, Cilycwm is surrounded by some of the wildest scenery in South Wales and is noted for the old wall paintings in its 15th-century church. The village chapel is claimed to be the first Methodist meeting place to have existed in Wales.

Continue through Rhandirmwyn on the main route. Farther up the valley on the left is a signposted footpath leading to Twm Sion Catti's Cave.

TWM SION CATTI'S CAVE, Dyfed SN74
A short nature trail up Dinas Hill leads to the one-time hideout of Twm Sion Catti, a famous early 16th-century outlaw whose modern reputation has a lot in common with England's tales of Robin Hood.

Continue through a wooded gorge to reach the carpark and viewing area at Llyn Brianne Reservoir. A narrow but excellently surfaced road may be taken through magnificent scenery to the reservoir's farthest arm and Towy Forest.

LLYN BRIANNE RESERVOIR, Dyfed & Powys SN85
The creation of this huge reservoir in the early 1970s was greeted with mixed emotions, as the area flooded had previously been considered one of the most remote and beautiful in Wales – if not all Britain. New roads to the lake have made it easily accessible, and the spectacular scenery that surrounds its great expanse can be enjoyed by all. The ast British nesting sites of the kite exist in closely-guarded and highly-secret locations in this area.

TOWY FOREST, Dyfed & Powys SN85
On the northern slopes of Llyn Brianne, accessible via the new reservoir road, are the coniferous anks of Towy Forest. The Afon Tywi has its source some miles north in the wild moors of central Wales.

Return along the Llyn Brianne access road to the main route at Llandovery. Turn right and then left on to the A40 SP 'Brecon'. Take the next turning ght on to the A4069, SP 'Llangadog', nd continue along the Tywi Valley to each Llangadog.

LANGADOG, Dyfed SN72
Llangadog was once an important own, with a 12th-century native Welsh castle unusual in that it was robably using defensive techniques earned from the Norman onquerors. The overlords, ever wary f opposition, completely destroyed in 1277. All that remains today is a mound sited about $\frac{1}{2}$ mile south of he village. Carn Goch, the largest on-age hillfort in Wales, lies 3 miles outh-west at OS SN689243.

ontinue to a T-junction and turn left, P 'Brynamman'. Follow the pretty fon Sawdde Valley with the river on e left and ascend on to the slopes of e Black Mountain. Continue to the 600ft viewpoint.

Associated in legend with one of King Arthur's knights, Carreg Cennen Castle is perched dramatically on a limestone cliff overlooking the Black Mountain.

BLACK MOUNTAIN, Dyfed
West from the A4069 viewpoint the Black Mountain falls away in ridges to the fertile Tywi Valley. In the middle distance Carreg Cennen Castle can be seen perched on its craggy limestone cliff, and to the east the grass-covered peaks of 1,987ft Foel Fraith and 2,076ft Gareg Las rise against a long backdrop provided by the ridge of Bannau Sir Gaerfyrddin – The Carmarthen Van. Geologically the Black Mountain is made up of very ancient red sandstone in the north and younger millstone grit in the south, the two beds being separated by a band of limestone. It is a lonely windswept land inhabited only by sheep and a thriving population of indigenous wild animals.

Descend, with views over a partly industrial area, to Brynamman. Turn right for Gwaun-cae-gurwen and on the nearside of the ensuing level crossing turn right again on to the A474. Drive through Garnant and Glanaman to Ammanford.

AMMANFORD, Dyfed SN61
Until the late 19th century the Cross Inn at the centre of this town was almost the only building here, but discovery of a local anthracite coalfield quickly brought the mixed blessing of industrial prosperity. Nowadays the area is dotted with slag heaps from the workings, but the essentially agricultural character of the local countryside remains.

Drive to traffic signals in Ammanford and turn right on to the A483 SP 'Llandeilo'. Proceed to Llandybie.

LLANDYBIE, Dyfed SN61
This small town stands on the edge of the local coalfield and is justifiably proud of its splendid early Victorian railway station. The church preserves a medieval barrel roof and carries an imposing battlemented tower. Inside are a number of interesting monuments. A lane leads east from Llandybie to beautiful river scenery and the waterfall of Glynhir.

Llyn Brianne serves as a storage reservoir for the Afon Tywi water supply scheme.

Continue to Ffairfach. A slight detour for splendid Carreg Cennen Castle can be made by taking a right turn on to an unclassified road, then turning right again and ascending. Follow the subsequent descent and keep left at the edge of Trapp.

CARREG CENNEN CASTLE, Dyfed SN61
No description of this most romantic of castles can better that given by A C Bradley, who wrote: 'It looks for all the world like an Arthurian Castle one might see in dreams. . . .' A steep approach via a farmyard leads to the imposing pile of walls and turrets perched on a limestone cliff which drops a breathtaking 200ft into the attractive valley below. The existing building fabric dates from the 13th century, but a fortress existed here long before that. The atmosphere of permanence about the castle inspired Dylan Thomas to refer to it reverently, in the prayers of one of his characters, as 'Carreg Cennen, King of Time'.

Return to Ffairfach (on the main route) and return to Llandeilo with views to the left of Dynevor Castle.

DYNEVOR CASTLE, Dyfed SN62
As Llandeilo is approached from the south, the ivy-clad tower of a castle can be seen rising from trees on a hill directly west of the town. This is Dynevor – or more properly Dinefwr – Castle, which was once the seat of Welsh princes. Ruins comprising the keep and part of the curtain wall are situated in a private park near a 19th-century mansion. It is expected that these remains will be adopted by the DoE and made accessible to the public.

THE STONEHENGE QUARRY

Between placid Cardigan and bustling Fishguard is a jagged coast backed by the craggy, rock-strewn block of Mynydd Prescelly. In prehistoric times the great bluestones of Wiltshire's Stonehenge were hewn from these slopes and somehow hauled to Salisbury Plain.

FISHGUARD & GOODWICK, Dyfed SM93
Lower Town, as the oldest part of Fishguard is called, is a delightfully unspoilt fishing village. It was chosen as the setting for the film version of Dylan Thomas' *Under Milk Wood*, and is connected to Upper Town by a steep hill. The square in Upper Town features a Market Hall and the attractive Royal Oak Inn. During the 18th century Fishguard witnessed the signing of a treaty that ended the last invasion of British soil. In reality the so-called 'invasion' was a fiasco perpetrated by a motley band of French soldiers and convicts bent on pillage. Unable to reach and destroy Bristol, which had been their mission, they landed at Carregwasted Bay and quickly discovered large amounts of alcohol from a recent shipwreck. Incapably drunk, the invaders were easily captured by the local militia – aided (it is said) by stout-hearted Welsh women dressed in traditional costumes that the French took to be soldiers' uniforms. Goodwick, almost joined to Fishguard, is a resort with sandy beaches; it is also the embarkation point for one of the principal ferry services to Eire. East and west of Fishguard is the breathtaking seaboard and shore scenery of the Pembrokeshire Coast National Park.

PEMBROKESHIRE COAST NATIONAL PARK (NORTH), Dyfed
Two outstanding features of the northern part of this superb national park are its grand coastal scenery and its rugged upland typified by the Mynydd Prescelly range. Pencaer Peninsula, to the west of Fishguard, is characterized by a wind-torn landscape and precipitous cliffs that make it as daunting as it is exhilarating. Much of Pencaer Peninsula and the northern part of Mynydd Prescelly are made up of volcanic rocks, but farther east at Dinas Head and Cemaes Head are gentler sedimentary rocks from a less traumatic period of the earth's history. National Park information is available in Fishguard.

Leave Fishguard by the A487 'Cardigan' road. Descend from Upper to Lower Town with views across the old harbour to Fishguard Bay. Continue to Dinas.

DINAS, Dyfed SN03
This small village features the handsome Tabor Chapel and is connected to the cove and cliff scenery of Dinas Island by several little roads and footpaths. The 'island' is isolated only in name nowadays, but at the end of the ice age it was separated from the mainland by a true channel. The local church, at Cwm-yr-eglwys, was built in 1860 after its predecessor was destroyed in a violent storm. The cove here is considered one of the most beautiful in Wales and the tip of the headland falls away in the impressive 500ft cliffs of Dinas Head. Strange impressions found on a slab of rock here are traditionally held to be the Devil's footprints. Seals are very numerous along the coast. Pwllgwaelod, on the west side of Dinas Island, is a quiet bay with an old lime kiln and an inn.

Continue on the A487 for 1½ miles to reach Cerrig-y-Gof.

CERRIG-Y-GOF, Dyfed SN03
Overgrown though this important prehistoric monument may be, it is worth exploring because it is the only one of its kind in England and Wales. It is in a field off the main A458 road (OS ref SN037389), and comprises the remains of five rectangular burial chambers set in a circle. The name can be translated into English as 'Blacksmith's Stones'.

Continue on the A487 to Newport.

NEWPORT, Dyfed SN03
Ever since the 13th century, when this pretty little town received its first charter, the Lord (or Lady) Marchers of Cemais have had the right to select the town mayor. Remains of the original Norman castle were incorporated into a mansion during the 19th century. Newport, as its name implies, was once an important seaport, but today its main function seems to be as a quiet resort taking full advantage of its superb sands. To the west lies Parrog, which once received coastal trade at a quay whose crumbling remains are still visible. Newport is surrounded b[y] reminders of man's prehistoric past, including the remains of an iron-ag[e] fort above the town on the peak of Carningli, and a cromlech called Carreg Coetan Arthur, upstream from Gwaun bridge.

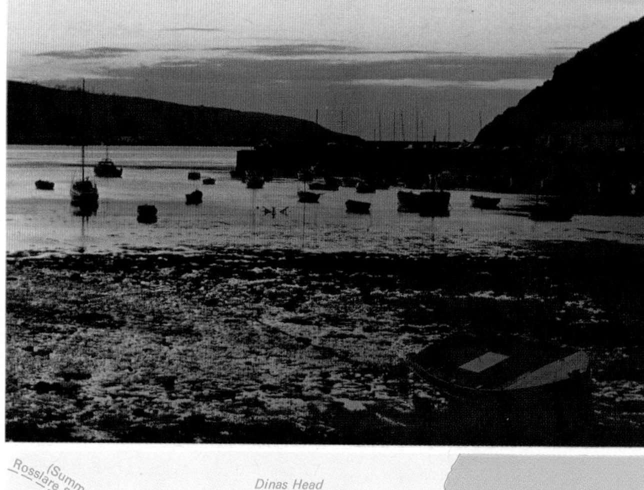

Once a haven for sm... picturesque Fishguard H... Lower Town, now provides s... holiday craft.

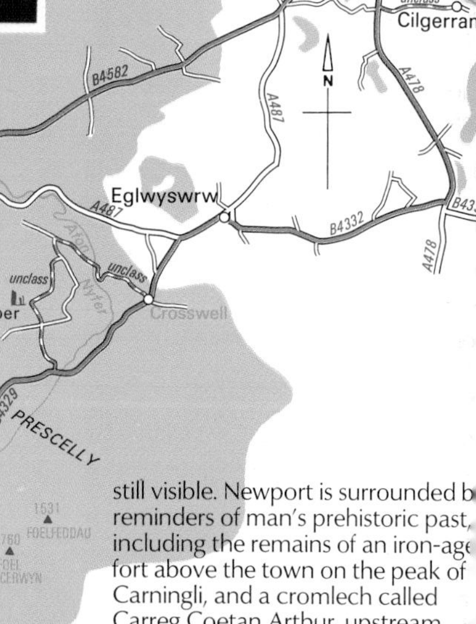

The huge stones which make up the distinctive outline of Pentre Ifan burial chamber were originally covered by a large cairn that has long since disappeared.

By tradition the first cuckoo of spring sings from Nevern's ancient cross.

Continue on the A487 for 2 miles and meet crossroads. Turn left on to the B4582, drive through woodlands, and cross the Afon Nyfer to enter Nevern.

NEVERN, Dyfed SN04
Not only is Nevern one of the most attractive and beautifully-set villages in Wales, it is also the guardian of a great treasure in the shape of a Celtic cross which stands outside the local church. Almost 13ft high and carved with intricate patterns, the cross carries a number of obscure inscriptions that have never been deciphered. Also in the churchyard is an avenue of Irish yews leading to the rugged old building itself, which contains other carved stones. One of the trees exudes a blood-like sap and is known as the 'Bleeding Yew'.

Follow the 'Cardigan' road between high banks for 5 miles, then meet the A487 and turn left. Descend into Cardigan with panoramic views. Shortly before entering the town the route allows a detour to be made to St Dogmaels via a left turn on the B4546.

T DOGMAELS, Dyfed SN14
he old Welsh county of ardiganshire was named after the fluential Ceredig, whose escendant St Dogmael founded a ermitage here in the 6th century. ne abbey was established in 1115 y Robert Fitz-Martin, Lord of emais, and the ruins (AM) that rvive today comprise fragments ating from the 14th to 16th nturies. A collection of carved ones is housed on the site of the rmer abbey infirmary, and other amples may be seen in the ljoining 19th-century parish urch. One of these, known as the granus Stone, was inscribed in th Latin and Ogham and proved invaluable key to mid-19th- ntury historians working to cipher the ancient Ogham script. e road to St Dogmaels can be owed beyond the village to the cellent beach at Poppit Sands. od walks from here lead through ely countryside to the wild cliffs of maes Head.

er Cardigan.

CARDIGAN, Dyfed SN14
Poets of all periods have waxed lyrical over the beautiful Afon Teifi, which flows into the sea at Cardigan. The salmon and sea trout that thrive in its tree-shaded waters are fished for from coracles, small traditional craft that have continued to use the river while relative newcomers have been forced elsewhere by the silting of Cardigan's port. The town is no longer of major maritime significance, but the observant visitor will find many reminders of its sea-faring past. A fine 17th-century 6-arched bridge spans the Teifi beneath the remains of a Norman castle. Cardigan nowadays has a mainly Victorian character and appearance typified by its notable 19th-century guildhall, the venue for a regular market held among its basement arches.

Recross the Teifi bridge and leave Cardigan on the A478 'Tenby' road. After 2 miles note a left turn leading to fascinating Cilgerran Castle.

CILGERRAN, Dyfed SN14
Legions of artists, some famous and many just enjoying themselves, have been inspired by the craggy situation and romantic air of Cilgerran Castle. The Afon Teifi, itself the subject of poetry and song, flows beneath the castle walls and once a year is the scene of competitive bustle and the display of ancient skills in a picturesque coracle regatta. The pretty little village of Cilgerran is somewhat overshadowed by its 13th-century guardian.

On the main route proceed along the A478. After 3 miles turn right on to the B4332 'Eglwyswrw' road and continue with fine views of the Prescelly Mountains. Drive into Eglwyswrw.

EGLWYSWRW, Dyfed SN13
In medieval times the body of St Wrw was entombed in a chantry chapel of the local church, after which the parishioners would allow nobody else to be buried there because they believed that the virgin saint 'would not have any bedfellows' – even in death.

In Eglwyswrw meet a T-junction and turn left on to the A487 SP 'Fishguard'. After ¾ mile turn left again on the B4329 SP 'Haverfordwest' and drive to Crosswell. At Crosswell the route allows a detour to be made to Pentre Ifan burial chamber: turn right on to an unclassified road and follow a stretch of the wooded Afon Nyfer, then in 1½ miles turn left.

PENTRE IFAN BURIAL CHAMBER, Dyfed SN03
Undoubtedly one of the finest megalithic monuments in Britain, Pentre Ifan (AM) stands on a slope overlooking vast tracts of the Pembrokeshire National Park and the distant waters of Cardiganshire Bay. To the west is 1,138ft Mynydd Carningli, on which St Brynach is said to have been ministered to by

Nest, whose beauty was legendary in medieval Wales, was abducted from Cilgerran Castle by one of her admirers.

angels. The monument itself consists of a 16-ton capstone supported by three spindly uprights and is thought to be some 5,000 years old.

On the main route, leave Crosswell and continue along the B4329. Climb steadily on to high moorland and reach a 1,328ft road summit. This viewpoint affords fine panoramas of the Mynydd Prescelly range.

MYNYDD PRESCELLY, Dyfed
Gentle moorland slopes dotted with outcrops of stone typify the scenery of Mynydd Prescelly, an ancient mountain range which culminates in 1,760ft Foel Cwmcerwyn east of the B4329. Beyond Foel Cwmcerwyn and 1,531ft Foeleddau is 1,200ft Foeldrygarn, whose slopes are said to have provided the famous blue stones of Stonehenge, in Wiltshire.

The slopes of Mynydd Prescelly rise to rock-strewn summits from 1,535ft Foeleryr.

Descend to Greenway and meet crossroads at the New Inn. Opposite is Rosebush Reservoir.

ROSEBUSH RESERVOIR, Dyfed SN02
Completed in 1932, this reservoir holds 170 million gallons and is an excellent leisure amenity for fishing and boating enthusiasts.

At the crossroads in Greenway turn right on to the B4313 'Fishguard' road. After 1 mile pass an unclassified right turn leading to the delightful countryside of the Gwaun Valley.

GWAUN VALLEY, Dyfed SN03
Words like magical, secret and enchanting come easily to mind when describing the Gwaun Valley. Its little river flows through a thickly-wooded coomb, which rises on the northern side to the lower slopes of the Prescelly Mountains.

Return to Fishguard on the B4313, passing through attractive countryside.

LAMPETER, Dyfed SN54
Neat rectangular fields bounded by hedges cover the gentle hills around Lampeter like a giant patchwork quilt. The town itself preserves a distinctive Welsh character coloured by its own personality. Small shops interspersed with dapper private houses, two Georgian hotels, and a proud Victorian town hall occupy the main street under the eye of the parish church. The latter was rebuilt in 1869, but contains memorials from earlier ages. Lampeter is best known for St David's College, which was founded in 1822 so that Welsh students (prohibited by expense from attending Oxford or Cambridge) could acquire a university education. The founder was Thomas Burgess, Bishop of St David's and the son of a Hampshire grocer. Although integrated with the University of Wales in 1971, the college remains a complete university in miniature.

Leave Lampeter on the A482 SP 'Aberaeron'. Drive through pleasant hill country and join the Aeron Valley at the combined villages of Felin Fach and Ystrad Aeron. Continue with the river through wooded country to reach Aberaeron.

ABERAERON, Dyfed SN46
Lampeter is not alone in being connected with that most English of counties, Hampshire. At the turn of the 18th century an Aberaeron heiress called Susannah Jones married a widowed Hampshire curate. Some years later the couple inherited a fortune and commenced to plan and build Aberaeron. The Development, which included the construction of harbours, quays, stores, a town hall, and numerous dwellings, continued well into the middle of the 19th century and resulted in an extremely pleasing Georgian-style town with a charm enhanced by the Welsh habit of highlighting architectural details with brightly-coloured paint. Aberaeron's days as a busy seaport are long gone, and today it performs a useful service as an elegant and unspoilt holiday resort.

Leave Aberaeron on the A487 'Aberystwyth' road. Drive through Aberarth, with glimpses of coastal scenery to the left, and continue to Llanon.

LLANON, Dyfed SN56
Memories of Dylan Thomas' *Under Milk Wood* are awoken here. Like the setting for that famous play, the village seems to be a retirement place for old sea captains with shipshape little cottages named after the craft they once commanded. Llanon is certainly of the sea and grew from the nearby fishing village of Llansantffraid, where the remains of fish traps said to have been constructed by the monks of Strata Florida Abbey can still be seen in places on the beach.

Continue to Llanrhystud.

TOUR 43 75 MILES

WESTERN BAYS

Retired seamen favour the quiet towns and villages of Cardigan Bay, and their neat cottages fit in well with the pastel shades of the omnipresent Welsh chapels. Inland is neat farming country crossed by small streams that suddenly waken into angry rapids and waterfalls.

LLANRHYSTUD, Dyfed SN56
No less than three castle mounds, the best of which is Caer Penrhos, survive near this attractive 19th-century village.

Climb inland and descend through Llanfarian to the Ystwyth Valley. Continue through Rhyd-y-Felin and cross the Afon Rheidol to reach Aberystwyth.

ABERYSTWYTH, Dyfed SN58
Seat of government and a holiday resort with a shopping area that serves a large locality, Aberystwyth grew to real importance with the establishment of its Norman castle by Edmund Crouchback in 1277. It is still a place of significance, and opposite the ruins of the castle is a Victorian hotel building that was bought in 1870 to form the nucleus of the University of Wales. Modern university buildings stand east of the town on Penglais Hill and include the National Library of Wales, which houses an incomparable collection of early Welsh manuscripts. Also of interest are the varied exhibits of the Ceredigion Museum. Notable among the many superb 18th- and 19th-century buildings preserved in the town are the fine houses that stand in Laura Place. A Victorian funicular railway operates on Constitution Hill, and echoes from the more distant past are evoked by the well-preserved iron-age earthworks that lie south of the town on Pen Dinas. The church at Llanbadarn Fawr – now a suburb of Aberystwyth – was founded in the 6th century by St Padarn, but the building that now occupies the site dates from the 13th century. Two beautiful Celtic crosses are preserved inside.

VALE OF RHEIDOL LIGHT RAILWAY Dyfed
British Rail's only line still to make use of steam locomotives runs 12 miles along the lovely Rheidol Valley between Aberystwyth and the spectacular river scenery of Devil's Bridge. Originally opened in 1902 to carry local lead ore and the occasional passenger, the line's rout through the breathtaking scenery of the 'Vale' has ensured success as a major tourist attraction and probably assured its future as a centre for steam-engine nostalgia. See also tour 45.

To leave Aberystwyth, return over Afon Rheidol on the A487 'Aberaeron' road and after $1\frac{1}{4}$ miles keep forward on to the A4120 'Devil's Bridge' road. Climb steadily, pass through Capel Seion, then 5 miles beyond the latter reach a 990ft road summit affording splendid views into the thickly-wooded Rheidol Valley. Continue to Devil's Bridge.

DEVIL'S BRIDGE, Dyfed SN77
A spectacular wooded gorge, tremendous waterfalls, and three bridges stacked on top of each oth in a 700-year sequence are to be seen here. For fuller details see the entry in tour 45.

Leave Devil's Bridge on the B4343 'Tregaron' road. Continue through hilly country and descend into the Ystwyth Valley. Cross a river and en Pontrhydygroes.

PONTRHYDYGROES, Dyfed SN7
The neat cottages in this village we once occupied by employees of th important local lead-mining indust Ruins of the mine buildings stand empty and useless on the surrounding hillsides – a comment on 'robber' mineral industries.

Continue, then after $\frac{1}{4}$ mile pass the Miners Arms (PH) and bear right on to an unclassified road SP 'Trawscoed'. Drive along a thickly-wooded valley and pass the Tyn-y-Bedw picnic site. After a short dista turn left on to the B4340 and proce to Ystrad Meurig.

Whitewashed farm buildings dotted amongst gentle hills typify the countryside of old Cardiganshire.

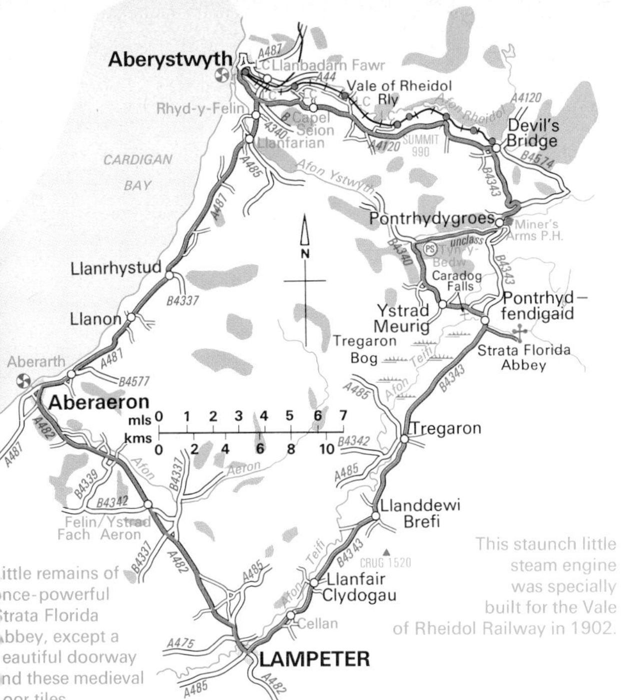

This staunch little steam engine was specially built for the Vale of Rheidol Railway in 1902.

ittle remains of
nce-powerful
trata Florida
bbey, except a
eautiful doorway
nd these medieval
oor tiles.

STRADAMEURIG, Dyfed SN76

ocal St John's College has been a mous educational establishment ıce the mid-18th century. Also of terest here are the slight remains of Norman castle.

ontinue to Caradog Falls, with the tensive Tregaron Bog to the right.

ARADOG FALLS, Dyfed SN76

ese picturesque falls are situated a tributary stream of the Afon ifi, just south of the tour route.

ontinue to Pontrhydfendigaid.

NTRHYDFENDIGAID, fed SN76

quaint old bridge spans the Teifi re. Once a year the village is the ue of a popular and well-dowed eisteddfod – a traditional elsh festival of poetry and music.

ve Pontrhydfendigaid on the 343 'Tregaron' road. Cross the on Teifi and shortly turn left on to unclassified road for a detour to ta Florida Abbey.

STRATA FLORIDA ABBEY, Dyfed SN76

Low foundations and a beautiful west doorway (AM) opening on to grass are all that remain of the once great and noble abbey of Strata Florida. In the 13th century, when the abbey was at the height of its power, it ran huge flocks of sheep on the vast upland areas of Mid Wales under its control. The Welsh prince Rhys ap Gruffydd started the abbey in 1184; an extensive group of attractive 18th-century farm buildings now covers much of the site eventually occupied by the abbey buildings. The refreshingly plain, early 19th-century parish church of Pontrhydfendigaid stands in the abbey grounds. Its yard is said to contain the grave of Dafydd ap Gwilym, who lived during the 14th century and is considered one of the greatest Welsh poets.

Return to Pontrhydfendigaid and turn left on to the B4343. Skirt Tregaron Bog.

TREGARON BOG (CORS TREGARON), Dyfed SN66

The 1,898-acre extent of this National Nature Reserve makes it the largest peat bog in Wales. In spring it is loud with the cries of curlew and plover, in summer it is white with the fluffy tufts of bog cotton grass, and in winter its sedges turn the glowing red that must have inspired its full Welsh name – 'Cors Goch Glanteifi', or the 'Red Bog Along the Teifi'.

Continue to Tregaron.

TREGARON, Dyfed SN65

Dominating the square of this unspoilt Welsh town is a bright-green statue of Henry Richard. Born in 1812, he became the Liberal MP for Merthyr and was such an outspoken supporter of disarmament that he became known as the 'Apostle of Peace'. The church of St Caron dates basically from the 14th century, but was restored during the 19th century. On Tuesdays Tregaron fulfils its prime function as a market town and fills with farmers, traders and sheep.

Leave Tregaron with SP 'Llanddewi Brefi, B4343'. Drive along the Teifi Valley to reach Llanddewi Brefi.

LLANDDEWI BREFI, Dyfed SN65

A great synod was held here in AD 519 to debate the *Heresy of Pelagius*, which denied the biblical doctrine of original sin. One of those refuting Pelagius was St David, beneath whom the ground is said to have risen so that those around could hear what he was saying. The village's 13th-century church stands on a mound which tradition holds to be the same miraculous eminence that provided the saint with his vantage point. Several interesting old stones can be seen inside the church.

Continue on the B4343 SP 'Lampeter' to reach Llanfair Clydogau.

LLANFAIR CLYDOGAU, Dyfed SN65

Sarn Helen, a Roman road, passes through this scattered little parish. The local church stands within a circular graveyard and contains a strangely-carved font. Other features of the village include a handsome bridge and an elegant chapel.

Drive through Cellan, and within 2 miles meet a junction. Turn right on to the A482 and return to Lampeter.

Aberaeron's brightly painted Georgian cottages overlook Cardigan Bay.

TOUR 44 63 MILES

AMONG THE BEACONS

High moorland that sweeps north from the industrial valleys of South Wales culminates in the sandstone peaks of the Brecon Beacons. Huge reservoirs built to satisfy industry lie to the south, and the crumbling towers of castles rise above the woodlands of the Usk Valley.

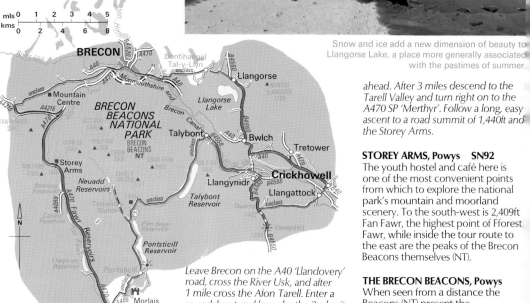

BRECON, Powys SO02
Streets lined with Georgian and Jacobean houses add much to the beauty and character of Brecon, a mid-Wales town that was raised to the status of cathedral city in 1923. It is an ideal centre from which to explore the Brecon Beacons National Park. The cathedral is situated on the northern outskirts and was originally the church of a Benedictine priory. Dating mainly from the 13th and 14th centuries, the building is cruciform in plan and displays a number of outstanding architectural features. Several priory buildings, including a fine tithe barn, have been restored. A charming walk extends along the banks of the Afon Honddu beyond the cathedral. Remains of Brecon Castle have been incorporated into the Castle Hotel, and parts of the medieval town walls can be seen at Captain's Walk, an area named after French prisoners who exercised there during the Napoleonic wars. St Mary's Church is a greatly restored medieval building in the city centre. The fascinating Brecknock County Museum stands in Glamorgan Street, and the Museum of the South Wales Borderers is sited on The Watton. Across the 16th-century bridge which spans the River Usk is Christ College, which was originally built as a Benedictine friary. It was restored in the 19th century and is now in service as a public school.

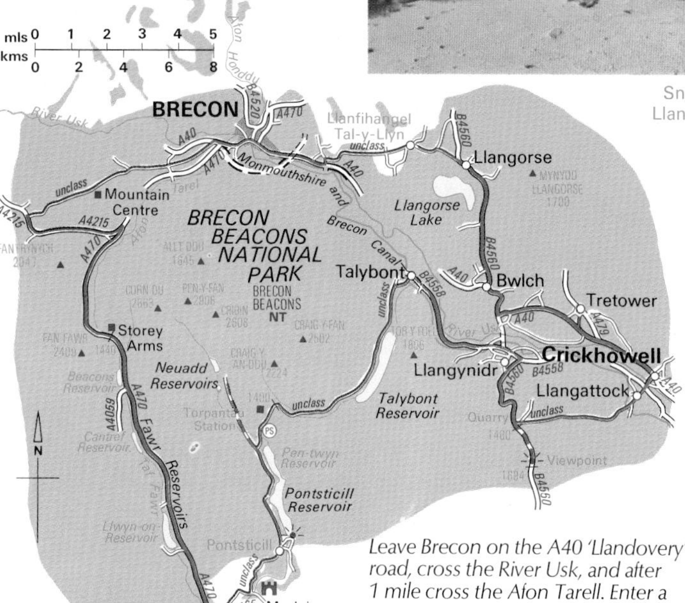

BRECON BEACONS NATIONAL PARK, Powys
From the Black Mountain in the west to the Black Mountains in the east are the 519 square miles of mountain, moor, and pastoral countryside that make up this valuable conservation area. Much of the underlying rock here is Old Red Sandstone, but to the west and south the landscape is built on younger limestones and grits.

Leave Brecon on the A40 'Llandovery' road, cross the River Usk, and after 1 mile cross the Afon Tarell. Enter a roundabout and leave by the 2nd exit. Continue, and take the next turning left on to an unclassified road SP 'Mountain Centre'. Ascend to moorland and reach the Mountain Centre.

MOUNTAIN CENTRE, Powys SN92
Magnificent views can be enjoyed from the centre, which functions as a meeting place, refreshment room, lecture theatre and comprehensive information office.

After $1\frac{3}{4}$ miles meet crossroads and turn left on to the A4215 (no SP), with 2,047ft Fan Frynych rising straight ahead. After 3 miles descend to the Tarell Valley and turn right on to the A470 SP 'Merthyr'. Follow a long, easy ascent to a road summit of 1,440ft and the Storey Arms.

Snow and ice add a new dimension of beauty to Llangorse Lake, a place more generally associated with the pastimes of summer

STOREY ARMS, Powys SN92
The youth hostel and café here is one of the most convenient points from which to explore the national park's mountain and moorland scenery. To the south-west is 2,409ft Fan Fawr, the highest point of Fforest Fawr, while inside the tour route to the east are the peaks of the Brecon Beacons themselves (NT).

THE BRECON BEACONS, Powys
When seen from a distance the Beacons (NT) present the extraordinary appearance of long, grass-covered swells that break at their apex like frozen waves and fall away to the north in stunning precipices. The highest point is 2,907ft Pen-y-fan, which affords views to the Bristol Channel.

Continue to the Fawr Reservoirs.

THE FAWR RESERVOIRS, Powys
Strung out along the west side of the A470 and fed by the Taf Fawr river are the three Fawr reservoirs – namely Beacons, Cantref, and Llwyn-on. They were constructed during a period between 1892 and 1927 to supply Cardiff with water.

Continue past the reservoirs and after a short distance reach Cefn-coed-y-cymmer.

CEFN-COED-Y-CYMMER, M Glam SO00
The great Cyfarthfa Ironworks were founded here in 1766 by the Crawshay family and Watkin George, one of the foremost of the early ironmasters. Also here is a fine 19th-century railway viaduct of 15 stone-built arches.

To visit Cyfarthfa Castle continue on the A470 for $1\frac{1}{4}$ miles.

CYFARTHFA CASTLE, M Glam SO00
Built in 1825 for 'Iron King' William Crawshay, this rather extravagant latterday castle now houses a museum and art gallery.

Crickhowell's beautiful 17th-century bridge is framed by an encircling ring of peaks, including the flat summit of aptly named Table Mountain.

From Cefn-coed-y-cymmer turn left ɔn to the unclassified 'Pontsticill and Talybont' road. Continue, with the ;orge of the Taf Fechan on the right. n 1¼ miles pass under a railway ɔridge and turn left. A detour can be nade to Morlais Castle by turning ight beyond the railway bridge.

ΛORLAIS CASTLE, Λ Glam SO00

plendidly situated on a 1,200ft hill vhich affords excellent views of the recon Beacons, Morlais Castle was a orderland stronghold built and efended by Gilbert de Clare.

On the main route, continue through ontsticill and at the end of the village eep left to follow the shores of ontsticill Reservoir.

ONTSTICILL RESERVOIR, owys SO01

xcellent views can be enjoyed from viewpoint at the south end of this xtensive reservoir, which was ɔnstructed at the beginning of this entury as part of a system designed supply nearby coalfields.

ontinue for 2¾ miles and turn right. detour ahead leads to the Neuadd eservoirs.

ruined keep of Tretower Castle saw on in the strife that bedevilled Wales ng the middle ages.

JADD RESERVOIRS, vys SO01

two Neuadd Reservoirs form t of the large Taf Fechan system are beautifully set in the heart of Brecon Beacons.

the main tour route, continue ɔss a river and shortly pass a picnic on the right. Ascend past the ner Torpantau Station to reach a 0ft road summit offering views of g-y-fan-ddu and Craig-y-fan. cend through woodland to the bont Valley. Proceed to the bont Reservoir.

YBONT RESERVOIR, ys SO01

e numbers of waterfowl and er aquatic wildlife may be seen his 2-mile long reservoir, which plies Newport with water.

tinue for 1¼ miles beyond the rvoir and turn right (no SP) into ɔont village.

Panoramic views of the magnificent Brecon Beacon mountains are opened up on the roads which follow the Usk Valley between Llangattock and the cathedral city of Brecon.

TALYBONT & THE MONMOUTHSHIRE AND BRECON CANAL, Powys SO12

Winding serenely from Brecon to Pontypool, the Monmouthshire and Brecon Canal offers a leisurely route from which to enjoy the scenery of the Usk Valley. It was built between 1799 and 1812, principally to supply the iron mines of old Monmouthshire (now Gwent), and was originally planned to stretch from Pontypool to Abergavenny. Within months of its commencement the decision was made to extend it to Brecon. Talybont has a modern bridge crossing the canal and makes an ideal centre from which to walk the towpaths and explore the surrounding countryside. East of Talybont the canal passes through the 375-yard Ashford Tunnel.

Cross the canal bridge at Talybont and turn right on to the B4558. Beyond the village keep forward SP 'Llangynidr and Crickhowell'. Drive along the wooded Usk Valley to reach Llangynidr.

LLANGYNIDR, Powys SO11

A fine old bridge of c1600 spans the Usk at Llangynidr, and five of the Monmouthshire and Brecon Canal's six locks are in this village.

Drive 1 mile beyond the canal bridge at Llangynidr and turn right on to the B4560 'Beaufort' road. Climb through sharp bends to 1,460ft for magnificent views. Continue past a quarry and turn left on to an unclassified road SP 'Crickhowell'. (For a detour to 1,694ft with superb views continue the ascent on the B4560 for another 1 mile.) Continue on the main route to Llangattock.

LLANGATTOCK, Powys SO21

St Catwg's Church, on the edge of the village, carries a massive 15th-century tower and contains some interesting memorials. Old limestone quarries exist south on the slopes of Mynydd Llangattock, where there is also a National Nature Reserve.

Keep forward to the end of Llangattock and turn left on to the A4077. Turn right to cross the Usk into Crickhowell.

The graceful 15-arched viaduct at Cefn-coed-y-cymmer was built in 1866 to carry the Brecon and Merthyr Railway. Today it stands as an impressive example of 19th-century invention and engineering skill.

CRICKHOWELL, Powys SO21

A magnificent 13-arched bridge dating from the 17th century spans the River Usk at Crickhowell. All that remains of the local castle is a mound and some battered-looking masonry, but there are some attractive houses in the town and the church has a pleasing 19th-century broach spire. On the western edge of Crickhowell is a fine 15th-century gatehouse called Porthmawr, which led to a long-vanished mansion.

Leave Crickhowell on the A40 'Brecon' road. After 2¾ miles pass a turning to the right which leads to Tretower and its castle.

TRETOWER, Powys SO12

A sturdy keep surrounded by a many-sided stone wall comprises the remains of Tretower Castle (AM), which was usurped as a habitation in the 14th century by nearby Tretower Court (AM). The latter is considered a very fine example of a fortified mansion and was the home of the Vaughan family for three centuries. Henry Vaughan, who spent most of his life in this area, was one of the outstanding metaphysical poets of the 17th century.

Continue on the A40 to Bwlch.

BWLCH, Powys SO12

Fine views of the Usk Valley and the surrounding mountains are afforded from the road as it approaches this little hamlet. The name 'Bwlch' means 'The Pass'.

Drive beyond the war memorial and turn right on to the B4560 'Talgarth' road. Continue to Llangorse.

LLANGORSE, Powys SO12

Restoration and so-called improvement during the 19th century destroyed much of the character of the little local church, but its 15th-century wagon roof has survived. An ancient inscribed stone has been preserved here.

Continue to the end of the village and turn left on to an unclassified road. Proceed towards Brecon and after a short way pass a road leading to the lovely expanse of Llangorse Lake.

LLANGORSE LAKE, Powys SO12

This, the largest natural lake in South Wales, is a haven for many kinds of flora and fauna. It is also a centre for many water-based leisure activities, including fishing and boating.

On the main route, continue for 1½ miles and turn left across a bridge. Drive through Llanfihangel Tal-y-Llyn, and after 2½ miles turn left. After ½ mile turn right on to the A40 and return to Brecon.

TOUR 45 60 MILES

THE WELSH LAKES

At one time the valleys of the Elan and its tributaries were noted for their beauty, but now they lie under the surface of a massive water storage scheme that has turned the area into the Lake District of Wales. Down-stream on the Afon Rheidol are the stupendous falls of Devil's Bridge.

RHAYADER, Powys SN96
This little market town retains a 19th-century atmosphere even though many of its shops have been modernized and given new fronts. Its old inns include The Triangle, a partly weather-boarded building across the Wye in the Cwmdeuddwr district, and, on the town side of the bridge, the Cwmdeuddwr Arms. Both are grand old institutions with histories that stretch back several centuries. All that remains of Rhayader's castle is a large mound set in the angle between Church Street and West Street, high above a reach where the river flows over boulders and rocky platforms to dash under the bridge in pretty falls. Rhayader was one of the centres of the Rebecca Riots in the first half of the 19th century, when men dressed as women and calling themselves Rebecca's Daughters smashed turnpike gates as a protest against heavy tolls. Some light industry has been introduced into Rhayader in an attempt to curb the depopulation which has bedevilled the region in recent decades.

Leave Rhayader on the B4518 'Elan Valley' road and continue to the edge of Elan village. Keep forward on to an unclassified road and ascend to Caban Coch Dam and Reservoir.

ELAN VALLEY & CABAN COCH RESERVOIR, Powys SN96
Late in the 19th century the Corporation of Birmingham constructed a reservoir system in an area now unofficially known as The Radnorshire Lake District. The new landscape is very beautiful and highly popular, but the scheme called for the drowning of a whole valley complete with attractive waterfalls, meadows, farms, houses and a church. Beneath the placid surface of the new lake is a house in which the poet Shelley lived for some time. He wrote appreciatively about the splendid local scenery in a letter to his friend Hogg, suggesting that it had impressed him even though his mind was on higher, less substantial things.

Continue to the Garreg-Ddu viaduct and turn left to cross it. Proceed through pleasant woodland, with the remains of the Dol-y-Mynach Dam on the left, and enter the attractive Claerwen Valley. At an AA telephone box turn right to reach Claerwen Dam.

CLAERWEN RESERVOIR, Powys SN86
The Claerwen project, officially opened by Queen Elizabeth II on 23rd October 1952, is a vast 600-acre lake held back by a massive dam. The Afon Teifi rises in the high moorlands to the west of the reservoir, and the route of an ancient road used by monks travelling from Strata Florida Abbey to Abbey Cwmhir runs through the area.

Return across Garreg-Ddu viaduct and turn left. Follow the wooded shores of Garreg-Ddu Reservoir.

GARREG-DDU RESERVOIR, Powys SN96
A unique submerged dam separates this reservoir from Caban Coch Reservoir. The entire Elan Valley complex supplies Birmingham with an amazing 60 million gallons of water a day and provides a haven for many forms of aquatic and marginal wildlife, including various plants.

From the end of Garreg-Ddu Reservoir ascend a short winding stretch of road to Penygarreg Dam and Reservoir.

PENYGARREG RESERVOIR, Powys SN96
Some 124 acres of lake, unbroken except where a tiny fir-covered islet rises at the centre, backs up the Elan Valley from yet another of the project's great dams. This and the other reservoirs can be fished for trout by permit holders.

Continue alongside Craig Goch Reservoir.

CRAIG GOCH RESERVOIR, Powys SN87
Topmost of the Elan Valley dam and reservoir complex, Craig Goch has a surface area of about 200 acres and may soon be extended. Plans are being laid to increase the capacity of the lake by allowing it to back up the valley all the way to the source of the Afon Elan – the river that was originally restricted to form this large and essential system.

Ascend and turn left on to the 'Aberystwyth' road. Continue along the wide moorland valley of the Afon Elan to a road summit of 1,320ft. Descend into the deep and wild Ystwyth Valley, and within 4 miles reach Cwmystwyth.

CWMYSTWYTH, Dyfed SN77
Ruins of mine workings, buildings and cottages in the neighbourhood of this village illustrate the 19th-century's insatiable desire for mineral wealth, but the village itself – no longer a centre of the mining industry – has settled into attractive retirement. Beyond Cwmystwyth, off the Pontrhydygroes road, is a pile of rubble that once stood as the proud mansion of Hafod, built by one Thomas Johnes in the late 18th century. The building was twice burnt down, and each blaze destroyed many priceless works of art and irreplaceable manuscripts. Johnes improved the estate by planting over 2 million trees and introducing new farming techniques, but the fires and the death of his beloved daughter Marianne in 1811 turned the innovator into a broken old man. A charred monument to Marianne in Hafod Church testifies to a final irony – the gutting of the church by fire in 1932.

Beyond Cwmystwyth keep forward to join the B4574 'Devil's Bridge' road. Ascend a wooded slope and reach The Arch Picnic Site.

THE ARCH PICNIC SITE, Dyfed SN77
Thomas Johnes of Hafod erected an arch over the road here in 1810 to commemorate the Golden Jubilee o[f] George III. Three Forestry Commission trails lead from the picnic site into wild countryside.

Descend with the Mynach Valley on the right and enter Devil's Bridge.

DEVIL'S BRIDGE, Dyfed SN77
Cwm Rheidol narrows to form a spectacular 500ft-deep wooded gorge at Devil's Bridge, where Afon Mynach adds its own 300ft of impressive waterfalls to the grandeu[r] of the Afon Rheidol's Gyfarllwyd Falls. Excellent views into the gorge can be enjoyed from the road bridge, but the full scenic splendour of the area can only be fully appreciated by a descent into the valley bottom. A flight of 91 steps known as Jacob's Ladder zig-zags down to river level, where a small bridge and platform afford views of five separate waterfalls which make up a superb 300ft cascade. Water erosion has resulted in the formatio[n] of curious cavities known as punchbowls at the bottom of the

Penygarreg Reservoir is one of a series created to supply Birmingham with wa[ter]

The spectacular 300ft Mynach Falls are set amid trees festooned with moisture-loving ferns and mosses.

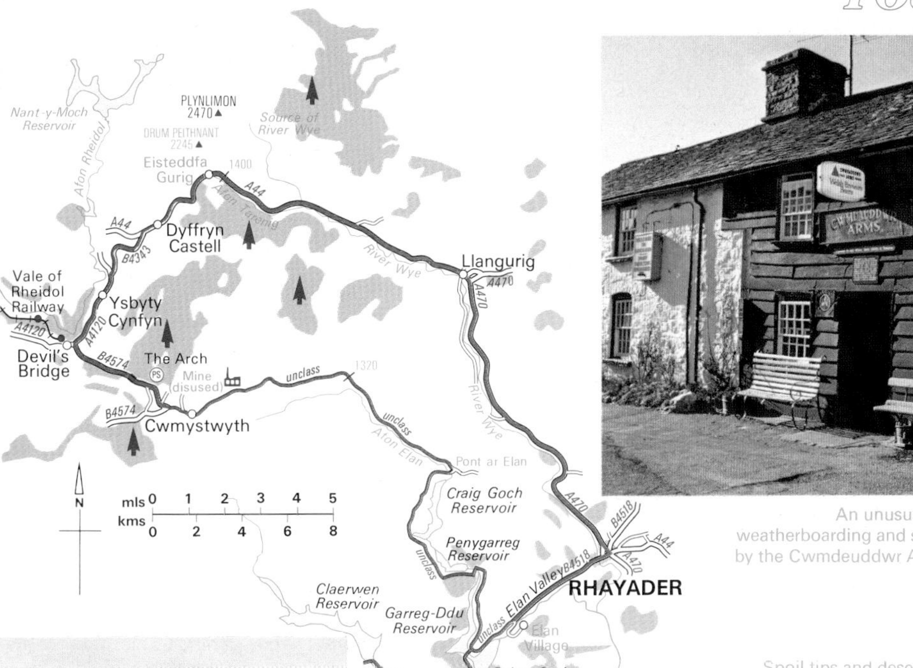

An unusual combination of weatherboarding and stone is displayed by the Cwmdeuddwr Arms at Rhayader.

e elegant dam which separates Craig ›ch Reservoir from Penygarreg servoir.

Spoil tips and deserted buildings are reminders of once-thriving mineral workings at Cwmystwyth.

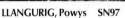

ries. Similarly magnificent views e available from a terrace in front the Hafod Arms Hotel, which was built in the 1830s. Of the three dges stacked on top of each other Devil's Bridge the oldest is – turally – the lowest, and is thought have been built in the 12th ntury by monks from Strata rida Abbey. Legend has it that the vil built it as a complex trick to n a soul, and abandoned it after he ed. The second bridge was built in 53, and an iron bridge was built ove the other two much later in early part of this century.

LE OF RHEIDOL LIGHT RAILWAY, fed

s narrow-gauge railway is the only ish Rail line to operate steam omotives. It is an unfailing tourist raction, and its Devil's Bridge minus is a charming miniature asting all the usual station lities, set amid dense dodendron thickets. See also npeter tour 43.

ve Devil's Bridge village by crossing Devil's Bridge on the A4120 nterwyd' road. Continue high ve the Rheidol Valley and after a rt distance reach Ysbyty Cynfyn.

YSBYTY CYNFYN, Dyfed SN77

Several stones of the prehistoric circle in which this immaculate, evergreen-shrouded church stands have survived in place. Many gravestones in the churchyard bear Cornish names and are reminders of the days when West Country miners came to Wales in search of better opportunities. A path leads from the church to a wooded gorge featuring a waterfall and the 'Parsons Bridge', so called because it was built for the convenience of a travelling parson who held services both here and at Llanbadarn Fawr.

Continue and turn right on to the B4343 'Dyffryn Castell' road. Meet the A44, bear right, and reach Dyffryn Castell.

DYFFRYN CASTELL & PLYNLIMON, Dyfed SN78

A path leads from here to the slopes of Plynlimon, a 2,470ft mountain which appears as a rounded hill from many directions, only a little higher than its neighbours. On wet days the vast expanse of bog and moor on its flanks tends to be depressing, but the views afforded by its summit are spectacular enough to make the ascent easily worth the effort involved. On a clear day the view encompasses virtually the whole of Wales, from Snowdonia in the north to the Brecon Beacons in the south. Plynlimon, famous for its wetness, is the source of the mighty Severn, the lovely Wye, and several lesser but equally vigorous rivers. Ascents to the summit can also be made from Eisteddfa Gurig (a little north of Dyffryn Castell) and from Nant-y-Moch Reservoir, which is on the west side of the mountain. The banks of the reservoir afford views of low crags that give Plynlimon a more mountainous aspect than is obvious from other vantage points. It should be stressed that although the ascent of Plynlimon is not difficult, the would-be explorer should wear sensible clothing and beware of the mountain's mercurial moods.

Ascend to Eisteddfa Gurig and a 1,400ft road summit. Continue alongside the Afon Tarenig and reach its confluence with the River Wye. Enter Llangurig.

LLANGURIG, Powys SN97

Small and beautiful Llangurig is delightfully set in the upper valley of the River Wye, amid high mountain ranges with thickly-wooded flanks. The church of St Gurig owes much of its appearance to J W Lloyd of Llandinam, who commissioned Sir Gilbert Scott to restore the building. Lloyd, famous for his inconstancy, began his career as a curate in Llangurig but later became a Catholic and eventually aspired to become a Knight of St Gregory. In later life he returned to the Anglican faith. Stained-glass windows show scenes from the life of St Gurig, relate incidents associated with the royal families of Wales, and depict members of the Lloyd family.

Leave Llangurig on the A470 and drive down the attractive Wye Valley, accompanying the river itself for much of the way, and return to Rhayader.

TOUR 46 56 MILES

MOORLANDS OF CENTRAL WALES

Towns are few and far between in mid Wales, and villages tend to be scattered round chapel or church buildings. Much of the area is open moorland scored by the occasional river valley, a wild, underpopulated region haunted by the cries of curlews and buzzards.

LLANIDLOES, Powys SN98
Tree-lined streets, a happy blend of old and new architecture, and a few venerable shop fronts combine to form Llanidloes' unique character. The 16th-century Market Hall in the centre of the town is a rare survivor of a type of building that was once common all over the country. Its arcaded lower floor is open to the street and once sheltered market stalls. The floor above now houses a folk museum, but has variously functioned as an assize court, Quaker meeting place, Wesleyan and Baptist premises, public library, and working men's institute. John Wesley preached from a stone preserved beside the hall. A beautiful arcade of five bays in the parish church was brought from Abbey Cwmhir at the time of the Dissolution of the Monasteries, and was installed in 1542. Also from the abbey are the timbers of the hammer-beam roof, but the gilded angels are not original and were added to the ends of the beams at the time of their transfer. Llanidloes stands at the confluence of Afon Clywedog and the River Severn.

Leave Llanidloes on the B4518 'Llyn Clywedog' road. Cross the Severn and turn left to follow the Clywedog Valley. After 2 miles, with views of 1,580ft Fan Hill on the right, turn left on to an unclassified road. Cross the valley and ascend to Clywedog Dam.

LLYN CLYWEDOG RESERVOIR, Powys SN88
Excellent views of the reservoir can be enjoyed from the dam, whose curving 237ft wall is the highest of its kind in Britain. The reservoir itself was opened in 1968 and is a popular sailing venue. Nearby Fan Hill commands extensive views to Plynlimon Mountain and south into the old county of Radnorshire.

Continue with the Clywedog Reservoir on the right and Hafren Forest on the left.

HAFREN FOREST, Powys SN88
Comprising large plantations between Clywedog Reservoir and the slopes of Plynlimon Mountain, this forest was started by the Forestry Commission in 1937, and is named from the Welsh equivalent of 'Severn'. The River Severn flows from the eastern flank of Plynlimon, where it rises in company with the Wye and several other vigorous waters. A picnic site is situated in the forest opposite the extreme western arm of the reservoir.

Continue to a T-junction and turn right on to the 'Llanbrynmair' road. After $2\frac{1}{4}$ miles reach the edge of Staylittle.

Bare moorland slopes crossed by winding roads typify the scenery of the mid-Wales wilderness, a place of rolling hills and deep, lake-filled valleys.

The once bare slopes of Plynlimon are gradually being covered by the dark coniferous plantations of Hafren Forest, which was begun in 1937.

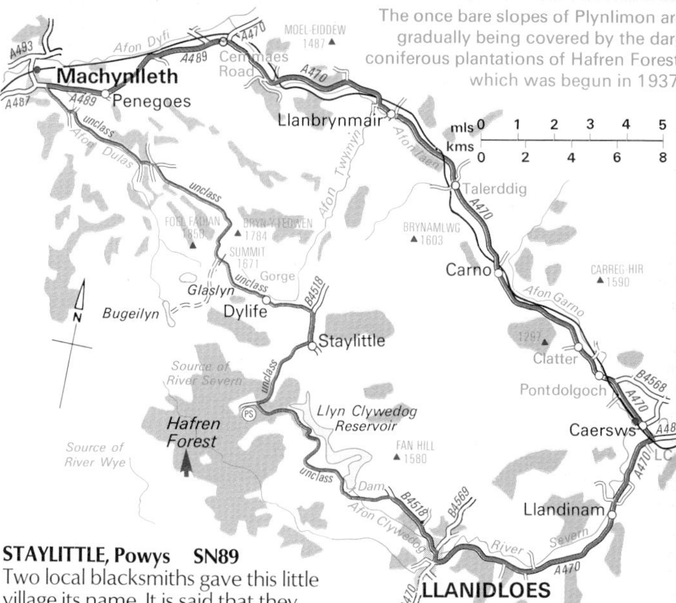

STAYLITTLE, Powys SN89
Two local blacksmiths gave this little village its name. It is said that they used to shoe horses so quickly that customers only needed to stay-a-little. On the hillside above the village is a Quaker burial ground with a nearby chapel overlooking the Clywedog Reservoir.

At Staylittle turn left on to the B4518. After $\frac{3}{4}$ mile turn left on to the unclassified 'Machynlleth' road, which is unguarded and must be driven with care. After a short distance pass high above the deep gorge of the Afon Twymyn, and continue to Dylife.

DYLIFE, Powys SN89
A few haphazard ruins, spoil tips, and an air of desolation are all that remain of an enormous lead-mining community that once flourished at Dylife. Huge numbers of men lived and worked here under awful conditions until the 1870s, but all that exist now are an inn and a tiny group of houses set back off the road. A little east of Dylife the infant Afon Twymyn plunges down spectacular Ffrwyd Fawr waterfall.

Continue for about 2 miles to a track leading left from the route to lakes Glaslyn and Bugeilyn.

ES GLASLYN & BUGEILYN, ys SN89
should be taken to stay on the path access to these two lakes, e area is made dangerous by peat bogs and several ipitous drops. This is a wild and ly landscape, once extensively ed for lead, but now inhabited by sheep, birds, and the sional fox. Glaslyn lies on private , and Bugeilyn (which means herd's Lake), is situated in the ills of the Plynlimon range. ll flint arrowheads, presumably used by people now buried in by prehistoric cairns, have been d washed out of the peat.

inue towards Machynlleth and ly reach a 1,671ft road summit. s south and east from here take tensive moorland, with 1,850ft Fadian to the left and 1,784ft -y-Fedwen to the right. Descend, impressive views north-west to r Idris and Aran Fawddwy, then down a long descent and keep ard at all road junctions to reach ynlleth.

CHYNLLETH, Powys SH70
narket days Machynlleth's ngwyn Street is packed with selling a wide variety of wares. he north side of the same street Owain Glyndwr Institute, h stands on the site of a building e Welsh revolutionary Owain dwr held Wales' last pendent parliament in 1404. On other side of the street is the ered Court House, with an iption dated 1628. The road as a e is dominated by an ornate orian clock tower which was ed by public subscription to the coming of age of Lord ereagh, heir to the Marquess of onderry. The marquess owned Machynlleth, a 17th-century

Situated in the Dyfi Valley, Machynlleth is the principal market town for this part of Mid Wales and has associations with the popular Welsh folk hero, Owain Glyndwr.

mansion which stands at the end of Pentrerhedyn Street and now houses the council offices. The grounds in which the house stands have been adopted as a public park.

Leave Machynlleth on the A489 'Newtown' road and proceed to Penegoes.

PENEGOES, Powys SH70
A tradition that the head of a Welsh chieftain, executed in this village, is buried under a local tree has proved so tenacious that in 1950 there was a serious proposal to dig for the skull. Penegoes once had a tiny curative bath that was fed from a spring whose waters were said to bring relief from rheumatism. Richard Wilson, painter of landscapes, was born in the village in 1714. His birthplace is said to have been the Rectory, but the building occupying this site now dates only from c 1800.

Follow the Dyfi Valley to Cemmaes Road and turn right on to the A470 'Newtown' road. Continue along the Twymyn Valley to Llanbrynmair.

LLANBRYNMAIR, Powys SH90
Roughly divided into half old and half new, this small scattered village enjoys a rural setting threaded by little rivers and was the site of an important castle during the 12th century. Only the castle mound survives today. The local church is sited in the old part of the village and contains ancient oak timbers. Abraham Rees, preacher and scholar, was born in the village in 1743. In 1778 he embarked on the preparation of information for *Chambers' Encyclopaedia*, a mammoth task that took 9 years to complete and won Rees election as a Fellow of the Royal Society. He was later made a Doctor of Divinity by Edinburgh University for his work on a further encyclopaedia.

Continue through the wooded gorge of the Afon Iaen to reach a road and rail summit at Talerddig, where there is a natural arch beside the road. Continue to Carno.

Left: the valley at Dylife was once exploited for its mineral wealth. Below: this statue of engineer David Davies stands at Llandinam.

CARNO, Powys SN99
Opposite Carno's church, which contains an ancient cross-incised slab that saw many years' service as a gatepost, is the Aleppo Merchant Inn. This unusual title was given to the pub by a retired sea captain who had been in charge of a ship of that name. A Roman fort was situated here, and later in history several fierce battles between the ruling princes of north and south Wales were fought near Carno.

Drive along the broad valley of the Afon Carno and pass through Clatter and Pont-dolgoch to reach Caersws.

CAERSWS, Powys SO09
Earthworks of a large Roman installation may be seen near the railway here, forming a hub from which the raised causeways of ancient roads still radiate in recognizable form. The village itself is laid on a typically Roman grid-iron pattern at the meeting of two rivers with the Severn. John Ceiriog Hughes, a famous 19th-century bard, was manager of a narrow-gauge railway here for many years. A memorial plaque marks the house where he lived, and his remains lie north-west at Llanwnog. The latter boasts a fascinating old church.

Continue on the A470 and after $\frac{3}{4}$ mile meet a T-junction. Turn right on to the 'Llangurig' road and shortly go over a level crossing, then follow the River Severn to reach Llandinam.

LLANDINAM, Powys SO08
Green hills rising to the lower slopes of mountains spread from the Severn Valley site of this pretty village. Close to a handsome iron bridge that spans the river is a statue of Llandinam's most famous native, David Davies. After starting from a modest beginning Davies worked to become a railway contractor, then went on to make a fortune with the construction of Barry Docks. The local church has been extensively restored and stands on the site of a hillfort which is still faintly visible. Ancient carvings preserved in the church include an interesting illustration of Adam and Eve.

Remain on the A470 for the return to Llanidloes.

TOUR 47 78 MILES

CASTLES ON THE BORDER

South from one of the tortuous meanders carved by the River Severn runs the border between England and Wales – a contentious division guarded by medieval fortresses at Powis, Montgomery, and Clun.

WELSHPOOL, Powys SJ20
Prior to the 19th century this 'English town in Wales' was known simply as Pool, a name derived from the marshy nature of the area in which it stood. The 'Welsh' prefix, ironic in the light of the town's hotly disputed position in the borderlands between England and Wales, was added in 1835 to distinguish it from Poole in Dorset. Many of the haphazard narrow streets which characterized the town until recently have been sacrificed to commerical interests, but enough remain to kindle an imaginative picture of Welshpool as it was. Opposite the town hall is a half- timbered building with a Jacobean staircase, one of several such examples in the town. Severn Road leads to a splendid railway station incorporating many gables, end towers, and a platform canopy resplendent with wrought-iron arcading. Powysland Museum stands in Salop Road and was started in 1874 by Morris Jones, who had previously founded the Powysland Club – claimed to be the oldest archaeological society in Wales.

POWIS CASTLE, Powys SJ20
Approached from Welshpool through a magnificently-wooded park, Powis Castle dates originally from the 13th century. Subsequent alterations which continued right up until the end of the last century have changed the building beyond all past recognition, and it now appears as a vast mansion. As an historic treasure Powis is very special because it has been continuously occupied, its present form having gradually evolved through the centuries in response to the tastes of various owners. The 18th-century terraced gardens that complement the building are especially noteworthy, and the interior of the castle is rich with curios including mementos of Clive of India. In 1952 the castle and park were passed over into the protection of the National Trust.

Leave Welshpool on the A483 'Newtown' road and follow the Shropshire Union Canal past the grounds of Powis Castle. After 4 miles turn right on to the B4390 to reach Berriew.

BERRIEW, Powys SJ10
Recipient of an award for the best-kept village in Wales, Berriew is a picturesque combination of black-and-white cottages and a few more recent buildings interspersed with trim flower gardens. Pretty falls can be seen near by on the Afon Rhiw, which joins the Severn $1\frac{1}{2}$ miles east.

Leave Berriew by turning left on to the B4385 and cross the Rhiw. Shortly turn left again. Later meet a T-junction and turn right to rejoin the A483 'Newtown' road. Continue to Garthmyl and turn left on to the B4385. Shortly cross the Severn and continue to Montgomery.

MONTGOMERY, Powys SO29
Montgomery's superficially Georgian character is shown in the red-brick town hall that dominates Broad Street, an aptly-named thoroughfare almost as wide as it is long. Away from the centre the 18th century has less hold, and fine examples of Tudor and Jacobean architecture make surprise appearances round secretive corners or at the tops of quaint slopes and steps. The parish Church of St Nicholas was built just before Henry III granted Montgomery's Royal Charter in 1227. Its best features include 15th-century nave roofs, a double screen, and monuments to the Herbert family. Poet George Herbert was born in the now-ruined castle (AM), built by Henry III above the remains of a Norman stronghold that stood at the foot of Castle Hill.

Continue on the B4385 SP 'Bishop's Castle', with views across the River Camlad valley – the only river to flow from England into Wales. Enter Bishop's Castle.

BISHOP'S CASTLE, Salop SO38
This hillside market town stands on the edge of Clun Forest and preserves a number of interesting old buildings, the most picturesque of which is the 16th-century House on Crutches. Its Victorian church retains a Norman tower, and the 18th-century town hall stands over a medieval lock-up.

Follow SP 'Clun', and after $\frac{1}{2}$ mile meet crossroads. Turn right on to the A488. Continue through wooded hill country to Clun.

CLUN, Salop SO38
Thousands of flint implements displayed in the museum at Clun's 18th-century town hall demonstrate that man has lived in this area for a very long time. Attractive almshouses of 1618 enliven the somewhat stolid appearance of the town. Access to the church is through an old lych gate. Remains of a Norman castle overlook the River Clun from a small hill, and the large expanse of Clun Forest stretches west as a patchwork of treeless uplands and recent afforestation.

Leave Clun on the A488 'Knighton' road and ascend Clun Hill to a summit of 1,150ft. Slowly descend and cross the River Redlake, then ascend again before skirting Kinsley Wood to reach Knighton.

KNIGHTON, Powys SO27
The Offa's Dyke long-distance footpath was officially opened here in 1971. The dyke itself, built by a king of Mercia in the 8th century, runs through the town. Built largely of local stone, Knighton occupies a delightful hillside position in the Teme Valley and has scant remains of a Norman motte-and-bailey castle. Knighton Railway Station stands on the Central Wales line an[d] is a little gem of Victorian-gothic railway architecture. Knighton's livestock sales are famous.

Leave Knighton on the B4355 SP 'Newtown'. After $\frac{1}{4}$ mile turn right to follow the River Teme. Continue to Knucklas.

KNUCKLAS, Powys SO27
Crowning the hill above Knucklas a[re] the remains of a 13th-century castl[e] which is connected in legend with Gwynhwyfar (or Guinevere), whom the heroic folk figure King Arthur married. A beautiful 75ft-high railwa[y] viaduct which can also be seen her[e] is of Victorian date and carries crenellated towers.

Continue through pleasant valley scenery to Beguildy.

A ruined keep and two 13th-century towers are the most outstanding features of Clun's impressively sited castle.

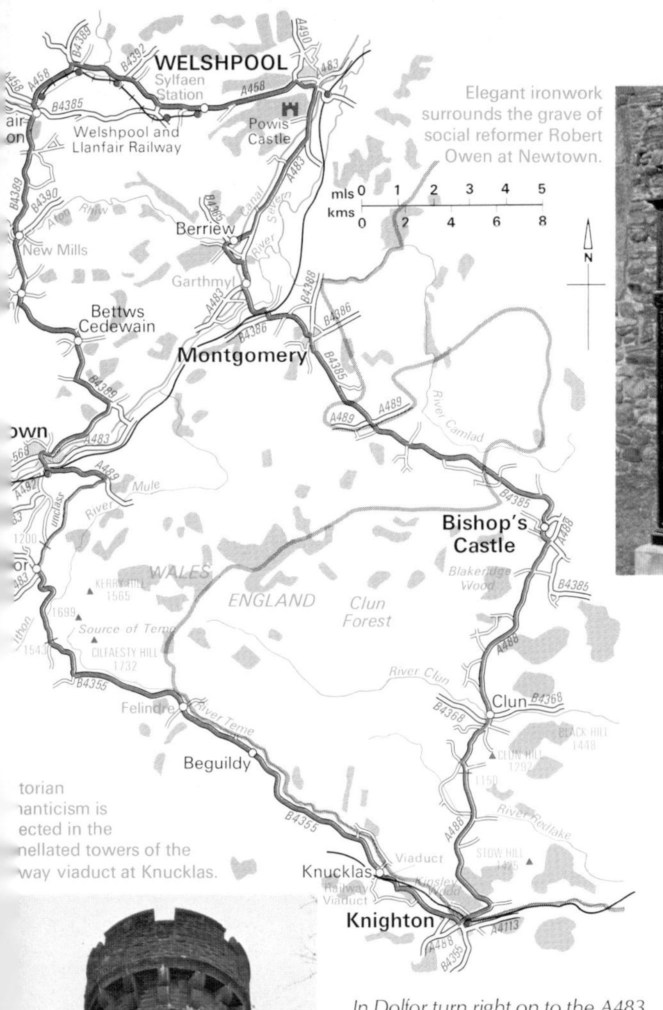

Elegant ironwork surrounds the grave of social reformer Robert Owen at Newtown.

torian
ıanticism is
ected in the
nellated towers of the
way viaduct at Knucklas.

UILDY, Powys SO17
ıe years ago a would-be efactor offered to donate a large ı of money to the local school on dition that the village should ert to its correct Welsh spelling of ail-dy meaning the 'Shepherd's se'. The offer was declined. ures of the local church include od screen with fine tracery and a bean pulpit and altar.

e on through Felindre and ascend) open moorland; to the right v 1,732ft Cilfaesty Hill is the e of the Teme. Descend into or.

FOR, Powys SO18
or stands at an altitude of 1,000ft affords extensive mountain s to the north west. Views south e Brecon Beacons range can be yed from the 1,565ft summit of oy Kerry Hill. The rivers Teme, ı, and Mule all rise in the area.

In Dolfor turn right on to the A483, then right again (no SP) on to a narrow unclassified road. Beyond the local church keep forward to a 1,200ft road summit, offering splendid views north over Newtown and the Severn Valley. Continue down a long descent and turn left on to the A489. Proceed to Newtown.

NEWTOWN, Powys SO19
Robert Owen, a social reformer who became known as the father of trade unionism, was born in Newtown and is buried in the churchyard of the old parish church. Some of the reasons why Owen was such an assiduous campaigner for workers' rights can be understood by a visit to the Newtown Textile Museum, and a museum dedicated to his memory is situated over the Midland Bank. The 15th-century rood screen from the old church has been preserved in a handsome 19th-century successor. Newtown was originally established in 1279, but the 20th century has incorporated it in a designated development area and made it into a new town all over again. Extensive new building has given the community two new bridges over the River Severn plus a theatre and various civic buildings.

Leave Newtown on the B4568, cross the River Severn, enter a roundabout, and leave by the 3rd exit SP 'Bettws Cedewain and Gregynog'. After $2\frac{1}{2}$ miles turn left on to the B4389 'Llanfair Caereinion' road. Enter Bettws Cedewain.

BETTWS CEDEWAIN, Powys SO19
Close-knit round a stone bridge spanning the little River Bechan, this attractive village boasts an interesting 14th-century church which carries a timbered and louvered tower typical of the area. A barrel organ and a pre-Reformation brass, depicting a priest vested for mass, can be seen inside.

Continue for 2 miles and turn right to enter Tregynon. After $1\frac{1}{2}$ miles cross the Afon Rhiw and enter New Mills. Turn left and make a winding ascent to a road summit of 980ft. Descend into Llanfair Caereinion.

LLANFAIR CAEREINION, Powys SJ10
The river at the foot of the hillside on which this quiet little greystone town is built has two names – Banwy and Einion. In the local church, which was rebuilt in 1868, is the 14th-century stone figure of a knight. The ancient doorway of the church is a good example of medieval building.

The charming House on Crutches in Bishop's Castle straddles a passage between the High Street and Market Place.

To leave Llanfair turn right, bear left and cross the Banwy-Einion, then turn right on to the A458 'Welshpool' road. After $\frac{1}{4}$ mile note the terminus of the Welshpool and Llanfair Railway on the right.

WELSHPOOL AND LLANFAIR RAILWAY, Powys SJ10
Opened in 1903, this narrow-gauge railway was the only line of its type built in Wales to carry general goods. Passenger services ceased in 1931, but the railway continued to fulfil its original function until it was completely closed down in 1956. Four years later in 1960 the Welshpool and Llanfair Light Railway Preservation Co was formed, and by 1973 was large enough to purchase the line outright. At the time of publication trains operate from Llanfair to Sylfaen Station, but plans are afoot to eventually re-open the line all the way to Welshpool. A wide variety of locomotives and rolling stock is used to operate the railway.

Continue through pleasant scenery, with the railway to the right, and return to Welshpool.

TOUR 48

THE FOREST OF DEAN

Carpets of daffodils in spring and a leafy canopy in summer provide a backcloth for the one-man craft industries for which the forest is famous. West are the silvery coils of the majestic River Wye, which borders this outstanding region and divides England from Wales.

The Forest of Dean is a place of beauty and interest at all times of the year.

ROSS-ON-WYE, Herefs & Worcs SO62

High above the roofs of this attractive town rises the splendid 208ft spire of St Mary's Church, the topmost part of which was rebuilt in the 17th century with money donated by the philanthropic John Kyrle. Inside the main church, which dates mainly from the 13th century, are numerous interesting monuments. An important feature of the High Street is the red-sandstone Market Hall (AM) of 1670, which features a Charles II medallion set into the gable overlooking Man of Ross House – where Kyrle lived. The most conspicuous reminder of Kyrle's many benefactions is the Prospect – a garden with excellent views over the river. Several ancient and attractive groups of buildings are preserved in the town, including a number of almshouses and the 16th-century Wilton Bridge.

Leave Ross-on-Wye with SP 'Monmouth A40'. After $\frac{3}{4}$ mile cross the River Wye and continue to Wilton roundabout.

WILTON, Herefs & Worcs SO52

The splendid 16th-century bridge that spans the Wye here features a curiously inscribed sundial which was added in the 18th century. Near by are a group of old buildings and the picturesquely overgrown ruins of a 13th-century castle.

Enter the Wilton roundabout, leave by the 1st exit, and ascend to Pencraig. Continue for $\frac{1}{2}$ mile, then turn left on to an unclassified road. Proceed to Goodrich.

GOODRICH, Herefs & Worcs SO51

Imposing ruins of moated Goodrich Castle (AM), built in the 12th century as a defence against Welsh raiders, stand on a wooded hill overlooking the beautiful River Wye.

Branch right with SP 'Symond's Yat' and join the B4229. After $\frac{3}{4}$ mile turn left on to an unclassified road SP 'Symond's Yat East' and cross Huntsham Bridge. After 1 mile keep left and steeply ascend a narrow road to reach Symond's Yat.

SYMOND'S YAT, Herefs & Worcs SO51

This famous beauty spot lies in a narrow loop of the River Wye. An AA viewpoint at the summit of 473ft Yat Rock affords magnificent views over the Yat (gap or 'gate') itself, and of the river as it winds through the rich woodlands of its deep valley.

Join the B4432 and continue to Christchurch, then turn right on to the B4228 SP 'Coleford'. After $\frac{1}{2}$ mile meet crossroads and turn right on to the A4136 SP 'Monmouth'. Proceed to Staunton.

STAUNTON, Glos SO51

Fine views of the River Wye can be enjoyed from many vantage points around this old village. The local church has Norman origins and is often referred to as the 'Mother Church of the Forest of Dean'. An isolated rock known as the Buckstone makes a fine viewpoint. It used to move to the touch, but after having been dislodged in 1885 it was firmly fixed in its original position.

Descend into Wales through beautifully wooded scenery and after $4\frac{1}{2}$ miles turn left on to the A466 SP 'Chepstow'. A short detour to Monmouth can be made by remaining on the A4136.

MONMOUTH, Gwent SO51

Strategically placed where the rivers Wye and Monnow meet, this ancient town played a vital role in subjugating South Wales from the Roman period till the middle ages. The outstanding reminder of these troubled times is a unique fortified bridge (AM) which has spanned the Monnow and guarded the town since 1260. The once-powerful castle preserves an interesting 12th-century building among its remains. Near by is the Great Castle House (exterior AM), a 17th-century structure noted for its fine interior decorations. Many other historic buildings survive in Monmouth, including a ruined priory, several fine churches, an 18th-century shire hall, and venerable houses of the Tudor and Georgian periods. East of the town is wooded Kymin Hill (NT), an excellent viewpoint which carries an 18th-century Naval Temple at its summit.

Shots from a cannon called Roaring Meg battered Goodrich Castle into submission during the Civil War.

Continue along the Wye Valley and pass through Redbrook, where the river forms part of the border between England and Wales. East of the road are traces of Offa's Dyke.

OFFA'S DYKE, Gwent etc

King Offa of Mercia constructed the banks and ditches of these extensive earthworks some time during the 8th century. The dyke, broken in places, stretches from Chepstow to Prestatyn and for many centuries was accepted as the boundary between England and Wales.

Cross Bigsweir Bridge and drive through Llandogo. Continue to Tintern Abbey.

TINTERN ABBEY, Gwent SO50

Set amid the soft mountains of South Wales and surrounded by the remains of ancient monastic buildings is the beautiful roofless church of Tintern Abbey. This once-important Cistercian foundation was created in 1131, and its size gradually increased along with its influence and importance – mainly in the 13th and 14th centuries. Close by is the little village of Tintern Parva.

Continue along the A466 and after 3 miles pass a path on the right leading to Wyndcliff Viewpoint. Drive through St Arvans and pass Chepstow Racecourse on the left. Enter a roundabout and take the first exit. Proceed into Chepstow.

CHEPSTOW, Gwent ST59

Spectacularly perched above a bend of the Wye are the extensive remains of Chepstow Castle (AM), a massive fortification that was begun in stone only a year after the Norman invasion of England. A path through pleasant gardens leads from the castle into the quaint old town, which includes many old houses built along switchback streets.

Leave Chepstow on the A48 SP 'Gloucester' and cross the River Wye into England. Ascend, and after $\frac{1}{4}$ mile turn left on to the B4228, SP 'Coleford'. Continue to the edge of Hewelsfield.

HEWELSFIELD, Glos SO50

Norman workmanship is evident in the fabric of Hewelsfield Church, which is said to be one of the oldest in the Forest of Dean.

Continue, with views of the River Severn to the right, and later bear left into St Briavels.

ST BRIAVELS, Glos SO50

During the middle ages this quiet little village was the administrative centre for the Forest of Dean. Its church was built in 1089 and maintains a custom in which small cubes of bread and cheese are scattered among the parishioners after evening service on Whit Sunday. This practice is probably 70 years old. St Briavels Castle, now a youth hostel, has a magnificent 13th-century gatehouse and a 12th-century great hall.

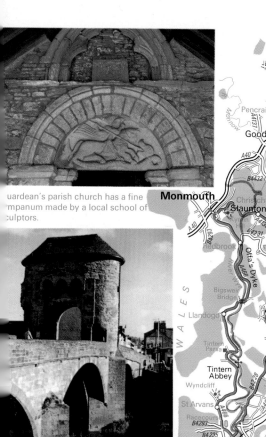

uardean's parish church has a fine ˙mpanum made by a local school of :ulptors.

Chepstow was one of the earliest stone castles to be built in Britain.

ɜ tower on Monnow Bridge was built ɜ fortified entrance to Monmouth.

The writer C S Lewis was so moved by the majestic roofless ruin of Tintern Abbey that he wished all churches were open to the sky.

ɜp forward through St Briavels and ɹr $\frac{1}{4}$ mile reach crossroads and turn . After $1\frac{3}{4}$ miles join the B4231. ɜp forward and after $\frac{1}{4}$ mile turn ıt to rejoin the B4228. After $\frac{3}{4}$ mile ı right on to an unclassified road 'Parkend', and after 1 mile meet a ınction. Turn right on to the B4431 ' continue to Parkend.

:KEND, Glos SO60
rather undistinguished village an interesting 'gothicky' church ıg from 1822. Close by is the .n Forest Railway.

ɴ FOREST RAILWAY, s SO60
s are afoot to open a working m railway line from Lydney to end in the near future. A ɛction of locomotives and ciated railway equipment is kept ırkend, and is accessible to the ic.

tinue on the B4431, and after niles turn left on to an unclassified SP 'Speech House'. Approach ch House through the Forest of ı.

ST OF DEAN, Glos
in the boundaries of this historic – the first National Forest Park created in England – is some of nest woodland scenery to be l anywhere in Britain. Since the forest has been Crown property (although it is now cared for by the Forestry Commission) and it is famous for a number of privately run industries, including coal mining and traditional charcoal burning. Specially laid-out forest trails and a forest drive help visitors appreciate the best that the area has to offer.

SPEECH HOUSE HOTEL, Glos SO61
This handsome building succeeded St Briavels to become the administrative centre for the Forest of Dean, on its completion in 1680. It now serves as an hotel, but the old Verderers Court of Foresters is still held there.

Turn right on to the B4226 and pass a picnic site on the left. Continue to the edge of Cinderford.

CINDERFORD, Glos SO61
Typical of early 19th-century development, this village was largely created to house the workforce required to operate the Forest Vale Ironworks.

Leave Cinderford and continue on the B4226. After $\frac{3}{4}$ mile join the A4151 and proceed to Littledean.

LITTLEDEAN, Glos SO61
Features of this small place include an attractive old church, an 18th-century gaol which now serves as a police station, and the Red House – a building showing features that may be of Norman origin.

Meet a T-junction in Littledean and turn right SP 'Newnham' on to an unclassified road. Descend into Newnham-on-Severn.

NEWNHAM-ON-SEVERN, Glos SO61
Many old houses survive in this pleasant little town, which has a grassy bank down the centre of its high street. The local church affords enchanting views across the River Severn to the Cotswold Hills.

Leave Newnham on the A48 'Gloucester' road. After 2 miles turn left on to an unclassified road SP 'Flaxley and Mitcheldean'. Continue to Flaxley.

FLAXLEY, Glos SO61
Unspoilt Flaxley is a cluster of houses with an unpretentious church and an historic abbey. The latter was originally created in the 12th century, but after a great fire in 1777 much of the monastic complex was rebuilt in the Georgian style. It is now used as a private dwelling.

Leave Flaxley, and after 3 miles cross a main road to enter Mitcheldean.

MITCHELDEAN, Glos SO61
The beautiful 18th-century spire of Mitcheldean Church rises grandly over the roofs of much older half-timbered cottages in the village.

At Mitcheldean Church turn left for Drybrook. Meet crossroads and drive straight across, then keep left. In $\frac{3}{4}$ mile meet a T-junction and turn right on to the B4227. Continue to Ruardean.

RUARDEAN, Glos SO61
Above the inner doorway of Ruardean's notable church is a beautifully-preserved Norman tympanum depicting St George's battle against the dragon.

Continue on the B4227 SP 'Ross', and after $1\frac{1}{2}$ miles join the B4228. Follow the River Wye and drive through Kerne Bridge to reach Walford.

WALFORD, Herefs & Worcs SO52
This Wye-side village has a 13th-century church and stands on the site of a Roman camp.

Continue on the B4228 to return to Ross-on-Wye.

TOUR 49 80 MILES

RIVERS OF THE SOUTH

After looping from its mid-Wales source the magical Wye swings in great curves down to Hay, Ross, and the cathedral city of Hereford. West of the Wye the River Dore flows gently through its fertile valley to join the Monnow, a Wye tributary guarded by ruined border fortresses.

HEREFORD, Herefs & Worcs SO54
Once the capital of Saxon West Mercia, this ancient town is at the centre of a rich agricultural district and is especially noted for the production of cider. There has been a cathedral in the city since the 7th century, but the present building dates mainly from the 12th and shows a variety of later alterations. It is dedicated to St Mary and to St Ethelbert, a king of East Anglia who was murdered near Hereford in AD 794. His tomb later became a famous shrine. Other notable relics in the cathedral are the 14th-century *Mappa Mundi* (Map of the World), King Stephen's 800-year-old chair, the best library of chained books in the country, and many monuments and tombs. Cloisters leading to the ancient Bishop's Palace contain a rare 12th-century timbered hall, and the College of Vicars Choral dates from the 15th century. There is another chained library in All Saints Church. The 11th-century St Peter's Church is the oldest in Hereford. A wealth of half-timbered buildings is preserved here, including the outstanding early-15th-century Old House, now a museum. In Widemarsh Street is the St John Coningsby Museum, which incorporates a 12th-century chapel and hall with 17th-century almshouses. Railwayana is shown at the Bulmers Railway Centre. The lovely Wye flows under the ancient Wye Bridge, past the cathedral grounds and castle ruins.

Leave Hereford on the A438 SP 'Brecon'. After 5 miles reach the Weir on the left.

THE WEIR, Herefs & Worcs SO44
Fine views of the Wye and the Black Mountains can be enjoyed from this steeply sloping riverside garden (NT, open). The house (not open) dates from the 18th century.

Continue to Letton, with occasional views of the Wye, and 1¾ miles beyond the village turn left and pass through Willersley and Winforton. Proceed to Whitney-on-Wye.

WHITNEY-ON-WYE, Herefs & Worcs SO24
For many centuries the district called Archenfield, a roughly triangular area bounded by Whitney, Hereford, and the River Monnow, was the subject of a bloody tug-of-war between Wales and England. The church here was rebuilt after flood damage in 1740. Cwmmau Farmhouse (NT) is a 17th-century timber-framed building situated north at Brilley.

Follow the Wye to enter the Welsh county of Powys. Continue, with views of the Black Mountains to the left, to reach the outskirts of Clyro.

CLYRO, Powys SO24
Francis Kilvert the diarist was curate of this quiet little village between 1865 and 1872. His notes and records paint a highly detailed picture of life in the Radnorshire hills during the 19th century, and have been the subject of a television series. The local church was rebuilt in 1853 but retains some of its original 13th-century structure.

Leave Clyro on the B4351, shortly cross the Wye, then turn right to enter Hay-on-Wye.

HAY-ON-WYE, Powys SO24
Book lovers are in their element here, for Hay has more than its fair share of book stores. Narrow streets winding through the old town are full of fascinating small shops, and on market day are alive with bustling activity. William de Braose, one of the most ruthless of the Marcher Lords, built a castle here to replace one burned down by King John. Folk hero Owain Glyndwr destroyed the later castle during the 15th century, but a fine gateway, the keep, and parts of the wall remain. Alongside the ruins is a Jacobean house.

From Hay turn left on the B4348 'Peterchurch' road and re-enter England. After 2¼ miles turn right and continue to the edge of Dorstone.

DORSTONE, Herefs & Worcs SO34
Thomas de Brito, one of the four knights who murdered Thomas à Becket in Canterbury Cathedral, founded the local church. Although largely rebuilt in 1889 it retains a 13th-century tower arch. A lane from Dorstone leads 1 mile north to Arthur's Stone, a prehistoric tomb (AM) dating from c 2000 BC. The view from here is magnificent.

Hereford Cathedral's massive sandstone tower was designed and built at the beginning of the 14th century.

Winding its way from its mountain source, the River Wye sweeps in great loops into the rolling farm and pasture lands at How Caple.

Continue and after ¼ mile meet crossroads and turn right. Drive along the Golden Valley to Peterchurch.

ETERCHURCH, Herefs & Worcs SO33
ituated in the heart of the lush Golden Valley, Peterchurch has a arge and exceptionally well-preserved Norman church. A wooden panel representing a fish with a chain round its neck hangs over the south door. Wellbrook Manor (open on application) is one of the best examples of a 14th-century hall-house in the county.

After 2 miles turn right on to the B4347 SP 'Pontrilas', still following the River Dore; later enter Abbey Dore.

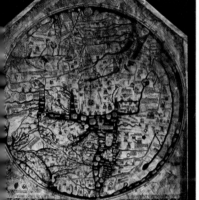

Jerusalem is the centre of the world on the *Mappa Mundi*, in Hereford Cathedral.

BEY DORE, Herefs & Worcs SO33
e meadows and orchards of the lden Valley surround this little age, which is famous for its parish urch. In 1174 an abbey was nded here, but after the solution of the Monasteries its dings were neglected. In 1633 d Scudamore commissioned the ant craftsman John Abel to uild the church. Much of the inal fabric was restored; additions Abel included the fine wooden een – a good example of his work.

ntinue to Ewyas Harold.

YAS HAROLD, Herefs & Worcs SO32
mportant Norman castle stood e during the 13th century, but the mound has survived to the ent day. The church, partly uilt in 1868, retains its impressive -century tower.

s a bridge. After ¾ mile cross the 5 and the River Dore, then turn . After 1½ miles turn right to re- Wales and ascend to Grosmont.

OSMONT, Gwent SO42
small old-world town, set amid utiful scenery by the River now, was a borough until 1860. e its massively towered church uge, flat-faced stone knight of nt origin. The castle (AM) here one of 3 erected in the ty to protect the border een England and Wales, the s being Skenfrith and White e. It is quite likely that the first is site was built as early as c 1070, but it was largely rebuilt during the reign of Henry III. Owain Glyndwr, the Welsh partisan, took the castle in 1410 but was ousted by Harry Monmouth (who was later to become King Henry V). This was Glyndwr's last recorded battle.

Continue through pleasant hill country and after 4¼ miles turn left on to the B4521 SP 'Ross'. Reach the edge of Skenfrith.

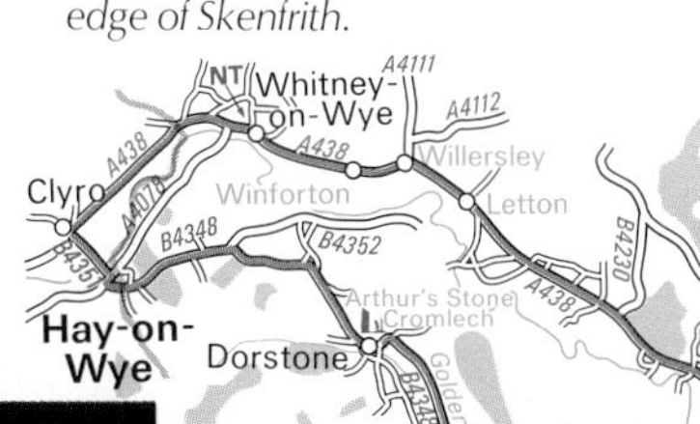

Ross-on-Wye is dominated by its 13th-century church.

Prehistoric Arthur's Stone is situated near Dorstone.

The craggy ruins of Skenfrith Castle stand near the River Monnow.

SKENFRITH, Gwent SO42
Remains of 13th-century Skenfrith Castle (AM, NT), one of a trio built to defend the English border, include a central keep enclosed by a four-sided curtain wall and a moat. In its western range is a flight of stone steps leading down to a central room which contains a fireplace with beautifully carved capitals. The local church also dates from the 13th century and has an impressive partially-timbered tower. Inside is the tomb of the last governor and guardian of the castle, John Morgan, who died in 1357.

Cross the River Monnow, re-enter England, and after 1 mile reach the Broad Oak Inn. Turn right on to an unclassified road SP 'Monmouth'. After 1½ miles reach the entrance to Pembridge Castle.

PEMBRIDGE CASTLE, Herefs & Worcs SO41
Dating originally from the 13th century, this castle (open sometimes) has a 16th-century chapel and a 17th-century hall. Some of the structure was restored during this century, and the buildings are partly used by a local farmer.

Leave Pembridge Castle, later reach the A466, and turn right. Take the next turning left on to an unclassified road SP 'Llangrove', and after 1¾ miles turn right to enter Llangrove. Descend into Whitchurch.

WHITCHURCH, Herefs & Worcs SO51
Roman remains were found on the outskirts of this village in the 19th century. The Church of St Dubricius is set beside the River Wye and contains a Norman font.

Follow SP 'Ross' to join the A40 and continue through Pencraig, with occasional views of the Wye. Later reach Wilton.

WILTON, Herefs & Worcs SO52
The splendid bridge and nearby buildings here are described in tour 48, from Ross-on-Wye.

Meet the Wilton roundabout and take the 3rd exit into Ross.

ROSS ON WYE, Herefs & Worcs SO62
A handsome market hall standing in the centre of this town is just one of many attractive buildings preserved here. Overlooking all is the fine 13th-century church. See also tour 48.

Follow SP 'Ledbury' and after 1 mile turn right on to the A449. Shortly enter a roundabout and leave by the 1st exit SP 'Worcester'. After 1¾ miles branch left to join the B4224 SP 'Hereford'. Continue for ¼ mile, turn left, and drive through How Caple to reach Fownhope.

FOWNHOPE, Herefs & Worcs SO53
Wooded hills, leafy lanes with grassy verges, and old timbered buildings exist in a magical combination in and around this picturesque Wye-side village. The church has a Norman tower and preserves a contemporary tympanum which depicts the Virgin and Child.

Continue to Mordiford

MORDIFORD, Herefs & Worcs SO53
Parts of the beautiful bridge that spans the Wye here date from the 14th century. Near by, making a delightful group, are the partly-Norman church and a Georgian rectory. Until 1811 the church tower carried a painting of the fearsome (and legendary) Mordiford Dragon.

Continue through Hampton Bishop to return to Hereford.

KIDDERMINSTER, Herefs & Worcs SO87
Carpets were the foundation of Kidderminster's prosperity, and the carpet-weaving industry that was introduced here in 1735 continues to be a major concern. The town's architecture is homely rather than distinguished, although handsome St Mary's Church and the cluster of Georgian buildings in Church Street have much to offer the eye.

Leave Kidderminster on the A456 'Leominster' road and shortly reach the West Midlands Safari Park.

WEST MIDLANDS SAFARI PARK, Herefs & Worcs SO87
Giraffes, elephants, and many other exotic beasts can be seen in the 200 acres of this interesting wildlife park. Other attractions include a pets' corner for the children, a 'boat safari', bird gardens, and a complete dolphinarium.

Cross the River Severn via Telford's bridge and enter Bewdley.

BEWDLEY, Herefs & Worcs SO77
Telford's fine bridge spanning the Severn at Bewdley was built in 1795. Severnside is a beautiful street lined with 17th- and 18th-century houses. An elegant parade of Georgian and earlier buildings line both sides of Load Street, which is eventually closed off by a large Georgian house and 18th-century St Anne's Church. Bewdley's more distant history is represented by several excellent half-timbered buildings. Overlooking the town is Tickenhill House, a period mansion refaced in 1738 and incorporating a royal palace. South of the town is a pleasant park shared by Ribbesford House and an interesting church which preserves 14th-century woodwork and Victorian stained glass by Burne-Jones. The house was rebuilt in 1820.

TOUR 50 76 MILES

ANCIENT TOWNS

From Kidderminster this tour visits the handsome Georgian streets of Bewdley, the purpose-built canal town of Stourport, and delightful Ludlow – an ancient gem in the English landscape. Scattered between are villages, each one unique in its character.

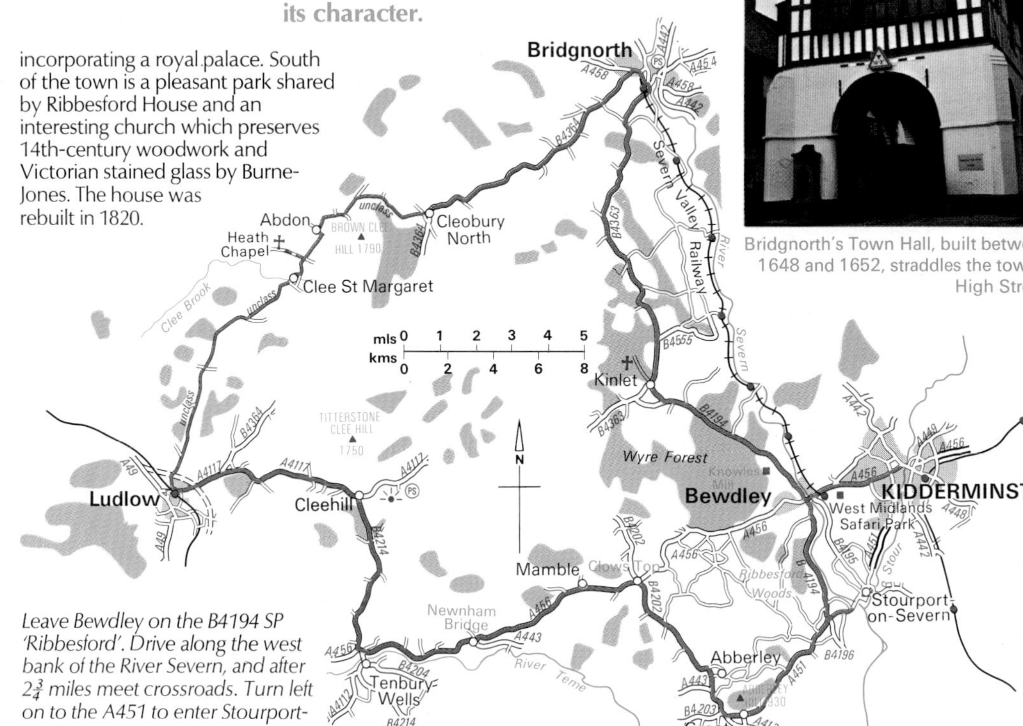

Bridgnorth's Town Hall, built betwe 1648 and 1652, straddles the towr High Stre

Leave Bewdley on the B4194 SP 'Ribbesford'. Drive along the west bank of the River Severn, and after $2\frac{3}{4}$ miles meet crossroads. Turn left on to the A451 to enter Stourport-on-Severn.

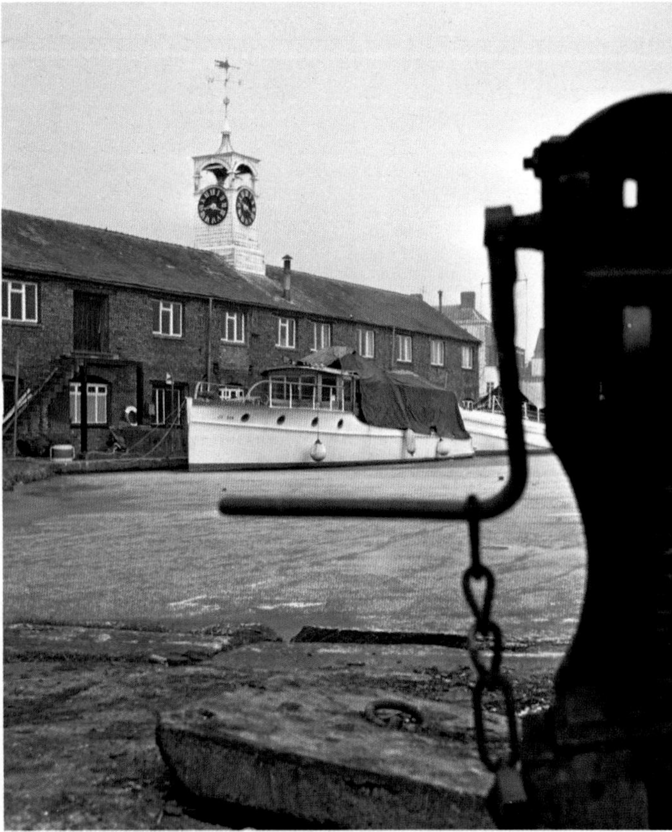

Winter holds the canal basin at Stourport-on-Severn in an icy grip. A Georgian warehouse stands in the background.

STOURPORT-ON-SEVERN, Herefs & Worcs SO87
After the opening of the Staffordshire and Worcestershire Canal, built by the engineer James Brindley in 1766, Stourport became a major canal port. It has survived to the present day as the only example of a purpose-built canal town in England.

Return along the A451 and recrosss the River Severn. After $4\frac{1}{2}$ miles reach Great Witley.

GREAT WITLEY, Herefs & Worcs SO76
Entry into Great Witley's Chapel of St Michael transports the visitor from the English countryside to some remote part of Italy. Rich rococo decoration completely alien to rural Britain assaults the eye – not unpleasantly – from skilfully-patterned walls and painted ceiling panels. Close to the chapel, which was consecrated in 1735, is the ruined shell of 17th-century and later Witley Court.

Drive to the end of the village and turn right on to the A443. After 1 mile branch right on to the B4202 SP 'Cleobury Mortimer'. Shortly reach the edge of Abberley.

ABBERLEY, Herefs & Worcs SO76
Overlooked by 930ft Abberley Hill, this peaceful little village is centre on the ruins of a Norman church that was replaced by a handsome Victorian successor. The clock tow of Abberley Hall is visible for miles.

Continue, and gradually ascend to Clows Top for good all-round view Meet crossroads and turn left on to the A456 SP 'Leominster'. Descen into Mamble.

MAMBLE, Herefs & Worcs SO6
Mamble's church dates almost entirely from the beginning of the 13th century and carries an unus timber bell turret.

Continue through Newnham Brid and along the Teme Valley to the edge of Tenbury Wells.

TENBURY WELLS, Herefs & Worcs SO56
Mineral springs discovered here i 1839 brought instant fame as a s town to Tenbury, and the Pump Room and Baths from this period still be seen. 'Taking the waters' h long since ceased to be fashiona and nowadays the town fulfils a quiet rôle as a little market centr the surrounding countryside. Ha timbered buildings make a pleas contrast with two fine churches dating from the 19th century.

Turn right on to the B4214 SP 'Cleehill' and proceed through hilly country to Cleehill.

CLEEHILL, Salop SO57
Just east of Cleehill on the A4117 is an AA viewpoint which affords superb views to the east and south. North is 1,750ft Titterstone Clee Hill, whose bare slopes rise to a summit crowned by a prehistoric hillfort.

Turn left on to the A4117 and descend into Ludlow.

LUDLOW, Salop SO57
Ludlow is a latterday Camelot on the banks of the Corve and Teme, among the gentle Shropshire hills. High above the town's roof tops soars the 135ft tower of the parish church, while on the ground the lovely River Teme adds its own enchantment to the picture-book quality of Ludlow Castle. The church, mainly of 15th-century date, is the largest in the county and preserves contemporary choir stalls. The ashes of poet A E Housman are kept here. lear by are the beautiful black-and-hite Reader's House (open on pplication), and the 17th-century eathers Hotel. These are possibly e best of many half-timbered uildings preserved in the town. eorgian architecture testifies to the ontinued popularity of Ludlow and epitomized in the elegant Butter ross, which now houses a museum. road Street, lined with many fine wellings from the same period, xtends from the Butter Cross to idlow's sole surviving medieval te, the Broad Gate. The town's rliest structure is, of course, the stle. From as early as 1085 this cupied a strategic position in the ntentious England/Wales border untry known as the Marcher nds. The town was actually nned round the castle in the 12th ntury. John Milton's 'Comus' was en its first performance here in 34. Ludford Bridge (AM) spans the me and is of medieval origin.

leave Ludlow return along the 117 'Kidderminster' road and pass der a railway bridge. Immediately n left into unclassified Fishmore ad and cross a new bypass (under nstruction at time of printing). After miles bear right SP 'Clee St rgaret'. Ascend, with views to ve Dale, Wenlock Edge, and the e Hills, and follow SP 'Clee St rgaret' to reach that village.

E ST MARGARET, Salop SO58
otely set in the Clee Hills by the e Brook, this little village is built nly of stone and is centred on a rch with a Norman nave.

ss a ford and turn left SP 'Abdon'. $\frac{1}{2}$ mile meet crossroads; a detour Bouldon') may be taken left from across pleasantly rural pshire countryside to visit Heath pel.

Scenes such as this, of the steam-operated Severn Valley Railway, were once commonplace throughout Britain.

HEATH CHAPEL, Salop SO58
This simple, barn-like building stands on its own in a field and is a perfect example of Norman ecclesiastical architecture. It contains a Norman font and various furnishings dating from the 17th century.

Continue on the main route to Abdon.

ABDON, Salop SO58
Bracken-covered slopes rise from this village to Abdon Burve, a tract of rough country that culminates in the dominating eminence of 1,790ft Brown Clee Hill. Excellent views across to Wenlock Edge are afforded by this high region.

Turn right SP 'Ditton Priors' and after $1\frac{3}{4}$ miles bear right SP 'Cleobury North'. Skirt the north side of Brown Clee Hill, and after $1\frac{1}{2}$ miles turn left and descend to a T-junction. Turn right and continue for $\frac{1}{2}$ mile, then turn left on to the B4364 SP 'Bridgnorth'. Enter Cleobury North.

CLEOBURY NORTH, Salop SO68
Wooded Burwarton Park adds much to the charm of this village, which boasts a large and picturesque Norman church that was carefully restored by architect Sir Gilbert Scott in the 19th century.

Continue on the B4364 to the outskirts of Bridgnorth, then turn right on to the A458 to enter the town.

BRIDGNORTH, Salop SO79
Shropshire has more than its fair share of lovely old towns, and Bridgnorth vies with the best of them. It is divided into two parts – Upper Town and Lower Town – by a steep ridge which is negotiated by a twisty road, several flights of steps, and a funicular railway with a breathtaking gradient of 1 in $1\frac{1}{2}$. In Lower Town is Bishop Percy's House, a fine half-timbered building of 1580 which is possibly the oldest structure in Bridgnorth. Upper Town is on the site of the original settlement and though much of it burned down during the Civil War the High Street is still straddled by its picturesque town hall (AM). The half-timbered upper storey of this building was made from a barn after the old town hall became a battle casualty. Many fine inns can be found in the High Street as it leads to the ancient North Gate, and at the other end are the elegant Georgian houses of East Castle Street. A precariously leaning tower (AM) is all that remains of Bridgnorth Castle. Nearby St Mary Magdalene's Church was built by engineer and architect Thomas Telford in 1794, and St Leonard's Church stands at the heart of a charming mixture of buildings dotted among grassy verges. The Hermitage (AM) is one of several local caves inhabited until fairly recent times. A terminus of the revived Severn Valley Railway exists at Bridgnorth.

THE SEVERN VALLEY RAILWAY, Salop
Steam locomotives operate between Bridgnorth and Bewdley on this privately-run railway, which follows the Severn Valley and provides a mobile viewpoint through the beautiful countryside of the area. Trains run most weekdays in the summer season.

Leave Bridgnorth on the B4363 'Cleobury Mortimer' road and drive to Kinlet.

KINLET, Salop SO78
In the heart of Kinlet Park is a Norman to 14th-century church which is notable for its beautiful monuments. The building was sensitively restored in 1892, and is open by request at the house next to the village school.

From Kinlet turn left on to the B4363 SP 'Bewdley', then shortly meet a T-junction and turn left on to the B4194. Continue through Wyre Forest.

WYRE FOREST, Salop, Herefs & Worcs
This one-time royal hunting forest covers an extensive area of mixed heath, scrub, and woodland. During the spring its many wild cherry trees make a picture of white blossom, and in summer the forest is a great attraction to walkers and picnickers. Knowles Mill, a National Trust property set in an orchard, stands close by off the B4194.

Enter Bewdley and turn left on to the A456 for the return to Kidderminster.

The impressive remains of Ludlow's stle are reflected in the waters of the River Teme near 15th-century Ludford Bridge.

TOUR 51 — 73 MILES

POETRY AND SHROPSHIRE IRON

Inspiration lives in the Shropshire hills and along Wenlock Edge. Housman captured its essence in the lovely poems of 'A Shropshire Lad', and the early ironmasters distilled it in a graceful bridge that was to herald the industrial revolution.

SHREWSBURY, Salop SJ41
Superbly set in a huge loop of the Severn, this beautiful and unspoilt town is famous for its half-timbered buildings and picturesque streets. Also here are many excellent examples of 18th- and 19th-century architecture. Traditionally founded during the 5th century by the Romans, Shrewsbury has been occupied by various peoples interested in its strategic position. Two notable 18th-century bridges span the Severn into the town centre, and the remains of a castle that defended the vulnerable north-eastern entrance dominate the imposing railway station. Fortification of the castle site was begun in the 11th century, but the remains date mainly from the 13th and were incorporated in a private house about 200 years ago. Near by are the 17th-century buildings of old Shrewsbury School, which now house the civic library, museum, and art gallery. Outstanding churches in Shrewsbury include the Norman and later Abbey Church, 12th- to 17th-century St Mary's, and mainly 18th-century St Julian's, with its ancient towers. Amongst the outstanding buildings are Rowley's Mansion, which houses a museum; Whitehall of 1582; the gateway of the Council House; the Lion Coaching Inn; and the small complex of 14th-century cottages, shops and lovely old hall called Bear Steps.

Leave Shrewsbury on the A49 'Leominster' road, and ½ mile beyond Baystonhill turn left on to an unclassified road to reach Condover.

CONDOVER, Salop SJ40
Pink sandstone was the predominant material used to build both the 17th-century local church and Condover Hall (open on application), a splendid example of Elizabethan architecture.

At Condover turn left SP 'Pitchford' and after ½ mile bear left. After 1½ miles meet crossroads and turn right to enter Pitchford.

PITCHFORD, Salop SJ50
Half-timbered Pitchford Hall (not open) is a perfect example of a 16th-century black-and-white building, and the adjacent church retains good Norman details.

Continue to Acton Burnell.

ACTON BURNELL, Salop SJ50
Edward I held what is said to have been the first English parliament here in 1283. Ruined Acton Burnell Castle (AM) dates from the 13th century and was built by Robert Burnell, Bishop of Bath and Wells, partly as a castle and partly as a palace.

Meet crossroads, turn right SP 'Church Stretton', and after 2 miles bear right. Enter Longnor.

LONGNOR, Salop SJ40
In a grove of trees here is a perfect 13th-century church with 18th-century furnishings. Longnor Hall (not open) stands in a large deerpark and dates from 1670. Near by is black-and-white Moat House.

Continue, and after a short way turn left on to the A49. Enter Leebotwood.

LEEBOTWOOD, Salop SO49
The finest of several half-timbered buildings in this village is the thatched Pound Inn. A 1,236ft hill known as The Lawley rises high above the village nearby.

Continue, with Caer Caradoc Hill to the left and the Long Mynd moorland to the right.

CAER CARADOC HILL, Salop SO49
Earthworks of an iron-age hillfort said to have been defended by King Caractacus crown this miniature mountain, which is only 1,500ft high.

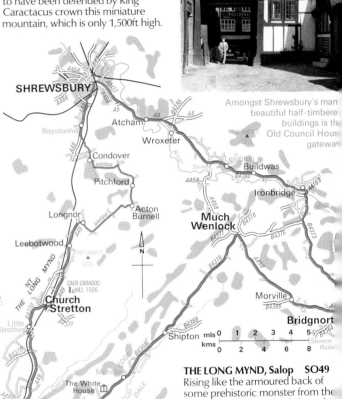

Amongst Shrewsbury's man beautiful half-timbere buildings is th Old Council Hous gatewa

THE LONG MYND, Salop SO49
Rising like the armoured back of some prehistoric monster from the ordered fields of lowland Shropshi the Long Mynd is a heather-cover mass of ancient grits and shales, largely owned and protected by th National Trust. Where the moorla hills fall towards Church Stretton they are scored by numerous ravines; the lovely Cardingmill Va is possibly the most beautiful.

Continue and meet crossroads. Tu right on to the B4371 SP 'Town Centre' and enter Church Stretton

CHURCH STRETTON, Salop SC
During the late 19th century the district around Church Stretton became known as 'Little Switzerland', and the town itself developed into a popular inland resort. Red-brick and half-timber Victorian villas mingle with older black-and-white buildings to cre pleasant character complement by the Church of St Lawrence, w has been adapted through many periods. Above the Norman nor doorway is a Celtic fertility symbol. There are three Stretton the valley – Church Stretton at t centre, All Stretton to the north, Little Stretton to the south. The has many half-timbered building

Winter sunshine on Wenlock Edge.

'Meet crossroads and turn left on to the B4370. Pass through the pretty village of Little Stretton. Turn right on to the A49, and continue to Craven Arms.*

CRAVEN ARMS, Salop SO48
Originally the hamlet of Newton, this 19th-century town development was renamed after a coaching inn that just preceded its expansion. Today it is an important centre for sheep auctions.

A detour of $\frac{3}{4}$ mile from the main tour route can be made by continuing on the A49 to Stokesay Castle.

STOKESAY CASTLE, Salop SO48
Wooden beams, overhanging walls, steep roofs, and decorated woodwork make Stokesay a picture-book castle where the imaginative visitor can easily slip into a world of Gothic fantasy populated by knights and dragons. Dating from c 1280, the castle (AM) is really a fortified manor house which owes its superb condition to a singularly uneventful history. Beyond the moat is a church that was damaged during the Civil War and subsequently refurbished during the Commonwealth. Interior furnishings and fittings of that time remain intact.

Leave Craven Arms on the B4368 SP 'Bridgnorth' and enter Corve Dale. Shortly reach Diddlebury.

DIDDLEBURY, Salop SO58
Diddlebury enjoys a picturesque setting beside the river in Corve Dale, beneath the high ridge of beautiful Wenlock Edge. Saxon masonry in the local church includes attractive herringbone work on the north wall.

Continue to the White House at Aston Munslow.

THE WHITE HOUSE, Salop SO58
Many periods are represented in the complex of buildings associated with the mansion, and the house itself has a 14th-century hall and 16th-century cross-wing. A fascinating museum of country life accommodated here displays a variety of farm relics.

Continue through Munslow, with Wenlock Edge to the left and the River Corve to the right. Reach Shipton.

SHIPTON, Salop SO59
Spacious and beautiful Shipton Hall (open sometimes) is the focal point of this Corve Dale village. Built in 1587 and enlarged at the back during the mid-18th century, it comprises a large range of buildings, including a fine stable block which dates from the 18th century.

From Shipton bear left on to the B4378 SP 'Much Wenlock' and continue to Much Wenlock.

MUCH WENLOCK, Salop SO69
A E Housman celebrated the beauty of this region in his collection *A Shropshire Lad*. The town is a charming little market centre with

The traceried stonework of Wenlock Priory is echoed in the symbolic design of Much Wenlock's attractive town nameplate.

many excellent half-timbered and other buildings, including such notable examples as Raynald's Mansion, the Manor House, and the Guildhall. Remains of Wenlock Priory (AM), which was founded in the 7th century and became a Cluniac house in 1080, include beautiful interlocking Norman tracery. Near by is splendid Priors Lodge of 1500.

Leave Much Wenlock on the A458 'Bridgnorth' road and continue to Morville.

MORVILLE, Salop SO69
Morville Hall (NT) was rebuilt in the 18th century, and the local church contains a wealth of details from many periods. The village as a whole is an attractive group amongst wooded rural countryside.

Continue to Bridgnorth.

BRIDGNORTH, Salop SO79
This ancient town, with its many interesting buildings, is fully described in tour 50.

Leave Bridgnorth on the B4373 and after $5\frac{1}{2}$ miles bear right SP 'Wellington'. Descend into the Severn Gorge and cross the river to reach a T-junction. Turn left on to the A4169 to enter Ironbridge.

IRONBRIDGE, Salop SJ60
Across the River Severn here is a splendid iron bridge that was built in 1779, the first of its kind in the world. This must surely be the most beautiful monument there is to the industrial revolution, which had its birth in this area. Thanks to the work of the Ironbridge Gorge Museum Trust, most of the important remains have been preserved and many can be seen in the Blists Hill Open-air Museum at Madeley. The streets and buildings of Ironbridge itself cling to the sides of the Severn Gorge.

Beyond Ironbridge keep forward on to the B4380 SP 'Shrewsbury'. Continue to Buildwas.

BUILDWAS, Salop SJ60
Concrete cooling towers looming from a local power station otherwise hidden by trees make a controversial counterpoint to the 12th-century remains of Buildwas Abbey (AM), near the River Severn. Stone from the ruin was incorporated in the local church. North of the hamlet is the 1,334ft bulk of The Wrekin.

Continue through Leighton, along the Severn Valley, to the edge of Wroxeter.

WROXETER, Salop SJ50
During Roman times the important town of *Uriconium* stood here. Excavated remains (AM) include the baths and fragments of other buildings. Near by is a church which incorporates Roman bricks and masonry in its fabric, and displays architectural features from many ages. Inside are several very fine monuments and memorials.

Continue on the B4380 and after $\frac{3}{4}$ mile turn left on to the A5. Enter Atcham.

ATCHAM, Salop SJ50
Spacious wooded parklands and two fine 18th-century bridges are the main features of this pretty village, which also has a church uniquely dedicated to St Eata. The Mytton and Mermaid Inn is of Georgian origin, and Longner Hall was built in 1803 to designs by John Nash. Humphrey Repton laid out the grounds of both Longner and nearby Attingham Hall (NT), a magnificent house of 1785.

Cross the Severn and return to Shrewsbury.

Right: Abraham Darby designed the revolutionary bridge at Ironbridge in the 18th century, unconsciously creating a memorial to the British industrial revolution. Below: a detail of the bridge's ironwork.

TOUR 52 60 MILES

TO THE VALLEY OF SONG

Walled Chester stands on the edge of England like the medieval guardian it once was. Across the border in Wales a natural wall of mountains encloses Llangollen, in a valley that rings with song during the International Eisteddfod.

Victorian architect W H Kelly designed this building, which stands in Park Street, Chester, in a convincing half-timbered style.

CHESTER, Cheshire SJ46
Founded nearly 2,000 years ago by the Romans, Chester boasts some of the richest archaeological and architectural treasures in Britain. It is the only city in England to have preserved its medieval walls in their entirety, and today they provide a 2-mile circular walk which affords excellent views of both the city and its surrounding countryside. The defences on the north and east side follow the line of the original Roman walls and are of largely Roman workmanship, but the original west and south defences were destroyed and later rebuilt in an extended form to take in the castle. At one point the walls overlook the Roodee, a racecourse where the Chester Cup has been run every May since 1540. Chester, or *Deva* as it was once known, remained a principal military station and trading town until the Romans withdrew from Britain at the beginning of the 5th century. For 5 centuries the site was deserted, then was probably re-occupied by the Saxons to prevent the Danes from using it as a stronghold. It gradually regained its position as a place of importance, and after it had fallen to the Normans in 1070 became the capital of a county Palatine whose earls were almost as powerful as the king. In 1237 the last earl died, and subsequently the eldest son of the reigning monarch has held the title. The medieval town flourished as a port until silting of the Dee during the 15th century brought a decline in trade prosperity. The city continued as a commercial centre, however, and its fortunes largely revived during the rich 18th and 19th centuries. Much survives from all periods of Chester's history, but the source of its distinctive character is undoubtedly the galleried tiers of shops known as The Rows. The beautifully restored sandstone cathedral dates mainly from the 14th century. It incorporates extensive Benedictine monastic remains, and is especially noted for its richly carved woodwork, the Lady Chapel, the refectory, and the cloisters. Partly ruined St John's Church retains excellent Norman workmanship. Most of Chester Castle now dates from the 19th century, but its 13th-century Agricola Tower is largely original. On the first floor is the vaulted Chapel of St Mary de Castro. Black-and-white buildings abound in Chester – God's Providence House, Bishop Lloyd's House and Old Leche House being outstanding – and there are also many timbered inns. Chester Zoo offers a variety of exhibits second only to London.

Leave Chester on the A483 SP 'North Wales' and cross the River Dee via Grosvenor Bridge. Reach a roundabout and take the 4th exit on to the A549 SP 'Saltney'. Reach Saltney and cross into Wales. Continue to Broughton Church, meet a roundabout, and take the 2nd exit. After $\frac{3}{4}$ mile turn left on to the A5104 SP 'Corwen'. After $1\frac{1}{4}$ miles turn left, and in 1 mile turn left again into Penyffordd. In $\frac{1}{4}$ mile turn right and after 2 miles cross the River Alyn to enter Pontblyddyn.

PONTBLYDDYN, Clwyd SJ26
Among several interesting houses that stand in this village is Plas Teg, a commanding Jacobean mansion with a bleak air which lends strength to its reputation for being haunted.

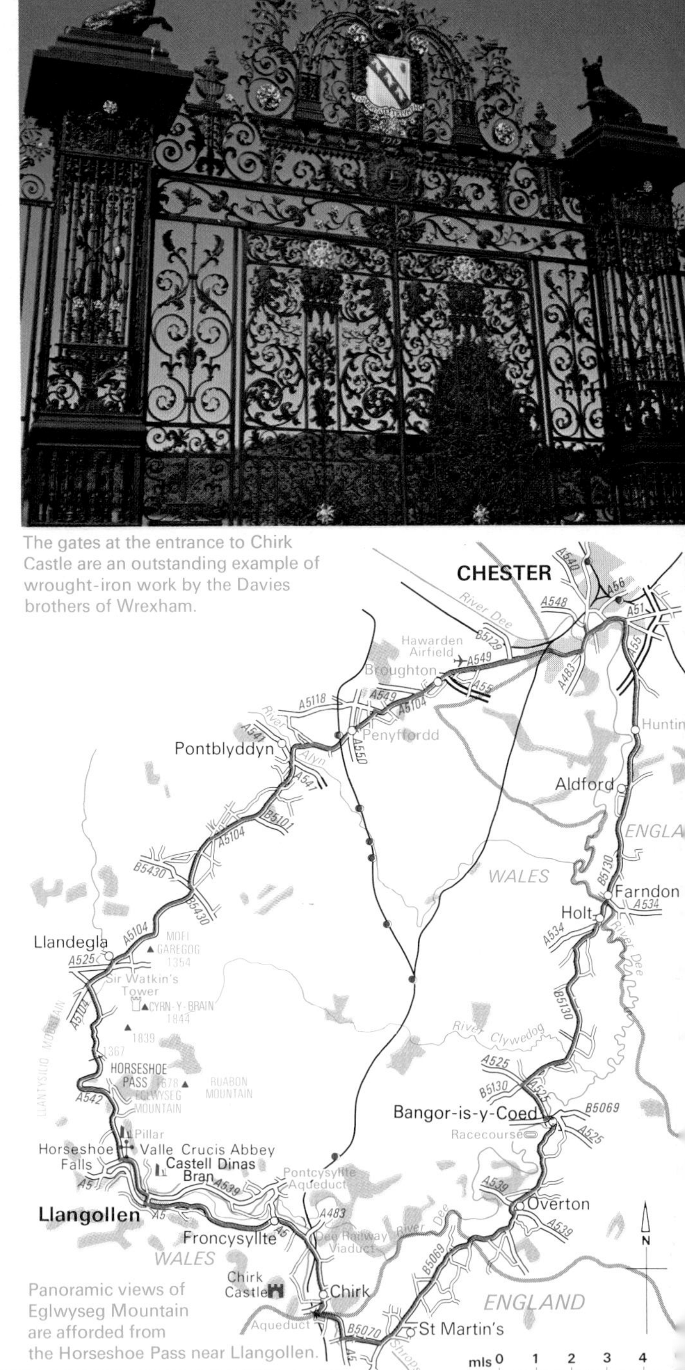

The gates at the entrance to Chirk Castle are an outstanding example of wrought-iron work by the Davies brothers of Wrexham.

Panoramic views of Eglwyseg Mountain are afforded from the Horseshoe Pass near Llangollen.

In Pontblyddyn turn left then right ascend. Proceed, with mountain views, to Llandegla.

LLANDEGLA, Clwyd SJ15
St Tecla's well, associated with ar elaborate ritual for the cure of leprosy, is sited here. At one time village was an important cattle droving centre.

Turn right then left, then after $\frac{3}{4}$ m reach a roundabout and take the exit on to the A542 'Llangollen' ro Reach Horseshoe Pass.

HORSESHOE PASS, Clwyd SJ14
Fine views of the surrounding mountain scenery can be enjoyed from this 1,367ft pass. North-east is 1,844ft Cyrn-y-Brain, topped by Sir Watkin's Tower, and west are the slopes of Llantysilio Mountain.

Continue along the Eglwyseg Valley to Valle Crucis Abbey.

VALLE CRUCIS ABBEY, Clwyd SJ24
Pleasantly wooded hills frame the view from the picturesque ruins of this ancient abbey, which was ounded in 1201 and has left xtensive remains (AM). 'Valle Crucis' neans 'Vale of the Cross' and lerives from nearby Eliseg's Pillar AM), which was erected to ommemorate a nobleman of ncient times.

After a short distance reach Horseshoe Falls.

IORSESHOE FALLS, Clwyd SJ24
lot a natural cascade but a eautifully curving weir with a fall of 8 inches, this lovely River Dee eature was built to feed water into ne Llangollen Canal.

ontinue, with Castell Dinas Bran to ne north-east.

ASTELL DINAS BRAN, lwyd SJ24
amparts of an iron-age fort partly irround this ruined 13th-century ronghold, which occupies a hilltop te overlooking the attractive little wn of Llangollen.

ırn right to cross the Dee and enter ngollen.

ANGOLLEN, Clwyd SJ24
is small town's world-wide putation as a centre of Welsh lture and music comes from the ernational Eisteddfod held here for e week in July. During this time e small streets are transformed by iot of colourful national costumes d chatter of foreign tongues, while e surrounding hillsides echo to the ınd of great international choirs d poets performing in a huge)0-seat marquee. Plas Newydd (open) is a black-and-white house on the edge of the town which was, for many years, the home of the 'Ladies of Llangollen'. This eccentric pair of spinsters, who arrived here in 1779, entertained a string of celebrities and generated endless gossip with their lifestyle. The house and grounds are attractive additions to the landscape.

Valle Crucis Abbey was founded by Madog ap Gruffyd, a prince of Powys, during the 13th century.

Follow the A5 'Shrewsbury' road through the winding valley of the Dee to Froncysyllte.

FRONCYSYLLTE, Clwyd SJ24
Thomas Telford's amazing Pontcysyllte Aqueduct is best approached from here. This, the longest in the United Kingdom, was built to carry the Shropshire Union Canal over the deep ravine of the River Dee. Downstream is a railway viaduct whose impressive design is almost as remarkable.

Continue to Chirk.

CHIRK, Clwyd SJ23
An interesting section of the Shropshire Union Canal in this well kept village includes a long, damp tunnel which opens into a wide basin before the canal is carried high across the Ceiriog Valley.

CHIRK CASTLE, Clwyd SJ23
Outside Chirk behind superb 18th-century wrought-iron gates (AM) is Chirk Castle, a 13th-century border fortress in a commanding position above the Ceiriog Valley. Unlike many of its contemporaries this stronghold has been continuously inhabited since it was built, and considerable structural changes have been made to suit the tastes of successive owners.

Poets, artists, and writers have praised Llangollen's hospitality since the early 19th century.

Cross the River Ceiriog into England, and after 1¼ miles turn left on to the B5070 SP 'Ellesmere and Overton'. Reach St Martin's.

ST MARTIN'S, Salop SJ33
The interior of the beautiful 13th-century local church preserves Georgian furnishings which include boxpews and a double-decker pulpit. Attractive almshouses stand near by.

Join the B5069 and cross undulating countryside to re-enter Wales. Reach the A528 and turn left to enter Overton.

OVERTON, Clwyd SJ34
Very old churchyard yews in this pleasant small town are traditionally held to be among the 7 greatest wonders of Wales.

Keep forward on the B5069, then turn right SP 'Bangor-is-y-Coed'. Continue with views of the Dee and Bangor racecourse, then enter Bangor-is-y-Coed.

BANGOR-IS-Y-COED, Clwyd SJ34
An ancient stone bridge is the dominating feature of this picturesque village. At one time a monastery stood near by, but the buildings were destroyed and its monks slaughtered by order of King Aethelfrith of Northumbria in AD 615. Little survives today.

Turn left and cross the bridge, then turn right on to the A525 SP 'Wrexham'. After 1¼ miles turn right on to the B5130 SP 'Wrexham Industrial Estate' and continue to Holt.

HOLT, Clwyd SJ45
Slight remains of a Norman castle can be seen near the 8-arched 15th-century bridge that spans the Dee here. The local church is a fine building which dates originally from the 13th century but was rebuilt in the 15th. Inside is an elaborately decorated font.

Join the A534 and cross the Dee to re-enter England. Continue to Farndon.

FARNDON, Cheshire SJ45
In Farndon attractive houses group round a large church that was rebuilt after Civil War damage. An unusual feature of the church is a stained-glass window depicting a troop of Royalist soldiers.

Turn on to the B5130 SP 'Chester' and continue through wooded scenery to Aldford.

ALDFORD, Cheshire SJ45
Earthworks of a Norman motte-and-bailey castle may be seen north of Aldford's Victorian church.

Return to Chester.

LLANDUDNO, Gwynedd SH78
Justifiably known as the 'Queen of Welsh Resorts', Llandudno developed in the 1850s from a cluster of fishermen's cottages to a Victorian seaside resort which is a classic of its kind. The town was the brainchild of Liverpool surveyor Owen Williams, who planned the great sweep of the Promenade and the majestically wide streets. Great Orme's Head, with its gardens, cable railway, an ancient church, and windswept grassy slopes, separates the resort's two superb beaches.

Leave Llandudno on the A546, SP 'Conwy'. After 2 miles reach a roundabout and take the 1st exit on to the A55 SP 'Betws-y-coed'. A detour may be made from the main tour route to Conwy by crossing the Afon Conwy from this roundabout.

CONWY, Gwynedd SH77
Three bridges span the Afon Conwy estuary for access to this walled town, which is squeezed between the mountains and the sea. The oldest of the bridges was built by Thomas Telford in 1826 to carry traffic previously forced to use the perilous ferry. In 1848 Stephenson built a tubular railway bridge across the estuary, and in 1958 a new road bridge took the load from Telford's original. All three bridges seem to lead straight into Edward I's magnificent castle, which, along with the town walls, is a supreme example of 13th-century defensive architecture (all AM). The original medieval street plan is preserved within the walls, but only a few old buildings survive. Outstanding amongst these are Aberconwy (NT), which was built in 1400, and the lovely Tudor house of Plas Mawr.

Continue on the main tour route through Llandudno junction. After $\frac{3}{4}$ mile reach a roundabout and take the 3rd exit on to the A470. Drive through Glan Conwy and after 2 miles reach the entrance to Bodnant Gardens.

TOUR 53 — 70 MILES

NORTHERN RESORTS AND MOUNTAIN LANES

Children's laughter is as common as the cries of gulls on the North Wales coast, but away from the sea the sounds diminish and change till all that is heard is the breeze through sedges and the murmur of mountain streams.

The weathered rock of Great Orme's Head is typical of limestone scenery.

BODNANT GARDENS, Gwynedd SH77
The finest garden in Wales, and one of the best in Britain, Bodnant (NT) occupies a superb terraced site on the east side of the Conwy Valley and is open from April to October. It is best seen early in the year when its celebrated azaleas and rhododendrons are in bloom. The gardens were first laid out in 1875 by Henry Pochin, and have been considerably extended since.

Follow the beautiful Vale of Conwy to Llanrwst.

LLANRWST, Gwynedd SH86
A graceful 3-arched bridge that spans the Conwy here is dated 1636 and (probably wrongly) attributed to architect Inigo Jones. Near by is Ty Hwnt i'r Bont, a 17th-century house (NT) which is open as a café. In the parish church are an elaborate 15th-century rood loft and screen which were brought from Maenan Abbey at the Dissolution. Attached to the church is the beautiful Gwydir Chapel of 1633, which houses memorials to one of Wales' greatest land-owning families – the Wynnes. Across the river is medieval Gwydir Castle (open), which was once the seat of the Wynnes.

Take the B5427, SP 'Nebo' from Llanrwst. Meet a T-junction and turn right on to the B5113. Pass through Nebo and descend into Pentrefoelas.

PENTREFOELAS, Clwyd SH85
Mountain scenery starts to give way to moorland near this hamlet. An 8ft-high inscribed pillar known as the Levelinus Stone marks the spot where Llywelyn ap Seisyll, a prince of Gwynedd, fell in battle in 1023.

Turn left on to the A5, and after $\frac{1}{4}$ mile turn left again on to the A543 'Denbigh' road. Continue across moorland with the Alwen Reservoir on the right.

ALWEN RESERVOIR, Clwyd SH95
A monster is said to guard the waters of this huge reservoir, which is 3 miles long and is one of the largest expanses of fresh water in Wales.

DENBIGH MOORS, Clwyd
Forestry plantations and huge reservoirs have dramatically changed the character of this moorland region in recent years. The latest enterprise is the construction of the vast Brenig Reservoir.

Continue past the lonely Sportsman's Arms – the highest inn in Wales – and drive through Bylchau to reach Denbigh.

DENBIGH, Clwyd SJ06
Overlooking the town's attractive streets are the ruins of Edward I's great castle (AM). It was begun in 1282 with the construction of town walls that have remained remarkably intact to the present da[y]. Perhaps the most impressive featur[e] of the fortress is its tripartite gatehouse. Inside the town walls ar[e] remains of St Hilary's Tower (AM), which formed part of the original garrison chapel, and Leicester's Foll[y] (AM). The latter is part of a church that was to have replaced the Cathedral of St Asaph, but was nev[er] completed. In the lower part of the town are the remains of a Carmelit[e] friary (AM), which was founded in 1284 by Sir John Salesbury; according to legend he had two thumbs on each hand.

Continue on the A525 'Rhyl' road, with the ridge of the Clwydian Rang[e] prominent to the right. Enter Trefna[nt]

Conwy Castle is arguably one of the greatest works by Edward I's military architect, Master James of St George

TREFNANT, Clwyd SJ07
Church, parsonage, and school here were built by architect Sir Gilbert Scott during the 19th century. The capitals of the columns inside the church are decorated with carved leaves typical of tree species found in the countryside round Trefnant.

Keep forward for St Asaph.

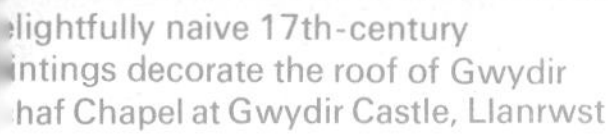

elightfully naive 17th-century intings decorate the roof of Gwydir haf Chapel at Gwydir Castle, Llanrwst

T ASAPH, Clwyd SJ07
oth a village and a city, little St saph stands beside the River Elwy d has a cathedral that was founded St Kentigern in AD 560. This has bsequently been rebuilt several nes, and major restoration work s carried out during the 19th ntury by architect Sir Gilbert Scott. e building, no bigger than a large rish church, is the smallest hedral in England and Wales.

low SP 'Rhyl', and after $\frac{3}{4}$ mile meet oundabout and keep forward. A our can be made from the main r route by turning on to the A55 onwy' road for Bodelwyddan.

DELWYDDAN, Clwyd SJ07
ng gracefully above the village f tops like the tip of a giant white ar is the 202ft spire of the parish rch. Its prominence as a dmark that can be seen miles und must have been planned by y Margaret Willoughby de Broke, o built it in 1856 as a giant morial to her husband. The rior of the building has earnt it name 'The Marble Church', for ess than 14 different kinds of that ne were used in its construction.

ntinue on the main tour route to ddlan.

JDDLAN, Clwyd SJ07
princes of Wales and their man conquerors recognised ddlan's position in the of Clywd as being of military ficance, and both forces built les here. The mound, or motte , of the first invasion stronghold still exists but it is the great castle of Edward I (AM) that really captures the eye. This was his headquarters whilst conducting the campaign to conquer Wales, and it was the Statute of Rhuddlan that confirmed his sovereignty in 1284. The parish church dates originally from the 13th century, and the bridge over the Clwyd has 16th-century arches.

Continue to Rhyl.

RHYL, Clwyd SJ08
'Sunny Rhyl' offers 3 miles of sandy beach and almost all the entertainments expected of a seaside resort as popular as this. Few other British holiday towns cater better for the family holiday, and Rhyl has been a confirmed success ever since its development from a pair of fishermen's cottages in 1833.

Leave Rhyl promenade on the 'Abergele' road and shortly turn right on to the A548. Follow the coast to Pensarn.

PENSARN, Clwyd SH97
Five miles of sandy beach ensure the popularity of this resort.

Reach a roundabout and turn left to enter Abergele.

ABERGELE, Clwyd SH97
No longer simply a market town but also a busy resort, Abergele is surrounded by caravan sites, chalets, and all the paraphernalia associated with the seaside. Its Tudor church features a double nave.

Follow the B5443 'Conwy' road to reach Gwrych Castle.

Fish eagles, hawks, and many other birds of prey can be seen at Colwyn Bay's Mountain Zoo.

The graceful lines of the bridge at Llanrwst have led to its being attributed to Inigo Jones.

GWRYCH CASTLE, Clwyd SH97
This mock-Norman extravagance with castellated walls and fairy-tale turrets was built in 1814. It now serves as a holiday centre, offering medieval banquets and jousting among its attractions.

Continue to Llanddulas.

LLANDDULAS, Clwyd SH97
Llanddulas is both a popular holiday village and a loading point for limestone worked in local quarries.

Join the A55 and continue to the 19th-century resort of Colwyn Bay.

COLWYN BAY, Clwyd SH87
Lovers of Victorian architecture will find much to please them in Colwyn Bay. The resort is hardly more than a century old, and is somewhat more restrained in character than many of its neighbours. Excellent parks soften the character of the town, and the Welsh Mountain Zoo is a post-war development featuring a good variety of wild animals.

Continue on the 'Conwy' road. After $\frac{3}{4}$ mile reach a roundabout and take the 2nd exit on to the A546. Cross Little Orme's Head and return to Llandudno.

Partial demolition after the Civil War reduced Rhuddlan Castle's 13th-century fabric to a picturesque ruin.

TOUR 54 85 MILES

LAKES AMONG THE FORESTS

Rarely level and often winding, the roads taken by this tour ascend the rocky clefts of mountain streams to summits that give panoramic views across forest-clad mountains and tree-bordered lakes. Everywhere is the sparkle and chatter of water.

BALA, Gwynedd SH93
Behind Bala's cheerful and unassuming tree-lined High Street is Tomen-y-Bala, the mound of a Norman castle. During the 18th century this was a popular spot for the local folk to do their knitting. Hand-knitted stockings from Bala were once famous, and George III would wear no others. In the High Street is a dramatic statue of Tom Ellis, a farmer's son who became Liberal Chief Whip and a tireless campaigner for Welsh home rule. His short but meteoric career was ended by an early death at the age of 40.

SNOWDONIA NATIONAL PARK
Much of this route is within the boundaries of the 845-square-mile Snowdonia National Park, which contains some of the most dramatic and beautiful scenery in Britain and is famous for its mountain ranges. The breath-taking valleys between mountains are often graced by lovely lakes and reservoirs, or enlivened with the sound of running water. In the south are old mine workings where prehistoric and modern men have searched for gold. See also tour 56.

Leave Bala on the B4391 'Llangynog' road and skirt the northern extremity of Bala Lake. Cross the River Dee and follow its valley for several miles. Climb on to open moorland and the slopes of the Berwyn Mountains.

THE BERWYN MOUNTAINS
Stretching from Llangollen to Lake Vyrnwy, this mountain range is gradually being changed in appearance as vast forests of conifers swallow up its slopes. Views from the two highest peaks – 2,712ft Cadair Berwyn and 2,713ft Moel Sych – open up outstanding panoramas in all directions.

Descend into the Eiarth Valley and enter Llangynog.

LLANGYNOG, Powys SJ02
Remains of once-important slate quarries and lead mines may be seen in this area. The church is dedicated to St Cynog, who was the eldest son of Brychan, a prince of one of the ancient Welsh kingdoms.

Follow the Tanat Valley to Penybontfawr.

PENYBONTFAWR, Powys SJ02
Picturesquely set on the southern slopes of the Berwyn Mountains, this village has a handsome Victorian church and a charming school building. All around is the beautiful countryside of old Merionethshire.

Turn right on to the B4396 SP 'Lake Vyrnwy' and continue along a narrow, winding road through wooded country to Llanwddyn.

The valley which romantic Lake Vyrnwy occupies was created by a glacier during the ice ages.

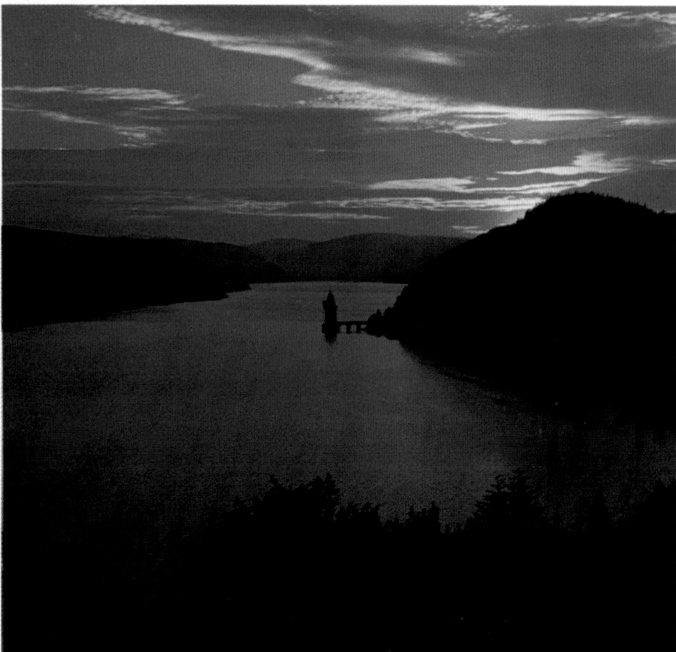

During the 16th century these hills near Dinas Mawddwy were the haunt of notorious brigands.

LLANWDDYN, Powys SJ01
Built to replace the old village of Llanwddyn, which now lies under the waters of artificial Lake Vyrnwy, this village stands in a countryside dominated by rank upon rank of dark green coniferous forest. Such rare creatures as the pine marten and polecat have been able to make a comeback because of the new habitats provided by afforestation, and are increasing in numbers.

Turn right on to the B4393 to reach Lake Vyrnwy. Turn left across the dam and skirt the wooded south shores of the lake.

LAKE VYRNWY, Powys
This lake is $4\frac{3}{4}$ miles long and was created in the late 19th century to supply Liverpool with water. The gothic water tower on its north-east side, and thick forests that clothe its banks to the water's edge, seem to suggest the depths of the German Black Forest rather than Wales.

Continue the circuit of the lake and return to Llanwddyn. Two alternative routes leading from the north end of the lake to Bwlch-y-Groes and through the Hirnant Pass to Bala respectively are described at the end of this tour. Follow the 'Llanfyllin' road for 4 miles. Turn right on to the B4395 and enter Dyfnant Forest. Cross the Afon Vyrnwy and continue to the edge of Llangadfan. Turn right on to the A458 'Dolgellau' road and climb gradually out of the Banwy Valley. Descend along the wooded Dugoed Valley to enter Mallwyd.

MALLWYD, Gwynedd SH81
Mallwyd is set beside the Afon Dyfi and is the haunt of both artists and anglers. The rib of a prehistoric animal hangs over the church porch

Continue north along the A470 from Mallwyd and reach Dinas Mawddwy

DINAS MAWDDWY, Gwynedd SH81
During the 16th century this very Welsh village was at the centre of a region notorious for its bandits. Remains of old mines and quarries dot the area, and one group of quarry buildings now houses a woollen mill. (An alternative route t Bala over the spectacular Bwlch-y-Groes Pass starts from Dinas Mawddwy and is described at the end of this tour.)

Continue on the A470 and climb th bleak 1,170ft Bwlch Oerddrws Pass. Descend, with views of Cader Idris mountain. Beyond the Cross Foxes Hotel a detour may be taken right o the B4416 to Brithdir.

BRITHDIR, Gwynedd SH71
The startling 19th-century church here was built in memory of Charl Tooth by his widow, and was designed so that it appeared to spring from the soil rather than sit solidly on it. The interior is simple, but glows with reflected light from the beaten copper of the altar and pulpit. Beyond the village is the beautiful Torrent Walk.

Descend into Dolgellau.

DOLGELLAU, Gwynedd SH71
Granite and boulder stone from the surrounding mountains are the principal materials from which Dolgellau is built. Its narrow, twisting streets are set in a fine position beside the Afon Wnion, and to the south green slopes rise to the craggy summits of Cader Idris. St Mary's Church was built in 1716 against a plain medieval tower. Wooden columns support the nave roof, and the interior is lit by windows with excellent stained glass. Beautiful Precipice Walk, which lies north of the town and is approached from the Llanfachreth road (off the A494), affords superb views throughout its 7-mile length round the rugged slopes of Moel Cymwch. Gold for the Queen's wedding ring came from old mines in the tree-clad hillsides above Dolgellau's rooftops.

olgellau's narrow streets re divided by the Afon Vnion, which is spanned ere by an ancient -arched bridge.

Leave Dolgellau on the A494 'Bala' road and climb the wooded Wnion Valley. To the west is 2,409ft Rhobell Fawr, beyond which lies most of the huge Coed-y-Brenin Forest.

RHOBELL FAWR, Gwynedd SH72
Composed of solidified lavas from ancient volcanoes, this 2,409ft mountain is the highest point in the wedge of land between the Wnion and Mawddach Valleys. Fine views afforded from its summit take in 2,155ft Dduallt to the north-east and 1,527ft Foel Ddu to the east.

COED-Y-BRENIN FOREST, Gwynedd SH72
This Forestry Commission enterprise embraces all the woodlands around and to the north of Dolgellau. It covers an area of nearly 16,000 acres, and access to the woodland and its varied mountain scenery is provided by 100 miles of forest roads; the public is warned against the dangers of leaving litter and especially, carelessly discarded cigarette stubs.

Descend to Llanuwchllyn and the southern end of Bala Lake.

LLANUWCHLLYN, Gwynedd SH83
A road-side memorial here commemorates two great champions of the Welsh language, Sir O M Edwards and his son Sir Ifan ab Owen Edwards. Sir Ifan founded the Welsh League of Youth in 1922. The nearby lakeside mansion of Glanllyn is used as a centre for the league's activities.

ALTERNATIVE ROUTES
At the north-western end of Lake Vyrnwy are 2 mountain roads. One of these can be taken through the Hirnant Pass to Bala, and the other leads up Cwm Eunant to Bwlch-y-Groes. The latter is described under the Dinas Mawddwy alternative route, which follows later.

HIRNANT PASS AND ABERHIRNANT FOREST, Gwynedd SH93
This alternative route is well worth driving for its scenery. From Lake Vyrnwy it climbs steeply along the valley of the little Afon Hirnant, which chatters among moss-grown rocks and gnarled trees alongside the road. To the west the landscape rises to the 2,055ft summit of Foel-y-Geifr, while east are the wide green expanses of Aberhirnant Forest.

From Dinas Mawddwy an alternative route may be taken back to Bala via Llanymawddwy and Bwlch-y-Groes. Leave Dinas Mawddwy by turning right on to an unclassified road and ascend the valley of the Afon Dyfi to Llanymawddwy.

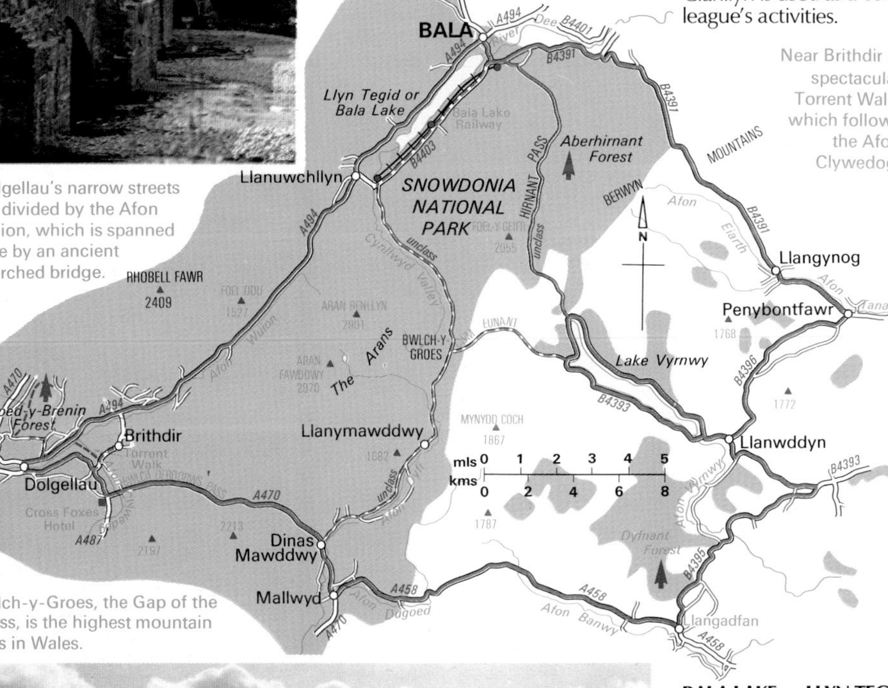

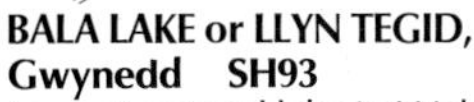

Near Brithdir is spectacular Torrent Walk, which follows the Afon Clywedog.

wlch-y-Groes, the Gap of the ross, is the highest mountain ass in Wales.

BALA LAKE or LLYN TEGID, Gwynedd SH93
Largest natural lake in Wales, Bala is over 4 miles long and in some places measures some 150ft in depth. It is surrounded by mountain scenery and is a popular venue for water-based sports. The narrow-gauge Bala Lake Railway runs along its south-eastern bank from Llanuwchllyn station to Bala, providing a mobile viewpoint from which to enjoy the superb waterside scenery. Originally this line was owned by British Rail, who closed it down in 1965 and sold it to the local council. The potential of the lake-side section was quickly recognised, and a number of steam locomotives were acquired to provide a tourist service. Plans are afoot to restore more of the track bed to working order.

Return to Bala.

LLANYMAWDDWY, Gwynedd SH91
This remote and mountain-encircled hamlet has a tiny church with an attractive old bellcote.

Ascend a 1 in 4 road to Bwlch-y-Groes.

BWLCH-Y-GROES, Gwynedd SH92
At 1,790ft this is the highest mountain pass in Wales. A road east descends to Lake Vyrnwy through Cwm Eunant, and the road to Bala follows the spectacular and precipitous Cynllwyd Valley.

THE ARANS, Gwynedd SH82
To the west of Bwlch-y-Groes rise the twin peaks – 2,970ft Aran Fawddwy and 2,901ft Aran Benllyn – of the Aran range. Aran Fawddwy is the highest mountain in Wales outside the Snowdon range.

Descend along the Cynllwyd Valley to join the B4403 and drive along the south-eastern shores of Bala Lake to reach the B4391 and Bala.

TOUR 55 66 MILES

AN ARM IN THE OCEAN

The coast of the lovely Lleyn Peninsula is a confusion of wide sands and massive cliffs. Vagrant lanes run through fields cut from the flanks of mountains, and ancient churches mark a pilgrim's way to Bardsey – burial place of a thousand saints.

THE LLEYN PENINSULA, Gwynedd
In many respects the Lleyn is similar to the other western peninsulas of St David's in South Wales and Cornwall in England. All three were settled by Iberian peoples in prehistoric times, and their cultures are still strongly Celtic in character. Their coastlines are rugged and invariably magnificent, and their inland hills are scored by numerous small river valleys. The great mountain barrier at the eastern end of Lleyn has enabled the peninsula to preserve more of its own special character than was possible for the others.

PWLLHELI, Gwynedd SH33
Seaside resort and market town, Pwllheli is the unofficial capital of the Lleyn Peninsula and has an old harbour that was once busy with sea-going craft. Even now it provides a safe haven for small boats, but is frequented more by holiday-makers than ancient mariners. Butlins Holiday Camp stands 3 miles east.

Leave Pwllheli on the A497 'Criccieth' road and continue to Llanystumdwy.

LLANYSTUMDWY, Gwynedd SH43
This village is assured of a permanent place in history because of its association with David Lloyd George, the small-town solicitor who became Prime Minister. His childhood was spent in a roadside cottage here (open), and his body was brought back to lie beside the River Dwyfor. Interesting items are displayed in the Lloyd George Museum.

Continue to Criccieth

CRICCIETH, Gwynedd SH53
Waves break constantly on the rocks beneath the ruins (AM) of a fortress built here by the princes of North Wales in the 13th century. The castle was enlarged by Edward I after he had occupied the region. Victorian charm and a relaxed atmosphere supplement the obvious amenity of the resort's excellent sun and sea-bathing beach.

Leave the town on the B4411 SP 'Caernarfon' and drive to the A487. Turn left and continue to Bryncir.

The eastern peak of Yr Eifl, a forked mountain on the north coast of the Lleyn Peninsula, is crowned by a magnificent hillfort called Tre'r Ceiri.

BRYNCIR, Gwynedd SH44
Good-quality cloth is sold from the working woollen mill in this Dyfach Valley village. A 6th-century tombstone stands at Llystyngwyn Farm.

Continue to Llanllyfni.

LLANLLYFNI, Gwynedd SH45
The Afon Llyfni flows north of this Victorian quarryman's village from its source at Llyn Nantlle Uchaf, among disturbingly derelict slate workings. Of the several old chapels in Llanllyfni, only Ebenezer has retained its 19th-century interior.

Continue to Penygroes.

PENYGROES, Gwynedd SH45
This colourful quarryman's town grew from its sister community of Llanllyfni with the development of the slate industry during the 19th century.

From Penygroes turn left on to an unclassified road SP 'Clynnog and Pwllheli'. After 2 miles meet a T-junction and turn left on to the A499. Drive through Pontlyfni and enter Clynnog-fawr.

Porth Dinllaen was considered as a possible rail terminus for Ireland in the 19th century.

CLYNNOG FAWR, Gwynedd SH44
St Beuno founded a monastery here in AD 616, and is buried in a chapel connected to the local church by a passage. His tomb was once reputed to hold great curative value. The church itself, a magnificent structure with a massive tower, was an important stopping place for pilgrims to the monastery on Bardsey Island. Between the main road and the sea is a well-preserved prehistoric tomb called Bachwen.

Continue for $3\frac{1}{2}$ miles and turn right on the B4417, SP 'Nefyn', and pass a lay-by under the slopes of Yr Eifl.

Welsh architect Clough Williams-[...] designed David Lloyd Geor[...] memorial at Llanystumd[...]

YR EIFL, Gwynedd SH34
Englishmen know the triple peaks [of] this 1,849ft mountain as 'The Riva[ls'] but a more accurate translation o[f] the Welsh name is rendered 'The Fork'. Footpaths lead to the summ[it.] The mountain is the haunt of

coos in spring, and its rock-
wn and heather-clad peaks
rd stunning views in the crystal
litions that often prevail at that
of year. One of the finest iron-
hillforts (AM) in Wales, with
hty stone walls defending an
rior crowded with hut circles, is
on the eastern peak. It is
ible that the complex was
bited until cAD 400.

cend through Llithfaen to Nefyn.

YN, Gwynedd SH34
ne time it was claimed that
n sent more of its men to sea
almost any other British town.
84 Edward I celebrated his
quest over the Welsh here, and
53 the Black Prince made the
n one of the 10 royal boroughs of
h Wales. Today Nefyn enjoys a
eel retirement from politics and
es the most of the resort
ibilities offered by its fine sands.

*right on to the 'Aberdaron' road
enter Morfa Nefyn.*

RFA NEFYN, Gwynedd SH24
ged headlands shelter a long
ep of sandy beach at Morfa
n, and an unclassified road leads
from the tour route to the
uresque hamlet of Porth
aen. This small community was
e considered as a rail terminus
t for Ireland; some might think it
a lucky escape.

*tinue on the B4417 and pass
ugh Edern to reach Tudweiliog.*

WEILIOG, Gwynedd SH23
coast near this village is indented
many small sandy coves, backed
ormidable cliffs pocked with
s. Architect Sir Gilbert Scott
gned the simple but effective
church in 1850.

*inue to a junction with the B4413
urn right. After $\frac{1}{4}$ mile the route
's a possible detour to Porth Oer:
right on to an unclassified road.*

TH OER, Gwynedd SH12
ous for its Whistling Sands,
h really do whistle when
den on, Porth Oer is a sheltered
bay offering cliff walks and fine
capes.

tinue to Aberdaron on the B4413.

RDARON, Gwynedd SH12
stop on the old route for
sey Island, Aberdaron is an
ctive village with a café reputed
ave been a pilgrim's halt. The
e of the café, Gegin Fawr, means
itchen. A large church on the
of a foundation established by St
yn in the 6th century probably
ered pilgrims as they waited for
at to take them across to the
d, the burial ground of saints.

CH-Y-PWLL, Gwynedd SH12
ectacular 500ft cliff dramatically
the Lleyn here. Views inland
nd along the whole peninsula to
wdonia, and a little over a mile
o sea is the holy island of
sey, destination of pilgrims since

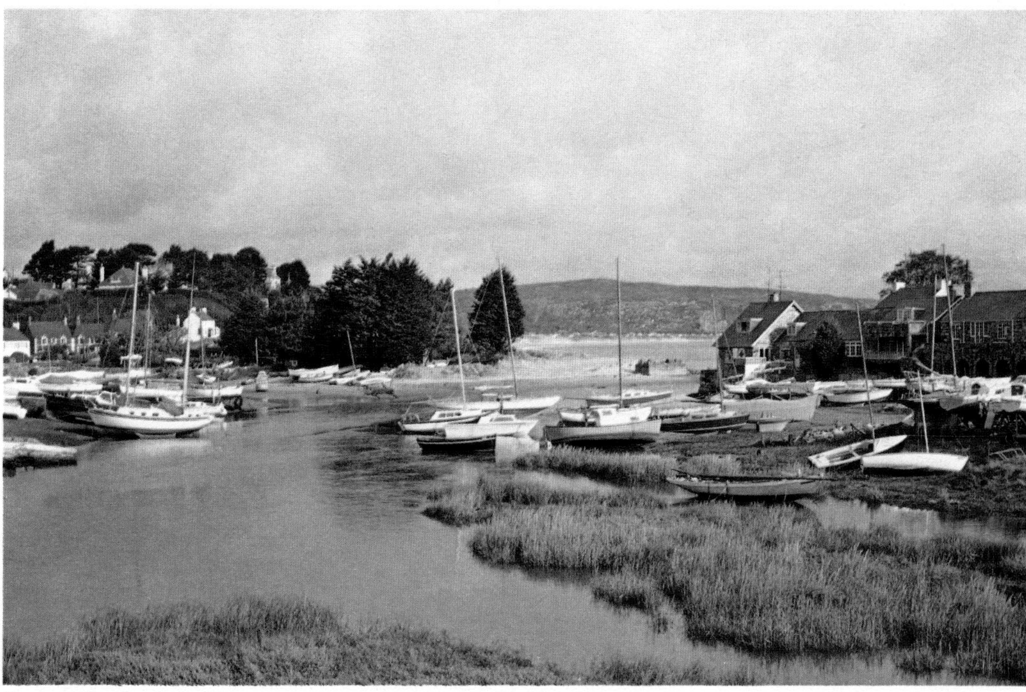

Abersoch is a popular holiday resort with a sheltered harbour.

the 6th century. Most of this magnificent coastline is protected by the National Trust.

Continue from Aberdaron on an unclassified road to Rhiw.

RHIW, Gwynedd SH22
The scattered cottages and 18th-century church of this village do little to obstruct views of the magnificent South Lleyn coast (NT). The village itself is windswept and exposed, but 1,000ft Mynydd Rhiw shelters the house and gardens of nearby Plas-yn-Rhiw from the Atlantic weather.

PLAS-YN-RHIW, Gwynedd SH22
This charming house, built in the 16th century and modernized in Regency times, is surrounded by nearly 60 acres of woodland and garden. The whole property and large areas of beautiful coastline were given to the National Trust in 1952 by the Misses Keating. Views from the house embrace an incomparable panorama extending across Hell's Mouth and Cardigan Bay to the enigmatic mountain of Cader Idris. The building is open by appointment only.

Keep forward on the 'Abersoch' road to reach Llangian.

LLANGIAN, Gwynedd SH22
Neat cottages with well-tended gardens full of flowers have helped this lovely place win the coveted Best-kept Village in Wales Award.

Turn left at Llangian, then ascend and turn right to descend to Abersoch.

ABERSOCH, Gwynedd SH32
Smart villas, expensive-looking yachts, and plush hotels are the typical signs of fashionable affluence displayed by this resort. Its popularity can be mostly attributed to its sandy beaches, mild climate, and safe bathing, but lanes leading to the windswept headland of Cilan are also a major attraction.

ST TUDWAL'S ISLANDS, Gwynedd SH32
Seen from the coast at Abersoch, these two grass-covered islands are named after a saint who came to live on one of them in the 6th century. They are privately owned, but trips can be made round their coasts by hired boats from Abersoch.

Follow the A499 along the coast to Llanbedrog.

LLANBEDROG, Gwynedd SH33
Excellent sandy beaches and attractive cliff walks have assured Llanbedrog's popularity as a resort. The parish church is embowered in trees and preserves a medieval screen. Fragments of ancient glass can be seen in the east window. Above the village is a hill which features a ruined mill (NT) and affords good views.

Continue through low-lying countryside and join the A497 for the return to Pwllheli.

Clynnog Fawr's magnificent church dates from the 16th century, and is the burial place of St Beuno.

TOUR 56 48 MILES

SNOWDON AND THE SEA

The name Gwynedd lives again as a modern county. Gwynedd the fortress, the strong land dominated by the great star of Snowdon and moated by the Menai Strait, has never died. It is still as majestically severe as it was under the Celtic princes.

CAERNARFON, Gwynedd SH46
Workaday Caernarfon is a comfortable small town which has become the most important tourist centre in Snowdonia. Above its jumbled roofs rise the massive towers of Edward I's 13th-century castle (AM), acknowledged as the finest of its type in Britain, while below in the streets is the settled life of a country community that wouldn't dream of trying to rival its own magnificent history. Although host to thousands, the town preserves a parochial 'Welshness' that is implicit in the gesticulating statue of Lloyd George opposite the castle balcony from which newly invested Princes of Wales greet their subjects. It is also acutely aware of its ideal position between the glittering Menai Strait and the mountains of Snowdonia. The sheltered waters of the Strait abound with small craft from the town's sailing clubs, and offer some of the finest fishing in Britain. Local pony-trekking centres offer a satisfying way to explore the superb countryside that encircles the town.

Leave Caernarfon on the A487 SP 'Bangor', and drive alongside the Menai Strait to Port Dinorwic.

PORT DINORWIC, Gwynedd SH56
Once a busy port concerned with the export of Dinorwic slate, this resort is now a well-known yachting centre with a large marina.

Continue, and after about 3 miles enter a roundabout and join the A5 for Bangor.

BANGOR, Gwynedd SH57
Visitors expecting the 'dreaming spires' of a university city are likely to be disappointed. Old Bangor should be enjoyed for what it is, a delightfully undistinguished maze in which the Cathedral of St Deiniol (claimed to be the oldest bishopric in Britain) crouches with unassuming modesty. The handsome buildings of the University College of North Wales were officially opened in 1911. On the seaward side Bangor's streets dip down to the city shore and a superb Victorian pier.

Leave Bangor on the A5 'Betws-y-coed' road and continue to the entrance of Penrhyn Castle Estate.

PENRHYN CASTLE, Gwynedd SH67
Although the site of Penrhyn Castle (NT) can lay claim to antiquity, the improbable extravaganza that rears its battlements above the park's

Caernarfon Castle, one of a series built to subjugate the Welsh, is arguably the finest example of medieval fortification in Britain.

wooded acres has its roots set firmly in 19th-century gothic fantasy. Parts of the edifice bear more than an accidental likeness to other great houses, and the combinations of revived styles favoured by architect Thomas Hopper are bewildering but effective. Inside are interesting exhibits, displays, and impressive chambers open to the public.

LLANDEGAI, Gwynedd SH57
Refreshingly simple after the staggering pretentiousness of Penrhyn Castle, this village was built to house local quarry workers in the late 1700s.

From traffic signals at the entrance to Penrhyn Castle Estate turn right, then right again, on to the B4409 SP 'Caernarfon'. After $4\frac{1}{2}$ miles enter a roundabout and turn left on to the B4547 SP Llanberis'. After 2 miles turn right and descend to Brynrefail. A detour can be taken from here by turning right on the A4086 to Llanrug, then left on to an unclassified road for the castle and grounds of Bryn Bras.

LLANRUG AND BRYN BRAS CASTLE, Gwynedd SH56
Bryn Bras Castle is a piece of 19th-century romanticism which presides over Llanrug village. It stands in grounds noted for their peaceful lawns and embowered walks through tranquil mature woodland.

From Brynrefail, continue the main drive by turning left on to the A4086 to skirt the shore of Llyn Padarn.

LLYN PADARN, Gwynedd SH56
Once part of a much larger water, Llyn Padarn is separated from its sister lake Peris by a natural dam formed by the gradual accumulation of material washed down in a mountain stream. Its north-eastern shore carries the narrow-gauge line of the steam-powered Llanberis Lake Railway, which originally transported slate from the Dinorwic slate quarries to Port Dinorwic. Nowadays it is a major tourist attraction.

Continue on the A4086 to Llanberis.

LLANBERIS, Gwynedd SH56
Terraced houses built on sites blasted from the rock huddle together to form Llanberis, a typical village of the slate-working communities of North Wales. A route which ascends to the main summit of Snowdon from here is considered the easiest of the mountain's 3 main paths. Close tc the village is the lower terminus o the Snowdon Mountain Railway.

SNOWDON MOUNTAIN RAILW Gwynedd SH55
Unlike its close neighbour, the Llanberis Lake Railway, Snowdon's hard-working little rack-and-pinio steam line was created as a touris aid and owes nothing to heavy industry. It was an enormous succ during the 19th-century tourist boom, and still carries a huge number of armchair mountaineer About $\frac{1}{2}$ mile or so from the lower terminus is Ceunant Mawr, one o the finest waterfalls in North Wale and by the second viaduct the Riv Arddu twists in a 120 ft fall from tł lip of a spectacular gorge.

Continue along the A4086. Pass Dolbadarn Castle and skirt Llyn Per

DOLBADARN CASTLE, Gwynedd SH56
The 13th-century castle represent by these gaunt, strangely attractiv ruins (AM) was a stronghold of the Welsh princes and has nothing to with Anglo-Norman design. Its tas was to guard the entrance of brooding Llanberis Pass; its bloody history testifies to the single-mindedness with which its native garrisons fulfilled this rôle.

LLYN PERIS, Gwynedd SH55
Smaller and narrower than Padarr Llyn Peris is a secretive place entir dominated by the moonscape devastation of the enormous Dinorwic slate workings.

DINORWIC SLATE QUARRY, Gwynedd SH55
The vast Dinorwic slate quarry rise terrace upon grey terrace from th

Llyn Padarn is one of many jewel lakes which encircle Snow

The Great Hall at Penrhyn Castle displays the mixture of styles favoured by romantic Victorian architects.

Radiating from the main peak of Snowdon are the knife-edged ridges of Crib Goch and Y Lliwedd.

This view from Snowdon's summit encompasses the lesser peak of Yr Aran and distant Moel Hebog.

Since it was opened in 1896 the Snowdon Mountain Railway has carried millions of passengers to the mountain's summit.

ore of gentle Llyn Peris, a huge onument to the scale of disruption used by man in his search for neral wealth. The effects of slate traction might be considered palling, but workings such as these ovided much-needed ployment. Buildings and chinery are in an excellent state preservation, and most of the site been turned into a museum owing the history of the slate lustry.

ntinue past Nant Peris and ascend he summit of Llanberis Pass.

NBERIS PASS, Gwynedd SH65
owdonia's great mountain masses ver above this narrow pass. To the th are the Glyders, whose highest nt is 3,279ft Glyder Fawr, and to south is the Snowdon massif, wned by 3,560ft Yr Wyddfa.

-Y-PASS, Gwynedd SH65
ated at the 1,169ft summit of the beris Pass, this is the starting t of the Miner's Track nature trail path to Snowdon.

OWDON, Gwynedd SH65
wdonia National Park covers e 845 square miles and prises large tracts of mountain moor divided by deep valleys. hin this area is the star-like wdon range, with Snowdon itself inating in the peak of Yr Wyddfa – the highest land south of the Scottish border. Radiating from the main peak are the knife-edged summits of Crib Goch and Y Lliwedd, which encircle lakes Glaslyn and Llydaw. Although all the paths to Snowdon are well trodden, no walker should set out without being properly dressed and equipped as sudden changes in the weather can prove fatal, even to the experienced.

Descend to Pen-y-Gwryd, which is situated at the head of the Gwryd Valley, and at the T-junction turn right on to the A498, SP 'Beddgelert'. Continue to the viewpoint above Llyn Gwynant.

LLYN GWYNANT AND NANT GWYNANT, Gwynedd SH65
From the viewpoint Llyn Gwynant appears as a jewel surrounded by the tree-covered flanks of mountains, with the craggy, waterfall-threaded slopes of 2,032ft Gallt-y-Wenallt on the north side. Nant Gwynant, which connects lakes Gwynant and Dinas, is often described as the finest mountain valley in Snowdonia. From its northern side the Watkin Path winds up a wooded valley on to open mountainside to reach the summit of Snowdon.

Continue along the valley and reach Llyn Dinas.

LLYN DINAS, Gwynedd SH65
Beautiful Llyn Dinas derives its name from the ancient fort of Dinas Emrys, which stands at the lake's west end, and is traditionally associated with Merlin the magician. Legend has it that the true throne of Britain is hidden in the waters of the lake, and will one day be revealed by a youth treading on a certain stone. Rising to the north-west is 2,451ft Yr Aran, which is a superb pinnacle from which to appreciate the majesty of the Snowdon range.

Skirt the shores of Llyn Dinas and continue to Beddgelert.

BEDDGELERT, Gwynedd SH54
Perhaps the only genuine alpine resort in Snowdonia, Beddgelert is completely surrounded by mountains and echoes their permanence in the solid stone of its architecture. Its name (Gelert's Grave) refers to the legend that Welsh hero Llywelyn the Great killed his dog Gelert because he thought that it had savaged his son. In fact the dog had just saved the baby boy from wolves. Historians have thoroughly debunked this story, which has since been laid at the door of an inventive local innkeeper, but its telling rarely leaves a dry eye in the schools of North Wales. Moel Hebog–'The Mountain of the Hawk'–dominates the landscape to the south-west of Beddgelert.

Keep forward on the A4085 'Caernarfon' road and reach Beddgelert Forest and picnic site.

BEDDGELERT FOREST, Gwynedd SH55
Attractive trails laid out by the Forestry Commission lead up through varied stands of conifers to tree-shrouded Llyn Llywelyn from the picnic site here.

Continue past Llyn-y-Gadair to Rhyd Ddu, where a path leads to Snowdon. Skirt Llyn Cwellyn and enter Betws Garmon.

BETWS GARMON, Gwynedd SH55
The Afon Gwyrfai flows through this village from Llyn Cwellyn and is known for its excellent game fishing. Near by is Hafodty Garden (open), where walks through the lovely rock and water gardens pass the Nant Mill waterfalls – cascades of water shrouded by flowering shrubs and overhanging trees.

Return to Caernarfon via Waunfawr.

THE ISLE OF ANGLESEY, Gwynedd
Isolated Anglesey, in which this tour is contained, is separated from the rest of Wales by the Menai Strait and presents a landscape of low, undulating hills unlike anywhere else in the Principality. First impressions are deceptive, however, for much of the coast is as wild and rugged as any to be found in the British Isles. The family holidaymaker will find good facilities and amenities here, and the lone wanderer can find all the solitude he desires. In prehistoric times the island was *Mona*, 'The Mother of Wales', and visible remains of the cultures that flourished here are everywhere.

MENAI BRIDGE, Gwynedd SH57
This largely Victorian town, named after Thomas Telford's superb bridge, is clustered round the Anglesey end of the crossing. Places of interest here include the Tegfryn Art Gallery and a fascinating Museum of Childhood, in which many rare and valuable exhibits illustrate the interests of children over the last 150 years.

Leave Menai Bridge on the A545 'Beaumaris' road and drive along the Menai Strait.

MENAI STRAIT, Gwynedd
This 14-mile stretch of water, flowing from sea to sea between Anglesey's wooded shoreline and the sloping pastures of the mainland, might be considered the major geographical feature of North Wales. Its beauty matches the splendour of Snowdon, and its sheltered reaches provide a testing venue for the water-sports enthusiasts who flock here in the summer months. Both banks – island and mainland – offer superb walking country where seabirds and rabbits are more common than people. Above Port Dinorwic are the remains of Stephenson's amazing 19th-century tubular rail bridge; farther up is the graceful suspension bridge that has carried the A5 road since 1826.

Continue to Beaumaris

TOUR 57 80 MILES

THE ISLE OF ANGLESEY

Today Anglesey is known for its quiet resorts and sandy beaches, its spectacular cliffs and a gentle interior threaded by narrow lanes. At one time it filled the bellies of North Wales with wheat and was known, almost reverently, as 'Mona', the Mother.

Beaumaris Castle is one of the best examples of concentric fortification in Britain.

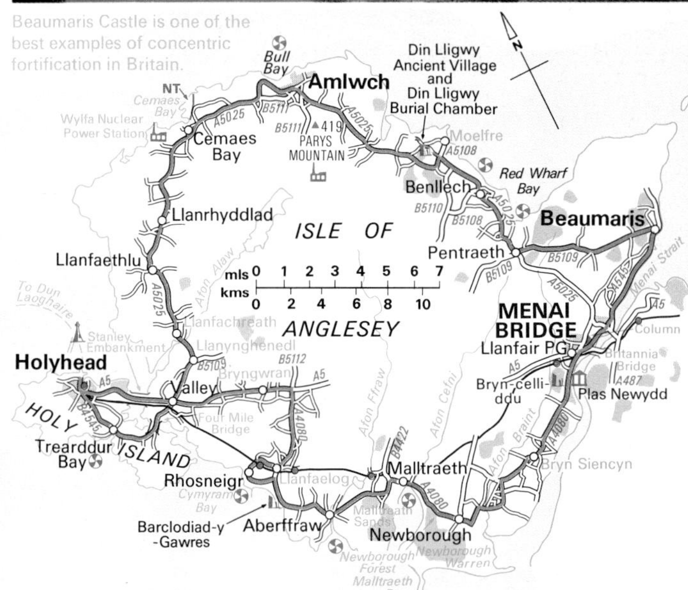

BEAUMARIS, Gwynedd SH67
The biggest attraction of Beaumaris is undoubtedly the castle (AM), an unfinished masterpiece that was the last in a chain built by Edward I to subjugate the Welsh people. A measure of the success with which this aim was achieved is the fact that the castle has never seen any military action and was never completed. The town contains much of interest, including the early 17th-century Court House and 15th-century Tudor Rose House. Several excellent inns include the Bull's Head, which was visited by Dr Johnson and Charles Dickens. The church is of 14th-century origin.

Turn inland on the B5109 'Benllech' road and cross rolling countryside to Pentraeth.

PENTRAETH, Gwynedd SH57
Land reclamation has left this village stranded 1 mile from the sea, but it was once situated at the head of Red Wharf Bay.

Turn right on to the A5025, and continue with fine views of attractive Red Wharf Bay.

RED WHARF BAY, Gwynedd SH58
More than 10 square miles of sand are revealed here at low tide, so it is not particularly surprising that the bay was once famous for its cockles. During the last century a small local shipyard built boats for the Amlwch copper trade.

Continue to Benllech.

BENLLECH, Gwynedd SH58
Perhaps the most popular seaside resort on the island, Benllech offers 2 miles of golden sand and safe bathing.

Continue, then after 2 miles enter a roundabout and leave by the 1st exit. A detour from the main route can be made by keeping forward on to an unclassified road for Din Lligwy.

DIN LLIGWY BURIAL CHAMBER, Gwynedd SH58
This important stone-age tomb (AM) consists of a huge capstone resting on a number of uprights and horizontals. Much of the chamber is cunningly hidden in a natural fissure adapted for the purpose.

DIN LLIGWY ANCIENT VILLAGE, Gwynedd SH48
Some of the ancient enclosed dwellings on this remarkable site (AM) still stand to a height of 6ft, though all of them were constructe before the Roman invasion. The surrounding wall was built subsequently. Near by is the beautiful ruin of a 14th-century chapel.

Continue on the main drive to Amlwch, with Parys Mountain rising to the left.

One of engineer Thomas Telford's fin works, this suspension bridge carries the London to Holyhead road over th Menai Strait and has a central span o 579ft.

PARYS MOUNTAIN, Gwynedd SH49
Now desolate and scarred, 419ft Parys Mountain was exploited for its copper in a small way by the Romans, but in 1768 came a boom. Fortunes were made and for a while Anglesey was the copper centre of the world, but by 1820 it was all over. Falling prices and the exhaustion of the ore forced the industry into collapse.

AMLWCH, Gwynedd SH49
At the height of the copper boom Amlwch was big enough to boast a staggering 1,025 ale houses. Today the derelict harbour, gouged out of the granite cliffs, wears a sad and contemplative frown.

Drive on to Bull Bay.

BULL BAY, Gwynedd SH49
Sheltered rocky coves and a good beach are the main attractions of this little holiday resort.

Continue to Cemaes Bay.

The Marquess of Anglesey's tall statue overlooks the Menai Strait.

EMAES BAY, Gwynedd SH39
ottages cluster round a small arbour in this quaint little fishing llage. Spectacular cliff walks lead in oth directions from the bay, and on e headland to the west is Wylfa uclear power station (open).

ortly enter Llanrhyddlad

ANRHYDDLAD, Gwynedd SH38
n Llygeirian and a large number of ehistoric sites are situated north of is hamlet. The nearby coast is lented by many lovely bays.

ter Llanfaethlu.

ANFAETHLU, Gwynedd SH38
stant views of Snowdonia can be joyed from this village, and luded bays and rocky headlands features of the nearby coast.

ntinue through Llanfachreath and nynghenedl to Valley.

LLEY, Gwynedd SH27
ne spotting enthusiasts can see F trainer aircraft and the casional rescue helicopter erating from the base here.

et traffic signals, turn right on to the and cross the Stanley bankment to Holy Island.

HOLY ISLAND, Gwynedd
The silhouette of a giant aluminium plant dominates the approach across the Stanley Embankment these days, but 720ft Holyhead Mountain still exercises a compulsive attraction as the highest point on the island. Many prehistoric monuments survive here.

Continue to Holyhead.

HOLYHEAD, Gwynedd SH28
This, the largest town in Anglesey, is a major ferry terminal for Ireland and is constantly busy with the jostling of travellers, seamen, and holidaymakers. The old parish church of St Cybi is built within the walls of a Roman fort, and the flank of Holyhead Mountain – which towers over the town – is scattered with the remains of prehistoric huts. Beyond the mountain a yawning chasm separates South Stack Lighthouse from the rest of the island.

Return along the A5 and shortly branch right on to the B4545 to reach Trearddur Bay.

TREARDDUR BAY, Gwynedd SH27
This fashionable Anglesey resort has fine sandy beaches broken up by occasional rocky outcrops.

Cross Four Mile Bridge and return to Valley. Meet traffic signals and turn right on to the A5. Pass through Bryngwran, and after 1 mile meet crossroads. Turn right on to the A4080, continue through open country, and at Llanfaelog turn right for Rhosneigr.

RHOSNEIGR, Gwynedd SH37
Cheerfully unpretentious, Rhosneigr is an ideal spot for holidaymakers who like the quiet life.

Continue on the A4080 to Barclodiad-y-Gawres.

BARCLODIAD-Y-GAWRES, Gwynedd SH37
The carved stones of this megalithic passage grave (AM) are among the finest of their kind in Britain.

Continue to Aberffraw.

ABERFFRAW, Gwynedd SH36
Aberffraw is a grey, somnolent village which has little to show of its historic past. Between the 7th and 13th centuries it was the capital of the Kingdom of Gwynedd, but no trace of the palace or associated buildings survives. A rocky islet near by features an ancient church which is accessible at low tide.

Reach Malltraeth.

MALLTRAETH, Gwynedd SH46
In c1800 a high embankment was built here to stop the incursion of the sea. Before this the estuary of the Cefni penetrated far inland, nearly cutting Anglesey in two. The village is well known for its fine sands and bird-haunted salt marshes.

Skirt Malltraeth Sands and continue through Newborough Forest to reach Newborough.

Holyhead Mountain's 720ft height offers superb views over the island.

NEWBOROUGH, Gwynedd SH46
Former inhabitants of Llanfaes, ousted by Edward I, founded this English-sounding village in 1303. A national nature reserve covers 1,566 acres of duneland and rocky coast to the south of the village, and Newborough Forest is constantly being extended to fix the dunes in the north part of the sanctuary. Three nature trails enable casual visitors to see much of the natural beauty of the area, but access to unmarked parts of the reserve is by permit only. Nearby Llanddwyn Island is accessible except at times of very high tide.

Continue, and 2 miles beyond Bryn-Siencyn reach a road on the left which leads to Bryn-celli-ddu.

BRYN-CELLI-DDU, Gwynedd SH57
This is a magnificent prehistoric passage grave (AM) of a type more usually found in Ireland. It consists of a passage leading to a polygonal chamber beneath a large mound.

Continue on the A4080 and shortly reach the entrance to Plas Newydd.

Llanfair PG's full name contains 59 letters and is the longest in Britain.

PLAS NEWYDD, Gwynedd SH57
Rebuilt by architect James Wyatt in the 19th century, this mansion (NT) overlooks the Menai Strait and is famous for the Rex Whistler mural in its dining room.

Reach the outskirts of Llanfair PG.

LLANFAIR PG, Gwynedd SH57
English visitors get lockjaw trying to pronounce the full name of this village, which is Llanfairpwllgwyn-gyllgogerychwyrndrobwyllllan-tysiliogogogoch. It means 'Church of St Mary in a hollow of white hazel near to a rapid whirlpool and to St Tysilio's Church, near to a red cave' and was invented by a tailor who combined the business of tourism with this wry joke against the tourists. George Stephenson spanned the Menai Strait with his tubular rail bridge in the 19th century, and an unassuming tin hut in the village was where the indomitable Women's Institute formed its first branch in the early 20th century. Overlooking the bridge, the village, and the Strait is the splendid Marquess of Anglesey Column, which affords remarkable views for anybody with the stomach to climb it.

Return to Menai Bridge on the A5.

Tissington, which enjoys an idyllic situation in glorious Derbyshire countryside, is a traditional village grouping of cottages, hall, and church set round a delightful pond.

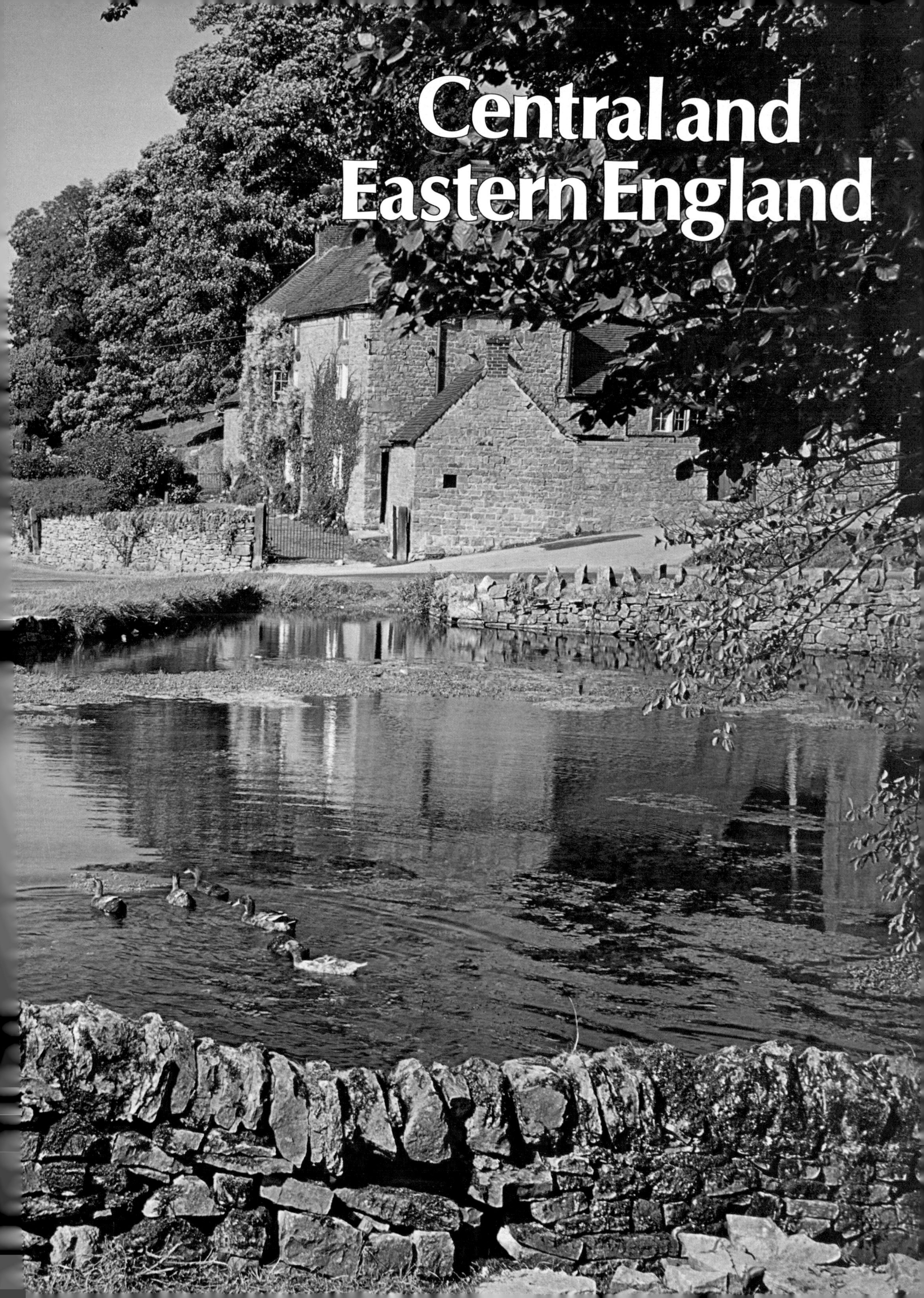

Central and Eastern England

WARWICK, Warwicks SP26
Imposing Warwick Castle is one of the finest medieval strongholds in Europe. It stands on a Saxon site above this compact River Avon town, and its exceptional Norman and later structure hides an interior completely rebuilt during the 17th century. The castle is still occupied, but visitors have access to the state rooms, torture chamber, silver vault, ghost tower, and Avon-side grounds that were landscaped by Capability Brown. Also in the town are the remains of town walls, two gates, and a great number of building styles ranging from half-timbered to the conscious starkness of the 20th century. Lord Leycester's Hospital was founded as a guildhall in 1383 and converted to almshouses in 1571 (open), and the 18th-century Shire Hall is considered an excellent example of its type. Elizabeth Oken's House contains a Doll Museum, and 17th-century St John's House features both a museum of crafts, costume, and furniture, and the Museum of the Royal Warwickshire Regiment. The 18th-century Court House is an Italianate building (open).

Leave Warwick on the A425 'Banbury' road and continue for $2\frac{1}{4}$ miles to join the A41. Proceed for $1\frac{1}{4}$ miles and turn right on to the B4087 SP 'Wellesbourne'. Continue to Wellesbourne.

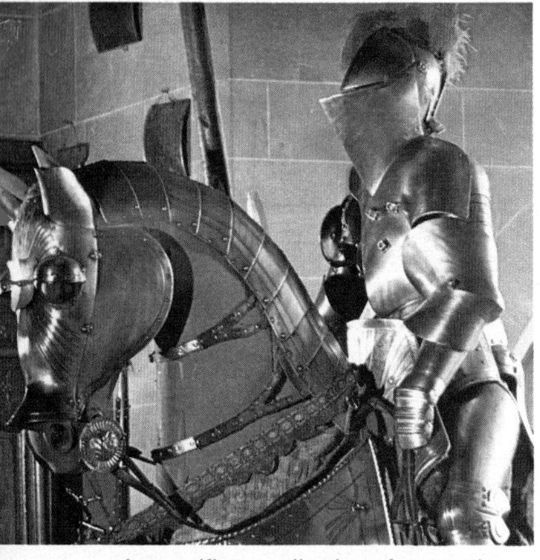

A magnificent collection of armour is housed in Warwick Castle.

WELLESBOURNE, Warwicks SP25
Georgian houses and a Hall dating from c1700 are the main features of this pleasant village.

Follow SP 'Stratford B4086' for 1 mile and turn right on to the B4088 SP 'Charlecote' to reach the village of Charlecote.

CHARLECOTE, Warwicks SP25
Charlecote Park (NT) is a fine Elizabethan house with a great hall and museum. The Avon flows through grounds where Shakespeare is said to have been caught poaching deer. Attractive old cottages survive in the village.

In Charlecote turn left on to the unclassified 'Hampton Lucy' road and cross the River Avon. Continue to Hampton Lucy.

TOUR 58 77 MILES

SHAKESPEARE COUNTRY

England's heartlands are watered by the Avon and Stour, great rivers that wind through charming Elizabethan villages, country estates graced by stately houses, and historic towns where Shakespeare drew inspiration from the comedy and tragedy in the lives of his contemporaries.

The River Avon formed an essential aspect of Warwick Castle's defences.

HAMPTON LUCY, Warwicks SP25
Of particular interest here is a cast-iron bridge that was built in 1829.

On entering Hampton Lucy bear left SP 'Stratford'. Proceed for $1\frac{1}{2}$ miles, bear left again, and in $\frac{3}{4}$ mile turn left on to the A46 for Stratford.

STRATFORD-UPON-AVON, Warwicks SP25
William Shakespeare was born here in 1564. His childhood home contains a museum relating to his life, and the old Guildhall that housed his school still stands. A picturesque Elizabethan knot garden can be seen near the foundations of New Place, where he died, and his remains lie in Holy Trinity Church. A lovely thatched and timbered cottage (open) in the nearby village of Shottery is where his wife Anne Hathaway was born, and gabled Hall's Croft (open) was the home of their daughter Susanna. Many of the great man's works are staged in the Royal Shakespeare Theatre, which was built on an Avon-side site in 1932; it incorporates a museum and picture gallery (open). Among many 15th- and 16th-century buildings preserved in the town are several lovely half-timbered houses and the 14-arch Clopton Bridge over the Avon. Harvard House is dated 1596 and was the home of John Harvard, founder of the US university of the same name. A waxwork exhibition in the town specializes in scenes from Shakespeare's plays, the Motor Museum preserves a number of veteran and vintage cars, and a model car museum exhibits some 1,400 individual miniatures.

Leave the town by the A34 'Oxford' road and later pass Alscot Park to the right. Proceed to Alderminster.

ALDERMINSTER, Warwicks SP24
Views across the Stour valley to Meon Hill and the Cotswolds can be enjoyed from the 13th-century church here.

The Guildhall schoolroom, where the poet and dramatist William Shakespeare took his first steps in learning.

Remain on the A34 to reach Newbold-upon-Stour. At the end of that village turn right on to an unclassified road and drive to Armscote. Turn right and continue to Ilmington.

ILMINGTON, Warwicks SP24
Situated at the east foot of the Cotswolds, this village has several picturesque cottages and an old tithe barn. The rectory and manor house both date from the 16th century. Above the village is 854ft Ilmington Down, one of the highest points in Warwickshire.

Turn left and follow SP 'Campden' to climb Ilmington Down. Descend, meet crossroads, and turn left to reach Ebrington.

EBRINGTON, Glos SP14
Delightful stone and thatched cottages complement a church with a fine Norman doorway in this lovely Cotswold village.

Join the B4035 and drive to Shipston-on-Stour.

SHIPSTON-ON-STOUR, Warwicks SP24
Once one of the most important sheep markets in the country, this mainly Georgian town lies at the edge of the Vale of Red Horse.

Follow SP 'Banbury', cross the River Stour, and proceed for $\frac{3}{4}$ mile to crossroads. Turn left on to the unclassified 'Honington' road, then in $\frac{3}{4}$ mile turn right SP 'Tysoe' and proceed for $2\frac{3}{4}$ miles. Meet crossroa and drive forward. In $\frac{3}{4}$ mile a detour from the main route can be made by turning right to reach Compton Wynyates.

COMPTON WYNYATES, Warwicks SP34
The estate in which this exceptional Tudor house stands has been in the same family since the 13th century. Sir William Compton built the magnificent red-brick extravagance that stands here today, and the interior has remained largely unaltered since Tudor times (open). Close to the house the wild hillside parkland has been cultivated as a modern topiary garden.

Continue to Upper Tysoe.

UPPER TYSOE, Warwicks SP34
One of a trio of villages named fror the Norse God Tiw, this little place has a 16th-century manor house a stands in the Vale of Red Horse. Th Vale itself derives its name from a turf-cut figure on Rising Hill, due ea of Lower Tysoe. Until 1800 this was scoured annually, but it is now scarcely visible.

In Upper Tysoe turn left SP 'Kineto then right SP 'Shenington' and 'Banbury'. Ascend Tysoe Hill, meet crossroads, and turn left to follow th ridge of Edgehill. Continue for 2 mi and drive forward on to the A422. A short detour from the main route c be made by continuing on the A42 for $\frac{1}{2}$ mile to Upton House.

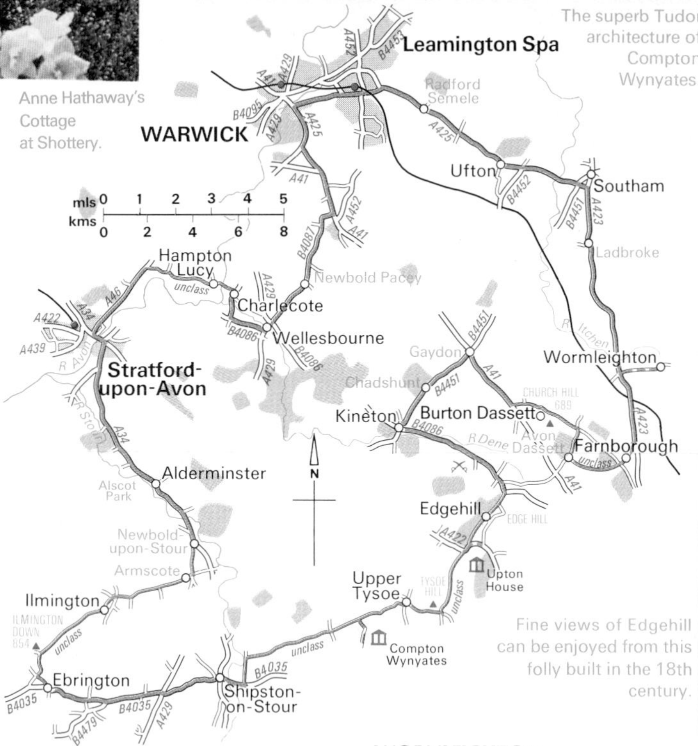

Anne Hathaway's Cottage at Shottery.

The superb Tudor architecture of Compton Wynyates.

PTON HOUSE, Warwicks SP34
ood views can be enjoyed from the vely terraced gardens of this npressive 17th-century house (NT). side are collections of porcelain, ctures, and various pieces of 18th-ntury furniture.

n the main route, continue for 1/4 ile after joining the A422 and bear t on to an unclassified road for gehill village.

DGEHILL, Warwicks SP34
n 18th-century folly which now rms part of a pub in the village fords extensive views over the untryside. North, on private ound by the B4086, is the field here the first major battle of the vil War was fought in 1642. Here e horizon is dominated by the ractively wooded 700ft ridge of gehill, which extends for 3 miles.

ave Edgehill village and in 1 mile ar left on to the B4086 SP 'Kineton'. scend to Kineton with the Edgehill ttlefield to the left.

NETON, Warwicks SP35
ar Kineton station are the remains a motte and bailey castle, and 3/4 e north west is a sail-less tower ndmill. The church has a splendid h-century doorway.

n right on to the B4451 SP uthamʼ and proceed to Gaydon. n right on to the A41 SP 'Banbury'. ceed for 2 miles and turn left on to unclassified 'Fenny Compton' d, then keep forward SP 'Burton s'. Ascend the Burton Hills (a ntry park) and pass the isolated ge of Burton Dassett to the right.

RTON DASSETT, rwicks SP35
urch Hill rises to 689ft above this ty village and is surmounted by a out tower that may once have n part of a medieval windmill. hill's summit was used as a con site to spread news of the le of Edgehill in 1642.

Continue for 1 mile to reach crossroads and turn right to descend to Avon Dassett. Drive to the end of the village and keep forward. Enter Farnborough.

FARNBOROUGH, Warwicks SP44
Notable Farnborough Hall (NT) dates from the 17th and 18th centuries and features excellent rococo stucco-work with panels of scrolls, rays, shells, fruit and flowers. Delightful grounds include landscaped terraced lawns which afford superb views to the ridge of Edgehill. A classical air is given the gardens by a small Ionic temple and an oval pavilion.

Keep left through Farnborough and at the end of the village turn left on to the A423 SP 'Coventry'. In 2 miles it is possible to make a detour from the main route to Wormleighton by turning right on to an unclassified road.

WORMLEIGHTON, Warwicks SP45
Prince Rupert slept at Wormleighton Manor the night before he gave battle to parliamentarian cavalry at Edgehill. The reputedly lovely house was destroyed later in the Civil War, but the imposing gateway survives, complete with its carved crests.

On the main route, proceed on the A423 to the edge of Southam.

SOUTHAM, Warwicks SP46
At one time this ancient town was famed for a mineral spring and healing well which were both claimed to have wide-ranging medicinal powers. The Reverend Holyoake, a rector of the local 15th- and 16th-century church, compiled the first dictionary of the English language.

At the edge of Southam turn left on to the A425 SP 'Leamington' to reach Ufton.

UFTON, Warwicks SP36
Views from this 380ft-high village extend beyond the ancient Fosse Way and River Avon to the distant Malvern Hills, known for their mineral springs. Inside the village church, which dates from the 13th century but has been extensively restored since, is a good 16th-century memorial brass.

Continue and pass through Radford Semele to reach Leamington Spa.

Fine views of Edgehill can be enjoyed from this folly built in the 18th century.

LEAMINGTON SPA, Warwicks SP36
In the 18th century it was claimed that mineral springs in this lovely old town were beneficial in the treatment of various complaints. As the high-society fashion for taking the waters blossomed so also did Leamington, and today it boasts many grand old buildings that recall the prosperity of those times. The Pump Room of 1814, rebuilt in 1925, is an excellent focus for the terraces of Regency, Georgian, and Victorian houses that grace the streets around it. Between the buildings are wide parks and open spaces, the carefully tended Jephson Gardens, and the vagrant windings of the River Lea. The Warwick Art Gallery and Museum exhibits a good selection of paintings and examples of 18th-century glass.

Continue along the A425 and return to Warwick.

TOUR 59 — 95 MILES

NORTHAMPTONSHIRE RIVERLANDS

Between the meanderings of the Welland and Nene are forests and farms, water meadows loud with the calls of wildfowl, and villages of stone and thatch clustered round elegant church spires. Much of the countryside was once held by squires, and many of their sturdy farms survive.

NORTHAMPTON, Northants SP76
One of the largest market towns in England, Northampton is the administrative centre of its county and is noted for its high number of fine churches. Among the finest is Holy Sepulchre, a rare round church that was founded in 1110 and has been variously adapted through the ages. Inside is a 6ft-tall brass which dates from the 17th century and is one of the largest in England. Other old buildings include 17th-century Hazelrigg Mansion, the 16th-century Welsh House, and the 17th-century Sessions House. Abington Park has ornamental and game birds in landscaped surroundings, and a 15th- to 18th-century house containing a museum. The Northamptonshire Record Office (grounds only open) is housed in Delapre Abbey, a 19th-century building on the site of a Cluniac nunnery. One of the Eleanor Crosses erected by Edward I in memory of his queen can be seen on the town's southern outskirts, at Hardingstone.

Leave Northampton on the A45 'Wellingborough' road and drive to Ecton.

ECTON, Northants SP86
Features of this village include a 13th- and 14th-century church, a gothic-revival hall, and an elegant 17th-century manor house.

From Ecton drive for 1½ miles and turn right on to the B573. Enter Earls Barton.

EARLS BARTON, Northants SP86
The magnificent Saxon church tower here was built about 1,000 years ago and may once have been incorporated in the defences of a nearby Norman castle.

Continue through Great Doddington and in 1½ miles meet traffic signals. Continue forward to Wellingborough.

WELLINGBOROUGH, Northants SP86
Situated at the junction of the rivers Ise and Nene, this old market centre is now a rapidly developing town serving numerous light industries.

Fotheringhay's church is an imposing survival of a much larger structure.

Follow SP 'Peterborough' to join the A510, and continue to Finedon.

FINEDON, Northants SP97
Curiously decorated ironstone houses and cottages gather beneath the graceful 133ft spire of an ironstone church in this large village. The church dates from the 14th century, but most of the houses were built by the village squire in Victorian times.

Proceed for 3¼ miles and turn right on to the A604. In 3½ miles cross the River Nene into Thrapston.

THRAPSTON, Northants SP97
The device from which the American Stars and Stripes were derived can be seen on a tablet to Sir John Washington in the village church. A nephew of Washington emigrated to America and was the great-grandfather of the first US president.

Return across the River Nene and turn right on to the A6116 to reach Islip.

ISLIP, Northants SP97
Brasses re-created by the Reverend H Macklin, author of a standard book on this type of memorial, can be seen in Islip Church.

Proceed to Lowick.

LOWICK, Northants SP98
Lowick's notable church has a 15th-century tower and 14th-century windows featuring 16 beautiful figures worked in stained glass.

Drive through Sudborough and on approaching Brigstock turn right on to a narrow unclassified road SP 'Lyveden'. Proceed for 2½ miles; ½ mile to the right of the road is Lyveden New Bield.

LYVEDEN NEW BIELD, Northants SP98
When Sir Thomas Tresham's family became involved in the Gunpowder Plot he had to stop building this ambitious house, which was begun in 1600 and still remains as a shell (NT). Its plan was meant to symbolize the Passion of Christ.

Continue for 2¼ miles and turn right on to the A427 to enter Oundle.

OUNDLE, Northants TL08
Set in pleasant countryside by the River Nene, this stone-built town is a place of narrow streets and alleys between rows of old houses broken by the occasional tiny cottage or inn. Its well-known public school was founded in the 16th century by William Laxton, a grocer who was born here and eventually became Lord Mayor of London. The Latham Almshouses date from 1611, but were altered and extended during the 18th and 19th centuries.

Leave Oundle and follow the A605 'Peterborough' road for 1¼ miles, then turn left on to an unclassified road SP 'Fotheringhay' and pass Cotterstock village on the left.

COTTERSTOCK, Northants TL09
The poet John Dryden wrote his *Fables* in an attic room of 17th-century Cotterstock Hall (open) while staying with his cousin, who owned it. Beautiful gardens lead from the house to the banks of the River Nene. In the village are a fine church, a 14th-century rectory, and an 18th-century mill with later mill cottages.

Drive through Tansor and continue to Fotheringhay.

FOTHERINGHAY, Northants TL09
A mound here once carried the grim castle in which Mary Queen of Scots was imprisoned before her execution in 1587. Nowadays the mellow old cottages and willow-hung banks of the Nene create a tranquillity in which such macabre associations become difficult to believe. The imposing church was a gift from Edward IV.

Take the 'King's Cliffe' road and pass through Woodnewton to reach Apethorpe.

The Welland Valley near Harringworth is dominated by a stupendous railway viaduct.

Duddington's famous watermill was built in 1664.

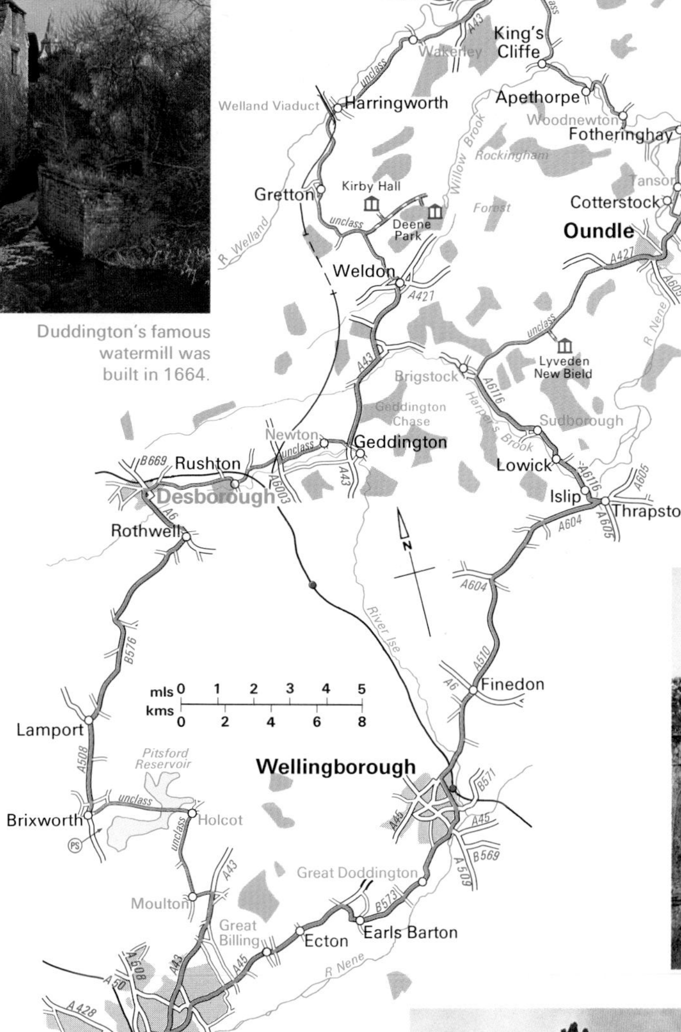

Return to the crossroads and drive forward on to the unclassified 'Newton' and 'Rushton' road. After Newton turn right then left under a railway. Continue to Rushton.

RUSHTON, Northants SP88
Triangular Lodge (AM), a famous curiosity in the grounds of 15th-century Rushton Hall, is far more than a mere folly. Its peculiar design, in which the number three is depicted time and again, is a devout symbolization of the Trinity, disguised to fool religious persecutors during a time of repression. The village is a cluster of golden ironstone houses on the banks of the River Ise.

In Rushton turn right SP 'Desborough'; at Desborough turn left on to the A6 to reach Rothwell.

ꟼETHORPE, Northants TL09
one-built Apethorpe boasts a very ge Tudor and later hall, and an posing 13th- to 17th-century age church.

oceed to King's Cliffe.

NG'S CLIFFE, Northants TL09
atures of this beautiful little village lude 17th-century almshouses, a urch with a Norman tower and h-century spire, and lovely roundings.

n right to follow the 'Stamford' d and later turn left on to the A47. mile turn right on to an classified road and drive to llyweston.

LLYWESTON, Northants SK90
ne roofing slates have been rried here for many years. The rch has a Saxon chancel wall, the village manor house dates n the 17th century.

n left on to the A43, and in 1 mile right then shortly left into dington.

DDINGTON, Northants SK90
tched cottages and a medieval ched bridge across the River land help to make this one of the tiest villages in the area. The ure is completed by a 17th-tury watermill and mansion.

e through Duddington to rejoin A43. In $\frac{3}{4}$ mile turn right on to the assified 'Wakerley' and ringworth' road. Drive past nsive ironstone workings to reach ingworth.

RINGWORTH, Northants SP99
ectacular feature of this village is 82-arch brick-built railway uct that spans the Welland ey here. This magnificent feat of neering was built between 1874 1879.

eed south to Gretton.

TTON, Northants SP89
ks and a whipping post still l on the green in this attractive p village, and fine views extend he Welland Valley. A few 17th-ury houses and a church with nan origins are reminders of its history.

along the 'Weldon' road for $1\frac{1}{2}$ and turn left. In $\frac{3}{4}$ mile a detour be made from the main route by g left; this leads to Kirby Hall in $\frac{3}{4}$ and Deene Park in $2\frac{1}{4}$ miles.

Edward I erected this cross at Geddington in 1290, as a memorial to Queen Eleanor.

KIRBY HALL, Northants SP99
This magnificent old house (AM) was begun in 1572 and bought by Sir Christopher Hatton, a favourite of Queen Elizabeth I. In the 17th century its appearance was completely changed by the architect Inigo Jones.

DEENE PARK, Northants SP99
A little farther along the detour route from Kirby Hall is the 16th-century mansion of Deene Park (open), which stands in a lake-watered estate known for its rare trees.

Proceed along the main tour route to Weldon.

WELDON, Northants SP98
The fine lantern tower carried by Weldon Church was once an invaluable landmark for travellers in thickly-wooded Rockingham Forest. An old lock-up once used for petty criminals stands on the green.

On entering Weldon turn left into Chapel Road then right on to the A43 for Geddington. Meet crossroads and turn left on to an unclassified road to enter the village.

GEDDINGTON, Northants SP88
One of the three surviving Eleanor Crosses stands in the main square of this lovely stone and thatch village, a reminder of the grief experienced by Edward I at the loss of his queen some 7 centuries ago. Of later date is the medieval bridge that spans the River Ise here, and $\frac{3}{4}$ mile south is 15th-century Boughton House (open), a monastery enlarged to its present magnificent proportions in the 16th and 17th centuries. Inside are art collections and sumptuous old furnishings, while all around are beautifully planned and tended gardens.

It is thought that Inigo Jones may have been responsible for the ornamental garden gateway of Kirby Hall.

ROTHWELL, Northants SP88
Inside the mainly 13th-century church of this old industrial town is a charnel containing thousands of bones. The centre of Rothwell is graced by the elegant 16th-century Market House (AM).

Turn right on to the B576 and proceed to Lamport.

LAMPORT, Northants SP77
Mainly 17th- and 18th-century Lamport Hall (open) is set in an attractive park featuring an early alpine rock garden. Inside the house are paintings by Van Dyck and other artists, and an excellent collection of china and furniture.

In Lamport turn left on to the A508 and drive to Brixworth.

BRIXWORTH, Northants SP77
Local Roman buildings were cannibalized to provide materials for a fine church raised here in the 7th century. The skill of the Saxon builders has been well proved, because today the church survives as one of the finest of its type.

Pass the Red Lion (PH) and turn left on to the unclassified 'Sywell' road. Later cross the Pitsford Reservoir into Holcot, meet crossroads, and turn right SP 'Northampton' to reach Moulton. In Moulton turn left and shortly right onto the A43 to return to Northampton.

CAMBRIDGE, Cambs TL45
This famous and attractive university town started life as a small Celtic settlement on the marshy banks of the Cam. In 1209 a split in the Oxford community resulted in a migration of students and scholars to Cambridge, and the establishment of a university that was to rival its unwilling parent in wealth and prestige. Traces of the first foundation – which was Peterhouse in 1284 – are largely disguised by later work, but 14th-century Clare College occupies buildings that were part of a 12th-century nunnery. Most of the other colleges show similar mixtures. King's College, founded by Henry VI in 1441, has an outstanding chapel that overlooks the Cam and is famous for some of the finest gothic fan vaulting in Europe. Corpus Christi is unique in having been founded by two town guilds, and lovely half-timbered Queens' of 1346 is by far the most picturesque. Much more can be learned about the university and its superb buildings, and the interested visitor is advised to invest in a guide booklet. The town itself is a delightful collection of old streets and houses alongside the river. Peaceful lawns and meadows slope down to the water's edge as grassy quays for summer punters, in marked contrast to the busy activity of the excellent shopping areas in the middle of town. Not surprisingly the city has several good museums. Extensive art and archaeological collections are housed in the Fitzwilliam, the Scott Polar Research Institute has many relics relating to famous expeditions, and the Sedgewick displays fossils from many different parts of the world. Cambridge and County Folk Museum is packed with domestic and agricultural bygones.

Leave Cambridge on the A45 'Bedford' road and drive for $2\frac{1}{2}$ miles to reach Madingley Postmill.

TOUR 60 79 MILES

BETWEEN THE OUSE AND THE CAM

West of Cambridge and the willow-shaded Cam a countryside of orchards and pasture stretches flatly to low Fenland horizons. Here and there the skyline is interrupted by a windmill or church tower, the roofs of an ancient riverside town, or the bushy crown of an occasional copse.

Trinity College Bridge in Cambridge leads to the famous 'Backs'.

MADINGLEY POSTMILL, Cambs TL36
The body of this restored windmill pivots on a central post so that the sails can be turned into the wind. Originally from Huntingdonshire, this interesting industrial relic was moved to its present site in 1936.

Continue for $\frac{1}{4}$ mile to reach the American Cemetery.

AMERICAN CEMETERY & CHAPEL, Cambs TL36
The War Memorial Chapel that stands here is a striking example of modern architecture. Inside is a 540-square-foot map showing Atlantic sea and air routes used by American forces during World War II.

Continue and shortly turn right on to an unclassified road to reach Madingley.

MADINGLEY, Cambs TL36
Just outside this attractive village is Madingley Hall, a fine Elizabethan house that stands in a wooded park and serves as a hostel for university students. Both Edward VII and George VI lived here when they were undergraduates at Cambridge.

Continue to the A604 and turn left. Proceed for 4 miles, turn right on to an unclassified road, and drive to Swavesey.

SWAVESEY, Cambs TL36
Attractively situated close to fenland, this long, narrow village has a good 14th-century church with notable window tracery. Inside the building are bench-ends with animal carvings.

Proceed to Over.

King's College Chapel, a medieval masterpiece, is one of the principal glories of Cambridge.

OVER, Cambs TL37
This pretty fenland village stands in orchard country to the east of the River Ouse, a popular venue for boating and angling. Its pleasant church contains a bell that was cast some 600 years ago.

Drive to Willingham.

WILLINGHAM, Cambs TL47
Two local windmills and the impressive tower of Willingham's 14th-century church are prominent landmarks in the flat farmlands that surround this village. The church nave has a notable 15th-century hammerbeam roof adorned with over 50 carved angels.

Turn left on to the B1050 and reach the River Ouse. Follow the river and turn left on to the A1123 to enter the village of Earith. Continue through Needingworth, and after $1\frac{1}{2}$ miles tur left on to the A1096 to enter St Ives.

ST IVES, Cambs TL37
In 1110 King Henry I granted St Ives the right to hold a fair. The town grew up around its fairground and i annual market became established as one of the largest in England. Overlooking the Market Place is a statue of Oliver Cromwell, who hac a farm in the rich countryside near by. The River Ouse runs through th town and is spanned here by a narrow 6-arched bridge (AM) that dates from the 15th century.

Follow the A1096 south and cross th river. After $\frac{1}{2}$ mile turn right on to an unclassified road and continue to Hemingford Grey.

HEMINGFORD GREY, Cambs TL2
A moated mansion in this lovely village dates back to the 12th century and is thought to be the oldest inhabited dwelling in Englan The 12th-century church is picturesquely sited in a bend of the River Ouse.

Turn left and shortly right, proceed Hemingford Abbots, and follow SP 'Huntingdon' to join the A604. Drive for 1 mile and branch left. Meet a roundabout and turn right on to an unclassified road to reach Godmanchester.

GODMANCHESTER, Cambs TL2
The site of this ancient town was once occupied by a Roman militar station. Nowadays it is a treasure-house of varied architectural styles from the homeliness of old timber and thatch to the aloof lines of Georgian facades.

Turn right on to the B1043, crossing 14th-century bridge (AM), and ente Huntingdon.

HUNTINGDON, Cambs TL27
Both Oliver Cromwell and the dia Samuel Pepys were born here and attended the town's former grammar school. Parts of the building date back to Norman tim and today it houses a museum of Cromwellian relics.

Leave Huntingdon on the A141 'Kettering' road and drive to Hinchingbrooke House.

The Great Ouse at Hemingford Grey.

Britain's oldest surviving postmill at Bourn resembles those seen in illuminated manuscripts.

HINCHINGBROOKE HOUSE, Cambs TL27
Now restored and in use as a school, this Tudor and later mansion (open) has been home to the Cromwells and the Earls of Sandwich. It ncorporates parts of a medieval nunnery.

Continue on the A141 'Kettering' road to Brampton.

BRAMPTON, Cambs TL27
Pepys House in Brampton is a lovely old gabled cottage that was the home of the diarist's parents, and was owned by him from 1664 to 1680 (open). The stalls in the local church display excellent carving.

Leave Brampton and in 2 miles join the A1 for the outskirts of Buckden.

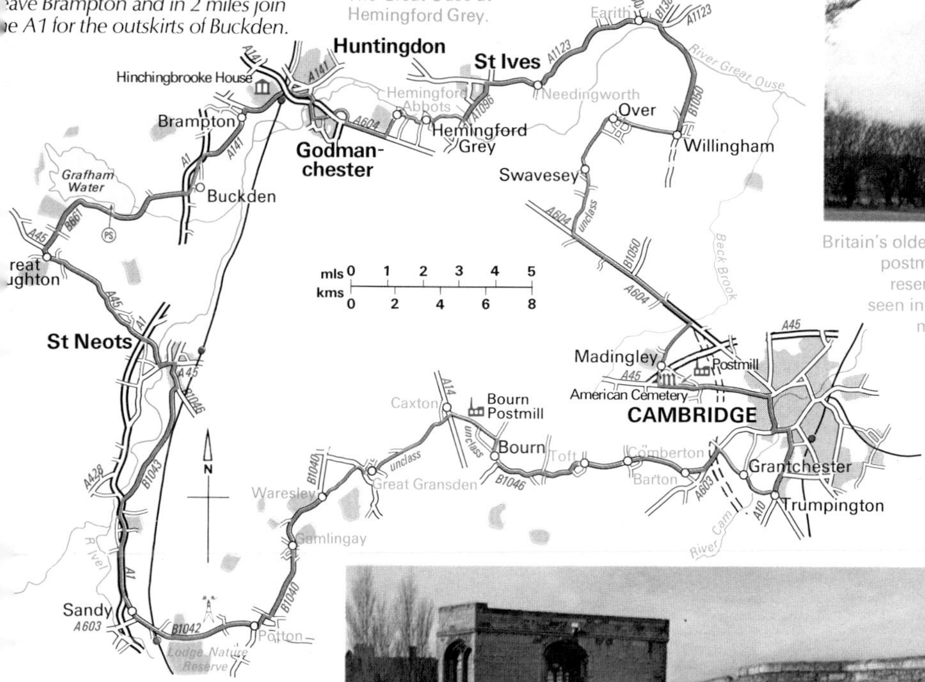

BUCKDEN, Cambs TL16
Considerable remains of Buckden Palace, a former residence of the Bishops of Lincoln, comprise a fine Tudor tower and an inner gatehouse of 1490 (open). The buildings are still restored and in use as a school. The local church is known for its notable spire and carvings.

Continue to a roundabout on the A1 and take the B661 'Kimbolton' road to reach Grafham Water.

GRAFHAM WATER, Cambs TL16
This $2\frac{1}{2}$-square-mile reservoir supplies drinking water for $1\frac{1}{2}$ million people and is a valuable leisure amenity offering long bankside walks and facilities for boating and trout fishing. Several picnic sites have been laid out around the edge.

Continue to Great Staughton.

GREAT STAUGHTON, Cambs TL16
Opposite 14th-century and later Great Staughton Church, which has a fine tower and contains good monuments, is a mansion with a pair of picturesque timber-framed barns. The village cross dates from the 17th century and features a sundial.

A rare medieval chapel survives in the centre of the 15th-century bridge over the Great Ouse at St Ives.

At Great Staughton turn left on to the A45 and continue for 4 miles, crossing the A1. Cross the River Ouse and enter St Neots.

ST NEOTS, Cambs TL16
The great charm of this ancient market town is its compactness. Interesting old inns can be found in many of its secretive back streets, and attractive buildings cluster round three sides of the Ouse-side market square.

Leave St Neots by turning right on to the B1043 and in 4 miles join the A1. After another 3 miles turn left on to the B1042 and drive through Sandy.

SANDY, Beds TL14
Low wooded hills that rise to the east of this large River Ivel village make a pleasant change from the flat countryside crossed by much of the tour. About 1 mile east is the 100-acre Lodge Nature Reserve, which is the HQ of the Royal Society for the Protection of Birds. A planned nature trail offers public access.

Continue along the B1042 and pass a TV mast to the left before reaching Potton. At Potton take the B1040 'St Ives' road through Gamlingay to Waresley, then drive forward on to an unclassified road for Great Gransden. Turn right, then shortly left into the village. Follow SP to Caxton and turn right then left for 'Bourn' to reach Bourn Postmill.

BOURN POSTMILL, Cambs TL35
Although the working parts of this remarkable windmill (open) have been replaced from time to time, the base and outer structure date back at least to 1636. It is claimed to be the oldest example in England.

Continue for 1 mile, meet a T-junction and turn right to reach Bourn.

BOURN, Cambs TL35
Red-brick Bourn Hall has Jacobean origins but has been restored. Between it and the attractive little Bourn Brook is a church with a fine 13th-century tower.

Drive through Bourn and join the B1046. Continue through Toft and Comberton to reach Barton, and turn left on to the A603. Proceed for 1 mile, turn right on to the unclassified 'Trumpington' road, and continue to Grantchester.

GRANTCHESTER, Cambs TL45
Rupert Brooke immortalized this beautiful village of thatched and lime-washed cottages in his poem *The Old Vicarage, Grantchester*. He lived here for a while after leaving King's College in nearby Cambridge, and wrote of the village as 'the lovely hamlet'.

Cross the Cam and continue to Trumpington.

TRUMPINGTON, Cambs TL45
Inside the elaborate local church is England's second oldest memorial brass. It is dated 1289 and was raised to Sir Roger de Trumpington, whose local associations are obvious in the name. Other features of the village include a 16th-century inn and two 18th-century halls.

Join the A10 and return to Cambridge.

TOUR 61 70 MILES

CONSTABLE LANDSCAPES

Here is the country of John Constable, who immortalized much of its rural beauty in his paintings. Here also are the ragged estuaries of the Stour and Orwell, which carve the coastline into a confusion of small bays, sheltered shingle beaches, and reed-covered marshes.

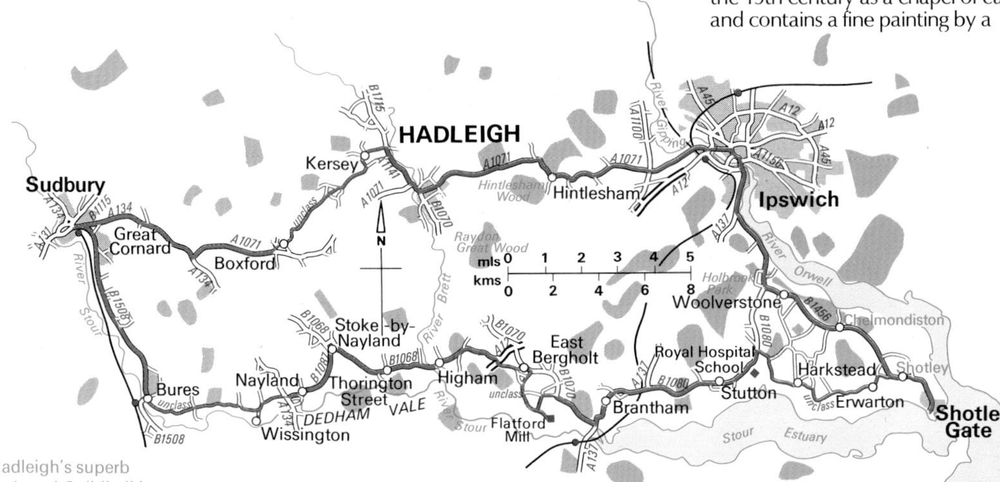

HADLEIGH, Suffolk TM04
Many fine Georgian and Victorian houses are preserved in this River Stour market town, and the High Street shows a remarkable architectural mixture of timber, brick, and plaster-faced buildings. Some of the plasterwork has been raised in decorative relief, known as pargetting, and most of the structures are excellent examples of their type. The fine 15th-century Guildhall (open) has two overhanging storeys and has been a school and an almshouse. Also of note is the imposing Deanery Tower, a remnant of the medieval palace of Archdeacon Pykenham. Features of the local 14th- to 15th-century church include a bench-end that depicts the legend of a wolf which found and guarded the decapitated head of St Edmund.

Leave Hadleigh on the A1071 'Sudbury' road. At the edge of the town turn right on to the A1141 'Kersey, Lavenham' road and follow the shallow valley of the River Brett for $1\frac{1}{4}$ miles. Meet crossroads and turn left on to an unclassified road for Kersey.

Hadleigh's superb timbered Guildhall has been well restored and extended. The ground floor originally formed almshouses.

KERSEY, Suffolk TM04
Shakespeare mentioned the cloth once made in this beautiful old weaving centre in his plays *Measure for Measure* and *Love's Labours Lost.* Nowadays Kersey's Brett Valley position, sloping streets, and numerous half-timbered buildings make it known as one of the most picturesque places in Suffolk. The local church is a gem of 14th- and 15th-century architecture on a site mentioned in the *Domesday Book.*

Drive to the church in Kersey and follow the 'Boxford' road. Continue to Boxford.

BOXFORD, Suffolk TL94
This quaint old village takes its name from an attractive stream that runs close to its timber-framed cottages. Its church features an unusual wooden porch that may be the earliest of its kind in the country, and contains an unusual 17th-century font with doors.

Leave Boxford on the A1071 'Sudbury' road and continue for $2\frac{1}{2}$ miles. Turn right on to the A134 and drive to Sudbury.

Wildlife of all kinds and restored Thames barges co-exist on the Orwell estuary.

SUDBURY, Suffolk TL84
Sudbury stands on the River Stour and is famous as the birthplace of painter Thomas Gainsborough in 1727. His house at 46 Gainsborough Street is now a local arts centre and museum containing a selection of hi work, and he is commemorated by a bronze statue on Market Hill. Novelist Charles Dickens referred to the town as 'Eatanswill' in *Pickwick Papers.* St Peter's Church was built ir the 15th century as a chapel of ease and contains a fine painting by a local artist named Robert Cardinall St Gregory's is much older, having been built on the foundations of ar old college by the Archbishop of Canterbury c1365. In 1381 he was brutally murdered in the Peasants' Revolt, and his skull is preserved as his memorial in the vestry. Other features of the building include beautifully carved choir stalls and one of the finest 15th-century font covers in the country. Also in the town are the notable Corn Exchan Chantry and Salter's Hall.

Leave Sudbury on the B1508 SP 'Bures' and continue to Great Cornard.

GREAT CORNARD, Suffolk TL84
Although almost a suburb of near Sudbury, the nucleus of this villag still centred on its charming churc and preserves an identity entirely separate from its large neighbour.

Stay on the B1508 and drive throu the Stour Valley to Bures.

BURES, Suffolk TL93
Fine half-timbered houses and an elegant church dating from the 1 to 15th centuries are the main features of this pretty little village, which stands on the banks of the River Stour. Inside the church is a font adorned with painted shields and a private chapel containing a monument dated 1514. Chapel B is an ancient thatched building th was once attached to the former Earl's Colne Priory.

Drive to Bures Church and turn le on to an unclassified road SP 'Nayland'. Follow the Stour Valley $3\frac{3}{4}$ miles to reach a right turn that be taken as a short detour to Wissington.

WISSINGTON, Suffolk TL93
Many people come to this attractive village to see the famous series of 13th-century wall paintings in St Mary's Church, a well preserved Norman building with later additions. Close by is an 18th-century house built by architect Sir John Soane.

On the main route, continue with the 'Nayland' road and in 1 mile meet staggered crossroads. Drive across on to the B1087 to enter Nayland at the start of Dedham Vale.

The Chapel Barn near Bures preserves several alabaster tomb chests.

NAYLAND, Suffolk TL93
Alston Court, an attractive half-timbered courtyard house, is one of many 15th-century buildings to be seen in this River Stour village. John Constable painted the altar piece in the local church.

DEDHAM VALE, Essex TM03
This area of outstanding natural beauty stretches from Nayland village to Flatford Mill, and is familiar to many people through the paintings of John Constable.

From Nayland continue on the B1087 to reach Stoke-by-Nayland.

STOKE-BY-NAYLAND, Suffolk TL93
Visitors who are also lovers of John Constable's paintings will recognise the lofty 120ft tower of Stoke-by-Nayland's handsome church. Entry at the south end of the building is through magnificently carved doors, and inside are many notable monuments. Close by are the timber-framed Maltings and the Guildhall, both superb survivals from the 16th century.

Leave Stoke-by-Nayland on the B1068 'Ipswich' road and drive to Thorington Street.

THORINGTON STREET, Suffolk TM03
18th-century additions are evident in the mainly 16th-century structure of Thorington Hall (NT), a house that completely dominates this tiny village.

Continue on the B1068 and later cross the River Brett to enter Higham.

HIGHAM, Suffolk TM03
Attractive St Mary's Church and 19th-century Higham Hall preside over this pleasant little village, which has a number of good timber-framed cottages.

Leave Higham on the B1068 and after 2 miles meet the A12. Turn right then immediately left on to the unclassified 'East Bergholt' road. Continue for 1 mile and turn right into East Bergholt.

EAST BERGHOLT, Suffolk TM03
In 1776 the great landscape painter John Constable was born here, and speaking of the area he once said 'These scenes made me a painter.' Clustered round the 14th-century church are mellow Elizabethan cottages set amid beautiful gardens. Separated from the church but close by is a unique timber-framed belfry. Stour, home of the late Randolph Churchill, stands near by in the gardens which he created (not open).

Drive to East Bergholt Church and bear right to reach Flatford Mill.

FLATFORD MILL, Suffolk TM03
Perhaps the most famous and admired of all Constable's landscape subjects, Flatford Mill (NT) is picturesquely situated on the River Stour and serves as a field-study centre. Both it and nearby Willy Lott's Cottage attract legions of artists every summer.

Leave Flatford Mill and bear right along a one-way street. After ½ mile meet crossroads and turn right. Continue for ½ mile to meet the B1070 'Manningtree' road, then drive forward and continue for another 1½ miles to the A137. Turn left here SP 'Ipswich' to reach Brantham.

BRANTHAM, Suffolk TM13
Inside Brantham Church is an altar-piece with a painting by John Constable.

Leave Brantham on the A137. Continue for 1 mile, reach the Bull Inn, and turn right on to the B1080 'Holbrook' road. Continue to Stutton.

STUTTON, Suffolk TM13
Architecture from many periods survives in the church, and there are a number of notable private houses in the neighbourhood. Among these is Stutton Hall (not open), which dates from 1553.

Drive forward for 1 mile and pass through the grounds of the Royal Hospital School.

ROYAL HOSPITAL SCHOOL, Suffolk TM13
An impressive tower with a white stone pinnacle that can be seen for miles around marks the location of the Royal Hospital School, which was founded in 1694 for the sons of seamen. The present group of buildings was occupied when the school moved from Greenwich in the early part of this century.

From the school continue for ½ mile and turn right on to an unclassified road for Harkstead.

Dark-framed and pastel-tinted weavers' houses line Kersey's pretty main-street, which runs down to a small ford.

HARKSTEAD, Suffolk TM13
Notable features of this solitary 14th-century church are its contemporary tower and fine Easter Sepulchre. The building as a whole is an interesting example of medieval architecture.

Continue on the winding 'Shotley' road and drive through Erwarton.

ERWARTON, Suffolk TM23
Red-brick almshouses are a striking feature of this pretty village, which also has an Elizabethan hall with a fine gateway.

Leave Erwarton and pass the gatehouse of Erwarton Hall. Continue to Shotley and turn right on to the B1456 for Shotley Gate.

SHOTLEY GATE, Suffolk TM23
Views of the busy shipping traffic into Harwich and Felixstowe can be enjoyed from this promontory. Close by is the former naval training centre *HMS Ganges*.

Return along the B1456 'Ipswich' road, pass through Chelmondiston, and reach Woolverstone.

WOOLVERSTONE, Suffolk TM13
Imposing Woolverstone Hall, built in the 18th century by William Berners, is beautifully situated overlooking the attractive Orwell estuary. It now houses a school.

Continue along the B1456 beside the River Orwell, then later turn right on to the A137 and drive to Ipswich.

IPSWICH, Suffolk TM14
Modern commercial development has made this major port and agricultural centre into the largest town in Suffolk. In spite of this it has managed to preserve a number of historic buildings. See tour 63 for fuller details.

Leave Ipswich with SP 'Colchester', then join the A1071 'Sudbury' road. Cross the River Gipping and proceed to Hintlesham

HINTLESHAM, Suffolk TM04
Every July Hintlesham holds a festival centred on its great hall (open during festivals and by appointment). The building itself has an Elizabethan core behind a fine Georgian façade and features a drawing room with an exceptional filigreed plaster ceiling. Inside the local church are notable monuments to the Timperley family.

Leave Hintlesham on the B1071 and return to Hadleigh.

The scene at Flatford Mill has changed little from the days when it was the subject of Constable's famous pictures.

TOUR 62 47 MILES

EAST ANGLIAN HEARTLANDS

The last king of East Anglia ruled from Bury St Edmunds in the 9th century. Today the town is an important market centre for east Suffolk, a focal point for farming communities made rich by a flourishing wool trade in medieval times.

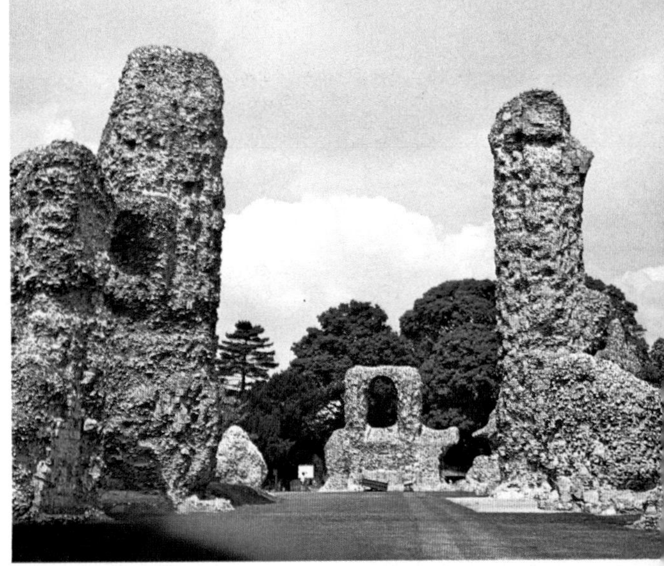

Once a rich and splendid monastery, the abbey
Bury St Edmunds is now an extensive rui

BURY ST EDMUNDS, Suffolk TL86
Edmund, the last king of the East Angles, was killed by the Danes c870 and was subsequently hailed by his people as a martyr. In 903 his body was moved from its resting place at Hoxne to Bury, then known as *Beodricsworth*, which became an important religious centre and place of pilgrimage. The abbey that grew here prospered until it was burned by the townsfolk in 1465. Its rebuilding resulted in one of the architectural glories of England, but it became too powerful and, like many of its contemporaries, was broken at the Dissolution. Today its former splendour can be judged by extensive ruins that form a focal point for a country park. Two gates still stand, and the precincts are made splendid by the Cathedral Church of St James. A large graveyard separates this fine building from 15th-century St Mary's Church, which is known for its magnificent hammerbeam roof and the grave of Mary Tudor. Mary's life is illustrated in a window given by Queen Victoria. Bury St Edmunds itself is an attractive market town which retains its 11th-century street plan and many fine old buildings. Moyse's Hall dates from the 12th century and contains a museum, and the lovely Guildhall and Cupola House are both of 15th-century origin. Excellent Georgian shop fronts are preserved in some streets, and the Town Hall of 1771 was designed by Robert Adam. Also from this period are a brick-built Unitarian chapel with an exceptionally well-preserved interior, and Angel Corner (NT) – now containing a display of old clocks and watches. Close to an outstanding 17th-century mansion in The Traverse is The Nutshell, which is thought to be the smallest pub in England. The 18th-century Angel Hotel was the scene of Mr Pickwick's meeting with Sam Weller in Charles Dickens' *Pickwick Papers*.

Some $2\frac{1}{2}$ miles south west of the town, off the A143, is Ickworth House.

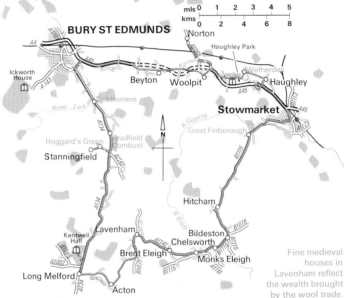

Fine medieval houses in Lavenham reflect the wealth brought by the wool trade.

ICKWORTH HOUSE, Suffolk TL86
Started by Frederick Harvey, 4th Ea of Bristol and the Bishop of Derry, this 18th-century house (NT) is one the most remarkable in England an an apt memorial to its builder's eccentricity. The Earl Bishop intended to fill it with works of art collected during his extensive trave but in Rome he was imprisoned by Napoleonic troops and his enormo collection confiscated. He died in 1803, with only half his dream actually realized in bricks and mortar. Visitors today can see the glory of the strange elliptical rotun that grew from plans by the Italian architect Asprucci. Inside the hous is a fine collection of 18th-century and French furniture. Part of the 2,000-acre grounds (NT) were landscaped by Capability Brown.

Leave Bury St Edmunds on the A13 'Sudbury' road. Drive through the villages of Sicklesmere and Bradfielc Combust, and $\frac{3}{4}$ mile beyond the latter pass an unclassified right turn leading through Hoggards Green t the village of Stanningfield. This offe a pleasant detour from the main route.

STANNINGFIELD, Suffolk TL85
Stanningfield Church has two fine Norman doorways, one within a timbered porch, and the 13th-century chancel preserves notabl features. West of the village is Elizabethan Coldham Hall, which a dovecote of the same period.

Continue on the A134 and appro Long Melford with the grounds of Kentwell Hall to the right.

KENTWELL HALL, Suffolk TL84
Access to this mellow Elizabetha manor (open) is through a 300-ye old avenue of lime trees and ove moat. The combination of water, tree-shaded grass, and old brick forms a tranquil beauty that is a rarity in the 20th century.

ONG MELFORD, Suffolk TL84
'erhaps the stateliest village in
uffolk, Long Melford has an
npressive main street lined by fine
ld buildings and dominated by a
nagnificent church. The latter dates
om 15th-century reconstruction
nd occupies the site of a Roman
emple. Its many windows give the
terior an airiness accentuated by
oaring columns and slender pillars.
he Lady Chapel of 1496 can almost
e considered as separate from the
ain building, though attached in
ortar if not in style to the east end.
he well-proportioned tower is a
nsitive addition dating from 1903.
teresting monuments include a
rved 15th-century piece in the
opton Chantry and a number of
ntemporary brasses that illustrate
othing and hairstyles of the period.
ading down towards the village
m the church is a triangular green
ged by the 18th-century wall of
e Congregational churchyard, the
th-century timber-framed Bull Inn,
d 16th-century Trinity Hospital.
e latter was founded by Sir
lliam Cordell and greatly restored
he 19th century. Dominating the
age is Melford Hall (NT), one of the
st Elizabethan manors in England.
ccupies three sides of a lovely old
urtyard and carries a splendid
ay of turrets.

*ve to the Bull Inn and turn left on
he unclassified 'Lavenham' road. In
miles continue forward to Acton.*

TON, Suffolk TL84
de Acton Church is an excellent
s, the most famous military
morial of its type in the country. It
raised to Sir Robert de Bures
2 and depicts a knight in chain
holding a shield. A notable
pture of a reclining man with his
at his feet carries the date 1722
has been attributed to Thomas
en of Camberwell.

*n Acton turn left with SP
nham'. In $2\frac{1}{4}$ miles join the B1071
continue to Lavenham.*

NHAM, Suffolk TL94
one of the most outstanding
es in East Anglia, Lavenham has
y changed in appearance since
yday as an important wool
in the 14th and 15th centuries.
zens of immaculately preserved
ings include timber-framed
es, the Guildhall (NT), and the
l Hall. Slightly apart from the
e is the local church, a superb
ng that is considered a
plete work of art in itself. It
s a 141ft tower resplendent
shiny knapped flint, and was
with money donated by a
of clothiers. Other reflections
sperous times are 15th-century
ere House, the old Town Cross
and Shilling Old Grange. An
century hand-operated fire
e is preserved in the village.

*Lavenham on the A1141
igh' road. After 2 miles turn left
n unclassified road and enter
Eleigh.*

One of the many superb old buildings preserved in Long Melford is Elizabethan Melford Hall.

BRENT ELEIGH, Suffolk TL94
Fine wall paintings have been discovered in the 14th-century Church of St Mary here, and Jacobean woodwork is much in evidence on the pulpit, south door, and box pews. Elizabethan Brent Eleigh Hall has modern additions by architect Sir Edwin Lutyens.

Return to the A1141 and turn left for Monks Eleigh.

MONKS ELEIGH, Suffolk TL94
This pleasant little village has a good church with a notable tower and a carved pulpit. An attractive weatherboarded mill and Georgian millhouse stand near by.

Drive to the end of the village and bear left on to the B1115 'Stowmarket' road. Continue to Chelsworth.

CHELSWORTH, Suffolk TL94
An attractive double hump-backed bridge spans the small River Brett here, and the village features many lovely timber-framed houses.

Stay on the B1115 and turn left for Bildeston.

BILDESTON, Suffolk TL94
Many notable half-timbered cottages survive here, and the village church is reached by a footpath across pleasant farming country.

From Bildeston continue on the B1115 to Hitcham.

HITCHAM, Suffolk TL95
A 15th-century hammerbeam roof can be seen in Hitcham Church, which is comfortable rather than outstanding and forms a natural focus for this delightful village. Many of the local cottages are half timbered.

Continue on the B1115 and drive through Great Finborough to reach Stowmarket.

STOWMARKET, Suffolk TM05
Poet John Milton visited this busy Gipping Valley market town many times to see his tutor Thomas Young, who lived at the vicarage. Most of the buildings are of fairly recent date, like the good Georgian and Victorian houses round the market square and the 18th-century workhouse of Stow Lodge Hospital. Inside the town church, which displays a variety of styles, are an old organ and a rare wigstand. Exhibits in the Abbot's Hall Museum relate to farming and country life in East Anglia.

Moated Kentwell Hall dates from the 16th century and stands in lovely grounds about 1 mile north of Long Melford.

Leave the town on the A1302 'Bury St Edmunds' road. In $\frac{3}{4}$ mile join the A45, and after another $1\frac{3}{4}$ miles branch left on to an unclassified road. Continue to the village of Haughley.

HAUGHLEY, Suffolk TM06
A Norman castle that once stood here has entirely vanished, but its mound remains as a monument to the village's previous importance. There are 30 18th-century leather buckets in the church porch, possibly a hangover from early fire precautions, and the nave has a good roof. New Bell's Farm is an experimental station of the Soil Association (open sometimes).

In Haughley turn left and continue to Wetherden. In the latter village turn left again, then in a further $\frac{1}{2}$ mile turn right and pass the grounds of Haughley Park on the left.

HAUGHLEY PARK, Suffolk TM06
Characteristic stepped gables and elegant octagonal chimneys are dominant features of this lovely old house, built in 1620 and restored in recent years. It stands in beautiful grounds and is open to the public on the occasional Tuesday.

After $1\frac{1}{4}$ miles rejoin the A45. In $\frac{1}{2}$ mile branch left, then turn left on to an unclassified road. A short detour can be made from the main route to the village of Norton by turning right on to the A1088 'Thetford' road and driving for $2\frac{1}{2}$ miles.

NORTON, Suffolk TL96
Excellent examples of old woodcarving, including misericords and a notable font, can be seen inside the local church. Near by are the partly 18th-century Rectory and Little Haugh Hall, both of which present good exteriors.

On the main route, continue to Woolpit.

WOOLPIT, Suffolk TL96
At one time wolves were brought here to be destroyed and buried, hence the name. A local legend tells of the Green Children, a boy and girl who suddenly appeared in some obscure period of village history and were remarkable for their distinctive colour. The story goes on to say that they claimed to be from underground St Martin's Land, a place of perpetual twilight, and that the boy died but the girl married and had a family. Inside the local church is a rare brass-eagle lectern and an impressive double-hammerbeam roof resplendent with carved angels.

Leave Woolpit on the unclassified 'Bury St Edmunds' road and in $\frac{3}{4}$ mile rejoin the A45 for Beyton.

BEYTON, Suffolk TL96
Good Norman features of Beyton Church include a pleasing round tower and an attractively simple doorway.

Continue on the A45 for the return to Bury St Edmunds.

TOUR 63 70 MILES

FARMLANDS OF SUFFOLK

This corner of rural Suffolk is the England of the romantics, an ideal of pastoral beauty hauntingly captured in the paintings of John Constable. It is a place of rolling meadows and tiny rustic villages, where life moves at an easy pace and the air of timelessness can almost be touched.

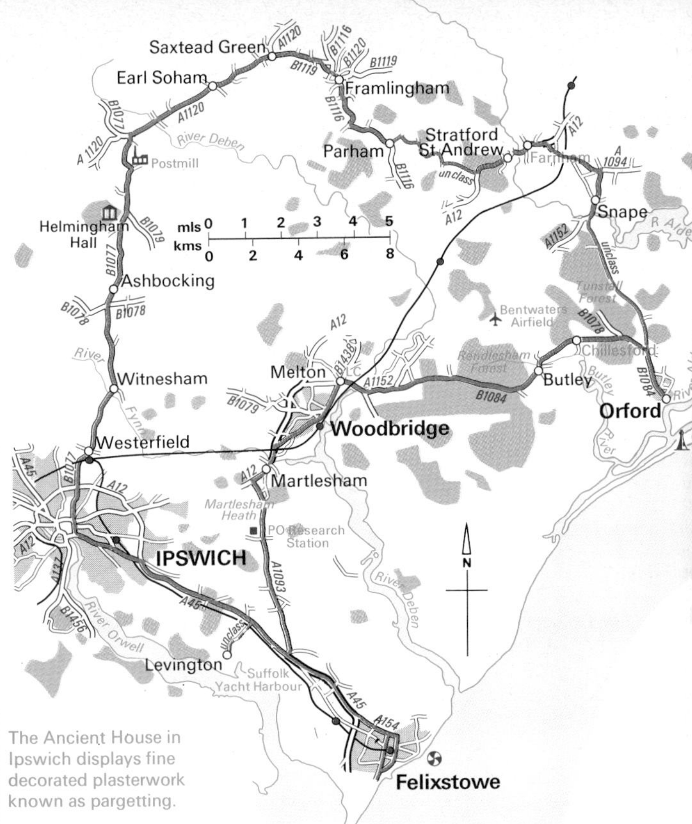

The Ancient House in Ipswich displays fine decorated plasterwork known as pargetting.

IPSWICH, Suffolk TM14
Centuries of development have made this major port the largest and one of the most successful towns in Suffolk. It is the main centre of employment in the eastern part of the county, and despite continued expansion has managed to keep many relics of its eventful past intact. A red-brick gateway bearing royal arms survives from the unfinished Cardinal College of St Mary, which was founded by Cardinal Wolsey – a native of the town – in the 16th century. The Ancient or Sparrowe's House of 1567 stands in the Buttermarket and is noted for its exterior decoration of intricate patterns and features carved in plaster, an outstanding example of the East Anglian art of pargetting. Original oak panelling and heavy carved beams can be seen by visitors to the bookshop which it now houses. Close by are the Great White Horse Hotel, which features in Charles Dickens' *Pickwick Papers*, and many old streets lined with well-preserved timber-framed houses. Christchurch Mansion (open) was built by a Tudor merchant and is isolated in an oasis of parkland near the centre of town. It contains fine collections of furniture and paintings. Exhibits relating to local history and wildlife can be seen in the Ipswich Museum of Archaeology and Natural History, which stands in the High Street. The number of good churches in the town reflects its former importance and prosperity. Among the best are: St Margaret's, with a fine hammerbeam roof; St Peter's, with an impressive black Tournai font; and St Mary-le-Tower, which boasts a lovely pulpit carved by Grinling Gibbons. A remarkable 16th-century Unitarian Meeting House stands in Friar Street.

Leave Ipswich on the A45 with SP 'Felixstowe' and in 5½ miles reach an unclassified right turn leading to Levington. A short detour can be taken to Levington from here.

LEVINGTON, Suffolk TM23
This attractive small village stands on the banks of the Orwell and is the base for the Suffolk Yacht Harbour. Its church dates from the 16th century.

On the main route, continue along the A45 and after 4 miles follow SP 'Town Centre' to enter Felixstowe.

FELIXSTOWE, Suffolk TM33
Towards the end of the 19th century this sheltered spot on the Suffolk coast was developed as a seaside resort. It attracted fashionable society, including the German Kaiser, and acquired a 2-mile length of promenade bordered by delightful flower displays and beautifully tended lawns. Long before this a 16th-century stronghold which became the Landguard Fort was defending the sea approach to Harwich. A later period of insecurity this time generated by Napoleon's hold on Europe, resulted in the building of a Martello tower *c*1810. Felixstowe Dock is an important tanker terminal, container port, and car-ferry terminus.

Leave Felixstowe on the A45 'Ipswich' road and in 4½ miles turn right on to the A1093 SP 'Woodbridge' and 'Gt Yarmouth'. After 4 miles reach a roundabout and go forward, passing the Post Office Research Station on Martlesham Heath. In ¾ mile turn right on to the A12 to reach Martlesham.

MARTLESHAM, Suffolk TM24
Martlesham village is picturesquely sited on a creek of the River Deben and features a church with an unusual 7-sided wagon roof. The local Red Lion Inn displays a curious sign that was taken from a Dutch ship in 1672.

Continue on the A12 to the end of Martlesham, drive under a railway bridge, then turn right on to the B1438 to reach Woodbridge.

This rare old mill on the river Debe[n at] Woodbridge is operated by the rise [and] fall of water between tides. Record[s of] East Anglian mills worked in this [way] date back as far as the 12th cent[ury].

WOODBRIDGE, Suffolk TM24
Attractive houses of major historic interest surround the old market square round which this port has grown. Many date from the 16th century, and the entire group is centred on the superb Shire Hall, which features work from the 16th to 19th centuries and picturesque Dutch-style gables. Multi-period Woodbridge Church carries a tall, flint-flushwork tower and contains a seven sacrament font. Two old m[ills], one a rare example which depend[s] on the tide, are being restored. The port's status as a busy centre of ocean trade declined a long time ago, but today it is a popular sailin[g] centre with a fine riverside park a[t] Kyson Hill (NT).

From Woodbridge continue on th[e] B1438 to Melton.

MELTON, Suffolk TM25
A small colour-washed brick building known as Friar's Dene was once the village gaol. Melton Church has a handsome tower with an attractive broach spire.

From Melton turn right on to the A1152 SP 'Orford'. Cross the railway line and the River Deben, then bear left and in $\frac{3}{4}$ mile keep forward on to the B1084. After a short distance enter part of Rendlesham Forest, which contains a picnic site, and continue to Butley.

BUTLEY, Suffolk TM34
An Augustinian priory founded here in 1171 has vanished but its superb 14th-century gatehouse has survived as one of the finest medieval buildings of its kind in Suffolk. Particularly notable are the heraldic designs cut into its stonework.

Leave Butley, remaining on the B1084, then skirt part of Tunstall Forest and pass through Chillesford. In $1\frac{3}{4}$ miles meet crossroads and turn right to reach Orford.

The finely-preserved postmill at Saxtead Green is typical of many in Suffolk.

RFORD, Suffolk TM45
1165 Henry II built a moat-circled castle with an 18-sided ep here in an attempt to establish orman power over the peoples of st Anglia. Today the building (AM) at developed from these early ginnings contains a collection of ms and affords excellent views of e picturesque houses and hermen's cottages below its walls. n the seaward side of the village e River Alde is separated m the sea by Orford Ness.

RFORD NESS, Suffolk TM44
is long strip of coastal marshland is cupied by the Orford Ness and vergate national nature reserve, e of the few places in England ere the rare avocet can be seen.

m Orford return along the B1084 d in $1\frac{1}{2}$ miles drive forward on to unclassified 'Snape' road. Skirt other part of Tunstall Forest for arly 4 miles and join the A1152. s The Maltings, cross the River e, and enter Snape.

Tudor Helmingham Hall's moat is spanned by two drawbridges.

SNAPE, Suffolk TM35
The magnificent Maltings concert hall, built on the site of old maltings where barley was stored prior to export, is the yearly venue for the famous Aldeburgh Music Festival. Its situation on the banks of the River Alde adds an extra dimension to its pleasing architecture. Snape Church houses a richly carved 15th-century font, and close to the village are slight remains of an ancient Benedictine priory.

Leave Snape, continue for $\frac{3}{4}$ mile, then meet the A1094 'Ipswich' road and turn left. In 2 miles turn left on to the A12 and pass through Farnham for Stratford St Andrew.

STRATFORD ST ANDREW, Suffolk TM36
Close to this pleasant little village is 17th-century Glemham Hall (open), an impressive red-brick mansion standing in 350 acres of beautiful parkland. Inside are panelled rooms appointed with fine paintings and Queen Anne furniture. The village church contains Norman workmanship and houses a 13th-century font.

Remain on the A12 and in 1 mile, at an entrance to Glemham Hall, turn right on to the unclassified 'Parham' road. In a further 1 mile turn right, then in a short distance turn left and continue to Parham.

PARHAM, Suffolk TM36
Tranquilly set in the upper valley of the River Alde, this little village has a church where the village stocks and a beautiful 14th-century screen are preserved. Just to the south-east is 16th-century Moat Hall, a picturesque timber-framed house that is encircled by a moat and nowadays serves as a farm.

Leave Parham on the B1116 and continue to Framlingham.

FRAMLINGHAM, Suffolk TM26
Framlingham's superb Norman castle (AM) was started in 1190 and represented an important advance in castle design. Fragments of the Great Hall are incorporated in picturesque 17th-century almshouses, and the towers carry distinctive Tudor chimneys. Monuments to the Howard family, who took possession in the 15th century, can be seen in the local church. The town itself is a historic market centre with many old houses and a well-known college.

From Framlingham follow the B1119 SP 'Stowmarket' to reach Saxtead Green.

Thames barges moored on the Orwell estuary near Ipswich are reminiscent of a maritime past when the elegance of sail was commonplace.

SAXTEAD GREEN, Suffolk TM26
One of the finest postmills in Suffolk stands here. It stopped working in 1947, but the stones and machinery inside the buck, or body, are in excellent working order. It was first recorded in 1706 and substantially rebuilt at least twice during its working life. Today it stands 46ft high and carries sails with a span of almost 55ft.

Leave Saxtead Green on the A1120 'Stowmarket' road and continue to Earl Soham.

EARL SOHAM, Suffolk TM26
Old cottages and Georgian houses face rows of allotments across a long street in this somewhat rambling village. The local church carries a 15th-century tower and contains several good monuments.

Drive to the end of Earl Soham village and turn left, then in 3 miles turn left again on to the B1077 'Ipswich' road. In 1 mile pass another fine windmill on the left, then in a further $1\frac{1}{4}$ miles reach Helmingham Hall on the right.

HELMINGHAM HALL, Suffolk TM15
Every night the two drawbridges that span the moat to this lovely manor house (open) are raised, though more for the sake of tradition than against rival lords or jealous monarchs. Home of the Tollemache family since the 16th century, the hall has Georgian additions with crenellations by John Nash and stands amid beautiful gardens in an ancient deer park. More than 500 red and fallow deer share the estate with herds of Highland cattle. Visitors may recognise parts of the grounds from John Constable's great landscape painting *Helmingham Dell*.

Continue to Ashbocking.

ASHBOCKING, Suffolk TM15
The medieval church in this village carries a 16th-century tower which is contemporary with Ashbocking Hall, an attractive timber-framed building near by.

Continue to Witnesham.

WITNESHAM, Suffolk TM15
Situated near a tributary of the River Deben, this peaceful little village has an Elizabethan hall and a good church. The hall includes a few Victorian additions and the church, which contains an 8-sided font, has an excellent hammerbeam roof.

Continue on the B1077 to Westerfield.

WESTERFIELD, Suffolk TM14
Westerfield Hall is a 17th-century building with attractive Dutch gables. The local church dates from c1300 and features a nave window in which pieces of a Norman doorway have been re-used. The roof in both the chancel and nave is of hammerbeam construction.

Leave Westerfield and drive through built-up areas to re-enter Ipswich.

AMONG THE NORFOLK BROADS

Close to the great cathedral city of Norwich are marshlands, meres, and lakes in a landscape dotted with the stark shapes of old wind pumps. Hidden canals link vast acreages of water drained from the local countryside, offering ideal highways by which to explore the broadlands.

NORWICH, Norfolk TG20
Once an important centre of the worsted trade, this county town stands on the River Wensum and boasts a cathedral with one of the finest interiors in the country. It dates from Norman times and contains the oldest bishop's throne still used in England. Other major features include a fine presbytery, a beautiful cloister, and a magnificent nave roof featuring many of the 800 roof bosses to be found in the cathedral. Access to the building is by two fine gates, the Erpingham of 1420 and St Ethelbert's of 1272 (both AM). Close to a former water gate on the river are Pull's Ferry and the Old Inn, two reminders of the city's antiquity, and amongst the many other fine old buildings are no less than 30 parish churches. The largest and finest of these is St Peter Mancroft, which carries a notable tower, but all the others have particular details that make them worth a visit. St Andrew's dates from the 15th century and displays a remarkable series of carved shields, and St Michael-at-Coslany has fine flintwork in the Thorpe Chapel. Norwich Castle (open) was started c1130, but its Norman origins have been heavily disguised by 19th-century refacing. Inside is an excellent collection of paintings by the Norwich School of artists – John Crome, John Sell Cotman, and their followers. Survivals from the medieval city and later are many. Flint-faced Bridewell is a 14th-century merchant's house that now contains a museum; the Cow Tower (AM) dates from the same period and formed part of a defensive system along the river bank. Slightly later is the St Peter Hungate Church, a 15th-century building which carries a fine hammerbeam roof and now houses a museum. In the 1920s a chapel was converted to house the well-known Maddermarket Theatre. The most famous of the city's many picturesque streets is Elm Hill, a cobbled road lined with old colour-washed shops and houses, while the most outstanding of its lay buildings are the 15th-century Suckling House and chequered-flint Guildhall. Many of the city's buildings show Dutch influence in the form of ornamental gables.

Leave Norwich on the A47 'Yarmouth' road and pass through Thorpe St Andrew to Blofield.

BLOFIELD, Norfolk TG30
Blofield Church, an impressive building that forms a landmark visible for miles round the village, is noted for its tall west tower. Inside is an 8-sided font ornamented with various scenes in relief.

Continue to Acle.

ACLE, Norfolk TG41
This well-known touring centre is within easy reach of the lovely Norfolk Broads and is a good base from which to explore the area. Its unusual church has a picturesque thatched roof and a round tower that dates from the 12th century. East of the village, on the tour route, are several windpumps that have survived from the days when many such machines were built to pump excess water from the reclaimed marshlands.

Continue along the A47 to Great Yarmouth.

Norwich Castle rises high above the city from a landscaped hilltop.

GREAT YARMOUTH, Norfolk TG50
Holiday amenities in this important oil and fishing port include 5 miles of seafront fringed by excellent sands and backed by colourful gardens. Its situation on Breydon Water, the combined estuaries of the Bure, Waveney and Yare, gives it a sheltered aspect that suits both the holidaymakers and the busy maritime traffic that uses its harbour. The town is very old and has managed to retain many historic features. Most of these can be seen in the South Quay area, where there are remains of the town walls and the notable Custom House. Leading from the town wall to the quay are the Rows, a number of narrow lanes where the 300-year-old Merchant's House (AM) can be seen. Close by is the 14th-century Greyfriar's Cloister (AM). The Elizabethan House Museum has a largely 16th-century interior disguised by a Georgian façade. Exhibits include furniture from that and later periods, and a fascinating collection of Victorian toys. The 13th-century building that houses the Tollhouse Museum is one of the oldest in Great Yarmouth and incorporates ancient dungeons. Close to England's largest parish church is Anna Sewell House, a 17th-century building that was the birthplace of the authoress of *Black Beauty*. The House of Wax museum features various historical figures and scenes , and the Maritime Museum of East Anglia illustrates life saving and marine oil exploration. Near Wellington Pier in an acre of landscaped garden is the quaint Merrivale Model Village.

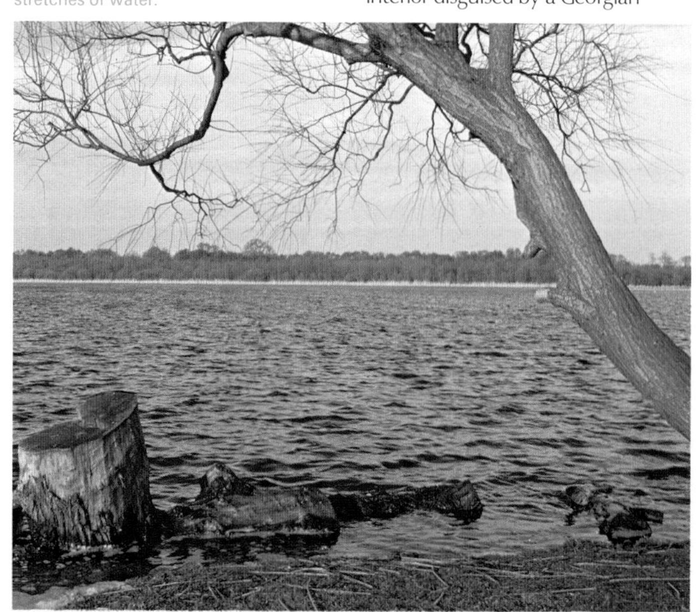

Ormesby, one of Broadland's loveliest stretches of water.

Leave Great Yarmouth on the A149 SP 'Caister'. In 2 miles meet a roundabout and drive forward to enter Caister.

CAISTER-ON-SEA, Norfolk TG51
Remains of town walls and a gateway (AM) survive from the time when this popular little resort was a Roman settlement. Much more recent is the 15th-century castle (open), whose remains now house a museum of veteran and vintage cars.

From the town centre turn left on to the A1064 'Acle' road and pass the remains of Caister Roman Town on the right. Meet a roundabout and tak the 2nd exit. In $\frac{3}{4}$ mile turn right on to an unclassified road SP 'Great Ormesby', and in 1 mile turn left on to the A149 to enter Ormesby St Margaret – at the edge of the Broads country.

THE BROADS, Norfolk
More than 30 large and very beautiful sheets of water, often linked by navigable channels, are contained in a triangular area between Norwich, Lowestoft, and Sea Palling. These, together with many rivers, lakes, and canals, provide some 200 miles of water for cruising and sailing. The essential character of the Broads can only be properly appreciated from a boat, and there are hire firms and tour operators in such centres as Wroxham, Horning and Potter Heigham. Angling permits are available from tackle shops in these and other towns.

A short and very pleasant detour fro the main route can be made by staying on the A149 and continuing to Ormesby Broad.

ORMESBY BROAD, Norfolk TG4
The main road between Ormesby S Margaret and Rollesby crosses this vast expanse of water and offers some of the best broadland views available to the motorist.

On the main route, drive to the war memorial in Ormesby St Margaret and turn right on to an unclassified road alongside the green, SP 'Scratb Meet a T-junction and turn right SP 'Hemsby'. At Hemsby, drive to the end of the village and turn left on to the B1159 SP 'Mundesley'. Continue along a winding road to Winterton.

WINTERTON-ON-SEA, Norfolk TG41
Much of the countryside round this little fishing village is included in a 260-acre nature reserve.

Continue to West Somerton.

WEST SOMERTON, Norfolk TG41
Situated at the weedy eastern end of Martham Broad, this quiet village is an excellent angling base and a good place to see how the marshes were drained. A maze of streams and man-made ditches still carries excess water into the main broads, and two windpumps that were used to pump from one level to another can be seen near by.

Continue with SP 'Cromer' to Horsey Mere.

Horsey Church is noted for its thatched roof and unusual stained-glass windows.

HORSEY MERE, Norfolk TG42
Access to this important breeding ground for marshland plants and animals is restricted to naturalists and permit holders. The mere's drainage windmill (NT) was built in 1912 and has been well restored.

Continue to Horsey.

HORSEY, Norfolk TG42
Despite frequent incursions of the sea since it was built, the thatched village church has retained its Norman round tower and a belfry dating from the 15th century.

Continue to Sea Palling.

SEA PALLING, Norfolk TG42
Although the smooth, dune-backed beach at Sea Palling looks inviting, the coastal waters here are dangerous and bathers are warned to be very careful.

In $1\frac{3}{4}$ miles turn right and continue to Lessingham, then Happisburgh.

HAPPISBURGH, Norfolk TG33
Offshore shipping is warned away from the treacherous Haisboro' Sands by a lighthouse, but the same sands provide sun and sea bathers with a superb dune-backed beach. The name of this pretty little fishing village is pronounced Hazeborough.

In $\frac{1}{2}$ miles meet crossroads and turn left for Walcott. Continue to Bacton.

BACTON, Norfolk TG33
Easy access to the broad local beach of shingly sand and pebbles is via a high sea wall. The village itself is an attractive little place that grew up alongside Broomholm Priory, a 12th-century foundation that claimed to possess a piece of the True Cross and became a great centre of pilgrimage. Remains of the priory, which was mentioned by Chaucer, include the gatehouse, north transept, chapter house, and refectory.

Drive past a windmill to Mundesley.

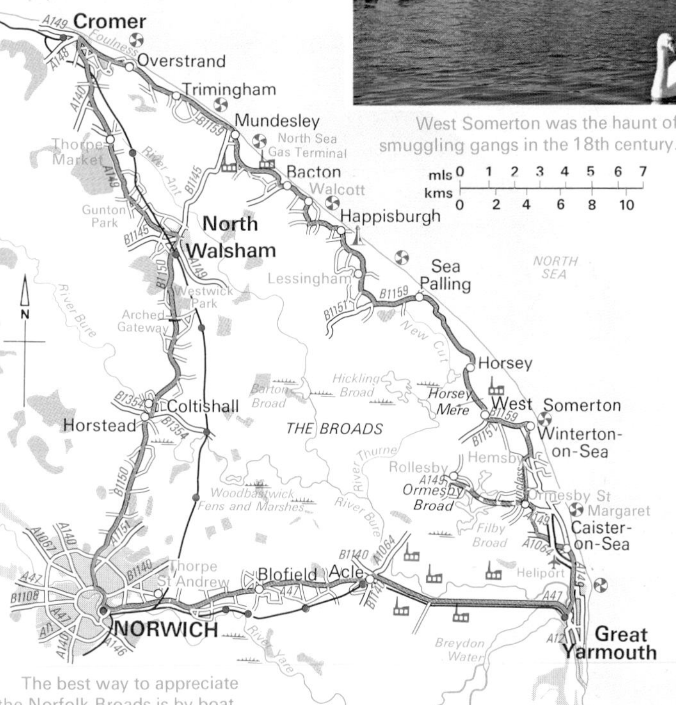

The best way to appreciate the Norfolk Broads is by boat.

West Somerton was the haunt of smuggling gangs in the 18th century.

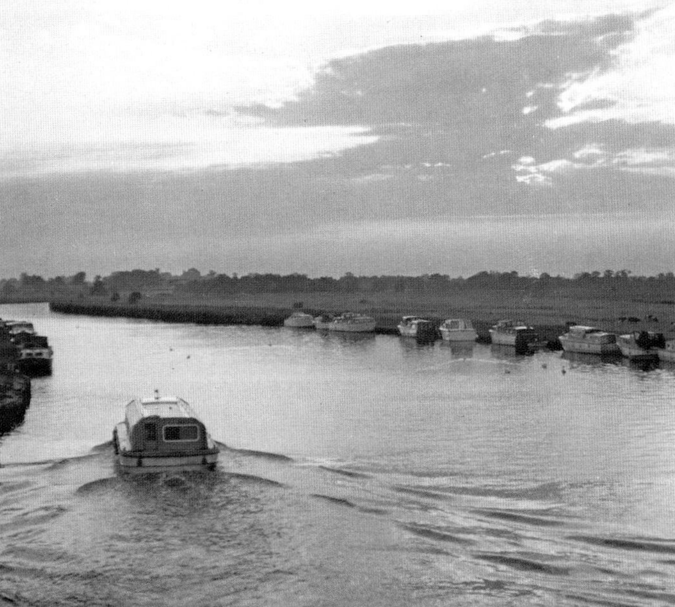

MUNDESLEY, Norfolk TG33
This quiet resort has a gently shelving sand beach backed by cliffs. It is associated with the poet William Cowper.

Continue to Trimingham.

TRIMINGHAM, Norfolk TG23
Some of the highest cliffs in Norfolk overlook a good bathing beach here. A painted screen can be seen in the local church.

Continue to Overstrand.

OVERSTRAND, Norfolk TG24
Pleasant cliff walks lead from here to the nearby resort of Cromer, and safe bathing can be enjoyed from the local sands. The 14th-century Church of St Martin was built after the old parish church fell into the sea.

Continue to Cromer.

CROMER, Norfolk TG24
Although a bustling resort mainly occupied with the needs of holidaymakers, Cromer still has a small fishing fleet and has the reputation for supplying the best crabs in England. Its sandy beach is backed by lofty cliffs, and its many amenities include a zoo and boating pool. The 15th-century parish church carries one of the tallest towers in Norfolk. Close to Cromer is Felbrigg Hall (NT), a fine house that dates from the 17th century.

Leave Cromer on the A149 'Norwich' road and in $2\frac{1}{4}$ miles bear left SP 'North Walsham'. Continue to Thorpe Market and North Walsham.

NORTH WALSHAM, Norfolk TG23
Homely buildings and winding little lanes make this beautiful market town well worth a pause in any journey. Its fine church is given an air of gothic mystery by a ruined tower that fell in 1724. Inside are a painted screen, a tall 15th-century font cover, and various monuments. The local grammar school was founded in the early 17th century.

Follow SP 'Norwich' on the B1150. Pass Westwick Park and drive beneath an arched gateway which spans the road; continue to Coltishall.

COLTISHALL, Norfolk TG21
This shooting and angling centre is situated on the River Bure and enjoys a genteelly relaxed atmosphere imparted by many 18th-century buildings.

Cross the River Bure to Horstead.

HORSTEAD, Norfolk TG21
Horstead Church carries a slender west tower that dates from the 13th century. The delightful village mill stands opposite the miller's house.

Drive through wooded countryside and return to Norwich.

TOUR 65 74 MILES

SALTINGS ON THE WASH

Along the sweeping coastline of the Wash are wide sandy bays backed by wild salt marshes populated by wildlife suited to the open surroundings. Here and there the flint tower of a medieval village church breaks the skyline, providing a landmark for travellers on both land and sea.

The creek at Burnham Overy Staithe is very popular with yachtsmen.

KING'S LYNN, Norfolk TF62
Two markets were founded here in Norman times, medieval merchants came here to build warehouses on the River Ouse, and 20th-century industry has continued the town's long history of commercial significance. Everywhere are survivals from periods that the settlement has grown through, and its medieval buildings are some of the finest in the country. Traces of the ancient walls show how the town has expanded since the troubled times in which they were built, and the superb Hanseatic Warehouse of 1428 recalls full-sailed barques laden with exotic goods. To complement the two market places are two guildhalls, both of which date from the early 15th century. The biggest of these (NT) is the largest medieval guildhall extant and is now used as a theatre. The other contains old town regalia, including a 14th-century vessel known as King John's Cup. Both the last-mentioned building and the much more recent Town Hall of 1895 display a striking flint-chequerwork design. The superb Custom House, perhaps the most outstanding building in the town, was built by architect Henry Bell while he held office as mayor in 1683. Many other of the town's old buildings have ancient roots but have been changed over the centuries. Clifton House dates originally from the 14th century but has later additions; Hampton Court shows period work from the 14th to 18th centuries; and Dutch-gabled Thoresby College of *c*1500 now reflects the tastes of the 17th century. The huge parish church contains two outstanding memorial brasses that are the biggest and most famous in England. Red Mount Chapel of *c*1485 is an octagonal building with beautiful fan vaulting.

Leave King's Lynn by the A47 'Swaffham' road and continue to Middleton.

Dutch influence is evident in King's Lynn's charming Custom House.

MIDDLETON, Norfolk TF61
Major Everard-Hutton, one of the famous Six Hundred who fought at Balaclava, is commemorated by a memorial in the local church. Some 3 miles north west is Middleton Tower, a splendid red-brick gatehouse of mainly 19th-century date.

Pass Walton Common, then cross the River Nar to enter Narborough.

NARBOROUGH, Norfolk TF71
Several fine brasses and a standing effigy can be seen in the local church.

Continue, and later pass Swaffham Heath to reach Swaffham.

SWAFFHAM, Norfolk TF80
Legend tells of the 'Pedlar of Swaffham', who travelled to London to throw himself into the Thames but was dissuaded by a man he met on London Bridge. This stranger related a dream in which he found treasure in a remote village garden – a garden that the pedlar recognised as his own. He hastened home to find two pots of gold; an image of the pedlar is now incorporated in the town sign. The triangular market place has a domed rotunda built by the Earl of Oxford in 1783 as a market cross. Features of the local church include a splendid angel-carved double-hammerbeam roof and a fine 16th-century west tower.

Leave Swaffham on the A1065 'Cromer' road. In $2\frac{3}{4}$ miles turn left on to an unclassified road for Castle Acre.

CASTLE ACRE, Norfolk TF81
This aptly-named village lies within the outer bailey of an 11th-century castle, of which only the earthworks and a 13th-century gateway remain. Impressive ruins of an 11th-century Cluniac priory, including fine Norman arcading (AM) and a Tudor gatehouse, can be seen near by.

Continue through the village and turn right SP 'Newton'. Rejoin the A1065 'Cromer' road and drive to Weasenham.

WEASENHAM, Norfolk TF82
Prehistoric barrows in all shapes and sizes, including bell, bowl, disc, and saucer types, can be seen in the countryside round Weasenham Plantation.

Continue to East Raynham.

EAST RAYNHAM, Norfolk TF82
Raynham Hall, a magnificent 17th-century building which has been ascribed partly to Inigo Jones, was once the home of the agricultural innovator nicknamed Turnip Townshend.

In $2\frac{1}{2}$ miles turn right SP 'Town Centre' for Fakenham.

FAKENHAM, Norfolk TF92
This attractive market town dates from Saxon times and was a Royal Manor until the 17th century. Its Market Place has two old coaching inns, both showing traces of earlier work behind Georgian façades, and the parish church has a commanding 15th-century tower.

From Fakenham town centre follow SP 'King's Lynn' to join the A148. In $\frac{1}{2}$ mile turn right on to the B1105 SP 'Walsingham' and descend into East Barsham.

EAST BARSHAM, Norfolk TF93
East Barsham is known for its brick and terracotta manor house, a splendid example of early Tudor work. Fine chimneys typical of the style rise high above the rooftops, and the approach is guarded by an imposing two-storeyed gatehouse.

Continue for 1 mile to Houghton St Giles.

HOUGHTON ST GILES, Norfolk TF93
On the far side of the Stiffkey river, about 1 mile south west of this attractive village, is the last in a chain of wayside chapels which once lined the Walsingham Way. It is known as the Slipper Chapel because pilgrims to the shrine of Our Lady at Walsingham would remove their shoes here before completing their journey barefoot. It is now the official Roman Catholic Shrine of Our Lady.

Continue to Walsingham, also known as Little Walsingham.

The legendary Pedlar of Swaffham is commemorated by the town sign.

VALSINGHAM, Norfolk TF93
he shrine at Walsingham, a place of aramount importance to the ilgrims of the middle ages, was ounded in the 11th century. irtually every English king from ichard I to Henry VIII came here, nd the last-named had the shrine obbed when he dissolved the onasteries. In the 19th century the lgrimages were revived, and a new hrine of Our Lady was built for the nglican Church in the early part of e 20th century. Remains of what as once a giant concourse of uildings date mainly from the 13th nd 14th centuries, and include the perb east wall of the priory.

ontinue on the B1105 'Wells' road d skirt Wighton to meet the A149. rn left, then right, with SP 'The ach'. Enter Wells-next-the-Sea.

ELLS-NEXT-THE-SEA, rfolk TF94
d houses and the picturesque ayside make a charming group in small resort and port. Bathing y be enjoyed in a nearby creek.

ve the resort on the A149 nstanton' road and drive to kham.

The Marble Hall in the Palladian mansion of Holkham exemplifies William Kent's lavish style.

HOLKHAM, Norfolk TF84
Holkham Hall (open), a vast Palladian mansion, is one of the show-pieces of the county. The present house was rebuilt in the 18th century to plans by William Kent, who also designed much of the furniture to be seen inside. Experts consider the entrance into the wonderful alabaster hall to show Kent's genius at its peak, and all the rooms are sumptuously decorated in the fashion of the day. An impressive art collection is displayed in the house, and the library has an excellent collection of 18th-century books. The lake-watered grounds were laid out by Capability Brown in 1762.

Continue to Burnham Overy Staithe.

BURNHAM OVERY STAITHE, Norfolk TF84
Close to this tiny village are a water mill (NT) and tower windmill (NT), both in a good state of preservation. Neither is open to the public at time of publication.

After a short distance cross the River Burn and continue to Burnham Deepdale.

BURNHAM DEEPDALE, Norfolk TF84
Inside the local church, which carries a rare Saxon round tower, is an outstanding Norman font.

Continue to Brancaster Staithe.

BRANCASTER STAITHE, Norfolk TF74
A boat service operates from here to Scolt Head Island, where there is a bird sanctuary (NT) and nature reserve.

Continue for ½ mile to Brancaster.

BRANCASTER, Norfolk TF74
This one-time Roman station is now a golfing resort. A lane leads from the church to a pebble beach which, though not as attractive as its large sandy neighbour, is far safer for bathing.

Continue through Titchwell to Thornham.

THORNHAM, Norfolk TF74
A rectangular earthwork on a slope overlooking the waters of the Wash here was excavated in 1960, revealing the remains of an iron-age village. The complex, thought to date from cAD40, measures 133 by 175ft and includes a defensive ditch cut into the soft chalk.

Drive through Old Hunstanton and ½ mile farther turn right on to an unclassified road SP 'Sea Front'. Continue into Hunstanton.

A peaceful atmosphere pervades Wells-next-the-Sea.

HUNSTANTON, Norfolk TF64
Hunstanton is the largest seaside resort in west Norfolk and the only East Anglian coastal town to face west. Great stretches of sand are backed by cliffs of mixed chalk and sand rising 60ft above the beach.

Pass the Pier, bear right into Westgate, and in ½ mile meet a roundabout. Take the 1st exit SP 'King's Lynn', then meet the main road and turn right on to the A149 to reach the outskirts of Heacham.

HEACHAM, Norfolk TF63
Pocahontas, the Red Indian princess who married John Rolfe at Heacham Hall in 1614, is commemorated in both the village sign and a memorial in the local church. Her son founded a line which was to include the wife of US president Woodrow Wilson.

Continue to Snettisham.

SNETTISHAM, Norfolk TF63
One of the finest churches in Norfolk stands here. Its lofty spire can be seen for many miles across the flat local countryside, and its superb west front is reminiscent of Peterborough Cathedral. Also in the village is attractive Old Hall, an 18th-century house with Dutch gables.

Continue through Ingoldisthorpe to Dersingham. Turn left on to the B1440 SP 'Sandringham'. Ascend through wooded country and in ½ mile pass the gates of Sandringham House.

SANDRINGHAM, Norfolk TF62
Included in this 7,000-acre estate, owned by the Royal Family, are a 19th-century house, the farms and woodlands of 7 parishes, and a 300-acre country park (open sometimes in summer). The park church is of exceptional note and contains an organ that was the last gift of King Edward VII. Many superb royal memorials enrich the interior, and the nave is roofed in English oak.

In 1 mile turn right on to the B1439 into West Newton. Continue to the main road and turn left to rejoin the A149. In 1 mile turn right on to an unclassified road for Castle Rising.

CASTLE RISING, Norfolk TF62
The sea has long withdrawn from this one-time port, but the Norman castle (AM) built to protect it still stands. It occupies a Roman site and has a great keep in which a fascinating sequence of rooms, galleries, and minor stairs are reached by a single dramatic staircase. The local Church of St Lawrence is famous for its Norman west front, which has a fine doorway on the lower level and houses a richly carved square font on a circular shaft. Bede House or Trinity Hospital dates from the 17th century and is an almshouse charity for elderly ladies.

Continue to South Wootton, meet traffic signals, and drive over crossroads. After another 1½ miles meet a T-junction, turn right, and return to King's Lynn.

TOUR 66 84 MILES

BULB FIELDS IN THE FENS

Spring in the Fens is an explosion of colour. Daffodils, tulips, and hyacinths cover acre after flat acre of reclaimed land, stretching away from the bulb towns in gloriously-variegated carpets reminiscent of the Dutch countryside rather than rural England.

SPALDING, Lincs TF22
This historic fenland town stands on the banks of the Welland in an area of drained marshland where market gardeners and bulb growers raise crops in soil of almost legendary richness. In springtime the district is glorious with tulips, daffodils, narcissi, and hyacinths that form a carpet of blazing colour comparable only with the bulb fields of Holland. Every May the town holds a spectacular Flower Festival that attracts visitors from all over the country. On the eastern outskirts are the beautiful Springfield Gardens, 25 acres of lawns and water features designed to show over a million bulbs to their best advantage. In summer the early freshness of the bulbs is replaced by the mature beauty of more than 80 species of rose in the magnificent Summer Rose Garden. The town itself has many old buildings in charming streets on both banks of the river, including several good examples of 18th-century design. One of the oldest is the greatly restored Ayscoughfee Hall, which dates from the 15th century and now houses a museum of British birds. Its mellow stone and graceful lines are complemented by well-kept lawns enclosed by yew hedges. The Museum of Antiquities, in Broad Street, was founded by the Gentleman's Society in 1710. Spalding has many good churches, but the best is the late 13th-century Church of SS Mary and Nicholas. This has an angel-carved hammerbeam roof in the nave and was extensively restored by the Victorian architect Sir G G Scott.

The area around Spalding is ablaze with tulips in the spring.

Leave Spalding on the A16 'Boston' road and drive to Pinchbeck.

PINCHBECK, Lincs TF22
Situated on the River Glen in a bulb-growing district, this village has preserved its old wooden stocks and has a restored church with a leaning tower. A fine 18th-century group of buildings includes the rectory and a stable block.

Continue on the A16 to Surfleet.

SURFLEET, Lincs TF22
The spire on the church in this fenland village leans 6ft out of true – considerably more than the tower at Pinchbeck. Naturalist Gilbert White described a local heronry in his early work *Natural History*, but this has since been abandoned.

Cross the River Glen and proceed along the A16 to Gosberton.

GOSBERTON, Lincs TF23
An outstanding feature of this pleasant little village is its cruciform church, which displays a curious tower gargoyle fashioned in the shape of an elephant.

Fleet Fen is part of Lincolnshire's extensive 17th-century drainage works.

Leave Gosberton, keep forward on the A152, and continue to Donington.

DONINGTON, Lincs TF23
In Roman times the area around Donington was drained in the first of many attempts to reclaim agricultural land from the Fens. Much later the town was a centre of the flax and hemp industry, and nowadays it is a popular touring base. Its cobbled market square is surrounded by pleasant Georgian buildings, and its church carries a fine tower surmounted by an elegant spire. Inside is a tablet commemorating Captain Matthew Flinders, a great sailor who was born in Donington and travelled with Captain Bligh after the *Bounty* mutiny. He became a pioneer of Australian exploration and wrote a book about his voyages. He died in 1814, on the day that his book was published.

Continue through fenland along the A52.

THE LINCOLNSHIRE FENS, Lincs
The Fens of Lincolnshire covered an area that is barely above sea level and have been reduced by centuries of land reclamation. The Romans built the first sea wall here and drained the land behind it; in subsequent centuries their work was continued, and much later the expertise of Dutch engineer Vermuyden was used to make many acres of ground into rich arable land. A giant reclamation scheme begun in the 17th century used the talents of such famous men as Rennie and Telford, and was largely responsible for the shape of the landscape as it exists today. Everywhere the flat fields and pastures are criss-crossed by drains and dykes that stretch away to an almost treeless horizon.

Continue along the A52, with Swaton Fen on the right and Horbling Fen to the left. In 4 miles turn left on to the B1177 'Bourne' road and proceed to Horbling.

HORBLING, Lincs TF13
Spring Well, situated a little way north of Horbling's Norman and later church, was once a communal washing trough. The village itself is a charming collection of mainly Georgian houses.

Proceed along the B1177 to Billingborough.

BILLINGBOROUGH, Lincs TF13
The local church carries a 150ft spire that can be seen for a long way over the surrounding flat countryside. An unusual façade is displayed by the George and Dragon Inn, which dates from the 17th century.

Continue for ¾ mile by Billingborough Fen and pass a track leading right to the site of Sempringham Abbey.

SEMPRINGHAM ABBEY, Lincs TF1
Sir Gilbert of Sempringham founded the Gilbertine order here c1130. He was the son of the local lord, and the Gilbertines were the only monastic order to have been founded in Britain. Close to the site an uneven area of grassland covers the remains of the village, but the superb Norman church survives as an outstanding example of its period.

Continue along the B1177 and drive through Pointon to Dowsby.

DOWSBY, Lincs TF12
Dowsby Hall was built c1603, and the local church contains many fine moulded arches.

Stay on the B1177 through Dunsby, passing Dowsby Fen and Dunsby Fen on the left. Join the A15, with Bourne North Fen to the left, and continue to Bourne.

The beautiful water gardens near ?eakirk are the home of various water birds, including trumpeter swans.

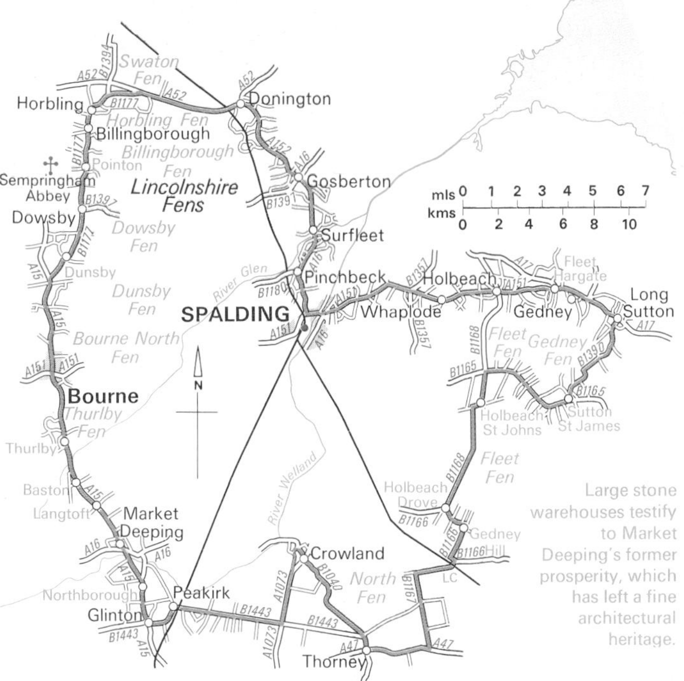

BOURNE, Lincs TF02

3ourne is an ancient market town ınd reputedly the birthplace ›f Hereward the Wake, the last ›axon to resist the invading Norman ırmy. Nowadays the town is well :nown as the home of the BRM acing car works, and is renowned ›r the purity of its water. The many vatercress beds in the area are mple proof of the latter. Good lomestic architecture in the town ıcludes attractive Tudor cottages in outh Street and a generous cattering of Georgian houses and ıops. The Burghley Arms Hotel was ıe birthplace of Sir William Cecil, ord High Treasurer to Elizabeth I, in 520. Other famous natives of the ›wn include Frederick Worth, ›under of the House of Worth in aris, and Robert Mannying, who ›unded an Augustinian abbey here the 13th century. Remains of the ıonastic buildings are incorporated the nave of the parish church. A oman canal known as the Car yke runs close to the town, and astle earthworks can be seen a little ay south.

ontinue along the A15 eterborough' road and drive rough Thurlby. Cross the River len and continue through Baston ıd Langtoft to Market Deeping.

ARKET DEEPING, Lincs TF11

›veral fine old houses testify to the ıe-time prosperity and importance this ancient market town, situated ı the River Welland at the edge of e Fens. Its restored church has an ıusual rood loft doorway, and the th-century parish rectory is ought to be the oldest inhabited rsonage in England.

ave Market Deeping on the A15, oss the River Welland, and pass the age of Northborough. Proceed to inton.

INTON, Cambs TF10

ıong the pleasant stone cottages this attractive village is a fine 17th- ıtury manor house; the entire up is centred on the slender spire he local church.

Leave Glinton and turn left on to the B1443 'Thorney' road. Continue to Peakirk.

PEAKIRK, Cambs TF10

A rare 14th-century lectern and numerous paintings can be seen in Peakirk's church, the only one in Britain dedicated to St Pega. Close to the village are fascinating gardens featuring a variety of waterfowl.

Leave Peakirk and continue east for 4 miles, then turn left on to the A1073. After another 2 miles turn left again on to an unclassified road and drive into Crowland.

CROWLAND, Lincs TF21

One of the most interesting features of this pleasant little town is its unique Triangular Bridge (AM), which was built in the 14th century to span several streams of the River Welland. Its three arches, which meet at an angle of 120 degrees, now stand on dry land. In 1720 a carved figure of the Virgin Mary was taken from the partly ruined abbey that now serves as the parish church and placed on the bridge. The original abbey was founded in 716 by King Ethelbald in memory of St Guthlac.

From Crowland follow the B1040 to Thorney.

THORNEY, Cambs TF20

It was here that the Saxon hero Hereward the Wake made his last stand against the invading Norman armies under William the Conqueror. Remains of a 12th-century abbey built by William after his victory can be seen near by, and the restored abbey church shows Norman and later workmanship. Abbey House is a largely 16th-century building with 17th-century additions. A good 18th-century windmill shares its grounds with a wildlife park.

From Thorney turn left on the A47 'Wisbech' road and in 1½ miles turn left again on to the B1167 SP 'Gedney Hill'. Continue for 4½ miles, drive over a level crossing, then turn left on to the B1166 to Gedney Hill. At Gedney Hill turn left and continue to Holbeach Drove, then turn right on to the B1168 with Fleet Fen to the right. Meet crossroads 1 mile beyond Holbeach St Johns and turn right on to the B1165 for Sutton St James. Drive to the end of this village, turn left on to the B1390 to Long Sutton.

LONG SUTTON, Lincs TF42

Many different architectural periods are represented in the fabric of this pretty market town's church, but the main feature is its detached, 162ft tower. This has a lead and timber spire that is considered one of the finest in Britain.

Leave Long Sutton on the A17 SP 'Sleaford', passing Gedney to the left.

Large stone warehouses testify to Market Deeping's former prosperity, which has left a fine architectural heritage.

GEDNEY, Lincs TF42

The fine marshland church in Gedney features a notable west tower and contains a 14th-century brass. Also inside are a number of alabaster effigies.

Leave the village and in a short distance turn left on to the A151 'Spalding' road, passing through Fleet Hargate into Holbeach.

HOLBEACH, Lincs TF32

One of the county's major bulb-growing centres, this ancient market town boasts many good Georgian houses and a 14th-century church with a lofty spire and fine traceried windows. William Stukely, a founder of the Society of Antiquaries, was born here in 1718.

Proceed along the A151 to Whaplode.

WHAPLODE, Lincs TF32

The splendid Norman and later church in this little marshland village has a presence that is out of all proportion to the size of the community that it serves. Inside is a notable 17th-century monument to Sir Anthony Irby.

Continue along the A151 for the return to Spalding.

Whaplode Church never came to the attention of 19th-century restorers, whose enthusiasm often outstripped their ability.

TOUR 67 82 MILES

LINCOLN AND THE WITHAM VALLEY

The proud triple towers of Lincoln Cathedral can be seen for many miles across the flat lands of the Witham Valley, a fertile area of farms and fens whose threatened monotony is relieved by picturesque villages of honey-coloured stone.

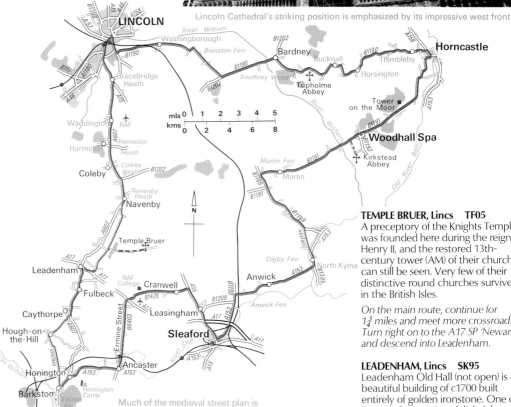

Lincoln Cathedral's striking position is emphasized by its impressive west front.

LINCOLN, Lincs SK97
Historic Lincoln rises majestically from the north banks of the River Witham, on a slope crowned by its beautiful triple-towered cathedral. This splendid building, the third largest of its type in England, completely dominates the city and overlooks miles of countryside. Its 11th-century origins are largely hidden by extensions and additions from subsequent periods, and its many ancient treasures include the best preserved of four existing copies of *Magna Carta*. In the Library are first editions of *Paradise Lost, Don Quixote*, and part of Spenser's *Faerie Queen*. Amongst many other interesting churches in the city are St Benedict's and St Peter at Gowt's, both of which include a great deal of Saxon work. Newport Arch (AM), the only surviving Roman gateway to span an English street, is a relic of the ancient walled city of *Lindum Colonia*. The Close, also known as Minster Yard, contains a superb collection of buildings including a fine tithe barn of 1440 and the ancient Bishop's Palace (AM). Lincoln Castle was founded by William the Conqueror in 1068 and over the centuries has grown into the impressive structure that occupies some 6 acres of city ground today. Its main features include 14th-century Cobb Hall, which was once a place of punishment, the Observatory Tower, and a fine Norman keep. Other old buildings in the city include the Jew's House, a fine example of 12th-century domestic architecture, and nearby Aaron's House – a product of the prosperous wool age and the oldest inhabited dwelling in England. Timber-framed 16th-century houses line the High Street as it crosses High Bridge, preserving in miniature the appearance of old London Bridge before it was destroyed in the Great Fire that razed the capital in 1666.

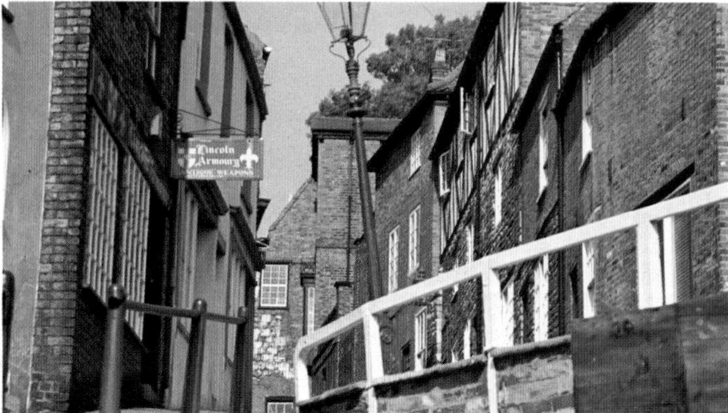

Much of the medieval street plan is preserved in Lincoln.

From Lincoln follow SP 'Sleaford A15' and ascend to Bracebridge Heath. Turn right on to the A607 SP 'Grantham' and after a short distance pass the large RAF base at Waddington on the left. Continue past Harmston Heath (on the left) and the village of Harmston in attractively wooded countryside to the right. After a short distance pass Coleby on the right, with Coleby Heath stretching away to the left.

COLEBY, Lincs SK96
Interesting old buildings in this pleasant village include the church and 17th-century Coleby Hall. The former is of Norman date and incorporates a Saxon tower, and the latter shares attractive grounds with the Temple of Romulus and Remus, by Sir William Chambers.

Continue on the A607 into Navenby, with Navenby Heath on the left.

NAVENBY, Lincs SK95
Stone and pantiled houses form charming architectural groups in this pleasant little village, and the restored church rises grandly above their rooftops to complete the picture. Inside the church is a notable Easter Sepulchre decorated with carved figures.

Beyond Navenby turn left on to an unclassified road SP 'Ancaster, Sleaford'. Continue for 2½ miles and meet crossroads. A detour from the main route can be made here by turning left and driving for 2¼ miles to Temple Bruer; access is via a road through Temple Farm.

TEMPLE BRUER, Lincs TF05
A preceptory of the Knights Templar was founded here during the reign of Henry II, and the restored 13th-century tower (AM) of their church can still be seen. Very few of their distinctive round churches survive in the British Isles.

On the main route, continue for 1¾ miles and meet more crossroads. Turn right on to the A17 SP 'Newark' and descend into Leadenham.

LEADENHAM, Lincs SK95
Leadenham Old Hall (not open) is a beautiful building of c1700 built entirely of golden ironstone. One of its main features is a delightful rustic doorway. The village itself is dominated by its lovely church spire and boasts a 19th-century drinking fountain beneath a hexagonal cano

Meet traffic lights in Leadenham and turn left on to the A607 SP 'Grantham'. Continue to Fulbeck.

FULBECK, Lincs SK95
A delightful combination of woods and farmland surrounds this pretty village, which has an old hall of 173 and a restored church containing many fine monuments.

Proceed on the A607, passing the edge of Caythorpe.

CAYTHORPE, Lincs SK94
The characteristically utilitarian appearance of Caythorpe's village architecture is lifted by the mellow gold of local ironstone. Notable Ivy House dates from 1684 and has projecting wings with gables. The local church features a good towe

Drive ½ mile beyond the Caythorpe crossroads and turn right on to an unclassified road for the village of Hough-on-the-Hill.

HOUGH-ON-THE-HILL, Lincs SK94
As its name suggests, this village occupies a lofty site that makes it an excellent viewpoint. The local church is noted for its tower, which features a curious Saxon turret containing a newel stairway.

Beyond the local church turn left SP 'Barkston, Grantham' and proceed to Barkston.

BARKSTON, Lincs SK94
Barkston Church features a good ironstone tower. Close by is a group of almshouses that reflect a style uniformly applied to the buildings of the local Belton estate.

From Barkston turn left on to the A607, with Syston Park ahead. After $\frac{3}{4}$ mile drive forward on to the A153, skirting Honington.

Iorth Kyme Fen typifies the Holland rea of Lincolnshire.

IONINGTON, Lincs SK94
About $\frac{3}{4}$ mile south-east of this village ; Honington Camp, one of the few najor hillforts built in this part of the ountry. It is of iron-age date and vas probably manned to defend the ncaster Gap. During the 17th entury an urn of Roman coins was ound here, which seems to suggest hat the inhabitants of nearby ncaster found the camp useful. Ionington Church contains some ood Norman work.

ontinue on the A153, passing onington Camp, and proceed for $\frac{1}{2}$ miles. Turn left on to the B6403 to ncaster.

NCASTER, Lincs SK94
:ted on the old Roman road of mine Street, this village is set in easantly wooded countryside and ands near the site of Roman ausennae. Remains of this ancient imp and posting station can be en near by, and relics excavated om the area can be seen in antham Museum – including osaic flooring and an altar. Some niles south of the village are arries where the famous Ancaster one was worked for many of colnshire's beautiful churches.

oceed along a modern road that ows the line of Ermine Street.

ERMINE STREET, Lincs SK94
This Roman road, built about 1,900 years ago between London and Lincoln, allowed the occupying forces to reach trouble spots in eastern England with comparative ease. The name is derived from a Saxon tribe who lived near by.

Drive for $3\frac{3}{4}$ miles beyond Ancaster and turn right on to the A17, then left on to the B1429 SP 'Cranwell', passing the RAF College. Continue to Cranwell.

CRANWELL, Lincs TF04
Traces of Saxon workmanship can be seen in Cranwell's mainly Norman church, which houses a fine old screen. West of the village is the well-known RAF college, which was founded in 1920 and includes a number of well-designed buildings.

In $\frac{3}{4}$ mile turn right on to the A15 'Sleaford' road and pass the edge of Leasingham.

LEASINGHAM, Lincs TF04
Notable buildings in this old village include the Ancient House of 1658, the 17th-century Old Hall, and Georgian Leasingham Manor. Later additions include Leasingham Hall and Roxholme Hall, both of the 19th century. The local church has a lofty west tower crowned by a spire.

Proceed along the A15 to Sleaford.

SLEAFORD, Lincs TF04
Charmingly situated on the banks of the peaceful River Slea, this pleasant little market town is dominated by a 12th- to 15th-century church with one of the earliest stone spires in England. The building's outstanding window tracery is arguably the best in the country. Early structures in the town include a 15th-century timber-framed vicarage and the Black Bull Inn; a carved stone at the latter is dated 1689 and 1791, and illustrates the old sport of bull baiting. Most of the town's workaday buildings date from the 19th century, including the Corn Exchange, Sessions House, Carre's Hospital, and a former workhouse.

Leave Sleaford on the A153 'Horncastle' road. After $2\frac{3}{4}$ miles turn right and proceed to Anwick.

Little survives to tell of the wealth and prestige that came to Bardney Abbey before its downfall and ruin.

ANWICK, Lincs TF15
Just south of Anwick's medieval church are adjoining cottages in the romantic gothic style. One houses the post office and the other is a smithy.

Continue with Anwick Fen on the right, and drive through the village of North Kyme. Beyond North Kyme continue forward on to an unclassified road SP 'Walcot', skirting Digby Fen on the left. In $1\frac{1}{4}$ miles turn left on to the B1189; proceed for 4 miles and turn right on to the B1191 SP 'Woodhall Spa', driving through Martin and later passing Martin Fen on the left. Cross the River Witham at Kirkstead Bridge, and after another $\frac{3}{4}$ mile pass a right turn leading to Kirkstead Abbey. It is worth making the short detour to this historic place.

KIRKSTEAD ABBEY, Lincs TF16
Scant remains of a rich Cistercian abbey founded by Hugo Brito in 1139 can be seen here, but the site is most famous for the 13th-century architectural gem of St Leonard's Chapel. This was built outside the abbey gates for lay worshippers, and has survived in a remarkably good state of preservation. Its wooden screen is thought to be the second oldest in England and includes timber work dating from 1210.

Like many of Sleaford's buildings, Carre's Hospital, in Eastgate, dates from the mid-19th century.

Continue along the main route and enter Woodhall Spa.

WOODHALL SPA, Lincs TF16
In Victorian and earlier times this inland resort was famous for its natural springs, and a fine pump room and bathing establishment remain from this period. Nowadays the town is well known as a golfing centre, with Lincolnshire's only championship-standard course.

Continue along the B1191 to Tower on the Moor.

TOWER ON THE MOOR, Lincs TF26
This impressive 60ft tower dominates the local countryside and is a well-known (if enigmatic) landmark. It is thought to have been built in the 15th century.

Continue along the B1191 to Horncastle.

HORNCASTLE, Lincs TF26
Roman *Banovallum*, the 'walled place on the River Bain', stood on the site now occupied by this pleasant little market town. Remains of the ancient fort that guarded the settlement have been incorporated in the modern town library. The local church dates from the 13th century and contains the fine Dymoke Brass of 1519, plus a 17th-century chest and various other relics. A 10-day horse fair still held in Horncastle every August is featured in George Borrow's *Romany Rye*.

Leave Horncastle on the A158 'Lincoln' road and in $\frac{1}{2}$ mile turn left on to the B1190 SP 'Bardney'. Drive through Thimbleby, Horsington, and Bucknall, later passing Tupholme Abbey to the left.

TUPHOLME ABBEY, Lincs TF16
Remains of a religious house that was founded c1160 can be seen here, including part of the refectory.

Continue along the B1190 for $1\frac{1}{2}$ miles and turn left into Bardney.

BARDNEY, Lincs TF16
Ethelred, King of Mercia, founded a Benedictine abbey here in the 7th century. It was rebuilt in Norman times by the Earl of Lincoln, and grew to become one of the country's most powerful centres of religion and education. Excavations conducted amongst the extensive ruins in 1912 uncovered many interesting relics, some of which can be seen in the local church.
The town itself is a typical fenland community on the River Witham, in an agricultural area.

Leave Bardney and cross the railway and the River Witham. Continue along the B1190, with Branston Fen to the right, and shortly bear right to skirt the Lincoln Edge. In 3 miles reach the Plough Inn and bear right SP 'Lincoln', then drive through Washingborough and return to Lincoln.

TOUR 68 78 MILES

BETWEEN THE WOLDS AND THE SEA

Attractive resorts and beaches of fine sand are interspersed with charming little fishing villages on Lincolnshire's holiday coast. Inland are picturesque hamlets clustered round greenstone churches, hills crowned by solitary windmills, and the enchanting lanes of the Wolds country.

SKEGNESS, Lincs TF56
In 1863 a rail service was begun at Skegness, with trains running to and from the teeming towns of the industrial Midlands. The result was a boom in seaside tourism, and the holiday crowds of today continue to enjoy the excellent sands and bathing facilities that prompted the transformation of this one-time fishing village into one of the east coast's most popular resorts. Magnificent seafront gardens border a long promenade where, in simpler days, Lord Tennyson and his brothers strolled to take the bracing sea air. A vast swimming pool and various first-class entertainments vie for attention with 6 miles of sandy beach and a 1,843ft-long pier, and batteries of hotels and boarding houses open their doors to increasing numbers of holidaymakers each year. At the southern end of the beach is Gibraltar Point, where there is a nature reserve and bird observatory.

Leave Skegness on the A158 'Lincoln' road and drive to Burgh-le-Marsh.

BURGH-LE-MARSH, Lincs TF56
One of the main features of this area is a fine 5-sailed tower windmill that is still in working order. The impressive local church has two porches and a tower with 16 iron crosses. Inside is a restored screen.

Drive for $2\frac{3}{4}$ miles beyond the village and approach a roundabout with Gunby Hall to the left.

GUNBY HALL, Lincs TF46
Lord Tennyson described this imposing red-brick building (NT) as 'a house of ancient peace'. It was built c1700 by Sir William Massingberd and shows the influence of Sir Christopher Wren. Features of the interior include an oak staircase, wainscoted rooms containing portraits by Reynolds, and various pieces of fine furniture. The house and its formal gardens are open by prior written appointment.

Continue along the A158 and drive through Candlesby, with Welton High Wood to the right. Proceed to Scremby.

SCREMBY, Lincs TF46
Notable features of the good 18th-century church in Scremby include a panelled chancel and a monument to Charles Brackenbury.

Beyond Scremby meet crossroads and turn right on to an unclassified road to Skendleby.

SKENDLEBY, Lincs TF46
Attractively set in the Lincolnshire Wolds, this pleasant village features a partly greenstone church and a mid 18th-century hall. Near by is a prehistoric site known as the Giant's Hill, where there are two long barrows. The most prominent measures 200ft long and stands 5ft high; the other has been severely reduced by ploughing.

Drive to the end of Skendleby and bear right SP 'Willoughby', then

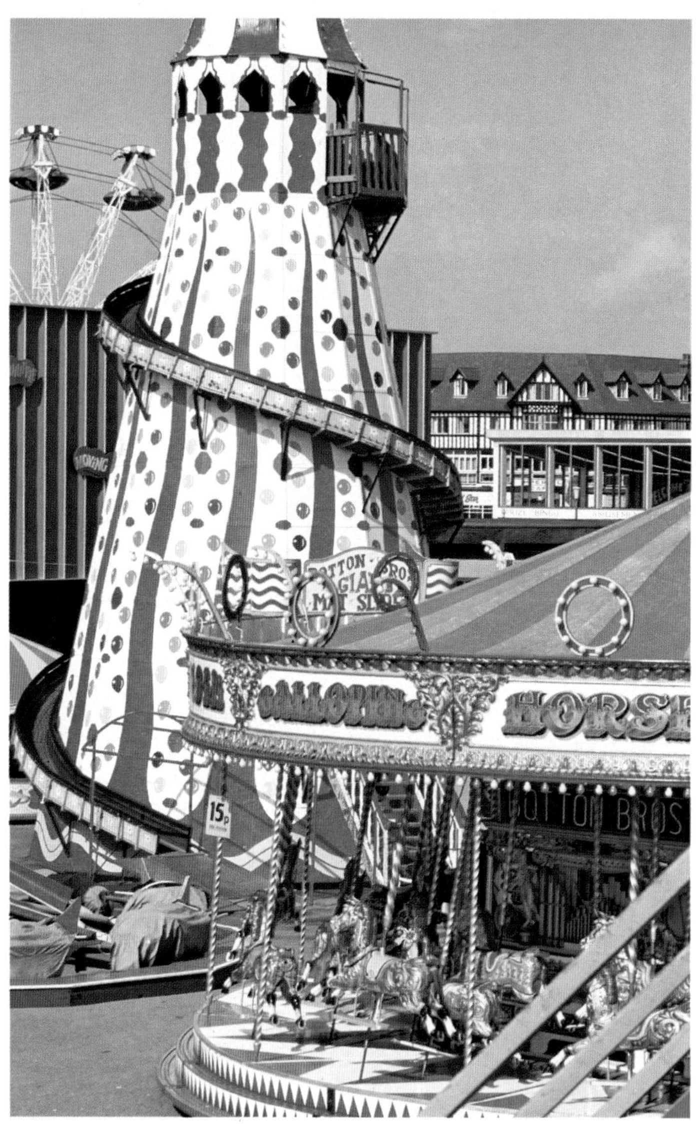

Skegness prepares for the holiday season.

ascend to cross a main road. Descend, and in $1\frac{3}{4}$ miles turn left on to the B1196 SP 'Alford'. Approach Alford, with Well Vale to the left, and turn sharp left on to an unclassified road to enter the village of Well.

WELL, Lincs TF47
Set on the eastern slopes of the Wolds, in the pastoral beauty of Well Vale, this tiny village takes its name from a spring that bubbles from the chalk to fill two lakes in a closely-wooded valley. Close to the village the beautiful Georgian red-brick building of Well Vale Hall stands in 170 acres of fine parkland.

Return to the B1196 and turn left to enter Alford.

ALFORD, Lincs TF47
One of Lincolnshire's finest windmills can be seen here. Its 6-storey brick tower carries five sails and is topped by an ogee cap. It dates from 1837 and, although intact, is no longer in use. Merton Lodge is a good example of the many Georgian and later houses to be seen in the town.

Leave Alford on the A1104 'Louth, Lincoln' road and ascend. Reach Ulceby; cross a roundabout and take the 2nd exit on to the A16, then in $\frac{1}{2}$ mile turn right on to the unclassified 'Harrington' road. Continue, with panoramic views, into Harrington.

HARRINGTON, Lincs TF37
Harrington Hall (not open) was rebuilt in 1673 and features a good Elizabethan façade. Interesting brasses can be seen in the local church.

Continue through pleasantly wooded countryside to Somersby.

Burgh-le-Marsh church clock urges a greater regard for time.

SOMERSBY, Lincs TF37
The poet Alfred Lord Tennyson was born in this tiny Wolds village. His house, which still stands but is not open to the public, was adapted by his father to include a dining room with high gothic windows that entirely suited that era of romanticism. Various memorials to the Tennyson family can be seen in the local church, and a fine carved cross stands in the churchyard.

Keep forward into a narrow road for Salmonby and turn left SP 'Horncastle'. Continue for 2 miles, then meet crossroads and turn right SP 'Belchford'. Climb to a road summit of 455ft, with good all-round views, then descend into Belchford and turn right SP 'Alford'. After a shor distance ascend Belchford Hill and meet a T-junction. Turn left SP 'Louth and continue, with magnificent views, to a road summit of 487ft. In $3\frac{1}{4}$ miles meet crossroads and turn right on to the A153, passing the entrance to Caldwell Park Motor Cycle Racing Circuit on the right. In $\frac{3}{4}$ mile branch right (no SP) on to an unclassified roa and continue to Tathwell.

TATHWELL, Lincs TF38
Attractively situated in a sheltered position above a lake, this village ha a good church that features a Norman tower and contains various interesting monuments.

Beyond Tathwell meet crossroads an drive forward SP 'Legbourne'. A shor detour from the main route can be taken by turning right at the crossroads and driving to Bully Hill.

BULLY HILL, Lincs TF38
Some of the finest prehistoric barro groups to have survived in the whol county of Lincolnshire can be seen here. The largest of seven measures 60ft in diameter by 10ft high, and they are thought to date from the late stone or early bronze age.

On the main route, drive $1\frac{1}{4}$ miles beyond the crossroads and turn right on to the A16. After another $1\frac{1}{4}$ miles turn left on to the unclassified 'Little Cawthorpe' road, descend through Maltby and Haugham Woods, and turn right at Little Cawthorpe. Reach the village church and turn left (no SP), then pass through a ford and meet a T-junction. Turn right, and in $\frac{1}{2}$ mile turn right again on to the A157. Continue to the end of Legbourne and bear right, then turn left on to the unclassified 'Manby' road. Continue to Little Carlton, turn left, and pass RAF Manby to reach Manby village.

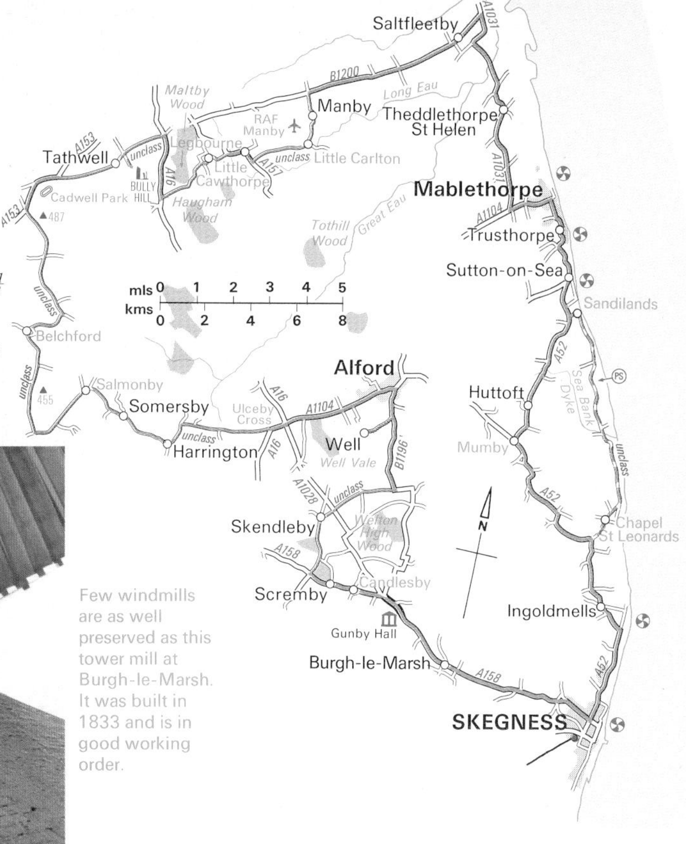

Few windmills are as well preserved as this tower mill at Burgh-le-Marsh. It was built in 1833 and is in good working order.

Gunby Hall's austere face conceals a wealth of fine decoration.

The solid Norman tower of St Vedast's Church, Tathwell, is well sheltered from the elements.

ANBY, Lincs TF38

e greenstone church of this easant little village has a tall tower d contains a remarkably well-eserved Saxon slab decorated th a distinctive rope design.

eet crossroads beyond Manby and n right on to the B1200. Continue Saltfleetby.

LTFLEETBY, Lincs TF48

ose to St Peter's Church in tfleetby is the isolated tower of a urch that the present greenstone ilding replaced. The recent ilding incorporates a few early-glish fragments from its decessor.

Meet a junction with the A1031, turn right, and continue to Theddlethorpe St Helen.

THEDDLETHORPE ST HELEN, Lincs TF48

This tiny coastal village is near a scrub-covered foreshore that forms part of a national nature reserve and is one of the few remaining habitats of the Natterjack toad. This curious amphibian runs instead of hops, and is easily identifiable by the pale stripe down its back. Signposts and warning flags mark the site of an RAF bombing range on the sands.

Proceed along the A1031 for 3 miles, then turn left on to the A1104 into Mablethorpe.

MABLETHORPE, Lincs TF58

Thanks to a highly expensive system of groynes this popular resort boasts a beautiful beach of firm golden sand. In normal weather swimmers can enjoy safe bathing here, but rough conditions make the water treacherous and red flags are flown to warn people away. Low tide reveals old stumps that are the sole remains of a woodland village swamped by the sea in 1289. All that survived was the fine old Church of St Mary, which contains various medieval relics. Today the village is guarded by a concrete promenade.

Leave Mablethorpe on the A52 'Skegness' road and continue to Trusthorpe.

TRUSTHORPE, Lincs TF58

Fine sands and good bathing facilities make this a popular resort, but it is also the base for Humber Radio – an important Post Office link with ships and oil rigs in the North Sea. The tall radio mast dominates the village.

Continue on the A52 and drive into Sutton-on-Sea.

SUTTON-ON-SEA, Lincs TF58

Safe bathing and a level sandy beach are the main features of this little coastal resort. The 4,500-year-old stumps and roots of a forest that was flooded by the sea can be seen at low tide.

From Sutton-on-Sea it is possible to take a pleasant detour from the main route, along the shore below the Sea Bank Dyke. In 1 mile meet a roundabout and turn left on to the unclassified road to Sandilands and drive straight on beside the sea wall. Reach Chapel St Leonards and turn left across a river bridge, then turn right with SP 'Skegness' to rejoin the A52 before Ingoldmells. On the main route, continue along the A52 to Huttoft.

HUTTOFT, Lincs TF57

A tall windmill of the tower type can be seen here, with an interesting early-Victorian grain store.

Continue along the A52 and drive through Mumby to Ingoldmells.

INGOLDMELLS, Lincs TF56

This little resort offers 3 miles of firm golden sand and a host of holiday diversions, including a funfair. Remains of an early iron-age salt-panning site between Ingoldmells and Chapel St Leonards include various structures that can only be seen at low tide.

Continue along the A52 for the return to Skegness.

TOUR 69 90 MILES

INSIDE OLD RUTLAND

Tiny Rutland has vanished in name but survives in fact. The towering spires of its churches rise from typically-clustered cottages of thatch and ironstone, and some of England's richest pasture is grown where the stag and hart were hunted in ancient times.

Market Harborough's old gram
school was founded in the 17th cer
and is a fine example of its t

MARKET HARBOROUGH, Leics SP78
A market was held here as early as 1203, and over the centuries the town has grown and prospered to become the mature community that exists today. The most recent developments have been industrial, but these have not been made at the expense of many fine buildings from previous, less intrusive periods. The most famous is the former grammar school, a lovely timbered and gabled building of 1614 that stands on wooden pillars above street level. The Three Swans is the largest of many old local inns and displays one of the finest wrought-iron signs in England. The parish church dates from the 13th to 15th centuries and is known for its tower, a beautiful structure crowned by a broach spire that is visible for miles around. Every November the church bells are rung to commemorate the rescue of a merchant lost in the Welland marshes in 1500, and the ringers traditionally receive one shilling for beer. Much of the town's present prosperity is due to the Symington family, who made liberty bodices in a Victorian factory behind the church.

Leave the town on the A427 'Corby' road to reach Dingley.

DINGLEY, Northants SP78
The most impressive feature of this small village is Dingley Hall (not open), an unforgettable building with a south gateway flanked by polygonal towers.

Continue, and in about $2\frac{1}{2}$ miles pass the village of Stoke Albany to the left.

STOKE ALBANY, Northants SP88
Features of the fine local church, which dates from the 13th century,include good doorways and windows.

Continue along the A427 beyond East Carlton, then turn left on to the B670 and proceed to Rockingham.

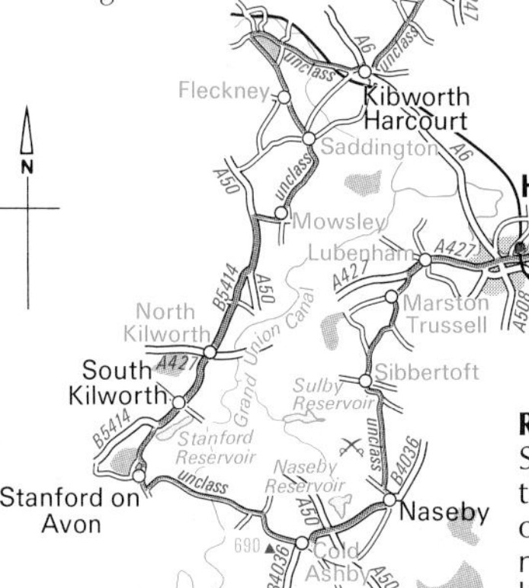

Naseby was the scene
decisive Civil War ba

Rockingham Castle's Panel Room is part of a rich collection of treasures.

ROCKINGHAM, Northants SP89
Set on a steep hillside overlooking the River Welland, this lovely village of flint-built thatched cottages has a number of new houses that have been built of traditional materials to harmonize with the whole. The summit of the hill is occupied by Rockingham Castle, which was originally built by William the Conqueror, and affords views into 5 counties. The site of the keep is now a rose garden surrounded by yew hedges, but surviving fragments of the old structure include the moat, foundations of the Norman hall, and the twin towers of the gatehouse. King John used the castle both as a fortress and as a hunting lodge for Rockingham Forest, a vast blanket of wood and heathland that once covered much of Leicestershire. The mainly Elizabethan house that stands here today (open) contains collections of paintings and furniture.

Turn left on to the A6003 'Uppingham' road, crossing the River Welland. (To enter Rockingham village turn right here into the A6003 main street.) Continue to Caldecott and drive forward on to the B670, then in $4\frac{1}{2}$ miles pass under the Welland railway viaduct.

WELLAND VIADUCT, Northants SP99
This 82-arch railway viaduct dates from 1874 and is a notable example of 19th-century industrial architecture. It spans the complet width of the Welland Valley and i well-known landmark.

In 2 miles turn right, then left, to jo the A6121; continue to Ketton.

KETTON, Leics SK90
One of the largest and most attractive of old Rutland's villages this picturesque collection of butt coloured buildings is a noted quarrying centre. The local stone greatly prized as a building mater and has been worked at least sinc Roman times. St Mary's Church h an exquisite spire that rises high above the village's sepia roofs of Collyweston slate, perfectly complementing one of the finest examples of church architecture the north Midlands. The west fror the building is an excellent examp of late 12th-century work, and th rest of the structure dates almost entirely from the 13th century.

Continue along the A6121 and dr through Tinwell to Stamford.

STAMFORD, Lincs TF00
Justly considered one of England's most beautiful towns, stone-built Stamford has a long history that can be traced back as far as the time of Danish settlement. In the 13th and 14th centuries it was important enough to have its own university, and the powerful influence of early Christianity is evident in many fine churches and other ecclesiastical buildings. All Saints' Place is the visual centre of the town and is noted for its outstanding, multi-period architecture. Browne's Hospital (open) has been described as one of the finest medieval almshouses surviving in England, and includes a beautiful Jacobean hall and chapel. Close to the Welland are the ancient Burghley Almshouses. he George Hotel was a coaching nn in the 14th century, and among ne buildings from many periods in t George's Square is a house that as been continuously inhabited nce c1350. Even older than that is ne Bastion in West Street, a section f the old town wall that has been ntouched for 700 years. Close to ne town is Elizabethan Burghley ouse (open) where the well-known urghley Horse Trials are held. The ouse itself is considered one of ngland's greatest mansions and ontains many superb rooms. It oasts over 100 works of art nd antique furnishings.

llow SP 'Grantham' and then akham' to leave Stamford by the 606. Continue to Empingham.

IPINGHAM, Leics SK90
ominating this large attractive lage is the handsome tower and ire of St Peter's Church, a well-oportioned building with a good est front. Features of the interior clude fragments of ancient glass d considerable remains of edieval colour.

ntinue, and 1 mile beyond hitwell reach Rutland Water on the . Turn right here on to the classified 'Exton' and 'Cottesmore' ad, entering an avenue of trees. er $1\frac{1}{4}$ miles reach a right turn that ers a pleasant detour to Exton. e main route skirts Exton Park.

TON, Leics SK91
uated in one of the largest nstone extraction areas in Britain, charming village of thatched estone cottages is well worth the all diversion needed to visit it. The ned Old Hall, probably built ing the reign of Elizabeth I, was ned down in 1810; the New Hall laced it some 40 years later. n's parish church is noted for its narkable range of monumental pture, which illustrates the gress of this art form in England n the 14th to 18th centuries.

the main route, drive to tesmore and turn left on to the 3. Continue to Burley.

This gateway forms an imposing entrance to the mansion at Burghley.

BURLEY, Leics SK81
Burley-on-the-Hill (not open) is considered by many to be the most beautiful country house in the county. Its fine colonnades and exquisitely restrained detail, the work of Joseph Lumley between 1694 and 1705, ornament a small hill that was once an ancient earthwork. The building is best appreciated from the south, looking down a long avenue of trees to the fine lines of the front.

Descend into Oakham.

OAKHAM, Leics SK80
Once the capital of the tiny and now defunct county of Rutland, this well-known hunting centre preserves memories of its former status in the Rutland County Museum. This is housed in the late 18th-century indoor riding school of the Rutland Fencibles. The town's church dates from the 12th to 15th century and features unusual nave capitals. It shares its churchyard with the original grammar school, which was founded in 1584. Remains of Oakham Castle include a beautiful Norman hall (open), where a unique collection of horseshoes is nailed to the wall. These were traditionally contributed to the household by members of the royalty or peerage visiting the lordship for the first time. An old butter cross with stocks has been preserved in the town.

Follow SP 'Melton Mowbray', drive over a level crossing, and turn left then left again on to an unclassified road for Braunston.

BRAUNSTON, Leics SK80
This lovely ironstone village stands on a hillside above the valley of the little River Gwash. Inside its distinctive church are traces of a previous building dating from the 12th and 13th centuries.

From Braunston follow the 'Leicester' road, and in $4\frac{3}{4}$ miles pass 755ft Whatborough Hill to the right. Access to the summit is by a nearby track. Continue to Tilton.

TILTON, Leics SK70
The early-English and later church in this high village is noted for its strange gargoyles.

Join the B6047 'Market Harborough' road and in 2 miles drive over a main road. After another 3 miles reach the top of an ascent and turn right on to an unclassified road SP 'Carlton, Kibworth'. Continue to Kibworth Harcourt.

KIBWORTH HARCOURT, Leics SK69
Examples of architecture from many periods can be seen in this village. Among the most notable are the Old House of 1678, the 18th-century Congregational Church, and 19th-century Kibworth Hall. Close to the village is the imposing tower of St Wilfred's Church.

Follow SP 'Leicester' to join the A6, then take the 1st unclassified road on the left SP 'Kilby, Wistow'. Cross the Grand Union Canal at a series of locks, continue to crossroads, and turn left for Fleckney and Saddington. Drive to Saddington, turn right, and continue to Mowsley. At Mowsley turn right and right again with SP 'Leicester'. In 1 mile turn left on to the A50, and after a further $1\frac{1}{2}$ miles turn right on to the B5414. Drive to North Kilworth and turn right on to the A427, then turn left with the B5414 for South Kilworth.

SOUTH KILWORTH, Leics SP68
South Kilworth's church is mainly of 19th-century design, although Norman and 14th-century work from a previous building can be seen inside. The font is of 12th- or 13th-century date.

Beyond South Kilworth pass Stanford Reservoir on the left, then turn left on to the unclassified 'Stanford on Avon' road. Descend to Stanford on Avon, passing Stanford Hall and Stanford Park on the right.

STANFORD ON AVON, Leics SP57
Divided between Leicestershire and Northamptonshire by the River Avon, this pleasant village has a good church with a pinnacled 15th-century tower. Stanford Hall (open) is impressively sited in open pasture and stands on the site of an earlier house. The present building dates from the reign of William and Mary, and has an imposing facade that adds a touch of grandeur to its pleasing design. Its rooms contain collections of costumes and furniture, and there is a motor museum in the stable.

In $\frac{1}{4}$ mile turn left on to the 'Cold Ashby' road and later re-cross the Grand Union Canal. In $1\frac{1}{2}$ miles climb 690ft Honey Hill. Continue to Cold Ashby and turn left on to the B4036, then drive to Naseby.

NASEBY, Northants SP67
A stone column $1\frac{1}{2}$ miles north of this village marks the field where the Battle of Naseby was fought in 1645. The Cromwellian victory heralded a new era of British government and sealed the fate of King Charles I. The Naseby Battle Museum at Purlieu Farm displays layouts of the battleground and various local relics. In Naseby Churchyard is a huge copper ball that is said to have been brought back from the Siege of Boulogne in 1544.

At Naseby turn left on to the unclassified 'Sibbertoft' road, and in 1 mile pass the site of the Battle of Naseby on the left. Reach Sibbertoft and turn right for the 'Theddingworth' road, and after 1 mile bear right to Marston Trussell. Return to Market Harborough via Lubenham and the main A427.

Local stone brings unity to Ketton's interesting old buildings.

LEICESTER, Leics SK50
Situated on the River Soar and Grand Union Canal, this county town and university city has been a thriving centre at least since Roman times. Relics from its very early history include Roman pavements under the former Central Station and below a shop fronting St Nicholas' Church. Other traces of the occupation have been found at the Jewry Wall site, including remains of 2nd-century Roman baths and the wall itself. Various relics from ancient times to the middle ages can be seen in the Jewry Wall Museum of archaeology. The Leicestershire Museum and Art Gallery stands in New Walk, a delightful promenade of elegant houses, mature trees, and carefully preserved Victorian lamp-posts. An ancient city gateway known as The Magazine houses the museum of the Royal Leicestershire Regiment, and the Newarke Houses Museum offers a vivid insight into social history from the 16th century to Victorian times. It is housed in an interesting old Chantry House of 1511, and its immediate neighbour dates from c1600. Wygston's House Museum of Costume is laid out in a 15th-century house, and the Leicestershire Museum of Technology preserves various items of industrial interest in the apt surroundings of Abbey Pumping Station. Among many interesting churches in Leicester is St Martin's, which stands on a Saxon site that was previously occupied by a Roman temple and now enjoys cathedral status. It was largely rebuilt in the 19th century and has a well proportioned tower and spire. Good Norman work is retained by the Church of St Mary de Castro. The city's Guildhall is a fine late 14th-century building with magnificent timbering, and the 17th-century Court House incorporates fragments of a Norman hall. There is also a Norman castle, but very little of it survives. Close to the university is a fine public park and cricket ground, and the University Botanic Gardens are of note.

Leave Leicester on the A46 'Newark' road and after 3 miles branch left on to the B667 into Thurmaston.

TOUR 70 68 MILES

THE CRAGS OF CHARNWOOD

Charnwood Forest is a huge upthrusting of rock whose wind-blasted heaths dominate miles of Leicestershire's gentle farming country. Now treeless and pitted with great quarries, it is an eerie place where open moorland flows round fascinating outcrops of rock and the lines of ancient forts.

The small brook at Rearsby is spanned by a quaint medieval bridge.

THURMASTON, Leics SK60
This large town stands on the east bank of the River Soar and has a number of developing industries. In its older quarter is a fine church with distinctive 13th century nave arcades.

Continue through the town on the B667, reach a roundabout at the far end, and take the 2nd exit on to the A607 SP 'Melton'. Drive through Syston.

SYSTON, Leics SK61
The tower buttresses of Syston Church display curious sculptures of a man and two women, possibly representations of the founder and his wives. Many of the houses in the area are brick-built structures of 18th-century date.

Continue to Rearsby.

REARSBY, Leics SK61
Situated on a tributary of the River Wreake, this village has a good 13th- and 14th-century church with an unusual drum-shaped font. To the east of the church is an attractive 6-arched medieval bridge, and a gabled house of 1661 stands in Mill Road.

Turn right on to the B674 for Gaddesby.

GADDESBY, Leics SK61
One of the largest and most beautiful of Leicestershire's many lovely village churches can be seen here. Its south side is richly decorated with stone carvings, and the south aisle is a showpiece. Inside is an equestrian statue of Colonel Cheney at Waterloo.

Charnwood Forest's windswept character is well appreciated from Beacon Hill.

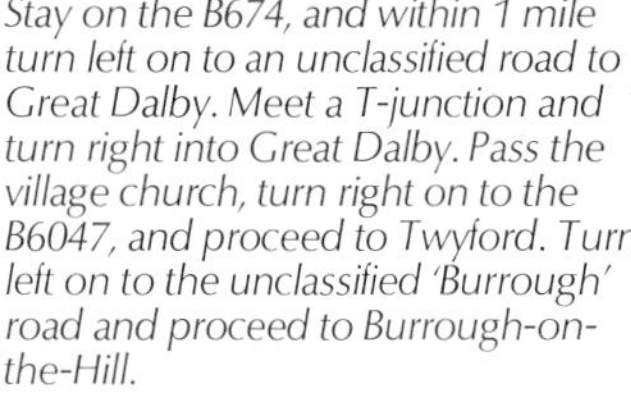

Stay on the B674, and within 1 mile turn left on to an unclassified road to Great Dalby. Meet a T-junction and turn right into Great Dalby. Pass the village church, turn right on to the B6047, and proceed to Twyford. Turn left on to the unclassified 'Burrough' road and proceed to Burrough-on-the-Hill.

BURROUGH-ON-THE-HILL, Leics SK71
Breached ramparts of an iron-age fort at Burrough Hill are thought to mark the site of a pre-Roman capital. The local church dates from the 13th century and has a good tower.

Continue to Somerby, meet a T-junction, and turn left SP 'Pickwell' and 'Melton'. In $2\frac{1}{4}$ miles cross the A606 and follow SP for Stapleford. To the right, on the approach to Stapleford, is Stapleford Park.

STAPLEFORD PARK, Leics SK81
Home of Lord and Lady Gretton, this fine old house (open) has an early wing dating from 1500 and was restored in 1633. Its exterior decoration includes an exceptional collection of stone sculptures depicting scenes from history, the scriptures, and legend; inside are rooms that have been attributed to John Webb. As well as fine pictures, tapestries and furniture, the house contains the famous Thomas Balsto collection of Victorian Staffordshire pottery figures (NT). In the grounds are a lake with an island bird sanctuary, a miniature steam passenger railway, and many other diversions for both children and adults.

From Stapleford proceed north and after a short distance turn left to join the B676. A short detour from the main route to the village of Saxby ca be made by turning right here on tc the B676.

SAXBY, Leics SK82
An ancient Saxon cemetery has been discovered at Saxby, and the local rectory and church both date from 1789.

On the main route, continue along the B676 to Melton Mowbray.

MELTON MOWBRAY, Leics SK7
No matter what various sections o public opinion feel about hunting i still a thriving tradition, and nowhe is it in better health than at Melton Mowbray. Three famous packs me here, and the district is often loud with the noise of horns, hounds, a horses. The town is internationally famous for Stilton cheese and por pies, and its attractive situation on the River Eye makes it a popular gc for summer visitors. St Mary's is arguably the stateliest and most impressive of all the county's churches, and beautifully illustrate the early-English, decorated, and perpendicular architectural perioc Anne of Cleves House is of ancier origin, and the 17th-century Bede House contains a museum illustrating local history. Attractive parks and gardens border the rive

eave Melton Mowbray on the A6006 Loughborough' road, pass Asfordby, nd in 3½ miles turn left on to the 3676. After 1½ miles pass beneath the \46, which follows much of the ourse of the ancient Fosse Way.

OSSE WAY

Certain stretches of this famous omanized road are mere tracks, but nuch of its diagonal route across ngland from Axminster to Lincoln is ollowed by modern main roads. xcavations have shown that the ourses of earlier paths were dopted by the Roman engineers who plotted the road. See tour 71.

ontinue to Burton-on-the-Wolds, rn left on to an unclassified road, en shortly join the B675 and drive to rrow-upon-Soar.

ARROW-UPON-SOAR, eics SK51

his attractive and popular village ands on the east bank of the River ar and has a curious village sign at depicts an uatic prehistoric

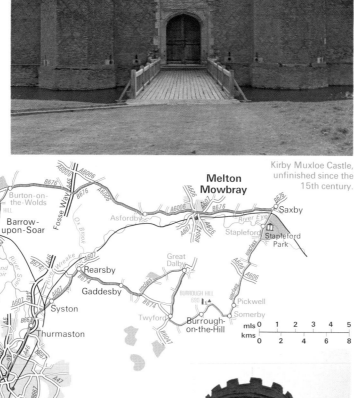

Kirby Muxloe Castle, unfinished since the 15th century.

Old John Tower in Bradgate Park is an 18th-century folly built on a 700ft hill.

ile. Good local dings include an old pital of 1694 and almshouses 825.

e to the end of Barrow-upon-Soar turn right, then cross a river ge into Quorndon.

ORNDON, Leics SK51

able Tudor relics are preserved e 14th-century Farnham Chapel uorndon's fine granite church, h also has a good Norman way. The village gives its name e most famous hunt in England, has a station on the Main Line n railway. The latter runs 5 miles veen Loughborough and Rothley ral. West of the village is rocky nwood Forest.

RNWOOD FOREST, Leics

e an important hunting ground, racken-covered summits of nwood Forest thrust their bare of ancient rock high above the wooded plains of stershire. Their presence in the ally unspectacular Midlands tryside is a startling scenic adiction, and the fascinating of geological beds that make up their bulk is a constant source of interest to geologists. Fine views can be enjoyed from the forest, and its sweeping barrenness gives an invigorating sense of freedom.

At Quorndon, turn left on to the A6 and drive for 200 yards, then turn right on to the unclassified 'Cropston' and 'Anstey' road to skirt Hawcliff Hill and Buddon Wood, on the edge of Charnwood Forest. After 2¼ miles meet crossroads and turn right towards Swithland. After a short distance cross the end of lovely Swithland Reservoir, a noted local beauty spot. Ascend through the village of Swithland.

SWITHLAND, Leics SK51

An attractive village associated with the traditional industry of slate cutting, Swithland stands near the eastern edge of Charnwood Forest in pleasantly wooded surroundings. Good monuments can be seen in the local church.

Drive 1 mile beyond Swithland and turn left for Woodhouse Eaves.

WOODHOUSE EAVES, Leics SK51

Several of the cottages in this picturesque hill village are made of rough stone taken from the slate pits at Swithland. To the west is 818ft Beacon Hill, an AA viewpoint and the site of an iron-age encampment.

Drive to the end of the village and turn left on to the B591; in 1¼ miles pass the Beacon Hill carpark and viewpoint, then in a short distance turn left on to the B5330 and meet crossroads. Drive forward on to the unclassified road for Newtown Linford, and pass the main entrance for Bradgate Park on the approach to the village.

BRADGATE PARK, Leics SK51

The 850 acres of untouched heath and woodland that make up this superb wild park were given to the city and county of Leicester in 1928 as permanent public space. The area, which extends from Cropston Reservoir to Newtown Linford, offers excellent walks through stands of cedar and oak, and alongside the course of a tiny stream. Bradgate House, now in ruins, was completed c1510. In 1537 it was the birthplace of the unfortunate Lady Jane Grey, who was the uncrowned Queen of England for nine days before being beheaded by order of Mary Tudor. At the highest point of the park is an 18th-century folly tower known as Old John, which was erected to the memory of a retainer who was killed by a falling flagpole.

Continue into Newtown Linford.

NEWTOWN LINFORD, Leics SK50

This village stands on the borders of Bradgate Park and has some attractive old houses, but it is a little too close to the suburbs of Leicester for comfort. Its 18th-century church features painted royal arms.

Follow the B5327 'Leicester' road to Anstey.

ANSTEY, Leics SK50

The 5-arched packhorse bridge that spans Rothley Brook in this Charnwood village is considered one of the finest in England. It dates from the 14th or 15th century and is complemented by some fine old cottages. Anstey was the birthplace of Ned Ludd, who as an apprentice initiated the infamous Luddite riots of 1812 by wrecking machinery that had been introduced to take over his job.

Meet a roundabout and turn right, crossing Rothley Brook with the old packhorse bridge to the right. Continue for 200 yards and turn right on to the unclassified 'Glenfield' road, then after a further 1 mile meet a roundabout and keep forward to enter Glenfield.

GLENFIELD, Leics SK50

Victorian St Peter's was built to replace the old Glenfield Church, which stands in ruins near by. Several architectural features salvaged from the interior of the older structure can be seen inside.

From Glenfield follow SP 'Kirby Muxloe' to Kirby Muxloe.

KIRBY MUXLOE, Leics SK50

Considered an excellent example of its type, this moat-encircled fortified manor (AM) was begun by Lord Hastings in 1480 – towards the end of the Wars of the Roses. The wars ended before the house was completed, and Hastings was executed for treason.

Meet crossroads at the edge of Kirby Muxloe and turn left towards Leicester. In 1 mile meet a roundabout and turn left on to the A47 for the return to Leicester.

TOUR 71 — 89 MILES

THE FORESTS OF SHERWOOD

Away from the industry of the coalfields is a picturesque countryside of forests, farms, and villages thick with legends of Robin Hood and his outlaw band. Great oaks grow in Sherwood, and fertile countryside follows the meandering course of the River Trent.

NOTTINGHAM, Notts SK54
The growth of this ancient city was influenced by the Saxons, Danes, and Normans, but it was the industrial revolution that made it a thriving commercial centre famous for fine lace. Early prosperity was aided by the natural highway provided by the River Trent, a strategic advantage that may have prompted William the Conqueror to build a strong castle here soon after his invasion of Britain. It was destroyed in the reign of Stephen, rebuilt by Henry II, and throughout the turmoil of the Wars of the Roses remained loyal to the cause of the Yorkists. When the Tudors came to the throne it fell into a slow decline and was reduced to ruins by the time it was bought by the Duke of Newcastle in 1651. The duke converted the soundest parts of the building into a house, but this was gutted by Reform Bill rioters in 1831. Nowadays the castle is the property of the Corporation and houses a museum and art gallery. Among several good churches in Nottingham is St Mary's, a splendid example of 15th-century architecture with excellent windows and a glorious Madonna and Child painted by Bartolommeo. Other notable buildings include the 18th-century Shire Hall, the partly-medieval Trip to Jerusalem Inn, and a wealth of Georgian domestic architecture. The city's natural history museum is in Wollaton Hall, a 16th-century building that stands close to the university campus.

Leave the city with SP 'Loughborough A60' and cross the River Trent. A pleasant detour from the main route to Holme Pierrepont can be made by turning left on to the A52.

HOLME PIERREPONT, Notts SK63
This early Tudor hall (open) was built to a medieval design c1500 and contains a fine collection of 17th-century English oak furniture. Its grounds include a formal courtyard garden of Victorian date, a country park, and a national and international competition and training centre for water sports.

On the main route, continue along the A60 and pass Ruddington and Bradmore to reach Bunny.

Victorian Belvoir Castle dominates the surrounding landscape.

BUNNY, Notts SK52
A great deal of this village was designed in the 17th century by Thomas Parkyns, who did as much as he could to improve the living conditions of his tenants by rebuilding farms and providing four charming almshouses. He lived at Bunny Hall, and his great love for sporting combat earned him the title The Wrestling Baron. This passionate interest is evident in his book *The Cornish Hugg*, and his self-designed graveyard monument shows him in an aggressive stance at the start of a bout. The local church dates from the 14th century and contains several good monuments.

Beyond Bunny turn right on to an unclassified road SP 'Gotham, East Leake' and skirt wooded Bunny Hill. Reach a railway bridge and after another ½ mile turn left. Continue to East Leake, meet a T-junction, and turn right for East Leake Church.

EAST LEAKE, Notts SK52
Inside the partly Norman church at East Leake is an unusual vamping horn, a type of trumpet that was once used during choir services to 'vamp up' or encourage the singers.

Return to the centre of East Leake and keep straight on to Costock. Cross a main road, continue through Wysall to Keyworth, then turn right and drive to Widmerpool.

WIDMERPOOL, Notts SK62
Some of the county's loveliest woodland scenery makes a perfect setting for this charming little village. The picturesquely ruined church has a 19th-century body with a 14th-century tower and contains an exquisite marble sculpture.

On the nearside of Widmerpool turn left SP 'Kinoulton', and in 1½ miles cross two main roads. The 2nd of these follows the old Fosse Way.

FOSSE WAY
Much of this ancient Romanized track is followed by modern main roads, though parts are still foot and bridle paths. See tour 70.

In a short distance descend and keep forward into Kinoulton.

KINOULTON, Notts SK63
Glorious views over the rich Vale of Belvoir and mature woodlands known as the Borders can be enjoyed from this high village, which claims to have one of the best cricket grounds in the county. The local church, built in brick by the Earl of Gainsborough c1793, stands opposite a forge.

Meet a T-junction and turn right to Hickling, then drive forward along a winding road for Nether Broughton. Continue with SP 'Melton' to turn left on to the A606, and in 1½ miles climb Broughton Hill at the northern end of the Leicestershire Wolds. Meet crossroads, turn left on to the unclassified 'Eastwell' road, then in ½ mile keep forward and meet a T-junction. Turn left SP 'Eastwell', and after 4 miles meet crossroads and turn left again, SP 'Harby'. After a short distance descend 524ft Harby Hill, and continue to Harby. Turn right SP 'Bottesford', and in 4 miles pass a right turn leading to Belvoir Castle. A worthwhile detour can be made from the main route to this historic building.

BELVOIR CASTLE, Leics SK83
Nowadays the superb site overlooking the Vale of Belvoir is occupied by a 19th-century 'castle' by architect James Wyatt, but originally this windy ridge was guarded by a strong medieval fortress that was occupied by the Manners family in the 16th century. This original castle was built in the late 11th century by Robert de Todeni. His coffin is on display in the present castle. The old castle was twice remodelled and finally much of it was destroyed by fire in the 19th century. Its rebuilding and refurbishment were supervised by Sir John Thoroton, friend and chaplain to the Manners family. The present structure (open) is renowned for its pictures, superb Gobelin Tapestries, and a regimental museum of the 17th/21st Lancers. The attractive grounds of the castle contain a number of interesting features including several statues, a mausoleum and a temple.

Continue to Bottesford.

BOTTESFORD, Leics SK83
The church in this village is one of the best in the county and contain an outstanding collection of monuments. Old stocks and a whipping post are preserved near the remains of an old cross, and attractive Fleming's Bridge dates from the 17th century.

In Bottesford turn left on to the A52 and continue to Bingham.

Bottesford still retains its old stocks and whipping post.

BINGHAM, Notts SK73
The most notable building in this village is the church, which boas fine tower capped by a spire. Sor of its windows date from the 14t and 15th centuries.

Meet traffic signals and turn right to the B687 SP 'Newark'. In 1 mile meet a roundabout and take the exit on to the A6097, then after a further 1 mile pass East Bridgford the right.

EAST BRIDGFORD, Notts SK64
Several good Georgian cottages houses can be seen in this villag which occupies an attractively wooded site above the River Tre

Descend and cross the River Tre then meet a roundabout and tak 2nd exit to skirt Lowdham. In 1¼ turn left on to the unclassified 'Woodborough' road. Continue Woodborough.

WOODBOROUGH, Notts SK
The broad upper windows in th terraced cottages of this village once filled by the frames of stoc knitters, for whom the terraces originally built. Inside the attrac 14th-century church is later monumental sculpture and car

Drive to the end of Woodborou turn left to reach high ground, a 1½ miles turn right SP 'Doncaste After another 1½ miles turn righ the A614, then in 3½ miles turn to the unclassified 'Kirkby-in-As road to enter Sherwood Forest.

SHERWOOD FOREST, Notts
All that remains of the 100,000-acre wood and pasture land that surrounded Nottingham in the 13th century are a few tracts between that city and the Dukeries District. The area is inextricably meshed with the legend of Robin Hood, the philanthropic outlaw who is popularly thought to have been born in Locksley c1160. Tradition has it that Robin of Locksley was the true Earl of Huntingdon, and the legend is perpetuated by many local

Magnificent old oak trees still survive in Sherwood Forest, part of which is now a country park.

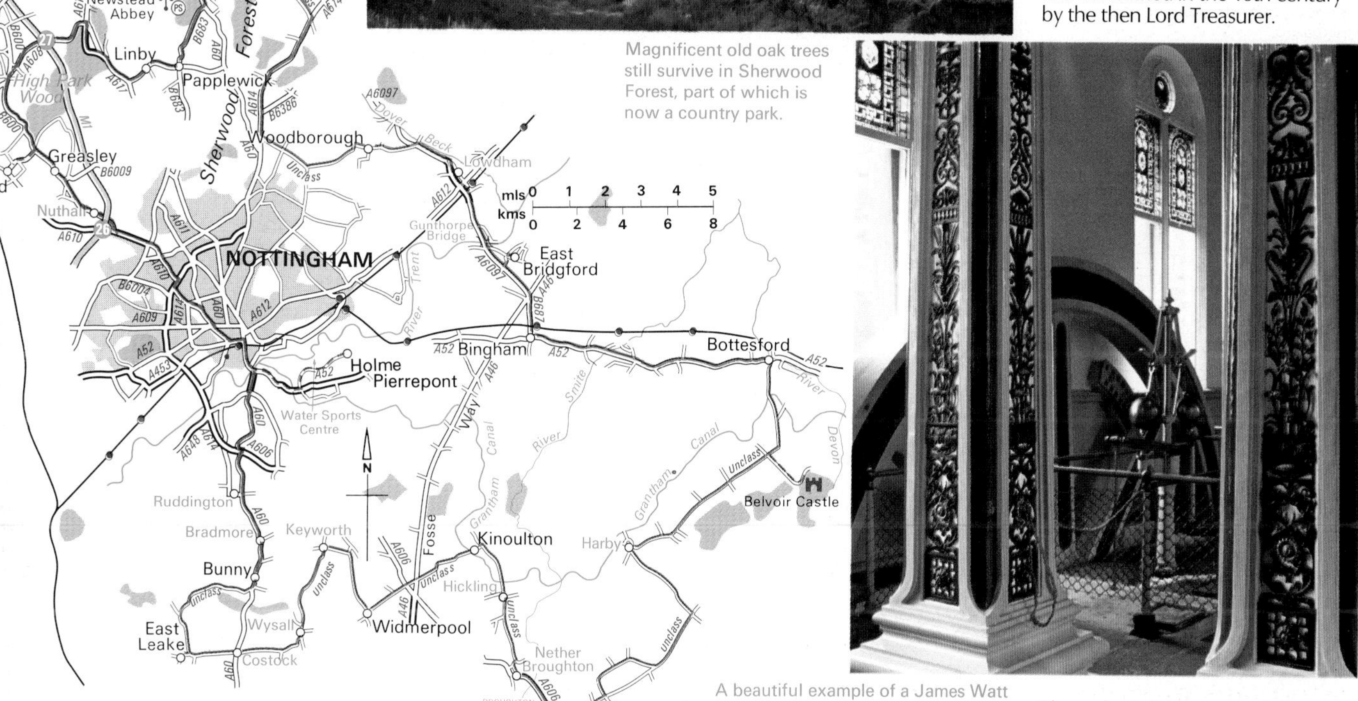

A beautiful example of a James Watt beam engine is preserved at Papplewick.

…rences. An old oak known as …in Hood's Larder stands within …boundaries of Sherwood, but the …st tree in the forest is claimed to …Green Dale Oak, which stands …h of Welbeck Abbey and is also … to be the largest in the district. …of the area has been preserved …e Burntstump Country Park.

… miles turn right SP 'Blidworth', …after a further ½ mile turn left on …e B6020 SP 'Sutton-in-Ashfield', …ng through the edge of …orth.

…WORTH, Notts SK55
…tion has it that this colliery …e was the home of Friar Tuck …Maid Marian, characters that …he essential ingredients of …our and romance to the Robin … legend. The fellow outlaw and … of Robin, Will Scarlet, is said to …ried in the local churchyard.

…miles meet crossroads and turn … to the A60 to pass the entrance …wstead Abbey on the right.

The superb lake provides a perfect setting for Newstead Abbey.

NEWSTEAD ABBEY, Notts SK55
An abbey founded here in the 12th century was converted into a house in 1550 and later was to be the ancestral home of the poet Lord Byron. In 1931 the house (open) was given to the city of Nottingham, and today it provides a fitting setting for relics of the poet, and of the explorer Dr Livingstone – who stayed here in 1864. Surviving features of the religious foundation include the west front of the priory church, the cloisters, and the Chapter House.

Continue along the A60 and in ½ mile turn right on to the B683. Continue to Papplewick.

PAPPLEWICK, Notts SK55
Papplewick Hall (not open) was built by the Adam brothers in 1787. An urn in memory of the poet Thomas Gray stands in the grounds, and there is a little temple to commemorate the writer William Mason.

Turn right on to the B6011 SP 'Linby'; continue to Linby.

LINBY, Notts SK55
The combination of red-roofed stone cottages with two crosses and a small stream flowing on each side of the main street makes this one of the county's prettiest villages. East of Linby is Castle Mill, which was rebuilt and castellated in the 18th century by the then Lord Treasurer.

After a short distance turn right on to the A611. Gradually ascend, skirting the southern part of Sherwood Forest, and after 1½ miles turn left on to the A608. Ascend, cross the M1 motorway, then after another 1½ miles join the B600 SP 'Nottingham' and continue through wooded country. In 2¼ miles pass an unclassified right turn offering a detour to Eastwood.

EASTWOOD, Notts SK44
Eastwood, the birthplace of author D H Lawrence, is a mining town set in the heart of an agricultural district. The ways in which the sharp contrast between pithead and countryside affected him is reflected in many of his novels.

On the main route, continue along the B600 to Greasley.

GREASLEY, Notts SK44
Handsome Greasley Church has a tall 15th-century tower that serves as a landmark for many miles around.

Drive into a built-up area, then meet a T-junction in Nuthall and turn left. After a short distance meet a roundabout and go forward on to the A610 for the return to Nottingham.

PEAK DISTRICT NATIONAL PARK
Some of England's wildest and most beautiful scenery is protected and made accessible to millions of people in the 542 square miles of this national park, which is mainly divided between the counties of Derbyshire, Cheshire, and Staffordshire. The high, craggy northern region includes gritstone Kinder Scout and various other lofty peaks, but in the south are gentler limestone landscapes that have been sculpted by water and softened by valley woodlands. The undulating White Peak area has thinly-grassed pastures separated by snaking limestone walls, and the lovely River Dove flows through its deep ravine past pinnacles, buttresses, and spires of weathered stone. East are the gritstone uplands and ridges of Millstone Edge, Froggat Edge, and Stanton Moor. See tours 73 and 74.

MATLOCK, Derbys SK36
This River Derwent spa town is situated on the eastern edge of the national park, in a high area of gritstone moors and ridges. During the 19th century it was a resort for people following the fashion for taking the waters, and a great hydropathy centre was built at Matlock Bank. This impressive building now houses Derbyshire County Council. Along the banks of the Derwent stretch lovely Hall Leys Gardens.

A detour can be taken from the main route to Matlock Bath by leaving Matlock on the A6 SP 'Derby' and continuing south for 1½ miles.

MATLOCK BATH, Derbys SK25
Regency visitors popularized the medicinal springs of Matlock Bath, and although the resort declined in Victorian times it remains one of the district's many attractive touring centres. Its Petrifying Wells are very famous and are hung with various objects left by visitors to turn to stone. Every autumn a parade of illuminated and decorated boats is staged on the River Derwent. The resort's charming setting among tree-covered hills is overlooked by the 1,000ft Heights of Abraham, which were worked for lead in Roman times. The Victorian Prospect Tower, on the crest of the heights commands excellent views. In the town is the Peak District Mining Museum, which traces the history of the Derbyshire lead industry.

On the main tour, leave Matlock on the A6 'Buxton' road and drive to Darley Dale.

DARLEY DALE, Derbys SK26
Stone from the quarries near here has long been prized as a building and sculpting material, and can be seen to advantage in many of Britain's large towns. The village church preserves ancient stone coffins and sections of an unusually decorated Saxon cross.

Leave Darley Dale and continue on the A6 to reach Rowsley.

TOUR 72 51 MILES

HILLS OF THE SOUTHERN PEAK

This part of the Peak District national park is of gentle aspect, a region of undulating limestone hills scored by the beautifully-wooded Derwent Valley and trout-rich races of the Wye. Curtains of rich foliage screen weathered outcrops, curious stone spires, and the dark mouths of caves.

ROWSLEY, Derbys SK26
Local examples of 17th-century domestic architecture include a fine old bridge over the River Wye and the pleasant Peacock Inn of 1652. More recent survivals include two obsolete station buildings, one of which was designed by Sir Joseph Paxton in 1849. See also tour 74.

Drive 1¼ miles beyond Rowsley and turn left on to the B5056 'Ashbourne' road. A pleasant detour from the main route to Haddon Hall can be made by keeping straight ahead on the A6 for ½ mile.

HADDON HALL, Derbys SK26
Medieval architecture can be seen at its best in the peaceful lines of this romantic old house (open). Parts of it date from the 12th century, and although it was originally built as a fortified manor house it has never seen military action. Among its many treasures is a chapel with a Norman font and lovely 15th-century wall paintings, and a long gallery with a painted ceiling and outstanding panelling. Terraced rose gardens are a striking feature of the grounds. See also tour 74.

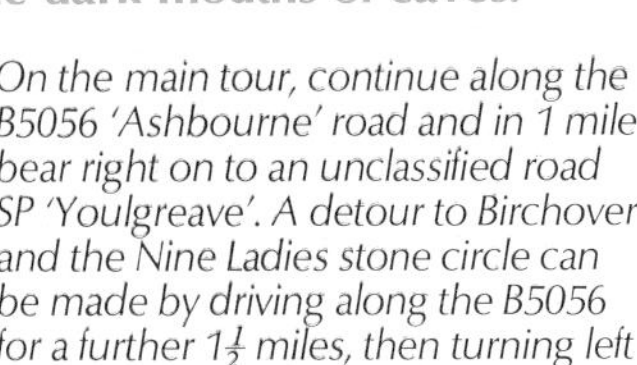

On the main tour, continue along the B5056 'Ashbourne' road and in 1 mile bear right on to an unclassified road SP 'Youlgreave'. A detour to Birchover and the Nine Ladies stone circle can be made by driving along the B5056 for a further 1½ miles, then turning left on to an unclassified road for Birchover.

BIRCHOVER, Derbys SK26
Heathcote Museum at Birchover (open by appointment) has an excellent collection of finds made during the excavation of bronze-age sites on Stanton Moor.

STANTON MOOR, Derbys SK26
The most remarkable of several fascinating prehistoric sites on the moor is the Nine Ladies stone circle (AM), which stands 900ft above sea level in an area that affords splendid views into the Derwent Valley.

On the main tour, continue along the unclassified 'Youlgreave' road, enter the Bradford Valley, and after ¾ mile pass the village of Alport to the left.

Dovedale is said to be the most beautiful of the Derbyshire Dales.

ALPORT, Derbys SK26
Pleasantly sited on a tumbling tributary of the River Bradford, attractive Alport is typical of the and preserves a number of old houses. The oldest is 16th-centu Monk's Hall.

Leave Alport and continue to attractive Youlgreave.

YOULGREAVE, Derbys SK26
Every June, on the Saturday near St John the Baptist's Day, the spr and wells of this charming village dressed with flower pictures as p of an ancient Derbyshire traditio Today the ceremony is Christian it is likely that the ornamentatior was once intended to appease t spirits of the springs.

Leave Youlgreave on the 'Ashbou road for 4½ miles and meet the A5012. Turn right here, then turn to join the A515 and continue to Newhaven Inn.

NEWHAVEN INN, Derbys SK1
This fine building, a black-and-w structure with 5 bays, was built b the Duke of Devonshire in the 1 century. About 2½ miles north is outstanding prehistoric stone cir of Arbor Low (AM).

Continue along the A515 to Also Plantation, with lovely Dovedale t the west of the road.

ALSOP PLANTATION, Derbys
The plantation on Alsop Moor is protected by the National Trust extends alongside the main A51 below a 1,253ft summit. Its prese is an attractive addition to the lo limestone scenery.

In 1½ miles pass the edge of Dove to the right.

DOVEDALE, Derbys & Staffs S
Here the lovely River Dove flows through a 2-mile ravine where spectacular limestone scenery c craggy buttresses and curiously weathered outcrops is clothed a softened by carpets of lush vegetation. Perhaps the most fa of many beauty spots in the nat park, the dale (NT) is also noted trout fishing.

In 2¼ miles turn left on to an unclassified road and continue t village of Tissington.

TISSINGTON, Derbys SK15
Greystone houses line two sides the attractive triangular green c which this exceptionally beauti village is centred; the third side occupied by a fine Norman anc church. Features of the latter in a good Norman font, an unusu decker pulpit dating from the 1 century, and various monumer Traditional Derbyshire well-dres ceremonies are enacted at five different wells on Ascension Da

Leave Tissington and turn right, drive through attractive parklanc meet the A515. Turn left and continue to Fenny Bentley.

autiful gardens surround
mantic Haddon Hall.

Many Derbyshire wells, such as this example at Tissington, are decorated for thanksgiving ceremonies.

Crich Museum houses many historic trams in working order.

Richard Arkwright's original cotton mill at Cromford was two storeys taller than the present building.

Y BENTLEY, Derbys SK15
res of this pleasant village
le the successful amalgamation
5th-century manor house with
mains of an ancient tower, and
d Derbyshire church. Inside the
is a macabre monument
nemorating Thomas Beresford,
'e, 16 sons, and 5 daughters.

Leave Fenny Bentley, drive for ½ mile, and turn left on to the B5056 SP 'Bakewell'. Continue through undulating countryside for 3¾ miles to reach an unclassified left turn. A detour from the main route can be taken by turning left here, then after ¼ mile turning right for the village of Ballidon.

BALLIDON, Derbys SK25
A well restored early-Norman chapel stands in a field near Ballidon.

On the main route, continue along the B5036 to Grangemill, meet the A5012, and turn right to descend the attractively wooded Via Gellia for Cromford.

CROMFORD, Derbys SK25
The world's first mechanized textile factory was built here by Richard Arkwright, a native of the village, in 1771. One of the key figures in England's industrial revolution, he lived in Willersley Castle and built the church in which he is buried. He also built many of the village cottages to house his millworkers. A fine old bridge that spans the River Derwent here carries a rare 15th-century bridge chapel (AM).

Leave Cromford and turn left, then turn right on to the A6 SP 'Derby'. Pass Cromford Canal on the left, then reach Shining Cliff Wood on the right.

SHINING CLIFF WOOD, Derbys SK35
This attractive area of woodland (NT) occupies 200 acres on the west bank of the River Derwent, and is a haven for many forms of wildlife.

Continue along the A6 to reach Ambergate and turn left on to the A610 SP 'Ripley'. Follow the Amber Valley, and after 2 miles turn left on to the B6013 SP 'Chesterfield'. In 3 miles turn left again on to the B5035 to reach South Wingfield Manor.

SOUTH WINGFIELD MANOR, Derbys SK35
Extensive remains can be seen of a fine 15th-century manor house where Mary Queen of Scots was imprisoned in 1584. Access to ruins is by permission from Manor Farm.

Continue along the B5035 to Crich and branch right on to an unclassified road SP 'Holloway' for the Crich Tramway Museum.

CRICH TRAMWAY MUSEUM, Derbys SK35
Vintage tramcars from all over the world have been restored to working order and are on display in this fascinating museum, which occupies a disused quarry. An air of authenticity is created by a period setting comprising the reconstructed façade of Derby's Georgian Assembly Rooms and a collection of Victorian Street furniture. An exhibition illustrates the history of lead mining in Derbyshire.

CRICH STAND, Derbys SK35
High above the Crich Tramway Museum is the 940ft summit of Crich Stand, a lofty vantage point crowned by a monument to the Sherwood Foresters – the Nottingham and Derby Regiment.

Descend to Holloway. Turn right SP 'Riber' and 'Tansley', then in ½ mile meet crossroads and drive straight on. In 2 miles meet a T-junction and turn left SP 'Riber Village', and after ¼ mile keep left to reach the Riber Castle Fauna Reserve on the right.

RIBER CASTLE FAUNA RESERVE, Derbys SK35
Near-natural surroundings are provided for comprehensive collections of European birds and animals in the 20 acres of this excellent reserve. Special features include a colony of lynx, and many breeds of domestic animals that have died out elsewhere. Picturesque ruins of 19th-century Riber Castle dominate 853ft Riber Hill.

Descend steeply through hairpin bends, turn right at the bottom, and in ¾ mile turn left on to the A615. Return to Matlock.

TOUR 73 67 MILES

AMONG THE HIGH PEAKS

Climbers and walkers come to this part of the national park for the stark ridges of weathered grit, towering rock outcrops, and refreshingly empty moorland. Villages of timbered cottages shelter in the valleys, making a contrast with the huge reflectors of Jodrell Bank's radio telescopes.

THE PEAK DISTRICT NATIONAL PARK
This tour starts west of the Peak District boundary and explores the brownstone towns and villages in the mid western part of the national park. In places massive limestone extraction has taken its toll of the landscape, but the sheep-cropped grass of high gritstone edges still rolls away to close horizons in areas of outstanding natural beauty that have been saved by the Peak Planning Board. Visitors should remember that although the region is protected it is not automatically accessible to the public. Some 40,000 people live and work in the park, and permission should always be sought from farmers and landowners before enclosed land is entered. Information centres are located in Buxton, Castleton, and Edale. See also tours 72 and 74.

Leave Congleton via West Street and West Road to join the A34 'Newcastle' road. Proceed to Astbury.

ASTBURY, Cheshire SJ86
Notable Jacobean and earlier woodwork can be seen in Astbury's 14th- and 15th-century church, and the fine village Rectory dates from the 18th century.

Continue along the A34 to pass Little Moreton Hall.

Little Moreton Hall is one of the finest medieval houses in Britain.

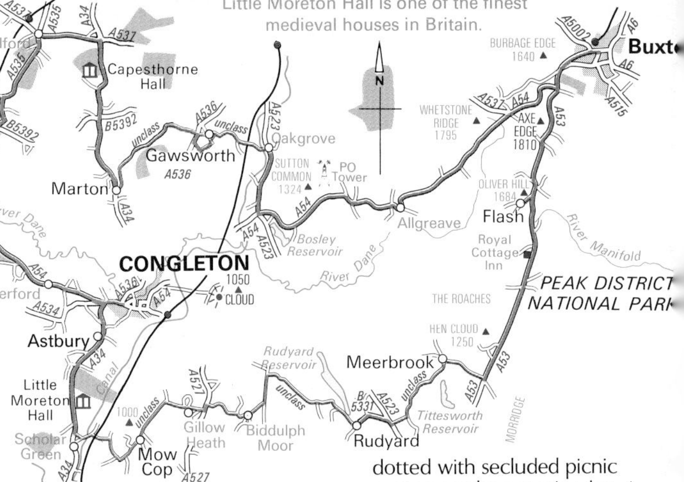

An attractive aqueduct carries the Macclesfield Canal over the road near Congleton.

CONGLETON, Cheshire SJ86
This market town stands on a bend on the River Dane and is a dormitory settlement for the vast industrial conurbations of Manchester and the Potteries. Its own industries include the manufacture of artificial yarn for the textile trade. Notable buildings in the town include three half-timbered inns and an 18th-century church with heavy woodwork that seems appropriate to Congleton's solid personality.

THE CLOUD, Cheshire SJ96
Some 3 miles east of Congleton a lofty hill known as The Cloud (NT) rises from farmed slopes to a 1,050ft summit offering magnificent all-round views. East are the Staffordshire hills, west the rolling Cheshire Plain, and south the towns and distinctively shaped chimneys of the Potteries.

LITTLE MORETON HALL, Cheshire SJ85
Beautiful carved gables and a distinctive black-and-white exterior of Elizabethan wood- and plasterwork have made this splendid 16th-century manor house (NT) one of the most famous examples in Britain. The dazzling effect of symmetrical timber patterns against brilliant white is increased by the reflection of the house in its own lovely moat. Inside are a long wainscoted gallery, a great hall, a chapel, and fine oak furniture.

Continue for $\frac{3}{4}$ mile to the edge of Scholar Green and turn left on to an unclassified road SP 'Mow Cop'. After $\frac{1}{4}$ mile turn left again, and after a further $\frac{1}{2}$ mile cross a canal bridge and drive beneath a railway before ascending Mow Cop.

MOW COP, Cheshire SJ85
Rough turf covers this stark limestone ridge for much of its 1,091ft height, but the rugged outcrop of rock known as the Old Man of Mow carries little but a sham ruin built in 1750. Known as Mow Cop Castle, this folly makes a picturesque addition to the distinctive outline of the Old Man.

Continue past a towered church and in 1 mile turn right (no SP) into Mow Lane. Descend through Gillow Heath to the main road and turn left, then in 300 yards turn right on to an unclassified road SP 'Biddulph Moor'. Climb to the village of Biddulph Moor and turn left SP 'Leek'. Take the next turning right, proceed for $\frac{1}{2}$ mile to reach a T-junction, and turn left. Continue for 1 mile and turn right. After $2\frac{1}{2}$ miles glimpse Rudyard Reservoir on the left and descend to Rudyard.

RUDYARD, Staffs SJ95
Rudyard Kipling's parents courted and became engaged in this lovely village, and when their talented son was born they named him after it. Attractive woodlands to the north border a 2-mile reservoir formed in 1793 to provide water for the Trent and Mersey Canal. Today the banks of this attractive lake are skirted by a 5-mile footpath dotted with secluded picnic spots near the water's edge. A section of the path follows the trackbed of an abandoned railway and its route passes caverns, unus rock formations, and the remains Roman copper workings.

Continue on the B5331 'Leek' road meet a T-junction, and turn right o to the A523. Take the next turning on to an unclassified road SP 'Meerbrook', continue for $\frac{1}{2}$ mile, turn left again. Approach Meerbro with Tittesworth Reservoir right.

MEERBROOK, Staffs SJ96
Wild upland country popular with climbers and fell walkers surroun this tiny moorland village. A curic aspect of the area is its naturalize colony of red-necked wallabies. T numbers some 30 strong and beg when several of the animals – natives of Australia – escaped fro private estate.

Turn right SP 'Blackshaw Moor, Le and after $\frac{1}{2}$ mile meet a main road turn left on to the A53 'Buxton' ro Climb on to open moors in the Pe District National Park, with a 2-mi stretch of rocky outcrops known the Staffordshire Roaches to the le The highest point of the Roaches 1,658ft; Merryton Low rises to 1,6 to the right. Pass the Royal Cottag Inn and reach an unclassified left leading to the village of Flash. A s detour can be made from the ma route here.

FLASH, Staffs SK06
Situated at 1,518ft, Flash is claimed to be the highest village in England and is itself dominated by 1,684ft Oliver Hill to the north.

ater enter Derbyshire and ascend to ,631ft below the distinctive summit f Axe Edge.

AXE EDGE, Derbys SK06
ising from an area of fine walking ountry, this 1,810ft summit is the ighest point in the moors from hich the rivers Dove, Manifold, Vye, Dane, and Goyt spring.

oceed to Buxton.

tremely faint signals from outer space can be detected by the advanced Jodrell Bank radio telescopes.

TON, Derbys SK07
ated some 1,007ft above sea l, this natural touring centre is highest town in England and has n known as a spa resort of one or another since Roman times. A rb legacy of 18th-century itecture has been left from its t popular period, and the tourists day are catered for by a large e of entertainment facilities. See tour 74.

e Buxton with SP 'Congleton' to n along the A53 'Leek' road, and 1½ miles turn right on to the A54. a winding ascent with 1,640ft age Edge visible to the right, and 1 mile enjoy views of 1,795ft tstone Edge on the same side. these ridges, in the deep Dane , is a junction of Derbyshire, hire, and Staffordshire daries in an area known as the Shire Heads. Descend from lating moorland to Allgreave for t views of a Post Office nunications tower, and after g close to the tower skirt Bosley voir and turn right on to the 'Macclesfield' road. Continue for s to Oakgrove and turn left on unclassified road SP worth', immediately crossing acclesfield Canal. Proceed to vorth.

GAWSWORTH, Cheshire SJ86
Spacious lawns and gardens watered by five lakes grace the grounds of Gawsworth Hall, a beautiful black-and-white timber-framed house (open) dating from Tudor times. Also in the park are rare traces of a tilting ground, where knights once displayed their prowess in jousts and mock battles. At one time the house was the seat of the Fytton family, whose daughter Mary was a favourite maid of Elizabeth I and may have been the 'Dark Lady' of Shakespeare's sonnets. Features of the village itself include the fine Old Rectory and an attractive church, both of the 15th century. The church carries quaint gargoyles and contains a notable range of monuments to the Fyttons. A nearby wood contains the tomb of 18th-century dramatist and eccentric Maggotty Johnson.

At Gawsworth turn left SP 'Gawsworth Church'. Continue to the end of the village and keep right, passing an attractive pond, with views of Gawsworth Hall. Continue along this unclassified road, pass the church, and at the Harrington Arms Inn turn right then right again on to the A536. After ½ mile meet crossroads and turn left on to an unclassified road for Marton.

MARTON, Cheshire SJ86
A famous oak tree in this village is said to be the largest in England. The local church is a quaint timbered structure dating from the 14th century.

Drive to a junction with the A34 and turn right SP 'Manchester'. Continue for 3½ miles to reach the entrance to Capesthorne Hall.

Rudyard's extensive reservoir has been planned to cater for a wide variety of leisure pursuits.

CAPESTHORNE HALL, Cheshire SJ87
A chapel which adjoins this lovely 18th-century house (open) may be the earliest surviving work of the architect John Wood of Bath. The house itself contains various relics, including pictures, ancient vases, old furniture, and Americana.

Continue along the A34 for 1 mile, meet traffic signals, and turn left on to the A537 'Chester' road. Continue to the Chelford roundabout and turn left on to the A535 SP 'Holmes Chapel' to reach Jodrell Bank.

Ramshaw Rocks are among the most striking gritstone crags in the Peak District.

JODRELL BANK, Cheshire SJ77
Manchester University made the name Jodrell Bank internationally famous by building a giant steerable radio telescope here in 1957. Now known as Mark I, the instrument has a 250ft reflector and is still one of the largest of its type in the world. The Mark II was built in the early 1960s and has a 125ft reflector with an advanced form of digital control. Regular presentations of the stars and planets are given in the Planetarium (open), and there are fascinating working models of both the telescopes on view.

Keep forward on the A535. In 3½ miles, near the outskirts of Holmes Chapel, turn left into unclassified Manor Lane (no SP). Continue to the A54 and turn left for the return to Congleton via Somerford.

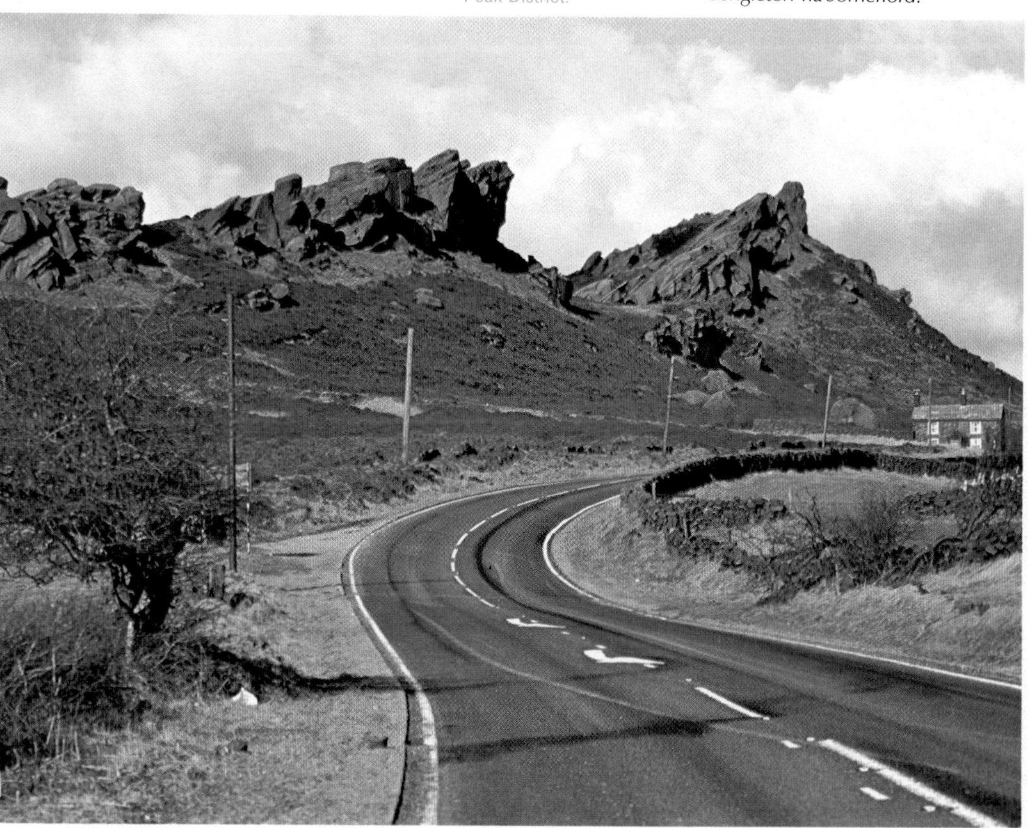

TOUR 74 46 MILES

THE PEAK DISTRICT DALES

Here the great River Wye and its tributaries have carved deep gorges in the soft limestone hills, making secluded pockets of outstanding beauty where the severity of naked rock is softened by water and foliage. The dales themselves are only accessible by foot.

BUXTON, Derbys SK07
Situated just outside the boundaries of the national park, this is the highest town in England and an ideal base from which to tour the moors and dales of the Peak District. It is sheltered by hills even higher than its 1,007ft site, yet is able to offer gentle scenery more typical of the lowlands alongside sedate reaches of the lovely River Wye. Grinlow Woods lie to the south of the town, Corbar Woods are a mere ½ mile away, and 1 mile east is the enchanting valley of Ashwood Dale. The town itself is built round a spa whose medicinal properties were discovered by the Romans and exploited to the benefit of the town towards the end of the 18th century, when Buxton rivalled the elegant supremacy of Somerset's Bath. The growth of the town during this period was largely due to the efforts of the 5th Duke of Devonshire, who built the beautiful Crescent and Pump Rooms opposite the town's hot springs. The pale blue mineral water of the area still bubbles up from a mile underground at a rate of ¼ million gallons per day and a constant temperature of 82 degrees Fahrenheit; it can be sampled from the Pump Rooms' elegant white marble basin. Spa treatment is available from the Devonshire Royal Hospital, which was originally built as the Great Stables and has a superb dome that was added in 1879. The Pavilion concert hall, theatre, and ballroom stand in 23 acres of lovely gardens featuring a boating lake, bowling and putting greens, tennis courts, and a children's play area. The local swimming pool is filled by the mineral spring, and the town boasts two fine golf courses. Fine collections of fossils and minerals can be seen in the local museum.

Leave Buxton on the A6 with SP 'Matlock' and descend through the wooded limestone gorge of the River Wye. Climb away from the valley, with Great Rocks Dale to the left, to reach the edge of Taddington. It is possible to visit this village by turning right from the main route on to an unclassified road.

Buxton built its reputation as a spa, but today it provides facilities for all tastes. The Pavilion Gardens offer a varied and relaxing landscape which enhance the town's appeal.

TADDINGTON, Derbys SK17
Taddington stands at an altitude of 1,130ft in attractive limestone country and is one of the highest villages in England. The slopes of Taddington Wood (NT) face lovely Monsal Dale some 1½ miles east, and to the south-west Taddington Moor rises to 1,500ft at the highest point in the hills south of the River Wye. Close to the summit of the moor is the Five Wells Tumulus, an unusual barrow with two burial chambers. Various interesting prehistoric remains can be found on the moors.

Descend wooded Taddington Dale, with Monsal Dale on the left, and pass Great Shacklow Wood on the right before crossing the River Wye. After ¾ mile turn left on to the A6020 to enter Ashford-in-the-Water.

ASHFORD-IN-THE-WATER, Derbys SK16
Two ancient bridges span the Wye in this delightful village, one dated 1664 and the other complete with a sheep-dipping enclosure at one end. An interesting well-dressing ceremony is held here on the Saturday before Trinity Sunday. Ashford marble was quarried near by.

Drive to the end of the village and turn right on to the B6465 'Bakewell' road, then after a short distance rejoin the A6 to reach Bakewell.

BAKEWELL, Derbys SK26
A busy cattle market and the largest town in the national park, Bakewell stands on the wooded banks of the Wye and is sheltered by hills on three sides. Many of its attractive brownstone buildings bear witness to a historic past, and its beautiful 12th-century church is famous for the superb Saxon cross (AM) preserved in its churchyard. The 5-arched medieval bridge (AM) that spans the river was widened in the 19th century, but is basically one of the oldest structures of its type in Britain. Holme Hall and the Market Hall both date back to the 17th century, and the Old House Museum is an early-Tudor house with wattle-and-daub interior walls. Inside the latter are exhibitions of costumes and domestic utensils. The name of the town will always b associated with the Bakewell tart, a dish apparently created by acciden when a harassed cook in the Rutlan Arms mistakenly poured the egg mixture meant for the pastry of a jam tart into the jam. The unusual dish was very well received by guests, and the cook was instructe to continue making her delicious mistake.

Leave Bakewell on the A6 'Matlock' road to pass Haddon Hall.

HADDON HALL, Derbys SK26
Although originally a fortified dwelling, exquisite 12th- to 15th-century Haddon Hall (open) was never fought over and survives as one of the finest examples of medieval architecture extant. Its peaceful history is reflected in its lovely wood and parkland setting the River Wye, and its beauty is enhanced by the enchanting rose gardens that ornament its grounds The romantic feeling of the place supported by its history, for it was from here that Dorothy Vernon eloped with Sir John Manners in th 16th century. See also tour 72.

Continue along the A6 and cross t Wye to enter Rowsley.

ROWSLEY, Derbys SK26
This charming little greystone villa stands on a tongue of land at the confluence of the rivers Wye and Derwent. The actual waters' mee a delightful spot beloved of artists and anglers alike. Sir Joseph Paxtc designed the earlier of two obsol but charming station buildings he and the beautiful old Peacock Inn was originally a 17th-century ma house. See also tour 72.

Pass the Peacock Inn on the left, th in a short distance turn left on to t B6012 SP 'Baslow'. Continue to Beeley.

BEELEY, Derbys SK26
From ancient times this little community was known for the grindstones fashioned by its craftsmen from the local hard gr tributary of the River Derwent, w is famous for its trout, runs throu the village.

Dramatic scenery found in the Peak District can be explored from Buxton by following the River Wye as it runs south through spectacular Chee Dale.

Chatsworth's superb apartments include the State Bedroom of the ill-fated Mary Queen of Scots.

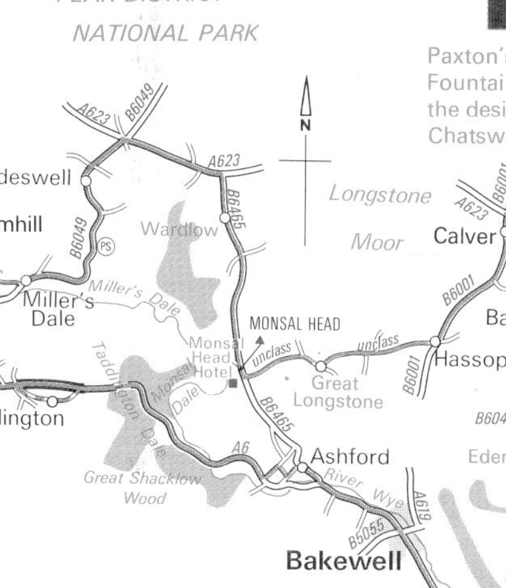

…yond Beeley skirt the grounds of …atsworth House, then cross the …er Derwent and enter the park to …s Chatsworth House itself.

…ATSWORTH HOUSE, …rbys SK27
…pularly known as the Palace of the …k, this magnificent mansion …en) stands in a superb park on the …er Derwent and is backed by …utifully wooded slopes. It was …t in the 17th century for the 1st …ke of Devonshire and is noted …ticularly for its superb state …rtments and great art collection. …earlier house that stood on the …e site was partly designed by the …Duke's ancestress Bess of …dwick, and was occasionally …ed by Mary Queen of Scots. …ains of the original Elizabethan … layout can be seen in the old …ting Tower, which vies as the …r focal point with a fountain … is the tallest in Britain. Features …e magnificent park include …ure chestnut avenues and the …m of ornamental waters.

…nd Chatsworth Park join the …) and enter Baslow.

…OW, Derbys SK27
…characteristic gritstone village …ds on the River Derwent and is … built round an old triangular …e green. Most through traffic is … across the river by a recent …e, but the old hump-backed …ing survives – complete with …use.

…low turn left SP 'Chapel-en-le- …to join the A623. Continue to …lage of Calver.

CALVER, Derbys SK27
Anglers come here for the fine Derwent trout, and the village boasts a good 18th-century cotton mill.

In Calver meet traffic signals and turn left on to the B6001 'Bakewell' road. Continue to Hassop.

HASSOP, Derbys SK27
Situated at the edge of wild Longstone Moor, this little village has a Jacobean hall that was the home of the Earls of Newburgh until 1853. Much of the local countryside has the tended appearance of parkland.

In Hassop turn right on to an unclassified road and drive to a T-junction in Great Longstone. Turn right for Monsal Head and continue to the Monsal Head Hotel, then turn right again on to the B6465 to pass a magnificent vantage point offering panoramic views across Monsal Dale.

MONSAL HEAD, Derbys SK17
This great rocky prominence affords superb views into Monsal Dale, where the River Wye threads its way between lush slopes punctuated by rocky crags and overhangs of weathered stone. The head and dale together form one of the national park's loveliest beauty spots.

Continue through Wardlow, turn left on to the A623, and in $1\frac{1}{2}$ miles turn left again to join the B6049. Continue into Tideswell.

TIDESWELL, Derbys SK17
Although this ancient town was granted a market as early as the 13th century, the only notable building to have survived the centuries is the superb Church of St John the Baptist. This is considered the finest building of its type in the county and is popularly known as The Cathedral of the Peak. Local wells and springs are dressed in a traditional ceremony held in Wakes Week, on the Saturday nearest June 24.

Continue with the 'Buxton' road, and after 1 mile pass the Tideswell picnic area (left). Descend into Miller's Dale.

Paxton's Emperor Fountain boldly reflects the design of Chatsworth House.

Native ashwoods fringe the River Wye in picturesque Monsal Dale.

MILLER'S DALE, Derbys SK17
Threaded by a narrow road to Litton Mill, this part of the Wye Valley is enclosed by craggy limestone cliffs that rise high above the river behind dense screens of shrub and woodland. The mill was once used for processing silk.

Beyond a railway viaduct and just before a bridge over the Wye turn sharp right on to an unclassified road for Wormhill. Pass Chee Dale on the left and continue to Wormhill.

WORMHILL, Derbys SK17
Situated high above the river curve that includes Chee Dale, this village is excellently situated for fine views across the River Wye and is popular with walkers. Narrow Chee Dale is only accessible on foot, but it is worth the exercise. One of the village's most notable buildings is a 17th-century hall with mullioned windows.

Pass Wormhill and bear left SP 'Peak Dale'. Continue for $\frac{1}{2}$ mile and turn right for the village of Peak Forest.

PEAK FOREST, Derbys SK17
The name of the medieval hunting ground that covered most of northern Derbyshire is preserved in this attractive little village. A chapel founded here in 1657 was extra-parochial and could issue marriage licences to anybody who applied. Before the building was demolished, Peak Forest gained something of a Gretna Green reputation as a goal for eloping couples. North of the village on the south side of Eldon Hill is a sheer-sided pothole known as Eldon Hole. For many years this was reputed to be bottomless, but modern potholers have discovered it to be a 186ft limestone shaft leading to two caverns which radiate from the bottom. On no account should an attempt be made to descend the hole without proper equipment.

Turn left on to the A623 SP 'Chapel-en-le-Frith', keep left at Sparrowpit, and within $1\frac{1}{4}$ miles turn left on to the A6. Proceed towards Buxton, passing limestone quarries on the left at Dove Holes. Black Edge rises to the right of the road.

DOVE HOLES, Derbys SK07
Not to be confused with a natural rock formation of the same name north-west of Tissington, this area is the site of vast limestone workings that extend some 4 miles south-east along Doveholes Dale, Peak Dale, and Great Rocks Dale. The quarries are 1,086ft above sea level. A railway tunnel penetrates $1\frac{1}{2}$ miles through bedrock deep beneath the main road here.

BLACK EDGE, Derbys SK07
This high prominence rises to 1,662ft and affords excellent views over much of the national park's finest countryside.

Descend and return to Buxton.

IN THE WOODLANDS OF CANNOCK CHASE

Nowadays the great chase, or hunting ground, of Cannock is a protected area of woodland famous for its superb stands of mature oak and birch. All around are the quaint black-and-white villages typical of the area, guardians of tradition.

LICHFIELD, Staffs SK10
A city of great age and architectural distinction, Lichfield has a fine red sandstone cathedral which carries three tall spires popularly known as the Ladies of the Vale. They form a well-known local landmark easily discernible above the rooftops of the town, and the grand west front of the building carries no less than 113 statues within its arcades and panels. Before the Commonwealth this type of decoration was reasonably common, but Cromwellian troops tracking down the sin of idolatry smashed such work wherever they could. Inside the building is preserved the 7th-century manuscript book of the *St Chad Gospels*, a rare treasure indeed. Other features include beautiful windows, a sculpted group by Chantrey, and numerous good memorials. The Bishop's Palace of 1687 is a lovely old example of its type, and restored Lichfield House dates from the 16th century. An old house in the Market Square was the birthplace of Dr Johnson and now serves as a Johnsonian Museum featuring, amongst other relics, his favourite silver teapot. The Swan Inn is also known to have associations with this famous man, and the city celebrates its connexion with him annually on the Saturday nearest September 18.

Leave Lichfield with SP 'Tamworth A51', passing the Barracks to the left on Whittington Heath.

WHITTINGTON BARRACKS, Staffs SK10
The official museum of the Staffordshire Regiment can be visited at Whittington Barracks, themselves evidence of Lichfield's long association with the military.

Pass a TV mast on the right and descend past Hopwas Hays Wood to Hopwas, then continue to Tamworth.

TAMWORTH, Staffs SK20
Tamworth's fine castle (open) displays an intriguing mixture of architectural styles ranging from the original Norman to the charming pretence of the 19th century. The 10ft-thick walls of the keep are typically Norman, but the less massive warden's lodge and beautiful banqueting hall both show the delicacy of Tudor workmanship. A frieze of 55 oak panels in the state dining room, which is in the north wing, is painted with the arms of the lords of the castle up to 1718. A museum of local history is housed in the castle. Tamworth Church has a unique square tower with a double-spiral staircase at one corner, and the red-brick Town Hall of 1701 is one of the prettiest in the country.

Follow the A513 'Burton' and 'Alrewas' road, and after 4 miles pass an unclassified left turn that can be taken as a detour from the main route to Elford village.

Tranquillity reigns today on the Trent and Mersey Canal, formerly an important route for the pottery trade.

Rich furnishings in Lichfield Cathedral include an ornate choir screen.

TRENT & MERSEY CANAL, Staffs
Designed by the great engineer Brindley to service the industrial heartlands of England, this canal was begun in the late 18th century and was the first safe means by which fragile goods could be transported from the Potteries district. Josiah Wedgwood, owner of one of the more famous Staffordshire china industries, worked in association with Brindley to produce this undoubted advantage to his interests. Just beyond Alrewas the canal actually joins the Trent by loc and leaves the river by the same method after 250 yards.

In $1\frac{3}{4}$ miles meet crossroads and turr left on to the B5016 for Barton-under Needwood. Continue forward SP 'Yoxall', then in 1 mile reach The Bel (PH) and turn right on to the unclassified 'Tutbury' road. In 3 mile cross a main road and continue to Tutbury.

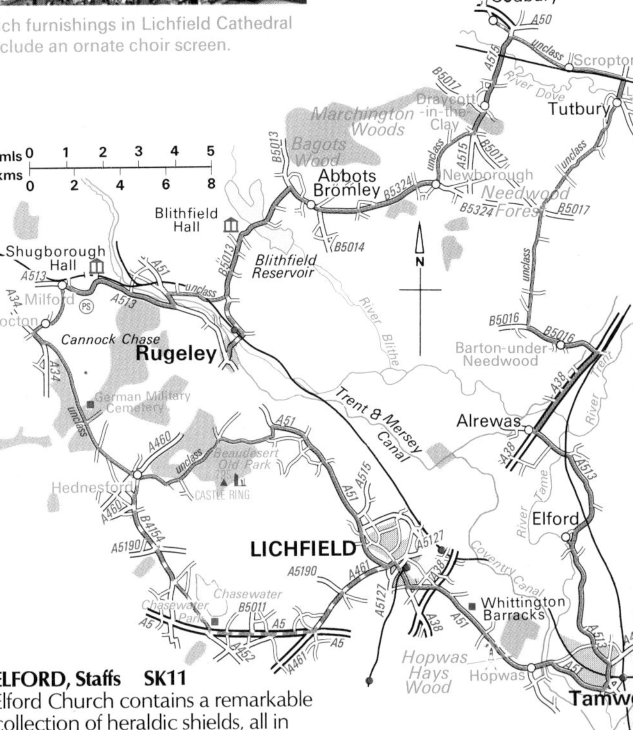

ELFORD, Staffs SK11
Elford Church contains a remarkable collection of heraldic shields, all in excellent condition, and the evocative monument to a child who is said to have been killed after being hit on the temple by a tennis ball in 1460. Many other fine memorials can be seen here.

On the main route, continue along the A513 to Alrewas.

ALREWAS, Staffs SK11
Famous for its River Trent eel fishing and basket-weaving industries, this charming little village of thatched black-and-white Tudor cottages is considered one of the prettiest in the county. Its 13th- and 14th-century church contains a fine font, and its situation on the Trent and Mersey Canal offers fine towpath walks.

Turn right on to the A38 SP 'Burton', and in 1 mile cross the River Trent before continuing alongside the canal.

TUTBURY, Staffs SK22
This picturesque old town stand the banks of the River Dove and claims to have the finest Normai church in the Midlands. The wes front of the building is certainly magnificent. Mary Queen of Sc was twice imprisoned in Tutbury Castle (open), and led a thoroug miserable existence in the cram surroundings of a high tower th stands. Nowadays this sad place visited for the outstanding view affords over Needwood Forest. Other remains of the castle, dramatically situated on an isol outcrop of rock, include 14th-century John of Gaunt's Gatewa The most striking building in the main street of the town is the o Dog and Partridge Inn.

Drive forward into the A50 High Street and cross the River Dove. Continue over a level crossing, then turn left on to an unclassified road SP 'Scropton' and 'Sudbury'. Continue for 2 miles beyond Scropton and turn left on to the A515. A short detour from the main route to attractive Sudbury can be made by turning right here on to the A515, then left on to an unclassified road leading to the village of that name.

Tutbury Castle offers excellent views over Needwood Forest.

;UDBURY, Derbys SK13
3uilt largely in the 17th century, this village is an excellent early example of unified design being applied to a :ommunity rather than being allowed to develop in its own andom fashion. Sudbury Hall (NT), eat of the Vernon family, contains xceptional carving by the sculptor ;rinling Gibbons. A stained glass vindow given by Queen Victoria an be seen in the village church.

)n the main route, continue along ie A515 and recross the River Dove. each Draycott-in-the-Clay and scend, then in $\frac{3}{4}$ mile meet rossroads and turn right on to an nclassified road for Newborough. ontinue to Newborough and turn ght on to the B5324 SP 'Abbots romley', then cross rolling ountryside and turn right on to the 5014 to enter Abbots Bromley.

BBOTS BROMLEY, Staffs SK02
eople from all over the country me to Abbots Bromley on the onday after September 4, when e curious and ritualistic Horn ance is performed through the reets and surrounding country les. Six of the twelve dancers carry cient reindeer antlers on their oulders, a seventh rides a hobby rse, a fool capers along the route multi-coloured costume, and the tourage is completed by a young l alongside a boy carrying a bow d arrow. The dance as it is seen day is thought to commemorate the anting of hunting rights to the local ople by the Abbot of Bromley in e 12th century. However, it is likely have been derived from a pagan remony with roots far back in ehistoric times. Features of the wn itself include many half-bered houses and a market place h an old butter cross. The 16th-ntury Church House and Bagot nshouses are of particular note.

Continue along the B5014 and in $\frac{1}{2}$ mile turn left on to the B5013 SP 'Rugeley'. In 1 mile cross the extensive Blithfield Reservoir.

BLITHFIELD RESERVOIR, Staffs SK02
The Queen Mother opened this 4,000 million gallon reservoir in 1953, and today it has become naturalized to such an extent that it is a valuable sanctuary for wildlife. Views can be enjoyed from the road, but a permit is required to visit the banks.

Pass a viaduct to reach Blithfield Hall on the right.

BLITHFIELD HALL, Staffs SK02
Set graciously in the peaceful Blithe Valley, this estate has been the home of the Bagot family and their ancestors for 900 years and includes a fine old house (open) of Elizabethan origin. Additions from later periods are evident in the design of the building, and inside is a magnificent staircase in carved oak. Of particular interest is a unique collection of relics from the Stuart period. Herds of black-necked Bagot goats roam the park.

Continue along the B5013 and in $1\frac{3}{4}$ miles turn right on to the unclassified 'Stafford' road. A short detour from the main route to the village of Rugeley can be made by keeping forward along the B5013 for a further $2\frac{1}{4}$ miles.

RUGELEY, Staffs SK01
During the 19th century this village became nationally famous as the home of notorious Dr William Palmer, who was found guilty of poisoning a bookmaker to whom he owed money. On its own this act is not sensational, but it appears that this unfortunate victim was the last in a long line of poisonings by Palmer, including many relatives and friends. The grave of the bookmaker, John Cook, can be seen in the local churchyard. The actual town is a pleasant little place that easily lives down its connexion with the Prince of Poisoners. About 4 miles south-south-east are fragments of Tudor Beaudesert Hall and a 19th-century park lodge.

On the main route, continue along the unclassified 'Stafford' road and in $1\frac{1}{2}$ miles meet crossroads. Turn left, then left again to join the A51, then cross the River Trent and turn right on to the A513 SP 'Stafford'. Follow the Trent Valley and pass the entrance to Shugborough Hall on the right before reaching Milford.

SHUGBOROUGH HALL, Staffs SJ92
Now run by Staffordshire County Council and housing the county museum, this great white mansion (NT) stands in beautiful grounds on the River Sow and contains fine collections of furniture and period bric-à-brac. Access to the gardens is by a bridge over a lovely ornamental lake, and the grounds are scattered with superb classical monuments and follies. The most notable of the latter are the Doric Temple and the Tower of the Winds.

Sudbury Hall is a typical example of 17th-century elegance.

Continue to Milford and turn left on to the unclassified 'Brocton' road. At Brocton drive forward SP 'Stafford', then meet a main road and turn left on to the A34 SP 'Cannock'. In $\frac{1}{4}$ mile turn left on to the unclassified 'Hednesford' road and climb to Cannock Chase.

CANNOCK CHASE, Staffs SJ91
Once the private hunting ground of the kings of England, the 26 square miles of wooded Cannock Chase form a designated area of outstanding natural beauty that is available for everybody to enjoy. Several pine and spruce plantations have been established in the area by the Forestry Commission, but a few of the majestic oaks that were once commonplace can still be seen in Brocton Coppice. The feather-like plumes of birches grace Black Hill, and to the west the bracken-clad forest glades give way to heather and gorse. Among many wild creatures to be seen here are deer and the rare native red squirrel. Good views are afforded by the hilltops of Seven Springs, which culminate in 795ft Castle Ring; the latter is crowned by the ramparts of a good iron-age hillfort.

Continue along the unclassified 'Hednesford' road and pass a German military cemetery on the left. Meet crossroads and ascend, then meet more crossroads and drive forward into the colliery district round Hednesford. In $\frac{1}{2}$ mile drive forward, descend to crossroads, and keep forward to cross a railway bridge. Turn right on to the A460, drive under a railway bridge, and turn left on to an unclassified road SP 'Rawnsley' and 'Hazelslade'. An alternative return to Lichfield, taking in the Chasewater Park Railway at Brownhills, can be taken by continuing with the A460 and following the route indicated on the tour map. On the main route, continue along the unclassified road and after $\frac{3}{4}$ mile turn left. Drive over a level crossing and climb through thick woodland to crossroads. Turn right into Startley Lane and descend. Continue, with Castle Ring rising from Cannock Chase to the right, and meet a main road. Turn right on to the A51 for the return to Lichfield.

The Abbots Bromley Horn Dancers performing outside Blithfield Hall.

A total of 48 enormous stones in two configurations make up the megalithic monument of Castlerigg Circle near Keswick. Lake District people have wondered at its significance for thousands of years, ever since its stone-age builders deserted it for reasons that can only be guessed at.

The North Country

BEVERLEY, Humberside TA03
The gothic completeness of medieval Beverley Minster has won it acclaim as one of the most beautiful churches in Europe. Its lovely twin bell towers can be seen for miles across the flat Humberside pastures, and its interior is packed with the monumental art of some 700 years. Here can be seen the full blossoming of the 14th-century stonemason's skill in the magnificent Percy Tomb, the ingenuity of 15th-century glassmakers in the great east window, and the craft of local men in the rich extravagance of carved wood. At the far end of the Main Street is St Mary's Church, a beautiful building that was started in the 12th century as a chapel for its more famous neighbour. Over the years it has been enlarged, with a wealth of excellent architectural detail, and is now independent. One of its more notable features is a 15th-century ceiling painting of the English kings. In early times the town was an important market centre and the capital of the East Riding of Yorkshire, a status that it had to defend with a stout wall pierced by five gates. Subsequent periods saw the community outgrow these confines, and all that remains today is the 15th-century North Bar. Evidence that much of the expansion was in the 18th and 19th centuries can be seen in the many Georgian houses and shopfronts that survive. The ornate market cross dates from c1714, and the Guildhall of 1762 displays a wealth of plasterwork and wood carving by local men. Inside 18th-century Lairgate Hall (open), which houses the council offices, is a Chinese Room with hand-painted wallpaper. Beverley's Art Gallery and Museum displays pictures and relics of local interest.

Leave Beverley and follow SP 'Hessle, A164'. Later reach Skidby Windmill.

SKIDBY WINDMILL, Humberside TA03
Well-preserved Skidby Windmill was built in 1821 and is the only example to have remained intact north of the River Humber and east of the Pennine Chain. Its black-tarred tower and white cap form a striking combination that makes it a prominent local landmark. An agricultural museum is being established inside (open).

At the windmill turn left on to an unclassified road SP 'Cottingham'. Later turn right on to the B1233 to reach Cottingham.

COTTINGHAM, Humberside TA03
Several halls of residence for the students from Hull University are established in this village, which is grouped round a large square. Inside the local church is a fine brass dating from the 14th century.

Continue along the B1233 and drive over a level crossing. Keep forward through 2 roundabouts, then ½ mile beyond the University of Hull turn right on to the A1079. Proceed to the centre of Kingston-upon-Hull.

TOUR 76 — 71 MILES

HUMBERSIDE AND HOLDERNESS

Between the River Humber and the sea is a flat peninsula famous for its magnificent churches, whose towers and spires stand high above the surrounding countryside of marshlands and drainage canals. Fishing fleets put out from Hull, and many of the coastal villages have become holiday resorts.

KINGSTON-UPON-HULL, Humberside TA02
Better known as Hull, this major industrial and commercial centre is an international port and a fishing base for deep-sea vessels. As such it suffered badly in World War II, but its rebuilding has included a fine shopping precinct scattered with flowerbeds and interspersed with parks and gardens. Docks stretch for a full 7 miles along the north side of the Humber, joined here by the little River Hull, and a suspension bridge being built to link with the south bank is expected to be the largest of its kind in the world. Despite these extensive new developments the city centre still has a few old buildings untouched by bombs or town planning, including the largest parish church in England and 18th-century Maister House (NT). An early 17th-century mansion in which the MP and anti-slavery campaigner William Wilberforce was born in 1759 is now preserved as the William Wilberforce Historical Museum. The Town Docks Museum relates to fishing and shipping, and the Transport and Archaeological Museum mounts interesting displays of both its somewhat disparate subjects. Paintings, sculptures, and visiting exhibitions of work can be seen in the Ferrens Art Gallery. Hull Fair, held every year in October, is claimed to be the largest in the country.

Leave Hull on the A165 with SP 'Hornsea' and 'Bridlington'. In 3½ miles reach a roundabout. Keep forward to another roundabout and take the 3rd exit on to the B1238 SP 'Aldbrough'. Continue for 1¼ miles and keep forward to reach Sproatley.

SPROATLEY, Humberside TA13
This village is in the heart of the Holderness area, where vast fields, golden with corn in summer, stretch flatly to the horizon or lap the fringes of small copses. Its 19th-century church, given an air of mystery by a cloak of ivy, contains an inscribed coffin lid of the 13th century.

Bear right, drive to the end of the village, and turn left on to an unclassified road to reach Burton Constable Hall.

BURTON CONSTABLE HALL, Humberside TA13
Grand 18th-century state rooms and 200 acres of parkland enchantingly landscaped by Capability Brown are features of this attractive Elizabethan house (open). Lakes covering some 22 acres provide plenty of scope for boating, and a model railway runs through the grounds.

Return to Sproatley and turn right to return along the B1238. Meet a war memorial and branch left on to the B1240 to Preston. At Preston turn left again to reach Hedon.

St Patrick's Church in Patrington has the grandeur of a small cathedral.

The Proud Pharisee is one of many carvings in the nave of magnificent Beverley Minster.

HEDON, Humberside TA12
At one time this small town was a major port connected to the Humber Estuary by canals. It was rich enough to start building the magnificent King of Holderness in the 12th century, and subsequent work on this church shows the prosperity to have lasted at least until the 15th century. Trade has long since filtered away to Hull, but the huge pinnacled tower of the 'King' remains in all its glory. Near by, the Ravenspur Cross commemorates a long vanished village of that name, where Bolingbroke (later Henry IV) landed in 1399 to claim the English throne for the House of Lancaster.

Turn left on to the A1033 SP 'Withernsea'. Pass through flat agricultural countryside crisscrossed by drainage canals to reach Keyingham.

KEYINGHAM, Humberside TA22
An attractive medieval church can be seen in this village, and just to the north west is a tower that was once a windmill.

Drive through Ottringham and continue to the edge of Winestead.

WINESTEAD, Humberside TA22
Features from the Norman and Jacobean periods jostle for attention with others less easy to define in Winestead Church. A good 16th-century brass can be seen inside.

Continue to Patrington.

PATRINGTON, Humberside TA32
Hedon's superb church has a rival here in the Queen of Holderness, a magnificent cruciform building in the decorated style of architecture. Its tower and spire are considered outstanding, and excellent craftsmanship of many kinds can be seen inside. At one time the village was an important market town in the manor administered by the archbishops of York.

A pleasant detour can be taken from the main route by following the B14 from Patrington to Easington (where there is a natural gas pipe terminal), and continuing through Kilnsea to Spurn Head and the Humber Shore

Hornsea Mere is famous for its huge pike and large flocks of coot.

The poet Andrew Marvell was MP for Kingston upon Hull from 1658 until his death in 1678.

Spurn Head Nature Reserve attracts huge numbers of migrant birds, as well as flocks of waterfowl and waders.

PURN HEAD, Humberside TA41
etween the North Sea and the lumber estuary is Spurn Head, a arrow hook of sand and shingle iat lengthens by about a yard each ear as silt from the Humber and ggregate from the Holderness cliffs deposited at its tip. At present it is bout $3\frac{1}{2}$ miles long and is gradually eing stabilized by the tough roots of arram grass. Many migrant species bird rest in the sanctuary at the ıd of the peninsula, and their omings and goings are watched om a special observatory Centuries go a beacon was burned here to iide shipping through the Humber tuary, but nowadays the steady eam of a lighthouse provides a ore dependable warning. A road retches for about three-quarters of e peninsula's length; the rest, cept parts of the bird sanctuary, ın be explored on foot.

ı the main route, drive from trington on the A1033 and ntinue to Withernsea.

WITHERNSEA, Humberside TA32
This quiet resort offers donkey rides, a reasonable sand and shingle beach, paddling and boating pools, a playground, and various amusement arcades – in fact, many of the diversions associated with family seaside holidays. Sports facilities include bowling greens, a putting course, and an open-air swimming pool. Inland the white 127ft bulk of a disused 19th-century lighthouse rises from a street of houses, and a quirky castellated gateway survives from a pier that stood here in the Victorian heyday of seaside holidays.

Drive to the Spread Eagle (PH) in Withernsea and turn left into Hull Road. Drive to the old lighthouse and turn right on to the B1242 SP 'Roos' and 'Hornsea'. Pass through Roos and in $\frac{1}{2}$ mile turn left. Continue for a further $\frac{3}{4}$ mile, then turn right and proceed to Aldbrough.

Withernsea lighthouse is now disused but still provides a focal point in this small resort.

ALDBROUGH, Humberside TA23
About $1\frac{1}{2}$ miles from this small village is a pleasant sand and shingle beach backed by small eroded cliffs. In the village itself is a 13th- to 15th-century church with a Norman arch and a sundial bearing a Saxon inscription.

Continue along a flat, winding road and pass through Mappleton to reach Hornsea.

HORNSEA, Humberside TA24
Hornsea has become very well known through its fine pottery, which is made in Marlborough Avenue and can be bought cheaply from a seconds shop. More can be learned about the processes and skills involved from a conducted tour, and the company has a special playground and mini-zoo for the children.The resort itself is popular with families and offers excellent sands divided from gardens and amusements by the fine Promenade. Behind the narrow streets and clustered houses of the old village is Hornsea Mere, a 2-mile lagoon formed during the ice ages. Today it is a popular boating venue with a reserve for wildfowl and a 5-mile walk round its wood and reed-fringed banks.

Skirt Hornsea Mere on the B1244 with SP 'Beverley'. Pass through Seaton and Catwick to reach Leven.

LEVEN, Humberside TA14
Between Leven and the River Hull is a 3-mile stretch of canal built in 1802. At one end of the waterway is the Canal House, a fine 3-bay building which incorporates a grand Georgian doorway from a house at Hull. Inside the dignified village church is the shaft of a Saxon cross.

Turn left on to the A165 then after 1 mile meet a roundabout and take the 2nd exit on to the A1035 SP 'Beverley'. Pass through rather featureless countryside and cross the River Hull, and the adjacent Beverley and Barmston drain; re-enter Beverley.

TOUR 77 73 MILES

FROM THE COAST TO THE MOORS

Every summer thousands of visitors flock to Scarborough and Whitby, bustling resorts with much to entertain the holidaymaker. Inland are the forest and heather-clad hills of the North Yorks Moors, where the colours are green and brown and silence is broken only by small natural sounds.

Pleasure craft throng Scarborough harbour.

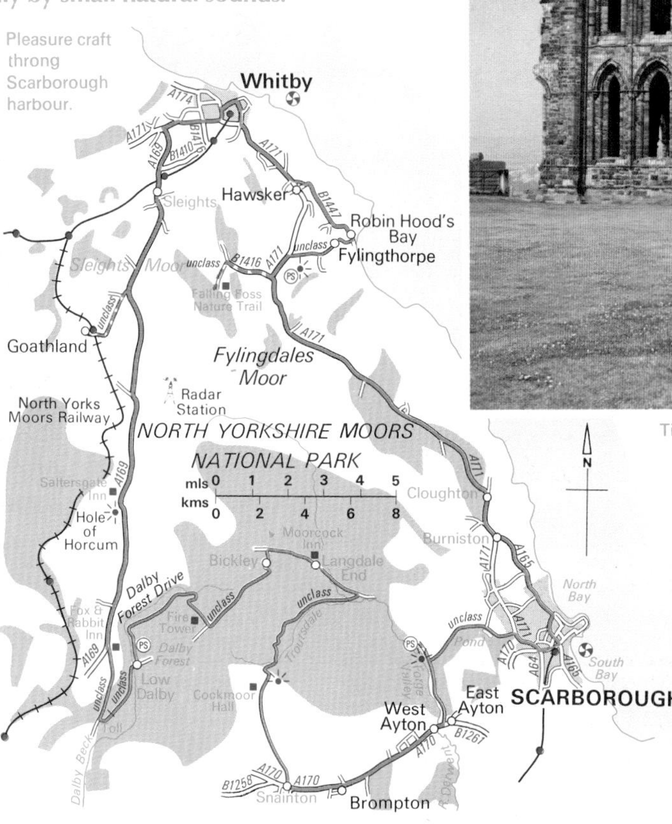

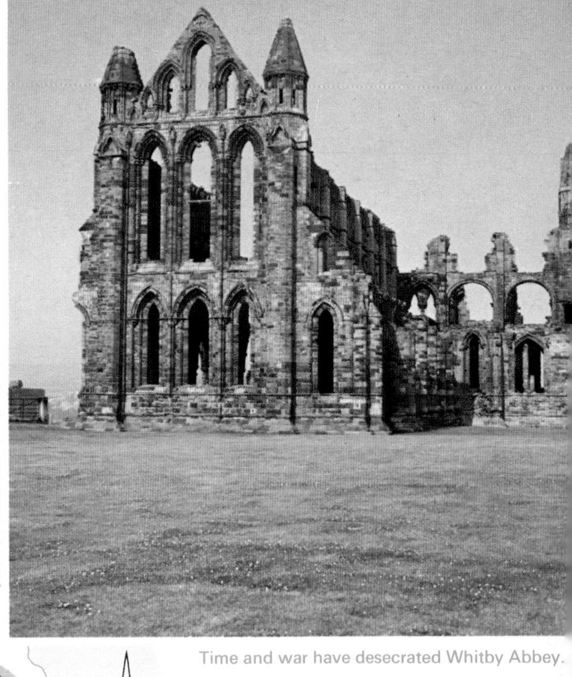

Time and war have desecrated Whitby Abbey.

Fylingdales Radar Station keeps a grim vigil on the desolate moor.

SCARBOROUGH, N Yorks TA08
An important conference centre and one of the most popular seaside resorts in Yorkshire, this charming old town overlooks two sandy bays divided by the massive bulk of a 300ft headland. In Roman times this excellent vantage point was the site of a signalling station, and the foundations of that ancient structure still exist amongst the magnificent 12th-century castle ruins (AM) that stand here today. Views from the 100-acre site, which is accessible through a 13th-century barbican, extend across the red roofs of the medieval old town to the harbour far below. Of particular note among the remains are the fine keep and three medieval chapels. During the 18th and 19th centuries the town became caught up in the fashion for seaside holidays and acquired several fine terraces of hotels and boarding houses, many of which still offer accommodation. The Natural History Museum, Art Gallery, and Medicinal Baths are housed in notable Victorian buildings, and a museum of general interest can be visited in Woodend, the one-time holiday home of the Sitwell family. Typical resort facilities and amusements offered to the visitor include fine promenades and well-tended seafront gardens, plus a good zoo with a dolphinarium. Views can be enjoyed from pleasant clifftop walks and the 500ft eminence of nearby Oliver Hill.

Leave Scarborough with SP 'North Bay' and join the A165, then in 1 mile meet a roundabout and take the A165 to reach Burniston. Meet a junction with the A171 and turn right SP 'Whitby'. Continue to Cloughton, bear left with the A171, and drive through an afforested area to Fylingdales Moor.

FYLINGDALES MOOR AND RADAR STATION, N Yorks SE99
The huge white domes of Fylingdales Early Warning Station seem a constant reminder of doom in the lonely desolation of the surrounding moor. At one time the area was inhabited, and the intrusive evidence of advanced technology contrasts strangely with prehistoric burial mounds and the Wade's Causeway, which is Roman.

Continue along the A171 for $8\frac{3}{4}$ miles. A detour from the main route can be made by turning left on to the B1416, driving $1\frac{3}{4}$ miles, then turning left again on to an unclassified road to reach Newton House and the start of the Falling Fosse Nature Trail. On the main route, continue along the A171 and in $\frac{3}{4}$ mile turn right on to an unclassified road SP 'Fylingthorpe' and 'Robin Hood's Bay'. Pass a viewpoint and picnic site on the right and descend (1 in 4) through hairpin bends to reach Fylingthorpe.

FYLINGTHORPE, N Yorks NZ90
This residential area of Robin Hood's Bay boasts the fine 17th-century Old Hall, which was built by the Chomley family of Whitby Abbey.

Keep forward to Robin Hood's Bay.

ROBIN HOOD'S BAY, N Yorks NZ90
Considered one of the most picturesque villages in England, this charming collection of old houses, shops, and inns occupies a precarious cliff-top site and was once a favourite haunt of smugglers. Its steep flights of steps and narrow passages recall unlit boats at the bottom of the cliffs, and furtive movements between houses where well-disguised hiding places waited to be filled with contraband. It is difficult to establish any real connexion between the village and the folk hero after whom it is named but it may be that the famous outlaw leader came here to escape by boat to Europe. During the last decade coastal erosion has destroyed two rows of houses, and the sea is so close that at high tide its waves lash the Bay Hotel. Superb sands are revealed at low tide.

Leave the village on the B1447 SP 'Whitby' and continue to Hawsker.

HAWSKER, N Yorks NZ90
It is thought that the well-preserved 10th-century cross shaft at Old Hall in Hawsker may mark the site of a medieval church. The intricate design of interlaced knot work and bird figures is typical of traditional Norse design.

Drive through the village, meet the A171, and turn right. Descend to Whitby.

WHITBY, N Yorks NZ81
Ruins (AM) of an abbey founded here by St Hilda in 657 can be seen above the town on the East Cliff. Close by is a huge carved cross that was erected in 1898 to commemorate Caedmon, the ancient poet whose *Song of Creation* is considered by some to mark the start of English literature. Below the abbey ruins the River Esk divides the old part of the settlement from the more recent West Cliff area, which is connected to the harbour via a rock-cut passage romantically named after the Khyber Pass. Whitby has always had a strong sea-going tradition and has been the home of many famous maritime figures, including Captain Cook. His house in Grape Street is identified by a plaque, and the stimulus that prompted his nautical career is still a persuasive element in the town's atmosphere – though the 18th-century colliers on which he worked have long since vanished. One of the finest buildings here is St Mary's Church, which stands at the top of a spectacular 199-step flight and contains superb 18th-century craftsmanship. The museum in Pannet Park illustrates fascinating episodes from the town's long history. Local craftsmen have been making ornaments and jewellery from jet, a particularly hard, shiny form of coal found in the area, for hundreds of years. One of the most unusual features of Whitby is a whalebone arch from Norway.

Leave Whitby on the A171 'Teesside' road and in $2\frac{1}{4}$ miles turn left on to the A169 SP 'Pickering'. Drive through Sleights and climb on to Sleights Moor, in the North Yorks Moors National Park.

Several restored steam locomotives run on the North Yorks Moors Railway.

NORTH YORKS MOORS NATIONAL PARK
Heather-clad moors occasionally scored by fertile valleys are the main ingredients in the startlingly open landscape of this 553-square-mile national park. To the west are the rounded heights of the Cleveland and Hambledon Hills, east the rugged beauty of the Yorkshire coast, and south the lush woodlands of the Vale of Pickering.

Continue across Sleights Moor for miles. A short detour from the main route to Goathland can be made by turning right on to an unclassified road and entering the village.

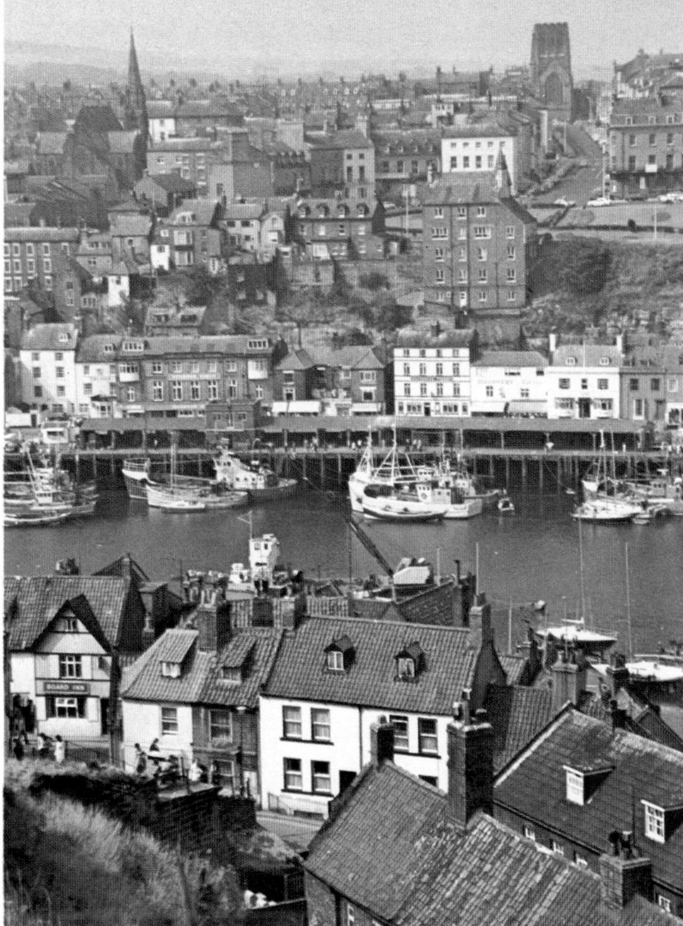
Old cottages line the hills on both sides of Whitby harbour.

GOATHLAND, N Yorks NZ80
All around this greystone moorland village are lovely walks leading past streams that suddenly plunge over rocky lips as spectacular waterfalls. Three superb examples in the immediate neighbourhood are Nelly Ayre Force, Mallyan Spout, and Thomason Force, and dozens of others in varying sizes can be visited by the rambler willing to venture a little farther. The village itself is well known for the Plough Stotts, a traditional group who perform sword dances in the area. A well-preserved stretch of Roman Road (AM) can be seen to the south, and the North Yorks Moors Railway is close by.

NORTH YORKS MOORS RAILWAY
Steam transport enthusiasts have restored and re-opened the old British Rail link that connected Grosmont with Pickering, and in doing so have provided a superb mobile viewpoint from which 18 miles of beautiful national park countryside can be enjoyed in comfortable conditions.

On the main tour, follow the A169 over bleak moorland, with views of Fylingdales Early Warning Station, then pass the lovely Saltersgate Inn and ascend to the Hole of Horcum.

HOLE OF HORCUM, N Yorks SE89
This vast natural hollow in the Yorkshire moorlands shelters the farms of High and Low Horcum, forming a lush oasis of pasture in the wilderness of Levisham Moor.

The Hole of Horcum is a vast bowl of rich grazing land.

After 4 miles reach the Fox and Rabbit Inn, then turn left on to an unclassified road SP 'Thornton Dale'. After another 2 miles turn left SP 'Low Dalby (Forest Drive)' on to a Forestry Commission toll road. Proceed to the hamlet of Low Dalby and turn left on to the Forest Drive SP 'Bickley'.

DALBY FOREST DRIVE, N Yorks SE88
Some 10 miles of well-surfaced roads offer the motorist a route through the beautiful woodlands of Dalby and Bickley Forests, where conifer plantations and stands of mature deciduous trees provide a vast haven for many species of wildlife. Red squirrels inhabit the conifers, the glades are full of wild flowers in spring and summer, and there is constant activity from such common woodland birds as jays, nuthatches, and the tiny goldcrest. A footpath which starts just beyond Staindale leads left to a curious formation of layered limestone known as the Bridestones. Planned amenities include numerous parking places, picnic sites, and forest trails, while many footpaths allow an uninhibited appreciation of the area. The Forest Drive is likely to be closed during periods of very dry weather, when the ever-present fire risk is abnormally high.

Continue along the Forest Drive to a fire tower and turn left, then drive for 2 miles to leave the Forestry Commission roads. Descend (1 in 8), and after $\frac{3}{4}$ mile meet a T-junction and turn right SP 'Scarborough'. Pass the Moorcock Inn at Langdale End and after 1 mile turn sharp right SP 'Troutsdale' and 'Snainton'. Continue along a winding road through Troutsdale; fine views can be enjoyed along the length of this valley, and there is a picnic site near a viewing spot at Cockmoor Hall (not open). Meet a T-junction in Snainton and turn left on to the A170 SP 'Scarborough'. Proceed to Brompton.

BROMPTON, N Yorks SE98
Brompton's greystone Church of All Saints features fine stained glass.

Leave Brompton and continue along the A170 to West and East Ayton.

AYTON, WEST AND EAST, N Yorks SE98
Situated on either side of the River Derwent, the twin villages of East and West Ayton are linked by an attractive 4-arched bridge which dates from 1775. The ruined pele tower of Ayton Castle makes a good counterpoint to the tower of East Ayton's church, on the other bank.

Immediately after crossing the Derwent to enter East Ayton turn left on to an unclassified road. In 2 miles turn right on to a road SP 'Private'. Keep forward at this junction to reach a picnic site and viewpoint. After 2 miles on the private road pass a pond on the right, then after another 1 mile meet a T-junction and turn right to re-enter Scarborough.

TOUR 78 68 MILES

IN THE VALE OF YORK

Away from the gothic completeness of York's superb minster are the rolling farmlands of the Vale of York and dry limestone ridges of the Howardian Hills. Everywhere are monuments to the skills of past generations, and close by are the untamed tracts of the Yorkshire Moors and Dales.

York Minster's magnificent proportions are difficult to appreciate except from a distance.

YORK, N Yorks SE65
Capital of a British province under the Romans in AD 71, this ancient centre is still the chief city of northern England and preserves many fascinating reminders of its historic past. The earliest surviving building is the Roman Multangular Tower, though parts of the city walls derive from the same period – particularly in the section south of Monk Bar. The walls themselves complete a 3-mile circuit round the medieval boundaries of the city and are among the finest examples of their type in Europe. Micklegate Bar, one of four main gates giving access through the defences, is traditionally the only one used by royalty. York's chief glory is its magnificent Minster, which towers over the little streets and houses of the old town. It is the largest gothic cathedral north of the Alps, and its fine windows contain more than half of all the medieval glass surviving in England. One reason for the purity of the Minster's architectural style is the speed with which it was built – between 1220 and 1470 – and the consequent absence of modifications brought about by changing ideas in church design. Many people consider the octagonal Chapter House to be the loveliest part of the overall medieval design; sadly, the last decade has seen rapid deterioration in the building's fabric, and urgent restoration is needed to preserve what must be one of the country's most valuable architectural treasures. As far as fine old churches are concerned, York probably has more than anywhere else in the country except perhaps Norwich. Holy Trinity is of 13th-century date and contains good box pews, All Saints' has medieval glass and carries a beautiful 15th-century tower, and St Mary's Castlegate has a rare Saxon dedication stone. Many of the city's buildings have been standing for 500 years and more, including the lovely Guildhall (AM), the Merchant Adventurers' Hall and Chapel (open), Taylors' Hall (open), and the lovely timbered front and picturesque courtyard of William's College. The latter shows work from later periods, and the 17th-century Treasurer's House (NT) preserves good collections of painting and furniture. Elizabethan King's Manor (open), once the home of the Abbot of St Mary's Abbey, is now owned by York University. It is not surprising that a city with as rich and well-documented history as this should have as many museums as York. Relics from the Roman occupation can be seen in the Yorkshire Museum, in the grounds of ruined St Mary's Abbey, and close to the 13th-century fragments of York Castle (AM) is the Castle Museum of Yorkshire life. Close by in the old Debtors' Prison are collections of dolls and militaria, and the National Steam Museum preserves great

(continues)

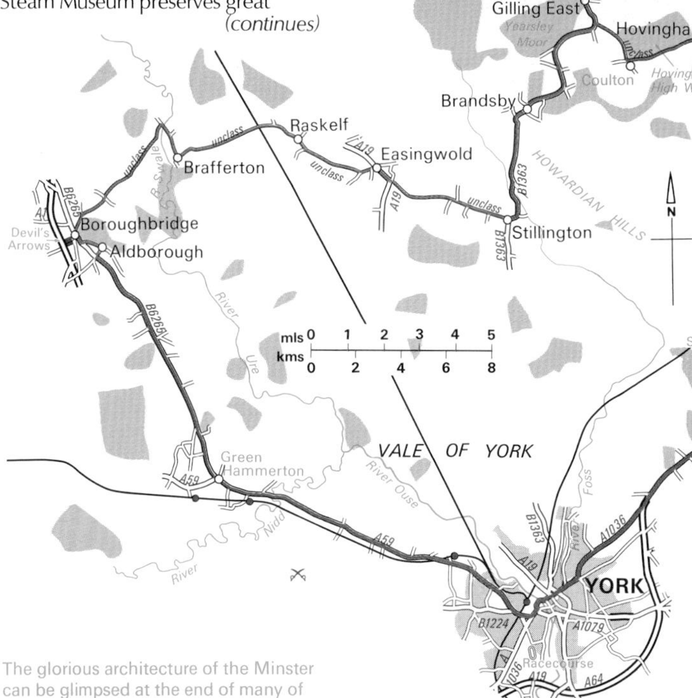

The glorious architecture of the Minster can be glimpsed at the end of many of York's old streets and alleyways.

(continued)
old locomotives such as the *Mallard*. St Mary's Heritage Centre, in Castlegate, uses audio-visual display and the work of contemporary artists to describe the city's architectural development. Over all is a sense of permanence fostered by the mellow stone of a city that is more medieval than modern.

Leave York on the A1036 SP 'East Coast' and 'Malton', then in 3 miles meet a roundabout and take the 1st exit on to the A64 SP 'Malton'. Drive through agricultural country and in 7 miles pass the Spittle Beck Inn. In 1½ miles it is possible to make a short detour from the main route by turning right on to an unclassified road SP 'Kirkham Priory,' descending over a level crossing and the River Derwent, and driving to the hamlet of Kirkham.

KIRKHAM, N Yorks SE76
Ruined Kirkham Priory (AM) includes a beautiful 13th-century gatehouse and a lavatorium, where the monks used to wash.

On the main route, continue along the A64 and in 1 mile turn left on to an unclassified road SP 'Welburn, Castle Howard'. Pass through Welburn, meet crossroads and turn right, then drive through an arch and wall gateway to reach Castle Howard

CASTLE HOWARD, N Yorks SE77
One of the most spectacular houses in Britain, Castle Howard (open) dates from the 17th and 18th centuries and is considered to be the greatest achievement of the architect Vanbrugh. A central dome forms the focal point of the house and is echoed in the 1,000-acre grounds by a circular mausoleum designed by Hawksmoor. Other garden follies include the lovely Temple of the Four Winds, and the huge gatehouse is crowned by a pyramid. Among many treasures inside the house is an extensive collection of period costumes.

The square wooden tower of Raskelf Church, a most unusual feature in this part of England, contrasts pleasantly with the masonry body.

Leave Castle Howard, cross the Howardian Hills, and descend to meet a T-junction at the edge of Slingsby. It 's possible to make a detour from the main route to Slingsby by driving forward at the village crossroads.

SLINGSBY, N Yorks SE67
Misnamed and never completed, the 17th-century house known as Slingsby Castle is a picturesque ruin that adds an air of gothic mystery to the countryside round the village. It was originally started for the soldier, philosopher, and mathematician, Sir Charles Cavendish. A feature of the village itself is its maypole, the scene of great celebrations every May 1.

On the main tour, meet the aforementioned crossroads and turn left on to the B1257 SP 'Helmsley'. Continue to Hovingham.

HOVINGHAM, N Yorks SE67
The stone cottages of this lovely little village cluster round the green under the Saxon tower of All Saints' Church and the stately presence of Hovingham Hall. The latter is an unusual building in distinctive yellow limestone, with a gatehouse that was designed as a riding school where horses could be exercised out of the rain (not open).

In Hovingham turn left on to an unclassified road SP 'Coulton' and 'Easingwold'. Drive through Hovingham High Wood and meet crossroads. Turn right SP 'Gilling' and follow a narrow road for $1\frac{1}{2}$ miles. Meet a T-junction and turn right on to the B1363 to reach Gilling East.

GILLING EAST, N Yorks SE67
It is thought that the architect Vanbrugh may have designed the west front of Gilling Castle (open), though most of the building is much too old for him to have had any hand in its construction. The keep dates from the 14th century, and a well-preserved ribbed plaster ceiling helps to make its dining room one of the finest in England. On either side of the village are the lovely Hambledon and Howardian Hills.

Return south along the B1363 to reach Brandsby.

BRANDSBY, N Yorks SE57
Features of this harmonious hillside village include a woodcarver's shop, an 18th-century hall, and an unusual church with a stone cupola. Neat terraces of cottages complete the picture.

Continue to Stillington, in the Vale of York.

STILLINGTON, N Yorks SE56
The 18th-century writer Laurence Sterne was vicar here for a time, and the lovely old church in which he served features a 12th-century priest's door.

VALE OF YORK, N Yorks
Numerous country lanes bordered by thick hedgerows criss-cross the fertile farmlands of the Vale of York, a large lowland expanse watered by the River Ouse and its many tributaries. Broad water meadows known as 'ings' border the rivers, providing an ideal habitat for marshland wildlife and water loving plants. Here and there large areas of heathland have survived uncultivated, providing ideal hunting grounds for nightjars and vipers.

The Devil's Arrows are a mysterious group of prehistoric standing stones near Boroughbridge.

Drive through Stillington village and pass the church. Keep forward on to an unclassified road SP 'Easingwold', then in $3\frac{1}{2}$ miles meet the A19 and drive forward to enter Easingwold.

EASINGWOLD, N Yorks SE56
An unusual bull ring can be seen in the market place of this pleasant town of red-brick houses and cobbled lanes. The local church contains an ancient parish coffin.

Meet crossroads in Easingwold and turn left on to an unclassified road to reach Raskelf.

RASKELF, N Yorks SE47
The 15th-century tower of local St Mary's church is made of wood and is said to be unique in Yorkshire. Parts of the building's main body date back to Norman times.

In Raskelf bear left then right SP 'Boroughbridge', and drive to Brafferton.

BRAFFERTON, N Yorks SE47
Brafferton Church was extensively restored in Victorian times, but still displays good examples of 15th-century workmanship.

In Brafferton village turn right and after 1 mile cross the River Swale and turn left. In $2\frac{3}{4}$ miles turn left then immediately right, then in 1 mile meet a T-junction and turn left. Continue to a roundabout and take the 1st exit on to the B6265. Cross the River Ure and enter Boroughbridge.

BOROUGHBRIDGE, N Yorks SE36
Three large monoliths known ominously as the Devil's Arrows stand a few hundred yards to the west of Boroughbridge. The largest rises to $22\frac{1}{2}$ft, and it is thought that the group may be some 3,000 years old. On the town side of a fine bridge that spans the Ure is a market place with a 250ft-deep well.

Turn left then keep left through Boroughbridge with SP 'York', and at the far end of the town branch left on to an unclassified road to reach Aldborough.

ALDBOROUGH, N Yorks SE46
This pretty village stands on the site of *Isurium*, the northernmost town to be built without any military motives during the Roman occupation. Remains (AM) revealed through excavation include sections of a boundary wall, two tessellated pavements, and a wide variety of coins, pottery, and artefacts on display in the small site museum. In the village itself are a striking maypole and a cross that probably commemorates the Battle of Boroughbridge, which was fought here in 1322.

Drive to the battle cross and bear right. Pass the church to reach the B6265, turn left to follow the old Ribchester Roman road, and continue to Green Hammerton. Join the A59, and in $1\frac{3}{4}$ miles cross the River Nidd. Drive through low-lying country for the return to York.

Castle Howard is a superb example of Vanbrugh's architectural genius.

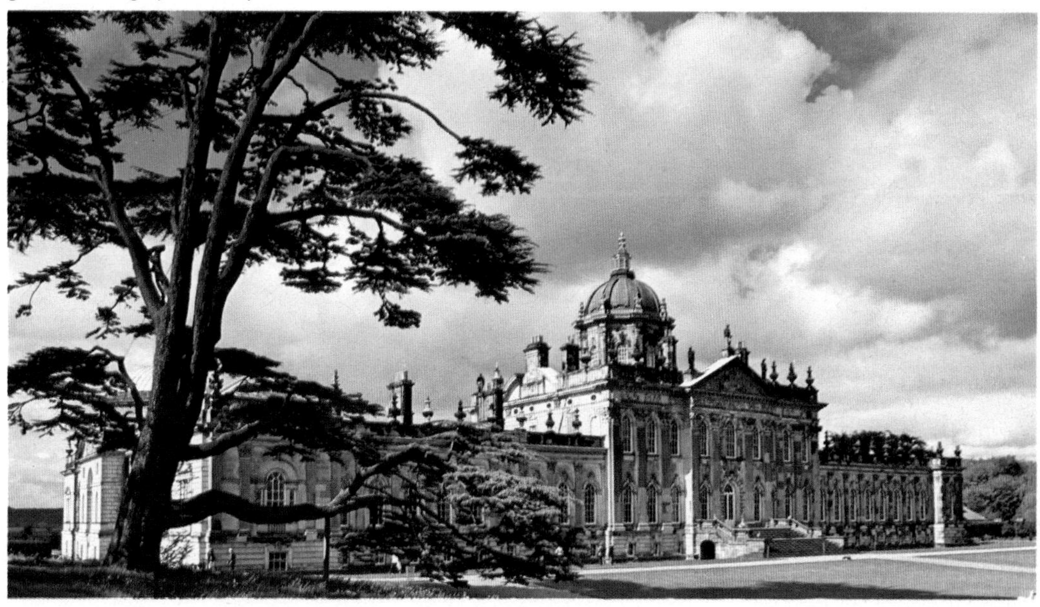

SKIPTON, N Yorks SD95
Attractively situated on the Airedale moorlands at the eastern edge of the Craven district, Skipton is dominated by a medieval castle (open) that was restored by Lady Anne Clifford in 1658. Founded in Norman times, the building was subsequently extended and was strong enough to resist a 3-year siege before falling into the hands of Cromwell's parliamentarian army in the Civil War. The Lord Protector dismantled the castle to make sure that it could never again be manned against him, but thanks to Lady Anne its six massive towers still punctuate the skyline of the town that grew beneath its walls. Opposite the massive castle gateway is the Craven Museum, where exhibits and displays illustrate the geology and folk history of the district. An old four-storey corn mill, on a site where similar buildings have operated since the 12th century, houses the George Leatt Industrial and Folk Museum, where working waterwheels and a collection of carts and horse traps can be seen.

Leave Skipton on the A59 'Harrogate' road, and in ½ mile reach a left turn leading to Embsay. A detour from the main route to the Yorkshire Dales Railway can be made here by turning left and driving to Embsay.

YORKSHIRE DALES RAILWAY, N Yorks SE05
Plans are under way to run track east from Embsay to Bolton Abbey, and the restoration of 13 steam locomotives is well advanced at the Embsay Steam Centre's 18-acre site. Existing facilities for visiting enthusiasts include access to the current work, a signal box, and a personalized saloon car.

On the main tour, leave Skipton via the A59 and drive through a countryside of drystone walls and quarries to Bolton Bridge. Reach the Devonshire Arms Hotel and turn left on to the B6160 SP 'Bolton Abbey', then continue to Bolton Abbey.

TOUR 79 75 MILES

THE YORKSHIRE DALES

Some of England's most impressive scenery can be seen in the rocky clefts of Airedale and Wharfedale, the superb natural amphitheatre of Malham Cove, and the breathtaking gorge of Gordale Scar. Underground are miles of water-worn tunnels, many resplendent with rock and ice formations.

Augustinian monks selected a magnificent site for their abbey at Bolton.

BOLTON ABBEY, N Yorks SE05
Woodlands and pastures in a bend of the River Wharfe make a fittingly peaceful setting for the remains of this once-powerful 12th-century priory (open). Most of the structure lies in ruins, but the nave has served as a parish church for hundreds of years and the old gatehouse was incorporated into a mansion during the 19th century. The little river can be crossed by stepping stones or a footbridge here, and attractive riverside walks extend from the ruins to The Strid.

Continue through a wooded stretch of Wharfedale to reach The Strid and later Barden Tower.

A man-made order is brought to parts of Wharfedale by a pattern of drystone walls.

THE STRID & BARDEN TOWER, N Yorks SE05
The modern translation of the old English word Strid is Turmoil, which is an apt description of the way in which the River Wharfe boils through a 12ft constriction of its gorge at this point. Farther north are the picturesque ruins of Barden Tower, a 12th-century structure that was restored by Lady Anne Clifford of Skipton Castle in 1659.

Reach Barden Tower and turn right on to an unclassified road SP 'Appletreewick'. Cross the river, and turn sharp right on an ascent with SP 'Hazlewood' and 'Storiths'. Continue along a gated road beneath Barden Fell, descend (1 in 5), and cross a ford. Ascend steeply (1 in 4) from the ford, passing The Strid again, and meet the A59. Turn left and ascend a winding road on to Blubberhouses Moor. Enter a narrow rocky valley and climb to the edge of Blubberhouses, at the end of Fewston Reservoir. Cross a river bridge and turn sharp left on to an unclassified road SP 'Pateley Bridge'. Continue over high moorland, and turn left on to the B6265. Stump Cross Cavern lies to the left of the road.

STUMP CROSS CAVERN, N Yorks SE16
Dramatic subterranean formations of ice and eroded rock can be appreciated from a pathway that extends ¼ mile into this cavern.

Continue, with views into beautiful Upper Wharfedale, to Grassington.

GRASSINGTON, N Yorks SE06
The lovely area in which this Upper Wharfedale village stands is rich in mineral deposits and has been settled since very early times. Many iron-age camps and barrows survive, and during the Roman occupation the area was extensively mined for lead ore. The village itself is a popular tourist centre with a cobbled market square reached via a picturesque medieval bridge.

Leave Grassington and follow an unclassified road SP 'Conistone' through wooded country, occasionally passing close to the River Wharfe. Reach Conistone and keep left to meet the B6160. Turn right and continue to Kilnsey Crag.

KILNSEY, N Yorks SD96
This village is completely dwarfed by the great limestone scar of Kilnsey Crag, one of the best-known landmarks in Yorkshire.

A pleasant detour can be made from the main route by continuing along the B6160 to Kettlewell.

KETTLEWELL, N Yorks SD97
At one time this attractive Wharfedale village was a small oasis of civilization in a great tract of forest, but nowadays the drystone-scattered expanses of the open moor extend right to its boundaries. Great Whernside rises to 2,310ft in the north-east.

On the main tour, leave Kilnsey on the B6160 and drive north. In ¾ mile branch left on to an unclassified road SP 'Arncliffe' and drive through Littondale to reach Arncliffe.

ARNCLIFFE, N Yorks SD97
Typical greystone houses of the Dales area nestle amongst clumps of mature sycamores in this secluded Littondale community. Evidence of long occupation is apparent in a clearly-defined Celtic field system in the immediate district, and the village church stands on the site of a building dated c1100. South of Arncliffe is the dramatic mile-long cliff of Yew Cogar Scar.

In Arncliffe turn right SP 'Halton Gill' and continue through Littondale.

LITTONDALE, N Yorks SD97
Once a medieval hunting forest, this lovely dale in the national park has avoided the depredations of the early lead miners. It retains extensive areas of wild woodland, and its farmlands show signs of having been cultivated since early times.

Reach Halton Gill and turn left on to a gated unclassified road. Continue, following SP 'Stainforth' and 'Settle', and ascend (1 in 5) to a road summit of over 1,400ft, with views of Pen-y-Ghent to the right.

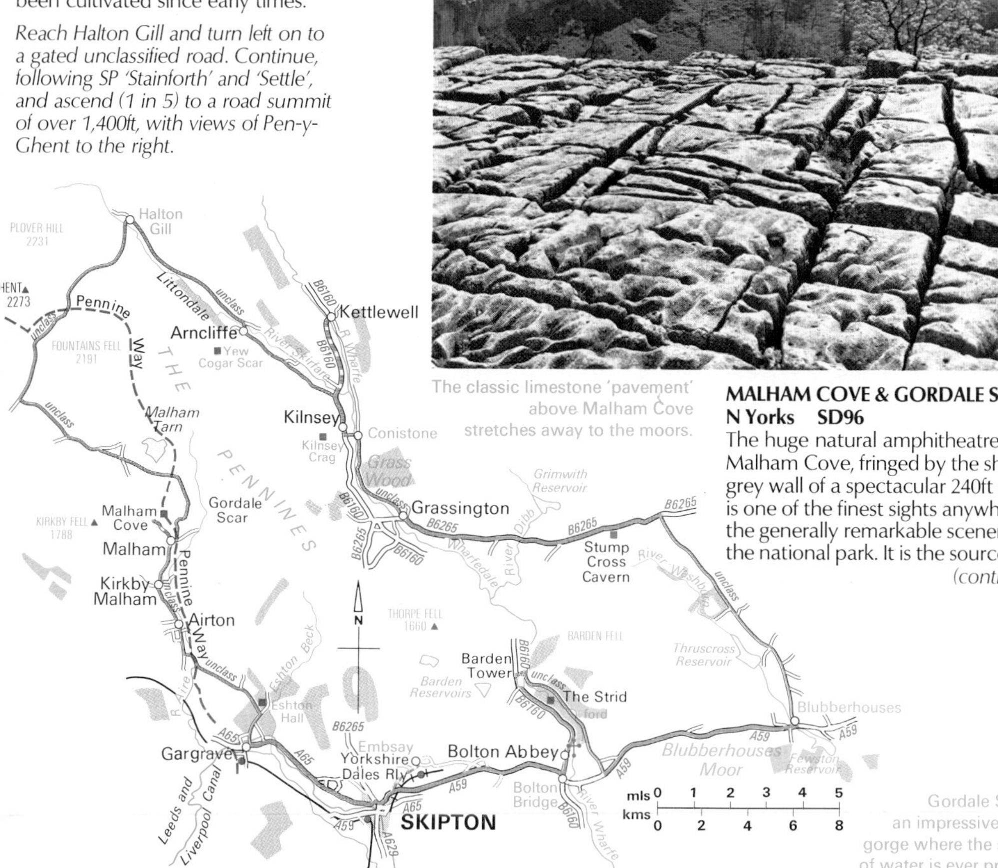

The classic limestone 'pavement' above Malham Cove stretches away to the moors.

PEN-Y-GHENT, N Yorks SD87
Potholing enthusiasts come here to dare the uncertainties of aptly-named Hell Pot and Hunt Pot, two entrances to the cave system that riddles Pen-y-Ghent. Above ground, this 2,273ft summit, one of the famous Three Peaks, affords wide views that extend more than 40 miles to Helvellyn in clear weather. See also tour 85.

Continue along the gated road and turn left on to the 'Malham' road. Ascend (1 in 5) to cross wild moorland, and in 3 miles bear right to meet crossroads. Drive forward on the gated 'Grassington' road to reach the Malham Tarn carpark.

MALHAM TARN, N Yorks SD86
All around the isolated waters of Malham Tarn (NT) are heathery moorlands and unusual raised bogs. The tarn itself is the habitat of many species of aquatic wildlife, and the serious naturalist can familiarize himself with the area at the Field Centre in Malham Tarn House, on the northern shore. Above the field centre are the high white cliffs of Highfolds Scar and a natural limestone pavement.

Leave the Malham Tarn carpark and descend steeply to pass Malham Cove and Gordale Scar.

MALHAM COVE & GORDALE SCAR, N Yorks SD96
The huge natural amphitheatre of Malham Cove, fringed by the sheer grey wall of a spectacular 240ft cliff, is one of the finest sights anywhere in the generally remarkable scenery of the national park. It is the source of *(continues)* the River Aire and forms part of a 22-mile fault that resulted from the intolerable stresses imposed by enormous glaciers during the ice ages. An energetic scramble leads to the moorland above and Malham Tarn. Gordale Scar, a precipitous, winding gorge filled with the sound of waterfalls and dashing cascades, can be reached from the cove via a $1\frac{1}{2}$-mile footpath.

Gordale Scar is an impressive 240ft gorge where the sound of water is ever present.

MALHAM, N Yorks SD96
In the height of the summer season this little stone village is inundated by visitors who flock to the area for its magnificent scenery. Information about the Malham district is available from the Yorkshire Dales National Park Interpretation Centre, which is based in the village. See also tour 81.

THE PENNINE WAY
From its southern extremity in Derbyshire, this 250-mile footpath follows the mountainous spine of England and passes through Malham before crossing Pen-y-Ghent on its way to Kirk Yetholme in Scotland. Prospective walkers should realize that this is a fairly rugged route, particularly in its northern sections, and can be positively hazardous in bad weather. See also tour 89.

Leave Malham with SP 'Skipton' and continue to Kirkby Malham.

KIRKBY MALHAM, N Yorks SD86
Close to the local 17th-century vicarage is the charming village church, containing a 12th-century font and family box pews of the Georgian period.

Drive through the village to Airton.

AIRTON, N Yorks SD95
Situated in Upper Airedale, this charming village is on the route of the Pennine Way and boasts several good 17th-century buildings. The most notable are the Manor House, the Friend's Meeting House, and the Post Office.

Leave Airton, continue for $\frac{3}{4}$ mile, and turn left. Drive through the grounds of Eshton Hall (not open) and turn right to reach Gargrave.

GARGRAVE, N Yorks SD95
Although Gargrave's parish church is mostly Victorian, it retains a 16th-century tower and fragments of several Saxon crosses.

Meet the A65 in Gargrave and turn left to cross the Leeds and Liverpool Canal.

LEEDS & LIVERPOOL CANAL
Wonderful scenery that can only be guessed at by the road-bound tourist is revealed to anybody who takes the trouble to hire a boat on this 127-mile canal. It is the longest waterway in Britain, and rises to 500ft above sea level as it crosses the high ridge of the Pennine Chain.

Continue along the A65 to re-enter Skipton.

RIPON, N Yorks SE37
Popularly known as the Gateway to the Dales, this attractive city stands at the meeting of the Rivers Ure, Skell, and Laver and boasts a small but impressive cathedral. The main features of this lovely 12th-century building include a Saxon crypt that may be the earliest Christian survival in England, a fine early-English west front, and a beautiful 15th-century screen. Excellent examples of local woodcarving are the finely worked misericords and curious Elephant and Castle bench. Every night Ripon's market square is the scene of a 1,000-year-old custom, when the town Hornblower or Wakeman strides out in his tricorn hat and sounds his ancient horn at each corner of a huge 18th-century obelisk. Years ago this sound indicated that the Wakeman had begun his night watch over the town, and that the townspeople could sleep secure in their beds. The half-timbered Wakeman's house, later used by the mayor, dates from the 13th century and now contains a museum. Near by is a good 18th-century town hall. Other buildings of the same period grace the town.

Before Ripon is left on the main tour route, a short detour can be made to Newby Hall: follow the B6265 SP 'Boroughbridge' to pass Ripon Racecourse and cross the River Ure, then turn right on to an unclassified road and in $\frac{1}{4}$ mile turn right again to reach Newby Hall.

NEWBY HALL, N Yorks SE36
Some of Robert Adam's finest work can be seen in his additions to this splendid Queen Anne House (open), which contains superb Gobelin tapestries and an important collection of classical sculpture. The beautiful grounds run down to the River Ure and contain a miniature railway.

To leave Ripon on the main tour follow SP 'Pateley Bridge B6265'. In $2\frac{1}{4}$ miles reach Studley Royal and Studley Royal Park.

STUDLEY ROYAL, N Yorks SE26
The fine house that once graced this lovely park burned down in 1945, and the present owner lives in a converted stable block that dates from the 18th century. Attractive estate cottages cluster round a 19th-century church that is considered the ecclesiastical masterpiece of architect William Burges and has a very rich interior. The park (open), landscaped in the 18th century, features many of the conceits of the period, including a temple folly and various statues. Its lakes and woodland combine in a sylvan beauty which is enhanced by grazing herds of deer and livestock, and at one point adjoins the magnificent ruins of Fountains Abbey.

Leave Studley Royal on the B6265 and after $\frac{3}{4}$ mile turn left on to an unclassified road to reach the impressive ruins of Fountains Abbey.

ALONG THE EDGE OF THE DALES

Between York and the deep Dales country is a gentler area of farmland. Here the landscape is dotted with curiously-weathered rocks rising from deep vegetation, peaceful reservoirs, and ancient ruins beside enchanting rivers. A foretaste of the Dales is given in How Stean Gorge.

Ripon's Town Hall reminds the citizens of the Wakeman's traditional role.

FOUNTAINS ABBEY, N Yorks SE26
Generally considered to be the finest in England, the remarkably well-preserved ruins of this 12th- to 15th-century Cistercian abbey (AM) are part of the Studley Royal estate (open) and clearly demonstrate the layout of a Norman and medieval monastic foundation. Particularly notable are the nave, tower, and lay-brothers' quarters. Opposite the ruins is Fountains Hall, which was built with stone taken from the abbey in the 17th century.

Return to the B6265 and turn left, drive through wooded countryside, and emerge on to Pateley Moor for views over Nidderdale. A short detour from the main route to Brimham Rocks can be made by driving to the road summit on the moor and turning left.

Fountains Abbey was once the wealthiest Cistercian house in England.

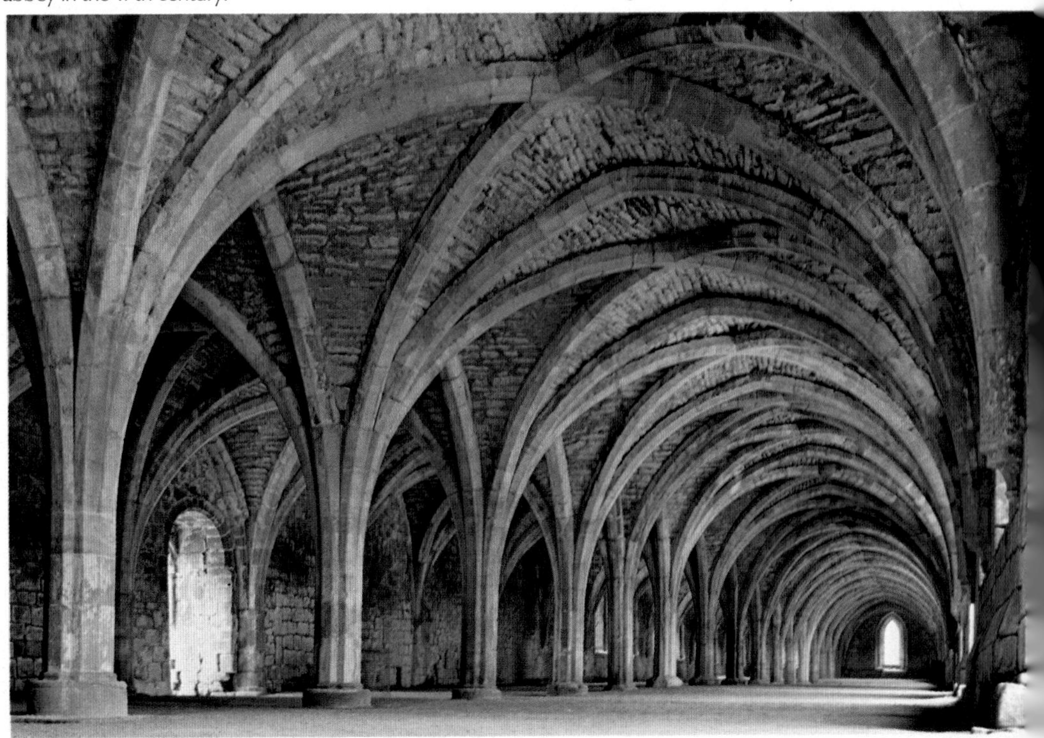

BRIMHAM ROCKS, N Yorks SE26
Thousands of years of wind and rain have sculpted the millstone grit of this group of rocks into a variety of weird and wonderful shapes. The surrounding moorland (NT) offers excellent views and is a popular site for picnics.

On the main tour, continue along the B6265 and later turn right to descend to Pateley Bridge.

PATELEY BRIDGE, N Yorks SE16
Since ancient times this pleasant market town has been a focus for the everyday life of Nidderdale, but nowadays its steep main street is busy as much with tourists as with local traffic. The picturesque ruins of Old St Mary's Church occupy a lofty hillside site, and the Nidderdale Museum displays over 3,000 items relating to life in the Yorkshire Dales. Of particular note are the Victorian Room and a replica cobbler's shop. West of the town are the fascinating Stump Cross Caverns – more than $\frac{1}{4}$ mile of natural passages and caves featuring many strange rock formations.

Leave Pateley Bridge and cross the River Nidd, then take the next turning on the right SP 'Ramsgill' to join an unclassified road. Drive for 1 mile to reach Foster Beck Flax Mill.

FOSTER BECK FLAX MILL, N Yorks SE16
Industrial archaeology enthusiasts will find this well-restored flax mill of considerable interest. Now a restaurant, it is built of local stone and features a huge 17th-century water wheel that is the second largest in the country.

Drive alongside Gouthwaite Reservoir and continue to Ramsgill and Lofthouse, at the head of Nidderdale.

NIDDERDALE, N Yorks
Part of the lovely valley of the River Nidd, Nidderdale is rich in mineral deposits and has been mined for lead and iron for many centuries. Its stone has also been in great demand for building, and the landscape is pitted with the overgrown remains of worked-out quarries. All along the river, from its high source in the rugged fell country of Great Whernside to the lush lower parts of its valley, the scenery offers plenty of incentives for the motorist to leave his car and explore on foot.

The huge water wheel at Foster Beck flax mill

LOFTHOUSE AND HOW STEAN GORGE, N Yorks SE17
The pretty Upper Nidderdale village Lofthouse is a good centre from which to explore the beautiful How Stean Gorge, a 70ft-deep cleft accessible by footpaths that thread their way along its rocky sides and over little bridges. The largest of two interesting caves here is Elgin's Hole, which penetrates nearly a mile into the roots of Middlesmoor Hill.

Return alongside Gouthwaite Reservoir to reach the B6265 and turn left to re-enter Pateley Bridge. Leave the town on the B6165 SP 'Harrogate' to reach Summer Bridge, then turn right on to the B6451 'Otley' road. Follow a long climb past Menwith Hill Wireless Station and turn right on to the A59 'Skipton' road, then proceed to Blubberhouses, at the north-west end of Fewston Reservoir. Drive to the village church, turn left on to the unclassified 'Timble' road, then take the next turning left SP 'Fewston'. Continue through pine forests, cross a dam separating Fewston and Swinsty Reservoirs, and continue to Fewston.

FEWSTON, W Yorks SE15
This charming village faces across Fewston Reservoir to the historic remains of a 16th-century hall (not open). The lovely village church dates from the 17th century.

Keep right through Fewston and cross the end of Swinsty Reservoir, then meet the B6451 'Otley' road and turn right across Sandwith Moor. Follow a long descent to Lindley Wood Reservoir and enter Otley.

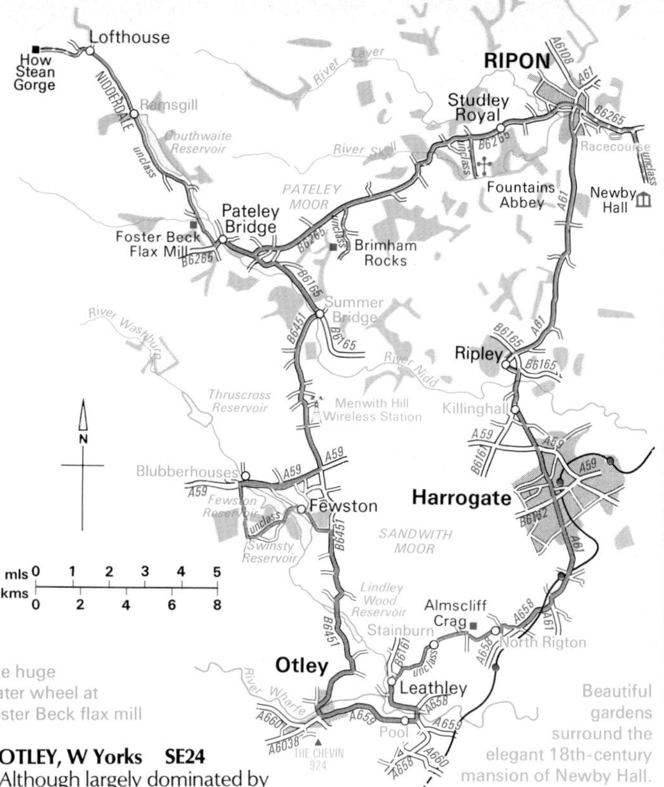

OTLEY, W Yorks SE24
Although largely dominated by modern industry, this old market town on the River Wharfe retains several good buildings as reminders of its long history. Among these are old inns and a fine cruciform church containing fragments of Saxon crosses and a good Georgian pulpit. A curious memorial in the churchyard commemorates the men who lost their lives while working on the Bramhope railway tunnel between 1845 and 1849. Close to the town are the fine Elizabethan halls of Farnley, where the artist Turner was a visitor, and Western. Above the town is the 925ft summit of Otley Chevin, from which panoramic views over the lovely countryside of Lower Wharfedale can be enjoyed.

Leave Otley on the A659 'Tadcaster' road and follow the River Wharfe to reach Pool. Turn left on to the A658 SP 'Harrogate', then cross the river and turn left again on to the B6161 to reach Leathley.

LEATHLEY, N Yorks SE24
Outside the Norman and later church in Leathley are the old village stocks and a mounting block. The local almshouses and hall date from the 18th century.

In Leathley turn right on to the unclassified 'Stainburn' road and follow SP 'Rigton' to reach lofty Almscliff Crag.

ALMSCLIFF CRAG, N Yorks SE24
This high crag affords superb views and has been the training ground for some of Britain's best-known rock climbers. The climbing faces should not be attempted without proper experience and equipment.

Continue to North Rigton and turn left, then right, to meet a junction with the A658. Turn left SP 'Harrogate' and in 1¾ miles turn left again on to the A61 to reach Harrogate.

HARROGATE, N Yorks SE35
One of the chief towns in Yorkshire's old West Riding, Harrogate achieved early fame as a spa resort and nowadays is an important conference centre. Its mineral springs were discovered in the 16th century, and the Royal Pump Room was built as the country's first public baths in 1842. From that time onwards the town's popularity steadily increased, resulting in a wealth of dignified stone buildings and beautiful gardens that have made it known as the Floral Resort of England. The Valley Gardens are particularly notable, and the Harlow Car Trial Gardens are used for experimental horticulture. Some 200 acres of commonland know as The Stray, a popular place for walking and picnics, borders the southern boundary of the town. An interesting museum of local history, Victoriana, and costumes is housed in the 19th-century Pump Room.

Leave Harrogate on the A61 SP 'Ripon' and drive to Killinghall. Continue for 1 mile beyond that village, cross the River Nidd, and meet a roundabout. Take the first exit on to an unclassified road and enter Ripley.

Beautiful gardens surround the elegant 18th-century mansion of Newby Hall.

RIPLEY, N Yorks SE26
Much of this attractive village was rebuilt during the 19th century, but it is largely unspoilt and retains an ancient market cross and stocks in its cobbled square. Ripley Castle (open), home of the Ingilby family since 1350, shows workmanship of mainly 16th- and 18th-century date and stands in beautiful grounds landscaped by Capability Brown. Its gatehouse is a fine building of c1450, and one of its floors was made from the timber of a British man-of-war. Oliver Cromwell stayed at the house on the eve of the Battle of Marston Moor in 1644, and armour from the opposing Royalist army is on view. Notable tombs and memorial brasses can be seen in the village church, and the churchyard features a curious weeping cross with eight niches in which sinners could kneel and repent.

Drive through Ripley, meet a roundabout, and take the 2nd exit to rejoin the A61. Return through undulating countryside to Ripon.

'Capability' Brown landscaped the grounds of Ripley Castle.

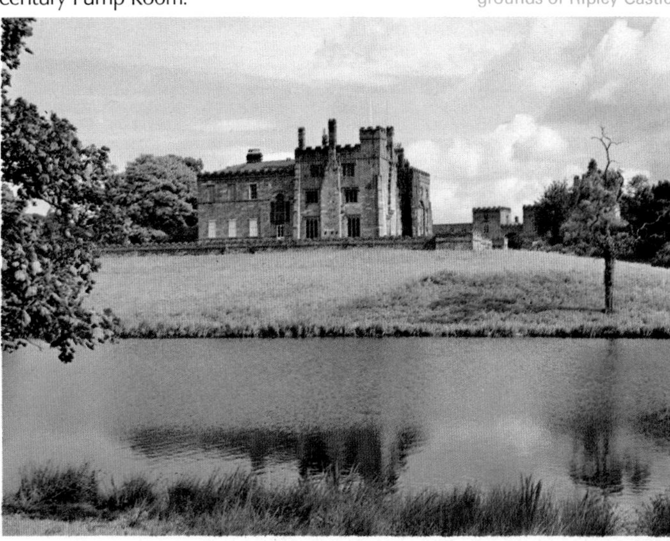

RICHMOND, N Yorks NZ10
Dramatically situated overlooking the River Swale, this attractive and historic town makes an excellent base from which to explore the lovely countryside of Swaledale. The dominant feature of the town is its massive Norman castle (AM), one of the earliest in Britain with 11th-century curtain walls round a splendid keep. In the shadow of its mighty presence are streets of lovely old buildings, all illustrative of important phases in Richmond's past. The cobbled Market Place is one of the largest in the country and is approached along little alleyways known as wynds. Greyfriars Tower is the remnant of an abbey that was founded here many centuries ago, and facing the Market Place is one of the strangest churches in England. Dedicated to the Holy Trinity, its main body and medieval tower are divided from each other by shops and offices actually built into its main structure. Other buildings in this area include several handsome Georgian and Victorian houses. The most outstanding Georgian building in the town is the Little Theatre (open) of 1788, beautifully restored and the oldest theatre in the country to have survived in its original condition. A Green Howards' Museum displays the colourful and fascinating history of that regiment. Many fine walks can be enjoyed in and around Richmond, but one of the closest and best is along the banks of the Swale to spacious parklands at Lowenthwaite Bridge.

Leave Richmond on the A6108 SP 'Scotch Corner' and branch left on to the B6274 for Gilling West. Ascend to high ground, turn left on to the A66 'Brough' road, and continue along a pleasant road to Greta Bridge, on the Rivers Greta and Tees, with views across moors and valleys.

GRETA BRIDGE, Durham NZ01
Among the many artists and writers who have recognized and recorded the beauty of this charming little hamlet are Dickens, Scott, and Turner. Just to the north is the junction of the Greta with the Tees, and south-west of Greta Bridge the river runs through the lovely woodland of Brignall Banks. Features of the hamlet itself include a picturesque river bridge dating from the 18th century, and the Morrit Arms public house, whose site was once occupied by a Roman fort.

Continue along the A66 'Brough' road for $\frac{1}{2}$ mile and turn right on to an unclassified road SP 'Barnard Castle'. In $1\frac{1}{4}$ miles are views ahead of Egglestone Abbey.

EGGLESTONE ABBEY, Durham NZ01
The waters of the River Tees add an extra dimension to the picturesque quality of these lovely remains (AM). See also tour 89.

Turn right and cross the River Tees to reach the Bowes Museum.

TOUR 81 — 71 MILES

THE NORTHERN DALES

In the northern part of the Yorkshire Dales national park are the great ice-scoured valleys of Wharfedale and Swaledale, carved out to their present size by huge glaciers that flowed across the Pennines over a million years ago. On the moors above are greystone villages and steep, sheep-cropped slopes.

Below the huge bulk of Richmond's 11th-century castle are picturesque streets displaying an attractive mixture of architectural styles. The abundance of Georgian design is particularly noticeable.

BOWES MUSEUM, Durham NZ01
Built in the style of a French château, the building that houses this museum is an architectural surprise to eyes that have come to expect the solid little stone houses of the area. Inside is one of the finest art collections in Britain, featuring fine European paintings, furniture, porcelain, tapestries, jewellery, and dolls. See also tour 89.

Continue to Barnard Castle.

BARNARD CASTLE, Durham NZ01
Ancient houses and several inns line the main street of this enchanting town, which has grown up round the walls of its ruined medieval castle (AM) and is a busy market centre for its area. See also tour 89.

Leave Barnard Castle with the A67 SP 'Brough, Bowes', re-cross the River Tees, and turn left on to the B6277 SP 'Scotch Corner'. Drive through woodland to meet the A66, turn right, and in $\frac{1}{2}$ mile turn left on to an unclassified road SP 'Reeth'. A short detour can be made from the main route to Bowes Castle by continuing along the A66.

BOWES CASTLE, Durham NY91
Close to the ruined keep of this Norman castle (AM) are the military remains of the Roman fort of *Lavatrae* (AM), which preceded it.

On the main tour, continue along an unclassified moorland road, with occasional steep hills (1 in 4), and drive through the pines of Stang Forest before climbing to a road summit of 1,677ft. Breathtaking views extend into lonely Arkengarthdale, in the vast and very beautiful Yorkshire Dales National Park.

YORKSHIRE DALES NATIONAL PARK
The boundaries of this national park encompass nearly 700 square miles of high dells scored by literally dozens of lovely river valleys that have collectivey come to be known as the Yorkshire Dales. Many great dales exist in the region, but Wharfedale and Airedale are probably the most famous. The desolate rocky scenery in the high part of the first mentioned gradually softens towards its lower reaches, and Airdale opens out into spectacular limestone scenery as it drops towards the village of Malham. In the south are the Three Peaks, well known for their dangerous potholes, while the length of the park is threaded by the Pennine Way long-distance footpath. Movement and sound is brought to the region by delightful waterfalls and lakes fed by rapid streams that rise in the rocky countryside of the high fells. This is the main dales tour, but the region is also visited by tours 79, 80, and 89.

ARKENGARTHDALE, N Yorks NZ00
Lead mining was carried on in this lovely valley from the 13th to 19th centuries, and traces can be seen today. The dale itself is a lovely valley that follows the course of the Arkle Beck to impressive Swaledale in the south-east.

Cross Arkle Beck and drive along Arkengarthdale, passing through Langthwaite to reach Reeth.

REETH, N Yorks SE09
During the 19th century this one-time market town became a busy centre of the lead-mining industry o nearby Arkengarthdale. Nowadays i is a peaceful village charmingly grouped round its large green, withi easy reach of some of the wildest country in the national park.

In Reeth turn left on to the B6270 'Richmond' road. Continue through pleasant countryside to Grinton.

GRINTON, N Yorks SE09
Grinton Church is a splendid buildir that has come to be known as the Cathedral of the Dales. It was founded in Norman times and contains an ancient font that is probably its original. Other features include beautiful screenwork and a Jacobean pulpit.

Gradually descend along Swaledale, between moorland heights that rise steeply to over 1,400ft from the rive

SWALEDALE, N Yorks SE09
Among the many relics of 18th- an 19th-century lead mining that still litter this wild and deep valley are remains of some of the 20 smelt mi that were used to process the ore. The valley itself is a deep cleft that runs west from Richmond, and is connected to Wensleydale via the bleak Buttertubs Pass.

Enter woodland and meet the A61C turn right and follow SP 'Leyburn' to reach Downholme.

DOWNHOLME, N Yorks SE19
This tiny village stands high above the River Swale and has an attracti church that features Norman workmanship.

Proceed along a winding moorlan road, passing through Bellerby to reach Leyburn.

Arkengarthdale is one of Yorkshire's nore secluded dales.

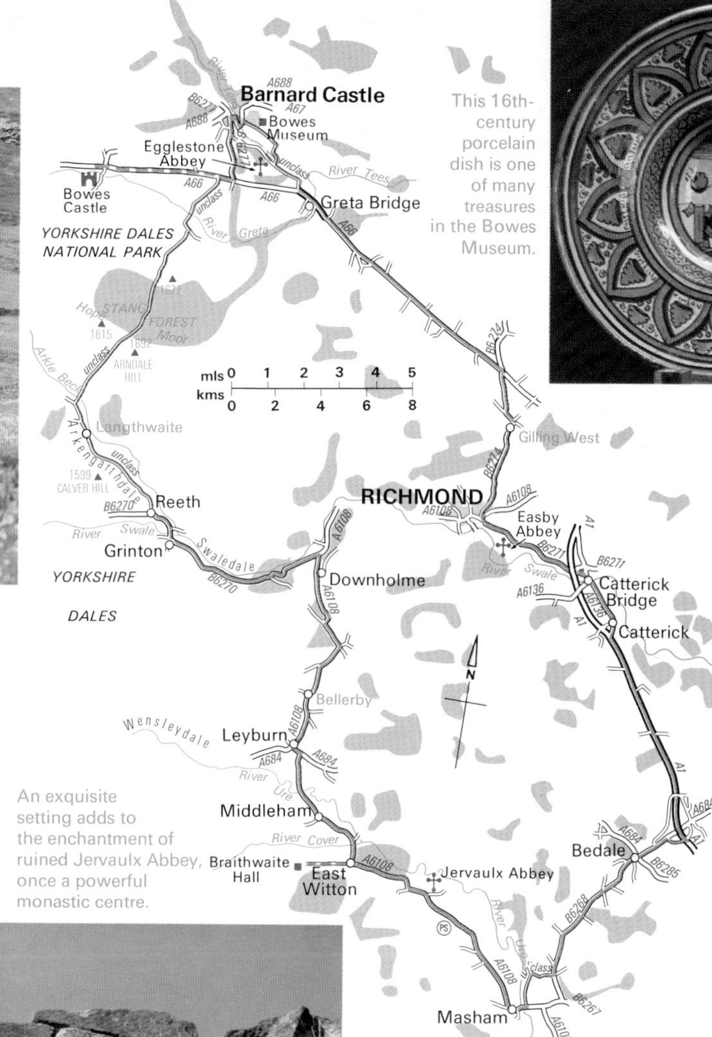

This 16th-century porcelain dish is one of many treasures in the Bowes Museum.

.EYBURN, N Yorks SE19

'he sloping market place in this old own is an appropriate example of he switchback landscape of the ocal countryside. Its Wensleydale osition, above the River Ure, makes an ideal touring base. Within easy valking distance of the town centre a 2-mile limestone scar known as he Shawl, which affords excellent iews into Wensleydale.

An exquisite setting adds to the enchantment of ruined Jervaulx Abbey, once a powerful monastic centre.

ENSLEYDALE, N Yorks

iry herds from the many farms attered along the length of this tile valley convert the freshness of lush pastures into rich milk from ich the distinctive Wensleydale eese is made. The villages of the e are generally small and without eption charming. Here and there pastoral solitude is emphasized by sound of falling water.

leave Leyburn follow SP ddleham' to the end of the town I turn right on to the A6108. scend and cross the River Ure via inusual bridge to reach the ge of Middleham.

MIDDLEHAM, N Yorks SE18

Once the chief town of Wensleydale, this scenic village is now an important horse breeding and training centre and a good touring base. Its impressive ruined castle (AM) was the seat of the powerful Neville family, who controlled much of the area from the massive keep that still stands at its full height behind well-preserved 13th-century curtain walls. Close by is the curious Swine Cross.

Continue along the A6108 'Masham' road, with moorland to the right and gentle riverside pastures to the left. Continue to East Witton.

EAST WITTON, N Yorks SE18

Most of the houses in this compact village are contained in two main rows facing two 19th-century churches and an attractive 17th-century bridge.

A detour can be made from the main route to Braithwaite Hall by turning right in East Witton and driving in partly-wooded country for 2 miles.

BRAITHWAITE HALL, N Yorks SE18

Now in use as a farm, this fine 17th-century house (NT) stands in attractive pastoral countryside and is open by appointment. Near by a large hillfort occupies a $2\frac{1}{2}$-acre site.

On the main tour, continue along the A6108 to reach Jervaulx Abbey.

JERVAULX ABBEY, N Yorks SE18

Cistercian monks chose this beautiful riverside site as a fitting setting for their abbey in the 12th century. Although it was destroyed in the 15th century, enough remains to show today's visitors the exquisite proportions of their achievement. Particularly notable are the remains of the monks' dormitory, which features a hall and beautiful lancet windows of the period.

Continue along the A6108 and pass the Ellington Firth Picnic Site before entering Masham.

MASHAM, N Yorks SE28

Masham's former importance as a market town can be judged from the huge square, which is dominated by a traditional maypole. In the churchyard of St Mary's are important remains of a Saxon cross, and the mainly-Norman church carries a beautiful 15th-century spire.

Leave Masham on the A6108 'Ripon' road. Cross the river, then immediately turn left on to the unclassified 'Bedale' road. Follow the river and in 1 mile turn right, then continue for $\frac{3}{4}$ mile and turn left on to the B6268. Continue to Bedale.

BEDALE, N Yorks SE28

This mainly Georgian town features an old stepped market cross in the main street, and an unusual church whose first floor is reached by a stair guarded by a portcullis. These elaborate precautions were taken against the very real possibility of Scottish raids. Opposite the church is Georgian Bedale Hall (open), a fine house with a museum and a complete ballroom wing.

Continue along the A684 'Northallerton' road and later turn right, following SP 'Scotch Corner' to join the A1. Continue on a fast section of dual carriageway on the Great North Road and meet a roundabout. Join the A6136 to reach Catterick.

CATTERICK, N Yorks SE29

Known mainly for the military training area on its borders, this delightful little grey-stone village has a good church of c1500. Inside the church are two 15th-century brasses.

Drive through Catterick to Catterick Bridge, on the Swale.

CATTERICK BRIDGE, N Yorks SE09

Most people come here to watch horse racing on the famous local course, but the lovely little local bridge that spans the Swale dates from 1422 and is worth attention. The local scenery is superb.

Turn right and cross the River Swale, then turn left SP 'Richmond' and meet the B6271. On the left are the river and Easby Abbey.

EASBY ABBEY, N Yorks NZ10

Picturesque ruins of an abbey founded in 1155 grace the beautiful surroundings of this Swaleside site. The remains (AM) are considerable.

Continue along the B6271 for the return to Richmond.

TOUR 82 — 74 MILES

TO THE WEST PENNINES

Between the elegant seaside resort of Southport and the wild western slopes of the Pennines is the Lancashire Plain, an area of farm and parkland where much of the county's folk history is preserved in picturesque villages, great houses in fine grounds, and fascinating small town museums.

The village cross guards a picturesque approach to St Michael's Church, Croston.

SOUTHPORT, Merseyside SD31
Particularly well known for its beautifully laid out gardens, this attractive and elegant resort is also noted for its wide range of sporting facilities. It is the home of the Royal Birkdale Golf Club, which has been the venue for Ryder Cup competitions, and is host to county cricket matches, horse jumping trials, and lawn tennis matches. The annual flower show is also a popular event. Amenities for holiday-makers include 6 miles of excellent sands, the largest pier in England, a model village, and boat hire on the 91-acre Marine Lake. The Victorian heyday of seaside holidays is recalled by old salt-water swimming baths and a room of the Botanic Gardens Museum. An interesting collection of fine buildings and shops can be found in Lord Street, which is considered one of the finest thoroughfares in the north of England. Churches in Southport include St Cuthbert's, which displays fine woodwork and a clock of 1739, and a curious red and yellow building in the suburb of Crossens. The latter building shares its churchyard with a very ornate neo-Norman mausoleum. The rapidly expanding Steam Transport Museum boasts a fine collection of locomotives, buses, traction engines, and various commercial vehicles. It is planned to become the largest centre of its type in the north of England, and will be a valuable aid to the understanding of industrial archaeology in transport.

Leave Southport on the A565 SP 'Preston', passing through Crossens. After 3 miles turn right on to the B5246 SP 'Rufford'. Continue through Mere Brow, Holmeswood, and Rufford, and meet the A59 SP 'Preston'. Turn left, and after $\frac{1}{2}$ mile reach the entrance to Rufford Old Hall on the right.

RUFFORD OLD HALL, Lancs SD41
This superb timber-framed Tudor building (NT) stands in $14\frac{1}{2}$ acres of beautiful grounds and is one of the finest examples surviving in England today. Built by the Hesketh family in the 15th century, it was slightly extended during Victorian times but has not been spoilt by 19th-century over restoration. The exterior is a startling combination of decorative black timbers infilled with brilliant white plaster, and the great hall carries an extremely ornate hammerbeam roof. Inside the house is a rare 15th-century screen, and one of the wings contains the Philip Ashcroft Museum of folk crafts and antiquities.

Leave Rufford Old Hall and continue along the A59 for 1 mile, then turn right on to the A581 'Chorley' road. Continue along the A581 to the Leeds and Liverpool Canal.

Unusual 17th-century windows at Astley Hall dominate the exterior.

LEEDS AND LIVERPOOL CANAL, Lancs
As it crosses the rugged Pennine Chain this 127-mile waterway between two of northern England's major cities reaches an amazing 500ft above sea level. The canal took 40 years to build and has many features of interest to naturalists and industrial archaeologists.

Proceed along the A581, crossing the River Douglas, and later turn left over a bridge to reach Croston.

CROSTON, Lancs SD41
Picturesque countryside following the twisting course of the River Yarrow makes a fine setting for this tiny village. Among its most notable buildings are 17th-century almshouses and a 15th-century church containing a curious memorial brass.

From Croston, turn right and in $\frac{1}{4}$ mile meet a war memorial. Turn left here and in 1 mile meet a T-junction. Turn right and continue along the A581 for $3\frac{1}{2}$ miles. Cross the M6, then meet the A49 and turn left. Turn right on to the A581. Drive for a short distance to reach Astley Hall on the left.

ASTLEY HALL, Lancs SD51
Charmingly set in nearly 100 acres of wood and parkland, this fine 16th-century and later house (open) has a drawing room with lovely tapestries depicting scenes from the legend of the Golden Fleece. Throughout the house are fine collections of furnishings, pottery and paintings, and special exhibitions are frequently mounted in its rooms.

Leave Astley Hall and proceed along the A581 into Chorley.

CHORLEY, Lancs SD51
Industry is this old textile centre's way of life. It was once known for cotton weaving and calico printing, but in recent years these traditional concerns have been largely replaced by a variety of modern enterprises. The town stands at the edge of farming country close to the foot of the Pennines. The area is dominated by the imposing height of 682ft Healey Nab which rises to the east.

Meet traffic signals in Chorley and turn left on to the A6 SP 'Preston'. In 1 mile cross a railway bridge, meet a roundabout, and take the 2nd exit on to the A674 SP 'M6' and 'Blackburn'. Continue, with Healey Nab rising to the right, and drive through Higher Wheelton. In 2 miles meet a roundabout; a detour from the main route can be taken here by following the 1st exit on to the A675 to reach Hoghton Tower.

HOGHTON TOWER, Lancs SD62
Ancestral home of what is claimed to be the oldest baronetcy in England, this fine 16th-century mansion occasionally opens its stat rooms, ballroom, Tudor wellhouse, and dungeon to the public. The gardens can also be visited at certai times. In 1617 King James I stayed here, and is said to have been so taken with a loin of beef prepared by the house kitchen that he drew his sword and knighted it, ever sinc which that particular cut has been sirloin – a charming, if dubious, tale

On the main tour, take the 2nd exit from the roundabout and continue for $\frac{1}{2}$ mile to meet a T-junction. Turr right to reach Fensicowles, then me the A6062 and turn right SP 'Darwe In $\frac{1}{2}$ mile drive under a railway bridg and immediately turn right on to an unclassified road, then turn left. Continue for 1 mile to the Black Bull (PH), meet crossroads, and drive forward. In 1 mile meet the A666 ar drive forward on to the B6231 SP 'Accrington'. In $\frac{1}{2}$ mile pass a railway bridge and ascend to Guide, then meet crossroads by the King Edwar VII (PH). Turn right on to the B6232 'Bury', then keep left and after 2 mil reach the Grey Mare Inn; turn right to an unclassified road SP 'Edgwortl Drive to Edgworth, meet crossroad and continue forward to reach Turt Bottoms. Meet a T-junction with th main road and turn sharp right on t the B6391 SP 'Darwen'. Turton Tow stands to the left.

Turton Tower features ornate 19th-century timbering.

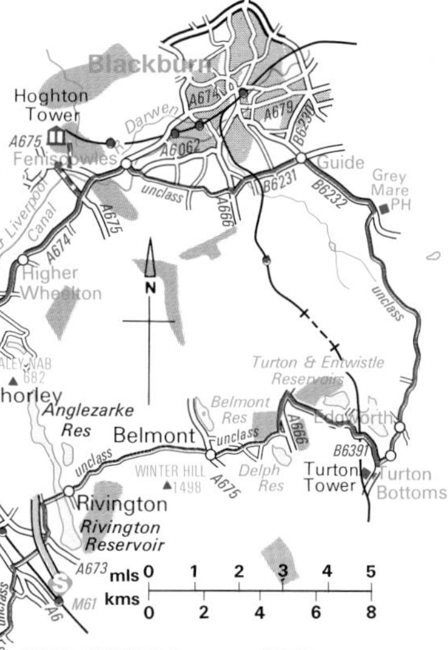

URTON TOWER, Lancs SD71
he core of this L-shaped building pen) is a 15th-century pele tower, a pe of fortified dwelling that was nce common in the north of ngland. Two wings were added in he 16th century, and the house now ontains fine collections of paintings nd furnishings, plus a fascinating lk museum.

Continue north along the B6391 with views of the Turton and Entwhistle Reservoirs on the right. In 1 mile meet a T-junction and turn left on to the A666 SP 'Bolton'. In ½ mile turn right on to an unclassified road SP 'Belmont', then take the next turning right and descend with views of Delph Reservoir to the left and Belmont Reservoir to the right. After 1 mile drive over crossroads to reach Belmont.

BELMONT, Lancs SD61
Belmont Church is a good example of 19th-century architecture that has been built to serve rather than impress. Its main feature is an attractive 6-light window.

At Belmont meet a T-junction and turn right on to the A675. Take the next turning left on to an unclassified road SP 'Rivington', and drive through open moorland with views of 1,498ft Winter Hill on the left. Descend to a T-junction and turn right, then meet another T-junction and turn left to reach Rivington.

RIVINGTON, Lancs SD61
Rivington Pike rises to a 1,190ft summit above this attractive little moorland village. It is crowned by an 18th-century stone tower and commands excellent views over miles of countryside. In the village itself is a good church housing a fine screen and a 16th-century pulpit. Rivington Hall, which stands in 400-acre Lever Park, was rebuilt in 1744 and contains a general interest museum. Close to the village are the Rivington and Anglezarke Reservoirs.

RIVINGTON AND ANGLEZARKE RESERVOIRS, Lancs SD61
These broad sheets of water add an extra dimension of beauty to the somewhat severe moorland countryside around them. They were built in the 19th century to supply Liverpool with water, and have naturalized into perfect habitats for many types of wildlife.

Leave Rivington and drive forward SP 'Adlington', crossing the Rivington Reservoir. Meet a T-junction, turn left SP 'Horwich', and in ¾ mile meet a junction with the A673. Turn right on to the A673 and take the next turning left on to an unclassified road SP 'Blackrod'. In 1 mile meet the A6, drive forward, and in ½ mile turn right. Continue for 1 mile, meet a T-junction with the B5239, and drive forward SP 'Standish'. In 1½ miles meet a T-junction and turn right on to the A5106, then in 200 yards turn left on to the B5239 and continue to the town of Standish.

STANDISH, Gt Manchester SD51
This colliery town stands on the line of a Roman road and features a good church that was rebuilt in the 16th century. Inside the building, particularly in the roof, are good examples of woodwork. The old village stocks are preserved on the steps of a modern town cross.

Meet traffic signals in Standish and drive forward on to the A5209. In 1¼ miles turn right to follow SP 'M6', then meet a roundabout and take the 2nd exit to cross the M6 motorway. Continue to Parbold.

PARBOLD, Lancs SD41
Parbold Hall is a splendid stone-built Georgian house (not open) with a Venetian-style doorway. Excellent views of the surrounding countryside can be enjoyed from the summit of Parbold Hill, which is crowned by the impressive 19th-century building of Christ Church.

Leave Parbold and cross the Leeds and Liverpool Canal, then the River Douglas, to reach Newburgh. Continue to Burscough.

BURSCOUGH, Lancs SD41
Slight remains of a priory lie to the south-west of Burscough, which has a Victorian church with four attractive pinnacled buttresses.

From Burscough, join the A59 SP 'Southport' and in ¾ mile turn right on to the B5242. Continue through Bescar, meet traffic signals, and turn right on to the A570 to reach Scarisbrick and its hall.

SCARISBRICK, Lancs SD31
Designed by the architect Pugin in 1837, ornate Scarisbrick Hall (open on application) is an excellent example of the opulence favoured in the Victorian period. It is gothic in style and was the architect's first major work, taking 4 years to complete. The 150 rooms of the house are now occupied by a school.

Leave Scarisbrick and continue along the A570 for the return to Southport.

ood views of Turton and Entwhistle eservoirs can be enjoyed from the ırton to Belmont road.

TOUR 83 79 MILES

BEACHES AND THE BOWLAND FELLS

Blackpool is more than the most popular holiday resort in the north; it is also an ideal place from which to tour the rolling, windmill-dotted landscape of the Fylde, its austere little villages, and the high wild moors of the Forest of Bowland.

Blackpool's Tower dominates the crowded beach.

The packhorse bridge near Hurst Green

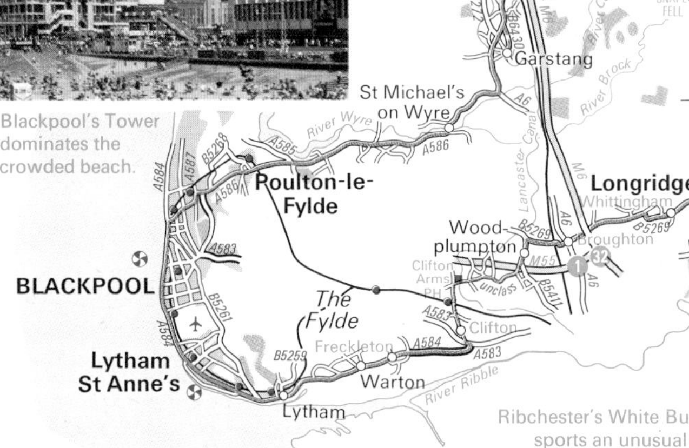

BLACKPOOL, Lancs SD33

Every summer Lancashire shuts down its industry for the annual wake, or holiday, and for a brief period Blackpool's resident population of about 152,000 is swelled by an influx of 8 million trippers eager to be entertained. Until the seaside-holiday vogue of the 18th century the town was little more than a cluster of cottages, but it has developed from these small beginnings to become one of the premier resorts in Great Britain. Everything is geared up to the boisterous, fun-fair atmosphere of high summer, and the natural asset of a beautiful sandy beach is supplemented by three fine piers and the splendid dominance of the famous 519ft tower. In the latter are a ballroom that is often the scene of dance festivals and beauty contests, an aquarium and butterfly farm, and various facilities for children. The traditional heart of the 7-mile Promenade is the famous Golden Mile, a bewildering collection of novelty shops, ice-cream vendors, and seafood stalls. Blackpool Zoo is the most modern in Britain and features a unique free-flight bird hall. Some of the other animal enclosures can be visited by miniature railway, and the entire complex is laid out to the best advantage of both visitors and animals. The East Drive area is well known for its richly-planted gardens, and the town's many other parks and public open spaces are green islands of peace amongst the bustle and noise of streets packed with tourist and local traffic. Sporting events held here every year include county cricket, league football, and various other championships associated with the amenities available. As well as being a resort Blackpool is a good touring centre.

Leave Blackpool and follow the A584 SP 'Lytham St Anne's' along the coast to reach Lytham St Anne's.

LYTHAM ST ANNE'S, Lancs SD32

No less than four championship courses make this popular seaside resort a mecca for golfing enthusiasts. Sand yachting and safe bathing are offered by 6 miles of sandy beach, and the British Sand Yachting Championships are held here every May. The residential part of the resort is laid out on garden-city lines, with many beautiful parks and gardens between streets of pleasant houses. Ashton Gardens and Lowther Gardens are of particular note, and the fascinating Alpine Gardens offer fine walks in landscaped surroundings where little bridges span water and cool hollows. In and between these gardens are many good half-timbered buildings, including the attractive 18th-century structure of Lytham Hall.

Drive through the town to Lytham.

LYTHAM, Lancs SD32

Lytham and St Anne's are incorporated in the borough of Lytham St Anne's, but this is where the similarity stops. The former is a quiet residential town with few of the holiday amusements and entertainments offered by the St Anne's area. A white windmill on picturesque Lytham Green near the shore is typical of many that once operated in the area.

Ribchester's White Bull Inn sports an unusual sign.

THE FYLDE, Lancs SD33

Between the Wyre estuary north of Blackpool and the Ribble estuary in the south is a flat, wind-blown area of land known as the Fylde. This area was once known for its many windmills, and several of these fascinating old structures have survived intact.

Continue along the A584 SP 'Preston' to reach Warton.

WARTON, Lancs SD42

There is a small aerodrome here, an the town has a good church of Victorian date.

Continue along the A584 to Freckleton, then in $2\frac{3}{4}$ miles meet traffic signals and turn left on to the A583. Take the first turning right on t an unclassified road SP 'Clifton'. Skirt Clifton, and in 2 miles reach the Clifton Arms (PH). Turn right SP 'Broughton' and cross the Lancaster Canal. In $1\frac{1}{2}$ miles meet a T-junction and turn right, then after another $\frac{1}{4}$ mile turn left. In $1\frac{1}{4}$ miles join the B5411 and continue to Woodplumpton.

WOODPLUMPTON, Lancs SD43

The 20th-century navigator Henry Foster was born in this village, and his memorial can be seen in the loc church. This warm, honey-coloure building is mainly of 15th- to 19th-century date.

Drive to the end of the village and turn right SP 'Broughton', then in a short distance turn right again on to the B5269. Continue to Broughton, meet traffic signals, and drive forwar SP 'Longridge'. Proceed through Whittingham to Longridge.

LONGRIDGE, Lancs SD63

High above the roof tops of this pleasant village is the fine steeple o 19th-century St Wilfrid's Church, a symmetrical counterpoint to the nearby craggy bulk of 1,148ft Longridge Fell.

Leave Longridge on the B6243 SP 'Clitheroe' and in $\frac{1}{2}$ mile turn right with the B6245 SP 'Blackburn'. Later bear left into Ribchester.

RIBCHESTER, Lancs SD63
In Roman times the wild country hereabouts was guarded by a fort that stood on this site for 300 years. Known as *Bremetennacum*, its remains (AM, NT) have been excavated and many of the finds installed in the local Museum of Roman Antiquities. A model displayed here shows what the building must have looked like in its complete state, and among the exhibits are gold coins, pieces of pottery, brooches, oil lamps, and a rare bronze parade helmet. Other remains from the same period have been incorporated in some of the village buildings. Two Roman columns support the oak gallery in 13th-century St Wilfred's Church, and the pillars at the entrance of the White Bull Inn are said to have come from a Roman temple. Just to the north of Ribchester is the Norman Stydd Chapel and a neat row of attractive 18th-century almshouses.

A detour from the main route can be made to Longridge Fell by leaving the centre of Ribchester on an unclassified road SP 'Chipping', then driving for - miles to the excellent road summit and viewpoint of the fell. On the main tour, leave Ribchester by continuing along the B6254 and in $\frac{1}{2}$ mile turn left on to an unclassified road SP 'Hurst Green'. In $1\frac{3}{4}$ miles reach the top of an ascent and turn right on to the B6243 'Clitheroe' road and continue to Hurst Green.

HURST GREEN, Lancs SD63
An attractive feature of this village is the Church of St John the Evangelist, which was built in 1838 and has a stellated tower in keeping with the romantic leanings of the period. In magnificent grounds close to Hurst Green is the imposing building of Stonyhurst, a famous school that was founded in the 16th century.

Leave Hurst Green and continue along the B6243. In $1\frac{3}{4}$ miles cross the River Hodder, with a 16th-century packhorse bridge visible to the right. In $1\frac{1}{4}$ miles meet a junction with the unclassified 'Bashall Eaves' road. A short detour can be taken from the main route to Clitheroe by turning right here and driving along the B6243.

CLITHEROE, Lancs SD74
After the Civil War the small Norman keep of Clitheroe Castle (open) was presented to General Monk, and today it still stands in a dominant position on a limestone knoll above the town. Inside is an important collection of fossils from the surrounding district. The town itself is an industrial centre that grew to prosperity through cotton, and at one time it was full of the clatter and noise of textile milling. Sinister Pendle Hill, associated with the notorious trial of several Lancashire women who were said to be witches and accordingly executed, rises to 1,831ft on the east side of Clitheroe. George Fox, practically the founder of the Society of Friends claims to have drawn his inspiration from the same hill.

Refreshing solitude is discovered near Blaze Moss in the Trough of Bowland.

On the main tour, keep forward at the junction and follow the unclassified road to Bashall Eaves. After 1 mile drive over crossroads and follow the Hodder Valley, with Longridge Fell on the left. To the right are views of 1,296ft Waddington Fell and 1,300ft Easington Fell. At Bashall Eaves keep forward, then after 1 mile reach Browsholme Hall.

BROWSHOLME HALL, Lancs SD64
Altered and extended during the 18th century, this basically Tudor mansion contains fascinating collections of tapestry work, armour, furniture, and pictures. It is open by appointment and stands in beautiful gardens that were landscaped in honour of the Prince Regent and Mrs Fitzherbert.

Continue for 1 mile and turn right SP 'Whitewell' via Hall Hill. After $\frac{1}{4}$ mile an unclassified right turn offers a short detour which ascends for 1 mile to a 960ft viewpoint.

VIEWPOINT, Lancs SD64
One of the best parts of the tour, this high road summit affords magnificent views south to the Hodder Valley, Longridge Fell, and Pendle Hill, with the dark peaks of the Pennine Range in the distance. North and west are the hills of the Forest of Bowland, with 1,629ft Totridge Fell and 1,415ft Burn Fell particularly prominent.

On the main tour, climb to a road summit of 750ft and descend into the Hodder Valley at Whitewell. Turn right SP 'Lancaster' and enter the Forest of Bowland.

FOREST OF BOWLAND, Lancs
In the days when the word 'forest' meant 'hunting ground' this area was the preserve of the kings of England, who regarded the local deer as their own property and were particularly hard on anybody caught poaching. Today the forest is a largely treeless expanse of moorland and steep-sided fells which has been designated as being of outstanding natural beauty. It lies partly in Lancashire and partly in what used to be the West Riding of Yorkshire, and offers excellent riverside walks.

Cross the River Hodder and Langden Brook. Drive through Dunsop Bridge into a deep, narrow valley and climb to the Trough of Bowland.

TROUGH OF BOWLAND, Lancs SD65
Here the road climbs to more than 1,000ft above sea level via steep gradients (1 in 6) through lonely moorland that was once the haunt of highwaymen. Views from the summit encompass 1,383ft Blaze Moss to the south, 1,651ft Whin Fell in the north-east, and 1,567ft Hawthornthwaite Fell in the distance.

Descend from the road summit of the Trough of Bowland to reach the village of Marshaw. After $1\frac{3}{4}$ miles reach a chapel and turn left on to the 'Preston' road and descend (1 in 5) to Abbeystead. Follow SP 'Preston' and in $3\frac{1}{4}$ miles reach Dolphinholme. After $\frac{1}{4}$ mile reach a church and bear right, then in $1\frac{1}{4}$ miles meet a T-junction and turn left SP 'Garstang'. The revolving restaurant tower of Forton Service Area can be seen on the left as the route reaches Forton village. After the village drive for $1\frac{1}{2}$ miles and turn left on to the A6 SP 'Preston', then continue for $2\frac{1}{4}$ miles. A detour from the main route to Garstang can be made by turning left here on to the B6430 and driving into the town itself.

The Forest of Bowland is a lonely area of great beauty.

GARSTANG, Lancs SD44
Among the fine Georgian buildings in this little town, which stands on the Lancaster Canal, are the Town Hall and elegant St Thomas' Church.

On the main tour, continue along the A6 for another $2\frac{1}{2}$ miles and turn right on to the A586 SP 'Blackpool'. Follow the course of the River Wyre to St Michael's-on-Wyre.

ST MICHAEL'S-ON-WYRE, Lancs SD44
Situated at the junction of the Rivers Calder, Brock, and Wyre, this pleasant village has a lovely church which preserves fragments of 14th-century wall paintings. The rural nature of the community is emphasized by a shearing scene in the church's 16th-century stained-glass window.

Continue along the A586 to reach Poulton-le-Fylde.

POULTON-LE-FYLDE, Lancs SD33
Old fish stones where the prices of fish caught by local boats were once fixed survive here, and the old market place features a set of stocks. Alongside the latter is a whipping post and a stepped Jacobean pillar. Georgian St Chad's Church features a beautiful carved screen and chairs that are prime examples of the wood craftsman's art.

Continue along the A586 to re-enter Blackpool.

TOUR 84 74 MILES

SOUTHERN LAKELAND

Characterized by narrow switchback lanes and tranquil lakes that recede far into the distance, this part of the Lake District was a favourite haunt of famous poets and artists. Relics of them remain, as does the timeless and indefinable quality of peace that first attracted them.

GRANGE-OVER-SANDS, Cumbria SD47
This quiet seaside resort is situated on Morecambe Bay. Its shingle and rock shore is scattered with fascinating rock pools at low tide, and is backed by lovely wooded fell scenery that sweeps right down to the sea. Bathing is dangerous. The mile-long promenade offers bracing walks, and the mild local climate has allowed the establishment of flourishing ornamental gardens throughout the town.

Leave Grange on the B5277 'Lindale, Kendal' road and drive through well-wooded countryside with views across Morecambe Bay to the right. Continue, with the Lakeland fells visible ahead, to Lindale.

LINDALE, Cumbria SD48
John Wilkinson, the 18th-century iron master, is appropriately commemorated by a cast-iron obelisk in this pretty village.

In Lindale turn right SP 'Lancaster', and in $1\frac{1}{4}$ miles meet a roundabout. Take the 2nd exit on to the A590, later pass the craggy cliffs of Whitbarrow Scar on the left, and continue for $1\frac{1}{2}$ miles. Immediately before a river bridge turn left on to the A5074 SP 'Bowness' and follow the lovely Lyth Valley. Continue, with views of the Lakeland fells ahead, and ascend a winding road through picturesque countryside. Drive through Winster, continue for 2 miles to reach crossroads, and turn left on to the B5284. In $\frac{1}{4}$ mile turn right on to the A592 to reach the town of Bowness-on-Windermere.

LAKE WINDERMERE, Cumbria SD39
The largest and one of the most beautiful lakes in England, Windermere measures $10\frac{1}{2}$ miles long and is only 1 mile wide. Its surface is studded with charming little islands, and its steep banks are cloaked with dense masses of attractive woodland. Water-sports enthusiasts find it suitable for most of their requirements, and at one time it was the regular venue for world water-speed record attempts.

BOWNESS-ON-WINDERMERE, Cumbria SD49
In summer the quaint narrow streets of this pleasant little Lakeland town are busy with anglers, sailors, walkers, and tourists who have come here just for the beauty of the surroundings. Its fine 15th- to 19th-century church has superb examples of medieval stained glass in the east window, and the picturesque quality of local stone can be seen everywhere. Motor launches operate from Bowness Pier to Belle Isle, an enchanting 38-acre island in the middle of Lake Windermere. The house (open) on this unusual estate was the first completely round building of its type erected in England and contains interesting collections of furniture, portraits, and miscellanea.

Return along the A592 SP 'Barrow' and in $\frac{3}{4}$ mile pass a right turn leading to Lake Windermere Ferry. An alternative route that shortens the tour by 15 miles can be followed by taking the ferry and rejoining the main route at Far Sawrey, on the other bank. On the main route, drive through thick woodland along the east shore of Lake Windermere to reach Fell Foot Park.

FELL FOOT PARK, Cumbria SD38
Attractively situated on the shores of Lake Windermere, this 18-acre park (NT) offer facilities for bathing, boating, picnicking, and many other outdoor pursuits.

Meet a T-junction and turn right on to the A590 to reach Newby Bridge.

NEWBY BRIDGE, Cumbria SD38
This unusual stone bridge dates from the 17th century and spans the River Leven at the southern extremity of Lake Windermere. It is an attractive ingredient of the beautiful local scenery.

Turn right on to an unclassified road SP 'Lakeside, Hawkshead' and follow a winding road along the west shore of Lake Windermere to Lakeside.

LAKESIDE, Cumbria SD38
Steam locomotives run south from here to Haverthwaite on the Lakeside and Haverthwaite Railway, which connects with passenger ferries operating from Ambleside and Bowness-on-Windermere.

Leave Lakeside and after $\frac{3}{4}$ mile bear right. In $2\frac{1}{2}$ miles reach Graythwaite Hall Gardens.

GRAYTHWAITE HALL GARDENS, Cumbria SD39
In spring and summer the 7 acres of this landscape garden are glorious with the blooms and foliage of many different plants. The Elizabethan hall round which they were created was sympathetically re-modelled in the 19th century.

Leave Graythwaite Hall and branch right SP 'Sawrey'. In $\frac{3}{4}$ mile descend steeply, then in $1\frac{3}{4}$ miles bear left and ascend to Far Sawrey. If the alternative route via the ferry has been taken, resume the main tour here.

FAR SAWREY, Cumbria SD39
This beautiful Lakeland village is situated between Lake Windermere and tranquil Esthwaite Water.

Keep left in Far Sawrey, then turn left on to the B5285 SP 'Hawkshead'. Continue to Near Sawrey.

NEAR SAWREY, Cumbria SD39
In 1943 Beatrix Potter, creator of Peter Rabbit and a host of other engaging animals in her children's books, bequeathed Hill Top Farm (open) and about half the village to the National Trust. The 17th-century farmhouse was her home up until her death, and the lovely surroundings of the village must have influenced her enchanting and essentially rural tales.

Lake Windermere is a popular centre for boating and sailing as well as being a magnetic scenic attraction.

Continue along the B5285 and follow the north shore of Esthwaite Water.

ESTHWAITE WATER, Cumbria SD39
Rowing boats can be hired by those wishing to explore this picturesque small lake by water, and its shores offer mountain views in which the 2,631ft peak of the Old Man of Coniston is prominent.

Continue to the edge of Hawkshead. A detour can be made from the main tour route to the Grizedale Wildlife Centre by driving forward, turning left on to an unclassified road SP 'Newby Bridge', then continuing for $\frac{1}{4}$ mile and turning right SP 'Grizedale'; proceed across Hawkshead Moor to reach Grizedale.

GRIZEDALE, Cumbria SD39
The variety of wildlife to be seen in this region is superbly illustrated in the Forestry Commission's Visitor and Wildlife Centre at Grizedale. The deer museum is of particular note, and among the best of several planned walks in the area is the 1-mile Millwood forest trail. Take care against fire in dry weather.

On the main tour, turn right to skirt the village of Hawkshead.

HAWKSHEAD, Cumbria SD39
Hawkshead's distinctive charm comes from its unspoilt stone cottages, courtyards, and narrow winding alleys. The 16th-century grammar school numbers Wordsworth among its past pupils. The poet lodged in Ann Tyson's cottage while he studied there. The cottage still stands and is noted for its unusual outside staircase. The picturesque Courthouse (NT) house the Folk Museum of Rural Crafts.

Keep forward on to the B5286 SP 'Ambleside' and follow a winding road that affords fine views of the loc countryside. Drive through Out Gat and in 2 miles reach an unclassified right turn offering a detour to impressive Wray Castle.

WRAY CASTLE, Cumbria NY30
Lovely grounds (open) surround th 19th-century extravagance of Wra Castle (not open) on the banks of Lake Windermere, sweeping right down to the water's edge. The cast estate, and much of the attractive local countryside are protected by the National Trust.

On the main route, continue to the village of Clappersgate.

CLAPPERSGATE, Cumbria NY30
Magnificently situated at the northern end of Lake Windermere Clappersgate is best known for th beautiful floral displays that can b enjoyed in the White Craggs Gard (open) during spring and summer. See also tour 86.

Leave Clappersgate and turn right to the A593. Continue, with fine vi of Wansfell and 1,581ft Wansfell Pi ahead, and cross a river bridge. Tu left to enter Ambleside.

AMBLESIDE, Cumbria NY30
Features of this very popular Lakeland tourist centre include a National Trust information office in tiny Bridge House. Excellent walking and climbing areas are nearby. See tour 86 for more details.

he area around Skelwith Bridge is raced by several lovely waterfalls.

eturn along the A593 SP 'Coniston' nd pass through Clappersgate. Cross kelwith Bridge and continue along n undulating road with all-round ountain views. Tilberthwaite High ells rise to the right, dominated by e strangely-shaped peak of 2,502ft Vetherlam. Continue, later driving elow the steep slopes of the oniston Fells with the Old Man of oniston towering in the ackground, to Coniston.

ONISTON, Cumbria SD39
nis cluster of whitewashed cottages the tip of lovely Coniston Water a bright spot in a landscape ominated in the west by the 2,631ft ld Man of Coniston. A little farther est is the 2,555ft peak of Dow Crag, nose testing faces are popular with mbers. Features of the village itself clude Coniston Old Hall, with its pical round Lakeland chimneys, d the Ruskin Museum. John skin, the 19th-century writer and ist, loved this area and is buried in e local churchyard. Although the useum is devoted mostly to him, ts of it recall the death of the nous Donald Campbell.

ve Coniston and turn left on to the 285 SP 'Hawkshead' to skirt the rthern end of Coniston Water.

ONISTON WATER, mbria SD39
e shore of this tranquil 5½-mile- g lake is cloaked in the woodlands Grizedale Forest, and the lake itself amous as the place where Sir nald Campbell died while trying better the world water-speed ord in 1965. Conditions were not al during the attempt, but its ure may not have been entirely to the choppy surface and is still atter for conjecture.

p left and climb through odland, then in 1½ miles turn left o an unclassified road SP 'Tarn vs'. In ½ mile turn left again and nd steeply to reach Tarn Hows.

Evening gives a dramatic aspect to Morecambe Bay.

Marvellous views of the Langdale Pikes and other famous Lakeland features can be enjoyed from the peaceful shores of picturesque Tarn Hows.

TARN HOWS, Cumbria SD39
Arguably the most outstanding of many beautiful areas in the Lakeland region, Tarn Hows (NT) is a group of lakes and woodland in an area ringed by the peaks of mountains. Visitors are catered for with carparks and picnicking facilities.

Descend steeply along a narrow road SP 'Coniston', meet a T-junction, and turn right on to the B5285. Take the next turning left on to an unclassified road SP 'East of Lake' and follow the eastern shore of Coniston Water. In 1½ miles reach Brantwood.

BRANTWOOD, Cumbria SD39
This house (open), once the home of writer and artist John Ruskin, is now a museum containing examples of his work and a variety of personal possessions. The grounds feature fine gardens, a deer trail, and one of the best nature trails in the Lake District.

Continue along a winding road that hugs the shore of the lake, with views of several waterfalls to the right. Above the road to the left are the steep wooded slopes of Grizedale Forest. On the far side of the lake descend into the Crake Valley, passing the wooded Furness Fells on the left, and meet a T-junction. Turn left to reach Spark Bridge, then turn left again and in ½ mile drive forward over a main road SP 'Newby Bridge'. Meet another T-junction and turn left on to the A590 SP 'Bowness', then in 1¼ miles meet crossroads and turn right on to the B5278 SP 'Cark'. A detour from the main route to Rusland can be made by turning left at the crossroads instead of right.

RUSLAND, Cumbria SD38
Rusland Hall (open) was built in 1720 and nowadays houses a museum of mechanical musical instruments and early photographic equipment. Its elegant landscaped grounds are the home of white peacocks.

On the main tour, continue along the B5278 to reach Haverthwaite.

HAVERTHWAITE, Cumbria SD38
Steam-hauled trains on the standard-gauge Lakeside and Haverthwaite Railway connect with passenger steamers on Lake Windermere, at the other end of the line, and run 3½ miles through some of Lakeland's finest scenery.

Drive beyond Haverthwaite and bear right, then continue along the B5278 through thickly wooded countryside to reach Holker Hall.

HOLKER HALL, Cumbria SD37
Originally built in the 16th century, this house (open) contains fine furniture and exquisite woodcarvings by local craftsmen. Parts of the building were restored in the 19th century, and the grounds include a deer reserve featuring a number of different species. During the summer Holker Hall is the scene of many local shows and events.

Proceed to Cark.

CARK, Cumbria SD37
One of the main features in this pleasant little village is its 16th-century hall, which has mullioned windows and a grand 17th-century doorway.

Drive to the Rose and Crown Hotel and branch left on to an unclassified road. Continue to Cartmel.

CARTMEL, Cumbria SD37
Little remains of the great priory (NT) that made this pleasant old town one of the most important religious centres for miles around, but the exceptionally beautiful priory church has survived. This large building was extended at various times up until the dissolution of the monasteries, after which it was left to decay until its restoration in 1618.

Keep forward, pass a school, and turn right SP 'Grange'. In 1 mile turn left into Grangefell Road and descend, with fine views over Morecambe Bay, for the return to Grange-over-Sands.

TOUR 85 82 MILES

AROUND THE THREE PEAKS

High fells and isolated dales sheltering the stone houses and outbuildings of hill farms surround Yorkshire's Three Peaks, rugged summits whose flanks are riddled with caves and pounded by the constant drop of lovely waterfalls. The roads are narrow and hilly, but the scenery is spectacular.

SEDBERGH, Cumbria SD69
This market town lies below Howgill Fells, a range of rounded bracken-topped hills which links the Yorkshire Dales with the edge of the Lake District. A famous public school for boys was founded here in 1525, but the majority of the town's buildings are 19th-century and the general feel of the place is very Victorian. Permanent displays relating to the topography of the area can be seen in the National Park Centre.

Leave Sedbergh on the unclassified 'Dent' road and follow the River Dee through beautiful Dentdale. Continue through pleasant countryside to Dent.

DENTDALE, Cumbria SD78
Lower Dentdale is a broad and well-wooded valley that narrows to a gorge and mountain pass beyond Dent village. Dent marble, a particularly hard form of limestone prized as a building material, is found in small quarries along its length, and beautiful fell scenery rises from both banks of the Dee.

DENT, Cumbria SD78
In the heart of Dentdale is the attractive old village of Dent, a picturesque collection of houses and cottages centred on the twisting course of a cobbled main street. The village drinking fountain commemorates Alan Sedgewick, a pioneer geologist born here in the 19th century.

Drive to the George and Dragon Inn in Dent, turn right, and after 1 mile turn right again SP 'Ingleton'. Follow a narrow winding road into Deepdale, with Whernside rising on the left.

WHERNSIDE, Cumbria & N Yorks SD78
Whernside, the cave-riddled flanks of Pen-y-Ghent, and lofty Ingleborough are neighbouring summits of a massive millstone-grit formation known as the Three Peaks. The first-named rise to 2,419ft above sea level. The area's many potholes and tunnels should not be entered by any but the most experienced and well-equipped explorers. See also tour 79.

Ascend steeply along a gated road to White Shaw Moss and a road summit of 1,553ft. Descend through Kingsdale, on either side of which runs a lofty limestone scar, and reach Thornton-in-Lonsdale. Turn left over a railway bridge, then left again. After a short distance turn left to enter the Dales centre of Ingleton.

Great Shunner Fell towers over the village of Muker.

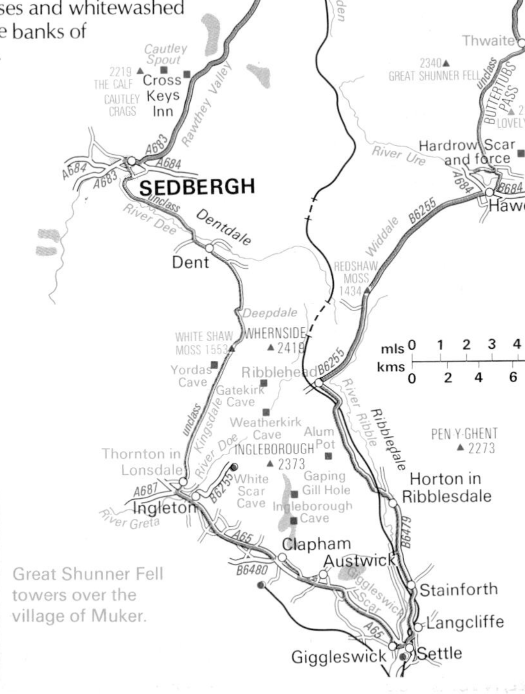

INGLETON, N Yorks SD67
This popular dales centre is a good rambling and touring base situated close to several beauty spots. Waterfalls in the area include 40ft Thornton Force and Pecca Falls, and lovely rock and river scenery can be enjoyed on a $2\frac{1}{4}$-hour round walk that follows the enchanting Doe Valley and returns alongside the River Twiss. The summit of Ingleborough is less than 4 miles from the village.

INGLEBOROUGH, N Yorks SD77
Ingleborough is the second highest of the Three Peaks, and its 2,373ft summit forms a curious 15-acre plateau that was once guarded by an ancient stronghold. All that remains of the fortification today is a low rampart pierced by three openings. A well-known section of the massive cave systems that riddle the local limestone is known as the White Scar Caves (open). Potholers come from all parts of the country to explore its tunnels, where an underground river flows amongst strange rock formations into a sunless lake. Farther east is Gaping Ghyll, an awesome pothole whose 360ft shaft leads to a main chamber that extends a full 500ft below ground. It has the longest shaft in Britain and is a severe test of nerves and skill for the experienced climbers that attempt it.

Leave Ingleton and follow SP 'Settle' to join the A65. Drive through farming country and after 4 miles turn left on to the B6480 to enter Clapham.

CLAPHAM, N Yorks SD76
A Yorkshire Dales information centre is based in this attractive little village, and the local caves attract potholing enthusiasts from all over Britain. About 1 mile north is the entrance to Ingleborough Cave (open), which runs for 900 yards and is noted for its splendid stalagmites and stalactites. The village is a charming collection of greystone houses and whitewashed cottages on the banks of Clapham Beck.

The windswept character of the Yorkshire Dales is particularly striking near Muker.

Leave Clapham on the 'Settle' road to join the A65, then in $\frac{1}{4}$ mile turn left on to an unclassified road for Austwick village. In $\frac{3}{4}$ mile reach Austwick.

AUSTWICK, N Yorks SD76
Many of the Craven District's outstanding geological features lie close to this village. Of particular interest is a series of perched boulders, huge rocks left in precarious positions by the melting glaciers of the ice ages.

Leave Austwick by returning to the A65 and later pass beneath Giggleswick Scar to reach the edge Giggleswick.

GIGGLESWICK, N Yorks SD86
A well-known public school found here in 1553 occupies impressive 19th-century buildings, but the ea history of Giggleswick is best represented by its old market cros stocks, and tithe barn. The local church features an ancient readin desk and a carved pulpit of 1680.

Leave Giggleswick and proceed to the town of Settle.

TLE, N Yorks SD86
› charm of this small Ribblesdale ·ket town is in its narrow streets ınpretentious buildings and luded courtyards. Folly Hall, also ›wn as Preston's Folly, is an nished 17th-century house with ›laborate front that contrasts erely with a very plain back. In ıy ways this sudden difference ›cts the startling changes of the l countryside. Close by is the 'ature peak of Castleberg Crag, ch towers 300ft above the town.

ırn through Settle along the A65 turn right on to the B6479 SP ton in Ribblesdale' to begin a › through scenic Ribblesdale. · a short distance reach Langcliffe.

GCLIFFE, N Yorks SD86
338 a chance discovery of the ıre now known as Victoria Cave › the retrieval of many nating prehistoric remains, ding the bones of animals long ct in the British Isles.

› Langcliffe and proceed on the 9 to reach Stainforth.

NFORTH, N Yorks SD86
:h-century packhorse bridge spans the River Ribble here is › have replaced a similar :ure built by monks in the 14th ıry. Some 300 yards ıstream is the impressive 'fall of Stainforth Force. The · Ribblesdale Valley extends and south along the river's ing course.

From Stainforth, continue to Horton in Ribblesdale.

HORTON IN RIBBLESDALE, N Yorks SD87
Alum Pot, one of the best-known potholes in the Craven district, lies 4 miles north-west of this picturesque moorland village.

Continue past Horton-in-Ribblesdale, with views of Pen-y-Ghent (right).

RIBBLESDALE, N Yorks SD87
This long, wide valley of the Ribble cuts through a varied landscape and is popular with walkers, climbers, and potholers. The railway line from Settle to Carlisle runs through Ribblesdale and is considered one of the most scenic routes in the country.

PEN-Y-GHENT, N Yorks SD87
One of the famous Three Peaks, this mountain rises to 2,273ft and is known for its potholes. In clear weather the views from its summit extend as far as Helvellyn, some 45 miles away. See also tour 79.

Continue along the B6479 through desolate countryside beside the Leeds–Carlisle railway line to Ribblehead. A fine railway viaduct can be seen on the left, and 2,419ft Whernside rises straight ahead. Meet a T-junction and turn right on to the B6255 SP 'Hawes'. Ascend Redshaw Moss to a road summit of 1,434ft, then later descend through the steep fell country of Widdale. Meet the A684 and turn right to enter Hawes.

Adventurous visitors can follow a footpath behind the stupendous Hardrow Force waterfall.

HAWES, N Yorks SD88
This sheep-marketing centre is the focal point of Upper Wensleydale life and a major supplier of the distinctive Wensleydale cheese. Its name means a 'pass between the mountains', and it stands between 1,900ft Fleet Moss and 1,726ft Buttertubs.

In Hawes turn left on to the unclassified 'Muker' road and cross the River Ure. Reach a T-junction and turn left, then take the next turning right. A short detour can be made from the main route to Hardrow Force waterfall by keeping forward with SP 'Hardrow Force'.

HARDROW SCAR & FORCE, N Yorks SD89
Considered one of the most spectacular in England, this magnificent waterfall plunges 90ft over the limestone rim of Hardrow Scar into a glen that was once used for brass band contests because of its superb acoustics. Access to the falls is by foot only, through the grounds of the Green Dragon Inn.

On the main tour, climb through the fine scenery of Buttertubs Pass.

BUTTERTUBS PASS, N Yorks SD89
This 1,726ft pass links the lovely valleys of Swaledale and Wensleydale, and is named after deep limestone shafts that pock the countryside a short distance from the road. It is thought that these may have been dug by farmers and used to cool and harden butter that had got too warm on the way to market.

Continue along Buttertubs Pass and meet the B6270. A detour from the main route to Muker can be made by turning right here and driving for $1\frac{1}{4}$ miles through fell country.

Pen-y-Ghent, one of the impressive Three Peaks that rise above the national park.

MUKER, N Yorks SD99
Set among the high moors and fells of Upper Swaledale, this remote little cluster of greystone houses is attractively set below the 2,340ft summit of Great Shunner Fell.

On the main tour, turn left on to the B6270 to Thwaite and later skirt the village of Keld.

KELD, N Yorks NY80
Lovely Kisdon Force is one of several attractive waterfalls to be seen near this village, and the desolate area of Birkdale Common lies to the west.

Beyond Keld drive along a narrow hilly road through Birkdale Common, climbing to a road summit of 1,698ft on the Cumbrian border. Descend steeply (1-in-5) with views over the Eden Valley to reach Nateby, and turn right on to the B6259. Later turn right on to the A685 to enter Kirkby Stephen.

KIRKBY STEPHEN, Cumbria NY70
This picturesque little market town is attractively set amongst moorland in the Eden Valley, and features a fine parish church containing several ancient carved stones. To the south the River Eden rises from its remote source in the wild Mallerstang Valley.

Leave Kirkby Stephen on the A685 SP 'Kendal' and after 2 miles turn left on to the A683 'Sedbergh' road. Continue among high fells along the attractive Rawthey Valley to reach the Cross Keys Inn.

CROSS KEYS INN, Cumbria SD69
Originally built c1600, this inn (NT) was altered somewhat in the 18th and 19th centuries but is still a fine building. The impressive 600ft waterfall of Cautley Spout is accessible by footpath from here.

Leave the Cross Keys Inn and continue along the A683 to re-enter Sedbergh.

AMBLESIDE, Cumbria NY30
This popular tourist centre of grey slate houses stands near the northern end of Lake Windermere and is popular with anglers, fell walkers, and climbers. The waters of the lake are alive with fish large enough to satisfy the most discriminating fishermen, and the rugged countryside of the Coniston Fells is only 3 miles away. The beautiful scenery of the lake shores is best appreciated from the water, and regular boat tours can be joined at Waterhead. In the town library are various relics discovered on the site of a 2nd- to 4th-century Roman fort excavated in Borrans Park. Tiny 18th-century Bridge House contains a National Trust information centre. About 1 mile south of Ambleside is the enchanting woodland garden of Stagshaw (open) which offers superb views of the lake from informal surroundings. In early times the floors of domestic and public buildings were covered with dried rushes that were replaced as they became soiled, and every July the town has a rush-bearing ceremony as a reminder of the days when everybody in the community collected rushes for the church floor. This very practical idea may have stemmed from Roman harvest thanksgiving celebrations.
See also tour 84.

Leave Ambleside with SP 'Keswick' to join the A591 and drive through pleasant mountain scenery to reach Rydal, near the Rydal Water.

RYDAL, Cumbria NY30
Close to Rydal is the little River Rothay, which links the east end of peaceful Rydal Water with the vast expanse of Lake Windermere. The poet William Wordsworth lived at Rydal Mount (open) from 1815 until his death in 1850, and must have been inspired by the glorious views over two beautiful lakes that can be enjoyed from the 4½-acre gardens. Nowadays the house is a sort of historical shrine to the poet, preserving many personal relics from his lifetime. Dora's Field was given by Wordsworth to his daughter, and is famous for its daffodils. Nearby Nab Cottage is associated with the writers Thomas de Quincey and Hartley Coleridge. The whole area is dominated by the rugged heights of Nab Scar and Loughrigg Fell.

Leave Rydal and drive past the shores of Rydal Water and Grasmere, with Rydal Fell rising to the right. Continue for ¼ mile beyond Grasmere to reach Dove Cottage.

DOVE COTTAGE, Cumbria NY30
After William Wordsworth had lived in this tiny 17th-century cottage from 1799 to 1808 it became the home of the writer Thomas de Quincey, who occupied it for 26 years. A Wordsworth Museum which now adjoins the house preserves several manuscripts and first editions of the poet's work.

Leave Dove Cottage and turn left on to the B5287 to reach Grasmere.

TOUR 86 47 MILES

HIGH LAKELAND PASSES

Fell and dale scenery at its most impressive can be enjoyed from this route, but it should be remembered that the roads in this part of Lakeland are particularly severe. Hard Knott and Wrynose passes have gradients up to 1 in 3 and should not be attempted unless both car and driver are fit.

Tranquil Rydal Water contrasts with the constant bustle and activity of Lake Windermere. Both waters are renowned for their excellent fishing, and are the homes of many wildfowl.

GRASMERE, Cumbria NY30
The idyllic setting for this tiny stone village is between the tranquil waters of Grasmere Lake and the jagged heights of Helm Crag and Nab Scar. Close by is a beautiful natural arena where the famous Grasmere Sports are staged every August, perpetuating such traditional events as Lakeland wrestling and the guides footrace. The latter follows an arduous course up a steep crag and along a ridge before descending through rough country to end in the arena. Important sheepdog trials are held in the village at about the same time, and the two events make a colourful high spot to the summer. A local rush-bearing ceremony involves the carrying of elaborately decorated bundles of rushes to the church, after which each of the bearers is rewarded with a piece of delicious local gingerbread.

In Grasmere turn left on to an unclassified road SP 'Langdale' and follow a winding, bumpy road along the west side of Grasmere Lake. In 1½ miles begin the ascent of Red Bank passing through woodland, and climb to the summit. Turn right here, descend through picturesque moorland, and at Chapel Stile bear right SP 'Dungeon Ghyll' to join the B5343. Drive along Great Langdale, passing through magnificent mountain scenery below cliffs that tower high above the road. Ahead are Langdale Pikes.

Dove Cottage in Grasmere, once the simple home of poet William Wordsworth, is now a museum containing examples of his work and various personal belongings.

Among the many traditions preserved ir Grasmere is that of gingerbread making

LANGDALE PIKES, Cumbria NY20
Harrison Stickle and Pike O'Stickle soar to respective heights of 2,403ft and 2,323ft above the secluded green dales and sparkling little tarns of the area. Collectively known as Langdale Pikes, they are separated by a deep cleft which contains the roaring waters of Dungeon Ghyll Force. This spectacular Lakeland feature is well worth a visit and can be easily reached by footpath from the New Hotel.

Drive ¾ mile beyond the New Hotel and turn sharp left on to an unclassified road. Continue through narrow pass with several steep climb and a number of hairpin bends. View from the road extend back to Great Langdale, and the lovely waters of Ble Tarn can be seen from the summit c the pass. Descend steeply, with view of the picturesque Little Langdale Valley, then turn very sharp right to climb the steep Wrynose Pass.

WRYNOSE PASS, Cumbria NY20
All around this high pass are the steep sloping peaks of the Cumbri Mountains. Just below the 1,281ft summit is the Three Shires Stone, where the boundaries of Lancashir Cumberland, and Westmorland used to meet before the national county reorganization. The summ itself affords spectacular views ove the surrounding hills and moors.

CUMBRIAN MOUNTAINS, Cumbr
Lakeland's highest passes cross the ancient Cumbrian Mountains, a range made up of several major groups separated by deep lake an river-filled valleys. At the geographical centre of the district are 3,210ft Scafell Pike, which is t highest mountain in England, the 3,162ft bulk of Sca Fell, and 2,960 Bow Fell. To the north-west rise t Great Gable and Pillar groups, an Langdale Pikes to the east. Climb parties test their skills on many o the peaks, and the high country holds many scenic rewards for th energetic fell walker.

Descend sharply from the summit Wrynose Pass. Views ahead exten over the valley to Hard Knott Pass, where the mountain road can be seen snaking across ridges and dropping away into hidden folds i the landscape. Continue along Wrynose Bottom alongside the R Duddon, with steep scree slopes either side.

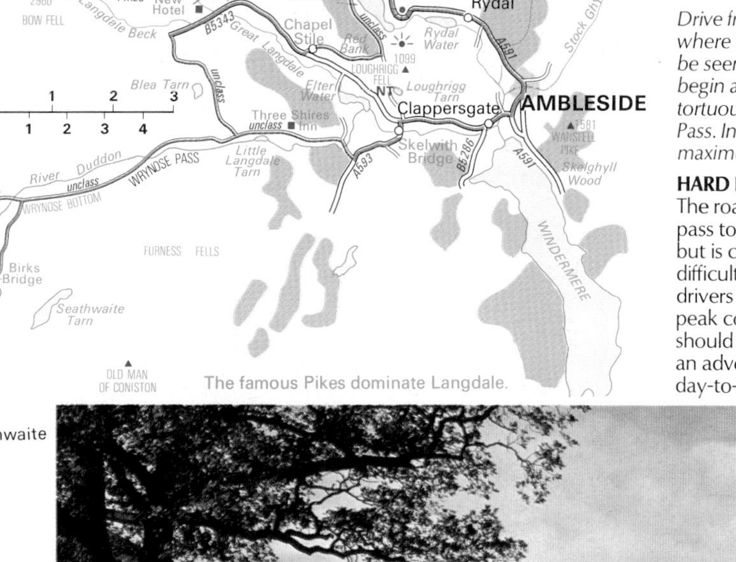

The famous Pikes dominate Langdale.

Drive from Boot to the Woolpack Inn, where the waterfall of Birker Force can be seen to the right, and in $1\frac{1}{2}$ miles begin a steep ascent through the tortuous hairpin bends of Hard Knott Pass. In places the road reaches a maximum gradient of 1 in 3.

HARD KNOTT PASS, Cumbria NY20
The road that runs through this high pass to its 1,291ft summit is surfaced, but is considered one of the most difficult in the Lake District. Cars and drivers who attempt it should be in peak condition, and its passage should be regarded as something of an adventure rather than ordinary day-to-day driving.

…typical Lakeland cottage at …lea Tarn, one of the wilder and less …equented areas of Lakeland.

…IVER DUDDON VALLEY, …umbria SD29
…lose to the Three Shires Stone in …Vrynose Pass is the source of the …iver Duddon, a beautiful water that …hatters down to Wrynose Bottom, …hrough Seathwaite and the …unnerdale villages to Ulpha. Its …ntire course is through attractive …cenery immortalized by …Vordsworth in no less than 35 …dividual sonnets.

… 2 miles turn left SP 'Broughton, …uddon Valley', with 2,129ft Harter …ell prominent to the right. Continue …ast a deep river gorge on the right. …ass the Dunnerdale Picnic Area, with …e 2,631ft Old Man of Coniston to …e left, and continue to Seathwaite.

…UNNERDALE FOREST, …umbria SD29
…alks from a riverside carpark …ovided by the Forestry …ommission lead through the lovely …d secluded countryside of …unnerdale Forest, a haven for many …fferent species of wildlife. A …articularly scenic path leads to …129ft Harter Fell, providing …cellent views over the Duddon …alley, Eskdale, and the Hard Knott …ss from its high route. Just below …k's Bridge the Duddon flows …rough an impressive gorge.

SEATHWAITE, Cumbria SD29
A remote Dunnerdale village in attractive surroundings, Seathwaite is well known as a walking centre and was beloved of the poet Wordsworth. His *Excursion* describes both the village and its 18th-century parson Robert Walker, whose grave can be seen in the local churchyard. About $\frac{1}{2}$ mile north of Seathwaite is the Walna Scar Track, which leads 5 miles across the fells to Coniston.

Leave Seathwaite and continue, passing the peak of 1,735ft Caw on the left, to reach Hall Dunnerdale. At Hall Dunnerdale turn right and drive under a thickly wooded ridge, then in $1\frac{1}{2}$ miles at Ulpha turn right with SP 'Eskdale' and ascend through more thick woodland. Follow a narrow winding road over Birker Fell for magnificent views to Sca Fell, Scafell Pike, Bow Fell, and the cone-shaped bulk of Harter Fell. Reach the King George IV Inn and turn sharp right with SP 'Boot, Langdale'. Follow the picturesque valley of Eskdale to reach Dalegarth Station, on the Ravenglass and Eskdale Railway.

RAVENGLASS AND ESKDALE RAILWAY, Cumbria NY10
Established in 1875 to carry iron ore, this fascinating little narrow-gauge railway has been revived to carry passengers through 7 miles of enchanting countryside between Dalegarth in Eskdale to Ravenglass, on the coast. Other stations allow the line to be joined at Eskdale Green and Beckfoot. The railway operates both steam and diesel locomotives, and provides a very convenient way by which to enjoy some of the district's best scenery.

ESKDALE AND STANLEY FORCE, Cumbria NY10
At its lower end this beautiful valley has a pastoral aspect, with bankside footpaths following the course of the River Esk through gentle farmlands. Beyond the villages of Eskdale Green and Boot it turns north and becomes wilder as it forges between the rocky flanks of Sca Fell and Bow Fell. Opposite Dalegarth Station is the starting point for the Stanley Ghyll Nature Trail, which leads to a lush valley and the stunning 60ft cascade of Stanley Force. Many of the paths in the dale are more suited to climbing than walking.

Leave Dalegarth Station and continue on an unclassified road to Boot.

BOOT, Cumbria NY10
A good starting point for walks along the heathery foothills of Eskdale, this beautifully situated village is surrounded by some of the highest mountains in the Lake District. Lovely Dalegarth Hall is a quaint old farmhouse with round chimney stacks that were once typical of the Lakeland region in general.

HARD KNOTT CASTLE, Cumbria NY20
Just before the summit of Hard Knott Pass are the remains of a Roman fort (AM) known as Hard Knott Castle. Built in the 2nd century AD, the ruins include surviving fragments of corner watchtowers and a bath house. It was sited in this improbable and isolated position to guard a route from the port of Ravenglass.

Begin the steep descent from the summit of the pass, negotiating very sharp hairpin bends, and in 1 mile bear left and drive along Wrynose Bottom before climbing over the steep Wrynose Pass. Descend, with excellent views over Little Langdale, and follow the valley with Little Langdale Tarn visible to the right. Pass the Three Shires Inn, and in 1 mile meet a T-junction and turn right SP 'Coniston'. In $\frac{1}{2}$ mile turn left on to the A593 SP 'Ambleside', and drive through Skelwith Bridge to reach Clappersgate.

CLAPPERSGATE, Cumbria NY30
Magnificent views are afforded by the White Craggs Garden (open) in Clappersgate, and the gardens themselves have splendid displays of heathers, rhododendrons, azaleas, and many other plants. See also tour 84.

Leave Clappersgate and cross the river bridge, then turn left for the return to Ambleside.

TOUR 87 61 MILES

THE NORTHERN LAKE DISTRICT

This is a district of beautiful mountains and lakes, heathery slopes dotted with sheep and boulders between valley woodland and the misty blueness of windswept crags. Much of the countryside is owned or protected by the National Trust, whose codes of conduct should be respected.

Derwent Water is known as the queen of the lakes, deriving much of its beauty from the many islands.

KESWICK, Cumbria NY22
This touring centre is close to some of Lakeland's finest scenery and attracts thousands of visitors every year. In Victorian times it was beloved of poets and artists, including such notables as Wordsworth, Coleridge, Southey, Ruskin, and Walpole. Many of their works and personal possessions are preserved in the fascinating Fitz Park Museum, which also features an impressive scale model of the Lake District and a variety of exhibits relating to the local area. Both Coleridge and Southey lived in Greta Park at different times, and there is a memorial to John Ruskin close to the town on the spectacular viewpoint of Friar's Crag (NT). Moot Hall is a handsome building that was reconstructed in the early 19th century. The superb 529ft viewpoint of Castle Head (NT) is within easy reach of Keswick.

Before starting the main route it is possible to take two rewarding detours to interesting areas close to the boundaries of Keswick. The first of these can be taken to Crosthwaite by driving through Keswick on the A5271 'Cockermouth' road before keeping forward on to the B5289 to reach the village.

CROSTHWAITE, Cumbria NY22
Keswick's lovely 11th-century and later parish church is sited here, and is well worth a visit. Among its many treasures are several fine monuments, 21 consecration crosses, and the churchyard grave of poet and writer Robert Southey.

For the second detour, continue along the B5289 from Crosthwaite for ½ mile, bear left, then turn left to join the A66. Again a further ¼ mile turn left again on to an unclassified road SP 'Portinscale' to enter Portinscale village. Here turn right to reach Lingholm Gardens.

LINGHOLM GARDENS, Cumbria NY22
The superb landscaped gardens of Lingholm (open), the home of Lord Rochdale, are laid out in a charming situation on the wooded western shores of Derwent Water. In spring the ground is golden with the famous Lakeland daffodils, and later in the year the banks of rhododendron bushes and azaleas blaze with colour.

DERWENT WATER, Cumbria NY22
Typical of everything that is beautiful in the Lake District, this broad lake is ringed by mountain peaks and dotted with mysterious little tree-clad islands. It measures 3 miles long by 1½ miles wide at its widest point, and is best appreciated from the lofty Friar's Crag Viewpoint (NT), back along the route. At the foot of the crag is the start of a nature trail that runs for about 2 miles along the shoreline of the lake.

To start the main tour, leave Keswick on the B5289 'Borrowdale' road and pass the Friar's Crag Viewpoint (NT) on the right. Drive beneath Castle Head (NT) on the left and reach the eastern shores of Derwent Water. Steep wooded slopes rise to the left, and farther on the road runs beneath the cliffs of the Falcon Crag Viewpoint. A detour can be taken from the main route to Ashness Bridge and Watendlath by reaching Falcon Crag and then turning left on to a winding unclassified road.

ASHNESS BRIDGE, Cumbria NY21
Thousands of visitors come here every year to admire the unique and enchanting combination of a single-arched packhorse bridge with beautiful falls on the little mountain stream which it spans.

Continue this detour by following the unclassified road to Watendlath.

WATENDLATH, Cumbria NY21
A small beck which rises close to this delightful little hamlet (NT) threads its way through a pretty valley and joins Watendlath Tarn, which lies in the shadow of 1,588ft Armboth Fell.

On the main tour, drive forward on the B5289. Continue, with excellent views of the lake, and in 1 mile reach the Lodore Swiss Hotel and the impressive Lodore Cascade.

LODORE CASCADE, Cumbria NY21
Views of this spectacular waterfall, which is situated at the southern extremity of Derwent Water, can be enjoyed from the carpark of the Lodore Swiss Hotel.

Drive through the short, green valley of Borrowdale, keeping to the left bank of the River Derwent, and in 1½ miles pass Grange village on the righthand side of the road.

GRANGE, Cumbria NY21
A double-arched bridge spans the River Derwent in this lovely little Borrowdale village. Superb views of the dale can be enjoyed from the summit of Grange Fell, which is known as King's How (NT).

Leave Grange and in ½ mile pass a track leading left to the Bowder Stone.

BOWDER STONE, Cumbria NY21
Although this remarkable 2,000-ton boulder (NT) seems about to fall from its precarious perch at any moment, it is quite firm and makes a good vantage point from which to survey the surrounding countryside.

Continue through Borrowdale to Rosthwaite.

The lush countr
around Seatolle
suffers highe
than average rainfal

ROSTHWAITE, Cumbria NY21
As Borrowdale opens out on the approach to this tiny village the views widen into a spectacular panorama of the mountains ahead. Massive Castle Crag (NT) dominates a narrow pass known as the Jaws of Borrowdale, rising high above the valley floor to a 900ft summit.

BORROWDALE, Cumbria NY21
Much of Borrowdale, the beautiful valley through which the last sectio of tour has just passed, is owned or protected by the National Trust. Its impressive crags and fells offer a challenge which draws climbers an walkers from many parts of the country, and its tiny unspoilt village are an essential part of the tranquillity that underlies its scenic grandeur. The southern end of the dale is dominated by the summits c 2,560ft Glaramara and 2,984ft Grea End, and the north by high fells.

Continue along the B5289 to reach the village of Seatoller.

Set amid mountains in one of Lakeland's most beautiful areas, Buttermere Lake is famous for the reflections that crowd its surface on calm days.

EATOLLER, Cumbria NY21
During the 17th and 18th century this village was the centre of a busy mining industry. Seatoller is now known as a base from which walkers can ascend to the Sky Head Pass, in the south. Also south of the village is eathwaite Farm (NT), one of ngland's wettest inhabited places.

detour from the main route to eathwaite Farm can be made by urning left in Seatoller on to an nclassified road and following a eep, steep-sided valley to the farm. On the main tour, continue along the 5289 and ascend Honister Pass.

ONISTER PASS, Cumbria NY21
his part of the tour follows a steep, ifficult road but offers some of the ost spectacular scenery in the hole region. The summit of the ass is 1,176ft above sea level and fords distant eastern views of the raggy Helvellyn group, beyond the cturesque foreground of orrowdale. Left towards Buttermere e the outstanding peaks of 2,479ft ed Pike and 2,644ft High Stile.

escend between scree-covered opes to the village of Buttermere.

UTTERMERE, Cumbria NY11
Vell-situated between Crummock Vater and the lake (NT) from which derives its name, this pretty village ands in the heart of a spectacular ndscape and is a popular base for alkers and climbers. Opposite the llage curiously-named Sour Milk hyll tumbles down the flanks of ty Red Pike. Scale Force, the ghest waterfall in the Lake District, accessible via a footpath.

detour from the main route to wlands Hause and Moss Force can made by driving to the outskirts of village, turning right on to an classified road SP 'Keswick', and mbing steeply.

WLANDS HAUSE AND MOSS RCE, Cumbria NY11
re the road climbs through the ectacular pass of Newlands Hause a summit of 1,096ft, with an nost sheer drop plunging away o a deep valley on the left.

the main tour, leave Buttermere ige with the B5289 and follow the east shore of Crummock Water with views of the Loweswater Fell peaks on the far side of the lake. Leave the lakeside and after 2 miles meet a T-junction. Turn right SP 'Lorton, Cockermouth' and enter the broad expanse of Lorton Vale. Continue to the edge of Lorton and turn right on to an unclassified road SP 'Keswick'. Continue to High Lorton, turn left into the village, and at the end of the village turn right. Meet a T-junction and turn right again on to the B5292 and begin to ascend Whinlatter Pass.

WHINLATTER PASS, Cumbria NY12
Drivers will find this one of the less taxing Lake District passes. Its gradients are reasonable and its bends are not quite as sharp as the others, but its 1,043ft summit affords views that are every bit as enjoyable as elsewhere.

THORNTHWAITE FOREST, Cumbria NY12
Woodland walks planned by the Forestry Commission help the visitor to get the most out of this lovely area, the longest established national forest in the Lake District. Detailed information about all aspects of the forest is available from the Interpretative Centre near the summit of Whinlatter Pass.

Descend from the forest with fine views over Bassenthwaite Lake to the left. At the foot of the descent keep left into Braithwaite.

BRAITHWAITE, Cumbria NY22
Climbers heading for the slopes and faces of 2,593ft Grizedale Pike generally start from this attractive village, which lies at the head of Coledale Valley.

Leave Braithwaite and take the 2nd turning left SP 'Cockermouth'. In ¼ mile turn left again on to the A66 and drive to the western shore of Bassenthwaite Lake.

BASSENTHWAITE LAKE, Cumbria NY22
Opposite this wooded shore, towering above the peaceful waters of lovely Bassenthwaite Lake, are the stern slopes of 3,053ft Skiddaw.

After 2½ miles turn right on to the B5291 SP 'Castle Inn', then turn right again to follow the northern end of Bassenthwaite Lake. In 1 mile turn right SP 'Bothel', cross Ouse Bridge, and continue to Castle Inn. Meet a T-junction and turn right on to the A591. Take the 2nd turning left on to an unclassified road SP 'Bassenthwaite' and approach that village.

BASSENTHWAITE, Cumbria NY23
Close to the lake in charming surroundings is the village church, which was restored in Victorian times and has a Norman chancel arch.

Do not enter the village on the main tour, but on its approach keep left (no SP) on to a narrow road and drive through pretty woodland. In 1½ miles meet a T-junction and turn left SP 'Caldbeck', then ascend a winding road to pass Over Water and smaller Chapelhouse Reservoir on the left. After 2½ miles cross open moors and meet a T-junction. Turn right, and in ¾ mile keep forward on to the B5299. In 1¼ miles cross a cattle grid, and in ¼ mile keep left to reach Caldbeck.

CALDBECK, Cumbria NY33
In 1854 the local folk hero of nursery song fame, John Peel, was buried in Caldbeck churchyard. According to tradition he was ruined by his obsessive love of fox hunting.

Drive forward on to an unclassified road and proceed to Hesket Newmarket.

HESKET NEWMARKET, Cumbria NY33
At one time this charming village on the northern flanks of Skiddaw was an important market town. Nowadays it rests in quiet retirement as yet another of the Lake District's picturesque communities.

Drive to the end of the village and bear right SP 'Mungrisdale'. Continue through agricultural country and in ½ mile bear right. In 1 mile turn left on to a winding road and continue to the Horse and Farrier (PH). Just beyond the PH bear right on to moorland and drive below the sheer rock face of 2,174ft Carrock Fell. Continue through Mungrisdale, pass below Souther Fell, then meet a T-junction with the A66 and turn right SP 'Keswick'; 2,847ft Saddleback rises to the right. Continue to the outskirts of Threlkeld; the main village lies just off the main road to the right.

THRELKELD, Cumbria NY32
No less than 35 local huntsmen are commemorated by a monument in the local churchyard, and it seems likely that the fanatical John Peel would have made many friends here. The village itself stands at the head of St John's Vale, on the banks of a stream that threads its way along the valley floor. North is the unusually shaped peak of Saddleback.

Continue along the A66 and pass the junction with the B5322. In ½ mile turn left on to an unclassified road SP 'St John's in the Vale Church', and in 1 mile turn left again SP 'Stone Circle'. In ¼ mile turn left and ascend to the Castlerigg Stone Circle.

CASTLERIGG STONE CIRCLE, Cumbria NY22
Situated in a superb mountain setting some 700ft above sea level, this prehistoric circle (AM, NT) measures over 100ft in diameter and is made up of 38 stones. An oblong space on the site contains another 10 stones.
Continue past the stone circle and descend to meet the A5271. Turn left and re-enter Keswick.

Castlerigg Stone Circle probably dates back to the bronze age.

TOUR 88 53 MILES

BOUNDARY OF AN ANCIENT EMPIRE

Here the monumental ruins of Hadrian's Wall undulate across the rocky spine of Britain, still proclaiming the might of the Roman Empire many centuries after its collapse. South are the soft woodlands of the beautiful South Tyne Valley, the heart of rural Northumberland.

CARLISLE, Cumbria NY45
During the Roman occupation Carlisle, then known as *Luguvalium*, was a strategic centre of the frontier that separated the largely Romanized peoples of the south from the wild northern tribes. Continued excursions from Scotland prompted William Rufus to build the town's sturdy castle (AM) in 1092; Queen Mary's Tower contains a fascinating museum devoted to the Border Regiments. During the Civil War the six western bays of Carlisle's small medieval cathedral were demolished to repair the town wall, but two surviving bays of the nave display Norman workmanship. The choir was restored in the 13th century and features a magnificent east window. In the cathedral grounds is a 13th-century pele tower known as the Prior's Tower. Tullie House Museum occupies a fine Jacobean mansion and contains exhibits relating to Hadrian's Wall.

Leave the centre of Carlisle with SP 'The South' on the A6 and in 3 miles reach the M6 junction roundabout. Take the 2nd exit SP 'Wetheral', and 1 mile beyond Cumwhinton pass a right turn leading to Wetheral Abbey. After a short distance enter the pleasant village of Wetheral.

WETHERAL, Cumbria NY45
An ancient abbey gatehouse in this attractive village faces across the River Eden to the impressive pile of Corby Castle. Fine monuments by the sculptor Nollekens can be seen inside the local church.

Follow the main road through Wetheral village and in $1\frac{1}{2}$ miles meet a T-junction. Turn right on to the A69 SP 'Newcastle' and cross the Eden. A detour from the main route to Corby Castle can be made by turning right immediately after the bridge on to an unclassified road and driving through pleasant countryside for $1\frac{1}{2}$ miles.

CORBY CASTLE, Cumbria NY45
In 1611 the local Howard family extended the old pele tower that had been guarding Great Corby since the 13th century, adding a long range that transformed it into a great L-shaped house. The present aspect of the building, set amid lovely grounds (open) in a particularly scenic area, owes much to further extension work carried out in the 19th century.

On the main tour, continue along the A69, skirt the grounds of Holme Eden Abbey, and enter Warwick Bridge.

WARWICK BRIDGE, Cumbria NY45
The two small communities of Warwick and Warwick Bridge are separated by a fine bridge of 1837. Most of the notable buildings are off the main route in Warwick, including a superb Norman church with an outstanding 12th-century apse.

Leave Warwick Bridge and after a short distance meet crossroads. Turn right on to an unclassified road SP 'Castle Carrock' and in 50 yards turn left. Follow a quiet by-road and in 1 mile pass Toppin Castle, which incorporates a pele tower. In a further $1\frac{1}{2}$ miles branch left SP 'Talkin', and 1 mile farther keep left, pass under a railway viaduct, and meet crossroads with the B6413. Drive forward over the main road and pass Talkin Fell on the right before entering Talkin.

TALKIN, Cumbria NY55
Close to the high fells whose ownership was so hotly disputed for many centuries, this village has a lovely little church that has managed to preserve surprising evidence of its Norman origins. Work from that early period can be seen in the nave, bellcote, and chancel, and there are even traces in the pulpit and altar rail. Some 4 miles south-south-east of Talkin the summit of Cold Fell is surmounted by a cairn measuring 4ft high and 50ft in diameter.

Leave Talkin, and in $\frac{1}{4}$ mile turn right SP 'Hallbankgate'. Ascend, with views which extend left over the tree-bordered waters of Talkin Tarn and the great expanse of the Cumberland Plain. Reach Hallbankgate and turn right on to the A689 SP 'Alston'. Continue through Halton Lea Gate, then in just over 1 mile turn left on to an unclassified road SP 'Coanwood'. Descend to the steep wooded banks of the River South Tyne, cross the river, and ascend past Coanwood to meet crossroads. Turn left on to the 'Haltwhistle' road, in $\frac{3}{4}$ mile enter the hamlet of Rowfoot, and turn left SP 'Featherstone Park'. After $\frac{1}{2}$ mile descend steeply to reach Featherstone Castle.

Carlisle Cathedral is impressive but sma

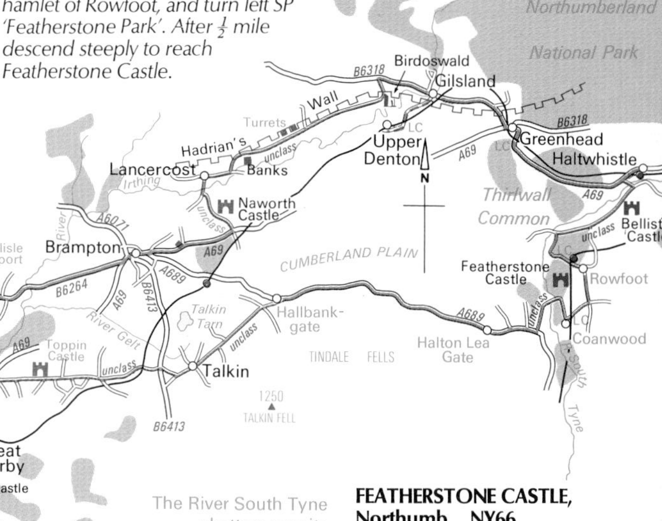

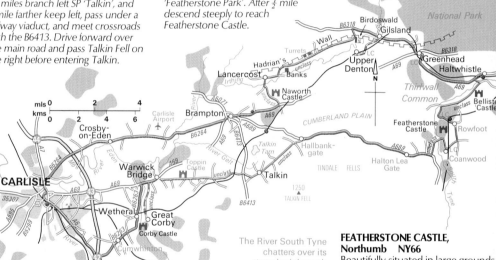

The River South Tyne chatters over its stony bed through the grounds of secluded Featherstone Castle.

FEATHERSTONE CASTLE, Northumb NY66
Beautifully situated in large grounds beside the River South Tyne, this fin house (not open) is built round a courtyard and dates from the 13th century.

Leave Featherstone Castle on a secluded, picturesque road along th east bank of the River South Tyne. Meet a bridge and keep forward SP 'Haltwhistle', then in $\frac{1}{2}$ mile ascend tc a T-junction and turn left. In $1\frac{3}{4}$ miles reach Bellister Castle on the right.

BELLISTER CASTLE, Northumb NY76
In the 16th century the ruined towe attached to this 3-storey building (not open) was known as a bastell house, which perhaps gives a clue t the origin of the name. The house itself dates from 1669 and displays a number of good architectural features from that time.

Leave Bellister Castle and after a shor distance turn left to cross a river bridge and reach the outskirts of Haltwhistle. Turn right on to the A69 to reach the town centre.

HALTWHISTLE, Northumb NY76
William the Lion founded this old mining town's church in 1178, and as it stands today the building is considered a particularly fine example of early-English architecture. There is no tower, and the sanctuary preserves three carved coffin lids which are thought to date from the 14th century.

Return along the A69 SP 'Carlisle' and follow the railway for $2\frac{3}{4}$ miles. Drive over a level crossing to reach Greenhead.

GREENHEAD, Northumb NY66
This little village lies south of Hadrian's Wall, close to a series of attractive ravines known as the Nine Nicks of Thirlwall. The route of a Roman track known as the Maiden Way extends from here to Penrith. See also tour 91.

Leave Greenhead, bear left, and in 50 yards turn right on to the B6318 SP 'Gilsland'. In $\frac{1}{2}$ mile pass a section of Hadrian's Wall on the left.

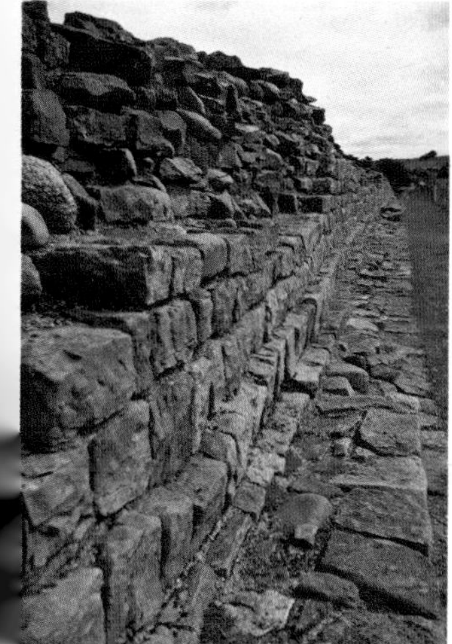

A section of Hadrian's Wall at Gilsland.

IADRIAN'S WALL, Cumbria
3etween AD 122 and 139 the Roman 'mperor Hadrian ordered that a lefensive wall should be built to liscourage the independent Scottish ribes from marauding into the argely pacified territory to the south. 'oday this major engineering ıchievement still stands as a emarkable monument to the ‹oman occupation of Britain, tretching 73 miles from Wallsend-n-Tyne to Bowness. Its course was lotted from one natural advantage ɔ the next, and it was built of the naterials most readily to hand – :one in the east and turf in the west. ılong its length were 20 or so major orts, interspersed with milecastles nd signal towers close enough ɔgether to allow the quick ansference of a warning by fire eacon. Much of the surviving ructure is protected under the ncient Monuments scheme. See so tour 91.

ontinue along the B6318 to Gilsland, ıd on the nearside of a railway ridge reach a left turn leading to the ɔman wall's Poltross Burn Milecastle.

The excavated milecastle at Haltwhistle was one of several built at intervals along the length of Hadrian's Wall.

GILSLAND, Northumb NY66
Gilsland has natural sulphur and chalybeate springs that once made it a popular spa resort, though it never developed to the rarefied fashionable heights achieved by its southern contemporaries. Part of the Poltross Burn Milecastle (AM) is incorporated in a railway embankment near by, and a section of the Roman wall (AM) stands east of the school. See also tour 91.

Meet a T-junction in Gilsland and turn right. A detour from the main tour can be made to Upper Denton by turning left at the T-junction.

UPPER DENTON, Cumbria NY66
It is thought that the Saxon builders of this fascinating little church may have used stone from Hadrian's Wall in its construction. Of particular note is the reconstructed Roman arch in the chancel.

Leave Gilsland by crossing the River Irthing. In $\frac{1}{4}$ mile turn left, and ascend with views of the Roman wall to the left. After 1 mile turn left on to an unclassified road SP 'Birdoswald, Lanercost', and in a further $\frac{1}{2}$ mile pass Harrow's Scar Milecastle (AM) to reach Birdoswald.

BIRDOSWALD, Cumbria NY66
The Roman fort of *Camboglanna* (AM) occupies a 5-acre ridge-top site overlooking the gorge of the River Irthing near Birdoswald. Access to the remains, which include a particularly well-preserved angle tower and postern gate, is controlled by the farmer. See also tour 91.

Leave Birdoswald and drive forward along the line of the Roman wall, passing two Roman turrets (AM) to reach Banks.

BANKS, Cumbria NY56
Notable Roman sites in the area around Banks include Coombe Crag, Pike Hill (AM) and Boothby Castle Hill, and there is a milecastle (AM) with a section of the Roman wall here. A converted farmhouse on the route of the wall contains the LYC Museum and Art Gallery, which has a permanent exhibition of Roman and Cumbrian folk art, crafts, and antiquities. See also tour 91.

Raiding parties from the Scottish side of the border inflicted heavy damage on Lanercost Priory during the 14th century.

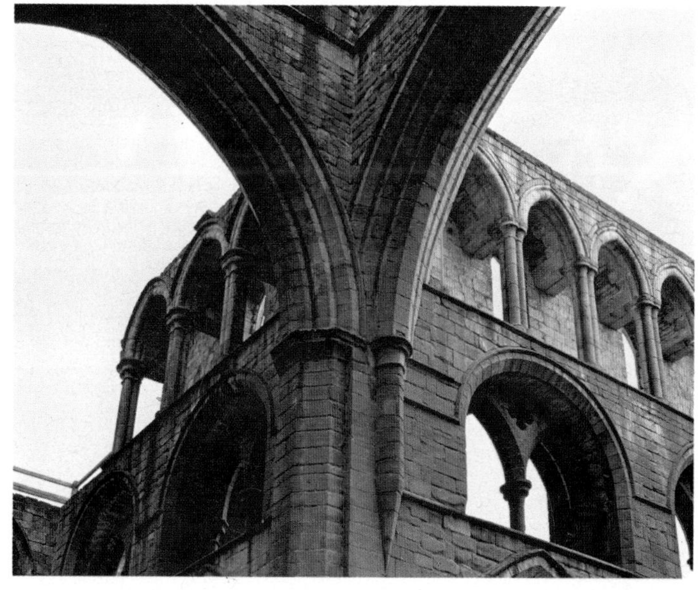

From Banks bear left, descend to the River Irthing, and continue to Lanercost.

LANERCOST, Cumbria NY56
Extensive remains of a priory (AM) that was built with stones taken from the Roman wall can be seen here, including parts of a gatehouse showing 16th-century adaptations. The 12th-century nave serves as the parish church.

Pass the entrance to Lanercost Priory, cross the river, then immediately beyond the bridge turn left and ascend. After a short distance cross Naworth Park to reach Naworth Castle.

NAWORTH CASTLE, Cumbria NY56
Pleasantly designed round a central courtyard, this 14th-century castle shows later additions and features a great hall, oratory, and rich tapestries. The building is open by arrangement.

At the castle entrance bear right and in $\frac{1}{2}$ mile meet crossroads. Turn right on to the A69 SP 'Carlisle' to reach Brampton.

BRAMPTON, Cumbria NY56
An unusual 8-sided moot hall stands in the cobble-flanked main street of Brampton, and the local church is the only ecclesiastical building known to have been designed by the inventive 19th-century architect, Philip Webb. The interior of the building is lit by a superb stained-glass window by the Victorian artist Burne-Jones.

Follow the A69 through Brampton, then keep forward on to the B6264 SP 'Carlisle Airport'. Proceed to Crosby-on-Eden.

CROSBY-ON-EDEN, Cumbria NY45
The windows of the local church show the striking and original use of cut clear glass instead of stained glass. Other notable buildings here include Crosby House and High Crosby Farmhouse.

In $3\frac{1}{2}$ miles turn left on to the A7 for the return to Carlisle.

TOUR 89 58 MILES

THROUGH WEARDALE AND TEESDALE

Deep in the wooded outriders of the eastern Pennines are beautiful river valleys and spectacular waterfalls, attractive little dales villages, and the stream-fed waters of placid reservoirs. Everywhere is the sound of water falling from ledges, tumbling over boulders, and cascading down hillsides.

The fast-flowing River Tees becomes even more rapid as it nears High Force Waterfall.

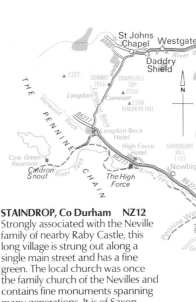

Raby Castle was considerably altered during the 18th and 19th centuries.

BARNARD CASTLE, Co Durham NZ01

The town of Barnard Castle stands in a picturesque setting on a clifftop overlooking the River Tees and is an ideal base from which to explore the lovely countryside of Teesdale. The first castle to stand here was built in the 12th century by Guy de Balliol, but this was rebuilt by his nephew Bernard – hence the Barnard element of the town name – and adapted throughout the centuries by various owners. During the Civil War it fell to the Cromwellian army, after which it was left to crumble away in peace. Today the site covers $6\frac{1}{2}$ acres, and the extensive remains (AM) include the 3-storey keep and parts of a 14th-century great hall. In the town itself is a medieval bridge that is still in use, and many old houses and inns. It is thought that Charles Dickens may have written *Nicholas Nickleby* while staying here. Close to the town is the fascinating Bowes Museum of Art and the local countryside is dotted with picturesque little villages. See tour 81.

A short detour before the main route begins can be taken to Egglestone Abbey by driving south on the B6277 and turning off with SP on an unclassified road.

Egglestone Abbey is now a romantic ruin.

EGGLESTONE ABBEY, Co Durham NZ01

These lovely ruins (AM) date from the 12th century and occupy a beautiful rural site beside the River Tees. Close by the Thorsgill Beck is spanned by a medieval packhorse bridge and an attractive 18th-century road bridge. See also tour 81.

On the main tour, leave Barnard Castle with SP 'Bishop Auckland' and at the edge of the town turn left to follow the A688 to Staindrop.

STAINDROP, Co Durham NZ12

Strongly associated with the Neville family of nearby Raby Castle, this long village is strung out along a single main street and has a fine green. The local church was once the family church of the Nevilles and contains fine monuments spanning many generations. It is of Saxon origin and carries a tower that was added in the 12th century, but its south aisle, porch, and nave all date from the 15th century. Inside is the only pre-Reformation screen surviving in County Durham.

Turn left by Staindrop Church and after 1 mile reach the entrance to Raby Castle.

RABY CASTLE, Co Durham NZ12

This impressive pile stands in a 270-acre deer park and exactly matches the popular conception of what a castle should look like, right down to its moat and nine great towers. It is known to have been in existence in one form or another from 1016, but its present distinctive appearance is largely due to 14th-century rebuilding and extension. Over the centuries Raby has played a major role in the politics of Britain. The huge Baron's Hall was the scene of plotting aimed at putting Mary Queen of Scots on the English throne instead of Elizabeth I, but when the scheme failed the castle was forfeited and passed into the hands of the Neville family. Later it became the property of the Vanes, Lords of Barnard; nowadays it is a valuable national asset which attracts many visitors each year. Inside are fine collections of furniture, paintings and ceramics, and among the many fine chambers is a curious octagonal drawing room. The kitchens display 14th-century rib vaulting and preserve a smoke-driven spit, while outside in the stables is a collection of carriages.

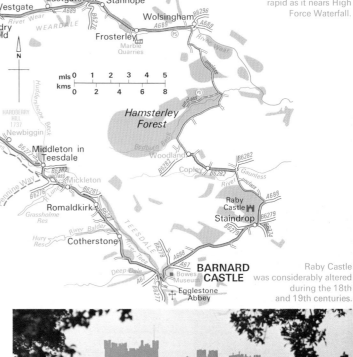

Leave Raby Castle and continue along the A688 for $\frac{1}{2}$ mile. Turn left on to an unclassified road SP 'Cockfield' and after $\frac{1}{2}$ mile keep straight on SP 'Butterknowle'. After another $2\frac{1}{4}$ miles turn left on to B6282 for Copley and continue to Woodland. Meet a T-junction and turn left, then after 300 yards turn right on to an unclassified road SP 'Hamsterley'. Descend, with good views over Hamsterley Forest.

HAMSTERLEY FOREST, Co Durham NZ02

Fast becoming known as one of the most beautiful countryside recreation areas in the county, this large state forest is crossed by a road that is open to motorists. It can be explored via dozens of footpaths, and parking space is virtually limitless. Visitors are catered for with three picnic sites, drinking water, forest picnic furniture, and a swimming pool. A special woodland trail has been laid out to help children identify various species of plants and animals, and the glades away from the busy areas are the homes of roe, fallow, and red deer.

After 3 miles turn left SP 'Wolsingham' and descend, then in $\frac{3}{4}$ mile meet a T-junction and turn left again to cross Bedburn Beck. After a short distance pass a left turn that gives access to Hamsterley Forest, and drive through woodland before emerging into open countryside and descending into Weardale. Cross the River Wear and continue to the edge of Wolsingham

WOLSINGHAM, Co Durham NZ03
A good base from which to explore beautiful Weardale, this typical Durham town of stone-built houses holds a precarious balance between the needs of industry and the preservation of its charm. The result is the type of contrast seen between giant steelworks on the outskirts and the historic 12th-century tower of St Mary's Church, more towards the centre of the town. North of Wolsingham is the lovely Tunstall Reservoir, which was formed by the constriction of Waskerley Beck and has become the home of many water birds and other wild creatures with a liking for aquatic surroundings.

Turn left on to the A689 SP 'Stanhope' and continue to Frosterley.

FROSTERLEY, Co Durham NZ03
A local stone known as Frosterley marble is much prized for building and monumental sculpture, but centuries of quarrying have almost exhausted the supply. What little is left is being saved for purposes considered important enough for such a rare material. Many of the county's churches have fonts, memorials, pillars, and various other features fashioned from the stone, which is not really marble but a grey limestone that becomes black and reveals hundreds of tiny fossils when polished. A particularly fine example of the material can be seen near the door of the local church, bearing the inscription 'This Frosterley marble and limestone, quarried for centuries in this parish, adorns cathedrals and churches throughout the world'.

Leave Frosterley and continue along the A689 to Stanhope.

An unusual feature of Stanhope Churchyard is the fossilized stump of a tree.

STANHOPE, Co Durham NY93
Stanhope churchyard features the fossilized stump of a tree that grew some 150 million years ago. The church itself dates from 1200 and contains a number of fascinating relics, including a Saxon font, two wooden plaques and a painting all thought to be Flemish. Close to the churchyard gate is the old town cross. West of Stanhope, in the high Weardale moorland, is a wooded gorge containing the famous Heathery Burn Cave. Bronze-age weapons and various artefacts proving the early domestication of horses in England were found here, and are now on display in London's British Museum.

Leave Stanhope on the A689 'Alston' road and continue to Eastgate.

The drama of Caldron Snout is well worth the difficult approach.

EASTGATE, Co Durham NY93
Attractive Frosterley marble is shown to advantage by the font in Eastgate's 19th-century parish church. A feature of the beautiful moorland countryside around the village is the Low Linn Falls, where a burn tumbles over rocks in an area that is of particular interest to geologists and botanists.

Leave Eastgate and continue along the A689 beside the River Wear to reach Westgate.

WESTGATE, Co Durham NY93
Both Westgate and Eastgate derived their names from the entrances to Old Park, which was once the hunting residence of the bishops of Durham. The village has a 19th-century church and an attractive watermill, and was once well known as a cock-fighting centre. Nowadays it has a strange claim to fame as the only place where a medieval thimble has been found.

Continue to Daddry Shield.

The high moorland of Weardale is within easy reach of Stanhope.

DADDRY SHIELD, Co Durham NY83
Another old centre of cock fighting, this attractive Weardale village stands just north of a mountain rescue post.

Continue to St John's Chapel.

ST JOHN'S CHAPEL, Co Durham NY83
This ancient market centre takes its name from the Church of St John the Baptist. The original foundation was probably created many hundreds of years ago, but the present building dates from 1752.

Turn left on to an unclassified road SP 'Middleton-in-Teesdale' and climb to 2,056ft on Langdon Common, part of the Pennine Chain.

THE PENNINE CHAIN
Popularly known as the Backbone of England, this great upland mass of hills, moorland, and mountains stretches north from Kinder Scout in Derbyshire to the Cheviot foothills on the Scottish border. A 250-mile footpath known as the Pennine Way traverses the range from end to end. See also tour 79.

Descend into Teesdale, meet a T-junction, and turn left on to the B6277. In ½ mile reach the Langdon Beck Hotel, where a short detour can be made from the main route by turning right and driving along a rough track to the picnic area at Cow Green Reservoir. A private road (locked) and footpath (open) lead from here to the waterfall of Caldron Snout.

CALDRON SNOUT, Co Durham NY82
More of a tiered cascade than a proper waterfall, beautiful Caldron Snout tumbles 200ft down a natural staircase formed by a hard rock known as dolerite. It used to be fed by a long winding pool called the Well, but this has now been incorporated in the Cow Green Reservoir. Downstream from the cascade is the spectacular High Force waterfall, and between the two are the remains of a slate mill.

Continue along the B6277 and after 2½ miles meet the High Force Hotel. A footpath opposite the hotel leads to the High Force waterfall.

HIGH FORCE, Co Durham NY82
Here one of England's loveliest waterfalls plunges 70ft over the menacing black cliff of the Great Whin Sill, to be caught in a deep pool surrounded by shrubs and rocks.

Continue along the B6277 through Newbiggin to reach the town of Middleton-in-Teesdale

MIDDLETON-IN-TEESDALE, Co Durham NY92
Strong Quaker influence is evident in the no-frills orderliness of this stern little town. This is because local lead mines, the mainstay of Middleton's economy until they were closed at the start of this century, were run by that denomination. The local church dates from the 19th century and shares its churchyard with various remains of a predecessor.

Leave Middleton-in-Teesdale and turn right on to a road SP 'Scotch Corner'. Cross the River Tees and in ½ mile keep left SP 'Barnard Castle'. Continue for ¾ mile, rejoin the B6277, and continue through Mickleton and attractive Romaldkirk.

ROMALDKIRK, Co Durham NY92
The attractive houses of this perfect little Teesdale village are interspersed with greensward that transforms an already good villagescape into a splendid one.

Leave Romaldkirk and continue along the B6277 to Cotherstone.

COTHERSTONE, Co Durham NZ01
Beautiful and dramatic scenery surrounds this pleasant village, which stands at the junction of Balder Beck and the River Tees. Close to the watersmeet are slight remains of a Norman castle.

Leave Cotherstone, recross the River Tees, and return to Barnard Castle.

TOUR 90 84 MILES

AN UNDISCOVERED COAST

Much of Northumberland's coast is unvisited and unspoiled. North of Alnwick it is designated an Area of Outstanding Natural Beauty, while to the south the lovely River Coquet meets the sea after winding past the religious foundations and mighty castles of bygone ages.

ALNWICK, Northumb NU11
This attractive and historic town is a convenient touring centre situated in attractive countryside only 4 miles from the coast. Its splendid castle was once a stronghold of the dukes of Northumberland, and over hundreds of years has been extended to cover some 7 acres of ground. It was founded by the Percy family in the 12th century, but was ruined during a particularly violent phase of border warfare and was not restored to military effectiveness until the 14th century. The major features of its design date from this time, although a great deal of maintenance work was carried out in the 18th and 19th centuries, and today it ranks as one of the most magnificent buildings of its type in the country. The gateway is guarded by an impressive barbican, and the outline of its massive keep, walls and towers completely dominates the town's horizon. Parts of the castle open to visitors are the armoury in Constable's Tower, a museum of British and Roman antiquities in the Postern Tower, the keep, and many of its beautifully furnished state rooms. The town itself has several good churches and several good Georgian buildings. St Michael's echoes the castle with its battlemented tower and is said to preserve some of the best 15th-century workmanship in the county. Among the treasures inside are numerous fine monuments and a Flemish carved chest that dates from the 14th century. Remains of Alnwick Abbey stand on the northern outskirts of the town and include a well-preserved 14th-century gatehouse. The 18th-century Town Hall has shops in its arcaded ground floor. Two well-known foundations are the Duke's and the Duchess's Schools, and the Old Ragged or Industrial School still exists for the education of needy children. Some 3 miles north-west of Alnwick in Hulne Park are the remains of 13th-century Hulne Priory.

Follow SP 'Morpeth', then 'Bamburgh B1340' and cross the River Aln via Denwick Bridge. Pass through Denwick, turn right on to an unclassified road SP 'Longhoughton', and after $2\frac{1}{2}$ miles turn left to join the B1339. Enter Longhoughton, then after another 1 mile turn right and in $\frac{1}{2}$ mile drive forward on to an unclassified road SP 'Howick'. Continue for 1 mile to pass the entrance to Howick Hall, then turn right and after another $\frac{1}{2}$ mile keep left to reach the edge of Howick.

HOWICK, Northumb NU21
Situated where the Great Whin Sill outcrop meets the sea in 120ft cliffs of black rock, this hamlet is also a good base from which to tour the local countryside. Howick Hall is a fine 18th-century mansion (not open) standing in beautiful grounds (open).

In $1\frac{1}{4}$ miles meet crossroads and turn right through an archway to the fishing village of Craster.

Crabbing boats at Craster are still built to the traditional Northumbrian design.

CRASTER, Northumb NU21
Craster is known for its oak-smoked kippers and splendid cliff scenery. The former can be sampled at many places in the district, and the latter is best appreciated from a $1\frac{1}{4}$-mile walk leading to Dunstanburgh Castle. Above the village is the Georgian house of Craster Tower, which incorporates the remains of a medieval building from which it takes its name.

DUNSTANBURGH CASTLE, Northumb NU22
The great rocky promontory that juts into the sea here would be impressive in any circumstances, but crowned with the picturesque ruins of Dunstanburgh Castle it is magnificent. Remains of this essentially 14th-century structure (AM, NT) cover 11 acres of ground and are enclosed by massive defensive walls. This particular section of coast is in a designated area of outstanding natural beauty.

Return from Craster for $\frac{1}{2}$ mile and turn right SP 'Embleton'. In another $\frac{3}{4}$ mile meet a T-junction and turn right for Embleton.

Restoration in the 19th century preserved Bamburgh Castle's imposing presence on the Whin Sill outcrop.

EMBLETON, Northumb NU22
One of the main buildings in this pretty village is the 14th-century fortified vicarage, which incorporates a pele tower. Military precautions in buildings ideologically devoted to peace are not uncommon in this area which was racked by war between Scots and English for centuries.

Keep left and drive to the church, then turn right on to the B1339. In $1\frac{1}{4}$ miles keep forward on to the B1340, and $1\frac{1}{4}$ miles farther turn right. In another $1\frac{1}{2}$ miles meet crossroads and turn right again for Beadnell.

BEADNELL, Northumb NU22
Close to this small fishing village are several 18th-century lime kilns (NT). Safe bathing and a sandy beach make it attractive as a resort, and the surrounding countryside is beautiful.

Continue to Seahouses.

SEAHOUSES, Northumb NU23
During the late 19th century a harbour was built here to serve Sunderland, and the village that grew up to house the port workers has changed little to the present day. It is a pretty place with plenty of boat traffic, including a service that runs to the offshore Farne Islands.

FARNE ISLANDS, Northumb NU23
It is said that St Aidan came to this group of 25 small islands (NT) to meditate in the 7th century, and that St Cuthbert stayed in a little hermitage here until he was reluctantly persuaded to become Bishop of Lindisfarne (see tour 92) in the same period. Nowadays the group is best known for its bird sanctuary, and ornithologists of the Bird Observatory study from a converted 16th-century pele tower.

At Seahouses turn right, reach a war memorial, and turn left to follow the coast road to Bamburgh.

BAMBURGH, Northumb NU13
Grace Darling was born in this unspoilt fishing village in 1815, and is buried in the graveyard of the mainly 13th-century church. She became instantly famous in 1838 when she sailed with her father from a lighthouse on Longstone Island, in the teeth of a gale, to rescue survivors from the wrecked ship *Forfarshire*. The RNLI has founded a local museum to her memory. Immediately obvious to the visitor is Bamburgh's huge Norman castle (open), once the seat of the kings of Northumbria and now restored to its original magnificence. During the 18th century it became a charitable institution, with schools, accommodation for shipwrecked sailors, a hospital, a granary, and many other facilities.

Branch right on to the B1342 SP 'Belford' and in $2\frac{1}{2}$ miles meet a T-junction. Turn left, then after another $1\frac{3}{4}$ miles reach Belford Station and drive over a level crossing. In 1 mile turn right on to the A1 for Belford.

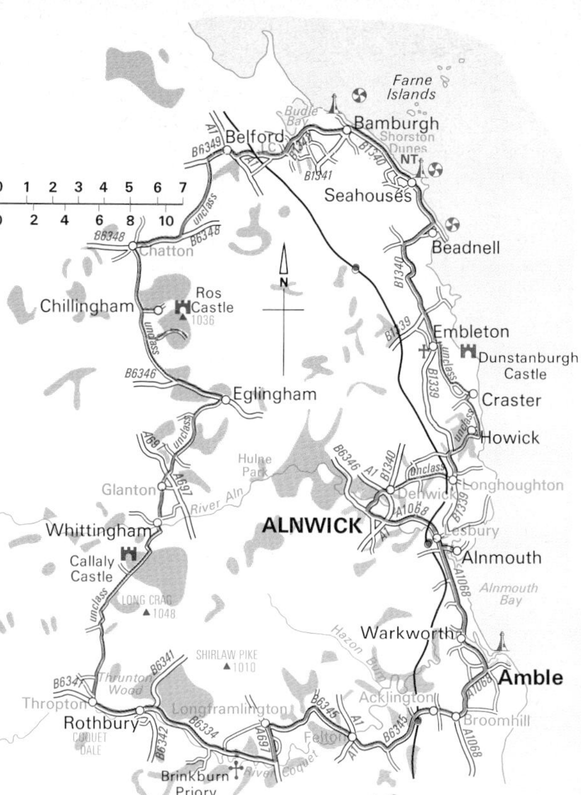

LFORD, Northumb NU13
coaching days this small market wn on the Great North Road was a pular stop where passengers uld stretch their legs and take reshment at local inns. Belford Hall ot open) is a large building signed by James Paine in 1756.

rn left on to the B6349 SP 'Wooler', d after another $\frac{3}{4}$ mile turn left again to an unclassified road SP atton'. In 3 miles meet a unction and turn right on to the 348, then descend from Chatton or to reach Chatton village. Drive he end of the village and turn left to an unclassified road SP illingham'. After another $1\frac{1}{2}$ miles ch Chillingham Post Office and n left; cross a ford into the village.

LLINGHAM, Northumb NU02
ing the summer months the unds of 14th- and 17th-century llingham Castle (not open) are essible for people wishing to see remarkable Chillingham wild tle. The animals in this herd are descendants of wild oxen eved to have been trapped when park was created in 1220.

urn to Chillingham Post Office turn left, then pass an unclassified urn leading to Ros Castle. This s a pleasant detour from the main e.

CASTLE, Northumb NU02
l people will insist, with some ce, that the views from this 6ft hill (NT) are better than any rs in the county. The nificent panorama stretches east he coast and the Farne Islands, to the Cheviot Hills, and races the romantic medieval nes of both Bamburgh and stanburgh Castles.

On the main tour, continue for 3 miles and drive forward to join the B6346 for Eglingham.

EGLINGHAM, Northumb NU11
The multi-period church in Eglingham is a charming, if heavily restored, asset to the villagescape. Eglingham Hall (not open) dates from the early 18th century.

On the nearside of Eglingham turn right on to an unclassified road SP 'Beanley' and 'Powburn', then in 1 mile bear left SP 'Glanton'. After another $2\frac{1}{2}$ miles cross a main road for Glanton, then turn right and take the next turning left for Whittingham.

Atlantic seals bask under Longstone lighthouse in the Farne Islands, offshore from Bamburgh.

Statues guard the barbican at Alnwick Castle.

WHITTINGHAM, Northumb NU01
Attractively grouped on both banks of the River Aln, this pretty village was once famous as the location of a large fair. A lovely stone bridge spans the river, and the local church shows evidence of Saxon origins in its tower and nave. A 15th-century pele tower survives here.

Cross the River Aln, turn right SP 'Callalay', and after 2 miles skirt the grounds of Callalay Castle.

CALLALAY CASTLE, Northumb NU00
The Callalays are the last of three families to have successively owned this estate since Saxon times, and the manor house is one of the best in the county. Most of the present building (open) dates from the 17th to 19th centuries, but the 15th-century pele tower which it incorporates is evidence of a much earlier building.

In $2\frac{1}{2}$ miles turn left SP 'Thropton', ascend, then descend into Coquet Dale at the edge of Thropton. Meet a T-junction and turn left on to the B6341 for Rothbury.

ROTHBURY, Northumb NU00
Popular with anglers and walkers, this historic village can trace its history to a time long before the Norman Conquest and the area is particularly rich in various prehistoric remains.

Keep forward and in $\frac{1}{2}$ mile bear right on to the B6334 SP 'Morpeth'. After $3\frac{1}{2}$ miles it is possible to take a short detour from the main route by turning right to Brinkburn Priory.

BRINKBURN PRIORY, Northumb NZ19
Beautifully set in a loop of the River Coquet, this 12th-century foundation was created by Augustinian Canons and has one of the best priory buildings (AM) in the country. This status is largely due to sensitive 19th-century restorers. Nowadays the priory is occasionally used for organ recitals.

On the main route, continue for $1\frac{1}{2}$ miles and turn left on to the A697 SP 'Coldstream'. Reach the edge of Longframlington and turn right on to the B6345, then continue to Felton. Turn right on to the A1, cross the River Coquet, then in $\frac{1}{4}$ mile turn left on to the B6345 SP 'Amble'. After another $1\frac{1}{2}$ miles turn left and continue through Acklington. Turn left again at Broomhill village on to the A1068 for Amble.

AMBLE, Northumb NU20
North of this attractive little resort is a stretch of coast that has been designated an area of outstanding natural beauty. Eider ducks breed on Coquet Island, which lies offshore from Amble.

Turn left and follow SP 'Alnwick', then in $1\frac{1}{2}$ miles meet a T-junction and turn right into Warkworth.

WARKWORTH, Northumb NU20
At the top of the main street in Warkworth are the impressive remains of a 12th-century and later castle (AM) that was probably built by the 1st Earl of Northumberland. Its keep, gatehouse, and hall are particularly notable. The view along the main street as it climbs towards the ruins between buildings of many periods is unforgettable. The mainly Norman Church of St Lawrence has an outstanding stone spire which is one of only two ancient examples to be found in the county, and the famous Warkworth Hermitage is a rock-cut chapel (AM) dating from the 14th century.

In $3\frac{1}{2}$ miles meet a roundabout and drive forward. A short diversion can be made from the main route by taking the 3rd exit from the roundabout and visiting Alnmouth.

ALNMOUTH, Northumb NU21
This holiday resort was once a major grain-shipping port, but nowadays it deals mainly with yachtsmen and other small-boat sailors.

On the main drive, return along the A1068 via Lesbury to Alnwick.

TOUR 91 — 90 MILES

AMONG THE BORDER FORESTS

The fascinating remains of Hadrian's Wall can be seen at their best over the vast coniferous plantations and wild moorlands of the Kielder and Redesdale Forests, parts of the Border Forest Park. Special Forestry Commission roads allow motorists to enjoy this area right up to the Scottish Border.

Bewcastle's ancient cross is decorated with intricate carvings and Runic inscriptions.

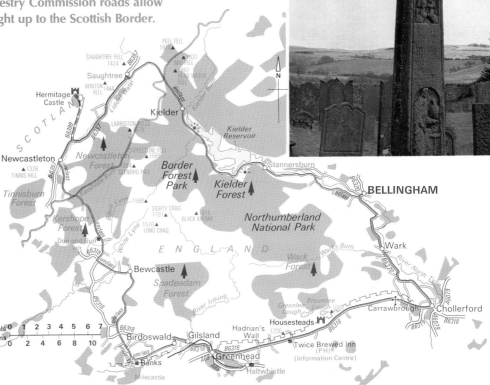

BELLINGHAM, Northumb NY88
The focus of life in North Tynedale, this small market town once had a flourishing iron industry but nowadays is best known as a gateway to the great moors and forests of Nortumberland. Its ancient Church of St Cuthbert has a unique roof, barrel vaulted with six-sided stone ribs instead of the usual timber, probably as a precaution against fire. In the churchyard is a well whose waters are traditionally held to have healing powers.

Leave Bellingham on the B6320 with SP 'Hexham', and in ½ mile turn left and cross a river bridge. Take the next turning right on to an unclassified road SP 'Kielder', then drive through picturesque North Tynedale.

NORTHUMBERLAND NATIONAL PARK, Northumb
Extending from Hadrian's Wall in the south to the Cheviot Hills in the north, this 400-square-mile national park occupies the whole western corner of Northumberland and joins the Border Forest Park along its western boundary. Much of the district is high moorland, with rugged hills and summits that afford superb views of the local countryside, but towards the east its character changes to a gentler landscape where the valleys of the Coquet, Redesdale, and North Tyne meander through beautiful woodland. Walking and pony-trekking are two popular ways in which visitors explore the park.

Continue for 4 miles, cross a river bridge, then turn right and continue to Stannersburn. After a while enter the Kielder Forest and drive to Kielder Reservoir.

KIELDER FOREST, Northumb
Really part of the Border Forest Park, this great sea of conifers blankets the slopes of the Cheviot Hills with the varied greens of larch, spruce, Scots pine, and lodgepole pine. It was planted by the state to meet the needs of industry and has matured as a valuable addition to the Northumbrian landscape.

BORDER FOREST PARK, Northumb, Borders
So called because it crosses the border into Scotland, this vast area of woodland incorporates three forests and is the largest area of its type in Britain. In the east its vast landscapes merge with the open moorland horizons of the Northumberland National Park, making a staggering 600 square miles of beautiful, wild, and essentially unspoiled countryside in all. Both parks are crossed by the 250-mile Pennine Way footpath, and the Kielder, Redesdale, and Wauchope forests offer many planned walks and nature trails. Various leisure activities are catered for. A converted 17th-century cottage near the Lewisburn camping site houses a forest museum.

KIELDER RESERVOIR, Northumb
The vast expanse of this new reservoir contributes the magic of water to the lovely countryside that sweeps down to its banks.

Continue through the Kielder Forest to the village of Kielder.

Much of the Border Forest Park has been planted with softwood species to supply the timber industries. Their dark ranks echo the forests of the past.

KIELDER, Northumb NY69
This and several other villages were developed as the area's forestry industry became established, and nowadays they make handy bases from which to explore the local countryside. Kielder Castle is an 18th-century shooting lodge that now serves as a Border Forest Park information centre.

Continue for 3 miles and cross the Scottish border, then in 3½ miles tur left on to the B6357 SP 'Newcastleto and follow the attractive Liddel Wat In 6½ miles reach a junction with th B6399. A detour from the main rou to Hermitage Castle can be made b turning right on to the B6399, drivir for 4 miles, then turning left on to a unclassified road.

HERMITAGE CASTLE, Borders NT49
Romantically associated with Mar Queen of Scots, this brooding cas (AM) punctuates the desolate moorland landscape with four gre towers and grim walls that entirel suit their windswept situation. It w a stronghold of the Douglas famil the 14th century, and much later became the property of Mary's lo Bothwell.

On the main route, bear left with the B6357 to reach Newcastleton.

NEWCASTLETON, Borders NY48
Before the forestry industry became such an important influence on local life this attractive village was a flourishing weaving centre. Its position affords views of beautiful Liddesdale from almost anywhere in or around the village, and beyond Newcastleton Forest are the magnificent 1,678ft Larriston Fells. This part of the Border Forest Park was planted in 1921.

Drive to the far end of the village and turn left on to an unclassified road (no SP). Cross a river bridge and turn right SP 'Brampton', then after 3 miles cross Kershope Burn to enter the English county of Cumbria. Ascend a winding road through the Kershope Forest, then after $\frac{3}{4}$ mile reach the Dog and Gun Inn and turn left SP 'Carlisle'. In 4 miles turn right, and in another $\frac{3}{4}$ mile drive forward on to the B6318. Take the next turning left on to an unclassified road and drive to Bewcastle.

BEWCASTLE, Cumbria NY57
Several ancient remains can be seen in the bleak open moorland that surrounds Bewcastle. Materials from a Roman fort that was once an outpost of Hadrian's Wall were used to build a castle (AM) here, but this too has succumbed to the ravages of time and cottage builders, leaving just a few fragments. In the village churchyard is the famous Bewcastle Cross, which dates from the 7th century and is intricately carved with Runic inscriptions and patterns.

At Bewcastle turn right (no SP) and cross a river bridge. In 5 miles cross the B6318, and in $2\frac{1}{2}$ miles meet a T-junction. Turn left SP 'Birdoswald' and follow the line of Hadrian's Wall for mile to reach Banks.

ADRIAN'S WALL, orthumb, Cumbria
his mighty engineering chievement was built in the 2nd entury AD and is the most npressive monument to the Roman ccupation in Britain. It runs for 73 iles across the entire width of orthern England and is remarkably ell preserved along several ections. It was part of a complex efence system designed to keep the arauding Scottish tribes out of the omanized south, and included two road ditches and a series of ilecastles interspersed with turrets nd signal towers. The Romans nally abandoned the wall in AD 3, but it survived in a reasonably omplete state until quarried by road uilders in the 18th century. Well-eserved forts can be seen at hesters, Housesteads, Great hesters, and Birdoswald, while the ost complete section of wall stands the west of the River North Tyne. 'alks along the wall are most joyable and can be very structive. See also tour 88.

One of the best-preserved of the original 17 Hadrian's Wall forts has been excavated at Housesteads, revealing many facets of Roman life.

BANKS, Northumb NY56
A turret (AM) on the Roman wall here was once manned by troops garrisoned at the nearest milecastle. A footpath leads east to the Pike Hill signal tower, part of a beacon system by which a warning of attack could be sent the length of the wall with surprising speed. Many relics of the Roman occupation, various other antiquities, fine paintings, and sculpture can be seen in the LYC Museum and Art Gallery, which is housed in a converted farmhouse. See also tour 88.

Continue to Birdoswald.

BIRDOSWALD, Cumbria NY66
Large and impressive outer defences of a Roman fort (AM) known as *Camboglanna* can be seen here beside the River Irthing, and well-preserved sections of Hadrian's Wall (AM) extend east and west. Close by are the substantial remains of Harrow's Scar Milecastle (AM). See also tour 88.

In $\frac{1}{2}$ mile ascend, then turn right on to the B6318 SP 'Gilsland' and in 1 mile turn right to reach Gilsland.

GILSLAND, Northumb NY66
Sulphur and chalybeate springs brought brief fame to this small place as a spa resort, but it is much better known for its excellent Roman remains. Hadrian's Wall runs south of the village and includes the Poltross Burn Milecastle (AM), a fascinating and well-preserved survivor from the occupation. Close to the village is an attractive waterfall. See also tour 88.

From Gilsland turn left along the B6318 and in 2 miles meet a junction with the A69. Turn left to enter Greenhead.

GREENHEAD, Northumb NY66
Close to Greenhead is a dramatic series of ravines known as the Nine Nicks of Thirlwall. Near by are the ruins of Thirlwall Castle, which was built in the 14th century, and the route of a Roman track known as the Maiden Way runs through the area. See also tour 88.

The northern frontier of Roman Britain ill forms a barrier as it follows the high ridges of Whin Sill.

Turn left on the B6318, ascend, and in 5 miles reach the Twice Brewed Inn.

TWICE BREWED INN, Northumb NY76
Slightly away from the site of the original building, this famous inn now houses a useful Northumberland National Park information centre. Close by, at Winshields, the Roman wall (AM) reaches its highest point of 1,230ft above sea level.

Continue along the B6318 to reach Housesteads, where there is a reasonable carpark.

HOUSESTEADS, Northumb NY76
The best-preserved fort (AM, NT) on Hadrian's Wall can be seen here. Once known as *Borcovicium*, it follows the typical Roman pattern of rectangular walls with rounded corners, and was built to house up to 1,000 infantrymen. Relics found during excavations in the area are displayed in a well laid-out museum, and close to Housesteads the wall itself reaches its highest point as it follows the high ridges of the Great Whin Sill rock outcrop. Marvellous views from the ridge extend west and take in several little lakes, including the lovely Crag Lough.

Continue for 5 miles to reach Carrawborough.

CARRAWBOROUGH, Northumb NY87
One of the very few Mithraic temples to be found in Britain has been excavated here. Probably dating from the 3rd century, it was a very small building containing three dedicatory altars to the deity Mithras, and a figure of the Mother Goddess. Close by is the Roman fort known as *Brocolitia*.

Continue along the B6318 to reach Chollerford.

CHOLLERFORD, Northumb NY97
Housesteads may be the best preserved of the Roman wall's forts, but *Cilurnum* (or Chesters) is by far the most interesting and best excavated. It was a large stronghold housing 500 troops. Digging has revealed fascinating details of the fort itself, plus the remains of a bath house and central heating system. Relics from this and other sites can be seen in the interesting local museum, and traces of the Tyne bridge that the fort was built to guard have been found downstream of the present 18th-century crossing.

Meet a roundabout and take the 1st exit on to the B6320 SP 'Wark, Bellingham'. Enter the North Tyne Valley to reach Wark.

WARK, Northumb NY87
Access to this picturesque huddle of cottages and houses is by an iron bridge over the River North Tyne. The woodlands of Wark Forest stretch away to the west.

Continue along the B6320 for the return to Bellingham.

TOUR 92 88 MILES

PEACE IN THE BORDER LANDS

Green rounded hills and unspoilt miles of coastline betray nothing of the centuries of human violence that once made this lovely area a place to avoid. Now the only battles are between nesting gulls, and the only invasions are of migrant birds seeking the haven of a largely unpopulated countryside.

BERWICK-UPON-TWEED, Northumb NT95
A busy seaport and now England's northernmost town, Berwick was alternately held by Scottish and English forces during the bitter border struggles that began with the Romans and persisted until the 15th century. Remains of a castle built here by the Normans in the 12th century include three towers and ancient sections of wall that were later incorporated in the medieval town defences. During Elizabethan times the town walls (AM) were restored to full defensive effectiveness, and they have survived as a complete 2-mile circuit round old Berwick. Their rebuilding was done with gun warfare very much in mind, and in their present condition they represent the earliest examples of their type in northern Europe. The approach to the town itself is dominated by three famous and attractive bridges over the River Tweed. Berwick Bridge dates from the 17th century and has 15 elegant arches, the Royal Border Bridge of 1880 was built to carry a railway into the town, and the Tweed Road Bridge is a good example of modern architecture dating from 1928. It is said that the town has more buildings scheduled for preservation than any other place of comparable size in England, and a walk round the lovely old streets would certainly seem to confirm that. The parish church, one of the few to be built during Cromwell's Commonwealth, is of exceptional architectural interest and was extended in the 19th century. In 1717 Vanbrugh built Britain's earliest barracks here, and today these incorporate the well laid out Museum of the King's Own Scottish Borderers. The Georgian period is represented by the Town Hall (open by arrangement) and several fine houses attractively sited by the quay. Relics from the town's past can be seen with collections of paintings and ceramics in Berwick Museum, and the lovely local countryside includes a coastal area of outstanding natural beauty. Every May Day the traditional ceremony of Riding the Bounds, reaffirming the parish boundaries, takes place here.

Leave Berwick on the A1 with SP 'Edinburgh', and in $\frac{1}{2}$ mile bear left on the A6105 SP 'Kelso'. In a further $\frac{1}{2}$ mile bear left on to the B6461, then after $2\frac{3}{4}$ miles enter the old Scottish county of Berwickshire. In $\frac{3}{4}$ mile keep left, and after another $1\frac{1}{2}$ miles turn left on to an unclassified road SP 'Norham'. Later cross the River Tweed by the Union Suspension Bridge and re-enter Northumberland. In $\frac{1}{2}$ mile meet a T-junction and turn right, then in $1\frac{1}{4}$ miles turn right again and continue to Norham.

Berwick's 17th-century bridge was built across the estuary in 1611 to connect the town with Tweedmouth.

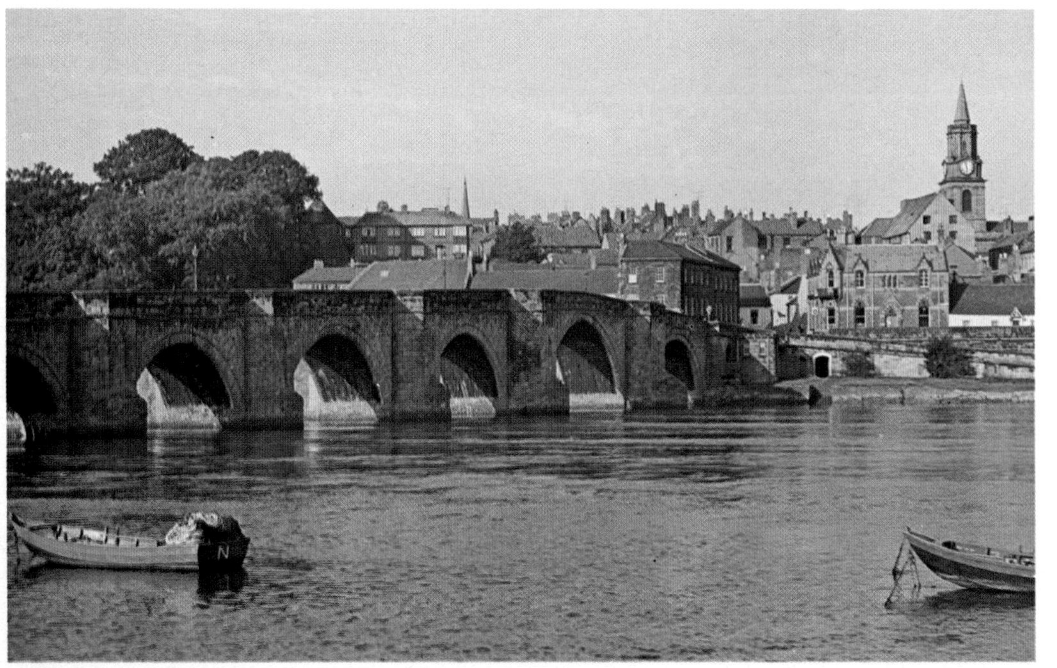

NORHAM, Northumb NT94
One of the two triangular greens in this attractive village features a 19th-century cross, and together they form a focal point for the solid little stone-built houses that surround them. At the east end of the main street the massive Norman keep of a 12th-century castle (AM) towers above the River Tweed from a rocky outcrop, proclaiming a strength that resisted the efforts of Scottish forces for many hundreds of years. The army of Robert the Bruce unsuccessfully assaulted its walls for nearly a year, and 12 months later the castle resisted a siege that was immortalized by Sir Walter Scott in the poem *Marmion*. The hero of the occasion was Sir William Marmion, an English knight who accepted a lady's challenge to take command of the most dangerous place in Great Britain as proof of his love. On February 13 the opening of the salmon season is marked by a ceremony known as the Blessing of the Nets, after which the Tweed can be fished for salmon by anyone with the right or money to do so.

Leave Norham, meet a main road, and turn left on to the B6470 SP 'Cornhill'. In $\frac{1}{2}$ mile turn right on to an unclassified road, then in $\frac{3}{4}$ mile turn right again on to the A698. After a further 2 miles cross (with care) the picturesque Twizel Bridge.

The keep of Norham Castle dates from c1160

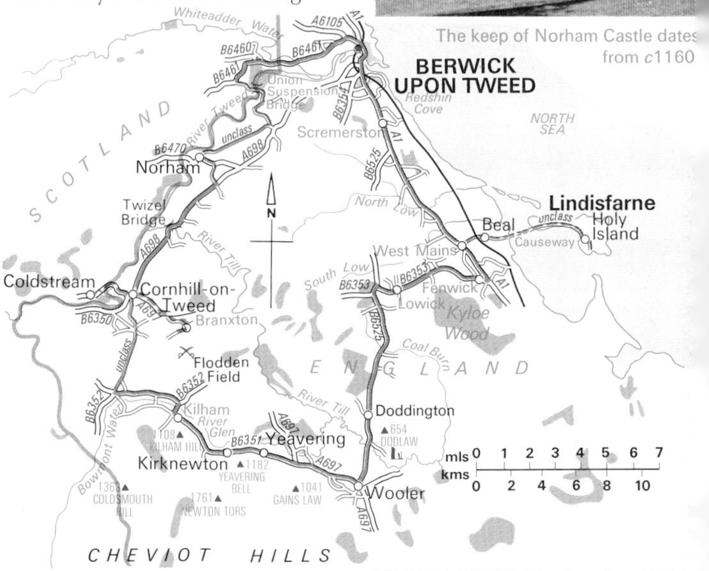

TWIZEL BRIDGE, Northumb NT84
This beautiful 15th-century bridge spans the River Till with a single elegant arch of 90ft. Views from the bridge into the deep wooded glen are enchanting, and the ivy-covered folly of Twizel Castle enhances the scene from a nearby ridge. Many such 18th-century conceits were left unfinished, but this was genuinely never completed.

Leave Twizel Bridge and continue to Cornhill-on-Tweed.

CORNHILL-ON-TWEED, Northumb NT83
The Scottish poet and folk hero Robert Burns entered England for the first time when he crossed the River Tweed here in 1787. This and other events are recorded on a plaque at nearby Coldstream.

A detour can be made from the main route to Flodden Field from Cornhill: meet a roundabout in the village and take the 1st exit on to the A697, then after $1\frac{1}{2}$ miles turn right on to an unclassified road and proceed to Branxton for Flodden Field.

FLODDEN FIELD, Northumb NT83
In 1513 one of the bloodiest battles ever witnessed on English soil was fought at Flodden Field, just a few hundred yards south of Branxton village. A monument inscribed 'To the brave of both nations' now marks the spot where James IV of Scotland was killed when the English army of 26,000 defeated a huge invading force of 40,000. Both sides suffered appalling casualties, with as many as 1,600 deaths between them.

A second detour from the main route at Cornhill to the village of Coldstream can be followed by taking the 2nd exit at the roundabout on to the A697 and driving for 1¾ miles.

COLDSTREAM, Borders NT84
ohn Smeaton built the 5-arched oridge over the RiverTweed here in 1766 to replace a ford that had been ısed for many hundreds of years, often by the armies of Scotland and ngland. A plaque on the bridge ecords the poet Burns' first crossing of the river into England, and one near the market commemorates the aising of the Coldstream Guards to ght in Cromwell's New Model Army.

On the main tour, meet the oundabout in Cornhill and take the nd exit on to the A697. Take the first urning left on to an unclassified road P 'Learmouth', then in 1¼ miles meet rossroads and drive forward. Take he 2nd turning left SP 'Yetholm' and 1 2½ miles meet crossroads. Turn left n to the B6352 SP 'Wooler' and in mile bear right to follow the owmont Water, then 2 miles farther urn right on to the B6351. Cross a ver bridge, meet a T-junction, and urn left to follow the foot of the heviot Hills. Pass the edge of Kilham nd drive to Kirknewton.

IRKNEWTON, Northumb NT93
irknewton's church has a chancel nd south transept that were bviously built for defensive as well religious purposes, a reminder of e centuries of unrest suffered by is and many other border villages. he valley of the College Burn leads om the village to the 2,676ft ımmit of The Cheviot via a narrow onstriction known as Hen Hole. The vely countryside hereabouts is best ppreciated on foot.

ontinue along the B6351 to eavering.

AVERING, Northumb NT93
e Saxon King Edwin had his capital re in the 7th century, and cavations in a field near the River en have revealed traces of wooden lls and amphitheatres from his cient town. It was Edwin who, cording to tradition, allowed the onk Paulinus to convert the people Northumbria to Christianity. One the largest hillforts in the border untry can be seen to the south of village, on the 1,182ft summit of avering Bell.

m Yeavering continue along the t of the Cheviot Hills.

Winter in the Cheviot Hills can be a beautiful but lonely season.

THE CHEVIOT HILLS, Northumb
Much of this lonely range forms the border between Scotland and England. Its grassy flanks and mountainous summits are cropped smooth by the famous Black Face and Cheviot sheep, hardy breeds that can find food in the most unlikely places and survive with the minimum of interference from man. The countryside between the hills and Hadrian's Wall forms part of the Northumberland National Park, and the arduous northern section of the 250-mile Pennine Way brings the footpath to an end here. North-east of the great mass that is The Cheviot itself lies the picturesque College Valley, and the equally attractive Harthope Valley lies to the east. Auchope Cairn, rising to 2,382ft, straddles the border between England and Scotland.

After 1½ miles turn right on to the A697 to reach the edge of Wooler.

WOOLER, Northumb NT92
Situated north-east of the Cheviot, this attractive little place makes a natural base from which to explore the open landscapes of the Cheviot Hills. Close to the village is a stone which commemorates the Battle of Hamildon Hill, when an English army led by Henry Percy defeated a huge Scottish army under the command of the Earl of Douglas.

Leave Wooler, turn left on to the B6525 SP 'Berwick' and continue to the village of Doddington.

The Priory at Holy Island was an important religious centre for centuries.

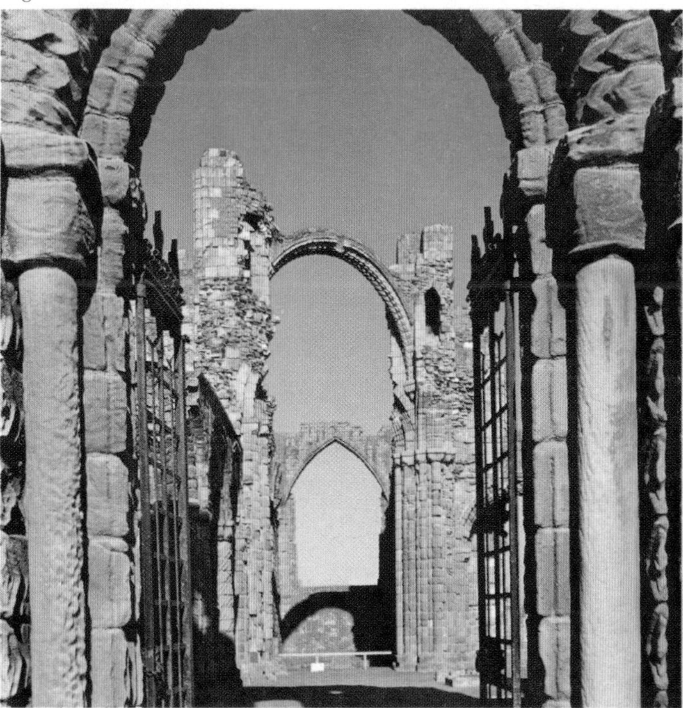

DODDINGTON, Northumb NT93
Features of this village include a ruined pele tower of 1584 and a 13th-century church containing a Norman font. The local countryside is very rich in prehistoric remains, including earthworks and stones bearing the enigmatic cup-and-ring marks of ancient cultures. South is the iron-age hillfort of Dod Law, where a natural crag known as the Lateral Stone features curious carvings and vertical grooves. Below this is a cave known as Cudy's Camp; Rowting Lyn Camp is situated in a miniature gorge near by.

Leave Doddington and drive forward for 5 miles, then branch right on to the B6353 to reach Lowick. Pass Fenwick, meet the A1, and turn left to reach the Plough Hotel in West Mains; a detour from the main route can be taken by following a side road to the right by the hotel and driving to the village of Beal.

BEAL, Northumb NU04
Most of the beautiful coastline near Beal is included in a national nature reserve, and the horizon to the south-west is dominated by the low summits of the gentle Kyloe Hills. A causeway exposed at low tide leads to Holy Island, but visitors should take careful note of the tide tables displayed all round the village to avoid being cut off.

To continue the detour, cross to the Holy Island of Lindisfarne via a causeway that is exposed for about 2 hours before and from approximately 3½ hours after high tide.

HOLY ISLAND (LINDISFARNE), Northumb NU14
Historically known as Lindisfarne, this Cradle of Christianity is only an island at high tide but offered sufficient isolation to please the missionaries who were led here from Iona by St Aidan in the 7th century. About 150 years later their monastic foundation was sacked and destroyed by Danish marauders, but in 1082 the Benedictine order built a fine priory on the same site. Its gaunt ruins (AM) still stand today, and various relics found during excavations can be seen in a local museum. The island's restored 16th-century castle (NT) contains antique oak furniture. Examples of the needlework for which the islanders are justly famous can be seen in the 13th-century parish church. Christianity has been at Lindisfarne for a long time, but a reminder of more ancient days is the Petting Stone. A legend attached to this was that brides who jumped over the stone would have a happy marriage – a tradition with more than a hint of paganism. The nature reserve on Holy Island is an important haven for an enormous variety of wildfowl and wading birds.

On the main tour, leave the Plough Hotel in West Mains and continue along the A1. Pass through Scremerston, cross the River Tweed, and return to Berwick-upon-Tweed.

Scotland

The awe-inspiring Black Cuillin mountains dominate the view from the old bridge at Sligachan on Skye. Some of Scotland's finest and most spectacular scenery is formed by the wild loch and mountain landscapes of this, the largest offshore island in Scotland.

TOUR 93 76 MILES

SIR WALTER SCOTT'S COUNTRY

A romantic glow cast by the great novels of Sir Walter Scott suffuses the wild and beautiful landscapes of the Border country. High in the Eildon Hills is the viewpoint from which he drew particular inspiration, and all round are tiny hamlets, remote castles, and the magnificent ruins of ancient abbeys.

KELSO, Borders NT73
This bustling Border town was described by Sir Walter Scott, who lived and went to school here, as 'the most beautiful, if not the most romantic, village in Scotland'. Its abbey (AM) was the largest and probably the most splendid of the Border abbeys. Fine Norman workmanship can be seen in the surviving fragments of the abbey church. The cobbled town square features the elegant Town House of 1816, and John Rennie built the town's splendid Tweed Bridge in 1803. Not far from the bridge is the distinctive Turret House (NTS). Floors Castle (open), the largest inhabited house in Britain, stands about 1 mile to the north-west of the town.

Leave Kelso on the A699 'St Boswells' and 'Selkirk' road, cross the River Tweed, and turn right. Cross the Teviot and in ½ mile reach Roxburgh Castle.

ROXBURGH CASTLE, Borders NT73
Roxburgh's Royal Burgh was a major town in the 13th century, but the town has completely disappeared and only traces remain of the castle.

ROXBURGH, Borders NT63
Roxburgh's famous name now belongs to a small hamlet lying 2½ miles south-west of the castle site, on the banks of the River Teviot.

From Roxburgh Castle drive on the A699 for 7 miles to reach Maxton.

MAXTON, Borders NT63
Maxton Church has been considerably altered and restored, but originally dates back to the 12th century. A curious old cross shaft in the village marks the spot where the men of the barony assembled for war. A ruined tower remains from an old seat of the Ker family.

From Maxton continue on the A699 for 1½ miles and meet the A68. Turn right, then right again on to the B6404 to enter St Boswells.

ST BOSWELLS, Borders NT53
Once a famous centre for livestock sales, this village faces across a 40-acre common to St Boswells Green, centre of the Buccleuch Hunt.

Continue on the B6404 and in 1 mile cross the River Tweed. In ¼ mile turn left on to the B6356 SP 'Dryburgh', then drive through pleasant riverside scenery and in 1¾ miles reach Dryburgh Abbey.

DRYBURGH ABBEY, Borders NT53
One of a famous group of 12th-century Border monasteries founded by David I, Dryburgh (AM) was repeatedly attacked by the English and badly damaged in 1544. The cloister buildings have survived in a remarkably complete state, and though the church itself has not been so well preserved its west front, parts of the nave, and the chapter house can still be seen.

Return along the B6356 and in ½ mile turn left to pass the Wallace Statue.

WALLACE STATUE, Borders NT53
This massive statue to Sir William Wallace overlooks magnificent Lowland scenery from the slopes of Bemersyde Hill.

Proceed on the B6356 to reach Bemersyde House on the left.

BEMERSYDE HOUSE, Borders NT53
Traditional home of the Haig family, this house (not open) was frequently visited by Sir Walter Scott. It incorporates an ancient tower which was burned in a raid during 1545.

In ¼ mile turn left, then in ½ mile reach Scott's View.

SCOTT'S VIEW, Borders NT53
This AA viewpoint on Bemersyde Hill faces west across the winding Tweed to the three conical peaks of the distinctive Eildon Hills.

In ½ mile drive forward on to an unclassified road SP 'Melrose' and descend through woodland to cross Leader Water. In ¼ mile turn right SP 'Jedburgh' and meet the A68. Turn left to cross the River Tweed, then immediately right to join the B6361. Continue to reach Newstead.

Some of the original architectural splendour is preserved in ruined Melrose Abbey.

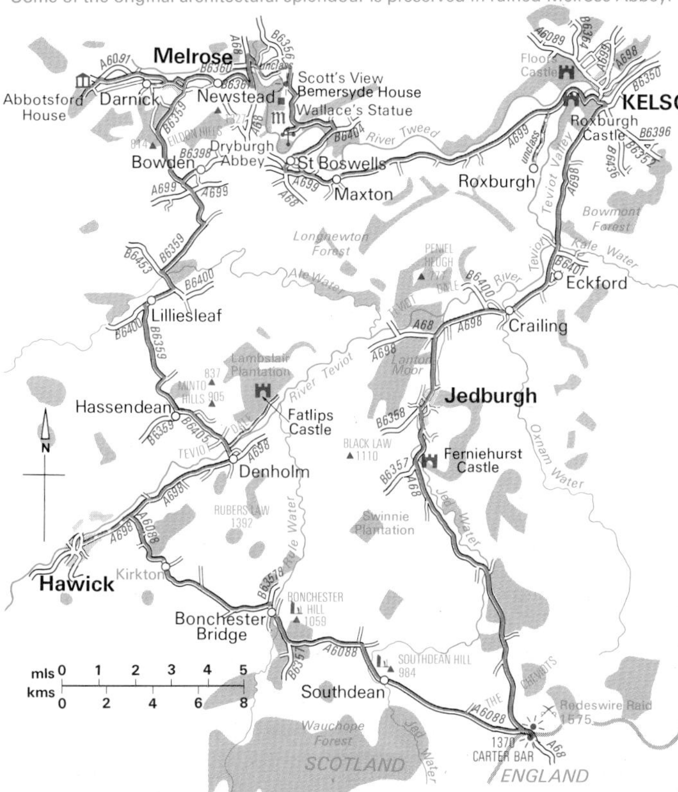

NEWSTEAD, Borders NT53
Standing on the south bank of the River Tweed, this old-world village faces across the water to the slopes of Leaderfoot Hill. Earlier in this century excavations there revealed the Roman complex of camps and fort known as *Trimontium*.

Continue on the B6361 to Melrose.

According to legend the Eildon Hills were cleft into three by a wizard.

MELROSE, Borders NT53
Border raids in the 14th and 16th centuries destroyed most of David I's beautiful Cistercian abbey (AM) at Melrose. Parts of the nave and choir remain, but the most spectacular survivals are the red sandstone windows with their rich tracery. The heart of Robert Bruce was buried in front of the altar. A nearby museum of carved stones and treasures from the abbey is contained in the 15th-century Commendator's House. The town preserves a 17th-century cross with the arms of Scotland.

From Melrose follow SP 'Galashiels' to join the A6091 and after ¼ mile reach the B6394 left turn leading to Darnick. This can be taken as a detour.

DARNICK, Borders NT53
The romantic Tweed-side setting of old Darnick Tower belies its turbulent past. Originally built in 1425, it was burned down by the English, and of the early structure only an old iron entrance gate has managed to survive.

On the main route, continue along the A6091 SP 'Galashiels' and in 1 miles meet a roundabout. Take the 1st exit to reach Abbotsford House.

BBOTSFORD HOUSE, orders NT53
ternationally famous as the home Sir Walter Scott, this fine building oen) was designed by the writer mself and he died here in 1832. It s been preserved in his memory, d the library contains a staggering llection of some 20,000 rare books.

turn to Melrose, meet a undabout, and turn right on to the 359 SP 'Lilliesleaf' and 'Hawick'. cend to a 814ft road summit, with ws ahead of the Cheviots. After 3 les meet the B6398 on the left, ich leads to Bowden.

tt's writing materials are preserved bbotsford House.

WDEN, Borders NT53
nteresting laird's loft can be seen e 17th-century church of this l town. The 16th-century market s serves as a war memorial.

he main tour, continue with the 9 and meet crossroads with the . Drive forward over the roads and continue for 3 miles. left to cross the Ale Water, and eed to Lilliesleaf.

ESLEAF, Borders NT52
parish church in this little village uilt in 1771, but since then has considerably extended. Some es south-west is a 19th-century on an old motte.

ng Lilliesleaf turn left with the SP 'Denholm'. Proceed to ndean.

ENDEAN, Borders NT52
ong *Jack o'Hazeldean* is ated with this small village.

sendean turn left on to the , passing the twin peaks of the Hills. In 1½ miles reach an sified left turn that offers a to Fatlips Castle.

PS CASTLE, Borders NT52
n the summit of the steep Crags stand the ruins of this sly-named castle, which was the 16th century for the art family.

main route, continue along 405 and cross the River Teviot r Denholm.

This typically ornate entrance hall was part of Sir Walter Scott's design for his home, Abbotsford House.

DENHOLM, Borders NT51
Two literary figures were born in this small River Teviot village. James Murray (original editor of the *Oxford English Dictionary*) and Scott's poet friend John Leyden. Westgate Hall is an attractive 17th-century building near the village green, and Text House is the weird creation of a local eccentric, Dr Haddon.

In Denholm meet the junction with the A698 and turn right SP 'Hawick'. After 3½ miles turn left on to the A6088 SP 'Bonchester Bridge, Newcastle'. A detour from the main route can be made by keeping forward on the A698 to the old woollen town of Hawick.

HAWICK, Borders NT51
John Hardie, a pioneer of Hawick's woollen industry, is buried in St Mary's Churchyard. The rebuilt church dates from the 13th century, and in Moat Park is the motte of a Norman castle built in the 12th century. The battle of Flodden Field was a disaster for Hawick in 1513, when nearly all the men of the town were killed; they are commemorated by the Horse monument in the High Street. Wilton Lodge Museum features the growth of the town's woollen industry.

On the main tour, continue along the A6088 through Kirkton to reach Bonchester Bridge.

BONCHESTER BRIDGE, Borders NT51
Rule Water flows under this bridge and beneath the slopes of 1,059ft Bonchester Hill, eventually to join the Teviot farther north. Wauchope Forest lies to the south.

Continue on the A6088, passing Bonchester Hill on the left, to reach Southdean.

SOUTHDEAN, Borders NT60
Souden Kirk stands in ruins to the south of Southdean, a little village beside the Jed Water. The building was a church in the 13th century, and the meeting place for Scottish leaders before the battle of Otterburn in 1388. A superb miniature altar only 9¼ inches long with fine carved crosses has been excavated from the site.

Jedburgh Abbey, although damaged and burned by the English, retains enough of its character to make it one of Scotland's finest medieval buildings.

Continue on the A6088 and ascend to the A68. Continue to Carter Bar.

CARTER BAR, Borders NT60
Scotland meets England at this 1,370ft viewpoint in the Cheviot Hills. Lush pastures and trim plantations spread out to the north, with the Eildon Hills in the distance, and the Roman camp and earthworks of Chew Green lie to the east. The lonely tree-clad Rede Valley and Border Forest Park provide a wild southerly prospect.

Return along the A68 SP 'Jedburgh' and descend to the wooded valley of Jed Water to reach Ferniehurst Castle.

FERNIEHURST CASTLE, Borders NT61
Scene of frequent Border skirmishes, this fine 16th-century castle was once the seat of the Border family of Ker. Their arms can still be seen on panels in the castle, but the most impressive part of the interior is the huge fireplace in the great hall. In today's more peaceful times the castle serves as a youth hostel.

Continue along the A68 to Jedburgh.

JEDBURGH, Borders NT62
A popular walking, climbing and riding centre, Jedburgh stands as a gateway to Scotland. Its finest attraction is the abbey (AM), which is roofless and in ruins but nevertheless magnificent. It was one of David I's Border abbeys and was burned in 1523. Mary Queen of Scots is associated with the town, and the 16th-century Mary Queen of Scots' House incorporates a museum devoted to her life. The castle at the top of Castlegate is a 19th-century construction on the site of the 12th-century stronghold built by Scottish kings. It houses a grisly gaol museum, where displays show the 'reformed' system of the early 19th century. The medieval custom of Candlemas Ba' takes place in Jedburgh every Shrove Tuesday, when a game of handball is played through the streets between Uppies born above the mercat cross – and Downies, born below it.

Leave Jedburgh on the A68 SP 'Edinburgh' and in 2 miles meet the A698. Turn right for Crailing.

CRAILING, Borders NT62
The fine Regency mansion of Crailing House is the main attraction in this pleasant small village.

Continue on the A698 and in 1 mile meet an unclassified road on the right. A short detour can be taken along this road to Eckford.

ECKFORD, Borders NT72
A pair of 18th-century jougs – iron collars used to punish wrongdoers – is preserved in the church. An old watch-house stands in the churchyard to guard against body-snatching, once a common crime.

On the main tour, continue along the A698 and re-enter Kelso.

BORDER VALES AND MARSHES

This lonely, unpopulated land was the scene of border strife and bloody warfare for many centuries, but it was also the inspiration for some of Burns' poetry and the goal of eloping couples. The peace of its river-threaded dales and gentle grandeur of its hills belies its turbulent history.

LOCKERBIE, Dumf & Gall NY18
In the late 17th century this pleasant little town was a major centre for horse and lamb trading. Lamb Hill takes its name from a market that has been held here since 1680, and everywhere there are signs of Lockerbie's agricultural affiliations. However, it has not always been as peaceful as it seems today. In 1593 one of the last Border family feuds ended in a fierce battle at which the Johnstones killed Lord Maxwell and some 700 of his followers. Wealth from the China tea trade came to local landowners and manifested itself in great mansions that appeared all round the town. Among them is Rammerscales House (open), an elegant building which stands in fine grounds and contains various paintings and antiquities.

Leave Lockerbie on the A74 'Glasgow' road and drive through Annandale. In 7 miles cross Johnstonebridge.

JOHNSTONEBRIDGE, Dumf & Gall NY19
This picturesque bridge spans the River Annan, which flows south through the lovely countryside of the Annandale valley.

In 6 miles turn left on to an unclassified road for Beattock.

BEATTOCK, Dumf & Gall NY09
Beattock stands in hilly country on the Evan Water, in lovely Upper Annandale. Close by are four prehistoric forts, and farther north along the Evan Valley are the picturesquely ruined towers of Blacklaw, Mellingshaw, and Raecleuch.

Turn left, pass under a railway bridge, and in 1 mile turn right on to the A701 'Dumfries' road. Continue to the hamlet of St Ann's and cross the Kinnel Water.

ST ANN'S, Dumf & Gall NY09
The bridge here dates from c1800, and the picturesque ruins of Lochwood Tower from 1592. A little to the north-west of the hamlet are the lovely Raehills Glens.

Continue to Amisfield Town.

AMISFIELD TOWN, Dumf & Gall NY08
Amisfield Tower is the ancestral home of the Charteris family, who have been associated with the area since the 12th century. It was built in the 16th century and is one of the best and most beautiful buildings of its type in Scotland.

Continue through rolling countryside to Locharbriggs and Lower Nithsdale, then proceed to Dumfries.

DUMFRIES, Dumf & Gall NX97
Affectionately known as Queen of the South by the Scots, this ancient Royal Burgh was combined with its sister community of Maxwelltown in 1919. The two districts are linked by five bridges across the River Nith, and they hold much of their history in common. The central point of the town is an 18th-century complex of buildings known as Mid Steeple, comprising the old municipal buildings, courthouse, and prison. An inscribed tablet of distances on the wall of the building is a reminder of times when Scottish cattle drovers herded their animals the length of England to reach the lucrative markets of London. The 15th- and 16th-century remains of Lincluden College (AM), including the fine collegiate church and provost's house, can be seen just outside the town. Relics from this and other periods of the burgh's history are preserved in Dumfries Museum. Many famous people have visited or lived in the town, but it is the two Roberts who are best remembered. Robert the Bruce changed the course of Scottish history when he stabbed the Red Comyn in the former Greyfriars monastery, and some 500 years later in 1791 the p Robert Burns made his home here Burns wrote some of his most famous songs while living in the town, and the house where he di has been made into a Burns Muse in his honour. On display are personal possessions and some o manuscripts, and the road in whi the house stands has been renam Burns Street. Other relics associa with the poet can be seen in the Hole in The Wa' Tavern and the Globe Inn. The family grave and mausoleum are together in St Michael's Churchyard.

Meet a roundabout and follow the 'Stranraer' road, then turn left SP 'Carlisle' and drive alongside the R Nith. Reach the end of the road ar turn left then right, SP 'Glencaple', continue along the B725 to Glenc

Ruthwell Cross, housed i special apse, has be exceptionally w preserved sir the 8th centu

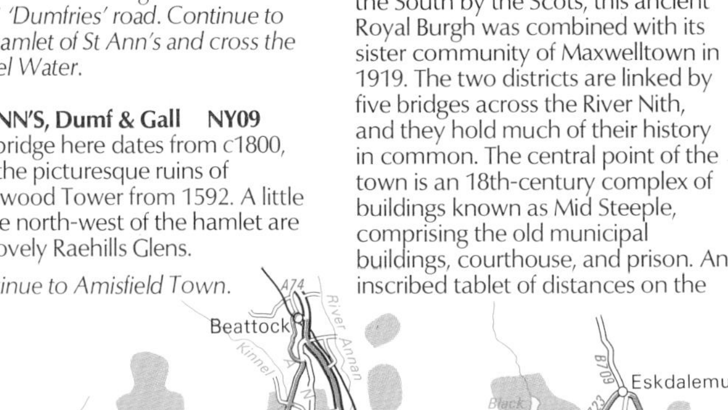

Devorgilla's Bridge, which was built in 1426, is one of five that span the River Nith at Dumfries.

;LENCAPLE, Dumf & Gall NX96
ı his novel *Guy Mannering* Sir Valter Scott refers to this little Nith-stuary village as Portanferry. To the ɔcal people it is the Auld Quay.

'ass the Solway Firth, with 1,868ft :riffell prominent across the water to ıe right; after 3 miles the ruins and state of Caerlaverock Castle lie $\frac{1}{4}$ mile) the right.

'AERLAVEROCK CASTLE & NATURE ESERVE, Dumf & Gall NY06
fortified building has stood here nce the early 13th century, but the iangular structure (AM) that ɔw occupies the site owes ost of its existence to the 15th entury. As a Maxwell stronghold aerlaverock had a stormy history. It as attacked by Edward I in 1300, ffered a 13-week siege in 1640, and ıded up in the hands of the ɔvenanters. In 1683 the interior was mpletely reconstructed, and the ilding has survived to the present y as a particularly fine example of Renaissance mansion. The Maxwell est and motto can still be seen tween two splendid towers over e gateway. The 6,200-acre estate is w a nature reserve with tstanding hide facilities and an servatory tower. The saltmarsh d sandy foreshore between the er Nith and Lochar Water is the ıter haunt of the barnacle goose d other wildfowl.

ntinue to Bankend and turn right 'Ruthwell'. Cross flat and often rshy countryside, and after miles turn right on to the B724. er $\frac{1}{2}$ mile an unclassified left turn rs a detour to Ruthwell Church.

ert Burns is commemorated in ıfries, where he died in 1796.

'HWELL CHURCH, nf & Gall NY16
18ft cross at Ruthwell Church s from the 8th century and is of the most remarkable dark-age ıuments (AM) to have survived in pe. This archaeological treasure eserved in a special apse and is vily inscribed with early written ıses in the Northumbrian dialect ıglish. These make up the *Dream e Rood*, which may have been en by the Saxon poet Caedmon; r inscriptions on the cross are in c characters.

Until 1940 English couples could be married in Scotland without their parents' consent. The blacksmith's shop at Gretna Green preserves the anvil over which the ceremony was performed.

Continues along the B724 to the village of Cummertrees.

CUMMERTREES, Dumf & Gall NY16
Scott describes the district around this village in *Redgauntlet*. The full devastating effect of the Solway Firth's notorious spring tides can be observed from here.

Continue for 3 miles and join the A75 to enter Annan.

ANNAN, Dumf & Gall NY16
Sited on the River Annan and the Solway Firth, this pleasant touring centre is noted for its shrimps and is within easy reach of beautiful countryside. Lovely Kinmount Gardens offer walks amongst superb arrays of shrubs, flowers, and trees, and views from the area take in Bowness in Cumbria and the Lake District peak of Skiddaw. Famous names connected with the town include Robert Stevenson, who built the fine bridge in 1826. Historian, essayist, and critic Thomas Carlisle attended the old grammar school and later described it as Hinterschlag Gymnasium in his *Sartor Resartus*.

Cross the River Annan, meet traffic lights, and turn left on to the B722 'Eaglesfield' road. In 2 miles turn left again on to an unclassified road SP 'Ecclefechan', then after $2\frac{1}{2}$ miles cross the Mein Water and turn right to Ecclefechan.

ECCLEFECHAN, Dumf & Gall NY17
In 1795 Thomas Carlisle was born in the local Arched House (NTS), which now contains a collection of his personal possessions.

In Ecclefechan turn right and continue to the A74 'Carlisle' road. After $2\frac{1}{2}$ miles pass a junction where a detour to Kirtlebridge can be taken.

KIRTLEBRIDGE, Dumf & Gall NY27
Close to Kirtle Water, a little to the south-east of Kirtlebridge, are several old towers. The one known as Robgill was built in the 16th century and now forms part of a recent mansion, and the ancient Irving stronghold of Bonshaw Tower still has its ancient clan bell. About $1\frac{1}{2}$ miles south-east is the fine Merkland Cross, an interesting wayside monument that dates from the 15th century.

On the main route, continue along the A74 and after 2 miles reach a junction where a short detour to Kirkpatrick Fleming can be taken.

KIRKPATRICK FLEMING, Dumf & Gall NY27
A cave which lies to the west of this village is popularly held to be the place where Robert the Bruce was given a lesson in perseverance by a spider. The event is also claimed by several other places in Scotland and Northern Ireland.

On the main route, continue along the A74 and after $3\frac{1}{2}$ miles branch left on to an unclassified road SP 'Gretna Green' to reach Springfield.

SPRINGFIELD, Dumf & Gall NY36
Founded by weavers in 1791, this village became famous for elopement marriages that were performed here in the 19th century.

A short detour can be taken from the main route here by turning right for Gretna Green and Gretna.

GRETNA, Dumf & Gall NY36
For 100 years Gretna Hall and the smithy at Gretna Green were the first places over the Scottish border where runaway lovers could be married without parental consent. Clandestine marriages of this nature were prevented in England by an 18th-century law, but in Scotland it was only necessary for the couple to make a witnessed declaration that they wished to become man and wife. A law passed in 1856 made it a requirement that either the man or woman should have lived in Scotland for a minimum of three weeks, and more legislation in 1940 prevented the village smith from performing the ceremony.

On the main route, continue along the unclassified 'Longtown' road into England and cross Solway Moss. In 1542 the Moss was the site of a battle in which the Scots were defeated by the English. After $\frac{3}{4}$ mile turn left on to the A6071 and continue to Longtown.

LONGTOWN, Cumbria NY36
At one time the main Carlisle to Glasgow road ran through Longtown, but this was superseded when the present A74 was built by way of Sark Bridge in 1830. To the north is Netherby Hall, made famous by the romantic elopement of the Graham heiress with Lochinvar in Sir Walter Scott's *Marmion*.

Return via the A6071 and turn right on to the A7 SP 'Galashiels'. Follow the River Esk and return to Scotland at Scots Dyke before entering the village of Canonbie.

CANONBIE, Dumf & Gall NY37
Before the Scots Dyke was built in 1552 the Debateable Land, an area close to Canonbie between the Rivers Sark and Esk, was held by anybody who had the force of arms to do so. The dyke formed an effective new boundary and put an end to the troubles. The village itself stands 3 miles from the present border and was once the site of an important priory. It was also a coaching stop, and an interesting old inn has survived from those days. Liddesdale, to the south, is associated with Scott's novels.

Continue through the wooded, narrowing valley of Eskdale to Langholm.

LANGHOLM, Dumf & Gall NY38
This angling resort and wool centre stands at the junction of Wauchope Water and the River Esk, with the lovely Ewes Water flowing in from the north. An annual border-riding ceremony that was instituted in the 19th century still takes place in the town. A monument to General Sir John Malcolm stands on 1,163ft Whita Hill, which rises to the east. The forbears of Neil Armstrong, the first man to walk on the moon, came from this area.

Leave the town on the B709 'Eskdalemuir' road and continue to the hamlet of Bentpath.

BENTPATH, Dumf & Gall NY39
The brilliant engineer Thomas Telford was born in a shepherd's cottage near Glendinning Farm; he is commemorated by a tablet standing 1 mile beyond the hamlet.

After 2 miles cross the River Esk and climb over moorland into the Castle O'er Forest. Continue to the hamlet of Eskdalemuir.

ESKDALEMUIR, Dumf & Gall NY29
Situated at the northern end of lovely Eskdale, this hamlet is on an important junction of roads in an area that abounds with prehistoric remains. The Eskdalemuir Observatory, which dates from 1908, lies 3 miles north.

At Eskdalemuir turn left on to the B723 SP 'Lockerbie', drive through the conifers of Castle O'er Forest, and beyond Boreland follow the valley of the Dryfe Water for the eventual return to Lockerbie.

TOUR 95 88 MILES

AMONG THE GALLOWAY HILLS

North of the empty beaches and bird-haunted estuaries of the Solway Firth are high forests, secret little lochs hidden between ridged outriders of the Galloway Hills, and dozens of green river valleys carved through hill flanks to the sea.

KIRKCUDBRIGHT, Dumf & Gall NX65
This ancient burgh stands in the heart of an area known as the Stewartry and was once a bustling port. Much of the local history is displayed in the Stewartry Museum, and the town is dominated by the handsome ruins of 16th-century Maclellan's Castle (AM). Close to the 17th-century mercat cross is the old Tollbooth, once a prison for John Paul Jones. A fine collection of pictures by E A Hornel can be seen in 18th-century Broughton House (gardens and library open). South of the town the wooded peninsula of St Mary's Isle separates the Dee estuary from Manxman's Lake.

Leave Kirkcudbright on the A755 Bridge Street and follow SP 'Gatehouse of Fleet' to cross the River Dee. Continue for 4½ miles, then turn left on to the A75 SP 'Stranraer' and follow a winding road to skirt the Fleet Forest. Continue along the A75 to Gatehouse of Fleet.

GATEHOUSE OF FLEET, Dumf & Gall NX65
This town was the inspiration for Scott's otherwise fictitious town Kippletringham, in *Guy Mannering*. In the town is a huge granite clock tower of 1871, and the local countryside includes isolated moorland where the poet Burns once composed some of his works. To the north-west the Water of Fleet runs through a beautiful glen, and south are the contrasting features of Fleet Bay and deciduous Fleet Forest. Cally House (not open), close to the town in fine parkland, was designed by architect Robert Mulne in 1763.

Continue along the A75 and after a short distance pass the ruins of Cardoness Castle to the right.

CARDONESS CASTLE, Dumf & Gall NX55
This section of the drive follows one of the most beautiful roads in the south of Scotland. The picturesque ruins of the 15th-century tower house at Cardoness (AM) stand in a superb situation overlooking Fleet Bay, Murray's Isles (NT), and the Islands of Fleet.

Continue, and ¾ mile beyond the castle reach an unclassified right turn that can be followed for a detour to the hamlet of Anworth.

ANWORTH, Dumf & Gall NX55
Anworth Church is a ruined 17th-century building which has retained a number of good features, including a medieval bell. In the churchyard are a cross from the dark ages and the remarkable 8ft-high tomb of a member of the Gordon family who was buried here in the 17th century.

On the main route, continue along the A75 to follow the scenic coastline, passing Barholm Castle to the right.

Kirkcudbright used to be one of Scotland's major ports, but it gradually declined in the 17th century. Today it is a small harbour at the mouth of the Dee.

BARHOLM CASTLE, Dumf & Gall NX55
Close to this ruined tower (not open) is Dirk Hatteraick's Cave, the hiding place of the smuggler captain in Scott's *Guy Mannering*. The castle itself was once a place of refuge for the religious reformer John Knox, and is beautifully set overlooking the waters of Wigtown Bay.

Continue, and after a short distance pass Carsluith Castle to the left.

CARSLUITH CASTLE, Dumf & Gall NX45
An unusual feature of this roofless 16th-century tower house (AM) is its L-shaped plan, brought about by the addition of a staircase wing in 1568.

From the castle continue along the A75 to reach Creetown.

CREETOWN, Dumf & Gall NX45
Portin Ferry in Scott's *Guy Mannering*, this sheltered and peaceful village overlooks the Cree estuary and the wide expanse of Wigtown Sands. To the north-east the Moneypool Burn runs through a charmingly wooded valley, and in the distant north is the 2,329ft mass of Cairnsmore of Fleet.

Continue through Creetown and after 3½ miles reach the hamlet of Palnure.

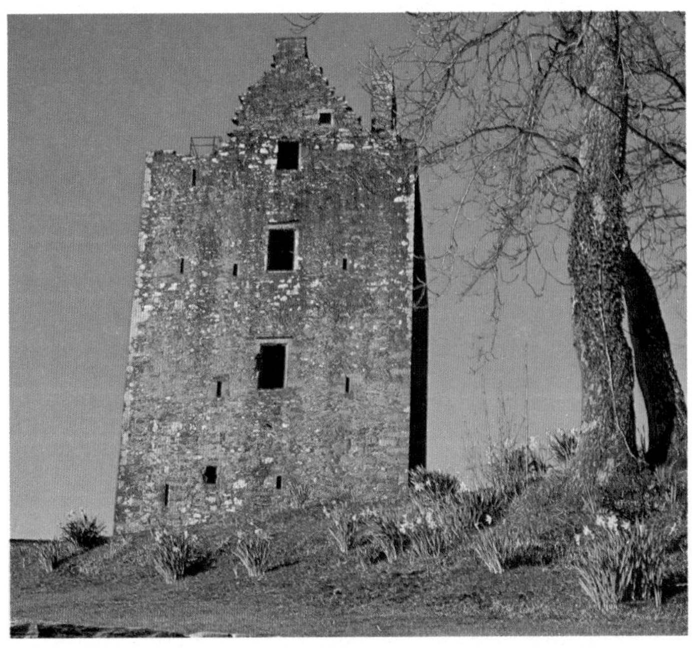

Cardoness Castle is a well-preserved tower house on the Big Water of Fleet.

PALNURE, Dumf & Gall NX46
A charming and worthwhile excursion can be made from this village to follow the clear Palnure Burn to Bargaly Glen.

Leave Palnure and continue on the A75, then after 4 miles meet a roundabout and take the 3rd exit on to the A714 to enter Newton Stewart.

NEWTON STEWART, Dumf & Gall NX46
In the 18th century this lovely Galloway market town was a centre for the weaving, spinning, and carpet-making industries. Nowaday these local skills are turned to the production of mohair rugs and scarves. Between Newton Stewart and Minnigaff the River Cree is spanned by a fine granite bridge bui in 1614 by John Rennie. Galloway Forest Park, famous for its many historical and archaeological sites a well as for its great natural beauty, lies to the north.

Leave Newton Stewart with SP 'New Galloway (A712)', cross the Cree Bridge, and enter the village of Minnigaff. Drive for 1 mile beyond th village and turn left on to the A712 'New Galloway' road. Continue through attractive woodlands of the Galloway Forest Park, with splendid views of the high Galloway Hills to th north and south. Continue along th A712 to reach Murray's Monument.

MURRAY'S MONUMENT, Dumf & Gall NX47
This obelisk on 2,329ft Cairnsmore Fleet commemorates Dr Alexande Murray, who grew up near by as a shepherd boy and eventually became Professor of Oriental Languages in Edinburgh University. The great rocky bulk of the hill was featured in John Buchan's spy nove *The Thirty Nine Steps*, and its lofty slopes afford good views of Kirroughtree Forest in the southerr part of the Galloway Forest Park. Near the monument a sparkling b plunges in two waterfalls collective known as the Grey Mare's Tail. No on the Crags of Talnotry is an interesting wild goat park.

Continue from the monument alor the A712 and after 4½ miles reach t shores of Clatteringshaws Loch.

CLATTERINGSHAWS LOCH, Dumf & Gall NX57
Part of the Galloway power schen this great reservoir was created by the obstruction of the Black Wate Dee. On the eastern shore is the battlefield of Rapploch Moss, whe a granite boulder (NTS) marks the spot where Robert the Bruce defeated an English force in 1307 hurling stones at them. The River Dee runs from the loch to eventu join the sea at Kirkcudbright, and views in this area are magical. To right of the main road is the 1,616 Black Craig of Dee, and the Fell of Fleet rises to 1,544ft in the south.

Continue along the A712 and afte 6 miles turn right on to the A762 t enter New Galloway.

NEW GALLOWAY, Dumf & Gall NX67
This noted angling centre on the River Ken is Scotland's smallest Royal Burgh. Kells Churchyard, sited a little to the north of New Galloway, features the grave of a Covenanter who was shot in 1685. Also here is the curious but attractive Adam and Eve Stone.

Continue along the A762 'Kirkcudbright' road and after 1 mile pass Kenmure Castle on the left.

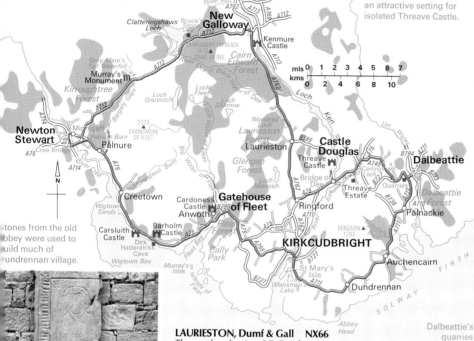

The River Dee provides an attractive setting for isolated Threave Castle.

…tones from the old …bbey were used to …uild much of …undrennan village.

…NMURE CASTLE, …mf & Gall NX67
…ttle of the original 16th- and 17th- …ntury work can still be seen in the …ns of this Gordon family …onghold, but most of the structure …nore recent than that. The hero of …Walter Scott's poem *Young …hinvar* sprang from this family.

…r a short distance reach the shores …och Ken.

…CH KEN, Dumf & Gall NX67
…med by damming the rivers Ken … Dee, this reservoir is surrounded …ich woodland and is a …uresque addition to the …dscape. Some 5 miles south-east …ew Galloway the Black Water of … enters the loch after flowing …ugh the lovely woodlands of …n Edward Forest.

…tinue along the A762 and skirt …shores of Woodhall Loch to reach …hamlet of Laurieston.

LAURIESTON, Dumf & Gall NX66
The works of writer S R Crockett are based on this area, and there is a monument to him in the village. Coniferous Laurieston Forest lies to the west, and south-west the waters of Loch Mannoch are overlooked by the Glengap Forest.

Continue through attractive hill country to Ringford.

RINGFORD, Dumf & Gall NX65
During his bloody campaign of persecution the notorious Sir Robert Grierson of Lairg murdered five Covenanters here in 1685. A memorial to the victims stands 2 miles north of the village, on the tour route.

At Ringford turn left on to the A75 'Dumfries' road. In 4 miles, shortly after crossing the River Dee, reach a track that leads left to Threave Castle.

THREAVE CASTLE, Dumf & Gall NX76
Built in the 1360s by Archibald the Grim, 3rd Earl of Douglas, this castle (AM) is beautifully sited on an island in the River Dee. The locally-forged and nationally famous Mons Meg cannon was used by James II to overcome the rebellious Douglas family here in 1455; this impressive piece of ordnance can now be seen in Edinburgh Castle. In 1640 the stronghold was captured by Covenanters, who sacked it and vandalized its interior.

Continue along the A75 towards Castle Douglas. Before the tour route enters this town it passes an unclassified right turn which offers a short diversion to the Threave Estate.

THREAVE ESTATE, Dumf & Gall NX76
Threave Estate includes the house and grounds, and is the National Trust for Scotland's School of Practical Gardening. The house is not open to the public, but the Wildfowl Refuge and lovely gardens are. Visitors flock here in the spring to see the estate's vast and very beautiful display of daffodils.

On the main route, pass alongside Carlingwark Loch and enter Castle Douglas.

CASTLE DOUGLAS, Dumf & Gall NX76
Once the commercial capital of its county, this pleasant old town is beautifully sited near the shores of Loch Carlingwark. In 1765 the loch was drained, revealing the remains of several prehistoric lake-dwellings known as crannogs, and a number of bronze-age artefacts.

Leave Castle Douglas on the A745 'Dalbeattie' road and after 5 miles descend past granite quarries to join the A711. Cross the Urr Water to reach Dalbeattie.

DALBEATTIE, Dumf & Gall NX86
In the 19th century the shiny grey granite of which this lovely place is built was shipped from quays on the Urr Water to all parts of the world. South of the town are the green ranks of Dalbeattie Forest, while 2½ miles north is the Mote of Urr—one of the finest Saxon fortifications anywhere in Britain.

Leave Dalbeattie by returning along the A711 and re-cross the Urr Water, then turn left and continue along the A711 to Palnackie.

Dalbeattie's quarries are famous for superb granite.

PALNACKIE, Dumf & Gall NX85
This attractive whitewashed village stands on a creek of the Rough Firth, which is an inlet of the Solway Firth. About 1 mile south on an unclassified road is 16th-century Orchardton Tower (AM), one of only two circular tower houses existing in the whole of Scotland.

Continue on the A711 to Auchencairn.

AUCHENCAIRN, Dumf & Gall NX75
A short way offshore from this Auchencairn Bay village is Hestan Island, which was featured as the Isle of Rathan in S R Crockett's book *Raiders*. It is the site of a lighthouse.

Continue on the A711 to Dundrennan.

DUNDRENNAN, Dumf & Gall NX74
Stone from the ruins of 12th-century Dundrennan Abbey (AM) was used to build many of the houses in this village. The foundation itself has sad associations with Mary Queen of Scots, for it was here that she spent her last night on Scottish soil before sailing from Port Mary to England and eventual imprisonment. The port is south of Dundrennan.

Continue along the A711 for the return to Kirkcudbright.

TOUR 96 108 MILES

THE LAND OF ROBERT BURNS

Scotland's most famous poet was born and raised in this area of cliff-fringed coast and lovely river valleys. His characters still seem to populate the stern little towns, charming villages, and enchanting countryside between the sea and the beautiful reaches of wooded Glen Trool.

Robert Burns was born in this cottage at Alloway in 1759. It now houses a commemorative museum.

AYR, Strath NS32
As well as being a popular resort with miles of safe, sandy beach, this Royal Burgh is also a fishing port and flourishing centre of industry. Here the spirit of Burns is never very far away. The poet was christened at the Auld Kirk, his statue stands near the station, and relics of his life and work can be seen in the Tam O'Shanter Museum. Ayr's famous Twa Brigs over the River Ayr were built in the 13th and 18th centuries respectively, but the later structure has been replaced by a modern road bridge. The early crossing was renovated in 1910 and is now used by pedestrians only. The town's oldest building is 16th-century Loudon Hall, which was extensively restored in 1938, but earlier incomplete fragments, such as ancient St John's Towers can be seen elsewhere in the area. Ayr is well known for its fine parks and gardens and has one of the finest racecourses in Britain.

Leave Ayr on the A719 'Maidens' road and climb past Butlin's Holiday Camp to a height of over 300ft. Skirt Dunure, which lies to the right below the main road.

DUNURE, Strath NS21
This attractive little fishing village is guarded by a ruined castle on a clifftop site, beneath the 913ft summit of Brown Carrick Hill. During the 16th century the stronghold was notorious for the cruel treatment to prisoners. Close by is an old dovecote in which pigeons were once raised to keep the castle supplied with fresh meat.

Continue for 2 miles to reach the Electric Brae.

ELECTRIC BRAE, Strath NS21
A curious optical illusion caused by the lie of the surrounding countryside makes the road through this area appear to be descending when it is actually climbing.

In 2 miles turn right with the A719 and follow a wooded valley to the entrance of Culzean Castle.

CULZEAN CASTLE, Strath NS21
An ancient tower that was once a Kennedy stronghold forms the centrepiece of this splendid castle (NTS), which was designed by the talented Robert Adam in 1777. Everything about the building prompts superlatives, but the Round Drawing Room and magnificent staircase are probably its finest features. Many of the rooms have beautifully decorated plaster ceilings. The grounds include the extensive Culzean Country Park.

CULZEAN COUNTRY PARK, Strath NS21
Scotland's first countryside park was created in the 565-acre grounds of Culzean Castle this century, but the lovely walled garden was established in 1783 and the buildings of the Home Farm were designed by Robert Adam while he was extending the castle. The farm has been adapted as a reception and interpretation centre for the park.

Continue along the A719 to reach the village of Maidens.

MAIDENS, Strath NS20
Just inland of this Maidenhead Bay resort is Shanter Farm, which was the home of Burns' Tam O'Shanter. The village itself has a fine bay sheltered by the curve of the bay's coast.

Leave Maidens on the A719 to reach the golf resort of Turnberry.

TURNBERRY, Strath NS20
Traces of Turnberry Castle guard Turnberry Point, an attractive promontory to the north of the resort's famous golf course. Legend has it that the castle was the birthplace of Robert the Bruce in 1247, and history records that he certainly landed here in 1307 to win his first battle against the English. On a clear day views extend 20 miles to lonely Ailsa Craig, a rocky little island that rises to 1,110ft from the sea.

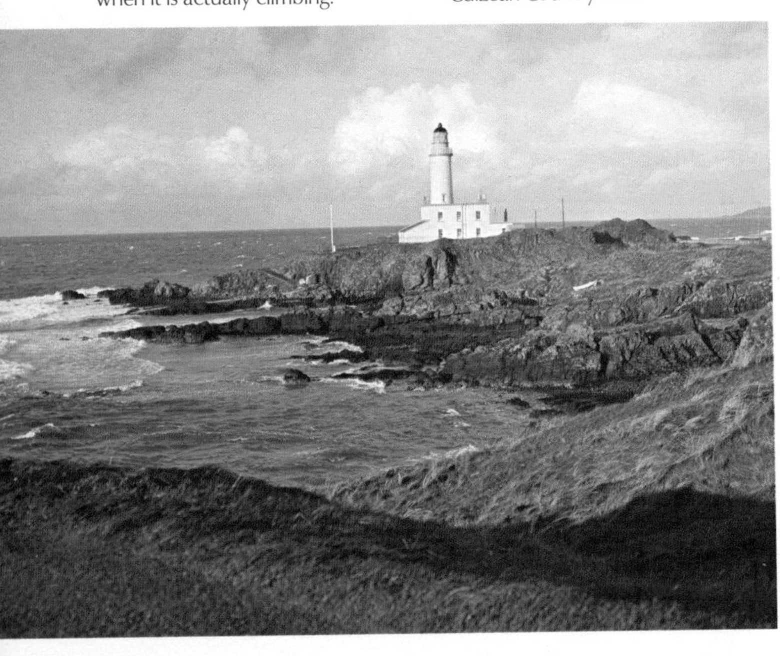

Views from the magnificent golf course at Turnberry extend past a lighthouse to distant Ailsa Craig.

In Turnberry village turn left on to the A77 'Ayr' road to reach Kirkoswald.

KIRKOSWALD, Strath NS20
Kirkoswald Churchyard contains the graves of two of Robert Burns' best loved characters, Tam O'Shanter and Souter Johnnie. In real life Tam was Douglas Graham of Shanter, who supplied grain to an Ayr brewery, and his crony 'Souter' was a village cobbler named John Davidson. Davidson's thatched 18th-century cottage (NTS) now houses a Burns' museum.

From Kirkoswald continue along the A77 to reach Crossraguel Abbey.

CROSSRAGUEL ABBEY, Strath NS20
Originally founded as a Cluniac monastery by the Earl of Carrick in the 13th century, this abbey (AM) was inhabited by the Benedictine order from 1244 to the 16th century. Many superb examples of 15th-century architecture can be seen amongst the extensive ruins.

Continue along the A77 and enter the town of Maybole.

MAYBOLE Strath NS30
Maybole was once the seat of the very powerful Kennedy family, who were the Earls of Cassillis. Their town house was 17th-century Maybole Castle, whose picturesque turret and oriel windows make a charming architectural contribution to the town's High Street. Nowadays it is used as administration offices for the Kennedy estates. Other family connexions exist with the Tollbooth, which was one of their mansions and incorporates fragments of a much older building.

From Maybole take the B7023 'Crosshill' road and drive to Crosshill village. Turn right here with the B7023 'Dailly' road, then in 1 mile join the B741 and continue through the Valley of Girvan. In 1 mile a short detour can be made from the main route to visit Kilkerran: turn left on to an unclassified road, cross the Water of Girvan, and turn right to reach Kilkerran.

KILKERRAN, Strath NS30
Part of the Kilkerran House estate, home of the Ferguson family since the 17th century, is being developed for riding and many other open-air sports and activities

On the main tour, continue along the B741 through the valley of Girvan, and in 2 miles meet an unclassified left turn SP 'Barr'. A detour can be taken from the main route to Dailly by continuing along the B741 for 1 mile.

DAILLY, Strath NS20
The 18th-century church in New Dailly features lairds' lofts, and the romantic 17th-century ruin of Dalquharran Castle stands to the north. Features of Old Dailly include the Bargany Gardens (open), where fine displays of flowers and shrubs can be enjoyed.

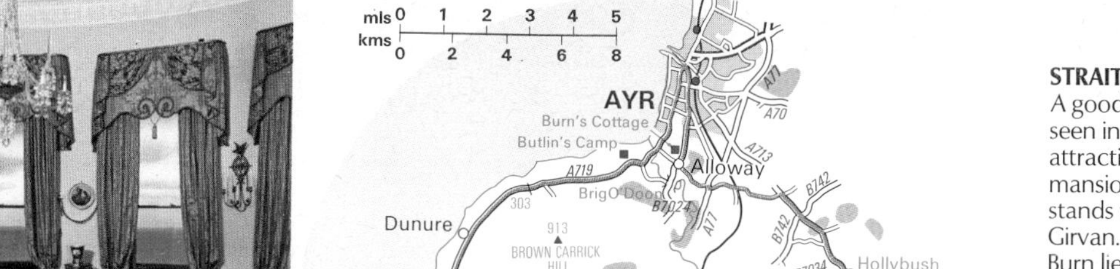

Culzean Castle's Round Drawing Room is a superb example of Georgian elegance.

)n the main tour, take the ınclassified road SP 'Barr' and drive hrough woodland for 5 miles, cross he River Stinchar and turn right to ɔllow the river to Barr.

ARR, Strath NX29

Changue Forest, part of the huge Galloway Forest Park, lies close to his little River Stinchar angling esort. Attractive Polmaddie Hill rises ɔ the south-east.

Aeet a T-junction in Barr village and ırn right then left on to the B734 SP arrhill'. In 6 miles meet the A714 nd turn left on to the 'Newton ewart' road to reach Pinwherry.

NWHERRY, Strath NX18

uins of a one-time Kennedy ronghold stand in the valley of the ver Stinchar, near Pinwherry.

ɔntinue along the A714 to Barrhill.

ARRHILL, Strath NX28

esolate, open moorland surrounds s pleasant little village, relieved ly by the green Duisk valley and een banks of the Cross Water of ce to the south.

ntinue along the A714 to grennan and turn left on to an classified road SP 'Straiton'. Drive ɔ the Galloway Forest Park.

LLOWAY FOREST PARK, mf & Gall

hird of this huge 110,000-acre k is planted with trees, and its ındaries encompass five nplete forests and 10 hills rising to r 2,000ft. Because this is a nmercial enterprise as much as thing else, the predominant cies of trees in the park are ıglas fir, Scots pine, Norwegian ıce, and other fast-growing ifers. This industrial aspect does detract from its scenic value vever, and each summer sees the val of more visitors to enjoy the quillity of its woodlands and larating openness of those places have not been planted. One of finest areas is Glen Trool Forest, ch is centred on enchanting Loch ol and the slopes of the Merrick. 764ft the latter is the highest mit south of the Highlands.

e through Glentrool village and t a right turn that offers a short ur from the main route to ctive Loch Trool.

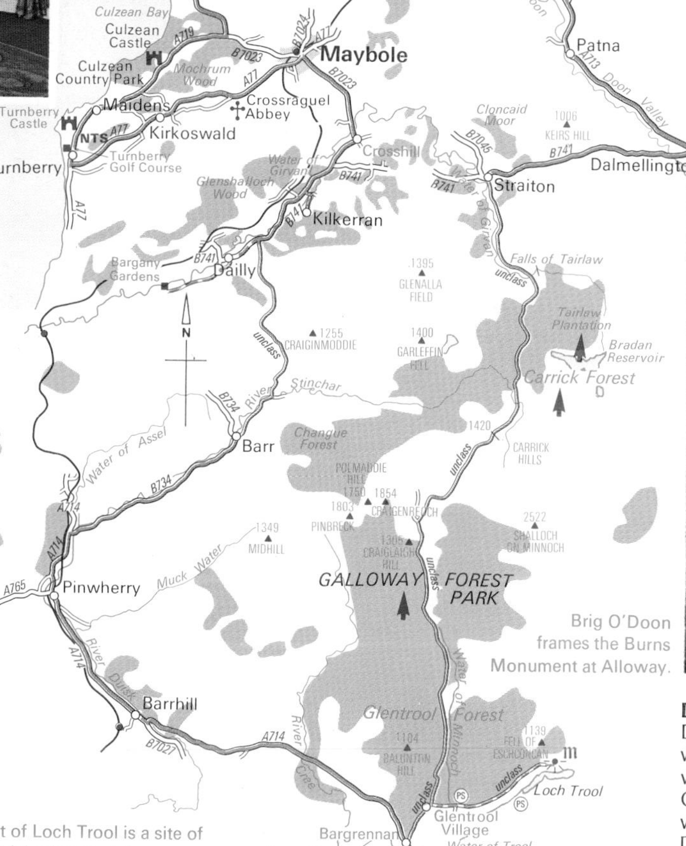

Part of Loch Trool is a site of special scientific interest.

LOCH TROOL, Dumf & Gall NX47

A campsite near the Martyr's Stone on the south-western side of this beautiful lake is the start of a $4\frac{1}{2}$-mile circuit of its pleasantly wooded banks. Woodland and water-margin wild life can be seen, and as the path rounds the east end of the loch it passes a granite memorial (NTS) that records the defeat of an English force by Robert the Bruce in 1307. Prominent to the north are the Rhinns of Kells and the Merrick, while Laurachan Hill rises to the south.

On the main tour, continue through the forest park and in 8 miles branch right. Climb to a road summit of 1,420ft, then descend through the Tairlaw Plantation of Carrick Forest into the Girvan Valley. Drive to the village of Straiton.

STRAITON, Strath NS30

A good pre-Reformation aisle can be seen in the restored church of this attractive little village, and the old mansion of Blairquhan (not open) stands west near the Water of Girvan. The glen of Lambdoughty Burn lies east of the Dalmellington road and is known for its lovely waterfalls.

In Straiton turn right on to the B741 'Dalmellington' road, and in 6 miles meet the A713 'Ayr' road. A detour can be made from the main route to Dalmellington by turning right here on to the A713 and driving for 1 mile.

Brig O'Doon frames the Burns Monument at Alloway.

DALMELLINGTON, Strath NS40

Dalmellington is a busy little iron-working town in an area well blessed with fine natural water features. Close by is the pretty Calcairnie Linn waterfall, and to the west the River Doon flows into Bogton Loch.

On the main tour turn left along the A713 'Ayr' road to reach Patna.

PATNA, Strath NS41

This River Doon town is deeply involved with the coal mining and steel industries.

Leave Patna and continue for $3\frac{1}{2}$ miles to pass through the hamlet of Hollybush. In $2\frac{1}{4}$ miles turn left on to an unclassified road SP 'Alloway', and in $1\frac{3}{4}$ miles meet the A77. Turn right then left to cross the A77 and enter Alloway.

ALLOWAY, Strath NS31

The thatched cottage in which Scotland's national poet was born in 1759 is now a Robert Burns Museum, and the Auld Brig described by Burns still spans the River Doon here. It is possible that the bridge dates from the 13th century, and above it is a Burns Monument that was built in the 19th century. Bibles belonging to the poet and Highland Mary are kept inside the memorial. A roofless building near by is the haunted Kirk Alloway mentioned in one of his many works.

From Alloway turn right on to the B7024, and after $1\frac{1}{2}$ miles join the A79 to re-enter Ayr.

TOUR 97 — 74 MILES

ON THE KINTYRE PENINSULA

The coast road of Kintyre opens up superb seascapes to the Western Isles and coast of Northern Ireland as it follows the peninsula's dramatic shore to the westernmost point in Scotland. Inland is a spine of rugged little hills scored by fertile valleys and dotted with the relics of ancient man.

KINTYRE, Strath
This tour is contained entirely within the Kintyre peninsula, a narrow tongue of wilderness that stretches south towards the Atlantic from the west coast of Scotland. At one point it is only 12 miles from Ireland's eastern shores. Down the middle of the peninsula is a backbone of rocky hills that culminate near Saddell with 1,491ft Beinn an Tuirc, and at its northern boundary Kintyre is almost completely divided from the Knapdale district by West Loch Tarbert. The farthest point south is the Mull of Kintyre, where there is a lighthouse.

TARBERT, Strath NR86
Situated on a tiny isthmus between East and West Loch Tarbert, this fishing town and resort is a centre of the Loch Fyne herring industry and one of the main towns on the lovely Kintyre peninsula. According to legend the Norse prince Magnus Barefoot dragged his ships overland from loch to loch here, claiming the whole peninsula as one of the Hebridean islands and therefore the property of his father King Olaf. Norse ownership ceased after the Battle of Lairgs in 1263, and Tarbert later acquired a 14th-century castle that was to become the stronghold of both Robert the Bruce and James II. Remains of the castle still overlook the harbour it once guarded, but the only invasion that threatens the town today is that of summer holiday-makers in search of the fine beaches and safe bathing.

Leave Tarbert on the A83 'Campbeltown' road and drive alongside West Loch Tarbert to reach Kennacraig.

KENNACRAIG, Strath NR86
Situated on beautiful West Loch Tarbert, Kennacraig is a terminus of car ferries that operate between the mainland and the islands of Islay, Jura, and Gigha. It is a good base from which to explore the 10-mile circuit of the loch, most of which is serviced by roads of varying difficulty. A section along the often hilly north shore offers glimpses of the Sound of Jura and Loch Caolisport, and passes impressive Kilberry Castle. This was the seat of the Campbells of Kilberry for 500 years and has fascinating sculpted stones dating from late medieval times. The piece of road which follows the loch's attractive south shore eventually joins the rugged west coast of Kintyre, affording views across the Sound of Gigha.

Continue towards Campbeltown on the west coast of Kintyre and reach Tayinloan.

TAYINLOAN, Strath NR64
A passenger ferry crosses the Sound of Gigha from here to the island of Gigha.

ISLE OF GIGHA, Strath NR64
Although only 6 miles long by $1\frac{1}{2}$ miles wide, this flat little island off the Kintyre coast has an impressive rocky shoreline and several interesting features. Among these is Achamore House (open) of 1884, which contains various works of art and 18th-century English furniture. The gardens were the inspiration of Sir James Horlick, who gave them to the National Trust, and seem to justify Gigha's claim to be the most fertile of all the Scottish Islands. High belts of trees protect azaleas, rhododendrons, hydrangeas, and a host of ornamental shrubs from the destructive Atlantic winds. Also on the island is the 13th-century ruin of Kilchattan Church, and Gigha parish was the birthplace of Gaelic scholar Dr Kenneth MacLeod. Just off the south tip of the island is the tiny islet of Cara, popular with seabirds.

Continue along the peninsula to Killean.

KILLEAN, Strath NR64
Close to the modern church in Killean are the remains of its ancient predecessor, from which it acquired its fine double window.

Continue to Glenbarr.

GLENBARR, Strath NR63
Beyond modernized Glenbarr Abbey the pretty Barr Water meets the sea, and inland the Barr Glen leads deep into isolated hill country.

Continue along the A83 to Campbeltown.

CAMPBELTOWN, Strath NR72
The chief town of southern Kintyre, Campbeltown stands at the head of a sheltered bay and has a rocky shore that is popular with sea anglers. Nowadays it is a resort known for its good facilities and unusually mild climate, but at the end of the 19th century it was a bustling centre of commerce and industry with 30 distilleries and a herring fleet of more than 500 boats. Reminders of the area's very early history, when lone Irish missionaries braved the Atlantic to lead Britain out of the dark ages, are everywhere in place names and ancient religious sites. About $3\frac{1}{2}$ miles south-east near Auchinhoan Head is St Kieran's Cave, which is a mere 25ft above high-water mark and may be the earliest Christian chapel in Scotland. It is thought that St Kieran, whose name can be recognized in the Kilkerran area of the peninsula, arrived in Scotland even before St Columba. Relics from these and prehistoric times can be seen in the town's museum, and an echo of Celtic culture is in the 16th-century cross standing at Old Quay Head. Offshore from the resort is isolated Davaar Island.

St Columba's footprints near Keil are said to mark the saint's landing place on Kintyre.

DAVAAR ISLAND, Strath NR72
Boats can be hired to cover the sho[rt] distance to this island, which is famous for the Crucifixion scene painted inside a natural cave by the 19th-century artist Archibald Mackinnon. It was designed so that the only illumination required is a shaft of light from a hole in the roc[k]. It was retouched by a local artist in the mid 1950s.

It is possible to make several detour[s] from the main route in Campbeltown, driving to such plac[es] as Machrihanish, Southend, Keil, an[d] the Mull of Kintyre, all of which are worth visiting. Details follow: to visit Machrihanish leave Campbeltown [on] the A83, proceed west to the B843, then drive for a further $5\frac{1}{2}$ miles.

MACHRIHANISH, Strath NR62
One of the main attractions in this one-time salt producing village is i[ts] beach, which offers $3\frac{1}{2}$ miles of san[d] on an otherwise rocky coast. Amo[ng] the resort developments prompte[d] by this natural asset is an excellent golf course that was laid out in 18[?]. Services from the nearby airport li[nk] with Glasgow and the Isle of Islay.

To visit Southend, Keil, and the Mu[ll] of Kintyre, leave Campbeltown on A83 and drive to its junction with t[he] B843 'Machrihanish' road and the B842. Turn left here on to the B842 and drive south to reach Southen[d].

The southern area of Kintyre is peat moss, partially drained for forestry.

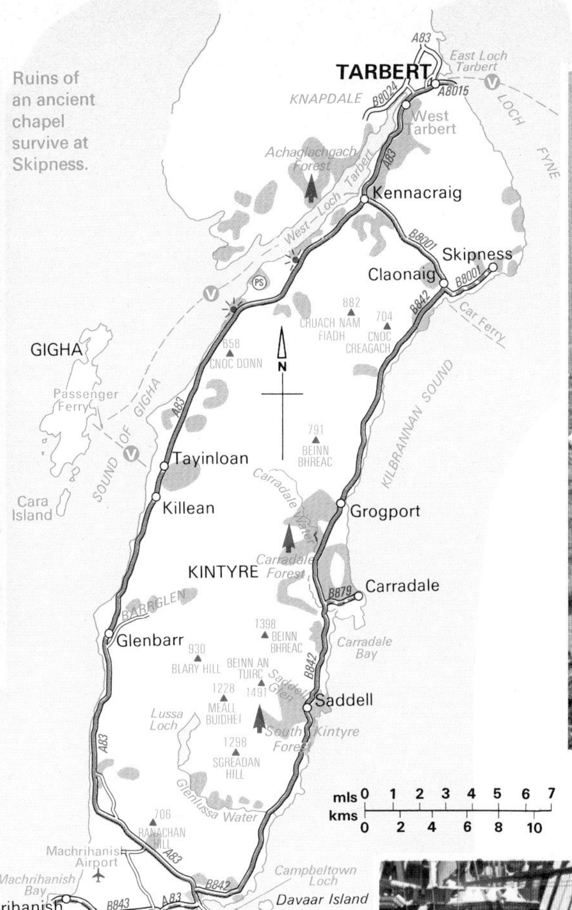

The early lighthouse at the Mull of Kintyre is Scotland's closest approach to Ireland.

A small fishing fleet uses Carradale's modern harbour.

SOUTHEND, Strath NR60
This small resort offers two sandy beaches facing Sanda Island across the narrow waters of Sanda Sound. Pleasantly isolated coastline is accessible by a short walk in either direction.

From Southend follow a narrow and hilly unclassified road through Keil to the Mull of Kintyre.

KEIL, Strath NR60
Tradition has it that a ruined chapel here marks the place where St Columba landed to begin his 6th-century mission in Scotland. He and his disciples were pledged to convert the Picts to Christianity; local evidence suggests that this site was a pagan place of sanctity long before the chapel was built. The impressions of two right feet on a flat stone known as St Columba's Footprints, may have been carved to mark the place where pagan chiefs took their initiation vows. Only 100 yards away are the remains of a druidical altar. Coarse remains of Dunaverty Castle, whose 300 occupants were slaughtered by Covenanters, survive in the neighbourhood.

MULL OF KINTYRE, Strath NR50
The southernmost tip of the peninsula and Scotland's closest point to the Irish coast, this wild headland offers some remarkable views. Rathlin Island rises from the sea a mere 12 miles away, and behind it is the dark line of the northern Irish coast. On both sides the shore has been torn ragged by the full force of the Atlantic Ocean, and inland the 1,405ft mass of Beinn na Lice isolates the headland from the rest of Kintyre. An early lighthouse built near the South Point in 1788 was later remodelled by Robert Stephenson.

On the main route, leave Campbeltown with the B842 and follow the east coast of the peninsula. Continue to Saddell.

SADDELL, Strath NR73
Interesting remains of an abbey and castle survive in this attractive village. It is thought that the former was founded by Somerled, the first Duke of the Isles, for Cistercian monks in the 12th century. Remains include boundary walls and sculptured Celtic tombstones in the churchyard. One of the recumbent effigies preserved here may be Somerled himself, the ancestor of the Clan Donald. Battlemented Saddell Castle dates from the 16th century and was once the residence of the bishops of Argyll. Lovely Saddell Glen is part of the South Kintyre Forest, a wild and beautiful area that merges with Carradale Forest farther north. To the west the Kintyre Hills are dominated by the peak of 1,491ft Beinn an Tuirc.

Continue through hill country where open stretches reveal fine views of the hills on the Isle of Arran; particularly prominent is 2,345ft Beinn Bharrain. Skirt the shore of Kilbrannan Sound and later reach the B879 right turn, which can be taken for a short detour to Carradale.

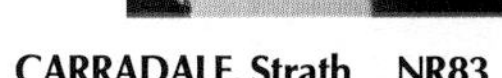

CARRADALE, Strath NR83
Situated opposite the Isle of Arran on the east coast of the peninsula, this small resort stands on a sheltered bay and has a fishing harbour. Close to the pier are the remains of Aird Castle, and the narrow spit of Carradale Point carries an oval vitrified fort. Such remains, not uncommon in Scotland, have had their stones and masonry fused into a glassy substance by fire.

Continue along the B842 and drive to the village of Grogport.

GROGPORT, Strath NR84
This small village stands on a secluded little bay in the Kilbrannan Sound, facing the Isle of Arran's mountainous outline.

Continue to Claonaig.

CLAONAIG, Strath NR85
During the summer this hamlet is the terminus for the Arran car ferry.

A short detour can be taken from the main route to Skipness in $2\frac{1}{2}$ miles by keeping straight on to join the B8001 and continuing to the village.

SKIPNESS, Strath NR85
Features of this charming little place include the remains of an ancient chapel and a large 13th-century castle. Local views extend seaward across the Sound of Bute to the northern part of Arran.

On the main tour, leave Claonaig and turn left on to the B8001. Climb, then descend with views of Knapdale and West Loch Tarbert. Continue to Kennacraig and turn right on to the A83 for the return to Tarbert.

TARBET, Strath NN30
Views to the east from this resort extend across Loch Lomond towards the fine 3,192ft peak of Ben Lomond. Ben Arthur, popularly known as The Cobbler, rises to 2,891ft beyond Ardgaten Forest and the expanse of Loch Long to the west.

LOCH LOMOND, Strath
Popularly known as the Queen of Scottish lakes, 24-mile Loch Lomond is the largest expanse of fresh water in Britain and is sheltered by wooded mountains that climb dramatically from its northern shores. In the south it is bordered by a gentler landscape of soft green hills, and the isolation of its many beautiful islands was as much of an attraction for 5th-century Irish missionaries as it is for visitors today. One particular example is Inchmurrin, which is believed to have been the site of St Mirren's monastery in the 6th century and now features the ruins of Lennox Castle. Five of the islands in the south-eastern corner of the loch are included in a national nature reserve, and much of the east shore is cloaked by the lovely Queen Elizabeth Forest Park. The famous song *Loch Lomond* is said to have been composed by one of Bonnie Prince Charlie's followers on the eve of his execution.

Leave Tarbet on the A82 'Crianlarich' road to reach Inveruglas.

INVERUGLAS, Strath NN30
Overlooked by 3,092ft Ben Vorlich and 3,004ft Ben Vane, Inveruglas is the site of a hydro-electric power station that receives its water by tunnel aqueduct from Loch Sloy.

From Inveruglas continue on the A82 to reach Ardlui.

ARDLUI, Strath NN31
Situated at the northern tip of Loch Lomond, this beautiful mountain village guards the entrance to picturesque Glen Falloch and features a curious pulpit hewn out of the rock face.

Continue from Ardlui through Glen Falloch, past the Falls of Falloch, to reach Crianlarich.

CRIANLARICH, Central NN32
The superb mountain scenery round Crianlarich has made it a natural resort for visiting walkers and climbers. Loch Dochart, with its pretty wooded island enhanced by the picturesque ruins of an old castle, lies to the east.

In Crianlarich turn left with the A82 'Fort William' road and drive along Strath Fillan. In 2½ miles reach St Fillan's Chapel.

ST FILLAN'S CHAPEL, Central NN32
Fragments of this 14th-century chapel can be seen to the east of Fillan Water. Robert the Bruce dedicated the place as a thanks offering for his victory at Bannockburn.

Continue on the A82 to reach the resort of Tyndrum.

TOUR 98 — 71 MILES

BESIDE LOCH LOMOND

Many centuries ago Irish missionaries were attracted to the enchanting isolation of Loch Lomond's tiny wooded islands. Today the loch, set against a backdrop of gentle hillsides and wooded mountains, is still acknowledged as one of Scotland's loveliest expanses of fresh water.

Beautiful Ben Lomond, seen from the shores of Loch Lomond.

TYNDRUM, Central NN33
Tyndrum is an angling and climbing resort in Strath Fillan, near its junction with Glen Lochy on the edge of the Grampian mountains. The legendary Brooch of Lorne was reputedly lost just south of the village by Robert the Bruce during an ambush at Dail Nigh. It is now kept at the Macdougall mansion of Dunollie, near Oban.

Leave Tyndrum and join the A85 'Oban' road. Drive through Glen Lochy to reach Dalmally.

DALMALLY, Strath NN12
The River Orchy flows through this Strath Orchy village on its way to Loch Awe. A monument has been erected to the Highland poet Duncan Ban MacIntyre, some 2 miles south-west of Dalmally, near a viewpoint on the old Inveraray road.

Leave Dalmally and after a short distance turn left on to the A819 'Inveraray' road. Continue to Kilchurn Castle.

Some of the finest views of Loch Lomond can be enjoyed from Tarbet.

KILCHURN CASTLE, Strath NN12
Beautifully situated in mountainous country at the upper end of Loch Awe, Kilchurn Castle (AM) dates from the 15th century and stands on ground that was once an island. Major additions were made in the 16th and 17th centuries, but in 1879 it was badly damaged by dreadful gales that also caused the destruction of the Tay Bridge. However, even in its ruined state the castle is one of the finest baronial strongholds in Scotland. (Castle closed for repair at the time of publication.)

Continue on the A819, following the shore of Loch Awe for 4 miles, then turn inland across open country and ascend through Glen Aray. Continue, and pass Inveraray Castle on the right to reach Inveraray.

INVERARAY, Strath NN00
Picturesque woodland surrounds this smart Royal Burgh, where white-walled buildings make an attractive cluster on the banks of lovely Loch Fyne. At one time the village site was near the ancient castle that can be seen near by, but after burning down it was replaced by the existing town and castle in the 18th century. The present castle (open), which had to be restored after another fire in 1975, houses many historic relics, including some of Rob Roy's possessions and several fine portraits. Architecturally the building is a very early example of the neo-gothic and Scottish baronial styles. A cannon from the sunken Spanish Armada vessel *Florida* is on display in the grounds. A fine Celtic burial cross, removed to the town from Iona, stands at the junction of Front and Main Streets. In the parish church is an unusual dividing wall which was built to allow simultaneous services in the English and Gaelic languages.

Leave Inveraray on the A83 'Glasgow' road to reach Glen Shira.

GLEN SHIRA, Strath NN11
A charming 18th-century ornamental bridge spans the little River Shira at the entrance to this beautiful glen. Although best appreciated on foot, the glen is also accessible by a narrow road that runs through forest at first and passes close to the pretty Falls of Aray. A memorial to local author Neil Munro can be seen here. At its higher end the glen opens on to moorland, a startling contrast to the dense woodland below, and the road terminates at the ruined house of Rob Roy.

Leave Glen Shira and continue on the A83, beside the shores of Loch Fyne, to reach Glen Fyne.

GLEN FYNE, Strath NN21
Threaded by the River Fyne, this picturesque glen leads north-east from the head of Loch Fyne. To the east are the impressive 1,278ft high summits of Eagles Fall.

Continue on the A83 along the shore of Loch Fyne to reach Cairndow.

Mighty snow capped summits dwarf Loch Awe and the once-isolated ruins of magnificent Kilchurn Castle.

The 'Rest and Be Thankful' stone.

AIRNDOW, Strath NN11
nnein an Fhidhleir dominates the wnship of Cairndow, and its 2,658ft ımmit is the popular goal of alkers. Just outside the town near ɔch Fyne is the excellent modern ıansion of Ardkinglas House, which as built by the Scottish architect Sir obert Lorrimer. The gardens (open) local Strome House feature a 190ft ee that is claimed to be the tallest owing anywhere in Britain.

ave Cairndow and continue on the 33 to make a long and easy ascent rough Glen Kinglas to the 806ft road ımmit and 'Rest and Be Thankful' one. An alternative route may be ken from Cairndow to the Rest and Thankful summit by leaving the wnship on the A83 and turning ht on to the A815. Continue for 2 les, then turn left on to the B839 d drive through Hell's Glen.

LL'S GLEN, Strath NN10
e rocky and lonely glen with this pleasant name is dominated by 92ft Beinn an Lochain, and affords ws down to the swirling waters of River Goil.

ntinue the alternative route on the 39 to meet the junction with the 28. A detour from the alternative ute to Lochgoilhead and Carrick stle can be taken here by turning ht with the B839 and driving to hgoilhead.

LOCHGOILHEAD, Strath NN20
Standing on the shingly shores of Loch Goil, this pleasing little Victorian burgh of whitewashed houses is set against the dark background of the Cowal Hills. Steamer trips down the loch start from the town's small pier.

To continue the detour, leave Lochgoilhead and join the unclassified road which runs west of Loch Goil. In 5 miles reach Carrick Castle.

CARRICK CASTLE, Strath NS19
Since the 17th century Carrick Castle has been a picturesque ruin, but it was once a royal stronghold. Splendid views of the castle can be enjoyed from the steamers which leave Lochgoilhead.

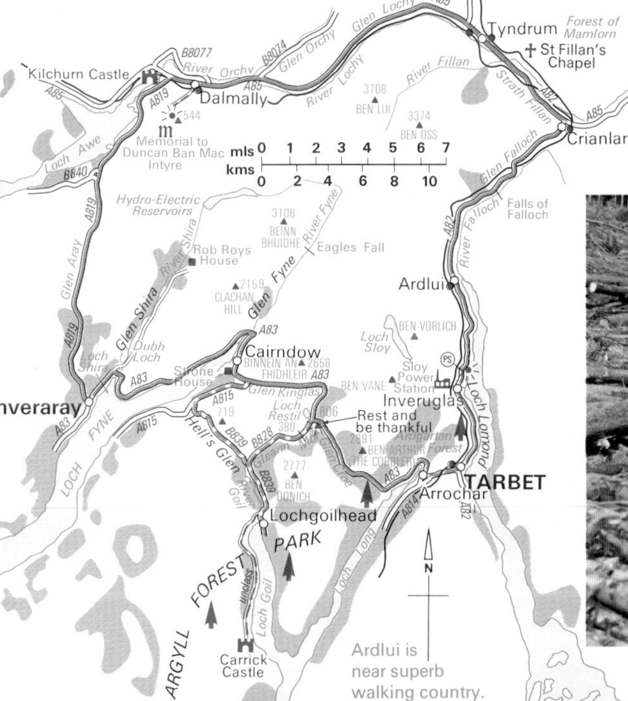

From Carrick Castle return to Lochgoilhead and thence to the junction with the B828 at the foot of Hell's Glen. From here continue the alternative route by following the B828 through Argyll Forest Park.

ARGYLL FOREST PARK, Strath
The huge forest park of Argyll covers 37,000 acres of beautiful mountain scenery from Ben Ime in the north to the Ben More ridge in the south. It is divided into two distinct areas: the large southern part stretches from Benmore Forest to Glenhanter Forest near Strachar, and the smaller northern section contains the Ardgoil and Ardgartan Forests between Lochgoilhead and Arrochar. The whole area is vast enough to provide an endless variety of gentle rambles, ambitious walks, and difficult climbs. It offers many things, from the pleasures of outdoor activities to the simple seeking out of solitude and peace in the mountains.

Continue the alternative by following the B828, to rejoin the main tour and reach Rest and Be Thankful.

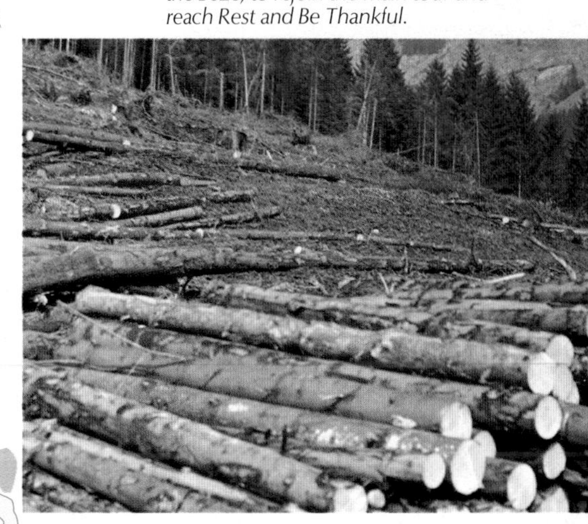

Forestry is a major industry in Argyll.

REST AND BE THANKFUL, Strath NN20
Near here the steep old road through Glen Croe, no longer used except for motor trials, reached a 800ft summit marked by a rough stone seat inscribed 'Rest and Be Thankful'. The seat has gone and the reconstructed road has been more gently graded for modern traffic, but the inscribed stone survives. The summit of 3,318ft Ben Ime can be reached by a long climb from the pass.

From Rest and Be Thankful continue along the A83, passing through Glen Croe and down Loch Long to reach the ferry port of Arrochar.

ARROCHAR, Strath NN20
Loch Long steamer trips that can be joined at Arrochar pier afford superb views of 2,580ft Brack, an impressive summit which rises in the west. Plenty of places exist for climbers to test their skills around Arrochar, and the village has become a popular centre for the sport.

Leave Arrochar and follow the A83 for the return to Tarbet.

TOUR 99 65 MILES

STRONGHOLDS IN THE HIGHLANDS

High above the fishing quays of Oban is an unfinished replica of the Colosseum, a fascinating folly built to relieve unemployment. Inland are the castles and towers of the Campbells and MacDougalls, grim ruins of serious intent in the spectacular loch and mountain scenery of the Highlands.

OBAN, Strath NM83
In the 200 years of its existence Oban has become a major centre in the West Highlands. Its busy port offers steamer services to the islands of Lismore, Mull, Colonsay, Coll, and some of the Outer Hebrides, making the town a thriving tourist resort. One of its most remarkable buildings is McCaig's Folly, which was begun in 1897 to relieve local unemployment but never finished. It was intended to be a replica of Rome's Colosseum and to house a museum and art gallery. The inside courtyard is landscaped, and the folly shines bravely in floodlights that bathe the summit of Battery Hill at night. Oban's museum is housed in Corran Halls, and the little granite St Columba's Cathedral near by was built by Sir Gilbert Scott. The Island of Kerrera stands just offshore from Oban and features the ruined MacDougall stronghold of Gylan Castle. The town is a popular golfing resort, and the fine 18-hole course lies to the east. Nearby Glencruiten House (not open) stands in a park which features the famous cathedral of trees. Macdonald's Mill, $\frac{1}{2}$ mile south of the town centre on the A816, mounts a fascinating display of the story of spinning and weaving.

Leave Oban on the A816 'Campbeltown' road and in $2\frac{1}{2}$ miles pass an unclassified right turn offering a detour from the main route to Kilbride village.

KILBRIDE, Strath NM82
Although the church has fallen into disrepair, Kilbride's 16th-century Lerags Cross has been well restored.

On the main tour, drive by the shores of Loch Feochan and in $2\frac{3}{4}$ miles reach a junction with the B844. A detour can be made to Kilninver by turning right and driving to the village.

KILNINVER, Strath NM82
This small village on Loch Feochan faces north-west across the wide Firth of Lorne to the mountainous Island of Mull.

This detour can be extended to Clachan Bridge and the Island of Seil; leave Kilninver on the B844 and shortly reach Clachan Bridge.

CLACHAN BRIDGE, Strath NM71
Telford built this attractive hump-backed bridge in 1792. It spans Seil Sound, a narrow arm of the Atlantic Ocean, to link with the Island of Seil.

ISLAND OF SEIL, Strath NM71
Slate is still worked at the local Balvicar quarry, and is much in evidence on the roofs of Seil's neat whitewashed cottages. The neighbouring island of Easdale provided slate in times past, but the supply has now been exhausted. Luing Island, lying to the south, is accessible via the Cuan Ferry.

On the main tour continue along the A816. After a short distance a detour can be made to Loch Scamadale by turning left on to an unclassified road through Glen Euchar to reach lovely Loch Scamadale.

LOCH SCAMADALE, Strath NM82
Surrounded by hills, this attractive loch lies in Glen Euchar some 4 miles from Kilninver.

Carnassarie Castle has been in ruins since the Argyll rebellion of 1685.

On the main tour, continue along the A816 and drive through wooded Glen Gallain. Descend to reach Kilmelford.

KILMELFORD, Strath NM81
A cluster of islands in the Firth of Lorne shelters this quiet angling village at the head of Loch Melfort. The Pass of Melfort, north of the village by the A816, is a picturesque area which includes a small hydro-electric dam. This type of industry has become common in Scotland.

From Kilmelford continue along the A816 to follow the shores of Loch Melfort. Continue towards the sea to reach Arduaine Gardens.

ARDUAINE GARDENS, Strath NM71
Many rare trees and shrubs have been collected in this 21-acre garden (open), which is especially famed for its spring displays of rhododendrons and azaleas. The attractive layout includes water and rock gardens, and superb views extend over Loch Melfort and the Sound of Jura.

Oban's busy port serves as the gateway to the Western Isles.

Continue on the A816 for $3\frac{1}{2}$ miles. A detour from the main route to the Lunga Wildlife Reserve at Ardfern and Craignish Castle can be taken here: turn right on to the B8002 and drive to Ardfern.

ARDFERN, Strath NM80
The Lunga Wildlife Reserve has a collection of European birds, mammals and plants in natural settings amongst Caledonian oak woodland and marshes.

Continue the detour on the B8002 to reach Craignish Castle.

CRAIGNISH CASTLE, Strath NM70
The 16th-century keep of Craignish Castle (not open) stands amid a fine rhododendron garden facing the Sound of Jura.

On the main tour, continue along the A816 to reach Kintraw.

KINTRAW, Strath NM70
This attractive little village offers magnificent views of the beautiful sea loch of Craignish, with its scattered islands.

Leave Kintraw and proceed on the A816 to reach Carnassarie Castle.

CARNASSARIE CASTLE, Strath NM80
Ruined Carnassarie Castle (AM) stands high on a hill about 1 mile north of the village of Kilmartin. It was built for the Bishop of the Isles in the 16th century, but was captured and partially blown up during the Duke of Argyll's ill-fated rebellion in 1685.

Near the castle turn left on to the B84 and proceed to Ford, passing Loch Ederline to the right.

FORD, Strath NM80
Sandwiched between huge Loch Awe and tiny Loch Ederline, Ford is a small angling resort and an embarkation point for steamboat trips on Loch Awe. The surrounding countryside is ideal for walking.

Reach the Ford Hotel and continue along an unclassified road bounded by Loch Awe on the right.

This isolated standing stone near Kintraw, stark against a background of ills, is thought to be of bronze-age date.

.OCH AWE, Strath
'he Campbells of Inveraray had nany occasions to be grateful for he protection given against attack rom the north by this long natural noat. Reminders of its part in scotland's turbulent history are cattered along the shores of the ch today. Ruins of a castle stand ear Fincharn at the southern end, nd the wooded islet of Fraoch lean in the north conceals remains f another. Early religious stirrings are ecalled by ancient chapels built on ome of Loch Awe's islands by holy nen seeking isolation. In the south is ne Innis-Sherrich Chapel, which was edicated to St Findoc c1257 and ands near several 14th- or 15th-entury carved slabs. Another undation can be seen on Inishail, in ne north. Today the loch forms part Scotland's largest hydro-electric heme and is a paradise for anglers d walkers. The lovely countryside Inverliever Forest borders the loch d features several marked nature ails, some of which lead to notable ewpoints. At its northern end the ch is dominated by the twin peaks 3,689ft Ben Cruachan.

ontinue through Inverliever Forest reach New York.

W YORK, Strath NM91
marked contrast to its famous mesake, this tiny hamlet faces ross the peaceful expanse of Loch ve to an ancient chapel at rtinnisherrich.

ave New York and continue to the w forestry village of Dalavich, then er a short distance cross the River ich. Continue through Inverinan est, meet the B845, and turn left to er Kilchrenan.

CHRENAN, Strath NN02
ranite block in the churchyard e commemorates 13th-century c Cailean Mor, clan hero and nder of the Argyll fortunes.

etour can be taken from the main te to visit the gardens at anaiseig by turning right on to an lassified road in Kilchrenan.

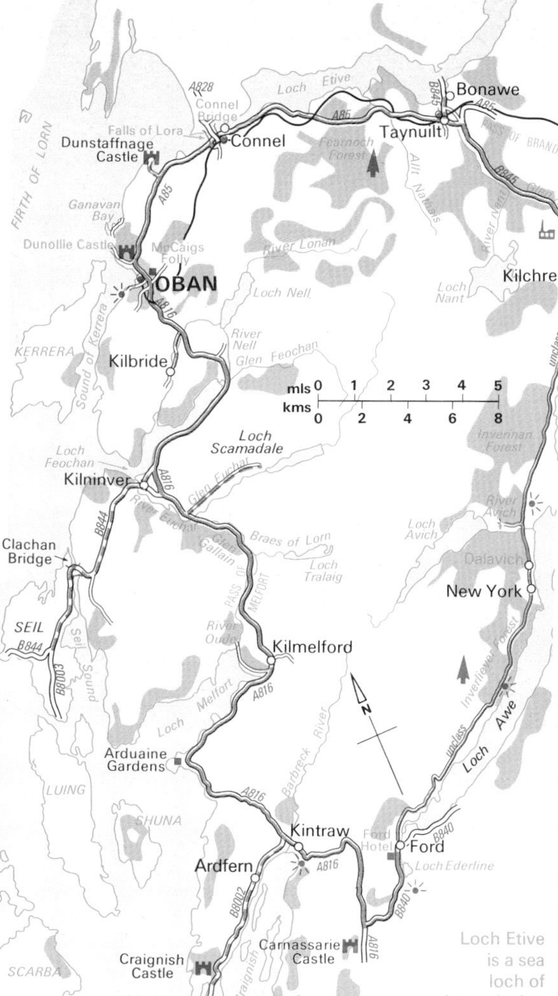

ARDANAISEIG GARDENS, Strath NN02
Superb views of Loch Awe can be enjoyed from these beautiful gardens (open), which are full of rare shrubs and trees. In the early part of the year banks of rhododendrons and azaleas burst into a magnificent display of colour.

On the main tour, continue on the B845 from Kilchrenan and drive through Glen Nant, passing Nant Power Station on the left. Meet the A85 and turn left to reach Taynuilt.

Loch Etive is a sea loch of quiet seclusion and home of many seabirds.

Telford's unusual Clachan Bridge is known as the 'Bridge over the Atlantic' because it actually spans a creek of that ocean.

TAYNUILT, Strath NN03
Taynuilt is a small resort at the head of Glen Nant, facing the lovely waters of Loch Etive. Ben Cruachan rises magnificently in the east, and the high situation enjoyed by the village affords marvellous views of the mountains which overlook Upper Loch Etive. Lord Nelson is somewhat unexpectedly commemorated by a standing stone at Muckairn Church, about 2 miles to the north-west of the village.

A detour can be made from the main route to visit Bonawe: in Taynuilt village turn right on to the B845, then after ½ mile turn right again on to an unclassified road and enter Bonawe.

BONAWE, Strath NN03
During the 18th century a thriving iron industry developed in the unlikely Highland setting of picturesque Bonawe. The furnace, casting house, and workmen's cottages used at that time have all been painstakingly restored.

On the main tour, continue along the A85 and follow the shores of Loch Etive to reach Connel.

CONNEL, Strath NM93
Cantilevered Connel Bridge is the largest of its kind in Europe, after the Forth Bridge, and is a splendid example of its type. Beside the bridge is a remarkable sea-cataract known as the Falls of Lora.

Continue on the A85 to reach an unclassified right turn leading to Dunstaffnage Castle.

DUNSTAFFNAGE CASTLE, Strath NM83
The Campbell clan built Dunstaffnage Castle in the 13th century, but many parts of the existing ruin (AM) date from a good 200 years later. Among the remains are two round towers, a curtain wall, and a gatehouse. The chapel near the castle is the burial place of the Campbells.

Continue on the A85 to re-enter the port of Oban.

EDINBURGH, Lothian NT27
Scotland's finest city and its capital since 1437, Edinburgh stands on seven hills between the waters of the Firth of Forth and the 2,000ft summits of the Pentlands. Until 200 years ago this great centre of culture and learning was little more than a cluster of houses along the Royal Mile, a cobbled slope that followed a windy ridge from Castle Hill to the Palace of Holyroodhouse. The foremost building here is the castle (AM), which overlooks the picturesque streets of the Old Town from its lofty summit and has a history that stretches back at least 1,000 years. Its old name *Duneadain*, meaning Fort on a Slope, aptly describes its site on Castle Rock and refers to a previous stronghold that may have had iron-age origins. Many of Edinburgh's oldest buildings stand on even older sites along the Royal Mile, which has been admirably restored in recent years and has a distinctive aura of age. Canongate Tolbooth dates from 1591, 15th-century John Knox's house was built by goldsmiths to Mary Queen of Scots, and 17th-century Gladstone's Land features rooms decorated with fine tempera paintings (all open). Lady Stair's House is a restored 17th-century building housing a museum, and off Canongate is 16th- and 17th-century Holyroodhouse (AM) – Scotland's finest royal palace. Ruins of the 12th-century Chapel Royal foundation adjoin the palace. Here and there the splendour of the city is relieved by more down-to-earth domestic architecture, like the old White Horse Inn and the mercat cross. The 14th-century stronghold of Craigmillar Castle is associated with Mary Queen of Scots, and the 17th- to 19th-century Parliament House is where the Scottish parliaments met before the Union of 1707. Famous George Heriot's School dates from 1628 and was founded by the Jingling Geordie of Scott's *Fortunes of Nigel*. Near the Castle Mound are the Royal Scottish Academy and the National Gallery of Scotland, where many fine paintings by artists from various schools can be seen, and in Chambers Street the Royal Scottish Museum exhibits one of the most comprehensive general displays in Britain. The National Library of Scotland comes close to Oxford's famous Bodleian in the richness of its contents, and the museum of the Scottish Register Office can be seen in West Register House, Charlotte Square. There are many other fascinating museums, galleries, workshops, and studios in the city, most of which will be listed in the local guides. Every year since 1947 Edinburgh's concert halls, theatres, galleries, and public halls have opened their doors to the arts of the world in the International Festival, a cultural extravaganza that takes place in late summer.

Leave Edinburgh city centre with SP 'Galashiels' and in 2 miles drive forward on to the A701 SP 'Penicuik' and 'Peebles'. Continue to Liberton.

TOUR 100 90 MILES

THE CITY ON SEVEN HILLS

Seven hilltops guarded by a massive castle carry Edinburgh, the Athens of the North. Just a few miles from its ancient heart are the rugged cliffs of the wild North Sea coast and the breathtaking scenery of mountains that were old before much of Britain was formed.

Edinburgh Castle stands high on a rock that may once have been the site of an iron-age hillfort.

LIBERTON, Lothian NT26
Almost part of the great city which developed on its doorstep, Liberton has a 15th-century tower that occupies a ridge-top position and was once a stronghold of the Dalmahoys. It overlooks the city and is a well-known landmark. Liberton House is an early 17th-century building with a sundial dated 1683.

Drive through Kaimes, then in 3 miles turn left on to the B7003 SP 'Roslin'. In $\frac{3}{4}$ mile turn right SP 'Rosewell'; a detour can be made from the main route by driving forward with the B7003 into Roslin.

ROSLIN, Lothian NT26
Scott mentioned this former mining village's famous chapel in the *Lay of the Last Minstrel*. It was founded in 1446 by William Sinclair and contains many fine stone carvings, including the exquisite Prentice Pillar. Nearby Roslin Castle (open) overlooks the North Esk River and picturesque Roslin Glen.

On the main route, continue to Rosewell, meet a T-junction, and turn right on to the A6094. In 2$\frac{1}{4}$ miles turn left on to an unclassified road and cross Cauldhall Moor. In 1$\frac{3}{4}$ miles meet crossroads and turn left on to the B6372, then 1$\frac{3}{4}$ miles farther turn right on to an unclassified road SP 'Peebles'. In 1$\frac{1}{4}$ miles pass a left turn leading to Gladhouse Reservoir.

GLADHOUSE RESERVOIR, Lothian NT35
This attractive reservoir is set amid beautiful scenery below the summits of the Moorfoot Hills.

On the main route, continue for 3 miles and descend, then turn left on to the A703 to reach Eddleston.

EDDLESTON, Borders NT24
This tiny hamlet lies in the valley of the Eddleston Water, with the 2,137ft summit of Blackhope Scar rising from the Moorfoot range to the east. On the Peebles road to the south of the village is a memorial to George Meikle Kemp, who served as an apprentice here in the 19th century and later designed the famous Scott Monument in Edinburgh.

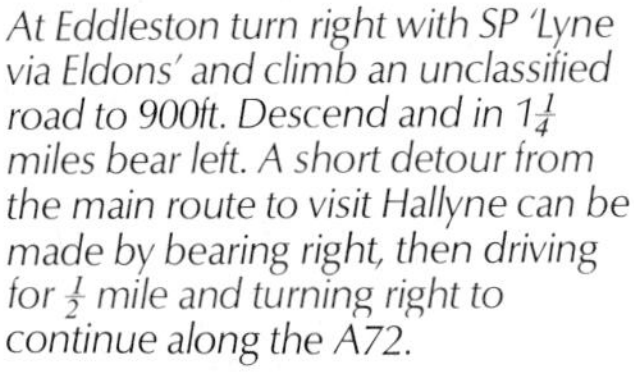

At Eddleston turn right with SP 'Lyne via Eldons' and climb an unclassified road to 900ft. Descend and in 1$\frac{1}{4}$ miles bear left. A short detour from the main route to visit Hallyne can be made by bearing right, then driving for $\frac{1}{2}$ mile and turning right to continue along the A72.

HALLYNE, Borders NT14
One of the smallest churches in Scotland can be seen here. Inside are a pulpit and two pews of Dutch workmanship. Close by are the remains of a Roman camp of AD 83.

On the main route, continue for $\frac{1}{2}$ mile and turn left on to the A72 SP 'Peebles', driving alongside the Lyne Water and the River Tweed. In 1$\frac{3}{4}$ miles a detour can be taken from the main route by turning right on to an unclassified road and crossing the Tweed to follow Manor Water to the village of Manor.

MANOR, Borders NT23
Made famous by Scott's work *The Black Dwarf*, this small village stands at the foot of the long and beautiful Manor Valley. A little churchyard near Manor Water preserves the tomb of David Richie, on whom Scott modelled his Black Dwarf or Bowed Davie character.

On the main tour, continue along the A72 and after a short distance pass Neidpath Castle on the right.

NEIDPATH CASTLE, Borders NT24
Originally a stronghold of the Fraser family, this 15th-century castle (open) is beautifully positioned above the River Tweed and is an attractive feature of the local countryside.

Proceed along the A72 to Peebles.

PEEBLES, Borders NT24
Anglers come here to fish for the great Tweed salmon, but this attractive old Royal Burgh also offers facilities for golf, tennis, and pony-trekking. It has been the home of such famous people as the author Robert Louis Stevenson and Mungo Park, whose exploration helped to open up Africa. William Chambers and his brother Robert, publishers of the first Chambers' encyclopaedias and dictionaries, were born here and donated the Chambers Institute, a library, and a museum to the town. Relics of the town's history include the ruins of 13th-century Cross Kirk and the old shaft of a former parish cross. Old local inns include the 17th-century Cross Keys and early 19th-century Tontine. The woodlands of the Glentress Forest lap the outskirts of Peebles.

GLENTRESS FOREST, Borders NT2
One of the first state forests to be established in Scotland, the Glentres comprises over 2,000 acres of fast-growing conifers such as Douglas fir Norway spruce, and Sitka spruce.

Continue along the A72 SP 'Galashiels' to Innerleithen.

Edinburgh's Charlotte Square is a gem of Georgian architecture.

Traquair House has seen centuries of beer-brewing.

Neidpath Castle was restored after severe damage by Cromwell's artillery.

INNERLEITHEN, Borders NT33
Sir Walter Scott popularized this small wool town in his novel *Ronan's Well*. To the south is the fine mansion of Traquair House (open), which can trace its history back to the 10th century and is the oldest inhabited house in Scotland. In its time it has played host to 27 English and Scottish monarchs, and its interior is packed with treasures and relics from many generations. A unique 18th-century brewhouse here is licensed to sell its own beer, and the grounds feature attractive woodland walks.

A detour from the main route can be taken by keeping forward on the A72 and driving to Walkerburn.

WALKERBURN, Borders NT33
Founded in 1845 for workers in the local textile industry, this tiny village stands in an area that has been settled since early times. Remarkable earthwork terraces can be seen north of Walkerburn on Purvis Hill.

On the main route, leave Innerleithen by turning left on to the B709 SP 'Heriot' and drive alongside Leithen Water for 4 miles. Leave the main river behind and climb to a road summit of 1,250ft over a narrow pass, then descend to the Dewar Burn. In 2 miles drive forward on to the B7007 and follow a gradual ascent to a 1,324ft summit at the back of the Moorfoot Scarp. In good weather views from here take in the Pentland Hills, the 1,900ft summits of Scald Law and Carnethy, Arthur's Seat in Edinburgh, and the waters of the Firth of Forth. In 1½ miles turn right on to the A7 SP 'Galashiels'; a short detour to Middleton can be made by turning left on the A7.

MIDDLETON, Lothian NT35
Middleton Hall and its acres of fine grounds are owned by the Scottish National Camps Association. This organization has founded the Middleton Camp School here with the aim of giving town-bred children the opportunity to continue and extend their education in country surroundings. The school is international in its scope.

On the main route, continue along the A7 with SP 'Galashiels' for 1¼ miles and turn left on to the B6367 SP 'Pathhead'. Continue to Crichton.

Peebles enjoys a delightful setting by the salmon-rich River Tweed.

CRICHTON, Lothian NT36
Crichton Castle (AM) stands south-west of the actual village and is more elaborate than is usual in Scotland. It overlooks the River Tyne from a high and desolate site, and the Italianate lines that were the legacy of the Earl of Bothwell in the 16th century are certainly out of keeping with the dour practicality of conventional castle design. The medieval church features a quaint bellcote.

Turn left, then right along the B6367 to Pathhead.

PATHHEAD, Lothian NT36
Close to this little village are two very fine houses. Oxenford Castle stands beyond the Tyne Water and now serves as a school, and 18th-century Preston Hall is open by appointment.

At Pathhead turn right then left SP 'Haddington'. In 2 miles turn right on to the A6093. In 1 mile a detour can be taken from the main route by turning left on to the B6371 for Ormiston.

ORMISTON, Lothian NT46
Situated on the Tyne Water, this village boasts a fine 15th-century cross (AM) mounted on steps.

On the main route, continue along the A6093 to Pencaitland.

PENCAITLAND, Lothian NT46
This village is divided into two parts. Wester Pencaitland has an old mercat cross, and Easter Pencaitland is centred on a notable 13th-century church.

Meet crossroads and turn left on to the B6355 SP 'Tranet', then take the next turning right on to the B6363 SP 'Longniddry'. In 3 miles a detour can be taken to the village of Gladsmuir by meeting crossroads and turning right on to the A1.

GLADSMUIR, Lothian NT47
In early times this area was notorious for witchcraft, but the village is more famous for its associations with the Battle of Prestonpans in 1745.

On the main route, drive over the crossroads on the B6363 and continue to Longniddry.

LONGNIDDRY, Lothian NT47
Between 1643 and 1647 John Knox, the religious reformer, was a tutor here. The village itself is attractively sited just inland from Gosford Bay.

Turn right on to the A198 and follow SP 'North Berwick'. In 1 mile meet a T-junction and turn left on to the B1348 to Cockenzie and Port Seton.

COCKENZIE AND PORT SETON, Lothian NT47
A large power station makes an unsightly blemish on the otherwise attractive appearance of Cockenzie, a quaint little fishing village close to the resort of Seton. Features of the latter include 2 miles of sandy beach, a fine 14th-century collegiate church (AM), and Robert Adam's Seton Castle of 1790.

After 2 miles pass the site of the Battle of Prestonpans on the approach to Prestonpans.

BATTLE SITE OF PRESTONPANS, Lothian NT37
In 1745 the forces of Prince Charles Edward defeated Sir John Cope's entire army here in an astonishing 10 minutes.

PRESTONPANS, Lothian NT37
Former prosperity is evident in this town's splendid 17th-century mercat cross (AM), Hamilton House (NT), and several other notable survivors from that period. The name Prestonpans originated from a salt-extraction industry operated by the monastic community from Newbattle Abbey in the 12th century.

Drive for 1½ miles beyond Prestonpans, meet a roundabout, and take the 3rd exit on to the A1. Return to Edinburgh through Musselburgh.

MUSSELBURGH, Lothian NT37
This manufacturing town on the sandy Esk estuary has a 16th-century Tolbooth which preserves an ancient clock given by the Dutch in 1496. Jacobean Pinkie House (open) incorporates a 14th-century tower but mainly dates from c1590. A fine painted ceiling can be seen in the Long Gallery, and the building now forms part of Loretto School.

TOUR 101 109 MILES

BETWEEN THE FORTH AND TAY

This narrow tongue of land between the Firth of Forth and Firth of Tay offers a contrasting landscape of exposed shores and sheltered estuaries. Here the rich farmlands of the Howe of Fife climb towards the high landward barrier of the Lomond and Ochil Hills.

St Andrews Castle.

ST ANDREWS, Fife NO51
Historically this ancient Royal Burgh is one of the most significant places in Scotland. The cathedral (AM), which was founded in 1160, had grown to become Scotland's largest church by the time the finishing touches were made in 1318. Sparse remains include parts of the east and west gables, a section of the south nave wall, and the Precinct Wall (AM). Close by is small St Rule's Church (AM), which was built c1130 and is one of the best of its type in Scotland. The Sessions House preserves reminders of harsher times in the form of two repentance stools and a barbaric scold's bridle. St Andrews University was founded in 1412 and is the oldest in Scotland. Its Chapel of St Salvator carries an octagonal broach spire and contains the tomb of its founder, Bishop Kennedy. Also to be seen here is the oldest Sacrament House in a Scottish church, and a pulpit from which John Knox preached while leading his Protestant Reformation. St Andrews Castle (AM) dates from the 13th century and overlooks the North Sea from a craggy eminence. The other reminder of the city's old defences is the West Port, which spans South Street on the course of the town walls. Today St Andrews is a popular summer resort on a cliff-girt coast, close to the four very famous golf courses of St Andrews Bay.

Leave St Andrews on the A91 SP 'Tay Bridge' and after a short distance pass the Royal and Ancient Golf Course on the right.

THE ROYAL AND ANCIENT GOLF COURSE, Fife NO51
Written records of the Old Course, which is the oldest in the world, date back to the 15th century. The Royal and Ancient was founded in 1754 and is the ruling authority on the game throughout the world.

Continue to Guardbridge.

GUARDBRIDGE, Fife NO41
One of the keystones of this attractive old bridge bears the shield of arms and pastoral staff of Bishop Wardlaw, who built it in the 16th century.

Cross the River Eden and turn right on to the A919 to reach Leuchars.

LEUCHARS, Fife NO42
The fine Norman church that stands here was built by the de Quincy family and is one of the best of its type in Scotland. Its chancel and apse are original, and it contains some good monuments.

Continue for $1\frac{1}{4}$ miles to St Michael's Hotel and turn right on to the B945 to the port of Tayport.

TAYPORT, Fife NO42
This one-time ferry port has a good church that was rebuilt in the 18th century. Some 47 acres of the local countryside have been taken over by the Tentsmuir Nature Reserve, including Morton Lochs.

The collapse of the original Tay railway bridge killed 75 people.

Leave Tayport on the B946 and drive beneath the new Tay Road Bridge into Newport-on-Tay.

NEWPORT-ON-TAY, Fife NO42
A 42-span road bridge, the second longest in Europe, links this busy small town with Dundee – on the other side of the Firth of Tay.

Continue to Wormit.

WORMIT, Fife NO32
The 2-mile railway bridge that spans the Tay here was built in 1885 to replace the famous one that collapsed, with great loss of life, during freak gales in 1879.

Continue inland on the B946 and after $\frac{1}{2}$ mile pass an unclassified right turn that offers a detour to Balmerino Abbey.

BALMERINO ABBEY, Fife NO32
Founded in 1226 and built by monks from the great religious centre of Melrose, this abbey was suppressed during the Reformation and is now in ruins (NTS). Among its remains is a 15th-century Chapter House.

On the main tour, shortly branch left on to an unclassified road SP 'St Andrews' and after another 1 mile meet a roundabout. Take the 2nd exit and in another $1\frac{1}{2}$ miles turn right on to the A92 to return to St Michael's Hotel. At the crossroads turn right SP 'Cupar' and continue through Balmullo, then after a further 2 miles join the A91 to enter Dairsie. Turn left on to an unclassified road SP 'Pitscottie', in 1 mile cross the River Eden, then turn right with views of Dairsie Castle on the north bank. Continue along the picturesque Dura Glen, which is noted for its fossils, to Pitscottie. Turn left and immediately right on to the B939 SP 'Kirkcaldy' and continue to Ceres.

CERES, Fife NO41
Some call this the prettiest village in Scotland. Old cottages surround a charming green, and the villagescap is completed by a medieval hump-backed bridge and the church.

After another $1\frac{1}{2}$ miles reach Craigrothie and turn right on to the A916, which passes the entrance to Hill of Tarvit Mansion.

HILL OF TARVIT, Fife NO31
Standing in spacious grounds overlooking the Howe of Fife, this fine mansion (NTS) contains collections of furniture, paintings, tapestries, and porcelain. It occupies the site of a 17th-century house anc is now partly in use as a nursing home. On a nearby hill is the ancien Scotstarvit Tower (AM).

Continue along the A916 and descend into the Eden Valley to join the A92 for Cupar.

CUPAR, Fife NO31
Cupar is a Royal Burgh and the market centre for the fertile Howe c Fife. Its parish church has a good 15th-century tower, and the merca cross in the town is picturesquely adorned with the figure of a unicorr

Follow SP 'Kincardine' to leave Cupar on the A91, and at the end of the town turn right on to the A913 SP 'Perth'. After another $1\frac{3}{4}$ miles turn right on to an unclassified road SP 'Luthrie'. Meet a junction with the A914 and turn left, then in $\frac{1}{2}$ mile turn right on to another unclassified road for Luthrie. After a further 1 mile bear left with the route, then later meet a T-junction and turn left to follow the Firth of Tay. Meet a junction with the A913 and turn right into Newburgh.

NEWBURGH, Fife NO32
Situated on the south shore of the attractive Firth of Tay, this small Royal Burgh is near the ancient remains of Lindores Abbey. Close to the water is 18th-century Mugdrum House, opposite a tiny island which preserves the 1,000-year-old Mugdrum Cross.

Continue along the A913 to Abernethy.

Burleigh Castle stands near Loch Leven.

BERNETHY, Tayside NO11
)ne of the main features of this one-me Pictish capital is the remarkable 2th-century round tower (AM) of its arish church. This type of onstruction is more commonly und in Ireland, and the 74ft-high xample standing here is one of only vo in Scotland.

ontinue past Aberargie and turn left to the A90 SP 'Forth Road Bridge'. ive through Glen Farg and later rn right on to the B996 to reach enfarg village.

ENFARG, Tayside NO11
enfarg is a popular tourist resort in heltered position, and makes a od base from which to explore the autiful scenery of Glen Farg.

$2\frac{1}{2}$ miles meet a T-junction and n right on to the A91, then turn left to the B919 'Glenrothes' road. In miles reach Balgedie and join the 11 for Kinnesswood, with Loch ven on the right.

NESSWOOD, Tayside NO10
et Michael Bruce was born here in 16, and his cottage is now a seum containing relics of his life l work. The landscape here is minated by prominent Bishop Hill l White Craigs.

The Chapel Royal at Falkland Palace was formerly a banqueting hall.

LOCH LEVEN, Tayside NO10
Romance and beauty mingle with an interesting history to make the very special atmosphere which surrounds Loch Leven. Its 14th- or 15th-century castle (AM), brooding on an island site, was the prison of Mary Queen of Scots until she made a sensational escape. The loch is often the venue for fishing competitions, and in winter its ice provides ideal conditions for curling. Some 300 acres of mixed habitats on the south shore make up the Vane Farm nature reserve, where there are nature trails and an official RSPB observation centre.

Continue to Scotlandwell.

SCOTLANDWELL, Tayside NO10
The springs that give this village its name bubble up into a 19th-century stone cistern at the end of the main street.

Turn left and continue to Leslie.

LESLIE, Fife NO20
A church on the green in this small industrial town is claimed to be the scene of a 15th-century poem entitled *Christ's Kirk on the Green.* Leslie House, a 17th-century seat of the earls of Rothes, stands east of the town.

Pass the church in the main street and after 300 yards reach the Clansman (PH). Turn left on to an unclassified road for Falkland.

Bishop Hill in the Lomonds rises behind the village of Kinnesswood.

FALKLAND, Fife NO20
Old weavers' cottages and charming cobbled streets characterize this lovely little Royal Burgh, but it is chiefly known for the historic Falkland Palace (NTS). This was a favourite seat of the Scottish Court from the reign of James V, who made considerable improvements to the building before his death in 1542. Scott used it for part of the setting in his *Fair Maid of Perth.*

Meet a T-junction and turn right on to the A912, and in $\frac{1}{4}$ mile turn left on to the B936 SP 'Freuchie'. Continue through Newton of Falkland to Freuchie, and at the end of that village meet crossroads. Drive straight across on to an unclassified road and meet a junction with the A92. Turn right here, then turn immediately left on to the 'Kennoway' road. In $4\frac{1}{2}$ miles turn left to enter Kennoway. Meet a main road and turn right, then immediately left SP 'Leven' and continue for 2 miles to reach the outskirts of Leven.

LEVEN, Fife NO30
Formerly a weaving village, this resort and maritime town on Largo Bay is well known for its golfing facilities.

Turn left on to the A915 'St Andrews' road and drive past Lundin Links.

LUNDIN LINKS, Fife NO40
Excellent fishing and sea bathing have made this a popular resort. Three prehistoric standing stones can be seen on the western outskirts of the town.

Continue to Upper Largo.

UPPER LARGO, Fife NO40
The 17th-century spire of the church at Upper Largo rests entirely on the arched roof of the chapel and is unique in Scotland.

Follow the A921 SP 'Crail' and in $2\frac{1}{2}$ miles turn right on to the A917 for Elie.

ELIE & EARLSFERRY, Fife NO40
Sailing, fishing, and fine sandy beaches are offered by these twin resorts. They lie between Chapel Ness and Elie Ness, and are known for their good golf courses.

Follow the A917 'Anstruther' road along the East Neuk coastline, passing St Monans.

ST MONANS, Fife NO50
Old houses cluster near the water's edge in this lovely little fishing port, and the beautiful Old Kirk of St Monance stands almost on the foreshore. This lovely old foundation dates from the 14th century but was restored in 1828. To the south-west of the village are the ruins of 17th-century Newark Castle.

Continue to Pittenweem.

PITTENWEEM, Fife NO50
Some of the best architecture in this picturesque little Royal Burgh has been restored by the National Trust for Scotland. The ruined priory dates back to the 12th century and the tower of the parish church is dated 1592. Some 3 miles from the town is Kellie Castle (NTS), a fine example of 16th- and 17th-century architecture.

Continue, with views of the Isle of May offshore, to Anstruther.

ISLE OF MAY, Fife NT69
Many species of sea bird use this isolated lighthouse station as a sanctuary.

ANSTRUTHER, Fife NO50
Anstruther Easter and Wester, both Royal Burghs in their own right, stand each side of the harbour and are famed for their herring fleets.

Continue on the A917 to Crail.

CRAIL, Fife NO60
The oldest Royal Burgh in the East Neuk district, this picturesque fishing town was once the haunt of smugglers. Its many lovely old buildings cluster round quaint streets and the harbour in a way that has attracted artists for generations. A curious weather vane depicting a salmon surmounts the 16th-century Tolbooth, and the mercat cross carries the figure of a unicorn.

Leave Crail on the A918 and drive through Kingsbarns.

KINGSBARNS, Fife NO51
A slender church spire rises high above the rooftops of this pretty little place, which is set on an inlet between Babbet Ness and Cambo Ness.

Continue along the A918 to return to St Andrews.

STIRLING, Central NS79
This Royal Burgh makes an ideal touring base as the Gateway to the Highlands, as it is popularly known, but is also worth visiting for its own sake. All round the foot of the rocky crag which carries its imposing castle (AM) are hilly streets of stone buildings, a quaint switchback area where it is difficult to find even the smallest patch of level ground. The castle itself seems to grow from the stone on which it is built. Its 250ft site has been fortified for many centuries, but the oldest parts of the present building date back about 500 years to the reign of James III. Magnificent views can be enjoyed from the viewpoints known as Queen Victoria's Lookout and Lady's Rock, extending far into the rugged Highlands in really good weather. Below the castle ramparts is the King's Knot (AM), one of the earliest ornamental gardens in Scotland. Down the hill in the Old Town are many good examples of 16th- to 18th-century domestic architecture, interspersed with such fine public buildings as the Guildhall, the Tolbooth of 1701, and the 15th-century and later church where Mary Queen of Scots and James VI were crowned soon after being born. The Argyll Lodging is a 17th-century mansion that became a military hospital in the 18th century. Its exterior (AM) is considered the most impressive of its style and period in Scotland. Unfinished Mar's Wark (AM) in Broad Street was begun in 1570 and intended as a town house for the Regent Mar, and the town's 15th-century Old Bridge (AM) was rebuilt in 1749 after having been blown up during the '45 Rising. About 1 mile east of Stirling are the beautiful ruins of Cambuskenneth Abbey (AM), which was founded in 1147 by David I and was the scene of Robert the Bruce's parliament in 1326. Stirling University (founded in 1967) is Scotland's newest university.

Leave Stirling on the A811 SP 'Erskine'. In $5\frac{3}{4}$ miles reach an unclassified left turn that can be taken as a short detour to Gargunnock.

GARGUNNOCK, Central NS79
Situated in flat countryside traversed by the serpentine course of the River Forth, this village is an attractive little place with a fine 16th- to 17th-century mansion (not open).

On the main route, continue for 3 miles and turn right on to the B882 SP 'Thornhill'. A short detour can be followed from the main route to visit Kippen by turning left on to the B822.

KIPPEN, Central NS69
An unusual aspect of this lovely south-facing village is the fame it attracted by the great Kippen Grape Vine. Claimed to be one of the largest in the world, it clearly liked the sun and soil conditions here and in its 70 years of life managed to cover an area of 50,000 square feet. The reason for its eventual demise is obscure, but before that time it managed to produce a staggering 1,000,000 bunches of grapes. A fine old dovecote (NTS) has been preserved in the village, and the local church of 1825 is considered one of the best examples of its period in Scotland. Treacherous Flanders Moss, a wild peat bog that is probably the site of an old forest, lies north of the River Forth.

On the main drive, continue along the B822 'Thornhill' road and in $\frac{1}{2}$ mile cross the River Forth. Later cross the Goodie Water, then at Thornhill join the A873. Keep forward with the B822 towards Callander, then pass the edge of Torrie Forest and join the A81. Continue to Callander.

TOUR 102 86 MILES

GATEWAY TO THE HIGHLANDS

Stirling stands in a bend of the River Forth and for years was the battleground of Scottish and English forces. Now it is a peaceful and historic centre from which to tour the beautiful Trossachs, the high country of the Campsie Fells, and the lovely Queen Elizabeth Forest Park.

Stirling Castle, home of Scottish kings, stands on a 250ft crag overlooking the Forth Valley.

CALLANDER, Central NN60
Callander's excellent position near the Trossach Hills and Loch Katrine makes it an ideal touring centre and resort. An inscribed sundial of 1753 is an attractive feature of South Church Street, and the Roman Camp Hotel has associations with the author Barrie. Other literary connections exist with Scott, who was a frequent visitor to the town. A road to the north-west leads through the beautiful Pass of Leny, where the River Leny rushes through a narrow gorge in a fine display of natural power. Close by is the Kilmahog Woollen Mill (open), where blankets and tweed cloth are made by hand. Some $3\frac{1}{2}$ miles from the town and easily accessible to climbing enthusiasts is the severe 2,873ft peak of Ben Ledi.

Follow the A84 'Crianlarich' road and in $1\frac{1}{4}$ miles turn left on to the A821 SP 'Trossachs'. Cross the River Leny, then drive alongside lovely Loch Venachar with Ben Ledi overlooking Brig O'Turk to the right.

BRIG O'TURK, Central NN50
This particularly beautiful Trossachs village is splendidly situated between Lochs Venachar and Achray, and is a popular base for anglers. The Turk or Finglass Water is spanned here by a rustic old bridge described in Sir Walter Scott's ballad *Glenfinglas*. In the early 19th century Queen Victoria often came here, and during her visits she enjoyed the company of a famous innkeeper called Kate Ferguson. Then, as now, the area attracted many artists who strove to capture the timeless quality of 'typical' Scottish scenery.

Leave Brig O'Turk and enter the Queen Elizabeth Forest Park by driving alongside Loch Achray. After a short distance reach the romantically-set Trossachs Hotel.

THE TROSSACHS, Central
A bewildering combination of mountains, lochs, rivers, and thick woodlands makes up the outstanding landscapes for which this beauty spot is famous. The name means Bristly Country, but the nature of the land is not as unfriendly as this would suggest and has inspired such romantic works as Scott's *Lady of the Lake*. Most of the area is in a wooded gorge between Loch Achray and Loch Katrine.

Continue for $\frac{1}{4}$ mile beyond the Trossachs Hotel. A detour can be made from the main tour route to visit Loch Katrine by keeping forward to a pier at the eastern end of the lake.

LOCH KATRINE, Central
There are no public roads to disturb the peace of lovely Loch Katrine, but summer steamers from the pier at its east end give visitors an appreciation of some of the Trossachs' most secret and beautiful places. After disembarking at Stronachlachar passengers can visit the birthplace of folk hero Rob Roy, but the area will always be most remembered for Scott's *Lady of the Lake*. The lady was Ellen Douglas, her lake was Katrine, and many of the places mentioned in the poem can still be identified. The modern world is not entirely shut out, however, and the 'Silver Strand' that was once opposite Ellen's Isle has been submerged since the water was raised to improve Glasgow's water supply. Ben Venue rises 2,393ft to dominate the whole scene, from Loch Katrine to the Pass of Achray.

On the main drive, continue on the 'Aberfoyle' road and drive through the Queen Elizabeth Forest Park.

Wooded Loch Achray leads gently into the mixed landscapes of lakes, rivers, mountains, and woodland which form the picturesque Trossachs.

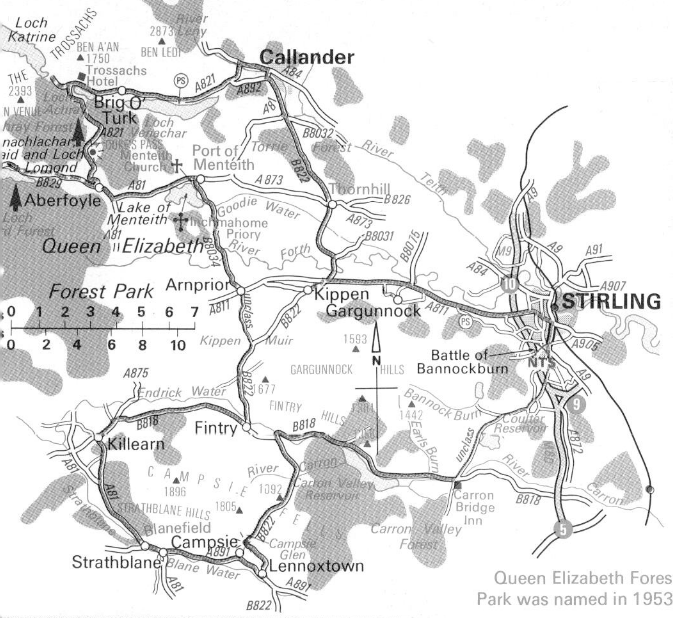

Queen Elizabeth Forest Park was named in 1953.

Salmon are sometimes seen jumping the Falls of Leny near Callander.

ʒUEEN ELIZABETH FOREST PARK, ;entral

'his National Forest Park covers ·1,454 acres of lovely countryside rom Loch Venachar to Loch omond, including the lofty summit of Ben Lomond. Both wild and planted areas can be enjoyed best by walking along the numerous marked trails that have been cleared or that purpose, though motorists re well catered for with carparks nd stopping areas. A viewing shelter as been built for visitors by the Carnegie Trust.

)escend to Aberfoyle, passing the AA iewpoint of David Marshall Lodge.

ABERFOYLE, Central NN50

'he tiny hamlet of Aberfoyle, associated with Rob Roy and Scott's poem of the same name, has little in common with the development of he present village. During the 19th century devotees of Scott's works came here in crowds, and the resort oon eclipsed what was left of its tiny neighbour. A plough coulter hanging rom a tree by the old site recalls a cene from the book.

'rom Aberfoyle it is possible to take n exceptionally scenic detour along he B829 for Inversnaid, on Loch omond: to follow it, drive alongside ochs Ard and Chon, and 2 miles beyond the head of Loch Chon meet T-junction. A brief visit can be made o the village of Stronachlachar by urning right here, but the main detour is left.

STRONACHLACHAR, Central NN41

A lonely path leads from this village to isolated Glengyle, where Rob Roy was born. This famous freebooter was immortalized by Scott in 1871.

On the main detour, turn left at the T-junction and continue to Inversnaid along an unclassified road, passing Loch Arklet.

INVERSNAID AND LOCH LOMOND, Central NN30

A fort built here in 1713 was once under the command of General Wolfe, of Quebec Heights fame, but this tiny village is best known for its spectacular surroundings. On the far side of lovely Loch Lomond are the towering summits of 3,318ft Ben Ime, and 3,092ft Ben Vorlich.

On the main tour route from Aberfoyle, continue with the A821 'Stirling' road and after 1 mile branch left on to the A81 SP 'Callander'. After another $2\frac{1}{2}$ miles reach the Lake of Menteith on the right.

LAKE OF MENTEITH, Central NN50

Inchmahome Priory (AM) was founded on one of three tiny islands in this lake during the 13th century, and for a time was a refuge for the infant Mary Queen of Scots. The lake itself is the only large expanse of fresh water in Scotland not called a loch, and on its west side it lies peacefully beneath gentle slopes of the 1,289ft Hills of Menteith. The Port of Menteith stands on its shore.

Drive for 1 mile beyond the lake and turn right on to the B8034 SP 'Arnprior'. After a short distance pass the passenger ferry terminus for Inchmahome Priory, on the right by Menteith Church. Continue to Arnprior.

ARNPRIOR, Central NS69

Here there is a fine Georgian mansion set in superb woodland gardens, which are unfortunately not open to the public.

At Arnprior turn right on to the A811, then turn left on to an unclassified road SP 'Fintry'. After 2 miles cross moorland below the Fintry Hills and turn right on to the B822 to Fintry.

FINTRY, Central NS68

Fintry occupies a central position in the ancient territory of Lennox, with the bare Fintry Hills to the north-east. The ancient Culcreuch tower, which stands a little north of the village, was extended in the 17th century.

From Fintry turn right on to the B818 'Killearn' road, then in $5\frac{1}{2}$ miles join the A875 'Glasgow' road to Killearn.

KILLEARN, Central NS58

George Buchanan, the historian and scholar who became tutor to James VI, was born here in 1506 and is commemorated by an obelisk. Killearn House is a 19th-century edifice $1\frac{1}{2}$ miles south-west.

Drive for 2 miles beyond Killearn, turn left on to the A81, and continue through Blanefield to Strathblane.

STRATHBLANE, Central NS57

This small resort is charmingly situated on the Blane Water, beneath the Strathblane Hills and the Higher Campsie Fells.

From Strathblane turn left on to the A891 and proceed to Campsie.

CAMPSIE, Strath NS67

All round this Campsie Glen village are the summits of the Campsie Fells, which offer good walking country to the energetic. Excellent views can be enjoyed from the Crow Road, which runs through the glen, and nearby Earl's Seat.

Continue along the A891 to Lennoxtown.

LENNOXTOWN, Strath NS67

Originally known as the Clachan of Campsie, this small industrial town stands in the ancient district that once came under the control of the Lennox family. The local churchyard features the Lennox vault and a number of 17th-century stones.

At Lennoxtown turn left SP 'Fintry' on to the B822, then climb out of the valley and pass the head of Campsie Glen. Cross the open moorland of the Campsie Fells, reaching a road summit of more than 1,000ft, and descend into the valley of the Endrick Water. Turn right on to the B818 SP 'Denny', then later run alongside the Carron Valley Reservoir. Drive for $1\frac{3}{4}$ miles beyond the dam and reach the Carron Bridge Inn, then turn left on to an unclassified road SP 'Stirling'. In $1\frac{3}{4}$ miles pass the small Loch Coulter Reservoir on the right, and after another $2\frac{1}{4}$ miles meet a T-junction and turn left. Later cross the M9 motorway, then in $\frac{3}{4}$ mile turn right then left to join the A872. Immediately to the left is the Battlefield of Bannockburn.

The bronze statue of Robert the Bruce at Bannockburn symbolizes Scotland's rebellion against English monarchy.

BATTLEFIELD OF BANNOCKBURN, Central NS79

It was this battle, fought in 1314 for the possession of Stirling Castle, that established Robert the Bruce on the Scottish throne. Bruce won against odds of nearly three to one, and earned the fear of his enemy as well as the respect of his people. An open-air rotunda encircles the Borestone, in which Bruce's standard is said to have been set, and the part of the battlefield just west of Bannockburn is owned by the NTS.

Return to Stirling via the A872 and A9.

TOUR 103 88 MILES

THE SIDLAW AND OCHIL HILLS

Scott immortalized the wild beauty of the countryside round Perth in his novels, and his praise is as justified today as it was then. Here the flanks of the Sidlaw and Ochil Hills sweep down to deep wooded straths, or valleys, where the enchantment of running water is never far away.

PERTH, Tayside NO12
Once known as St Johnstoun, the fair city of Perth is an old Royal Burgh set at the head of the Tay estuary between the meadows of the North and South Inch. In early times the area attracted the attention of English forces, and the town was taken and fortified by Edward I in 1298. Its single year as the capital of Scotland ended with the murder of James I at a former Blackfriars monastery in 1437. In 1559 John Knox effectively started the Protestant Reformation here with his emotive sermon against church idolatry. Cromwell's parliamentarian army took the city a little under a century later, and it came into the Jacobites' hands in the Risings of the 18th century. One of the most important buildings to have survived all this turmoil is famous St John's Kirk, a fine medieval and later church that has been attended by many members of English and Scottish royalty. Perth's associations with Sir Walter Scott are numerous. The 14th-century heroine of the *Fair Maid of Perth*, Catherine Glover, lived in a house on the site where the present Fair Maid of Perth's House now stands. Also of interest are the natural history museum, art gallery, and the regimental museum of the Black Watch, which is housed in Balhousie Castle. A survival of early industry exists in the city's 19th-century dye- and glassworks, and the bridge which spans the Tay here was built by Smeaton in 1771.

Before the main route begins it is possible to take a short detour on the A85 SP 'Crianlarich', to Huntingtower Castle.

HUNTINGTOWER CASTLE, Tayside NO02
Formerly known as Ruthven Castle, this great stronghold (AM) has a permanent place in Scottish history as the site of the Raid of Ruthven. In 1582 the 16-year-old James VI came here at the invitation of the Earl of Gowrie, ostensibly to hunt. When he tried to leave he found himself prevented by Protestant nobles, who demanded the dismissal of the young king's favourites. The conspirators held the young king for a year while they wielded power in his place. The 15th-century mansion that stands here today has been restored and contains fine painted wooden ceilings.

On the main route, follow SP 'Braemar' across the River Tay to leave Perth on the A93, and in 2 miles pass the grounds of Scone Palace.

SCONE PALACE, Tayside NO12
Scone Palace, the home of the Earl of Mansfield, is a 19th-century mansion that stands on the site of the old Abbey of Scone. This was founded c1114 by Alexander I, and before it was destroyed by a mob of John Knox's reformers in 1559 it was the coronation place of all the Scottish kings up to James I. By tradition the kings were crowned on a stone that was brought to the ancient mote-hill of Scone by Kenneth Macalpine in the 9th century. This, identified with both Jacob's Pillow at Bethel and the Stone of Destiny at Tara in Ireland, was removed from the site and placed under the Coronation Chair of Westminster Abbey by Edward I in 1297. This token of conquest did little to improve relations between the two countries. The present mansion (open) contains various relics and objects of art.

Continue to Old Scone.

OLD SCONE, Tayside NO12
As the abbey developed it attracted a little satellite community that grew into the village of Scone. In 1805 this was moved by the Earl of Mansfield to improve the landscape, and only the village cross and graveyard remain to mark its old site.

Continue through Guildtown, then after 1½ miles reach Stobhall.

Kinnoul Hill rises steeply above the Tay to the south-east of Perth, and provides outstanding views over the valley.

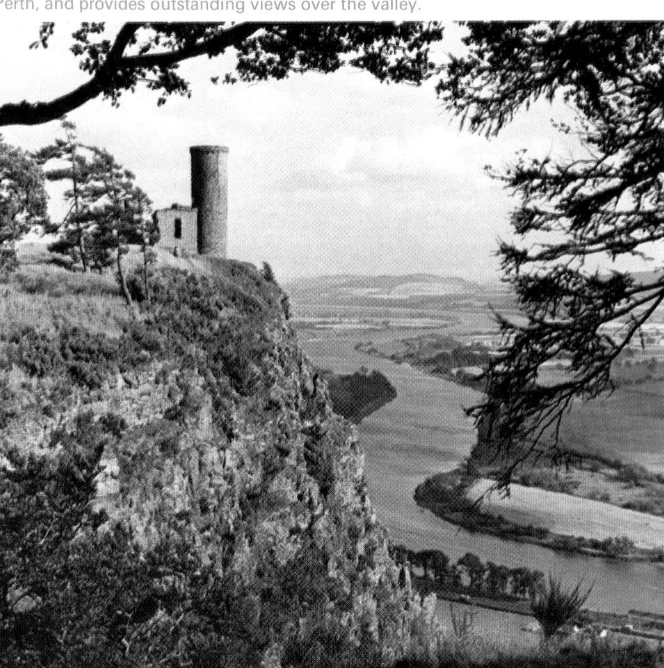

STOBHALL, Tayside NO13
This picturesque group of buildings (not open) is centred on a courtyard and was once the home of the Drummond family. It is picturesquely sited on the banks of the Tay and comprises the house, chapel, and tower. Much of the structure dates from the 15th century.

Later cross the Bridge of Isla to reach the grounds of Meikleour House, continue alongside the fine beech hedge that follows the estate boundary, and at the end turn left on to an unclassified road for Meikleour.

Meikleour Mercat Cros dates from 169

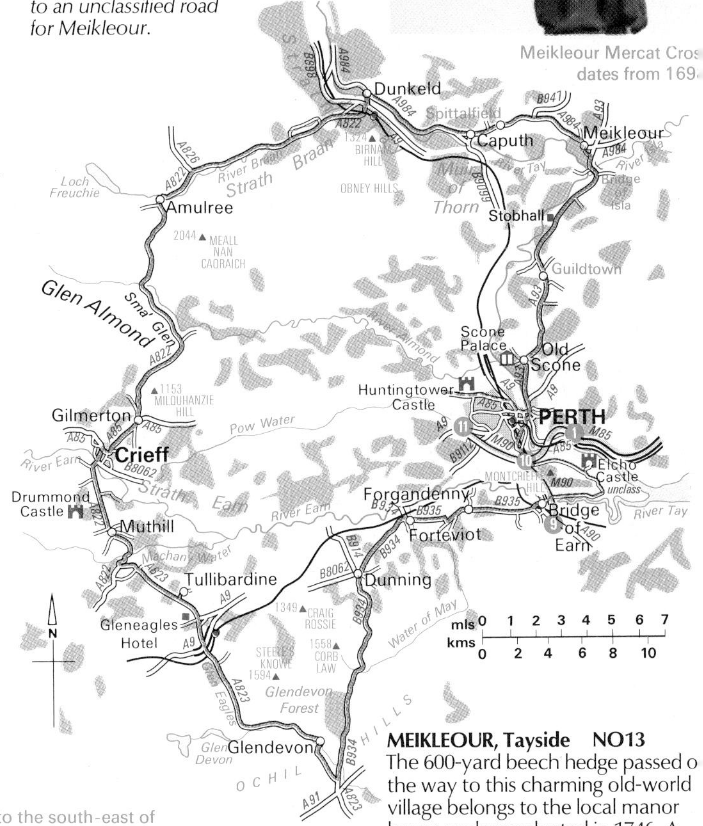

MEIKLEOUR, Tayside NO13
The 600-yard beech hedge passed o the way to this charming old-world village belongs to the local manor house and was planted in 1746. A focal point of the village is the mercat cross of 1698, opposite whic is an old place of punishment know as the Jougs Stone.

Join the A984 'Dunkeld' road and drive through Spittalfield to Caputh.

CAPUTH, Tayside NO04
An attractive bridge spans the salmon-rich Tay here, and across th river to the west is 16th-century anc later Murthly Castle in grounds which feature huge specimens of Sitka spruce and Douglas fir. Some miles east is the Roman camp of Inchtuthill.

Continue, driving through attractive and well-wooded Strath Tay to reach the town of Dunkeld.

DUNKELD, Tayside NO04
Telford spanned the Tay with a fine bridge here in 1809, but this delightful small town is best known for the lovely ruins of its ancient cathedral (AM). It was founded in th 9th century, was desecrated in 156 and considerably damaged in the 17th-century Battle of Dunkeld.

Nowadays the 14th-century choir has been restored and is in use as the parish church. East of the town is the Loch of Lowes Wildlife Reserve, where a variety of species can be watched from special hides, and 1 mile south-west is the restored 18th-century folly of Ossian's Hall. Near by the River Bran plunges over a rocky lip as the Falls of Bran, close to Hermitage Bridge (NTS). The whole area is good for walking.

:eave Dunkeld on the 'Crieff' road and cross the River Tay into Little Dunkeld. Turn right then left on to he A822 and ascend, then continue o Amulree.

Weaving is one of several cottage ıdustries which still thrive in Scotland.

MULREE, Tayside NN93
ıe lovely countryside around Lochs uaich and Freuchie, and in Glens ichill and Almond, can be explored om this handy base.

ıter Glen Almond and follow one of eneral Wade's military roads rough lonely Sma' Glen.

EN ALMOND, Tayside NN83
gged and mountainous at its ginning near Loch Tay, this autiful glen gradually widens out become a broad fertile valley after wton Bridge. One of its many eresting features is a large ehistoric burial cairn.

1A' GLEN, Tayside NN83
atherclad Sma' Glen is a famous auty spot that has attracted ıerations of admiring visitors. A rtly-vitrified fort tops 1,520ft Dun ır on the east side, and below it ween the river and the road is a ciated boulder known as Ossian's ne. Whether it has anything to do h the 3rd-century bard and rrior after whom it is named is a tter for conjecture.

ıtinue to Gilmerton.

MERTON, Tayside NN82
ıe $5\frac{1}{2}$ miles east of this little village sparse traces of 13th-century ıaffray Abbey.

ı right on to the A85 and skirt the park of Monzie Castle on the way rieff.

CRIEFF, Tayside NN82
Beautifully situated in a hillside position overlooking Strath Earn, Crieff is a popular touring centre in one of Tayside's most scenic areas. To the north of the town the River Earn is joined by Turret Water, which flows from lovely Loch Turret and plunges downhill in a series of picturesque waterfalls. The town itself is old, with many interesting features. Close to the Town Hall is an octagonal cross of 1688, and the old Market Cross incorporates a 10th-century cross-slab made of red sandstone and decorated with Celtic patterns. Iron stocks that were last used in 1816 are kept in the 17th-century Tolbooth. About 4 miles south-east of the town is the ruin of 17th-century Innerpeffray Castle, and near by in Innerpeffray Library (open) is one of Scotland's oldest and most valuable collections of books.

Leave Crieff on the A822 'Stirling' road, and in 2 miles reach the grounds of Drummond Castle on the right.

DRUMMOND CASTLE, Tayside NN81
Built by the 1st Lord Drummond in 1491, this fine castle (open) has been considerably altered over the centuries and shows the work of several periods. An armoury is housed in the square tower that survives from the original structure.

Continue to Muthill.

MUTHILL, Tayside NN81
Surviving fragments of Muthill's abandoned church (AM) include a splendid Romanesque tower that dates at least from the 12th century. Other remains are mostly of 15th-century date.

In $1\frac{3}{4}$ miles turn left on to the A823 SP 'Dunfermline'. In 3 miles a detour can be made from the main route by turning left on to an unclassified road and continuing to Tullibardine.

The elegant Long Gallery is the highlight of the 19th-century palace at Scone.

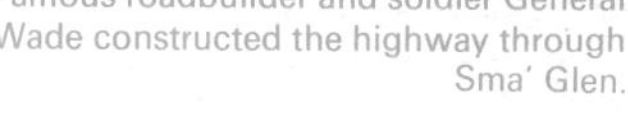

Famous roadbuilder and soldier General Wade constructed the highway through Sma' Glen.

TULLIBARDINE, Tayside NN91
Founded in 1446, the collegiate chapel (AM) at Tullibardine is one of the few in Scotland to have been finished and left unaltered.

On the main route, continue for 1 mile and pass the entrance to Gleneagles Hotel.

GLENEAGLES HOTEL, Tayside NN91
Gleneagles is situated on moorland near Auchterarder and is one of the best-known golfing resorts in Scotland, a country famed for its excellent courses.

Cross the A9 and follow the A823 through Glen Eagles, drive into the heart of the Ochil Hills and enter Glen Devon to reach the village of the same name.

GLENDEVON, Tayside NN90
An excellent touring base for exploring the lovely glen from which it takes its name, this village stands on a road that affords fine views north over Strath Earn to distant ranges of mountains.

After 2 miles turn left on to the B934 towards Dunning, then re-cross the Ochil Hills for Dunning.

DUNNING, Tayside NO01
The church in this pretty village has been rebuilt but retains a typical 13th-century tower.

In Dunning turn right with the B934, then keep left and follow SP 'Perth'. In $1\frac{3}{4}$ miles turn right with SP 'Bridge of Earn' on to the B935, then immediately keep left and continue to Forteviot.

FORTEVIOT, Tayside NO01
This village stands just south of an attractive waters-meet where the River Earn joins the Water of May. It was once a Pictish capital. To the north 19th-century Dupplin Castle stands in wooded grounds east of Dupplin Loch, and the splendid early-Christian Dupplin Cross can be seen close to Bank Farm on the summit of The Earn.

Continue to Forgandenny.

FORGANDENNY, Tayside NO01
Culteuchar Hill, also known as Castle Law, rises to a 1,028ft summit south of this village and preserves the remains of an old fort.

Continue to Bridge of Earn.

BRIDGE OF EARN, Tayside NO11
This large village is well situated for touring in the foothills of the Ochil range. Fragments of its original medieval bridge can still be seen, and the 16th-century mansion of Balmanno lies $2\frac{1}{2}$ miles south-east.

At Bridge of Earn turn left on to the A90 'Perth' road, then cross the River Earn and turn right on to an unclassified road towards Rhynd. In $2\frac{1}{2}$ miles meet a T-junction and turn left, then after 1 mile reach a track that leads to the right for Elcho Castle.

ELCHO CASTLE, Tayside NO12
More accurately a fortified mansion, ruined Elcho Castle (AM) was the ancestral seat of the earls of Wemyss and is noted for its tower-like wings. It dates from the 16th century.

Continue, with views of the River Tay and city of Perth from the road. Meet a junction with the A90, turn right, and return to Perth.

TOUR 104 82 MILES

ON THE ANGUS COAST

Fishing ports and popular holiday resorts fringe the surprisingly gentle North Sea coast of old Angus, where weathered cliffs of red sandstone guard sandy bays and narrow rock strands. Inland are the rugged heights of the Grampian Mountains and the fertile Howe of Mearns.

DUNDEE, Tayside NO33
One of the largest cities in Scotland, Dundee covers some 20 square miles of hillside above the north bank of the Firth of Tay. Clashes between English and Scottish forces punctuate its history. Its strong seafaring tradition dates back to when local men went whaling to Iceland and the north as early as the 12th century. The only surviving gate of the strong walls that protected the town in medieval times is the Cow Gate Port. One of the oldest buildings is 15th-century St Mary's Tower, which was built to house a bell and is now a museum. Also of interest are the Mills Observatory (open), the Spalding Golf Museum in Camperdown House, and the comprehensive local collections shown in the City Museum and Art Gallery. Exhibits relating to shipping and industry, particularly those aspects associated with Dundee, can be seen in the Barrack Street Museum. Victoria Dock contains 19th-century HMS *Unicorn*, the only floating wooden warship in the country. Nowadays the town is an important centre of industry, with 35 acres of dockland and a reputation for fine jam made with fruit from the fertile Carse of Gowrie. The renowned Dundee marmalade was first made by Mrs Keiller in 1797 and is still enjoyed on breakfast tables throughout the world.

Before leaving Dundee on the main route it is possible to make a 4-mile detour: leave the city on the A930 and drive to Broughty Ferry.

BROUGHTY FERRY, Tayside NO43
Originally an old fishing village, Broughty Ferry has developed into a residential suburb of Dundee and is a popular holiday resort. Broughty Castle (AM) stands on a rocky headland and houses a fascinating whaling museum, and Claypotts Castle is one of the most complete examples of an old tower house in existence. The dates on the tower of the latter are 1569 and 1588, and it still has its roof. Exhibits in the resort's interesting Ochar Art Gallery include many works by 19th-century Scottish artists.

On the main tour, leave Dundee on the A92 with SP 'Aberdeen', and drive through agricultural country to Muirdrum. A short detour can be made from the main route to Carnoustie by turning right on to the A930 and continuing for 2 miles.

CARNOUSTIE, Tayside NO53
As well as being a flourishing industrial area, Carnoustie is a popular holiday resort with sandy beaches and a championship golf course considered one of the best in the world. There is also another good course here, and the deep dunes of Barry Links offer lovely coastal walks south to Buddon Ness.

On the main route, continue with the A92 and in 5 miles turn right under a railway bridge to enter Arbroath.

ARBROATH, Tayside NO64
Best known for its smokies, delicious haddock flavoured and browned by smoke from an oak fire, this fishing port has a harbour at the mouth of the Brothock Water and has become a popular holiday resort. Various recreational facilities supplement the natural advantages of good sands and safe bathing, and the local countryside offers pleasant walks. Distinctive red sandstone cliffs known for their caves fringe the beach to the north-east. The town itself has been a Royal Burgh since 1599 and has an important place in Scottish history. After the Battle of Bannockburn, in 1320 Robert the Bruce signed Scotland's Declaration of Independence at Arbroath Abbey Considerable 13th-century remains (AM) of this important foundation have survived.

Continue along the A92 'Aberdeen' road to a point just north of the town. A short detour can be made by turning left on to an unclassified road and driving to St Vigeans.

ST VIGEANS, Tayside NO64
One of the finest collections of early-Christian and medieval memorial stones in Scotland is housed in St Vigeans' Cottage Museum (AM). Many of these beautiful monuments take the form of Celtic crosses, invariably carved with elaborate interlacing decorations on the front and groups of animals, figures, and symbols on the back.

On the main route, continue along the A92 for $\frac{3}{4}$ mile to a point where another detour can be made, this time by turning right on to an unclassified road and driving to Auchmithie.

AUCHMITHIE, Tayside NO64
Perched on a rocky sandstone cliff 150ft above a sandy beach, this precarious and exceptionally picturesque little fishing community can trace its history back to the 11th century. The cliffs extend north-east to impressive Red Head and Lang Craig, which overlook Lunan Bay. Dickmont's Den and the Forbidden Cave are just two notable examples of the many caves in the area.

On the main route, continue along the A92 to Inverkeilor.

INVERKEILOR, Tayside NO64
The main feature of this tiny place is its isolation from the rush of 20th-century life. Its church contains a good 17th-century pew, and the 15th-century and later pile of Ethie Castle stands to the south-east. Remarkable singing sands, whose grains vibrate against each other when walked on, lie to the east.

From Inverkeilor a $2\frac{1}{4}$-mile detour can be made to Lunan by turning right on to an unclassified road, driving for $1\frac{1}{2}$ miles to a T-junction, and turning left to Lunan.

A superb view of the city can be enjoyed from Dundee Law.

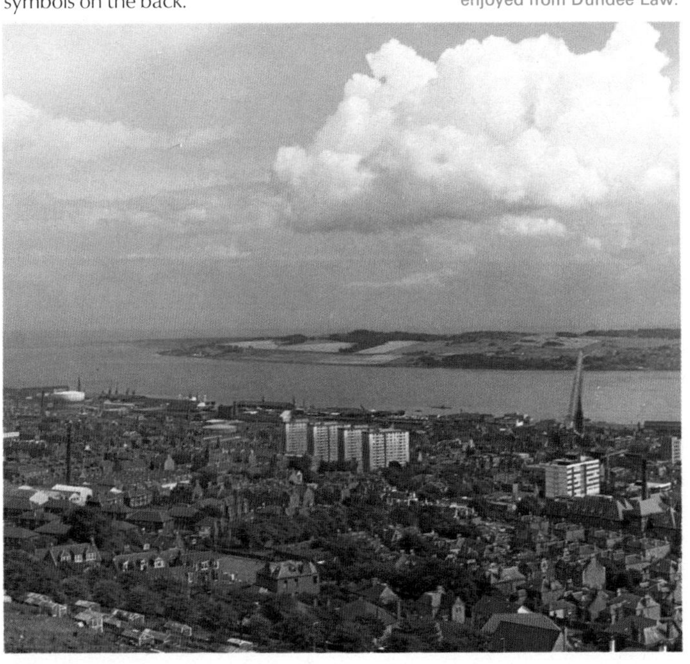

LUNAN, Tayside NO65
Ruined Red Castle stands beside the sandhills in Lunan Bay. It may have been built to counter raids from Danish pirates in the 15th century, but an earlier fort on the site was given by Robert the Bruce to his son-in-law in 1328.

On the main route, leave Inverkeilor on the A92 to cross Lunan Water. Continue, later enjoying views into the Montrose Basin before crossing the River South Esk to enter the town of Montrose.

MONTROSE, Tayside NO75
Here the South Esk River forms a 2-square-mile tidal lagoon known as the Montrose Basin, which is popular with many different species of wader all the year round and is a wintering place for pink-footed Arctic geese. The town itself is a pleasant market and holiday centre popular with sailors, golfers, and anglers. A fine sandy beach is complemented by a grassy belt that parallels the spacious High Street and is known as The Links. Leading from the High Street to the town's charming old heart are narrow, twisting 18th-century closes lined by quaint old houses.

Beyond Montrose keep forward with the A937 SP 'Laurencekirk'. Continue for $4\frac{1}{2}$ miles and turn right under a railway bridge before crossing the River North Esk to reach Marykirk.

MARYKIRK, Grampian NO66
Marykirk is well situated at the edge of the Vale of Strathmore, near the point where it merges with the Mearns country, and is a good touring centre for these lovely districts. Its own villagescape is enhanced by the North Esk River.

Turn left on to the B974 with SP 'Fettercairn', reach a junction with the A94, then turn right and left to stay on the B974. Continue for $3\frac{3}{4}$ miles and turn right to reach Fettercairn.

FETTERCAIRN, Grampian NO67
Set in woods and fields at the edge the Howe of Mearns, this 18th-century village boasts a great 19th-century royal arch that was built to commemorate an incognito visit made by Queen Victoria and Princ Albert. The village square has a 17th century cross which is notched to show the length of the Scottish ell, measurement that is roughly the same as the English yard. It remains to be seen if the memory of the ya will remain as strong as this in the age of metrication. Fettercairn Hou dates from the 17th century and w erected by the 1st Earl of Middleto who was Lord High Commissioner the Scottish Parliament. About 1 m south of Fettercairn is 16th-century Balbegno Castle.

Leave Fettercairn and turn left on to the B966 'Edzell' road. In $3\frac{1}{2}$ miles it possible to make a detour from the main route, adding 31 miles to the tour, by turning right on to an unclassified road and driving to beautiful Glen Esk.

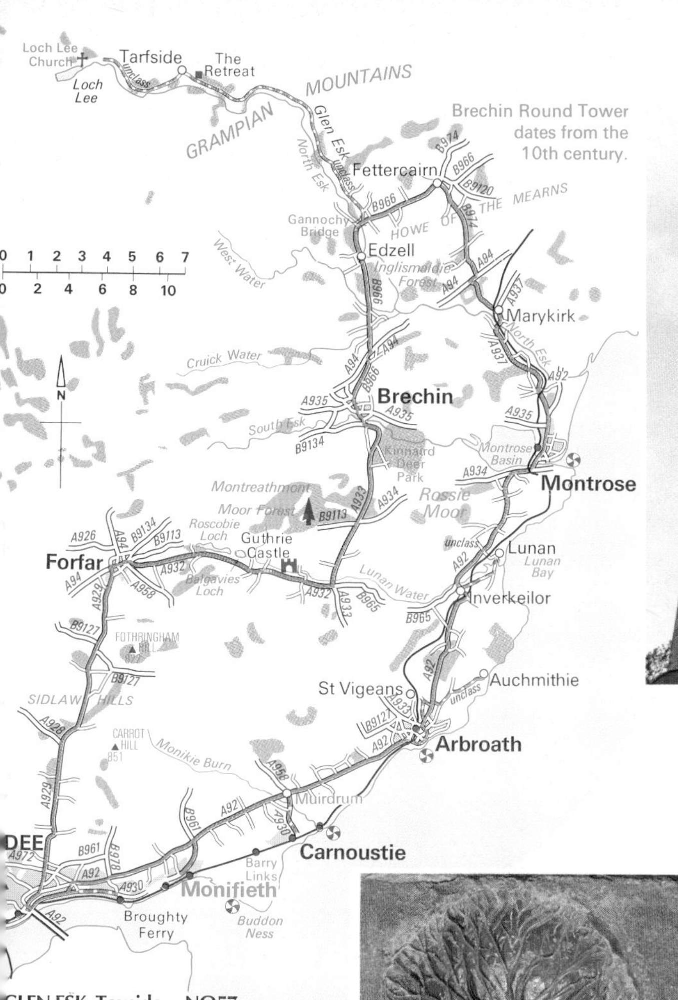

Brechin Round Tower dates from the 10th century.

GLEN ESK, Tayside NO57
The road through the superb scenery)f long Glen Esk accompanies the ?iver North Esk into the fastness of he Grampian Mountains. It is a truly nemorable drive for anybody who ias the time to take it. The following oute instructions and entries detail he countryside from end to end.

)n the detour, follow the unclassified oad for 9½ miles to reach The Retreat.

'HE RETREAT, Tayside NO57
his one-time shooting lodge is now museum of local country life and andicrafts.

till on the detour, continue to arfside.

The Medicine Well at Montrose was a popular 18th-century spa.

The River North Esk enters the Howe of Mearns at Gannochy.

TARFSIDE, Tayside NO47
Beautifully set in the foothills of the Eastern Grampians, this highly attractive village stands at the waters-meet of the North Esk River and the Water of Tar. Mount Battock rises to 2,555ft in the north.

Still on the detour, continue to Loch Lee Church and the end of the Glen Esk road.

LOCH LEE, Tayside NO47
Shortly before reaching the end of this lovely glen the road passes the picturesque ruins of Invermark Castle. At the end of the glen, south-west of the little local church, is the lovely expanse of Loch Lee. Queen Victoria and Prince Albert climbed the 3,077ft bulk of Mount Keen, which rises to the north-west of the glen, in 1861. Their visit is commemorated by the Queen's Well beside the Mounth Track, which follows a lovely route cross-country to Aboyne.

If the detour has been taken, rejoin the main route by returning along the entire length of Glen Esk to the B966. On the main tour, continue along the B966 and cross the River North Esk before reaching Edzell.

EDZELL, Tayside NO56
From the south this little inland resort is approached through a fine 19th-century arch raised to the memory of the 13th Earl of Dalhousie. Early 16th-century Edzell Castle (AM) lies to the west of the main village and was visited by Mary Queen of Scots in 1562. One of its major features is a fine 17th-century garden surrounded by a wall which displays unique heraldic and symbolic decoration. The village itself lies between the lovely countryside of Strathmore and the fertile Howe of Mearns, which is situated just west of the North Esk River.

Continue for 3½ miles and meet the A94 'Perth' road. Turn right here, then in ¼ mile turn left on to the B966 for the town of Brechin.

BRECHIN, Tayside NO56
Rising steeply from the banks of the South Esk River, this lovely old town of red-sandstone buildings stands against a backdrop of hills that gradually rise to the great dark chain of the Eastern Grampians. The old cathedral is now a parish church, and parts of the original 12th-century building still exist as proof of the foundation's great antiquity. It was partly rebuilt in the 19th century, but the lovely Maison Dieu Chapel (AM) is preserved as a particularly fine example of 13th-century workmanship. Attached to the church is an 87ft-high round tower (AM) that dates from the 10th or 11th century and is one of only two such examples existing in Scotland. The other is at Abernethy, and both buildings are similar in shape and decoration to those built by the Celts in Ireland. They were generally used as watchtowers and places of refuge for whole villages. Brechin Castle, the seat of the earls of Dalhousie, was rebuilt in 1711.

Follow SP 'Arbroath' to leave Brechin on the A933 and cross the River South Esk. Skirt the private Kinnaird deer park and Montreathmont Moor Forest, then after 7 miles meet the A932 and turn right SP 'Forfar'. Continue for 1¾ miles and pass the grounds of inhabited Guthrie Castle on the right.

GUTHRIE CASTLE, Tayside NO55
Very occasionally open to the public, this castle has been the home of the Guthrie family ever since it was built by Sir David Guthrie in 1468. The lovely Spring Garden is best seen in early spring.

Continue on the A932, passing Balgavies Loch and the larger Rescobie Loch, and enter Forfar.

FORFAR, Tayside NO45
Before the county reorganizations Forfar was the chief town of Angus, but it has now been absorbed into the new Tayside. It lies in charming surroundings in the flat Howe of Angus, between the little Lochs Forfar and Fithie at the north-east end of the Vale of Strathmore. In the 11th century there was a Royal residence here, and an ancient octagonal turret marks the site of the castle where King Malcolm conferred surnames and titles on the Scottish nobility at a parliament in 1057. The castle itself was destroyed many years later by Robert the Bruce. His son was buried near Loch Fithie in Restenneth Priory (AM), a 12th-century foundation in beautiful surroundings. Forfar's Town House preserves a gruesome pronged bridle that was used to silence victims before and during execution, and is associated with so-called witches who were burned here during the 17th century.

Leave Forfar on the A929 'Dundee' road, passing through agricultural country and crossing the low Sidlaw Hills on the return to Dundee.

GLEN LYON LANDSCAPES

On either side of the River Lyon's lovely and often spectacular glen are the wooded flanks and high rugged summits of the Breadalbane Mountains. Below them are the beautiful reaches of Loch Tay, attractive lochside villages in small river valleys, and the cascades and falls of numerous streams.

PITLOCHRY, Tayside NN95
Fine woodland graces the countryside round this attractive little resort and touring centre. It lies in the lovely valley of the River Tummel and is the site of a huge hydro-electric power station that, although built for obvious economic and practical reasons, has turned out to be a popular and unusual tourist attraction. When the station was built the river was blocked to form the artificial Loch Faskally, and a fish ladder had to be included to help springing salmon follow the old course of the river to their spawning beds in its upper reaches. Visitors can watch the brave efforts of these fish from an observation chamber by the ladder. Various plays and concerts are staged at the Pitlochry Festival Theatre, also known as the Theatre in the Hills, during the summer months.

Leave Pitlochry on the A9 'Perth' road and in ½ mile turn right on to an unclassified road SP 'Logierait'. Cross the new Aldour Bridge and turn right with SP 'Foss' on to a narrow road. Continue alongside Loch Faskally and pass the Clunie Memorial Arch.

CLUNIE MEMORIAL ARCH, Tayside NN95
A bronze, horseshoe-shaped memorial at the end of the 2-mile water conduit between Loch Tummel and the Clunie generating station, this arch is the same shape as the conduit and commemorates men who died during its construction in 1946.

Continue alongside Loch Faskally to reach the Linn of Tummel.

LINN OF TUMMEL, Tayside NN95
Once known as the Falls of Tummel, the Linn of Tummel (NTS) is a well-known feature where running water lends its own particular enchantment to lovely countryside. The name of the area was changed when the raising of the water level in Loch Faskally reduced the height and impressiveness of the waterfall. Walks starting from the Linn can be taken alongside the River Garry to the Pass of Killiecrankie, and to the magnificent viewpoint of Queen's View, named in memory of a visit by Queen Victoria.

Queen Victoria was particularly attracted to the beauty of Loch Tummel.

Meall Luaidhe, to the south of Bridge of Balgie, rises to 2,558ft.

Romantic ruins of Finlarig Castle stand just north of Killin.

Continue through magnificent scenery along the south bank of the River Tummel and Loch Tummel. After 12 miles turn left on to the B846 towards Aberfeldy. A detour from the main route can be made by meeting this junction and turning right to stay with the B846; follow the River Tummel to Kinloch Rannoch.

KINLOCH RANNOCH, Tayside NN65
Situated in an area of great scenic beauty, this little angling resort stands on the River Tummel at the south end of lovely Loch Rannoch. Magnificent views extend from the village to distant peaks that guard the entrance to Glencoe, and near the shores of the loch the famous Black Wood of Rannoch recalls the primeval Caledonian pine forests that covered the Highlands.

On the main drive, continue along the B846 'Aberfeldy' road and climb out of the Tummel Valley to a road summit of over 1,270ft. Continue along a section of road that follows the route of one made by General 'Roadbuilder' Wade in the 18th century and reach White Bridge.

WHITE BRIDGE, Tayside NN75
Situated at 1,000ft or more in the hil of old Perthshire, this bridge is a handy vantage point affording excellent views of the surrounding summits. Prominent to the right of the road is the mountainous peak o 3,547ft Schiehallion.

Continue along the B846 and descend through the valley of the Keltney Burn to reach the lonely Coshieville Hotel.

COSHIEVILLE, Tayside NN74
An old inn from which this area and its hotel take their names once stoo at the junction of roads from Aberfeldy, Fortingall, and Rannoch. was a favourite stopping-off place f 18th-century cattle drovers on their way to Falkirk and Crieff.

At the Coshieville Hotel turn right or to an unclassified road and continue to Fortingall.

FORTINGALL, Tayside NN74
Old thatched cottages and the attractive River Lyon are the main scenic features of this lovely little village, which is separated from the north end of Loch Tay by the wooded bulk of Drummond Hill. A huge yew standing in the local churchyard is thought to be the oldest living tree in Britain. Its girth was measured at 56ft in 1772, and the village tends its one remaining live stem with great care. Earthworks to the south-west of the village are often referred to as the Roman outpost of *Praetorium*, but they are more likely to have survived from a medieval fortified homestead. According to legend Pontius Pilate was born in the area.

Drive for $\frac{1}{2}$ mile beyond Fortingall and turn right SP 'Glen Lyon' to follow the River Lyon into its valley.

GLEN LYON, Tayside
Measuring a full 32 miles in extent, this is the longest and one of the loveliest glens in Scotland. Its Gaelic name means Crooked Glen of Stones, and there is a tradition that the heroic Fingal of Celtic mythology had twelve castles here. Some of the castles may be explained by the iron-age ring forts that survive in the area.

Continue through Glen Lyon to Innerwick.

INNERWICK, Tayside NN54
Isolated amongst the picturesque hills of Glen Lyon, this lonely village has a church which preserves an ancient bell.

Continue, and after 1 mile turn left towards Loch Tay and cross the Bridge of Balgie.

BRIDGE OF BALGIE, Tayside NN54
The attractive Bridge of Balgie is situated on the Glen Lyon road at a point where it meets the steep (1 in 6) mountain road to Killin.

Continue along the narrow Glen Lyon road and ascend through moorland to 1,805ft as the route crosses the Breadalbane Mountains. Descend, with views to the right of Lochan na Lairige and to the left of Ben Lawers.

BEN LAWERS, Tayside NN64
At 3,984ft this grand old mountain of the Breadalbane district is the highest for many miles around. About 8,000 acres of its flanks and summit are protected by the National Trust for Scotland, and the abnormally large number of Alpine plant species growing on its lower slopes makes it an area of considerable scientific interest. Views from the summit, which can be reached quite easily, extend over the whole of the Breadalbane country and much of the Grampian range. Local history and details of the area's many outstanding features can be studied at a visitors' centre.

Continue past the Ben Lawers Mountain Visitor Centre, then after 2 miles turn right to join the A827 along the north side of Loch Tay.

Killin, on the River Dochart, is dominated by Ben Lawers.

LOCH TAY, Tayside
Overlooked at its western end by Ben Lawers and surrounded on all sides by breathtaking scenery, this superb loch was a favourite place of the poet Sir Walter Scott. He composed a beautiful word picture that captures the essence of its loveliness in his poem the *Fair Maid of Perth*. Below Ben Lawers the 120-mile-long River Tay flows towards Aberfeldy, carrying the greatest volume of water of any British river and providing an inland route for the famous Tay salmon.

Continue along the A827 to Killin.

KILLIN, Central NN53
During spring and summer this all-year-round resort offers fishing and walking, while in the winter months it provides après-ski facilities for people who come here to ski on the slopes of Ben Lawers. The town is situated at the eastern end of mountain-encircled Glen Lochay, on the excellent game-fishing Rivers Dochart and Lochay. One of two small islands near Dochart Bridge is the traditional burial ground of the Clan MacNab, and their 17th-century seat of Kinnell House faces the village from the south side of the river. This mansion later came into the hands of the Breadalbane family. In its grounds is a well-defined circle of standing stones. Just north of Killin is ruined Finlarig Castle, a one-time Campbell stronghold described by Scott in his *Fair Maid of Perth*.

At the end of Killin cross the River Dochart, then keep right and take the next turning left on to an unclassified road SP 'Ardeonaig'. Continue along the south side of Loch Tay and pass through the hamlets of Ardeonaig and later Acharn. In $1\frac{1}{2}$ miles turn right on to the A827 SP 'Aberfeldy'. To the left of the route at this point is the small resort of Kenmore.

KENMORE, Tayside NN74
Robert Burns admired the lovely views from an 18th-century bridge that spans the Tay here, where the river leaves Loch Tay, and set his impressions down in verse. This little snippet of local history is recorded in the parlour of the hotel, a venerable establishment first licensed over 400 years ago. William and Dorothy Wordsworth left their beloved Lake District long enough to visit Kenmore, and nowadays the village is a charming and popular resort.

Salmon fishermen flock to the River Tay at Kenmore, a village praised by the poet Robert Burns.

Continue along the A827 in the Tay Valley, with views of Drummond Hill Forest to the left. Near by, also on the left, is Taymouth Castle.

TAYMOUTH CASTLE, Tayside NN74
Once the seat of the Breadalbanes, Taymouth Castle was visited by Queen Victoria in 1842. The present building dates from the early 19th century and houses a school.

Proceed on the A827 to Aberfeldy.

ABERFELDY, Tayside NN84
A 5-arched bridge that spans the River Tay in this little market town and touring centre was built by General Wade in 1733. The General built roads and bridges all over Scotland after the Rising of 1715, so that troops could be rushed to trouble spots with the minimum loss of time. Of all his works this bridge at Aberfeldy is thought to be among the finest still standing.

At Aberfeldy turn left on to the B846 towards 'Kinloch Rannoch'. Cross Wade's military bridge and continue to Weem.

WEEM, Tayside NN84
Weem Hotel, said to date back to 1527, displays a sign commemorating a visit by General Wade in 1733. Menzies Castle stands in fine grounds just west of the village, and monuments to the Menzies can be seen in the local church. This stronghold was the clan's chief seat. Overlooking the village is the 800ft viewpoint of the Rock of Weem.

Turn right on to an unclassified road SP 'Strathtay', and follow the north bank of the river to Strathtay. A detour from the main route can be made here by turning right to cross the Tay and driving into Grandtully.

GRANDTULLY, Tayside NN95
Grandtully Castle dates from the 16th century and is the ancestral home of the Stewarts of Innermeath. Canoe slaloms are held in the village, which is pronounced Grantly.

On the main route, keep straight on for $1\frac{1}{4}$ miles and turn left to join the A827 'Ballinluig' road. Continue to Logierait.

LOGIERAIT, Tayside NN95
Interesting sculptured stones can be seen in the churchyard here, plus reminders of the macabre body-snatching exploits of Burke and Hare in the shape of several mortesafes. These were once placed over new graves and locked. At one time the crime was common in Britain.

At Logierait turn left on to an unclassified road that leads towards 'Dunfallandy'. Follow the west bank of the River Tummel for 4 miles, then turn right to re-cross the Aldour Bridge. On the far side of the bridge turn left on to the A9 and return to the resort of Pitlochry.

BALLATER, Grampian NO39
The Ballater Highland Games are internationally famous and have been drawing large audiences for over a hundred years. Traditionally held in August, they include many old Scottish sports and the arduous Hill Race to the summit of Craig Cailleach. The town itself is a popular summer resort, even without the attraction of the games, set in beautiful Grampian countryside. Lochnagar rises to 3,786ft in the south-west, and just north of the town the pretty Pass of Ballater is threaded by the old Deeside road as it passes beneath the flanks of Craig-an-Darroch. The long and lovely valley of Glen Muick lies south-west below 3,268ft Broad Cairn, and was a favourite of Queen Victoria. Edward VII bought the fine 18th-century house that stands 1 mile south-west of Ballater in Glen Muick while he was the Prince of Wales, and it is now used by HM the Queen Mother. To the east of Glen Muick is the Forest of Glentanar, which includes the 3,077ft bulk of Mount Keen.

Leave Ballater on the A93 'Aberdeen' road and drive along the Dee Valley to the Cambus O'May Hotel. After 1 mile turn left on to the A97 SP 'Huntly'. Drive past Lochs Kinord and Davan, then turn left again to remain on the A97. Drive beyond Logie Coldstone and climb through rough moorland with the 2,862ft peak of Morven to the left. Eventually reach a road summit of 1,213ft, then descend to Deskry Water and later the River Don. Turn right with the A97 and cross two river bridges to run alongside the River Don. A short detour can be taken from the main route to visit Strathdon by turning left here on to the B973 and driving for another $2\frac{1}{4}$ miles.

STRATHDON, Grampian NJ31
Here the trout-rich River Don is joined by the Water of Nochty, which flows down from the Ladder Hills. The river and hill country round the village is particularly lovely, and the village itself is a charming place with a church spire that can be seen for miles around. A little to the south-west the Don is spanned by a fine 18th-century bridge, and nearby Colquhonnie Castle was begun in the 16th century but never completed. In mid-August Strathdon is usually the venue for the Lonach Highland Gathering.

On the main route, continue alongside the River Don on the A97 and after a short distance pass Glenbuchat Castle on the left.

GLENBUCHAT CASTLE, Grampian NJ31
Ruins of this ancient Z-plan tower house (exterior AM), considered one of the finest extant, form a major feature of lovely Castle Park. The building was erected in 1590 and is known for its variety of unusual architectural features.

Continue to Glenkindie.

TOUR 106 — 96 MILES

CASTLES OF THE LADDER HILLS

This is a place of large pine forests and purple moors, of windy summits and glens guarded by ancient castles that once symbolized the strength of their clans. Here in the picturesque valley of the Dee is Balmoral Castle, the private country home of the Royal Family.

Dufftown lies within easy reach of broad expanses of moorland.

GLENKINDIE, Grampian NJ41
Close to Glenkindie House in the upper Don Valley is a remarkable weem, or ancient Pictish house. In a churchyard about 1 mile away on the other side of the river, near the remains of Towie Castle, is an ancient sculptured cross.

Continue for $2\frac{1}{2}$ miles to pass the ruins of Kildrummy Castle on the left.

KILDRUMMY CASTLE, Grampian NJ41
Built in the 13th century and extensively repaired since, this ruined castle (AM) stands at 800ft above sea level and is guarded on two sides by precipitous ravines. It has seen more than its share of stormy Scottish history, and in 1306 was the scene of a famous and gallant defence by Sir Nigel Bruce. The remains are extensive and the most complete of this period in Scotland. One of its great towers is almost equal in size to the superb example at Bothwell, and it preserves a complete layout of domestic buildings, hall, kitchen, solar, and a chapel with a triple lancet window. There is a Japanese Water Garden in the lovely grounds.

Drive through the hamlet of Mossat and turn left, then continue to Lumsden. After 2 miles turn left on to the B9002 and pass Auchindoir Church, then Craig Castle, on the left.

AUCHINDOIR CHURCH, Grampian NJ42
One of Scotland's finest medieval churches, roofless but otherwise complete, can be seen here. The main features of the ruins (AM) are a carved 12th- or 13th-century doorway and an interesting Sacrament House.

Balvenie Castle is one of the largest in north Scotland.

CRAIG CASTLE, Grampian NJ42
Patrick Gordon, who was killed on the battleground of Flodden Field in 1515, built the tower that first stood on this site 3 years before his death. It stands on the attractive waters of the Burn of Craig.

From the castle climb across bleak moorland to 1,370ft and after $4\frac{1}{4}$ miles turn left on to the A941 'Dufftown' road. Gradually descend through the hamlet of Cabrach into the upper valley of the River Deveron.

CABRACH, Grampian NJ32
The countryside round Cabrach, dominated by the 2,368ft Buck of Cabrach in the south-east, is a place of contrasts. Flourishing deer forests fringe barren moorlands, and the lonely source of the River Deveron is hidden in the heathy slopes of the surrounding hills.

Continue along the A941 and drive alongside the River Deveron for a short distance before continuing over moorland. On the approach to Dufftown reach an unclassified right turn that offers a $\frac{1}{2}$-mile detour from the main route to medieval Auchindown Castle.

AUCHINDOWN CASTLE, Grampian NJ33
Prehistoric earthworks surround this ruined castle (AM), which occupies a pleasant site overlooking the River Fiddich. It is thought that the stronghold was originally founded as early as the 11th century but much of the existing structure was built by Thomas Cochrane in the reign of James III.

On the main route, continue to Dufftown.

DUFFTOWN, Grampian NJ34
This pleasant town was laid out by James Duff, the 4th Earl of Fife, in 1817. Its pleasingly symmetrical design is in the form of a right-angle cross, with four streets radiating from a central square to the four points of the compass. In the middle of the square is a Tolbooth tower. The area is well known for its many whisky distilleries, including the famous Glenfiddich plant (open).

Just north of Dufftown are the ruins of Balvenie Castle.

BALVENIE CASTLE, Grampian NJ
Originally built by the Comyn family this great moated stronghold (AM) later came into the hands of the Black Douglases and subsequently the Atholls. It was the latter family who created the appearance of the building as it stands today, by demolishing the entire south-east front and replacing it with a 3-storey Renaissance tower house known as the Atholl Building. Edward I visited the castle in 1304, and it was occupied by the Duke of Cumberland during the 18th-century Jacobite Rising.

Leave Dufftown on the B9009 'Tomintoul' road and follow Dullan Water through Glen Rinnes.

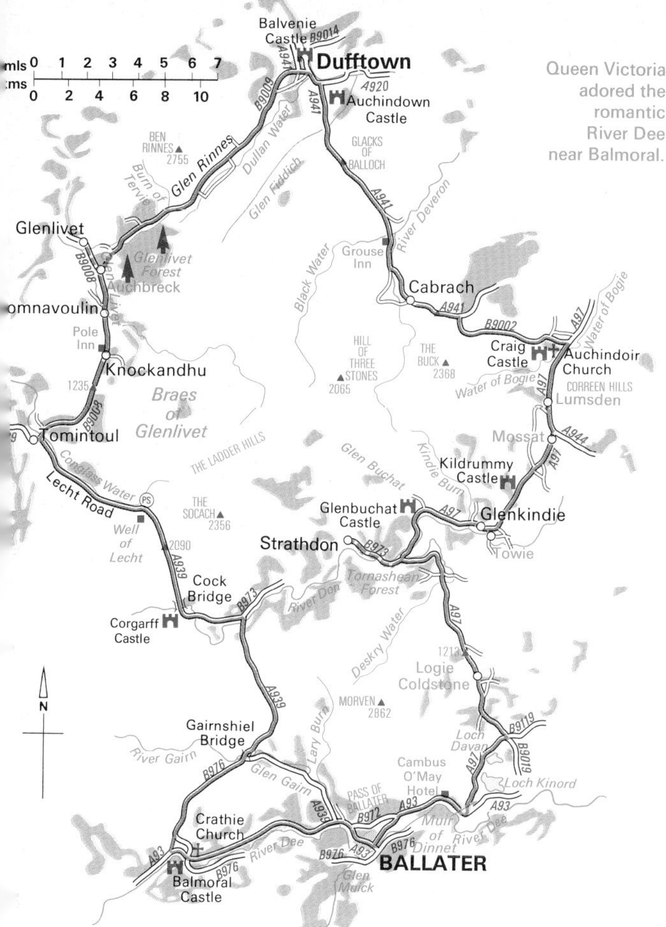

The Royal Family usually spends a summer holiday at Balmoral.

Queen Victoria adored the romantic River Dee near Balmoral.

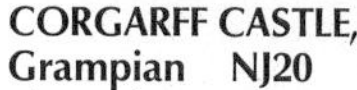

LEN RINNES, Grampian NJ23
his lovely glen is surrounded by fine ountain scenery. Ben Rinnes rises 2,755ft in the north-west, and the uth is dominated by 2,563ft orryhabbie Hill.

ter pass Glenlivet Forest to reach uchbreck. A 1¾-mile detour can be ken from here to visit the village of enlivet by turning right on to the 008.

LENLIVET, Grampian NJ13
hisky has been distilled in this area a great many years, and the mous Glenlivet distillery has been oducing its fine unblended malt ce 1824. The Glen itself stretches uth-east from the village towards e Ladder Hills and offers some od walks. Just south of the village the remains of Blairfindy Castle, d a picturesque ruined bridge ans the Livet Water north at dgend. See also tour 108.

the main route, leave Auchbreck d keep left on to the B9008 (no SP). ve through Glen Livet to mnavoulin.

MNAVOULIN, Grampian NJ22
mnavoulin is beautifully set ongst lonely hills and moorland in area that is best appreciated by walker. A road from the village to mintoul offers excellent views wever, and beyond the Braes of nlivet climbs to a high summit of 0ft.

tinue the climb out of Glen Livet each the Pole Inn at Knockandhu.

KNOCKANDHU, Grampian NJ22
Near here in the Braes of Glenlivet, some 3½ miles south-east of Chapeltown, is the old Scalen Seminary. This interesting Christian foundation was built in the mid-17th century and burned down during the Rising of 1745. Today its ruins form an interesting feature of the local landscape.

Continue across moorland at a height of 1,235ft and after 4½ miles turn left on to the A939 with SP 'Cock Bridge' and 'Braemar'. A short detour from the main route to Tomintoul can be made by keeping forward here.

TOMINTOUL, Grampian NJ11
Claimed to be the highest village in the Highlands, Tomintoul is stretched out along a 1,160ft sandstone ridge between the Glen of Avon and the Vale of the Water of Conglass. In summer it is popular with anglers, who come to fish here and south-west of the village, where the Avon is joined by the Water of Ailnack, near the Water of Caiplach. The last-mentioned streams flow through a series of spectacular gorges in a landscape dominated by 2,692ft Geal Charn. The A939 road from Tomintoul to Grantown-on-Spey is noted for the excellent views it affords of the Grampian foothills.

Continue along the A939 'Cock Bridge' road through a landscape that becomes bleak and desolate as the route crosses the Ladder Hills. Climb to a 2,090ft summit on the Lecht Road.

LECHT ROAD, Grampian NJ21
An old carved stone on the Well of Lecht commemorates the building of this military road by the 33rd Regiment under Lord Charles Hay in 1745. During the winter deep snow often makes it impassable.

Continue, and descend steeply to Cock Bridge.

COCK BRIDGE, Grampian NJ20
This picturesque bridge carries the Lecht Road across the River Don and is situated 1,330ft above sea level.

Pass Cock Bridge and continue, with ruined Corgarff Castle on the right.

CORGARFF CASTLE, Grampian NJ20
The 16th-century tower house (AM) of Corgarff played a large part in the 18th-century Jacobite Risings.

In 2½ miles turn right with the A939 SP 'Braemar' and cross the River Don. Cross open moorland and after 6 miles drive over the fine old Gairnshiel Bridge.

GAIRNSHIEL BRIDGE, Grampian NJ20
Lofty hills and moors surround this attractive old bridge, which spans the Dee in Glen Gairn.

Beyond the bridge branch right with the B976, then after 5 miles reach Royal Deeside and a junction with the A93. Turn left on to the 'Aberdeen' road. After a short distance pass Balmoral Castle to the right, across the River Dee.

BALMORAL CASTLE, Grampian NO29
In 1852 Prince Albert bought this beautiful Royal Deeside estate for £31,000, and had the existing castle rebuilt in the romantic Scottish baronial style. Later Queen Victoria added Ballochbuie Forest to the grounds (open sometimes), and since 1855 Balmoral has been the private holiday home of the Royal Family. It is beautifully situated in a curve of the River Dee in the district of Mar, with Glen Gelder leading to Balmoral Forest and the White Mounch hills in the south. The glen provided a picturesque route for Queen Victoria and Prince Albert when they climbed Lochnagar on ponies in 1848. Appropriately, the Gaelic rendering of Balmoral is *Bouchmorale,* meaning Majestic Dwelling.

Continue, and after a short distance pass Crathie Church on the left.

CRATHIE CHURCH, Grampian NO29
Queen Victoria laid the foundation stone of this church in 1895, and the Royal Family attend services here when in residence at Balmoral. The grave of John Brown, Queen Victoria's personal retainer for many years, lies in the churchyard of the present building's ruined predecessor.

Continue with the A93 alongside the River Dee and pass through attractive woodland on the return to Ballater.

TOUR 107 — 89 MILES

THE SCOTTISH RIVIERA

Crescents of firm sand backed by high sandstone cliffs arc between rocky headlands east of the sheltered Moray Firth. Busy resorts are interspersed with coastal villages and miles of empty shoreline, where local craftsmen come to gather the mineral serpentine for sculpting into souvenirs.

BANFF, Grampian NJ66
Built on a series of cliff terraces rising high above the old harbour, this ancient seaport stands at the mouth of the River Deveron and has become a popular holiday resort. Among its many fine buildings is the notable Duff House, which was built by William Adam in 1735 and eventually given to the town by the Duke of Fife. Its beautiful grounds now form a public park adjoining the Duff House Royal golf course. The 18th-century Town House incorporates an earlier tower, and the shaft of an old cross stands in the area known as Planestones. A few 17th-century houses and the remains of an old church can be seen elsewhere in the town, and an interesting cameo of local history is represented by the Biggar Fountain. This stands on the site of gallows where James Macpherson, a Highland freebooter in the 18th century, showed his contempt for authority by playing the fiddle as he was led to execution.

Leave Banff on the A98 'Inverness' road and after 1$\frac{1}{2}$ miles turn right on to the B9038 for Whitehills.

WHITEHILLS, Grampian NJ66
This little fishing village stands on a sandy and rocky bay sheltered by the scenic promontories of Stake Ness and Knock Head.

At Whitehills turn left (no SP) on to an unclassified road and in $\frac{1}{2}$ mile meet crossroads. Turn right on to the B9139 SP 'Portsoy' and continue to Boyne.

BOYNE CASTLE, Grampian NJ66
Beautiful woodland surrounds this picturesque ruin, which overlooks the Burn of Boyne. The stronghold dates from 1485 and was once held by the Ogilvie family.

In 1$\frac{1}{4}$ miles turn right on to the A98 to the village of Portsoy.

PORTSOY, Grampian NJ56
The prized Portsoy marble for which the area round this little fishing village is known is actually a variety of serpentine. When worked and polished the mineral reveals unsuspected shades of translucent green and pink. Louis XIV of France used it for two of the chimney pieces in the magnificent Palace of Versailles, and local craftsmen have been working it for centuries. Even today the area's shop windows are adorned with finely wrought serpentine paper weights, chessmen, and other small objects.

Buckie boatyards produce some of the finest vessels in the Highlands.

Continue along the A98, parallel to the coast, and pass the popular fishing village and resort of Sandend. Continue to Cullen.

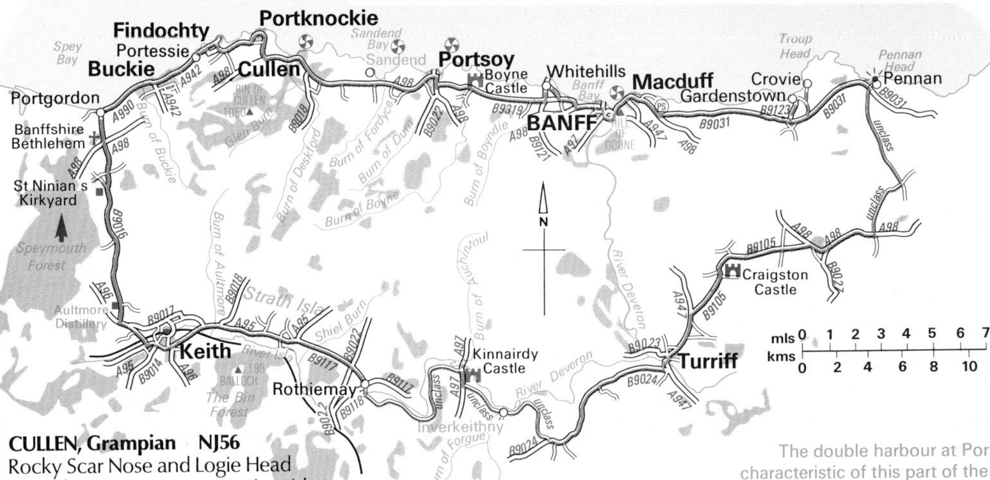

CULLEN, Grampian NJ56
Rocky Scar Nose and Logie Head extend out to sea on respective sides of this pleasant resort, sheltering the sandy beach and forming an attractive part of the local seascape. On the shore are three isolated rocks known as the Three Kings of Cullen. The town itself offers many holiday facilities and preserves a number of good features. A magnificent fireplace of Portsoy marble is a feature of Cullen House, a 16th-century building that was greatly extended in the 19th century, and its rooms afford excellent views out to sea. Close by is St Mary's Church, which was founded by Robert the Bruce and became collegiate in 1543. Inside is the laird's pew of the Seafield line of Clan Grant, and a large monument to a member of the Ogilvy family.

Continue along the A98 'Inverness' road for 1$\frac{1}{4}$ miles and turn right on to the A942 for Portknockie.

PORTKNOCKIE, Grampian NJ46
During the late 19th century a deep water harbour was constructed to service the flourishing local herring industry, but nowadays the fishing has declined and the quays are almost deserted. The village itself is a picturesque little place situated along the coast from Cullen Bay.

Follow SP 'Inverness Coast Road' and pass the village of Findochty.

The double harbour at Portso characteristic of this part of the co

FINDOCHTY, Grampian NJ46
On each side of this attractive village is a rocky, empty coastline that makes excellent walking country. The beach at Findochty is of fine sand and is ideal for bathing.

Continue to Portessie.

PORTESSIE, Grampian NJ46
Portessie is yet another of the many attractive little fishing villages for which this otherwise lonely coastline is justly famous. It is unspoilt and retains many of its old cottages.

Continue to Buckie.

BUCKIE, Grampian NJ46
High above the rooftops of this straggling port is the elegant and very prominent steeple of St Peter Catholic Church, acting as a landmark from both sea and land. The harbour here is the busiest on the Moray Firth, and many of the town's long maritime associations are recorded in the Buckie Museu and Art Gallery. Various seafaring exhibits and over 400 pictures of fishing vessels can be seen here.

Drive beyond the harbour and turn right with the A990. Continue for 2 miles to Portgordon.

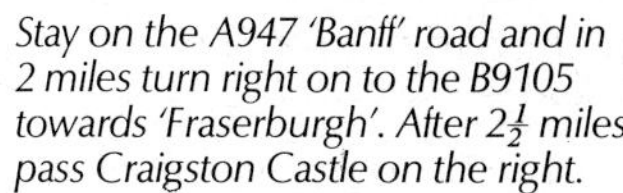

PORTGORDON, Grampian NJ36
The harbour here was built by the Duke of Richmond and Gordon in 1874, a fact commemorated in the village name.

Turn left with the A990 and after 1¼ miles meet a junction with the A98. On the right is a building which 's revered as the Banffshire 3ethlehem.

3ANFFSHIRE BETHLEHEM, Grampian NJ36
After John Knox's hysterical and often bloody Reformation, many Scots who had been Catholic changed to the Protestant faith under pressure from the new regime. n the old Banffshire area the nfluence of the Gordon Clan was uch that the local people clung persistently to the traditional faith, even when the clan chiefs played hem false and forsook the religion which they had supported for generations. Following the Jacobite isings Scotland was swept by a wave of hatred against anything Catholic, and the 1,000 or so faithful n Banffshire were hounded from one secret church to the next until they were given an old cottage-cum-byre hat had been converted for sheep. It as this property of the Laird of ynet that served as their place of worship through the troubled times nd became known as the Banffshire ethlehem. Even today the white alls under a grey slate roof appear be nothing more than a farm uilding, but the interior has been arefully restored and is still in use.

urn right on to the A98 then mediately left on to the B9016. In miles a short detour can be made turning right on to an unclassified ad and driving for ½ mile to St nian's Kirkyard.

NINIAN'S KIRKYARD, rampian NJ36
decade or so after the Protestant formation, before the Jacobites eated the need for such hideaways the Banffshire Bethlehem, the thful of this area built a new urch in an ancient churchyard dicated to St Ninian. This was the t Catholic place of worship to ve been built since John Knox's igious crusade, but after the obite Rising it was attacked by an ned band of Protestants and mpletely wrecked. Its site beside Tynet Burn is marked by a cross ed to the memory of 18th-ntury Bishop Nicholson, who was first Vicar Apostolic of Scotland.

the main route, continue with the 16 for 4¾ miles, meet a junction the A96, then turn left on to the erdeen' road and continue to town of Keith.

TH, Grampian NJ45
row lanes criss-crossing between three parallel main streets of this th Isla market centre give it a int, timeless character all of its . It stands on the River Isla, ch is spanned by two bridges

The seashore near Gardenstown is picturesque but rocky and precipitous.

connecting the town with its close neighbour Fife of Keith. The early crossing dates from 1609 and the later from 1770. At one time Keith was famous for its fair, but nowadays it is better known as the site of the Milton Distillery. This was founded in 1785 and is the oldest working malt whisky distillery in Scotland.

Leave Keith on the A95 with SP 'Banff' and follow Strath Isla. After 5 miles turn right on to the B9117 with SP 'Rothiemay'. In 2½ miles turn right then immediately left, and after ¾ mile follow the B9118 to Rothiemay.

ROTHIEMAY, Grampian NJ54
Remains of Rothiemay Castle stand beyond the River Deveron in fine gardens, and the river itself is spanned here by a fine old bridge. A monument at Milltown of Rothiemay commemorates James Ferguson, an early 18th-century astronomer.

Continue forward on an unclassified road, cross the River Deveron, and turn left. Continue along a narrow road through the well-wooded countryside of the Deveron Valley, and after 5½ miles turn right on to the A97 'Huntly' road. A detour from the main route can be made here by turning left on to the A97, crossing the River Deveron, and in ½ mile turning right on to an unclassified road for Kinnairdy Castle.

Macduff harbour is the base for the town's important herring fleet.

KINNAIRDY CASTLE, Grampian NJ64
This L-shaped tower house (not open) was finely restored by its owner Sir Thomas Innes of Learney. The titles and estates passed to his eldest son in 1971.

On the main drive, continue with the A97 'Huntly' road and in ½ mile turn left on to an unclassified road SP 'Inverkeithny'. After 1½ miles keep left and descend to Inverkeithny hamlet, at the junction of the Burn of Forgue and the River Deveron. Climb above the river, then leave the valley and cross open country to a junction with the B9024. Turn left on to the 'Turriff' road and in 6 miles turn left again on to the A947 towards 'Banff' for Turriff.

TURRIFF, Grampian NJ75
In 1639 this thriving little market town was the scene of the Trot of Turriff, when Covenanters met Royalists in battle. A church of the Knights Templar stood here, and the old Market Cross was re-erected in 1865. Pleasant woodland to the east of the town surrounds the great tower house of Delgatie Castle (open), a seat of the Clan Hay that has been in the family's possession for nearly 700 years. It was founded by the Hays of Delgatie in the 13th century and shows alterations up to the 16th century. Inside are various relics and pictures, but among its best features are its fine painted ceilings of c1590.

Stay on the A947 'Banff' road and in 2 miles turn right on to the B9105 towards 'Fraserburgh'. After 2½ miles pass Craigston Castle on the right.

CRAIGSTON CASTLE, Grampian NJ75
Remarkable woodcarvings are preserved in this 17th-century castle, which was built by John Urquhart and has hardly been altered since. It is open by appointment only.

Continue through Buchan countryside and in 3½ miles turn right on to the A98. In another 2½ miles turn left on to an unclassified road SP 'New Aberdour'. After another 2½ miles turn left again towards 'Pennan', then continue along a winding road to meet a junction with the B9031 at the coast. Drive over the crossroads and descend steeply into the village of Pennan.

PENNAN, Grampian NJ86
Pennan Head dominates the rocky and precipitous shore of Pennan Bay, and the pretty Troup Burn joins the sea near the village. Farther west is the bold outline of Troup Head. The village itself has housed generations of fishermen and is typical of many along this coast.

Return to the B9031 and turn right towards 'Banff'. Continue along a hilly road with occasional coastal views. Short detours from the main route towards the coast lead to the attractive villages of Crovie and Gardenstown.

CROVIE, Grampian NJ86
Crovie Head shelters this fishing community, which stands at the base of high red cliffs on Gamrie Bay.

GARDENSTOWN, Grampian NJ86
Picturesque cottages and houses rise in tiers above the lovely old harbour of Gardenstown, a fishing village on the shores of Gamrie Bay. To the west near Mhor Head, on the Hill of Gamrie Mhor, is a ruined church that was founded to commemorate a local victory over the Danes. The date given for this event is recorded on the gable of the building as 1004, but it is unlikely that the existing structure is as early as that. West and east of the village are ranges of spectacular cliffs.

On the main route, continue for 8¾ miles (from Pennan) and turn right on to the A98 towards 'Inverness'. Continue to Macduff.

MACDUFF, Grampian NJ76
Steep streets of attractive houses lead down to a superb harbour in Macduff, an important Banff Bay town known for its herring industry. Very fine views of the area can be enjoyed from the war memorial on top of the Hill of Doune, and the local coastline is impressive. Remarkable rock outcrops can be seen near a bathing pool on the foreshore.

Cross the River Deveron and return along the A98 to Banff.

TOUR 108 94 MILES

BELOW THE CAIRNGORM SUMMITS

Here are the best winter-sports facilities in Britain, mountain walks that are unequalled elsewhere in the country, and the forested depths of beautiful Glen More. Superb views are afforded by ski lifts that operate all the year round, riding high above granite crags and tree-shrouded lochs.

AVIEMORE, Highland NH81
In the 1960s the village of Aviemore, situated in the heart of the British winter sports area, became transformed into one of Scotland's major inland resorts. This amazing change was brought about by the building of the Aviemore Centre, a massive complex of shops, restaurants, luxury hotels, and entertainment facilities with a definite après-ski flavour. Superb sporting facilities include ice-rinks for skating and curling, a go-kart track, a dry ski slope, and a swimming pool. Various events are staged at the theatre and concert hall, and for people who dislike hotel rooms there are numerous well-appointed chalets. The local granite and timber of which the complex is built is in keeping with its site at the foot of the great rock of Craigellachie. Steam-hauled trains operate on a revived railway which runs along the Spey Valley to connect Aviemore with Boat of Garten, some 5 miles away. Another feature of the area is a 600-acre nature reserve.

Leave Aviemore on the A9 'Perth' road and continue to Lynwilg.

LYNWILG, Highland NH81
Situated in attractive woodland near Loch Alvie, Lynwilg is typical of many hamlets in the Highlands. To the south-west on Tor of Alvie Hill is the Waterloo Cairn and Monument to the last Duke of Gordon.

Skirt the shores of Loch Alvie and the village of Alvie.

ALVIE, Highland NH80
Alvie Church is a homely focal point for this pleasant village. Nearby Geal Charn Mor stands at 2,703ft and rewards anybody who climbs it with one of Scotland's finest views of the Cairngorm Mountains.

Continue through Kincraig to reach the Highland Wildlife Park.

HIGHLAND WILDLIFE PARK, Highland NH80
This was opened in 1972 and is based on an interesting historic theme, to illustrate the wildlife that has existed in Britain from the ice ages to the present day. Among the inhabitants displayed in one of the most fascinating collections in the country are bears, wolves, lynx, wildcats, and European bison.

Continue to Kingussie.

KINGUSSIE, Highland NH70
A popular pony-trekking centre surrounded by the wooded countryside of Strath Spey, Kingussie was chosen as the site for the superb Highland Folk Museum when it was moved from its place of foundation on Iona. Exhibits relate to the everyday life of the Scottish people and include farming implements, domestic tools, dress, tartans, relics of old crafts, and several much larger items such as a complete cottage furnished in traditional style, a mill from the Isle of Lewis, a traditional islander's black house, and a curious clack mill. A visit here will provide the type of understanding that can only enrich the tourist's enjoyment of Scotland in general, and the Highlands in particular. Some $2\frac{1}{2}$ miles north-east of Kingussie, off the Aviemore road, is the 18th-century mansion of Balavil. This was built by James Macpherson, who was born in the area and later became a translator of Ossianic poetry.

Before leaving Kingussie it is possible to take a detour from the main route by keeping forward on the A9 for 3 miles to Newtonmore.

Superb facilities for ski-ing exist around Aviemore, including a wide variety of nursery slopes and many more difficult runs.

NEWTONMORE, Highland NN79
Highland ponies can be hired for rides into the bleak Monadhliath Mountains from this town, which was the first place in Britain to offer pony-trekking as a recreation. Overlooking the site of a clan battle fought near by in 1386 is 2,350ft Craig Dhu, the ancient gathering place of the Clan Macpherson. Macpherson House features clan history and relics of the 1745 Jacobite Rising.

On the main tour, turn left at Kingussie on to the B970 Station Road and drive over a level crossing. Continue to Ruthven Barracks.

RUTHVEN BARRACKS, Highland NN78
Built in 1719 and added to by General Wade 'the road builder' in 1728, these old barracks (AM) were adopted to house anti-Jacobite troops between the Risings of 1715 and 1745. They were captured and demolished by the followers of Bonnie Prince Charlie in 1746.

After $1\frac{3}{4}$ miles cross the River Tromie at Tromie Bridge and turn left.

TROMIE BRIDGE, Highland NN79
Paths lead south from here to Grampian Gaick Forest, down the long and picturesque Glen of Tromi[e]. Features of the forest include Loch an't Seilich and Loch na Cuaich, which lie between its steep hillsides and are linked by a stream. Their combined waters flow across an aqueduct to Loch Ericht as part of the important Rannoch hydro-electric scheme.

Continue to the hamlet of Insh.

INSH, Highland NH80
A Celtic handbell that was once used to call people to worship is preserved in the 18th-century church at Insh. It pre-dates the building by at least 1,000 years, and the site occupied by the church is even older.

In $2\frac{1}{2}$ miles keep forward with the 'Rothiemurchus' road and later cros[s] the River Feshie at Feshiebridge.

FESHIEBRIDGE, Highland NH80
Excellent all-weather footpaths extend along the Glen of Feshie towards Deeside from here. Some of the most scenic areas are where th[e] valley penetrates the hill ranges of attractive Speyside.

Continue along the B970 and drive through attractive Inshriach Forest t[o] reach Rothiemurchus.

ROTHIEMURCHUS, Highland NH80
At one time the woodland round t[he] hamlet formed part of the primeva[l] Caledonian Forest that covered m[ost] of the Scottish Highlands. Much of [it] is contained within the boundaries [of] Rothiemurchus Forest, which is accessible by attractive paths and tracks. Part of the area is protected as a nature reserve.

Just beyond Rothiemurchus it is possible to make a short detour fro[m] the main route by turning right on [to] an unclassified road and driving to Loch an Eilean.

LOCH AN EILEAN, Highland NH8
Noted for its odd triple echo, this beautiful loch was once the bolth[ole] of the Wolf of Badenoch, a clan leader who was notoriously bloodthirsty. The island ruins of his castle add a sinister note to the otherwise innocent enchantment [of] the lochside area.

On the main tour, continue along t[he] B970 to Inverdruie and turn right o[n] to the A951 for Coylumbridge.

The splendid Cairngorm Mountains r[ise] to the north of attractive Loch Morlic[h]

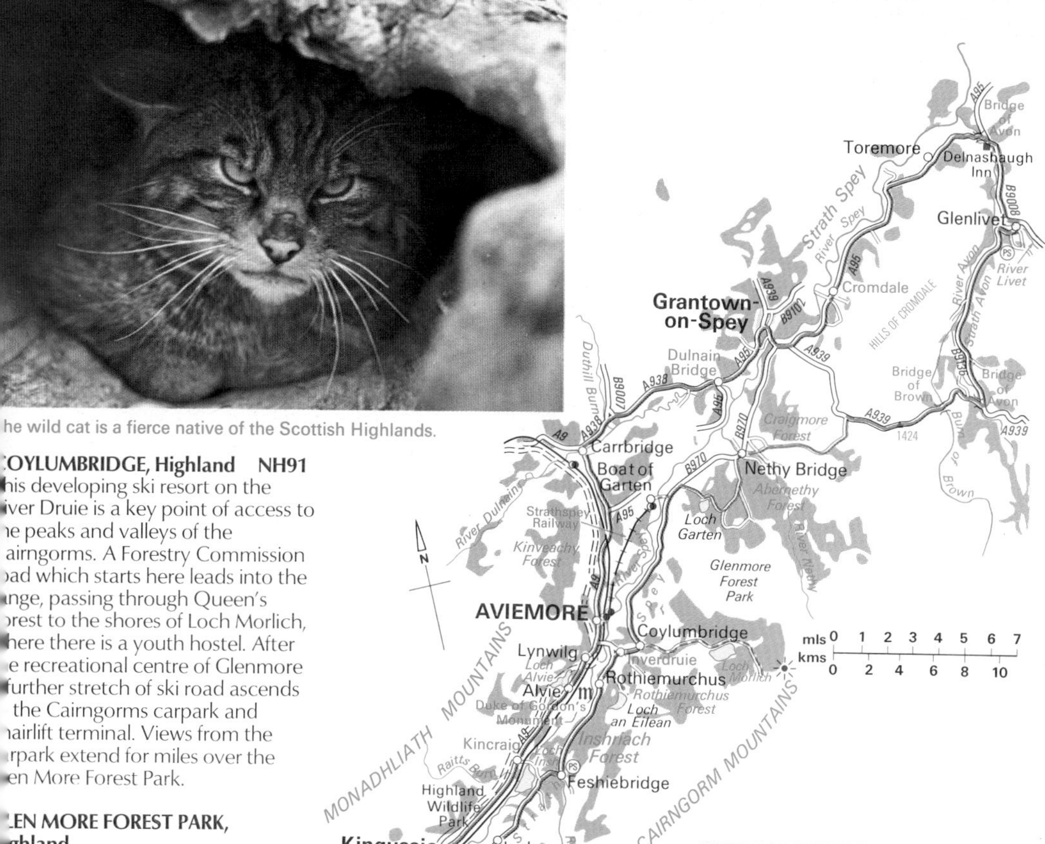

he wild cat is a fierce native of the Scottish Highlands.

:OYLUMBRIDGE, Highland NH91

his developing ski resort on the iver Druie is a key point of access to ie peaks and valleys of the airngorms. A Forestry Commission oad which starts here leads into the inge, passing through Queen's orest to the shores of Loch Morlich, here there is a youth hostel. After e recreational centre of Glenmore further stretch of ski road ascends the Cairngorms carpark and hairlift terminal. Views from the rpark extend for miles over the en More Forest Park.

LEN MORE FOREST PARK, ghland

me 3,300 acres of coniferous forest d 9,200 acres of mountainside ake up this beautiful and often ectacular national forest park. At heart is Loch Morlich, which lies in hollow 1,000ft above sea level and s sandy beaches fringed by scendants of the old Caledonian ies that once covered the ghlands. Rock and heather take er where the trees stop, and all ind the horizon are the serrated lines of mountain peaks. Rare dlife found nowhere else in Britain s here, and species that are common elsewhere abound. lkers using the Forestry mmission trails may see the blue e or stately red deer, the turkey- capercaillie that was re- oduced to the Highlands several rs ago, or the ptarmigan that er quite died out. Also here are use, golden eagles, the elusive rey, and roe deer. Reindeer are ig farmed in the area, so the ker who comes face to face with of these magnificent creatures uld not fear for his sanity.

n Coylumbridge follow SP 'Nethy ge' along the B970 to continue g Strath Spey. After 6½ miles a ile detour can be taken from the n route by following an assified left turn to Boat of Garten.

AT OF GARTEN, land NH91

curious name of this mountain ge is derived from a ferry that to cross the Spey from here re the present bridge was built in 9th century. It is the northern inus of a 5-mile steam-hauled ay which runs along Strath Spey e winter sports and recreation e of Aviemore.

On the main tour, continue along the B970 for a further ½ mile and turn right on to an unclassified road to enter the Abernethy Forest. Continue to the banks of Loch Garten.

LOCH GARTEN, Highland NH91

Visitors to the RSPB observation point here can watch many species of birds, including the rare osprey.

Pass Loch Garten and after ½ mile keep forward on to the 'Nethy Bridge' road. In 2½ miles turn right to rejoin the B970 and continue to the resort of Nethy Bridge.

NETHY BRIDGE, Highland NJ02

Winter-sports enthusiasts come here in early spring for the ski-ing, and later in the year it is a popular centre for walkers and anglers. North-east of the village on the B970 are the ruins of Castle Roy, a great fortress that was a stronghold of the Comyn.

Cross a tributary of the Spey, turn right on to an unclassified road towards 'Tomintoul', and in ½ mile drive over crossroads. Continue over bleak moorland, and after 4½ miles turn right on to the A939 towards 'Tomintoul'. Proceed, with the Hills of Cromdale on the left and the dark outlines of the Cairngorms to the right. Ascend to a road summit of 1,424ft, then descend to the Bridge of Brown. Climb again and descend to the Bridge of Avon, then turn left on to the B9136 SP 'Craigellachie'. Follow Strath Avon and in 8½ miles cross the River Livet at the hamlet of Glenlivet.

GLENLIVET, Grampian NJ13

Fine malt whisky has been distilled in this small village for many years, and although there is a modern distillery here the method has not changed much since the days of clandestine home-brewing. See also tour 106.

Beyond the Livet bridge turn left to join the B9008. After 4 miles reach the Delnashaugh Inn and turn left on to the A95 'Grantown' road.

DELNASHAUGH INN, Grampian NJ13

Close to this famous landmark is Ballindalloch Castle, which was begun in the 16th century and bears the arms of the Macpherson-Grants. Beyond its picturesque grounds is the junction of the River Avon with the River Spey.

After a short distance re-cross the River Avon, with the grounds of Ballindalloch Castle to the right, and continue to the hamlet of Toremore.

TOREMORE, Highland NJ13

In 1960 the first distillery to be built in the Highlands this century was opened here. The building, which at the time was described as 'the most beautiful industrial structure in the Highlands', was designed by Professor Sir Albert Richardson.

Continue along the south side of the Spey and pass through the hamlet of Cromdale. Continue to the resort of Grantown-on-Spey.

GRANTOWN-ON-SPEY, Highland NJ02

A local landowner planned this essentially residential resort in 1776, and the elegance of the 18th century has persisted to the present day. It is set in the lovely surroundings of Strath Spey and has become a major centre for anglers seeking the excellent Spey salmon. There is also considerable local involvement with the Scottish winter-sports industry. Castle Grant, a mansion that is the seat of the Earls of Seafield, stands about 2 miles north of the town.

Loch Garten is nationally famous as a breeding ground for the osprey.

Leave Grantown on the 'Perth' road and continue on the A95 to Dulnain Bridge. Keep forward on to the A938 and follow the valley of the River Dulnain to Carrbridge.

CARRBRIDGE, Highland NH92

The award-winning visitor's centre in this Highland resort is claimed to be the finest in Europe. It offers all kinds of information about the Highlands, including an exciting audio-visual display that covers some 10,000 years of history. In winter Carrbridge is a ski-ing centre.

Leave Carrbridge and follow the A9 'Perth' road for the return to the Aviemore centre.

TOUR 109 104 MILES

ROAD TO THE ISLES

Reminders of Bonnie Prince Charlie and the ill-fated Jacobite Rising are everywhere in the west Highland countryside. Ben Nevis towers over lochs and glens, moors and hillsides, known for the bloody battles and long-drawn-out feuds enacted there in the past.

Snow-capped Ben Nevis forms a popular excursion from Fort William. On a clear day views from the summit extend for 150 miles.

FORT WILLIAM, Highland NN17
The first fort built here was a wattle-and-daub structure erected by General Monk in 1655, but the town takes its name from a stone stronghold that replaced it by order of William III. It was besieged by Jacobites in the Rising of 1715, but they failed to take it and General Wade – of roadbuilding fame – was commissioned to strengthen it. His engineering talents were proved in 1745, when the second Jacobite Rising failed to capture it. The fort was garrisoned until the mid 19th century, by which time its redundancy was obvious and it was demolished. Relics from these and earlier days can be seen in the West Highland Museum including a curious picture of Prince Charles Edward that can only be seen in its reflection on a curved and polished surface. The town itself is a major resort and touring centre for the West Highlands, situated near the west end of Glen More and the head of Loch Linnhe. Towering above the town is the massive bulk of Ben Nevis, while the comparatively low summit of 942ft Cow Hill affords lovely views into lower Glen Nevis. One of the major features of the local landscape is the white quartzite peak of Sgurr a' Mhaim, which rises like a snow-capped Alp to the south.

BEN NEVIS, Highland NN17
An enormous expanse of countryside round Fort William and the Lochaber area, including a large part of Glen More, is dominated by 4,408ft Ben Nevis. It is the highest mountain in the British Isles, and round its south and west flanks is Glen Nevis, one of the most beautiful valleys in Scotland. At the far end of the glen the River Nevis rushes through a steep wooded gorge, but closer to Fort William its waters can be crossed to reach a mountain path starting at Achintee Farm. The mountain can be climbed from here, but the path is only suitable for walkers. The energetic explorer will find many enchanting and often impressive natural features to reward his efforts, such as the Allt Coire Eaghainn waterfalls plunging from their hidden corrie, the waterfall of Steall in its wild setting at the end of Glen Nevis, and the spectacular narrow arrête that links the Ben with the upper slopes of Carn Mor Dearg. Views from here extend to Ireland.

From Fort William follow SP 'Inverness' to take the A82 northwards out of the town. Continue, and pass Inverlochy Castle.

INVERLOCHY CASTLE, Highland NN17
Thought to date from the 13th century, this ruined Comyn stronghold (AM) stands by the River Lochy and is well-preserved. The largest of its circular towers is named after the family and has massive 10ft-thick walls enclosing rooms that are a full 20ft across. A Civil War battle between a royalist force led by the Marquess of Montrose and a Covenanters' army under the command of the Duke of Argyll took place near here in 1645. It resulted in a victory for Montrose after he and his men had completed a remarkable forced march through the rugged fastness of the Lochaber Mountains.

Beyond the castle turn left to join the A830 'Mallaig' road – the famous Road to the Isles. At one time this was notoriously difficult, but it has been improved recently. Cross the River Lochy, then the Caledonian Canal, and enter Banavie.

BANAVIE, Highland NN17
Telford came here in the 19th century to build a chain of eight lochs on the Caledonian Canal, and his brilliance in solving difficult civil engineering problems can still be seen in this 'Neptune's Staircase'.
Continue to Corpach.

CORPACH, Highland NN07
A little to the west of Corpach is Kilmallie Churchyard, where an obelisk was raised to Colonel John Cameron after he fell in the Battle of Quatre Bras during the Waterloo Campaign of 1815. Some say that the inscription on the monument was written by Sir Walter Scott, though this is difficult to prove.

Continue along the A830 and follow the picturesque shore of Loch Eil to Kinlocheil.

KINLOCHEIL, Highland NM97
Nowadays this is a peaceful little place, but it must have been full of tension when Prince Charles Edward came here after unfurling his father's standard at Glenfinnan in 1745.

Continue to Glenfinnan.

GLENFINNAN, Highland NM98
More than 1,000 clansmen mustered here under the red and white of the Stuart banner to begin the second Jacobite Rising in 1745. The place where the standard is said to have been unfurled is marked by a tall castellated tower (NTS) with an inner staircase leading to a 19th-century statue of a Highlander at the top. Each year Highland games are held on the site of the gathering in memory of those who died for Bonnie Prince Charlie. Views from here extend along 18-mile Loch Shiel.

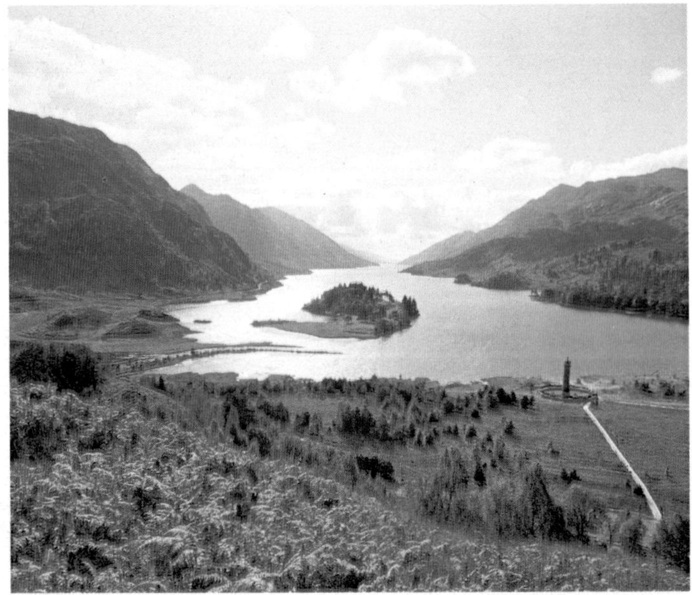

LOCH SHIEL, Highland NM87
Many visitors consider Loch Shiel to be the most picturesque expanse of fresh water in the Highlands. At its north end it is framed by spectacula mountain scenery, and parallel ranges of rocky hills border Glen Finnan to the north of the '45 Rising monument. Below the massive bulk of Ben Resipol are the narrows of the loch and the little island of Eilean Fhionain, which used to be a burial ground many centuries ago.

Continue, then pass Loch Eilt on the way to Lochailort.

LOCHAILORT, Highland NM78
Situated in a lovely position at the head of the sea loch Ailort, this isolated village stands against a backdrop of high hills in which 2,877ft Rois Bheinn is prominent. Close to the seaward end of the loc is the tiny island of Eilean nan Bobhar, where the French ship that brought Bonnie Prince Charlie anchored in July of 1745.

From Lochailort a 39-mile detour car be taken to Mallaig by continuing along the A830 alongside Loch Ailor then Loch nan Uamh.

LOCH NAN UAMH, Highland
Worth visiting for its own sake, this picturesque loch is best known for associations with Bonnie Prince Charlie and the Jacobite Rising of 1745. Borrowdale House was the scene of a fateful meeting when th whole issue of the Jacobite cause came into question, and although was burnt after the Battle of Culloden it still preserves much of original structure. After the '45 Risir had degenerated into a disorganiz bloodbath the Prince returned to Loch nan Uamh with a fortune on head, and he had to hide in the woods of Glen Beasdale before escaping to the isolation of the Outer Hebrides.

Still on the detour, continue to Arisa with views across the Sound of Aris to the little islands of Rhum and Eigg

Wild Loch Shiel echoes with memor of Bonnie Prince Charlie at Glenfinn

ARISAIG, Highland NM68
A memorial clock in the Roman Catholic church here commemorates the most revered of all Scots Gaelic poets, Alisdair MacMhaigstir Alasdair, who took part in the Rising of 1745. Near by are the gardens of Arisaig House.

Still on the detour, continue to Morar.

MORAR, Highland NM69
Loch Morar is the deepest inland water in Britain, and the Falls of Morar have been harnessed in a local hydro-electric scheme on the River Morar. The white sands of a bay formed by the river's estuary are famous. The hamlet itself is situated on a narrow neck of land between the loch and the Sound of Sleat.

Continue on the detour to Mallaig.

MALLAIG, Highland NM69
…cing the Isle of Skye from the …cky shores of north Morar, this …ge herring port stands at the …estern end of the Road to the Isles …d is the mainland terminus of the …ands' ferry. Cars can be taken from …re to Armadale, on Skye.

…the main route, leave Lochailort …the A861 and follow the eastern …ore of the loch and the Sound of …saig. Later turn south to reach Loch …oidart and Kinlochmoidart.

…LOCHMOIDART, …ghland NM77
…re, where the River Moidart flows …ough woodland to the head of …ch Moidart, are 7 beech trees that …re planted to commemorate 7 …al men who were among Bonnie …nce Charlie's most constant …mpanions.

…ntinue along the A861 and after 6 …es reach an unclassified right turn. …etour can be made from the main …e to Castle Tioram here.

CASTLE TIORAM, Highland NM67
One of the most romantic and beautifully situated ruins in the Western Highlands, this 13th-century castle is perched on a spit of land that becomes isolated when the tide rises. It was built by the Macdonalds of Clanranald who, after they realized that the '45 Rising was doomed to failure, burned it rather than let it fall into enemy hands.

Continue on the A861 to Acharacle.

Neptune's Staircase of 8 locks at Banavie raises the Caledonian Canal 64ft in 1 mile.

ACHARACLE, Highland NM66
This little angling resort stands on the west tip of Loch Shiel and is the embarkation point for cruises.

Continue to Salen.

SALEN, Highland NM66
The small fishing resort of Salen stands on Loch Sunart, a narrow ribbon of sea that separates Ardnamurchan from the traditionally MacLean territory of the Morvern district. It is little more than a cluster of cottages round a hotel, but its surroundings are a superb mixture of mountain, moorland, and pine plantations.

LOCH SUNART, Highland
At the head of this beautiful sea loch is an amphitheatre of hills where the Ardgour and Morvern districts meet.

A 43-mile detour can be made from Salen to Kilchoan and Ardnamurchan Point: take the B8007 (a narrow, winding road) west along the loch and drive inland through the Ardnamurchan Peninsula, returning to the coast at Kilchoan. To reach Ardnamurchan Point and lighthouse (a further 6 miles) continue along the B8007 for another 4 miles and turn left on to an unclassified road to Ardnamurchan Point.

During the season Mallaig harbour is packed with fishing boats.

KILCHOAN AND ARDNAMURCHAN POINT, Highland NM46
Situated on the rocky Ardnamurchan coast, this remote little village has a pier that is the starting point of a passenger ferry to Tobermory, on the Island of Mull. Ardnamurchan Point is a wild and lonely area populated by sea birds.

On the main tour, leave Salen and continue along the A861 beside the northern shore of Loch Sunart to the village of Strontian.

STRONTIAN, Highland NM86
Strontium, a rare mineral that used to be mined in the district, is named after this village. To the north the River Strontian carves its way between the mountains of Sunart and Ardgour before emerging from its glen to join Loch Sunart in an area that used to be mined for lead. Close by is the Ariundle Forest nature reserve, one of the few places where the true Scottish wildcat survives.

Continue along the A861 through Glen Tarbert and later pass through Inversanda to reach the shores of lovely Loch Linnhe.

INVERSANDA, Highland NM95
Here the wild country of Abhainn Coir ean Iubhair leads north from Glen Tarbert to the superb rock scenery of 2,903ft Garbh Bheinn, the Ardgour district's finest peak. Inversanda itself is a village on the wide bay of the same name, close to the east end of the glen and the north-western shore of Loch Linnhe.

LOCH LINNHE, Highland
Situated at the extreme west end of the Great Glen, or Glen More, Loch Linnhe is divided into the Inner and Outer Loch by the Corran Narrows. Loch Leven joins it beyond the Narrows, which are crossed by a car ferry between Ardgour and Corran.

Continue along the west shore of Loch Linnhe to Ardgour.

ARDGOUR, Highland NN06
This name applies generally to a wild and rugged district between Loch Shiel and Loch Linnhe, and particularly to a small village near the Corran Narrows.

Pass the ferry point at the Ardgour Hotel and continue along the west shore of Loch Linnhe to the head of the loch and Camusnagaul.

CAMUSNAGAUL, Highland NN07
Excellent views extend over Loch Linnhe to Fort William, dominated by the towering summit of Ben Nevis. Close by the loch bends west to become Loch Eil.

Continue along the A861 to follow the shore of Loch Eil, then round the head of the loch and turn right on to the A830 for Kinlocheil and the return to Fort William. An alternative route cutting 25¼ miles off the route can be taken to Fort William by crossing Loch Linnhe via the Ardgour Ferry to Corran, then following the eastern shore and the A82 to Fort William.

KYLE OF LOCHALSH, Highland NG72
This busy fishing and shipping village stands at the west end of Loch Alsh and is the railhead on a line from Inverness. It is also the main ferry stage for Skye, and the shores of that beautiful island lie just a few hundred yards away across the Kyle Akin waters. Fine views from Kyle of Lochalsh encompass the Cuillin range on Skye, the Crowlin Islands, and Raasay to the west. East is the vast Balmacara Estate (NTS).

Take the Skye ferry across the narrow strait to Kyleakin.

KYLEAKIN, Highland NG72
Ruined Castle Moil stands on the shore a little to the east of this island port. It is thought that its small Highland keep may have been built by the daughter of a Norwegian king but it is known to have served as a lookout post and fortress against Norse raiders for centuries. During most of this time it was a stronghold of the Mackinnons of Strath. Behind the village is the 2,396ft bulk of Beinn na Cailleach.

Drive along the A850 and pass through Breakish to reach Broadford.

BROADFORD, Highland NG72
Broadford is a convenient touring centre for south Skye. It stands by Broadford Bay on a junction of roads from the ferry ports of Armadale, Kylerhea, and Kyleakin, overlooked by the granite screes of the Red Hills. Prominent in the range is 2,400ft Beinn na Caillich, the site of the largest hill cairn in Scotland. Tradition has it that a Norwegian princess was buried here, where the winds of Norway could blow over her grave, in the 13th century. Offshore to the west is the Island of Scalpay.

From Broadford a detour can be made along the A881 to reach Torrin and Elgol.

TORRIN, Highland NG52
In front of this crofting township is Loch Slapin, and the majestic Red Cuillin range rises in the north-east. Across the loch on the Strathaird peninsula is the great Black Cuillin peak of 3,044ft Bla Bheinn and a precipitous rocky ridge known as Clach Glas. The latter is popular with experienced rock climbers.

Still on the detour, continue to Elgol.

ELGOL, Highland NG51
Magnificent views from this Loch Scavaig hamlet extend north to the Cuillins and south to the mountainous little islands of Canna, Rhum, and Eigg. Motor-boat trips can be taken from here to Loch Coruisk, which lies amongst the wild Cuillin peaks in a landscape of lochs and mountains more scenic than any other in the British Isles. The loch can also be reached by way of footpaths, one of which runs along the lovely and mountainous north shore of Loch Scavaig.

TOUR 110 — 142 MILES

THE ISLE OF MIST

History and legend join hands in the misty no-man's land that is Skye's romantic, often turbulent, past. Old castles guard the shoreline, and some of the most spectacular mountains in Scotland encircle the magical scenery of hidden inlets and unsuspected lochs.

Castle Moil at Kyleakin commands breathtaking views up Loch Alsh.

On the main drive, continue towards Portree and skirt Loch Ainort with views of 3,044ft Bla Bheinn left.

CUILLIN HILLS, Highland
Unrivalled for scenic splendour anywhere in Britain, the Black and Red Cuillins are the most famous landscape features of this outstanding island. A 6-mile arc of black peaks, 15 of which exceed 3,000ft in height, curves across the south-west part of the island as the Black Cuillin range; on the other side of Glen Sligachan, in spectacular contrast to its jagged neighbours, are the softly rounded summits and glowing pink granite of the Red Cuillins. The black peak of 3,309ft Alasdair and rough pinnacled mass of 3,167ft Sgurr nan Gillean attract experienced climbers, while the determined walker heads for the fastnesses of hidden corries and surprising little valleys in the red hills. Both ranges are prone to sudden mists and can be deadly, even to experienced people. Local advice should be sought before attempting to explore either.

Portree offers a pleasant harbour for steamers to Raasay.

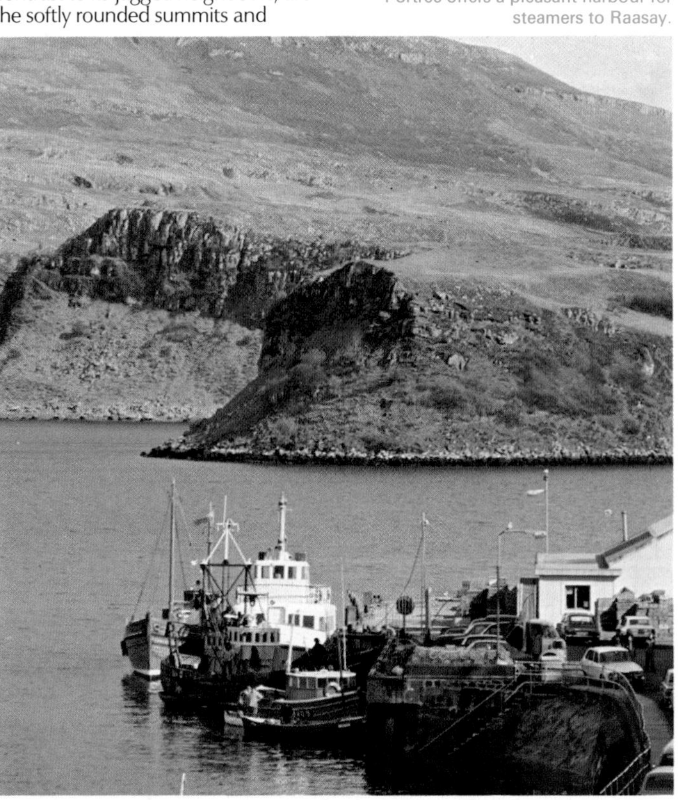

Ascend from Loch Ainort and continue, with Lord MacDonald's Forest and the Red Cuillin summits of Marco and Glamaig to the left of the road. Later descend with views of the island of Raasay on the right and continue to Sconser.

SCONSER, Highland NG53
Parts of an inn where Dr Johnson and Boswell stayed while visiting the island in 1773 have been incorporated in the Sconser Lodge Hotel. The hamlet itself is sited at the mouth of Loch Sligachan.

Proceed to Sligachan.

SLIGACHAN, Highland NG42
Well known for its salmon and sea trout, this hamlet stands on the River Sligachan near the head of the loch of the same name. The U-shaped glacial valley of Glen Sligachan extends south into the Black Cuillins, with the 3,167ft peak of Sgurr nan Gillean prominent to the left. Several high peaks and spectacular Loch Coruisk can be reached via a path through the glen.

Drive north along Glen Varragill and descend to Portree Loch to reach the harbour town of Portree.

PORTREE, Highland NG44
Skye's pleasant little capital town of whitewashed houses stands on Portree Bay, which is sheltered by high cliffs on three sides. Well situated as a touring centre for the island, the town has a charming harbour and receives all kinds of ligh boat traffic at its pier. Opposite, across the Sound of Raasay, is the wooded island of Raasay. This isolated place is of particular interest to botanists and geologists.

Turn right on to the A855 and later pass the reservoirs of Loch Fada and Loch Leathan, both of which are incorporated in a hydro-electric scheme. To the left are the Trotternis Ridge and the precipices of The Storr

THE STORR, Highland NG45
Extending the length of the wild Trotternish peninsula of Skye, this 10-mile backbone of rock is dominated by the 2,360ft Storr plateau. Here is a grand and disturbing landscape of sudden cliff and jagged crags, where the Old Man of Storr pinnacle rises to 160ft like a giant's tower in a child's story. It has posed a challenge for centuries, but was not climbed unt 1955. The Storr lochs are harnessed to a hydro-electric scheme.

Continue, passing Lealt Falls and the well-known Kilt Rock near Loch Mealt, to reach Staffin.

STAFFIN, Highland NG46
Opposite this village in the curve o sandy Staffin Bay is the gull-populated isolation of Staffin Island Close by is the Kilt Rock, so named because its columnar and horizont beds of basalt suggest the pleats in Highland kilt.

Continue, passing the Quiraing on the left.

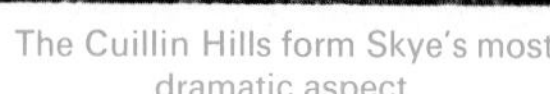
The Cuillin Hills form Skye's most dramatic aspect.

...unt ruins of Duntulm Castle stand ...posed on the headland.

...UIRAING, Highland NG46
...is strange wilderness of rocks is ...e of the most peculiar sights on ...ye. It is a remarkable group of ...one stacks and pinnacles bearing ...ch descriptive names as Needle ...ock, The Table, and The Prison, ...cluding a grassy natural ...phitheatre and a rugged group ...own as Leac nan Fionn.

...ntinue and skirt Flodigarry.

...ODIGARRY, Highland NG47
...ra Macdonald, known for her part ...Bonnie Prince Charlie's escape ...er the collapse of the Jacobite ...use at Culloden, spent the early ...ars of her marriage here. She ...corted the Prince, disguised as her ...id, from Benbecula in the Outer ...brides to Portree. Her house ...oins a local hotel.

...ntinue to Duntulm.

DUNTULM, Highland NG47
Crumbling Duntulm Castle dates from the 15th century and was once the seat of the Macdonalds of Sleat and Trotternish. A groove has been worn into the rock on the shore below the castle by the keels of the Macdonald galleys. The promontory of Rubha Hunish extends beyond the shore of Score Bay north of Duntulm, and views north-west across the waters of the Minch encompass the mountainous Outer Hebridean island of Harris.

Continue along the coast road to Flora Macdonald's burial place and the Skye Cottage Museum.

SKYE COTTAGE MUSEUM AND FLORA MACDONALD MONUMENT, Highland NG37
Traditional Highland furniture and relics from the island's past can be seen in a well-restored Black House here. This type of dwelling was traditional amongst the islands, though few good examples now survive. Close by is the old burial ground of the Macdonalds, Martins, Macarthurs, and Nicolsons. In 1790 Flora Macdonald was buried here, wrapped in a sheet in which Bonnie Prince Charlie had slept at Kingsbridge. Over her grave is a great Iona cross inscribed by Dr Johnson.

Proceed beyond Kilmuir and descend Idrigill Hill, with fine views over Uig Bay. Keep left on to the A856 to Uig.

UIG, Highland NG36
Situated on a fine bay, this picturesque little hamlet of scattered crofts faces across Loch Snizort and its islands to the Vaternish peninsula. The steamer pier is used by car ferries to the Outer Hebrides, but in 1746 Flora Macdonald and Bonnie Prince Charlie landed here after a much more difficult and dangerous voyage from those islands.

Continue to Kensaleyre on the shore of Loch Eyre, an inlet of Loch Snizort Beag, and in another ½ mile turn right on to the B8036. After another 1½ miles meet a T-junction and turn right on to the A850 to follow the shores of Loch Snizort Beag and Loch Greshornish to Edinbane. To the right of the road are views of the Outer Hebrides. Continue to Dunvegan.

DUNVEGAN, Highland NG24
Until 1748 the only entrance to the massive pile of moated Dunvegan Castle was by a sea gate. Seat of the Macleod chiefs, it dates from the 16th to 19th centuries and is claimed to be the oldest continuously inhabited castle in Scotland. Views from the ramparts extend across island-studded Dunvegan Loch to the distant ranges of Harris. Its greatest treasure is a fragment of silk which is known as the fairy flag and was probably woven on the Island of Rhodes in the 7th century. According to tradition a fairy gave the flag, and various magical properties, to the 4th clan chief in the 14th century. Other relics include the great broadsword of the 7th chief, the ancient Dunvegan Cup of Irish silver that was given to the 11th chief, and various items related to Bonnie Prince Charlie. Features of the building itself include a 15th-century dungeon with a high slit window opening on to the kitchen stairs, no doubt as an additional torture for the hungry prisoners. West of the castle is a pair of flat-topped basalt mountains known as Macleod's Tables.

Dunvegan Castle is steeped in legend.

From Dunvegan take the A863 'Sligachan' road, which affords good views of the Cuillins ahead, and on the approach to Struan pass Dun Beag on the left.

DUN BEAG, Highland NG33
Extensive remains of a 2,000-year-old Pictish broch stand here. Once a 40ft look-out post and refuge, the ruins include 12ft-thick walls, several rooms, and parts of a stone staircase.

Cross high ground above Loch Harport and descend to Glen Drynoch. A detour can be made from the main route here by turning right on to the B8009 and driving first to Carbost, then to Port-na-Long.

CARBOST, Highland NG33
The well-known Talisker Whisky Distillery is sited here, on the west shores of Loch Harport.

Still on the detour, continue to Port-na-Long.

PORT-NA-LONG, Highland NG33
This tiny weaving village has become famous for Harris Tweed.

On the main route, continue to Sligachan and turn right on to the A850 for the return to Kyleakin, where the ferry is taken back to Kyle of Lochalsh on the mainland.

TOUR 111 119 MILES

FROM THE CAPITAL OF THE HIGHLANDS

Close to Inverness are some of Scotland's best-known features. The Moray Firth offers sheltered boating and fishing, Loch Ness broods with mystery in the bottom of the Great Glen, and the engineering prowess of the 19th century is proved by the locks and cuts of the Caledonian Canal.

INVERNESS, Highland NH64
Often referred to as the Capital of the Highlands, Inverness has a magnificent setting. The oldest surviving building in the town is 16th-century Queen Mary's House, though as it stands today the building shows more restoration than original material. Just a little later is Abertaff House, which was built in 1593 for Lord Lovat and has a turnpike staircase. Nowadays it contains an exhibition detailing the origins and history of the Gaelic peoples, and is the headquarters of *An Comunn Gaidhealach* – an association dedicated to the preservation of Gaelic language and culture. Inverness Castle is modern.

Before leaving Inverness on the main tour it is possible to make a $6\frac{1}{2}$-mile detour to Culloden: follow SP 'Perth A9' and after 1 mile reach a roundabout; take the 2nd exit, meet another roundabout and take the 3rd exit. Continue for another 1 mile and turn left on to the B9006, then after $\frac{1}{2}$ mile branch left SP 'Croy' and continue to Culloden.

CULLODEN, Highland NH74
In 1746 the last battle to be fought in the United Kingdom took place here between Bonnie Prince Charlie's Jacobites and a Hanoverian army under the Duke of Cumberland. The Prince was defeated after 40 minutes by sheer weight of numbers, and subsequent atrocities earned the English leader the title Butcher Cumberland. Culloden Moor has altered since those bloody days. A plantation of new trees partly screens it from view, a road cuts through the battlefield itself, and a huge memorial cairn marks the site (NTS) where so many men died. There is an information centre in Old Lenach Farmhouse.

On the main tour, leave Inverness with SP 'Dingwall A9' and after 1 mile cross the Caledonian Canal.

CALEDONIAN CANAL
Created in the 19th century to provide passage between the Irish and North Seas, this $60\frac{1}{2}$-mile waterway uses 22 miles of canal to link 29 lochs and virtually splits Scotland in two. Without it the sailing boats of the day would have had to risk the passage round Cape Wrath.

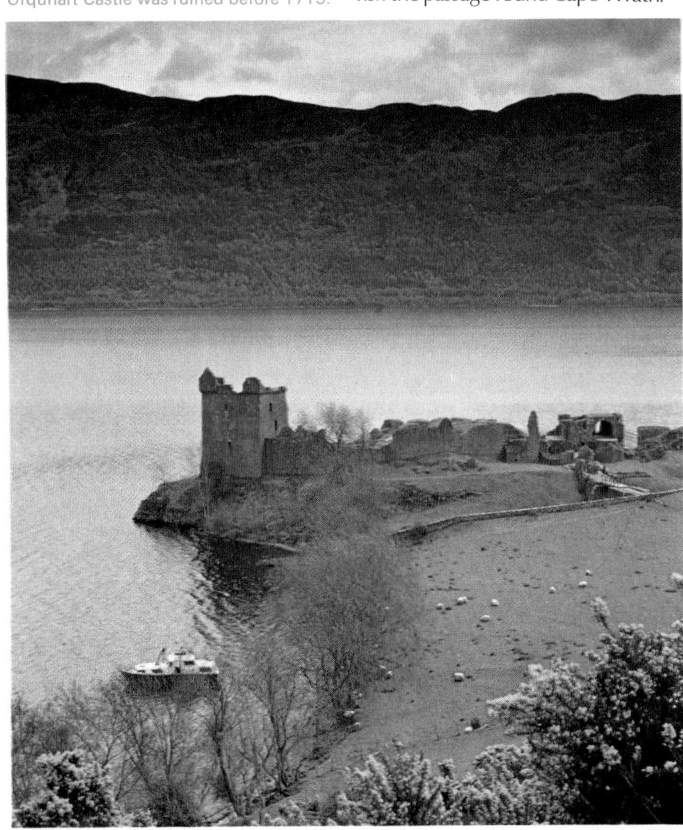

Urquhart Castle was ruined before 1715.

Early Victorian Inverness Castle occupies a commanding position above the town.

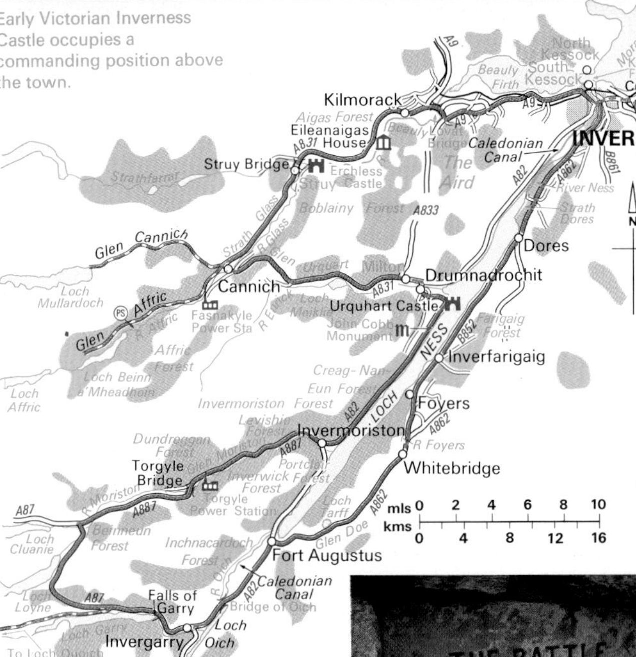

Continue along the A9 to skirt the south shore of Beauly Firth, and after 9 miles cross Lovat Bridge. Beyond the bridge branch left on to the A831 SP 'Cannich' and continue to Kilmorack.

KILMORACK, Highland NH44
South-east of this village is 19th-century Beaufort Castle, seat of the Chief of Clan Fraser. Near by are the ruins of an earlier stronghold. Although the castle is not open to the public it can be seen from foot and bridle paths that cross the Beauly River.

Continue along thickly wooded river banks and reach Crask of Aigas. Just past this hamlet, on the other side of the River Beauly, is Eileanaigas House.

EILEANAIGAS HOUSE, Highland NH44
Situated in lovely gardens between two arms of the River Beauly, this house (not open) was the home of Lord Lovat in 1697 and that of Victorian prime minister Robert Peel. It is also associated with the Sobiéski brothers, who claimed direct descendancy from Prince Charles Edward.

Continue along the Beauly Valley, passing Erchless Castle before crossing Struy Bridge.

The Culloden Cairn marks Charles Edward's final defeat.

STRUY BRIDGE, Highland NH44
Near this bridge the River Farrar joir the Glass to form the Beauly River. Beautiful walks along Glen Strathfarrar penetrate deep into mountain country from here, eventually reaching the lovely expanse of Loch Monar.

Continue through Struy and along Strath Glass to reach Cannich.

CANNICH, Highland NH33
Cannich is a charming stone-built Highland village in a beautiful woodland setting at the south end of Strath Glass. The area is popular wit walkers.

Pleasant detours from Cannich lead through Glen Cannich and Glen Affric, each of which is penetrated b about 10 miles of road. At the end c each glen turn round and return to the main route in Cannich.

GLEN CANNICH, Highland
The woodland scenery in this glen is outstanding. After passing under the slopes of 2,120ft Beinn a'Chairein the road enters densely forested hill country and follows the River Cannich to tiny Loch Carrie. After skirting the banks of Carrie the road reaches Loch Mullardoch, an attractive water which backs up behind the main dam of the Cannich hydro-electric scheme.

GLEN AFFRIC, Highland
In many ways Glen Affric is very much like its neighbour Cannich. After the hamlet of Fasnakyle, where a power station is to be sited, the road passes the Dog Fall and emerges amid birch and pine trees that surround Loch Beinn a'Mheadhoin. Magnificent scenery accompanies the road as it nears its end by the isolated expanse of Loch Affric, with 3,401ft Sgurr na Lapaich rising above the water.

On the main tour, continue along the A831 'Drumnadrochit' road to climb away from Strath Glass and enter Glen Urquhart. Pass Loch Meiklie and follow the River Enrick between pine-clad slopes, through Milton to Drumnadrochit.

DRUMNADROCHIT, Highland NH53
Situated on the River Enrick and the west side of Loch Ness, this village is a popular centre for walking, angling, climbing, and pony-trekking.

Turn right on to the A82 and pass Urquhart Castle on the left, at the mouth of the Great Glen.

URQUHART CASTLE, Highland NH52
Possibly built by the Lord of the Isles, Urquhart overlooks Loch Ness from a lonely promontory and is one of the largest castles in Scotland. It dates from the 14th century. Many sightings of the Loch Ness Monster have been reported from this part of the loch.

Continue along the shores of Loch Ness and pass a memorial to John Cobb on the left.

LOCH NESS, Highland
One of a chain of lochs connected by the Caledonian Canal in the Great Glen, Loch Ness extends from Inverness to Fort Augustus and in places is over 700ft deep. It is world famous as the reported home of the Loch Ness Monster, or Nessie as it has become known, and is occasionally kept under surveillance by teams from various scientific foundations. Sightings of the creature have been reported since the 7th century, but these have swelled from a trickle to a flood since the road along the wooded west shore was opened in 1933. Investigation is hampered by the almost opaque quality of the water, which is stained brown by the peat-laden streams that feed the loch from surrounding mountainsides.

Continue to Invermoriston.

Beautiful Glen Moriston forms part of a large hydro-electric scheme.

INVERMORISTON, Highland NH41
This small town at the east end of Glen Moriston faces Loch Ness and is bordered to the north by the Hills of Invermoriston.

Turn right on to the A887 'Kyle of Lochalsh' road, enter wooded Glen Moriston, and climb gradually beside the river to cross Torgyle Bridge.

TORGYLE BRIDGE, Highland NH31
The reach of the River Moriston spanned by this bridge is known for its fine rapids. Torgyle Power Station can be seen to the left.

Continue through open country to meet the 'Fort William' road and turn left on to the A87. Climb on to bare mountains beside Loch Loyne, and continue with spectacular views before descending beside Loch Garry. Here a single-track road to the right leads 22 miles west to Loch Quoich and Kinloch Hourn, passing through some of the wildest scenery in Scotland. On the tour, continue along the A87 to pass the Falls of Garry.

FALLS OF GARRY, Highland NH20
At the east end of Loch Garry the River Garry plunges over rocks and ledges in a series of beautiful waterfalls. It is now part of a hydro-electric scheme. The forests to the west of this area can be explored by means of planned walks, nature trails, and woodland paths.
Proceed to Invergarry.

INVERGARRY, Highland NH30
South of this little hamlet, on the shores of Loch Oich, are the impressive ruins of Invergarry Castle. It was once the seat of the MacDonells of Glengarry and replaced castles destroyed in 1654 and 1689. Bonnie Prince Charlie stayed here before and after the battle of Culloden, and the 'Butcher' Duke of Cumberland had the building burned in reprisal. Just north of the ruins the River Garry flows into Loch Oich, and the whole area is framed by spectacular Highland mountain scenery.

Turn left on to the A82, skirting the north end of Loch Oich.

LOCH OICH, Highland NH30
Small but beautiful, this is the highest of the Great Glen lochs in the Caledonian Canal chain. Bonnie Prince Charlie rallied his clansmen at Aberchalder Lodge, near the north end, before crossing the Corriveyairack Pass on his way to Edinburgh and England. The road that runs along the east shores of the loch was built by General Wade as a military way.

Continue to Fort Augustus, crossing the Caledonian Canal.

Telford spent from 1803 to 1847 building the Caledonian Canal.

FORT AUGUSTUS, Highland NH30
Wooded hill country surrounds this hamlet, which stands at the south-west end of Loch Ness in the Great Glen. It takes its name from a Hanoverian outpost that was built against the Jacobite Highlanders after the first Rising in 1715. General Wade built the first fort in 1730 and it was named after William Augustus, the Duke of Cumberland, who was later to become known as the Butcher of Culloden. In the second Rising of 1745 the Highlanders actually captured the fort and managed to hold it until the Prince's defeat at Culloden marked the end of the Jacobite cause. The site of the fort is now occupied by a 19th-century abbey and a Catholic boys' school. The Great Glen Exhibition in Fort Augustus relates the history and traditions of the area.

Leave Fort Augustus on the B862 'Errogie' road and follow a former military road which eventually leads to Inverness. Climb steeply through Glen Doe and enjoy magnificent scenery to the north, then pass Loch Tarff and cross lonely open moorland to reach Whitebridge.

WHITEBRIDGE, Highland NH41
Here the River Foyers is joined by the River Fechlin, which flows from remote Loch Killin in the hills rising to the south-east.

Proceed for 1 mile and turn left on to the B852 SP 'Foyers'. Descend through woodland to the east shore of Loch Ness to reach Foyers.

FOYERS, Highland NH42
This village on the eastern shores of Loch Ness is best known for the beautiful Falls of Foyers. The uppermost of these drops 30ft and the lower 90ft, but their scenic impact was considerably reduced when they were starved of water by the opening of Britain's first hydro-electric scheme in 1896.

Continue alongside Loch Ness, with fine mountain views to the west, and reach Inverfarigaig.

INVERFARIGAIG, Highland NH52
A permanent Forestry Commission display and several marked trails have been provided here to help the public understand the industry and wildlife of the area. Close to the village on the east side of Loch Ness is a steamer pier.

Continue to Dores.

DORES, Highland NH53
Dores stands in Strath Dores at the point where it meets Loch Ness and is well situated for walking and angling. Aldourie Castle lies 2 miles north off the B862 and has been a seat of the Frazers since 1750. The first castle was built here in 1626, but the earliest work evident today dates from the 18th century.

Join the B862 and follow Strath Dores, then the River Ness, for the return to Inverness.

TOUR 112 125 MILES

NORTH TO DUNNET HEAD

The rocky, wave-torn headland of Dunnet Head extends far into the stormy Pentland Firth to become the northernmost point on the British mainland. Along the coast are rocky cliffs and small sandy bays where seals bask in the sun, high dunes hiding smothered villages, and ferry points for the Orkneys.

HELMSDALE, Highland ND01
Situated between high moorland ridges, this small fishing village has a natural harbour which offers a safe anchorage and sandy beaches. The River Helmsdale flows into the sea at this point.

Leave Helmsdale on the A9 'Wick' road and climb on to moorland before descending steeply to the village of Berriedale.

BERRIEDALE, Highland ND13
Red-deer antlers decorate the post office and old smithy of this pleasant village, which has a small harbour and is situated at the mouth of Berriedale Water. Remains of a 14th-century castle stand here, and the house of Langwell stands in fine gardens where a variety of plants grow in exposed conditions (gardens only open). Langwell Water rises on a distant slope of the 2,313ft Morven and meets Berriedale Water.

Ascend from Berriedale and continue, with good views along the rocky coast. Pass Dunbeath Castle on the right and descend to Dunbeath.

DUNBEATH, Highland ND12
This scattered fishing village probably derives its name from an ancient Pictish broch which lies about ½ mile north-west and is called Dun Beath. The castle of the same name perches on a lofty promontory 1 mile south and, despite having been enlarged in the 19th century, retains much of its original 15th-century work. It was besieged and captured by Jacobites during the Risings.

Continue to Latheronwheel.

LATHERONWHEEL, Highland ND13
On the right-hand side of the road approaching this village is a curious archway made of whale bones. Latheronwheel itself is the residential half of a partnership with its sister community of Latheron. Both are situated on a natural harbour.

Continue to Latheron.

LATHERON, Highland ND13
Sister village of Latheronwheel, Latheron is at the centre of a district which is well known for its ancient remains. A homestead of early iron-age date is the latest of several ruins recently excavated about 1 mile away at The Wag. A hill above the local church is surmounted by a tower which houses the church bell.

Proceed to Lybster.

LYBSTER, Highland ND23
This is the largest of several attractive fishing villages that manage to make a living on this wild and rocky coast. Its church, built with locally dressed flagstones, has a west door and chancel entrance that are typical of an ancient design used in the area. A road east of the village leads to The Grey Cairns of Camster (AM), which are two chambered tombs from the prehistoric megalithic period.

Continue to Mid Clyth.

The small port of Helmsdale is famous for its lobsters.

MID CLYTH, Highland ND23
Appropriately named the Hill of Many Stones (AM), the slopes behind this village feature 22 prehistoric rows containing 192 stones. They are unique in Scotland, but similar structures exist elsewhere.

Continue along the A9 to Thrumster.

THRUMSTER, Highland ND34
Many prehistoric remains survive in the area round Thrumster, particularly in the vicinity of Loch Yarrows. These include brochs, cairns, and various scattered stones, and there is a standing stone just south of the village school.

Continue to Wick.

WICK, Highland ND35
Situated at the junction of Wick Water and Wick Bay, this ancient Royal Burgh is a thriving market town and herring port with two good harbours. One of these was initially designed by Thomas Telford and later improved by Stephenson. The ruined Castle of Old Wick (AM), also known as Castle Oliphant, stands 1½ miles south-east. Close by are the curious rock stacks known as Brig O' Tram and Brough.

A detour can be made from the main route by leaving Wick on the unclassified Ackergill Street and driving 3 miles, passing Wick Airport and the castles of Girnigoe and Sinclair to reach Noss Head.

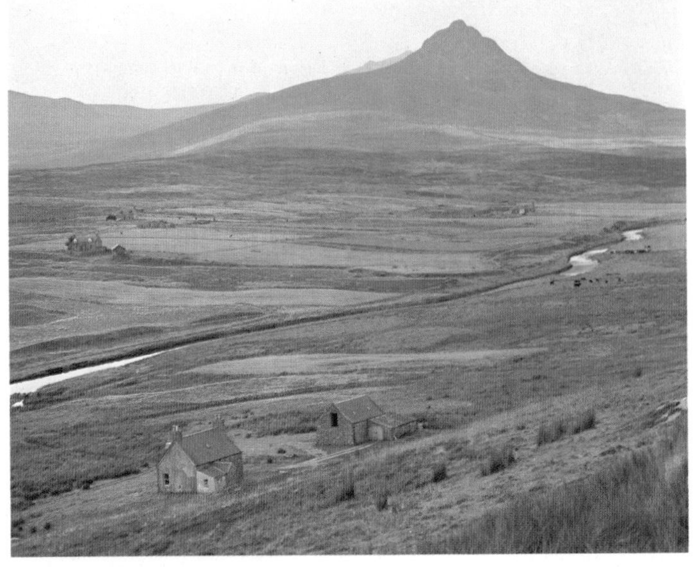

CASTLE GIRNIGOE AND CASTLE SINCLAIR, Highland ND35
Close together in a striking situation at Noss Head are these two picturesquely ruined castles, both abandoned in the mid 17th century.

On the main route, leave Wick on the A9 and continue to Reiss.

REISS, Highland ND35
Reiss stands at an important road junction a little inland from Sinclair's Bay, which boasts one of the longest stretches of sand on this coast. On the shore is modernized Ackergill Tower, which claims to be one of Scotland's oldest inhabited castles.

At Reiss turn right with the main road and skirt Sinclair's Bay to the right. Continue to Keiss.

KEISS, Highland ND36
The remains of the old Keiss Castle stand on the coast to the north of this Sinclair's Bay fishing village, near its modern replacement.

Continue to Freswick.

FRESWICK, Highland ND36
The transition from land to sea near this village is a gentle affair of green slopes and broad sands around Freswick Bay. Close by are the ruins of 15th-century Bucholly Castle.

Continue along the A9. On the approach to John O' Groats a short detour can be made from the main route by taking an unclassified right turn to Duncansby Head.

DUNCANSBY HEAD, Highland ND37
Here, at the extreme north-eastern point of the Scottish mainland, spectacular sandstone cliffs soar to over 200ft above the sea in a massiv display of strength that must have alarmed would-be invaders in time past. Remains of an ancient watch tower still stand on the head, close a lighthouse, and the great chasm c Long Geo runs inland from the sea.

On the main tour, continue to the end of the A9 at John O' Groats.

JOHN O' GROATS, Highland ND37
The shortest distance by road between this village and Land's Enc in Cornwall is exactly 877 miles. Its name is derived from that of a Dutchman who came to Scotland the 15th century, and its beach is famous for the attractive little seashells known as Groatie Buckies

Return along the A9 for ½ mile and turn right on to the A836. After 2 miles a detour can be made from th main route along an unclassified lef turn to Canisbay.

CANISBAY, Highland ND37
The 15th-century church in this village contains a number of interesting monuments, including one which commemorates memb of the de Groot family. Jan de Gro gave his name to John O'Groats.

Berriedale Water flows through a lon valley to join the sea.

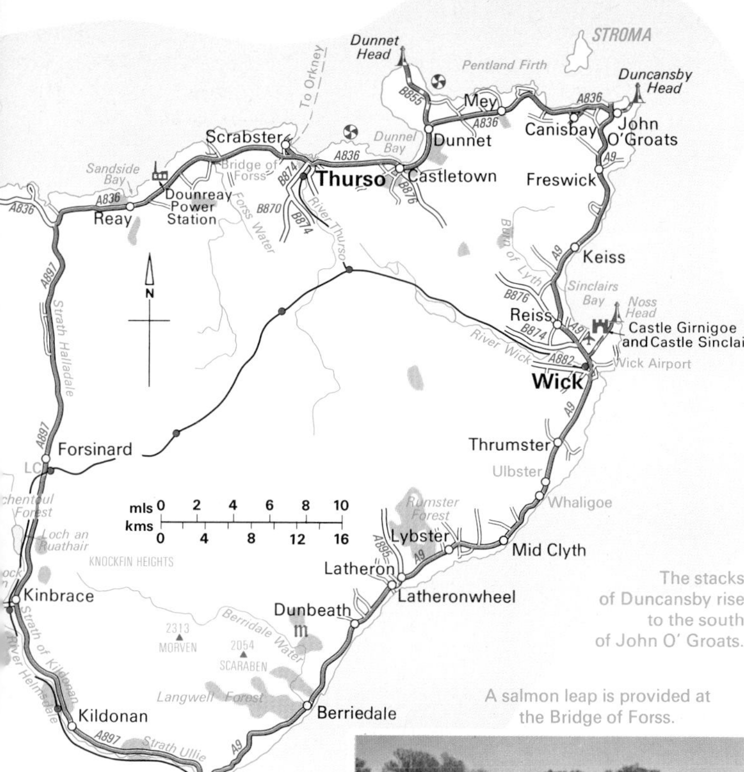

The stacks of Duncansby rise to the south of John O' Groats.

A salmon leap is provided at the Bridge of Forss.

)n the main tour, continue along the \836 to reach Mey, with views over ne Pentland Firth to the right. Various ccess roads lead to the shoreline 'om the tour route.

IEY, Highland ND27
irey seals are a common sight in the ttle coastal bays of the Pentland rth, and views across the water om this village take in the distant)rkneys. One of the best vantage oints in the area is in the gardens)pen) of the Castle of Mey, outside ne village. The building dates from 606.

'roceed to Dunnet.

UNNET, Highland ND27
unnet Church has a saddleback wer and is thought to date from e 14th century. The village itself verlooks Dunnet Bay to the south St John's Loch and is popular with out fishermen.

detour can be made from the main ute at Dunnet by turning right on to e B855 to reach Dunnet Head.

UNNET HEAD, Highland ND27
ne views from this, the most ortherly point in Britain, extend ross the rough seas of the ntland Firth to the Orkneys and e 450ft rock stack of the Old Man Hoy. A lighthouse stands on the adland.

the main route, skirt the sands of innet Bay to reach Castletown.

ASTLETOWN, Highland ND16
is village was founded in 1824 to use workers employed in a nearby arry development that produced ving stones. It has a picturesque e harbour and stands close to the omontory of Dunnet Head.

Continue to Thurso.

THURSO, Highland ND16
An expanding resort and residential town on the sandy shores of Thurso Bay, this charming place is the most northerly town on the British mainland. It stands on the River Thurso, which is well known for its salmon and flows into the bay between the craggy cliffs of Holborn Head and Clairdon Head. Close to the harbour are well-restored houses dating from the 17th and 18th centuries, and ruined St Peter's Church stands on a site occupied since the Vikings. The remains that stand here today are of a 17th-century building. Thurso's interesting museum maintains good collections of plants and fossils, and boasts a lovely little Runic cross. Roofless Thurso Castle, birthplace of the 18th-century statistician and agriculturalist Sir John Sinclair, stands 1 mile east of the town. Beyond this is Harold's Tower, which was erected over the 12th-century grave of Harold, Earl of Caithness, and has subsequently been used as the clan's burial place.

Continue along the A836 'Tongue' road and after a short distance reach the A882 right turn. This offers a detour to Scrabster.

SCRABSTER, Highland ND07
A ferry from Stromness in the Orkneys crosses the Pentland Firth to Scrabster, which stands on sandy Thurso Bay and is sheltered in the north-east by the remarkable Holborn Head. This headland is split from top to bottom by several chasms, the largest of which is open to the sea and spanned by two natural rock arches. Near by the precipitous rock of Clett rises 150ft from the sea.

On the main tour, continue along the A836 to reach Dounreay.

DOUNREAY POWER STATION, Highland NC96
Britain's first prototype fast-breeder reactor was constructed at the experimental nuclear power station here in the 1950s. The site is not open to the public, but an exhibition of its work is held in the summer.

Continue to Reay.

REAY, Highland ND96
Situated near the head of Sandside Bay, this village has a good 18th-century church that can be considered typical of the area. It has an external staircase leading to the belfry, and there is a carved Celtic cross slab in the churchyard. The bay's broad sands, appreciated by the holiday-maker today, were the death of the old village that stood here in the 18th century.

Continue for 3 miles and turn left on to the A897 'Helmsdale' road to enter lonely Strath Halladale. Continue to the resort of Forsinard.

FORSINARD, Highland NC84
This popular angling resort lies between Strath Halladale and Achentoul Forest, with 1,903ft Ben Griam Beg and 1,936ft Ben Griam Mor to the west.

Cross bleak moorland and pass little Loch an Ruathair to reach the edge of Kinbrace village.

KINBRACE, Highland NC83
Two burns meet near this lonely crofting village to form the River Helmsdale, and the local countryside is rich in prehistoric remains. Several chambered cairns can be seen near the Kinbrace Burn. In 1877 the 3rd Duke of Sutherland devised a local reclamation scheme to increase his holding of arable land.

Continue along the A897 beside the River Helmsdale and pass through the Strath of Kildonan to reach Kildonan.

KILDONAN, Highland NC92
At some time in the 19th century small quantities of gold dust were found in Kildonan Burn, but the minor gold rush that resulted from the discovery fizzled out when efforts to extract it failed. Prehistoric rows of stone stand north-west on Leirable Hill.

Descend through the Strath of Kildonan and return to Helmsdale.

The wild moorlands near Forsinard, in the sparsely populated far north of Scotland, are overshadowed by the peaks of rugged Ben Griam Beg and its lofty neighbour Ben Griam Mor.

INDEX

A

'Auld Lang Syne' manuscript at Burns' Cottage Museum, Alloway.

B

Amongst many treasures in Brecon Cathedral is this fine Norman font.

A magnificent old ship's figurehead in Buckler's Hard Museum.

C

Interior decoration at Watts Memorial Chapel, Compton.

D

E

The Clan graves at Culloden serve as reminders of a great battle.

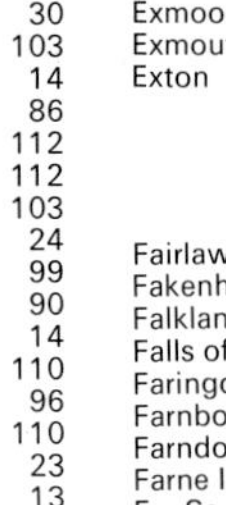

e Abbot's Kitchen at Glastonbury Abbey has been preserved intact.

H

Broken pillars can be seen at Housesteads Roman Fort.

I

J

K

L

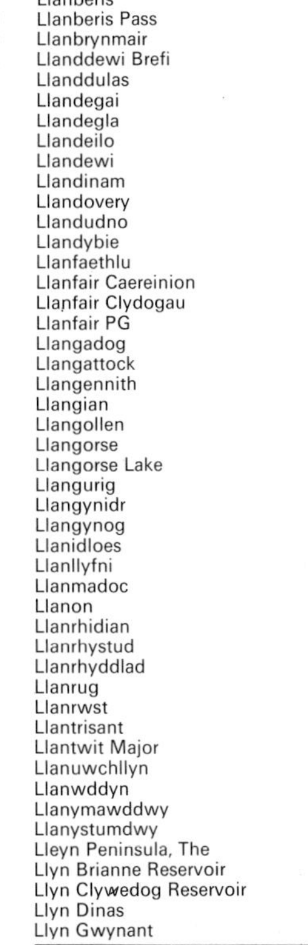

Ancient Eliseg's Pillar stands near Valle Crucis Abbey.

M

N

O

This field gun stands inside the walls of Pevensey Castle.

P

Q

R

St Mary's Church at Rye carries t[illegible] ornate clock.

S

T

U

V

W

Coverlet by Mary Queen of Scots at Traquair House, Innerleithen.

Y

Z

THE NATIONAL GRID

The National Grid map references which appear after the place and county names throughout this book can be used to pin-point those places on any Ordnance Survey based map.

Arisaig, situated on the Morar peninsula in northern Scotland, is the nearest mainland settlement to the islands of Rhum, Eigg, and Muck. When the sun sets on this part of the Scottish coast it is easy to imagine the predatory dragon-shapes of Viking longships gliding from rocky harbours to plunder coastal villages.